D1112095

Information, Organization and Management

Wiley Series in Information Systems

Information, Organization and Management

Expanding Markets and Corporate Boundaries

ROLF WIGAND
Syracuse University

ARNOLD PICOT
University of Munich

RALF REICHWALD
Technical University of Munich

JOHN WILEY & SONS
Chichester · New York · Weinheim · Brisbane · Singapore · Toronto

Baffins Lane, Chichester,
West Sussex PO19 1UD, England

National 01243 779777
International (+44) 1243 779777
e-mail (for orders and customer service enquiries):
cs-books@wiley.co.uk
Visit our Home Page on http://www.wiley.co.uk
or http://www.wiley.com

Other Wiley Editorial Offices

John Wiley & Sons, Inc., 605 Third Avenue,
New York, NY 10158-0012, USA

WILEY-VCH Verlag GmbH, Pappelallee 3,
D-69469 Weinheim, Germany

Jacaranda Wiley Ltd, 33 Park Road, Milton,
Queensland 4064, Australia

John Wiley & Sons (Asia) Pte Ltd, 2 Clementi Loop #02-01,
Jin Xing Distripark, Singapore 129809

John Wiley & Sons (Canada) Ltd, 22 Worcester Road,
Rexdale, Ontario M9W 1LI, Canada

Library of Congress Cataloging-in-Publication Data

Wigand, Rolf T.
Information, organization and management : expanding markets and corporate boundaries / Rolf Wigand, Arnold Picot & Ralf Reichwald
p. cm. — (Wiley series in information systems)
Includes bibliographical references and index.
ISBN 0-471-96454-9 (cloth)
1. Management information systems. 2. Information resources management. 3. Information technology—Economic aspects.
I. Picot, Arnold. II. Reichwald, Ralf, 1943– III. Title.
IV. Series: John Wiley series in information systems.
HD30.213.W54 1997
658.4'038'011—dc21 96–51946
CIP

British Library Cataloguing in Publication Data

A catalogue record for this book is available from the British Library

ISBN 0-471-96454-9

Typeset in 10/12pt Times from the author's disks by
Dorwyn Ltd, Rowlands Castle, Hants
Printed and bound in Great Britain by
Bookcraft (Bath) Ltd, Midsomer Norton, Somerset
This book is printed on acid-free paper responsibly manufactured from sustainable forestation, for which at least two trees are planted for each one used for paper production.

Contents

Preface and Acknowledgements

This book has a long history. The three authors' research foci are in related areas and they have worked together on numerous projects in organization research, organization design and the application of information and communication technologies. In addition they exchanged ideas for over 15 years. This occurred in the form of publications, at conferences in Europe and North America, by guest lectures and through visiting professorships at their respective universities. Toward the end of the 1980s the idea to write this book jointly and publish it simultaneously in German and English emerged from this cooperation. After numerous meetings, the authors were fascinated by the idea of utilizing new communication media in this project enabling virtual teamwork.

Transatlantic telecooperation, however, proved at times more difficult than anticipated: The complexity of this book project, the rapid development of the new technologies and their deployment resulted in substantial changes to the subject matter addressed and demanded intensive dialogue among the authors. The subsequent development of the concept and content of the book had to be clarified and discussed. The boundaries and limits of telecommunication and telecooperation, as well as the book project, reached a crisis stage.

During a most productive, week-long meeting in April, 1994 in the Brewster Inn at Casenovia Lake in New York the project was revitalized and the present new conceptualization together with a new work plan materialized.

Throughout these efforts we gained an experience that may also be a subject topic for this book: The authors encountered the boundaries and limits, but also the support potential of information and communication technology, especially the Internet and its e-mail and file transfer services. This technology enabled the formation of a *virtual team*, as well as the accomplishment of a complex project. All of this was only possible of course on the basis of commonly-shared values and trust which were developed initially through face-to-face interactions. The general recognition that complex projects have to pass through a serious crisis before they find a suitable and goal-directed conclusion can certainly be confirmed in our case.

The realization of our project may be attributed in part to the cooperation of our respective research teams. The innovative concept of the "boundary-less firm" and the opportunity to help shape the new "management leadership in the Information Age" excited and motivated them to contribute to this book in some fashion. These teams, too, were virtually connnected and thus contributed essentially to efficient geography- and time-expanding coordination of the final product. In this fashion we were enabled to combine knowledge and this cooperation approached the limits of co-authorship.

For conceptual and content contributions we thank in particular Prof. Robert Benjamin, Dr Wolfgang Burr, Dipl.-Ing. Dipl.-Wirtsch.-Ing. Juan-Ignacio Conrat, Dipl.-Inform. Burkhard Hermens, Dr Gerhard Hesch, Dr Claudia Höfer, Dr Wolf-Guido Lutz, Dr Donald A. Marchand, Dipl.-Inform. Kathrin Möslein, Dr Johann Niggl, Dipl.-Kfm. Hans Sachenbacher and Dr F. Dianne Lux Wigand. For their valuable editorial support we thank Dipl.Ing. Dipl.-Wirtsch.-Ing. Rudolf Bauer, Dr Hans Koller, Dipl.-Kfm. Barbara Kreis, Dr Rahild Neuburger, Dipl.-Kfm. Heiner Röhrl, Dipl.-Kfm. Sven Scheuble and Dr Birgitta Wolff. Dipl.-Wirtsch.-Ing. Carsten von Glahn, Ms Tanja Ripperger (MBA) and Ms Angela Shelley contributed in various translation efforts expertly and with much enthusiasm. Dipl.-Kfm. Markus Böhme, Dipl.-Kffr. Christine Bortenlänger, Dipl.-Phys. Martin Braig, Dipl.-Phys. Jorun Cramer, Dipl.-Inform. Hermann Englberger, Ms Christine Graap-Lippert, Mr Florian Haase, Dipl.-Phs. Guido Hertel, Ms Beth Mahoney, Dipl.-Ing. Florian Pfingsten, Dipl.-Kffr. Ulla Raithel, Dipl.-Ing. Dieter Riedel, Dr Peter Rohrbach, Dr Andrea Schwartz, Dipl.-Kfm. Eckhard Wagner, Dipl.-Ing. Axel Wiemers and Dipl.-Ing. Stefan Zeilner contributed and assisted in the creation and design of figures, as well as other editorial tasks. Last, but by no means least, the authors thank Dean Ray von Dran of the School of Information Studies, Syracuse University, for his continued support. We would like to thank them all sincerely for their excellent and much committed work and cooperation with the authors. The responsibility for content and potential errors remains of course with the authors exclusively.

A surprisingly difficult aspect turned out to be our desire to publish this book in English and German simultaneously, although the creation of both language versions was really fairly straightforward. Some portions of the book were written right from the beginning in German while others started in English. Consequently a "two-language" manuscript was available that in each case was further developed by the other authors and their teams and was translated. The English and German versions are therefore not literal translations of each other. They differ also content-wise as appropriate for the country-specific audience and their respective "textbook culture". Both versions are, therefore, not appearing simultaneously, but within a few months of each other.

We found it surprising that, in spite of all sorts of globalization in the publishing and media fields, apparently no model for tandem-solutions in the management literature exists within German and English language regions. Numerous discussions and meetings were necessary until two equally respected and expert publishing houses agreed to become cooperative partners for this project. John Wiley & Sons Ltd is publisher of the present volume for the English-language version and Gabler Verlag (Bertelsmann Group) is the publisher of the book for the German edition. We are very pleased with these arrangements and would like to thank especially Ms Diane Taylor (Wiley) and Dr Reinhold Roski (Gabler) for their consistently constructive and cooperative work.

We welcome any sort of feedback on this book and would like to thank our readers in advance. They can reach us at the addresses specified on preceding pages and, of course, via e-mail.

Rolf T. Wigand (rwigand@syr.edu)
Arnold Picot (picot@bwl.uni-muenchen.de)
Ralf Reichwald (reichwald@aib.wiso.tu-muenchen.de)

Syracuse and Munich, June 1997

List of Abbreviations

ACD	Automatic Call Distributor
ACS	Automatic Call Sequencer
ANSI	American National Standards Institute
API	Application Programming Interface
ARIS	Architecture of Integrated Information Systems
ATM	Asynchronous Transfer Mode
CATeam	Computer Aided Team
CBT	Computer Based Telelearning
CD-ROM	Compact Disc-Read Only Memory
CIM	Computer Integrated Manufacturing
CORBA	Computer Object Request Broker Architecture
CPU	Central Processing Unit
CSF	Critical Success Factors
CRS	Computer Reservation System
CSCW	Computer Supported Cooperative Work
CTI	Computer Telephone Integration
DQDB	Distributed Queue Dual Bus
DSS	Decision Support System
E-mail	Electronic Mail
EDI	Electronic Data Interchange
EDIFACT	Electronic Data Interchange for Administration, Commerce and Transport
EDP	Electronic Data Processing
FDDI	Fiber Distributed Data Interface
FTP	File Transfer Protocol

	GATTGeneral Agreement on Tariffs and Trade
GDSS	Group Decision Support System
GII	Global Information Infrastructure
GSM	Global System for Mobile Communication
IDN	Integrated Data Network
IEEE	Institute of Electrical and Electronic Engineers
INMARSAT	International Maritime Satellite Organization
IPX/SPX	Internetwork Packet Exchange/Sequencing Packet Exchange
ISDN	Integrated Services Digital Network
ISO/OSI	International Standard Organization/Open Systems Interconnection
IT	Information Technology
IS	Information Systems
JIT	Just In Time
LAN	Local Area Network
NAFTA	North American Free Trade Agreement
NC	Numerically Controlled
NII	National Information Infrastructure
ODA/ODIF	Office Document Architecture/Office Document Interchange Format
OMG	Object Management Group
OMT	Object Modelling Technique
OOA	Object Oriented Analysis
PaCT	PBX and Computer Training
PBX	Private Branch Exchange
PC	Personal Computer
PCMCIA	Personal Computer Memory Card International Association
PCS	Personal Communication Services
PCN	Personal Communication Network
POSDCORB	Planning, Organizing, Staffing, Directing, Coordinating, Reporting, Budgeting
PPS	Production Planning Systems
PTT	Ministry of Post, Telephone and Telegraph
R&D	Research and Development

RDA	Remote Database Access
RISC	Reduced Instruction Set Computer
SDW	Simultaneous Distributed Work
SIS	Strategic Information System
SNA	System Network Architecture
SNMP	Simple Network Management Protocol
SOM	Semantic Object Model
SONET	Synchronous Optical Network
SPARC	Systems Planning and Requirements Committee (within ANSI)
SQL	Structured Query Language
STEP	Standard for the Exchange of Product Definition Data
T/TTS	Task/Team Support System
TCP/IP	Transport Control Protocol/Internet Protocol
TQM	Total Quality Management
UCD	Uniform Call Distributor
VRU	Voice Response Unit
WAN	Wide Area Network
WWW	World Wide Web

1
Information, Organization and Management: Toward the Boundary-less Organization

INTRODUCTION

Traditionally, communication technologies, information and resources have been used as cost-displacement and labor-saving devices. With the emergence of customer-driven organizations, even flexible, efficient, high performance companies—and public sector organizations as well—cannot rely exclusively on such applications.

Companies in today's complex organizational world are experiencing rapid changes in ever-increasing competitive settings. With the need to respond quickly to changing market conditions new organizational forms and alliances are emerging that were inconceivable just a few years ago. We can observe the importance of such key concepts as just-in-time delivery enabled by newer information and communication technology and how this concept triggers new organizational arrangements and forms with supplier firms, in effect, blurring the traditional boundary of organizations. In turn, such arrangements suggest more the organizational form of a family of firms or the Japanese *Keiretsu*. More and more frequently, the innovative use and appropriate application of information and communication technologies make new alliances, value acceleration and entire new markets possible.

Amidst such accelerating change, blurring, as well as expanding boundaries, there are three certainties: ever-changing market demands, an uncertain economy and the omnipresence of international competition. With information and computers reshaping basic business structures and traditional hierarchies, competitive organizations must either use new information and communication technologies to improve products, services and internal processes, or create new ones.

CHANGES IN COMPETITIVE ENVIRONMENTS AND CORPORATE STRUCTURES

We are used to thinking of corporations as self-contained, integrated structures. They are physically located in office buildings and production plants, in which the corporation's members usually work and where the required machines, equipment, materials and information can be found. From the perspective of most observers from both theory and practice, these physical structures and the contractual relations between the corporations define a corporation's boundaries. Naturally, a corporation crosses its own boundaries constantly when transferring goods to and from markets, procuring input goods, selling finished products, and borrowing or investing capital. This type of boundary-crossing between the corporation and the market, however, corresponds to a clear perception of inside and outside, of membership and non-membership, and of interfaces between the corporation and markets.

In today's economy, many areas no longer correspond to this textbook model of corporate boundaries. Network organizations, telework, cooperative networks, virtual organizational structures and telecooperation are no longer simply buzzwords, but are often found in the practical world. They are reactions to new market and competitive environments under the influence of modern information and communication techniques. *The classical corporate boundaries are beginning to blur, to change internally as well as externally, and in some cases, even dissolve.* Multi-layer corporate hierarchies which function primarily through orders and obedience are increasingly replaced with decentralized, modular structures characterized by autonomy, cooperation and indirect leadership. Apparently, this development is connected with changes in competition and technology. Figure 1.1 illustrates this new situation for corporations and markets.

Changes in the Competitive Markets

For a variety of corporations *drastic changes in competitive terms can be observed.* Goods, labor and information markets are increasingly globalized. The use of new communication networks provides worldwide access to previously difficult to reach markets. Competition is intensified through the entrance of new competitors into formerly local or proprietary markets. The successful measures taken by East Asian

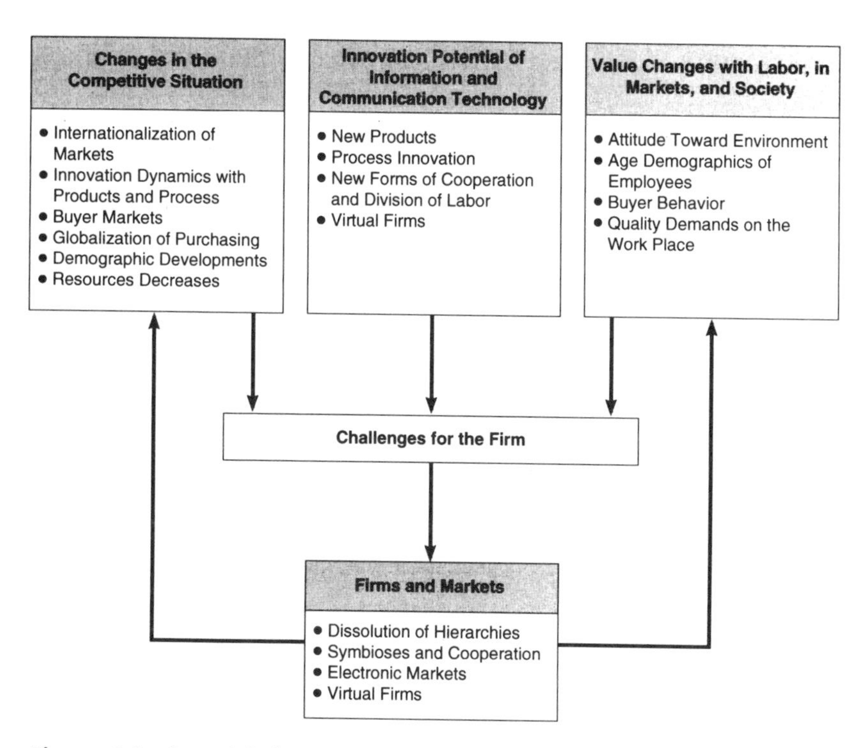

Figure 1.1 *Potential for innovation, competitive markets and innovation strategies*

suppliers, especially in the field of industrial mass products, are still impressive. Since the opening of the borders to the East European markets, suppliers have come into existence, whose national economies allow the production of industrial goods at substantially lower costs and who—while simultaneously improving the quality of their goods and services—increasingly gain access to the world market. Also qualified service providers offer their services worldwide over data networks.

In addition, we observe a change from seller to buyer markets. Buyers have become more demanding and are no longer willing to accept organization-related coordination problems such as long delivery times or interface problems for products. This new buyer behavior influences substantially the development of new goods and services under higher quality demands. This is true for the consumer goods industry, for investment goods, and for all types of services. *Many competing products are of very high quality, an attribute that is taken for granted today, and often real product differentiation occurs actually in the service offered after the product's sale.* Above all, buyer markets require customer orientation and flexibility from the corporation. Competitive strategies must fundamentally reevaluate the business-management goals of "flexibility", "time" (development and delivery times), "quality" and "costs". In especially turbulent markets, *time and flexibility are often the decisive criteria for competition*, when corporations have to adapt to changing demands in a quick and efficient manner.

Changes in Value Systems in the Work Place and Society

The development described in the above section is eclipsed by *radical changes in the work place and society*. These changes have taken place since the 1960s and find worldwide parallels, at least in highly developed industrial societies. Changes in the work world most obviously manifest themselves in an increasing reluctance to subordination, obligation and pure execution of tasks without some degree of autonomy. In the 1970s this led to the implementation of new forms of labor organization in industrial corporations, whose aim was to improve labor conditions in the sense of increased worker autonomy. However, these new forms did not have a lasting effect: numerous models for the humanization of the work place failed because of a superficial and narrow understanding of efficiency. Today, values such as self-responsibility, autonomy, self-realization and individuality gain in importance; simultaneously their potential for quality, flexibility and increases in efficiency of work and overall organizational performance is (re-)discovered.

On a much broader scale, in society these changes in the value system manifest themselves in a modified attitude towards resources, the environment, and a differentiated use of technology. One important factor for this value change in the work place is the increase in traffic concentration and decreasing availability of space in densely populated cities. Every day on their way to and from work, before and after an actual work day, millions of people experience mass transportation accompanied by risk, time loss and stress. Rental space costs in densely populated cities are increasing constantly and are, in turn, lowering the discretionary income. Ecological damage, stress, and the loss of valuable time present negative social costs which are not compensated through a recognizable utility gain. In turn, these changes in working conditions trigger serious discussion on the optimal location for industrial production, on services and their work places, and also about uncertainties concerning the market success of products and services.

Innovative Potential of Information and Communication Technology

Information and communication technologies play a special role in change and reorganization processes. The dramatic performance increase, miniaturization and integration of these technologies often lead to completely new application potentials at the product and process level for business and society. In conjunction with production, energy, material and transport technologies, drastic changes occur, whose most important features can be described as increases in capacity, mobility, cooperative work, integration, openness, distribution and globalization. With the help of these and other technologies, numerous new service markets develop in related fields.

On the other hand, these new technologies contribute greatly to the innovation dynamic in the area of product and process innovations. Microelectronics alters products and production processes and turns many machines into quickly aging ones, as new technologies with increased capacities and capabilities make their way more quickly to the market.

Due to the growing number of applications of these technologies and the related structural potential for change, increased awareness is given to the well-known and important fact that corporations, markets, industries, politics and society essentially constitute themselves through information and communication. It follows that new performance qualities and new design forms of economic processes evolve, which continually alter the abilities and the methods of business, science and management. Also, in order to meet these new demands, the altered consumer behavior, the changed value system, and the resulting challenges for the work place, new information and communication technologies offer a wide field for structuring new production forms based on the division of labor. New forms of cooperation within and between corporations, team concepts and group work, telework, work in mobile offices or in decentralized work places, modular organizations all the way to virtual corporations, are examples of new ways to work that is enabled by newer information and communication technologies.

The information society, which manifests itself above all in the connection and diffusion of individual and mass communication media, together with the intensification of competition through many suppliers, strengthens the buyer's position and turns customer value into the decisive factor for a corporation's market success. The fact that many services can be obtained globally today can be seen in software production, and procurement markets for immaterial goods, in particular, distribute their goods worldwide.

New Organizational Concepts: Overcoming the Boundaries

A variety of factors often limit corporate activities, especially such factors as physical distance and confinement, time scarcity, knowledge deficiencies, production bottlenecks, and lack of flexibility. The use of the application potentials of newer information and communication technologies in competitive processes gives the overcoming of these barriers and boundaries a focal attention. Moreover these technologies offer new solutions for various business innovations.

- *Due to facilitating communication and substituting transport*, regional or national borders play a decreasingly important role for the definition and organization of economic activity.
- *Easier communicative integration of a third party* when enabling entrepreneurial concepts, eradicates increasingly corporate boundaries in the sense of a clear differentiation between inside and outside.
- Locational constraints become less influential due to the *facilitated coordination in space and time.*
- Knowledge boundaries can be extended and overcome more quickly through the *worldwide access to knowledge carriers and knowledge bases.*
- Capacity restrictions are extended in a problem-oriented manner due to the *flexible integration of required resources.*
- Limits of traditional specialization and hierarchical organizations may diminish due to the new *combination and integration possibilities of processes and people*, as well as broader qualifications of participating and responsible individuals. These latter individuals are brought into these processes through information and communication technology.

The above described trends serve as examples. They will be analyzed in more detail in the subsequent parts of this book and demonstrate that a rethinking of traditional concepts about the construction and function of corporations is necessary. Today corporations are less often seen as self-contained, permanent, integrated, clearly defined structures, which are easily distinguishable from their environment. Fundamental organizational innovations are on the agenda, namely the transition to completely new entrepreneurial concepts and new forms of economic division of labor within and between corporations.

Such new organizational forms are observable in modularized, partially virtual enterprises. They are problem-specific and flexible within an open, symbiotic network and they enable value-added processes. Moreover, they utilize innovative technical and organizational potential of, for example, telecooperation, electronic markets and interorganizational system integration.

Barriers to Organizational Innovation

It is well known that especially organizational innovations diffuse slowly due to various *counteractive tendencies.* A lack of understanding of the new challenges and of the forces driving this change, lack of adaptability and readiness to change, as well as fears of the consequences of new structures are examples of such barriers. These prevent a speedy development of the corporation and lead to a change that is possibly too late. The deep permeation of change potentials and their driving forces contribute to the reduction of those barriers.

NEW MODELS FOR THE ORGANIZATION AND MANAGEMENT OF CORPORATIONS

The Tayloristic Industrial Organization: Productivity under Stable Conditions

The insights about the new competitive environments are well known. Modern concepts for suitable innovation strategies are proposed in a variety of ways, future courses of action are presented in numerous publications dealing with new competitive strategies. This insight, however, is difficult to translate into action. The experiences of traditional industrial organizations still dominate everyday corporate activities, since the "guidelines of successful management" are marked by the success story of Tayloristic factory organization. This type of organization was shaped to a high degree by the work (*Principles of Scientific Management*) of Frederick W. Taylor and influenced structure, firms, productivity and value chain conceptualizations, but also the classic management tools of leadership, incentive and control systems.

Hierarchy, the functional division of labor in the process organization, as well as the *one best-way*-conceptualization of labor organization were fundamental characteristics of classical industrial organization. The dominating formal principles of Tayloristic labor organization were:

- the focus of work methods on maximal work specialization;
- the personnel separation of managerial work from operative work; and
- the physical exclusion of all planning, steering and controlling tasks from the manufacturing area.

In this way the complex coordination problem in industrial production could be "optimally" solved through the provision and disposition of production factors. However, the individual was integrated into the production process as a functionable production factor, responsible for receiving and implementing commands. Communication relations followed the hierarchic structures, i.e. formalized, hierarchic communication, along official channels which was prescribed according to fixed rules. The communication behavior between superior and subordinate was characterized by the conceived roles in which the superior gave the orders which the subordinate followed.

Strategies to increase efficiency for the industrial production of goods, however, result essentially from classical concepts of management and organization, which were developed at the beginning of this century through the principles of scientific management. Such strategies focused mainly on mass production in large corporations. They achieved considerable success through the systematic development, perfection and application of methods for the optimization of manufacturing processes. However, this success was only achieved through an adequate utilization of the long-term, stable basic conditions of economic activity and through the appropriate translation of these basic conditions into clear guidelines for entrepreneurial action. The following are the *basic premises for the success of classical increase in efficiency strategies*:

- relatively long life cycles of products
- stable sales markets
- limited number of competitors with known strengths and weaknesses
- low costs of natural resources and low environmental burdens for firms
- extensive availability of highly motivated, well qualified or easily qualifiable workers.

As long as these economic and social conditions were valid, the classic principles—Burkhart Lutz calls them the "common wisdom of industrial innovation strategy"—guaranteed corporate success. Today, the basic conditions have changed and new principles are necessary. Moving away from these classic principles, however, is not an easy task. These fundamentals have been reinforced over decades and are today anchored in task design and definition of management's responsibility, in the design of educational programs, qualification and employee competence, in the selection and implementation of business information systems, as well as in the form of a firm's external relations.

The stable conditions in markets, the longevity of products and high productivity rates justified this type of industrial organization until the late 1970s. The industrial sociologist Konrad Thomas comments on this development:

> "The division of labor, assembly line production, and performance incentives have given industry a productivity boost which, together with the methods of rational corporate design, is correctly labeled as the second industrial revolution by G. Friedmann. Nothing makes more sense than to judge the legitimacy of the applied methods by their efficiency."

New Models: Flexibility and Capacity for Innovation

These differing competitive environments require corporate flexibility and capacity for innovation instead of inflexible productivity increases based on division of labor. The flattening or even the eradication of hierarchical structures is necessary. Classical departments and hierarchical levels are diminishing in importance. Strictly prescribed communication structures are replaced through direct group communication which cannot be channeled directly and specifically. The integration of managerial and operational tasks, the combination of services and the production of goods into self-contained value chains, have an additional consequence questioning a corporation's boundaries also in geographical terms: The stronger the principle of autonomous organizational units permeates the value chain and the more the autonomous units can be coordinated through information and communication technologies, the more the location debate becomes the center of attention. When economic advantage can be realized through a change in location, for example through closer market proximity, through the exploitation of cost advantages, through an increase in the employees' quality of life, through transport and supply advantages, then the trend towards geographic decentralization, meaning the change of location of organizational units, follows organizational decentralization. This concerns the location of entire corporations, of modular organizational units, groups or individual work places. Thus, it is no longer surprising that new forms of labor and division of labor, such as telecooperation and telework, are discussed intensely in the course of modularization and restructuring of corporate organization. Organizational forms enabling quick and permanent market orientation, new forms of networking improving the capability for internal and external cooperation, as well as new forms of human resources management providing for the development and utilization of workers' potential present models for new innovative strategies in today's competitive markets.

Decentralization and Modularization: A Call for Organizational Forms Enabling Quick and Permanent Adaptation

Only today can the side effects from Tayloristic industrial organization be fully realized. The variation in basic industrial environments and the importance of structural change for maintaining and securing competitiveness require above all distinct capabilities for adapting to market changes through:

- the reintegration of production and service functions into self-contained processes focusing on customer value as well as business value;
- direct communication in new forms of work organization among all participants of a value-creating process;
- the ability of employees to process market information, to interpret such information correctly and to act in a customer-oriented fashion;
- the capacity of employees to recognize their organizational unit's contribution to the total corporate value creation and market success, and to share their daily decisions accordingly;
- new roles for managers and employees in less hierarchic organizations.

Through the extensive reintegration of managerial tasks in industrial production processes, future industrial work will be organized in rather autonomous groups. The new concept of reengineering also propagates an integration (beginning at the outset with a market orientation) of industrial performance processes in teamwork, starting ideally with material supply and ending with the final assembly at the buyer's location.

Technical and Non-technical Forms of Integration: Capability for Internal and External Cooperation

Future forms of global collaboration within the corporation have been enabled through decentralized, but also physically distributed group organizations, as well as among organizations in a business world that is increasingly based on the international division of labor. These developments demand from the employee of the future a capability to act in technical as well as in non-technical networks.

Network membership implies a high value of social connections inside and outside of the organization, whose success and durability depends on the compliance to certain rules. These rules deal with the interaction with other team members stemming from varying societies and cultures, the communication with customers and market partners who live by different norms and rules, the handling of different expectations on managers in global teams, and also the evaluation of alternatives whose utility and costs depend on all network participants. Such a case for cooperation can be made for the areas of R&D, sales, marketing, logistics, assembly, etc., whenever service chains, alliances with competitors or other forms of vertical or horizontal cooperation are established.

It follows that employee qualifications pertaining to the difficult field of communication have to be developed. Due to increased deployment of networks, important questions relate to the creation of trust and the maintenance of interpersonal relations in a global working world. Also, evaluation methods need to include numerous new tasks in the area of cooperation. Among other issues, they must deal with questions concerning the utility and costs of cooperation, the measurement and accountance of joint effects in a cooperation or the agreement process with respect to budget definition and profit utilization.

New Forms of Human Resources Management for the Development and Use of Employee Potentials

Finally, holistic organizational structures are innovative corporate concepts which redefine the context between division of labor, coordination forms and effectiveness. The development and exploitation of employee capabilities and potentials are decisive for the realization of these corporate concepts. The new organization and work forms offer important points of departure. As long as autonomous groups and flexible problem-dependent networks are integrated sensibly into the value creation process, they possess all the necessary prerequisites to unfold the creativity and performance potentials of employees, to foster motivation and to create economic benefit. The insights gained from the work structuring debate substantiates that meaningful job content, a comprehensible work environment, quick feedback of work results, as well as sufficient qualification, autonomy and responsibility provide the individual with the possibility for self-realization and increased willingness to perform. These considerations may reconcile much of the previous friction and may harmonize the goals of the employee with the goals of the firm.

STRUCTURE AND SPECIAL FEATURES OF THIS BOOK

A New "Theory of Management"

This book deals with the causes, tendencies and forms of the above described changes at the corporate level and at the level of economic competition. In addition, these developments are seen in the light of opportunities and perspectives resulting from these changes, the

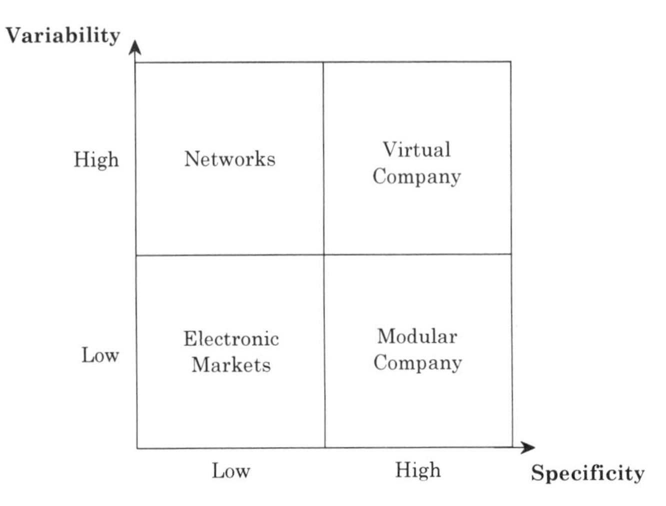

Figure 1.2 *Coordination forms and task structure*

difficulties in handling them, and the challenges they present for management. It shows the fundamental importance which changes in the price-performance relation of information and communication have for the economic organizational forms; meaning what effect the actual and future expected further decreases in information and communication costs, accompanied by a simultaneous increase in information and communication performances, have on the structures of division of labor within and between corporations and markets. Figure 1.2 depicts various arrangements of coordination forms *vis-à-vis* its dependence on underlying tasks.

In these efforts completely new design options, opportunities and requirements are created for corporate management. With this in mind, this book can be seen as a *new theory of management in the age of the information society.*

Overview of This Book's Structure

The following sections offer a brief overview of each chapter. Chapters 2 and 3 lay the theoretical foundation for all subsequent chapters and they deal with the *fundamentals and the explanations for changes in the competitive environment.* Chapter 4 explicates key concepts and describes the potential of newer information and communication technology. Chapters 5 to 8 take up directions for development and trends of corporations and markets, and Chapter 9 discusses the role of the human factor.

Chapter 2 is dedicated to the theoretical foundations of various exchange relationships in markets and in the corporation. Moreover, this chapter focuses especially on the *fundamental role of information and communication in market dynamics and competition*. It shows in which manner information and communication influence the dynamic corporate competition, as well as the division of labor and, thus, the organization. Organizational forms, interpreted as institutional structures of processes based on the division of labor, provide for a possibly frictionless and motivated task completion and, thus, for efficiency increases in the division of labor, information and communication. Market process theory and new institutional economics present important reference theories in this area.

A deeper discussion of processes based on the division of labor within and between corporations requires a more detailed analysis of the related information and communication processes. Chapter 3 prepares the basis for this by describing *fundamental information and communication models* that, in turn, enable *insights into communication and information behavior*. With the help of these basic theories and together with the discussed economic theoretical foundation of Chapter 2, possibilities and limits of new communication and information forms, as well as new organizational solutions can be derived. The reader is presented with fundamental social-scientific concepts of interpersonal communication, as well as empirical evidence of human information and communication behavior in organizations.

Chapter 4 deals with the potential of information and communication technologies for organization development within the market place. The focus is on development trends of these techniques at the levels of the technical infrastructure of information or information systems (hardware, software) and communication (networks, services). Both areas are increasingly integrated, offer new performance potentials, and provide support for different corporate structures and processes. Hypotheses about the reciprocal relationship between corporate organization and technology supply are further topics in this chapter.

The following chapters, Chapters 5 through 9, take a more detailed look at the new organizational forms in corporations and markets. These new organizational forms have emerged based on the general insights discussed in Chapters 2 and 3, as well as in connection with the technology potentials described in Chapter 4.

Chapter 5 deals with the *dissolution of hierarchies* under the influence of competition and technology. In the efforts pertaining to the modularization of firms, traditional, multi-layer hierarchical structures are replaced through relatively independent, process-oriented units, which are only loosely coordinated with each other. One prerequisite among others presents a suitable optimization of the performance strength and an appropriate design of information and communication systems. This trend can be observed at different organizational levels: at the macro-level (e.g., the holding company), at the intermediate level (e.g., business segments) and at the micro-level (e.g., the island principle, group work). In all cases, self-steering mechanisms are strengthened, hierarchies are flattened and integral processes are being supported through information and communication technology. All of this occurs in a unified fashion under one responsible person or group.

The *dissolution of corporate boundaries* within extended relationships that, in turn, lead to *symbioses and networks* present the focal point in Chapter 6. Intensified competitive dynamics and new communication possibilities lead to a more intense, problem-dependent collaboration with third parties, sometimes even in the areas of proprietary core competencies. Through this, classical entrepreneurial boundaries of organizations blur in favor of strategic networks or alliances, vertically or horizontally. Besides the causes and forms of this development, this chapter discusses the information and communication technical implications as well as the special challenges for management.

Not only the coordination forms "corporation" or "hierarchy", respectively, are impacted by the new information and communication possibilities, but "market" as a coordination form. *Electronic markets enable new forms of market coordination* and may open up new options to firms for the marketing of products and services. Chapter 7 presents types of electronic markets and describes the conditions for their emergence and functioning, as well as the requirements for management and technology.

Chapter 8 looks at forms of geographical decentralization. The degree of freedom in the design and application of the new information and communication technology not only relates to organizational aspects, meaning the choice of new coordination forms, but generally also to the physical dimension of completing labor-divided processes. These new technologies thus enable in many ways the *overcoming of physical and location boundaries* at the levels of the individual work place, the department and the entire corporation. This leads to the formation of telecooperation as a work form. Telework, telecooperation, site-independent work at local, regional and global levels and their technical-organizational prerequisites, as well as the resulting requirements for the management are therefore discussed in this chapter. These developments may be seen as prerequisites for the manifestation of the concept of *virtual enterprise.*

The *improvement of human performance boundaries* is an important concept for the organization without boundaries. Chapter 9 is dedicated to the new roles of managers and employees in the boundary-less organization. The above discussed change processes, all of which are enabled in an intensified competition through performance increases in information and communication technology, pose partially new requirements on participating individuals. Thus they are based on the premise, that all actors identify these new requirements and are able to fulfil them. Therefore, the *rediscovery of the human factor* accompanies these organizational changes. This refocusing of organization and management design on the role of the working individual results from the value system changes in the work place and society, from the need for new, interdisciplinary qualifications and from the changed roles of managers and employees in organizations with few hierarchic levels. These developments demand a new and holistic conceptualization of value-added processes.

Special Features of this Book

In addition to the overview, a few special features need to be highlighted:

- *Theoretical foundation*: The book is not limited to a descriptive inventory of certain phenomena. Without a solid theoretical foundation, many statements concerning the development process suggest at most a plausible *ad hoc* character and remain pithy or fashionable. Therefore, in a deliberate and relatively detailed manner, this book begins with a number of relevant basic theories that illuminate the role of information and communication in the competitive process and in the handling of the division of labor. Thus, a foundation is offered for the management and organization while utilizing new information and communication technology. These foundations are complemented with theories about the connection between technology and organization development, theories of organization and motivation, as well as with theories of organization change.
- *Linking of organization, information and communication technology, and management*: The book offers the appropriate insight into important information and communication technology developments, whose application potential enables the realization of new organizational and managerial forms. The linkage is made among the fields of management, information and organization (which otherwise is typically analyzed without referring to technology) under consideration of relevant technological developments.
- *Modular system*: The book treats a large amount of subject matter from various disciplines; starting from the general theoretical foundations of organization, information and communication, over

development trends of information and communication technology, up to different forms of restructuring and managing corporations, as well as personnel development. It can be assumed that the reader is aware of some problem fields discussed in this book, yet wants to study others in more detail. Therefore the text is structured in eight additional, relatively independent modules, which relate to each other through a cross-referenced system. According to the respective level of knowledge and interests, a reader can work with the individual models. Of course we would recommend a reader who is less familiar with the underlying theories to first read the chapters providing a theoretical foundation.

- *Applied orientation*: As well as having a theoretical foundation, the book focuses on the development of practical perspectives and provides an orientation for the person responsible in practical business life. Management has a special challenge: to identify and exploit opportunities in currently occurring change processes. Therefore all chapters contain summarizing statements for implementation-oriented management.
- *New models for competitive organization and leadership strategies*: Corporate management is currently in a process of reorientation and rethinking. The classical patterns of successful entrepreneurship are no longer valid. Therefore new models for successful entrepreneurship have to be found. Chapters 5 to 9 are dedicated to this task currently challenging business management. In each of these chapters, conclusions for management are derived. This means that guidelines for innovation strategies are developed, satisfying the changed conditions in the markets, in the working world and in society.

2
Market Dynamics and Competition: The Fundamental Role of Information

WHY CORPORATIONS AND MARKETS?

The *satisfaction of human needs* is the basic intention of economic activity. Human needs are unlimited, yet the resources for their satisfaction are scarce. This *scarcity of goods* in relation to endless needs has led to the formation of economic institutions which cannot eliminate, but at least minimize this scarcity. This scarcity predicament sets the stage for various phenomena in economic life, not only for abstract phenomena such as exchange, division of labor, and competition, but also for more plastic phenomena, such as markets and corporations. According to "modern" standards, there are few natural commodities appropriate for direct consumption, making a combined process necessary for the transformation of the largest portion of goods into consumable goods. This process is broken down into a variety of individual steps, resulting in a complex nexus of economic activities.

The effective pursuit of scarcity reduction entails the allocation of production factors in a manner maximizing need satisfaction. Economizing means making decisions in regard to scarce resources. *Attempts to diminish the scarcity problem* have been made through the emergence of the division of labor, the realization of advantages earned through specialization, and the use of *production detours*. Exchange activities between economic subjects are invariably tied to these forms of scarcity reduction. Hence, exchange is a fundamental phenomenon of economic activity.

Division of labor and *specialization* are mutually dependent. A human's limited temporal and cognitive ability to deal with comprehensive assignments on his own provide the motivation for these concepts. This leads to a systematic breaking down of complex assignments into single tasks until the completion of these partial tasks lies within the scope of an individual's capacities. In most societies a high degree of division of labor results from this process. Concentrating on single task components allows for the development of specific knowledge, abilities and processes with which these tasks can be completed in an efficient manner. The principle of creating and using specialized skills, known as far back as Aristotle as well as more recently by Adam Smith, leads to considerable productivity increases in the management of partial tasks. A more productive economizing of given resources implies the possibility of satisfying a larger number of needs. This mechanism can be observed at all levels of economic activity, beginning with personal, intrafirm or interfirm specialization, and division of labor all the way to sectoral, regional, national or international specialization and division of labor.

Another way to increase a resource's potential for need satisfaction lies in the *creation of production detours*. This expression stems from Carl Menger (Menger, 1871), the Austrian national economist. He classifies economic goods according to their proximity to end consumption. Consumer goods are goods of first order. They are produced from pre-products using explicit production means. These production factors represent goods of second order, which once again stem from pre-products and production means of a higher order. The expression production detour describes a good's placement in a higher order, bringing its productive use further away from end consumption (for example, the use of grain as seed instead of food; the use of materials and labor to produce tools). The production detour implies sacrificing present consumption for the sake of future productivity increases and in turn, an increase in future consumption options. Production detours lead to an increase in the potential of need satisfaction on the basis of given resources.

In order to combine partial tasks into specific production methods or consumer goods, actors' services must be exchanged with one another. Partial tasks which are carried out through division of labor must be reunited in a coordinated fashion in order to finish the complete job, for example, the production of a car. This process results in a *nexus of various exchange relationships*. This coordination of partial tasks does not happen automatically, but is a task in itself, also requiring resources. Exchanges between economic actors have to be initiated, negotiated and completed. For this purpose, the exchange partners require information.

In neoclassical microeconomic models, this fundamental basis for the coordination of economic activities was principally ignored. The assumption was made that prices reflect all relevant information and that these prices are determined without costing time or money. In turn, it was assumed that an actor's information search was frictionless and cost-free, allowing for identical information levels for all actors. However, the main stumbling block in coordinating economic activities lies in the unequal distribution of information and the considerable efforts involved in obtaining information (see von Hayek, 1945).

Experience, knowledge and abilities are different for each actor and are constantly changing. The human capacity to process information is limited. This accounts for the *continually changing information asymmetries* in all economic fields. These asymmetries are the starting point for all labor-divided activities and for all entrepreneurial initiatives. At the same time, the search and evaluation of information expends resources, for example, concerning the potential exchange partners' abilities and intentions.

The *coordination of economic activities* demands the employment of resources and generates costs, which are defined as coordination or transaction costs (see Coase, 1937; Williamson, 1975; Picot, 1982). Transaction costs are the "production" costs of coordination. As a rule, they comprise the partial tasks of initiation, negotiation, completion, control, and adaptation of a transaction relationship. They involve those information and communication costs requisite for the preparation, implementation and supervision of division of labor and exchange. The level of transaction costs is influenced primarily by the diverse transaction characteristics. These are explained on page 86. Therefore, the challenge of coordination lies in finding coordination patterns for partial tasks under consideration of various circumstances and allowing for a frictionless completion of task-related exchanges between participants, aiming to minimize transaction costs.

An empirical study by John J. Wallis and Douglass C. North (see Wallis and North, 1986) shows the considerable importance which transaction costs possess in the coordination of economic activities. These two researchers examined the total level of transaction costs in the American economy from 1870 to 1970. In this study, they differentiated between transformation services and transaction services. In order to identify transaction services, they analyzed those economic activities taking place in the context of market transactions. In doing so, they grouped diverse economic activities together as transaction industries, such as financial, insurance, as well as wholesale and retail activities. In addition, they evaluated the transaction services within companies in non-transaction industries (for example, manufacturing, raw materials and agriculture). Further, Wallis and North studied the contribution of public transaction services. In conclusion, they provided very impressive results, which are presented in Figure 2.1. These findings show the substantial increase in the national income realized through the provision of transactions services. Whereas in 1870 only a quarter of all economic activity was related to the provision of transaction services, this percentage amounted to over a half (54.71%) of the total realized income in that economy in 1970. A notable growth in corresponding governmental activities was also experienced in this time period. This percentage climbed from 13% in 1870 to 25% in 1970. This shows that the largest percentage of national income is spent on information and communication, meaning for coordination purposes. Furthermore, Wallis and North's study illustrates the growing strategic significance of the emergence of information and communication technologies.

An interpretation of this study clearly represents the *structural changes in the American national economy*, such as the transition from an agricultural to an industrial economy, the growth in services and government activities, the changes in the size of corporations, and the related distinction of economic coordination activities. This study emphasizes a further consequential aspect in respect to the fundamental economic purpose, namely the overcoming of the scarcity problem. Although division of labor and specialization have enabled, or still enable, progress in productivity through improving efficiency in transformation processes, these gains can only be realized through exchange activities. These exchange activities, however, expend economic resources themselves. The consequence is that transaction costs present a similar limiting factor for economic growth as do the costs for transformation processes. "Until economic organizations developed a way to lower the costs of exchange we could not reap the advantage of ever greater specialization" (Wallis and North, 1986, p. 121).

This implies nothing else than the need for weighing the advantages of further specialization against the related increase in those coordination costs. It is even imaginable that the advantages at a certain level of specialization could be exhausted by the required coordination costs. In such a case, the progress in productivity in transformation processes would inherently set its own economic limits through the increase in coordination costs. Thus, organizational or technological institutions and innovations assisting in the reduction of exchange costs are of great importance for total economic development. Parallels can be drawn to the intraorganizational exchange of services. The long-term analysis of production costs under varying company sizes is based on the exploitation of economies of scale, meaning that production costs decrease with growing company size and a simultaneous growth in specialization. This empirical insight, valid in the past, found justification under stable circumstances in the production of services and on markets. Coordination costs decrease relative to company output. The classical model of the

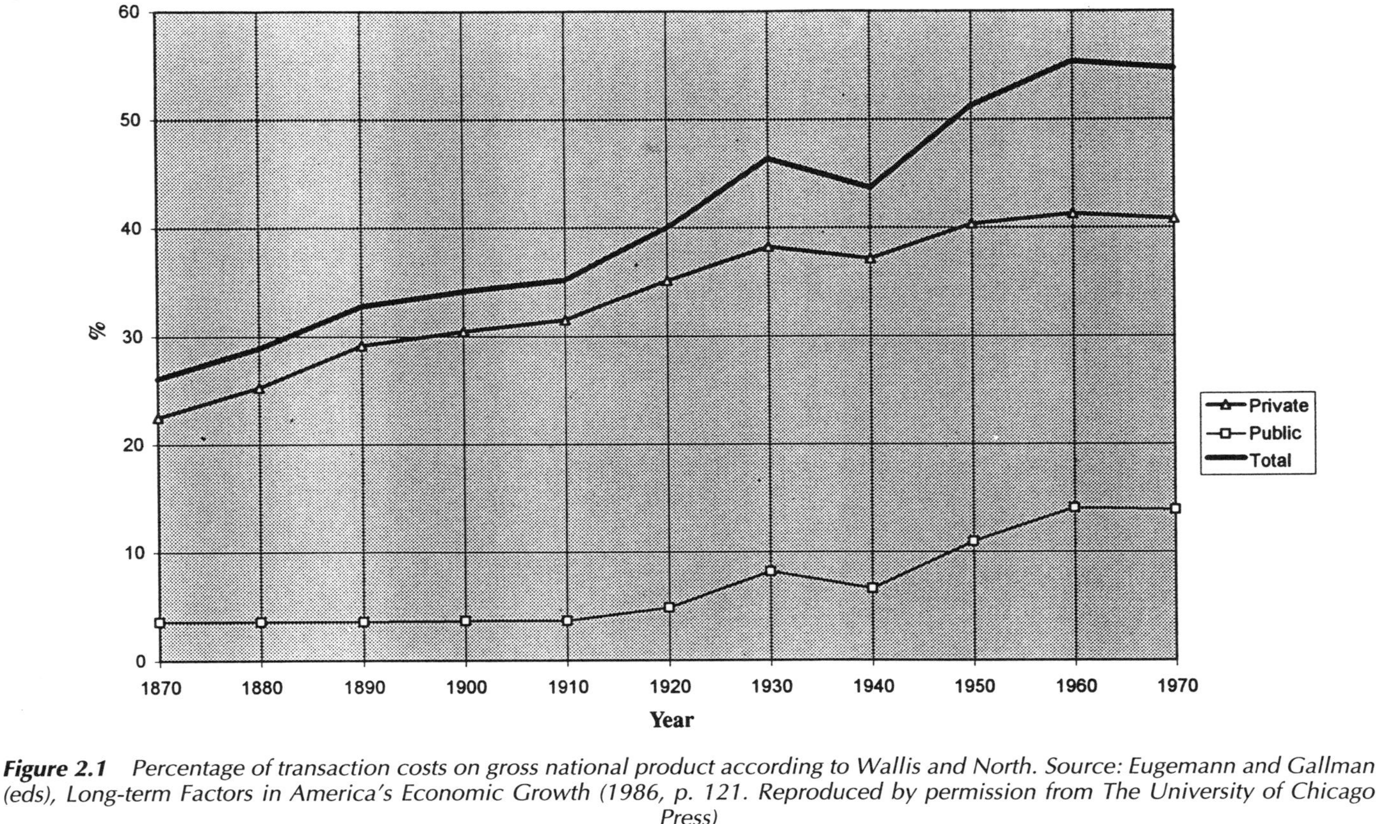

Figure 2.1 *Percentage of transaction costs on gross national product according to Wallis and North. Source: Eugemann and Gallman (eds), Long-term Factors in America's Economic Growth (1986, p. 121. Reproduced by permission from The University of Chicago Press)*

learning curve can be applied. But, under unstable circumstances, meaning when factors of change influence the production process as much as demand on the market, decreasing production costs are quickly overcompensated by the ever-increasing coordination costs, i.e. the costs of adaptation and modification. The producing companies no longer reach the economically attractive area of low unit costs.

Inevitably, these facts shift the focus towards the central importance of *various coordination mechanisms for economic activities*. Coordination mechanisms are to be evaluated and designed according to the degree to which they allow for the arrangement of economic activities yielding the lowest degree of friction. Corporations and markets can be identified as the two poles on a continuum of possible coordination mechanisms, presenting dichotomous organizational forms of economic activities. Based on their different properties, a variety of options for the design of minimal coordination forms arise. To recognize these options, the fundamental functions and effects of markets and corporations must be understood.

MARKETS AS PROCESSES

A *market is an economic location on which the supply of and demand for goods meet*, enabling exchange processes. The more similar the goods are on a market, the closer a market becomes to being considered as perfect or homogenous. According to neoclassical market theory, the price reflects all relevant information for that market. For this reason, this market theory is known as price theory.

The *neoclassical equilibrium theory* is founded on the central assumption that all actors possess perfect information. The actors decide autonomously based on equal information levels. This theory also includes models for the study of market efficiency, in which the number of economic subjects, the type of goods, the consumption and production quantities, individual preferences, and production technologies are determined. The corporation size and the location at which goods are produced with the help of production technologies remain undetermined. In this theory, goods are classified according to physical attributes, including their availability. The property rights on technologies and products are completely defined and can be carried through. Accordingly, no forms of external effects exist.

Through these model assumptions, only very few problems arise relating to the *distribution of market relevant information* between the economic subjects and the search for information essential for production, consumption and exchange decisions. The coordination of buying and selling intentions is explicitly carried out by the *auctioneer* (see Arrow and Hahn, 1971). All information needed for a coordination of the individual economic subjects' purchasing and production plans is conveyed through the price system. Homogenous goods are exchanged at standard prices and information is free, meaning that no transaction costs arise in the coordination of partial services. According to this theory, an equilibrium exists when all consumption and production plans are matched with the help of the price system. It has been proven that these equilibrium states are explicit and stable (see Arrow and Hurwicz, 1958).

The analysis of market processes is founded on the assumption of complete information. There is no need to curtail transaction costs, for example through the formation of certain institutions. In the case of given equilibrium prices, all individual decisions are made based upon their desired results, known *ex ante*. Due to complete information, the market events are fully organized at all times. This gives way for revealing insight: *under complete anticipation of all economic subjects' future decisions, there is no freedom of action.* This mechanistic market scenario (see von Hayek, 1952) retains a paralyzing effect, which would result from perfect anticipation of any economic activity. The "leveling of all differences in the individual availability of information" (Kunz, 1985, p. 32, translation by author) leads to a market interpretation in which all economic activities have ceased to take place.

These far-reaching assumptions about the economic subjects' information level block the view on numerous situations necessary for a more realistic analysis of economic activities (see Ernst, 1990). As previously stated, in reality more than half of all economic activities are allotted to transactions, meaning information and communication processes. Therefore, for a realistic observation of systems based on the division of labor, information activities are paramount and cannot be neglected. *Market process theory* differs from the neoclassical equilibrium theory in that the awareness, the exploitation, and the significance of information gaps and incomplete information present the foundation for the analysis of market processes. This theory is based explicitly upon imbalanced states. Market process theory was predominantly shaped by the Austrian economists Menger, von Mises, Schumpeter, von Hayek, Kirzner, and Lachmann, giving rise to the expressions "Austrian School" and "Austrianism".

The elemental point of this theory is the *(unequal) distribution of knowledge in society*, i.e. between participating actors. In his 1945 article "The Use of Knowledge in Society", von Hayek drew attention to this unequal distribution of knowledge and the distinct influence of the price system in contrast to that in the neoclassical equilibrium theory. Not only did von Hayek consider scientific insight as economically relevant knowledge, but above all the recognition of special circumstances of place and time. In these settings, the differing levels of information of economic subjects about markets or technical applications are revealed. The economy's ability to function and its efficiency depend upon the extent to which this scattered existing knowledge can be used in a sensible manner. It is impossible to convey all relevant information to a central planning authority. A planned economy would be overburdened. There must be a simpler way to provide the individual economic subjects with the pertinent information which they need to coordinate their activities.

In this context, the price system plays a weighty role. Through price changes, the applicable information is made available to the economic subjects, which is vital for their adjustment of activities under the altered circumstances. According to von Hayek, this is the key function of the price system, enabling economic subjects to carry out the relevant activity with relatively little knowledge. Should a certain raw material become scarce, a majority of economic subjects would be prompted to use this material sparingly on account of the higher price. Once again, neither a central authority is requisite nor have the economic subjects to be informed about the causes of this raw material scarcity. The market price system proves itself as an effective instrument for rationalization of information and communication for the purpose of coordination under fluctuating circumstances.

Von Hayek notes that the price system evolved "spontaneously", meaning without conscious planning or intention from individual economic subjects' activities. The *fictional character of the auctioneer* in the neoclassical equilibrium model is no longer necessary. The unequal distribution of information and the spontaneous coordination of economic subjects are no longer in agreement with the neoclassical model's assumption of stable equilibria. Moreover, all activities and agreement processes are subject to constant fluctuations. "The market is seen here as the result of mutually influenced decisions by consumers, entrepreneurial producers, and resource owners in a certain period of time" (Kirzner, 1978, p. 7). The market process results from the mutual influence which develops from the economic subjects' relative lack of information.

The closure of information gaps and the exploitation of imbalances occurs spontaneously, meaning without intervention from a central planning authority. The driving force described by Kirzner is the character of the *entrepreneur* (see Kirzner, 1978). The market plan adaptations constituting the market process happen through the market participants' realization that their plans were either too optimistic or pessimistic (see Kirzner, 1978). For example, buyers/sellers discover that they could have bought the goods at a lower price, and respectively could have asked a higher price for the goods sold. In this step-by-step process, entrepreneurs appear who discover these unused opportunities and realize the profit potential. They would buy goods at lower prices from those sellers who were unaware that certain buyers are willing to pay a higher price, and resell these goods at a profit. Thereby, entrepreneurs transfer market knowledge to other market participants who are not capable of acquiring that information on their own.

The consideration of information as a driving force behind market events manifests itself in the fact that specific markets for information have arisen in which information itself is traded as a good. Thereby, reciprocal effects between markets for information and markets for goods appear. For example, a less expensive availability of information in information markets might leverage informational disparities in markets for goods and vice versa. As a consequence, information markets exercise a considerable influence on the competitive situation in markets for goods and services.

In this market process, *competition* inevitably takes place. Enterprises must continually offer more attractive conditions to their market partners than do their competitors. In this effort to stay ahead of the competition, the market process causes market participants to push their abilities to the limit in order to succeed in the market process. Such competition never leads to a stable equilibrium. Rather, the market participants are under constant pressure to take advantage of the opportunities offered by the market in order to stay in the race for competitive advantages.

ENTREPRENEURSHIP

In the previous section, it was explained that the criticism of the neoclassical equilibrium theory focuses especially on the lack of consideration of information costs, entrepreneurship, and dynamic competition. In the model world in which every economic subject possesses the same level of information, there is no place for an entrepreneurial search for market advantages. Because of this, such advantages would be recognizable by everyone and in turn, would be anticipated by all economic subjects within their activities. Model assumptions which presume stable equilibria therefore overlook the role of entrepreneurs, entrepreneurship, and competition in the market process.

The *importance of entrepreneurship in the market process* is interpreted differently by Austrian School authors. All approaches are based on the lack of perfect knowledge and explain the functioning of the market process through the driving force of entrepreneurship. It is the lasting merit of the *Austrian School* to have introduced the entrepreneurial element associated with every economic activity into economic theory. In this entrepreneurial element, the unequal distribution of information is personified. Entrepreneurial ideas and entrepreneurial success result from an informational lead over other economic subjects. This information lead manifests itself in three notable functions of entrepreneurship in the market process: innovation, coordination, and arbitrage functions (see Picot, Laub and Schneider, 1989; Windsperger, 1991).

The *innovation function* was attributed to entrepreneurship by Schumpeter (see Schumpeter, 1926). According to Schumpeter, entrepreneurship comes about when individual economic subjects implement new production processes resulting either in new products or new production methods. By inventing new products or methods, such an innovator thereby intervenes in everyday production sequences and market exchange. He tries to realize profit through his information advantage which is expressed in these new combinations (see Schumpeter, 1926). This profit is created through the gap which Schumpeter's entrepreneur recognizes and uses between the prices for resources and the goods or services he produced. Through this, he can stay ahead of his competition for at least a short period of time. Profit realization is possible only until other enterprises imitate this innovation. The innovation then loses its uniqueness, hence decreasing the innovator's profit margin until it is completely eaten away. The innovator can realize profit until prices match costs because of imitators. An entrepreneur can decrease his selling price in comparison to the competition, for example, through an innovative production technology or through the use of information and communication technology, if this enables production at a lower cost. Through this he improves his competitive position. As long as an innovator recognizes the potential for profit due to lack of imitation by other enterprises, he will attempt to exploit this source of profit. In his later works, Schumpeter stresses the role of large corporations in the innovation process, which on account of their size possess distinct strengths in the research and development of new products (see Schumpeter, 1926).

The foremost characteristic of Schumpeter's entrepreneur lies in his appearance as a *creative destructor* of existing structures. The introduction of new products or methods brings about an imbalance (see Schumpeter, 1926). Under the consideration that imitation turns innovation into a standard routine, this leads to a new market equilibrium. This state of balance, however, will either never be reached or will be unstable, since an innovative entrepreneur can once again appear as a creative destructor and bring about another state of imbalance. According to Schumpeter, innovation is the motor for any economic development. On account of the inevitable creative destruction, a never-ending market process of approaching an unreachable state of equilibrium comes into being. Schumpeter's reflections can still be applied to the design of enterprises (see Chapter 5). The more an enterprise throws away the classical productivity-oriented strategies and applies new innovation strategies, the greater the role entrepreneurship plays in the recognition of innovation potential, the breaking down of innovation barriers, and the further development of methods and procedures which make the ability to change, to cooperate, and to innovate permanent topics.

A complementary aspect of this entrepreneurial function can be found in *Knight's profit theory* (see Knight, 1921). The emphasis is placed on the variety of individual risk inclinations. According to this theory, entrepreneurs are on average higher risk takers and to a certain degree, reduce the income uncertainty for their employees. As a bonus, they realize a profit. In this context, the entrepreneur functions as a risk carrier and an insurance surrogate. Knight stressed the uncertainty factor corresponding with the results of alternative actions, which result from the permanently changing structures of economic activities. Profit is, according to Knight, the residual remaining for the entrepreneur, stemming from the difference between market price and the factor inputs needed for the production of goods. The profit is not only compensation for dealing with uncertainty, but also is the difference resulting from the expected and the actual (unpredictable) value of marketable products.

This perspective is noteworthy and characteristic for entrepreneurial action, as it expresses that the profits realized by the entrepreneur are not only determined by his own abilities, but depend also on general measures of initiative, abilities and behaviors in the market (see Kirzner, 1978). "Market" describes, therefore, a processual event in which one's own economic activities can be limited by the other actors' actions. This not only leads to the previously discussed phenomenon of dynamic competition, but also opens the door for a later discussed question of possibilities in managing and reducing uncertainty in the framework of economic exchange and coordination processes. It will be shown to which extent the factor of uncertainty—meaning simply incomplete information—presents a measure for alternative forms of coordination of partial tasks. With this, it is possible to apply the concepts of Knight's profit theory and the corresponding issue of uncertainty to the *coordination function of corporations.*

As a further attribute for the description of the entrepreneurial position, the market process implicit in Knight's theory leads to the *arbitrage function of entrepreneurship* described by Kirzner. Knight personifies the entrepreneur as an enterprise's leader who carries the sole responsibility for entrepreneurial activity and the corresponding uncertainty. The leader concept is equivalent to Kirzner's concept of "highest knowledge" and with his abstract figure of entrepreneurial resourcefulness (see Kirzner, 1978).

Kirzner assumes that human action cannot be explained solely through the categories of economizing, maximizing and optimizing efficiency. He sees, in which he describes as entrepreneurial element (following von Mises), a further "non-economic" category which is decisive for the market process. He finds justification in the fact that under given conditions, exclusive economizing and maximizing often fail to explain the market process as it can be observed in reality. He regards entrepreneurship as a supplement in the analysis of market events. With this he expands the perspective of economizing activity into a more comprehensive term of human activity. This expansion no longer binds decision-makers to the pure allocation and economizing activities based on given means and purposes. An entrepreneurial decision-maker no longer limits himself to the efficient pursuit of set goals. In addition, he possesses the resourcefulness to set new goals, discover unknown resources, and to use them for economic gain.

This element of *resourcefulness* is regarded by Kirzner as the entrepreneurial element of human decision-making. It can be characterized by dynamic and creative activity. With this, human activity is no longer interpreted as passive and rather mechanistic reactive behavior simply following given patterns and expressing itself only in the course of economizing. Instead, decisions are made on the basis of learning processes in which increasing experiences of former decisions manifest themselves.

> "We have to consider the entrepreneurial element to understand, that by subsequent decisions the seemingly relevant means/purpose patterns might be the explainable result of an experience process in which the decision-maker's resourcefulness related to relevant new knowledge has brought about an ever-changing succession of decisions.' (*Kirzner, 1978, p. 29; translation by author*)

Two aspects have to be highlighted in this consideration. First, Kirzner stresses the active role of entrepreneurs in the market process, in that they do not simply react to given market data but develop a resourcefulness with which they can change these data and hence trigger a market process. Second, according to his theory, the differentiation can be made between the entrepreneur as a *function* and the entrepreneur as a *human actor*. This distinction seems to be important, because it distinguishes between entrepreneurs as human actors who influence the market process through their resourcefulness, and entrepreneurial activity as a mere function to accomplish economic tasks. This personalization of the entrepreneurial creativity does not necessitate a definite coordination pattern for economic activity (enterprise) or a position of ownership. Rather, the perspective is open for the development of entrepreneurial behavior and structures which do not necessarily presume enterprises respectively have to occur within such structures.

Kirzner's resourceful entrepreneur discovers profit sources stemming from price discrepancies between given procurement and sales markets. The entrepreneur plays the *arbitrage* role; his knowledge of how to use information leads to his economic advantage in dealing with these particular information spheres. Disparities in time and location as well as variation in the production structures can be responsible for the existence of arbitrage profits.

A supplier, as part of the procurement market, has incomplete information about the realizable profits on the sales market. His supply price P_S is lower than the demand price P_D. At the same time, his customers have incomplete information about the current supply price on the procurement market. Here the supply price is also lower than the demand price. The resourceful entrepreneur plays the arbitrage role when he detects a source of profit in the mediation between the procurement and sales markets. He calculates that a certain quantity of goods on the procurement market can be bought at a lower price than the customers are prepared to pay on the sales market. He will do this as long as the realizable price difference is enough to cover the necessary transaction costs.

Entrepreneurial resourcefulness, then, is based mainly on the discovery of unequal distribution of ability and knowledge in an economy. This unequal distribution opens the door for information leads and allows for entrepreneurial exploitation of informational divergences. *Entrepreneurship and dynamic competition comprise the recognition of economically relevant information respectively knowledge leads and in the practical exploitation of such divergencies.* The entrepreneurial arbitrage results from the *creative bridge* between formerly incompletely connected information spheres with the help of entrepreneurial ideas. Figure 2.2. illustrates this relationship.

This entrepreneurial activity is probably obvious in trading. Goods are purchased from suppliers and eventually sold under consideration of time, location and quantity in order to satisfy customer demands (Picot, 1986). This principle relationship is also valid for industrial

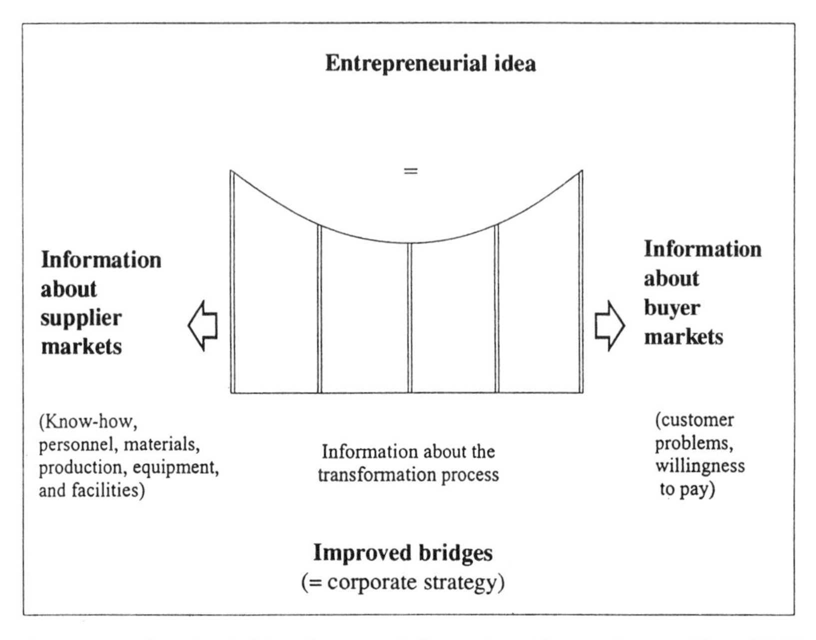

Figure 2.2 *Creative bridges between information spheres. Source: Picot (1989a, p. 4)*

entrepreneurial activity. Between procurement and sales, the production of goods exists as an especially intensive transformation step (i.e. Cheung, 1983). In both cases, information leads and knowledge differences between two information spheres are recognized and used for economic gain.

Without this entrepreneurial activity, market partners could not optimize the use of available resources to satisfy demands. In a dynamic competitive system, such advantageous entrepreneurial positions are repeatedly eliminated through imitation or further innovation, so that entrepreneurial activity is constantly challenged with discovering, developing and applying of economically relevant information and knowledge disparities. The characteristic of competition in the dynamic market process is expressed in this challenge.

The process of continual innovation and permanent change, which is insolubly connected with the image of entrepreneurship, is also displayed in the modification of organizational forms. In this context, coordination forms do not represent fixed structures. Rather, they must be able to adapt to the informational changes in the market process and to reduce the inefficiencies of existing organizational forms through the search for innovative coordination forms. This search itself can assist in the construction of a creative bridge between two informational spheres. The abilities for permanent market and organizational change place demanding requirements on the participating human actors. Organizational innovations lead to altered assignments, shake the traditional perceptions which participants have of themselves, and force the alteration in forms of human interaction.

ORGANIZATION THEORIES

The scarcity of economic goods and the inevitable corresponding economic problems as well as the possibilities of reducing them through division of labor form the *core of the business and economic problem of organization*. With that, the determination of tasks based on the division of labor and the selection of appropriate coordination forms present central issues related to organization in and between corporations as well as in the economy as a whole. The field of economics offers numerous theoretical instruments and models to provide solutions for this organizational problem. Pages 22–24 discussed the contributions of market process theory, which deals principally with the significance of information in the creation of and the activity in markets. As a field of research, *New Institutional Economics* has recently received noteworthy attention to academic literature and in the practical world. New institutional economics also emphasizes the significance of information and communication for the coordination of economic activity. Institutions stand in the center of its analysis and serve the rationalization of information and communication processes. Institutions are ". . . socially sanctionable expectations, related to actions and behaviors of one or more individuals" (Dietl, 1991, p. 37; translation by author). They function as mechanisms for stabilizing expectations, in turn facilitating the coordination of production based on the division of labor.

New Institutional Economics deals with the effects of institutions (e.g. contracts, organizational structures, language and money) on human behavior as well as with possibilities for the efficient formation, respectively evolutionary development, and with the rational design of institutions (see Richter, 1994; Douma and Schreuder, 1991), With that, new institutional economics is based upon *two fundamental assumptions*: "Institutions (1) matter and (2) are susceptible to analysis." (Matthews, 1986, p. 903).

The creation of institutions can also be explained with the help of game theoretical reflections: Ullmann-Margalit (1977) differentiates between self-maintaining institutions and those requiring supervision. *Self-maintaining norms* are formed wherever participants attain a higher utility level through the creation and observation of institutions than through behavior not mandated through institutions. The compliance with such a norm which proves beneficial for the participants does not have to be controlled, since a divergence itself would cause disadvantages for the actors. Examples for self-maintaining norms are presented through rules of language for interpersonal communication (sentence structure, grammar), money or basic traffic rules such as driving on the right side of the road in continental Europe. On the contrary, conflicts of interest between participants can arise through the creation and expected compliance of institutions requiring supervision. Norms which must be monitored are characterized in that individuals may behave as rational actors, i.e. from these actors' focal perspective, by not respecting the created norms. The creation of standards is a prime example for norms requiring supervisions (see Besen and Saloner, 1988).

The emergence of self-maintaining norms and norms requiring supervision can be explained with the help of game theoretic models. For example, *the creation of self-maintaining games can be modeled as cooperative games*, where all participants can improve their position through group-conforming behavior (see Figure 2.3).

Norms requiring supervision and their creation and compliance can be described with the help of what is known as the prisoner's dilemma (see Axelrod, 1984). *Prisoner's dilemma situations* are characterized by the fact that the actors can choose freely between alternative plans of action and that the constellation of expected action results is designed in such a

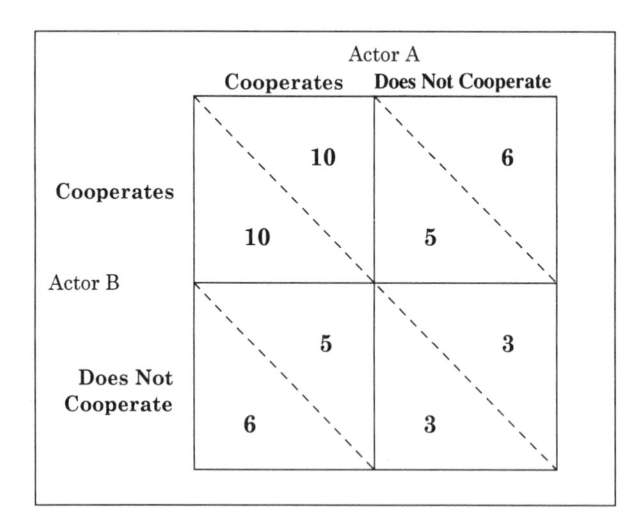

Figure 2.3 *Cooperative game–utility values for alternative actions*

way that the optimal solution will be systematically missed. This happens because each actor tries to maximize his individual results, eventually at other actors' costs. Because every partner anticipates these possible behaviors, cooperation cannot take place. The prisoner's dilemma belongs to the category of non-cooperative games. As a consequence, a final situation is reached bringing about worse results for all participants than there could have been through cooperative behavior. A typical example for the prisoner's dilemma is shown in the following situation: Two thieves are arrested by the police and are separately interrogated. Each thief has the option to either refuse testimony or to admit to the crime, i.e. to tell on his fellow thief. If both of them should refuse testimony, they can each expect a maximum of three years imprisonment. If both testify, they'll each receive a sentence of ten years. If only one of the thieves testifies, he can expect a sentence of one year (principal witness program), whereas the other thief will receive five years imprisonment. Since each thief would assume that his fellow thief would betray him in order to minimize his punishment, the strategy which would be optimal for *both* of them (not testifying and each receiving a three-year sentence) will not be taken. Instead, each thief would testify in an attempt to prevent the other one from improving his own situation at the other's cost. Thus a less than optimal situation will be realized (see Figure 2.4).

The *creation of institutions* such as mutual trust and social norms (e.g., the crooks' honor in the above example) can help in overcoming such

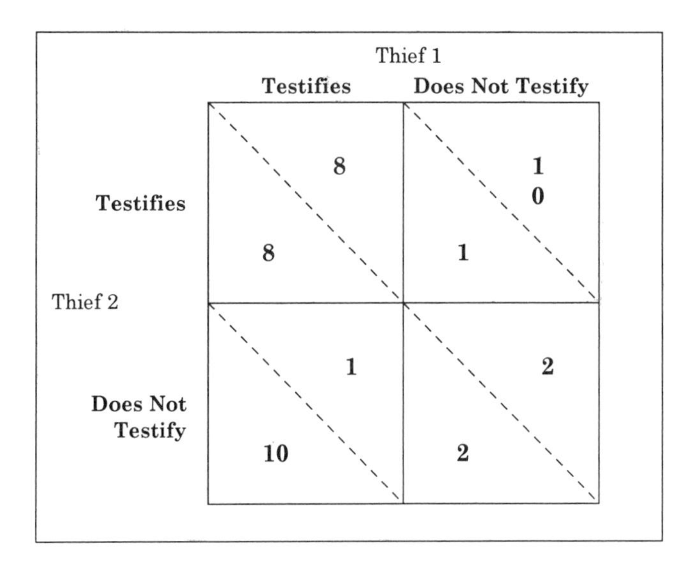

Figure 2.4 *Pay-off matrix for the prisoner's dilemma situation*

prisoner's dilemma situations. The creation of those norms and institutions might possibly constitute a prisoner's dilemma situation itself. In general, it can be said that the creation and observance of norms and rules can also be analyzed from an institutional economic as well as from a game theoretic perspective. At this point, two research branches flow together, namely institutional economics and game theory, both having gained in importance in recent years.

The New Institutional Economics does not present a unified theoretical framework. Rather it is composed of different methodologically-related approaches which are mutually overlapping, complementing and partially based on one other. All institutional economic approaches are characterized by identical assumptions about human behavior in that individual utility maximization, bounded rationality and opportunistic behavior describe and guide the actors' activities. In addition, all institutional economic approaches are based on the research concept of methodological individualism, that means social constructs such as business organizations or government are analyzed and explained from the single individual's perspective and his decisions (see Wolff, 1995; Chapter 3). Included in the list of new institutional economics' theoretical approaches are the *transaction costs theory*, the *property rights theory*, *principal-agent theory*, and in a comprehensive sense, also *economic contract theory*. An overview of these theories is presented in the following section. Their relevance for the determination of corporate boundaries, for the explanation of dissolving corporate boundaries, and for the evolution of new organizational forms will be shown.

Property Rights Theory

Property rights theory, which primarily goes back to Coase (1937); Alchian and Demsetz (1973), is generally presented as an extension of neoclassical theory, but is clearly contrary to the statements and research methods of neoclassical theory. Property rights theory is based principally on four elements:

- behavioral assumption of individual utility maximization;
- existence of property rights;
- existence of transaction costs;
- appearance of external effects.

The *assumption of individual utility maximization* implies that each actor attempts to follow his own goals and to realize his self-interest within the possibilities and restrictions perceived by him and according to his own preferences. In contrast to neoclassical microeconomic theory, which assumes profit maximization as the guiding rule for entrepreneurial activity and utility maximization as the aim of private households, the property rights theory is characterized by less specific objectives of the actors. It is undetermined, which arguments with regard to content are brought into the utility function of the economic subjects. Utility maximization is no longer limited to the attainment of material advantages, but the individual can also maximize his individual utility through altruistic deeds. Hence, the expression of individual utility maximization is not interpreted *ex ante* as negative or positive.

In the core of the *property rights theoretical analysis* are the so-called property rights on goods, especially questions concerning their specification and distribution, including the resulting incentive structure influencing individuals' behaviors. Property rights are connected with a good and attributed to economic subjects on the basis of contracts and legal systems. These property rights have aspects which are related to the object as well as to the person. They define the individual rights in dealing with a good and, in turn, delimit the individual rights on this good between one another. The assignment of property rights creates rights for the beneficiaries and activity restrictions for those individuals having no property rights on the respective good at their disposal. The property rights on a good can be divided into four single rights:

- rights to use a good (*usus*);
- rights to change the form and substance of a good (*abusus*);
- rights to reap the profits resulting from a good, respectively the responsibility to carry the losses resulting from a good (*usus fructus*);
- rights to sell the good to a third party (*right of liquidation*).

These rights can be attributed to a sole individual (meaning completely specified) or can be shared among different individuals (meaning diluted).

Transaction costs arise through the creation, assignment, transfer and implementation of property rights (see Tietzel, 1981, p. 211). They comprise especially costs of information and communication, as well as time and effort spent on the initiation and completion of a service exchange. Transaction costs present the efficiency criteria for the evaluation and choice of different property rights distributions.

External effects arise when all property rights on a good are not held by one individual. In this case, the individual does not feel the full effect of all the negative or positive economic consequences of his resource utilization. As a result, positive or negative external effects arise, meaning side effects on a third party from individual consumption and production activities which are neither compensated for on the market nor accumulated as costs for the individual in another manner. Positive or negative external effects present further efficiency criteria for the evaluation and choice of property rights structures.

From a property rights perspective, the most efficient property rights distribution is the one which *minimizes the sum of transaction costs and the residual loss caused by negative external effects*. The creation of high transaction costs and high negative external effects indicates the necessity of new institutional solutions, leading to a complete specification and to an eventual reallocation of property rights. In accordance, the organizational recommendation of property rights theory is to allocate distribute property rights in such a manner that the most complete bundle of rights is connected with the use of economic resources and attributed to the actor, in order that he receives incentives for responsible and efficient use of resources.

The empirical evidence strongly supports this approach of economic organization theory (see, e.g., Picot, 1981, 1991; Kaulmann, 1987). The essential contribution of property rights theory to questions in business economics is the differentiated view of the business organization. According to *methodological individualism*, this perspective is considered as a multiple person construct and a dynamic nexus of contractual relations. The efficiency effects of various property rights distributions, which have been determined, for example, in the frame of corporate constitutions between shareholders and stakeholders (owners, managers, employees, government) present a central application field for this theory. Aside from an economic analysis of corporate constitutions, the business application of property rights theory comprises the analysis of all decisions leading to a shift of property rights within the corporation. With this, property rights theory can provide valuable recommendations for further internal organization design questions.

For this, a more detailed classification of property rights might be necessary. A corporation's efforts, for example, to decentralize and modularize their internal organizational structures by forming independent task fields through the bundling of competencies and functions, as well as through the delegation of responsibility, can be interpreted as a reallocation of property rights in the form of modified allocation of competencies and resources. A stronger assignment of task-related property rights, that means decision and implementation competencies, to a single area of responsibility leads to a reduction of division of labor and specialization and can increase motivation and responsibility for an efficient task completion (see Chapter 5). The aim of organizational design must be to allocate property rights through organizational rules within the corporation in a manner which optimizes the corporation's efficiency.

The protection and implementation of property rights play an important role for economic activity. To the degree to which an actor can realize personal benefit resulting from his action, his willingness to act increases. This phenomenon is particularly significant for R&D (Research and Development) activities. Various institutional rules exist that guarantee the protection of knowledge, meaning the right to its exploitation, such as copyrights, registered designs or patents. Without these institutions, meant to define property rights on information and facilitate their implementation, an innovative production of knowledge would be inhibited.

Transaction Cost Theory

The fundamental unit for research in *transaction cost theory* (see Coase, 1937; Williamson, 1975, 1985; as well as Picot, 1982a; Picot and Dietl, 1990) is the single transaction, defined as the transfer of property rights. The costs of information and communication resulting from initiation, negotiation, settlement, adaptation and control of a service exchange perceived as fair are called transaction costs. The level of transaction costs depends on specific characteristics of the services to be rendered, on economic actors' behavioral characteristics, and the chosen coordination respectively organization form (see, for example, Picot and Franck, 1993, p. 188). Corporations as integrated constructs based on division of labor have the right to exist only if they are able to solve the coordination problems related to the production processes internally more efficiently than through a completion with external partners on the market. Transaction costs serve as a *measure of efficiency for the evaluation and selection of various institutional arrangements*. Market, hierarchy, and all hybrid forms such as long-term cooperation present possible coordination forms. For the selection of appropriate coordination mechanisms, Williamson developed a transaction cost model which has found widespread acceptance as an *organizational failure framework* (see Figure 2.5).

Essential *elements of the organizational failure framework* include human factors, environmental factors (especially the characteristics of the service to be coordinated), and the transaction atmosphere. Particular transaction problems arise when opportunistically acting economic subjects endowed with bounded rationality enter transaction relations with a high degree of uncertainty and when information and knowledge is asymmetrically distributed among the transaction partners (*information impactedness*). In this case, pure market forms of exchange coordinated over the price mechanism become too transaction cost intense. In order to limit transaction costs, alternative organizational forms guaranteeing

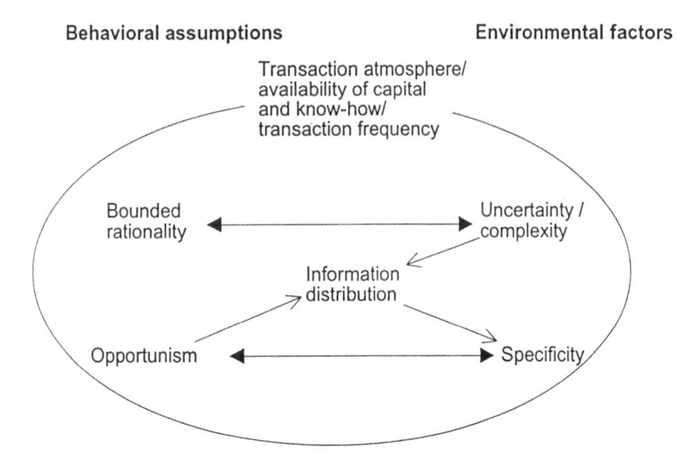

Figure 2.5 *Influence factors on transaction costs. Source: Williamson, 1991. "Comparative Economic Organization: The Analysis of Discrete Structural Alternatives", in Administrative Science Quarterly (1991), 36. Reproduced with permission from Administrative Science Quarterly*

a more intense integration of transaction partners and inhibiting opportunistic behavior have to be implemented, that is, if they don't evolve spontaneously by themselves. Noteworthy in this context are hierarchical corporate structures which, through long-term integration such as incentive, control and sanction systems, can better restrict the possibilities for opportunistic behavior under certain conditions than would be possible with a pure market coordination mechanism. In the scope of transaction cost theory, the task characteristics specificity and uncertainty, the behavioral assumptions of opportunism and bounded rationality, and the possibility of asymmetric information present central influences. From these factors, *specificity is generally regarded as the main influence on the dissolution of corporate boundaries*. A transaction's degree of specificity is relative to the value reduction caused when the input factors are not used for the original purpose, but are used for a second best employment. Thereby the specificity can stem from the requisite know-how, the investments to be made, the location and logistic requirements, certain secrecy and protection needs and/or other characteristics particular to the production process.

Task specificity only becomes a problem in conjunction with the behavioral assumption of *opportunism*. Opportunism implies a tightening of the concept of individual utility maximization. Opportunistic behavior exists when economic subjects do not only behave in a cooperating manner, but often act strategically, by attempting to realize their own interests eventually at others' costs and under disobedience of social norms.

Uncertainty as an environmental factor is expressed in the number and extent to which unforeseeable task modifications occur. In an uncertain environment, the settlement of a contract is complicated through recurrent changes in scheduling, prices, conditions and quantities requiring frequent contract modifications, and hence the acceptance of higher transaction costs.

The uncertainty of environmental conditions only becomes a problem under the assumption of *bounded rationality*. This behavioral assumption is based on the insight provided by Simon (1955), according to which a person wants to act rationally, but is limited in doing so by his restricted information processing capacity and by problems which arise in communicating tacit knowledge.

With the expression *information impactedness*, Williamson describes situations of asymmetric information distribution in which the danger exists that one transaction partner exploits his information lead in an opportunistic manner. This constellation of asymmetric information presents the focal point of the principal agent approach (see pages 42-45).

Aside from these four influence factors and the possibility of information impactedness, three further, less important variables, although having a noteworthy influence on the selection of an efficient coordination form, demand consideration. The *transaction frequency* determines the amortization time and in turn the economic advantage of hierarchic corporate structures or long-term cooperation. Frequently recurring transactions make the creation of internal production capacities or the settlement of long-term cooperation contracts appear more profitable than sporadic exchange relations which should be coordinated over the market.

To a considerable degree, the *transaction atmosphere* also influences the transaction costs of various coordination forms. It comprises all social, legal and technological environments which are relevant for a coordination of services. These include value systems and mutual trust between transaction partners, as well as all underlying technical infrastructures which facilitate the interaction of transaction partners and hence decrease transaction costs. Mutual trust and similar value systems among transaction partners decrease the probability of opportunistic behavior and make transaction cost intense contractual safeguards superfluous. Modern information and communication systems can broaden the possibilities for rational behavior, alter a transaction's degree of specificity, and generally decrease the costs of information transfer. Consequently, trust and efficient information and communication systems foster market or cooperative forms of task completion.

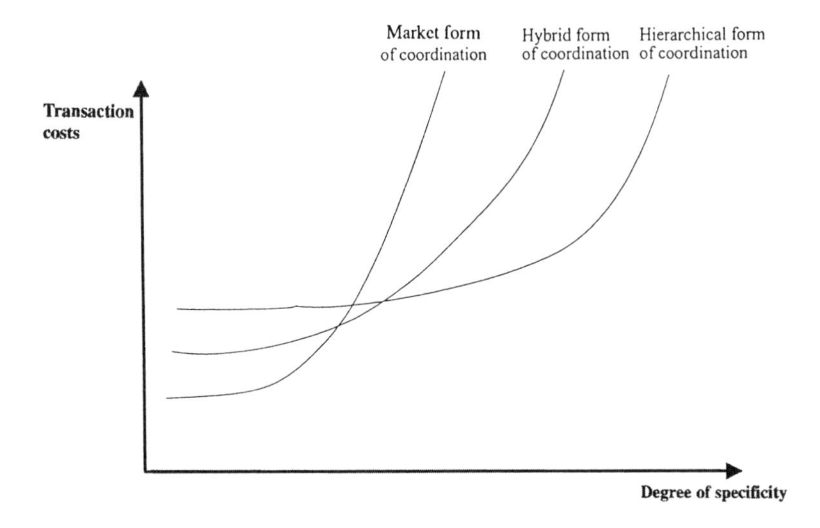

Figure 2.6 *Coordination forms and specificity. Source: Williamson (1975, p. 40) and Michaelis (1985, p. 103). Reproduced by permission from Simon and Schuster.*

The third accompanying variable in the determination of efficient coordination mechanisms is the *availability of know-how and capital.* When a corporation does not possess the required capital and know-how for the internal production of specific and uncertain services and can acquire them only under the acceptance of high transaction costs, then it can not produce internally the respective services. In such a case, it has to enter a long-term cooperation relationship with external partners having the appropriate capital and know-how at their disposal. In Figure 2.6 the respective correlation between the level of transaction costs and the appropriate institutional integration form is illustrated.

Figure 2.6 illustrates how the selection of the efficient coordination form varies with the degree of specificity related to the service to be rendered: for services with a low degree of specificity, markets minimize transaction costs; for services with a high degree of specificity, however, hierarchical coordination forms provide the transaction cost minimal solution, thus the most efficient solution.

The above discussions indicate the existence of a spectrum of a large variety of hybrid forms between market and hierarchy as extreme forms. These hybrid forms unite elements of market as well as hierarchical coordination. They include, for example, long-term cooperation between firms, strategic alliances, joint ventures, franchising systems, licensing to third parties, networks, as well as long-term procurement and sales contracts. In transaction cost theory, more intense research has

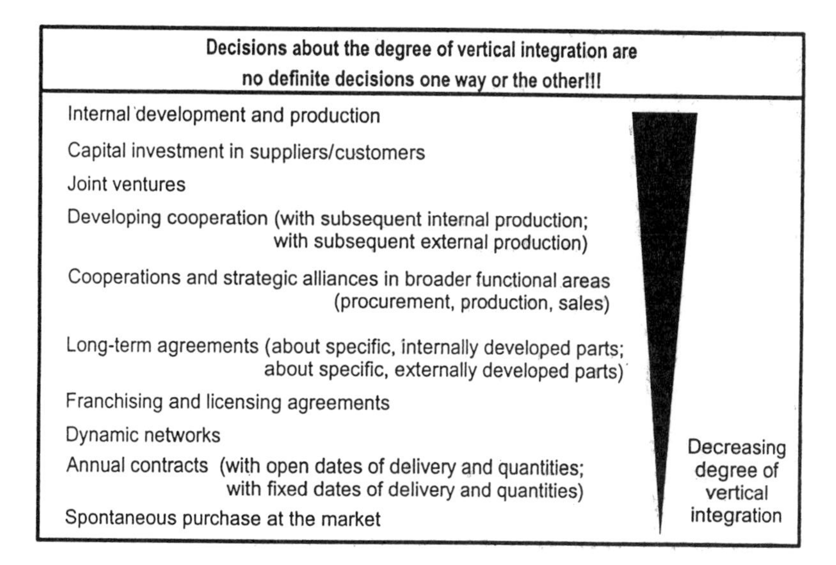

Figure 2.7 *Alternative decisions for the optimal degree of vertical integration (examples)*

only recently been undertaken on these hybrid organizational forms. Through their acknowledgment, it becomes possible to span a continuum of organizational forms between the two extreme poles of pure market coordination with short-term spot-market contracts and the pure hierarchical coordination based on employment contracts for an unlimited period of time. Transaction cost theory helps to select the most efficient organizational form from this continuum relative to a given task. This seemingly simple choice between internal and external production turns out to be a complex optimization assignment within a broad continuum of possibilities (see Figure 2.7).

This *process of transaction cost analysis* is as follows: After having determined an exchange relation's degree of specificity and uncertainty, the coordination form has to be selected which brings about the comparably minimal transaction costs. This selection must be made under the consideration of respective transaction atmosphere, expected transaction frequency, and availability of know-how and capital.

With the help of the theoretical framework of transaction costs, both the emergence of corporations (see Coase, 1937), as well as the observable phenomenon of blurring and even dissolving corporate boundaries can be explained (see the discussion in Chapter 6).

Also for the questions concerning the internal organizational design (see Chapter 5 for more on decentralization and modularization) or the physically decentralized, interorganizational completion of tasks, which could not be possible without transaction cost decreasing information and communication systems (see Chapter 8 on virtual corporations), valuable suggestions for design can be derived from transaction cost theory. For this purpose, the term specificity should be eventually further refined. Specificity could be further classified as technical specificity and specificity of infrastructure and with that, the decentralization of internal corporate structures could be analyzed (see Picot, 1990).

Principal-Agent Theory

The *principal-agent theory* (see Jensen and Meckling, 1976; Pratt and Zeckhauser, 1985; Ross, 1973; and Wenger and Terberger, 1988) deals with the principal-agent relation based on the division of labor, characterized through asymmetrically distributed information and through uncertainty about the occurrence of certain environmental situations as well as the contract partner's behavior. Principal-agent relations are entered into when one party (principal) delegates decision and implementation competencies to another party (agent). In a principal-agent relation, the agent makes decisions which not only have an impact on his own welfare, but also influence the utility level of his principal (see, for example Wenger and Terberger, 1988, p. 506). The agent is the informed partner. Principal-agent theory studies the contract underlying this relation, respectively the metaphor of an underlying contract, if not explicit between the parties. Hence, the contract between principal and agent forms the central unit of analysis and the principal-agent approach focuses on the determination of the optimal contractual design required to steer and control the principal-agent relation.

Important elements of principal-agent theory include the principal-agent relation, the agency costs, the typology of informational asymmetries, and the determination of appropriate institutional integration forms as possibilities for the organizational design of principal-agent relations.

Principal-agent relations exist, for example, between owner and manager, between supervisory board and board of director, and also between doctor and patient, student and professor, or between auctioneer and auction participants. Whoever holds the position of the principal, respectively of the agent, meaning who is the "poorly-" or "well-" informed transaction partner, can only be judged according to the particular situation: For example, a doctor employed by a hospital holds the agent position relative to the patients, to the hospital board, and to the health insurance. He finds himself in an agent relation with several people and institutions. In addition, however, he can also hold the position of the principal, for example, in relation to his assistants or to his tax consultant. Organizations such as corporations can be interpreted as a nexus of principal-agent relations. Principal-agent theory can therefore be considered as a theory of the internal relations of an institution.

This does not mean that principal-agent theory can only explain events occurring internally in a corporation. Its scope of explanation also comprises interorganizational structures, such as symbiotic arrangements, when one considers the cooperation contract as an institution and studies the inner relation of this cross-corporate institution. In recent years, principal-agent theory has been increasingly applied to cooperation and alliances between legally and economically independent corporations (see, for example, Reichwald and Rupprecht, 1992).

If complete information could be obtained at no charge by all participants, principal-agent problems would not exist in this world of complete information and certainty. Since all future environmental situations and partners' possible reactions could be specified *ex ante* in a contract, the so-called first-best solution could always be achieved in each cooperative relation based on division of labour. None of the partners would have leeway for behavior not in conformance with his contractual obligations without the other partner knowing how to prevent such behavior. In reality, however, a partner's knowledge in a contract relationship is incomplete and unequally distributed between the actors. In addition, the search for further information to support and improve decision-making generates costs. As a result of the incompleteness and unequal distribution of information, the agent's discretional scopes of action are broadened, which he can use to his own advantage. As a consequence, deviations from the first-best solution described above occur and with this, so-called *agency costs* arise, which measure the difference between the first-best solution under complete information and the second-best solution under asymmetric information (see Spremann, 1988, p. 617).

Agency costs comprise (according to Jensen and Meckling, 1976, p. 308) the principal's costs of monitoring and control, the agent's guarantee costs, as well as the remaining welfare loss (residual loss). Trade-off relations exist between these three types of costs. The residual loss can be limited, for example, through increased efforts in monitoring and control, whereas the latter again can be reduced through credible guarantees by the agent. Principal-agent theory contributes to the explanation (positive analysis) as well as to the design (normative analysis) of principal agent relations. It recommends that institutional arrangement for the settlement of a service relation which minimizes agency costs. Agency costs present the efficiency criterion in principal-agent theory. An important role is played by the classification of the principal-agent relation under analysis according to the underlying *information asymmetry between principal and agent.* As a rule it is assumed that the information asymmetry exists to the principal's disadvantage, implying the agent's possession of an information advantage. With respect to the sources of an information asymmetry, three different problem types are distinguished: hidden characteristics, hidden action and hidden intention.

Hidden characteristics exist before the contract is signed. The problem stems from the fact that an agent's characteristics or those of the services offered by him are *ex ante* unknown to the principal. The danger resulting from hidden characteristics is manifested in the possible selection of unfavorable contract partners (*adverse selection*). This problem is most probable in the employment of new co-workers or in the relation between creditor and debtor.

In contrast, the problem of *hidden action* only arises after the contract has been signed, meaning after a successful contract partner selection. Hidden action implies that the principal is not able to observe the agent's actions or, despite his ability to observe the agent's actions, he lacks the expert knowledge required to adequately evaluate them. The danger of *moral hazard* resulting from this hidden action involves the possibility of an agent opportunistically exploiting his scope of action and not behaving in accordance with the principal's interest, for example by employing less care and/or effort than required.

In the case of *hidden intention*, the principal has already brought preservices in the form of sunk costs. Through this specific investment in the transaction relation, the principal becomes dependent upon the agent after signing the contract, since he now needs the particular services. This danger of opportunistic exploitation of existing dependencies is characterized as "hold up". The correlation between principal-agent theory and transaction cost theory becomes apparent in the hold up situation: in both cases, the investment specificity is the source of the problem.

Principal-agent theory provides concrete design recommendations for managing problems which stem from asymmetrical information distribution. For the design of institutional integration forms, suggestions are derived based on the informational asymmetry underlying the principal-agent relation. As an example, for avoiding adverse selection problems, it suggests the implementation of signaling or screening mechanisms or the design of self-selection situations. *Signaling* means that the agent signals his qualities, consequently the qualities of his services, to the principal in the attempt to enter into a principal-agent relation. Letters of reference or diplomas may have such a signaling function for the potential agent. In contrast, *screening* implies that the principal takes the initiative to search for further external information in regard to the qualities of the agent, with respect to the services offered by him. The use of employment tests or requests through credit inquiry agencies serve as examples for screening activities. *Self-selection* takes place when the agent is confronted with a situation which has been designed by the principal so that the agent's decision gives valuable insight into the qualities of his personality or services. For example, the principal could demand an unusually long guarantee period for the agent's services. Agents supplying products of inferior quality would shy away from a contract under these conditions. In order to limit the danger of moral hazard, principal-agent theory recommends the design of *information and control systems to monitor* the agent (e.g. budget systems, report systems, management by objectives, boards and other control organs—see Eisenhardt, 1989, p. 61; Picot, 1989b) or of *profit sharing systems dependent on performance*, with the goal of reaching *an alignment of interests* between principal and agent. To manage hold up related problems, the assignment of ownership on unique and withdrawable resources is recommended, for example through means of vertical integration, the settlement of long-term supply and service contracts, or the creation of mutual dependencies through safeguards (hostage exchange) (see, for example, Spremann, 1990, p. 563). A clear, stable attribution of institutional integration forms to certain information asymmetries, however, is hardly possible (Spremann, 1990, p. 577). Since the above described information asymmetries also often arise simultaneously in the practical business world, an efficient solution of the problems resulting from asymmetric information will in many cases be possible only through a combination of different institutional integration forms.

Important business applications of principal-agent theory can be found in the field of design of incentive systems as well as information and communication systems, which gain in importance, for example, in the internal decentralization of organizations in the frame of task and modularization (see Chapter 5) or in physically distributed task completion in the frame of the virtual corporation concept. Especially through physically decentralized task completion (telecooperation, telework) information asymmetries between principal and agent, in particular the problem of hidden action, drastically increase (see Chapter 8). Further fields of application present questions related to vertical integration, governmental regulation and determination of internal transfer prices and so on (see Eisenhardt, 1989, p. 59).

Contract Theory

"A contract in the economic sense is any explicit or implicit binding agreement concerning the exchange of goods and services between people, who agree on this arrangement because they expect an improvement of their situation." (Wolff, 1995, p. 38, translation by author; see also Milgrom and Roberts, 1992, p. 127). The design of efficient contracts is a central issue in contract theory. One can distinguish between different branches of contract theory. The *economic* contract theory considers legal-sociological aspects of different types of contracts and their possible application fields (e.g. MacNeil, 1978; Schanze, 1991), as well as the contract theoretical movements within the New Institutional Economics, in particular Williamson's extension of transaction cost theory through contract theoretical aspects (see Williamson, 1985, p. 77, and Hart, 1995) and the principal-agent theory. Aside from the formally oriented economic contract theory in this concentrated sense, *constitutional contract theory* forms the second branch of this research direction, which has further developed the thoughts of Hobbes, Locke, Rousseau and Kant to the social contract supporting the formation of government and has put it on an economic foundation (see in particular Buchanan, 1984; Nozick, 1974; and Rawls, 1979). Both branches of contract theory can be integrated and enable a comprehensive organizational analysis founded on contract theory (see Wolff, 1995).

In the context of contract theory *various typologies of contract* have been developed. For example, the American legal sociologist MacNeil has developed a classification of different contract types which, since its reception through Williamson in the framework of transaction cost theory, has gained widespread acceptance (see, for example, Picot and Dietl, 1993). MacNeil categorizes classical, neoclassical and relational contracts.

Classical contracts are characterized through the synchronous occurrence of service and service in return, in accordance with the traditional legal understanding of a contract. The contract partner's identity is not important, whereby neither preceding nor subsequent relations exist. This orientation to a point in time underlying classical contract relations can be maintained even then, when service and service in return occur at different points in time, but can be clearly foreseen in the moment of closing the contract and can be determined in the contract, that means, can be visualized in the presence, under consideration of all possible environmental situations. Classical contracts are usually related to standardized goods and are closed for the purpose of a short-term services exchange between anonymous contract partners. Service and service in return are specified *ex ante* in the contract. Spot-market exchanges are very similar to the ideal of classical contracts. Another everyday example for a classical contract is buying gas at a filling station. Disagreements arising during the settlement of classical contracts are decided based on formal criteria, where neither personality nor future interests of the contract partners are considered.

Neoclassical contracts, in contrast, relate to a fixed time period. Although the contract relation is restricted by time, it exists over a longer period of time. For this reason, it is no longer possible to contractually determine all eventualities at the point of the contract's closure. Hence, neoclassical contracts remain partially incomplete. When disagreements arise between contract partners during the settlement of a contract, a third party can be involved in this bilateral exchange relationship as a mediator (specialist, court of arbitration). Supply contracts with a supplier over several years or a rental contract are examples of neoclassical contracts. Also, long-term cooperations between firms can be founded on neoclassical contracts.

Relational, long-term contracts differ fundamentally from classical and neoclassical contracts. Whereas classical and neoclassical contracts are based on explicit arrangements which are as contractually defined as possible, these arrangements are replaced in relational contract law to a high degree through implicit agreements which are primarily based on mutual trust. The contract partners' identities as well as the developed quality of their mutual relations play a dominant role: the exchange relationship evolving over time, the common value systems, the mutual trust and the solidarity between the contract partners gain in importance for the relational contract's closure and its settlement according to the agreement. Relational contracts underlie most employee-employer relations and also particularly intense cooperation agreements between firms. An efficient elimination of disagreements, not detrimental for the relationship, can only occur through the participants themselves. The involvement of a third party, be it as judge or as mediator, is seldom helpful and as a rule impossible, since the purpose of relational contracts is in general too specific to be described or even verified by a third party.

With his concept of *symbiotic contracts*, Schanze (1991) develops an extension of the idea of relational contracts. With this term he describes long-term contracts with specific ties, which are manifested in one-sided and consequently especially critical dependencies and intensive relations between the partners. Successful symbiotic contracts are characterized through sophisticated incentive schemes, which are especially effective for the selection and control of the contract partner (Schanze, 1991, p. 69). Schanze names franchising agreements or specially designed joint ventures as examples of symbiotic contracts.

A further important classification of contract types presents the distinction between *complete and incomplete contracts*. When contract partners desire to write a complete contract, their capacity to predict events and to process information will be seriously challenged in many cases (especially in long-term contracts): the contract partners would have to anticipate all future environmental situations relevant to the result of their exchange relationship even while writing the contract. In addition, they would have to specify beforehand the measures to be taken and the distribution of activity gains for any possible future environmental situation. These conditions are so restrictive that they cannot be fulfilled in many cases. Therefore, many business relations are arranged through incomplete contracts, that are more able to take into account the actors' bounded rationality in many complex, economic transactions reaching far into the future. In addition, they reduce information and communication costs compared with complete contracts:

> "The recent development of the theory of incomplete contracting is a concession to the unfeasibility of comprehensive *ex ante* contracting. Although frequently unexpressed, bounded rationality has become the operative behavioral assumption out of which the economics of contracting increasingly works." (*Williamson, 1990, p. 11*)

An incomplete contract, however, opens the door for a larger scope of undefined behavior, and this can be opportunistically exploited. Precautions against opportunistic behavior have to be taken in incomplete contracts through a careful selection of contract partners and appropriate protection mechanisms (e.g., through signaling and screening of contract partners or hostage exchange). Thereby, aside from protection mechanisms against opportunistic behavior, incentive mechanisms should be implemented, which channel the interest of the single contract partner in such a way that by working for his own interests he simultaneously maximizes the total interest of all participants to the contract. Only an incomplete contract which is safeguarded against opportunistic behavior and provided with positive incentive mechanisms is also efficient. Typical examples of incomplete contracts are employment contracts and long-term cooperation contracts (see Wolff, 1995).

Links can be established between the typology of contracts according to MacNeil and Schanze on the other hand, and the distinction in complete and incomplete contracts on the other hand: generally classical contracts strive for completeness; neoclassical and relational contracts, as well as Schanze's symbiotic contracts, can be usually attributed to the category of incomplete contracts.

A further important distinction exists between *explicit and implicit contracts*. Explicit contracts, meaning those which are exactly specified and documented, are in many cases (especially with specific investments and a high degree of environmental uncertainty) not at all or only possible under the acceptance of very high transaction costs, because of the actors' bounded rationality. Essential contract contents often escape the contract partners' constructive design intention. For this reason, contract partners often have to rely on informal and legally nonsanctionable practices, similar to contracts, resulting in the closure of implicit contracts. Such implicit contracts can contain, for example, a reputation mechanism (see Wagner, 1994, p. 13): that partner, on whose services other partners are dependent, obtains a premium in addition to the price for his services, which rewards his good behavior, meaning the renunciation of exploitation. If the dominant partner exploits his opportunistic scope of action, the premium is no longer paid. Hence, implicit contracts are based on the compliance to certain implicit rules and norms, which are known to the contract parties, but cannot/should not be fixed in writing. In particular they take into account the evolutionary element in the business world. If one establishes connections to the contract types discussed above, it is seen that classical and neoclassical contracts are primarily explicit contracts, whereas relational and symbiotic contracts have in the main an implicit character.

According to contract theoretic interpretation, market and hierarchy do not present two essentially different organizational forms (see Wolff, 1995, p. 33). Both coordination mechanisms are based on contracts. Contracts form the foundation for market (buying and selling contracts), hierarchical (employment contracts), and hybrid coordination forms (cooperation, franchising, licensing contracts). Hence, different types of contract form the foundation of all organizational forms. All economic production and exchange processes are organized through contracts. Contracts are the instruments and the means for the organization of exchange relations based on the division of labor. From the perspective of contract theory, each organizational form for the completion of tasks based on the division of labor is considered as a nexus of contracts. *The corporation is interpreted as a nexus of internal, long-term bilateral contracts* (see Aoki et al, 1990) between economically dependent individuals. This nexus of contracts representing and constituting the corporation can be modeled for theoretical analysis in two ways. First, it can be assumed that every employee signs a contract directly with the owner and closes subcontracts with the other co-workers to form a coalition. Second, the corporation can be modeled in such a manner, as if every co-worker would enter an explicit or implicit contractual relation with his co-workers (see Crémer, 1990; Wolff, 1995). Markets can be analogously considered as nexuses of short-term contracts between economically and legally independent economic units, whereas for example cooperations and strategic alliances can be interpreted as nexuses of mid-term to long-term contracts between legally independent, yet economically partially dependent partners (see Figure 2.8).

The appropriate contract type to be chosen is dependent on the task to be completed. "Interfirm contracting is well suited for some transactions; intra-firm contracting is well suited for others. Hybrid modes are

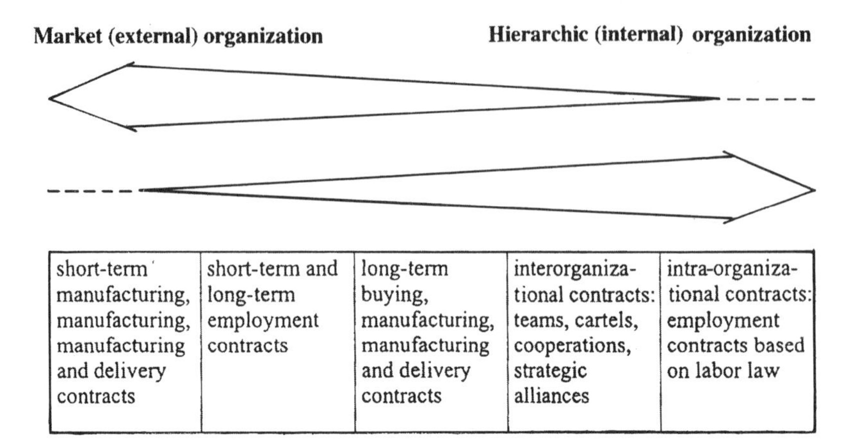

short-term manufacturing, manufacturing, manufacturing and delivery contracts	short-term and long-term employment contracts	long-term buying, manufacturing, manufacturing and delivery contracts	interorganizational contracts: teams, cartels, cooperations, strategic alliances	intra-organizational contracts: employment contracts based on labor law

Figure 2.8 *Contractual forms of organizing partial tasks*

superior in still others." (Williamson, 1990, p. 8). These contracts constituting organizations will be incomplete in many cases due to the actors' bounded rationality and the uncertainty of future environmental situations, meaning that not all future transaction relations, environmental situations and reactions of the partners will be comprised. The consideration of all these future parameters in the contract, implying the completion of a complete contract, would either be impossible due to the actors' limits of rationality or require too much effort in an economic sense. Incomplete contracts, however, open the door for the opportunistic exploitation of existing behavioral scopes, for which safeguards through efficient contract design have to be implemented.

It has been shown that all approaches presented in this section are closely related to one another. Only the perspective of analysis distinguishes property rights, transaction cost, principal-agent, and contract theory. The common theoretical framework, however, which they fill out together, is presented through the New Institutional Economics.

CHANGES IN THE MARKET AND CORPORATE BOUNDARIES THROUGH IMPROVEMENTS OF INFORMATION AND COMMUNICATION POSSIBILITIES

The preceding reflections include several important consequences for the further contemplation of coordination forms of economic activities. From a theoretical perspective, the fundamental significance of information and communication for economic activity became apparent. On the one hand, a growing degree of division of labour and specialization increases the requirements for coordination and hence transaction costs, which essentially represent costs of information search and processing. This is valid analogously for the service exchange in corporations (see Chapter 5). On the other hand, market activity itself is based, as has been shown, on the unequal distribution of information between economic actors. Entrepreneurial resourcefulness, driving the market process, is based on the realization and the exploitation of economically relevant information asymmetries. Entrepreneurial ideas and resourcefulness are aspects of human capacities and behaviors. The way in which economic activity takes place and is coordinated, including entrepreneurial action, is not determined *ex ante* and in itself presents a phenomenon worthy of explanation.

Economic reality shows that there exist a *variety of different forms for the organization of economic activity*. Market and hierarchic completion mechanisms represent only the extreme forms on a continuum of hybrid coordination forms (e.g. long-term contracts, cooperations). Depending on various factors, economic activities are at times organized in a way similar to markets and at other times as if within a corporation. Because of the central importance of information and communication aspects for the development and coordination of economic activities, it seems plausible that changed conditions in information search and processing as well as in forms of communication, let changes in economically efficient coordination mechanisms be expected. New information and communication potentials also let new configurations of processes based on the division of labor be expected (see Chapter 5). They enable different scopes of action for the design of innovative organizational forms (see Chapter 9).

At this point, the conditions under which coordination forms appear more efficient shall not be analyzed, but it shall be expressed that these changes have an impact on existing coordination structures. An improvement of information and communication possibilities leads to a *modification of previously appropriate coordination forms*. Scopes and limits of markets and corporations as typical coordination forms change under the influence of new information and communication possibilities.

New information and communication possibilities, however, are not the sole reason for these changes. First, due to faster and less expensive space and time bridging message transfer and information processing, certain new information and communication technologies enable new organizational forms which might have been desired before, but could not be realized. Examples for this are the integration possibilities of cross-corporate data streams through innovative communication technologies such as *Electronic Data Interchange (EDI)*. Thereby, new possibilities of inter-firm cooperation arise, for example in the form of just-in-time (JIT) cooperations or strategic networks. On the one hand, these developments have an immediate impact on the change of classical corporate boundaries. Organizational change is, to a certain measure, technically induced (see Picot, Ripperger and Wolff, 1996). On the other hand, a more intense competition for scarce resources and buying decisions, which can be observed in many fields of the economy, produces a pressure to adjust to efficiency increasing information and communication technologies between single corporations, and between regional centers of economic activity. In this case, the organizational pressure to adapt is induced by competition. New information and communication techniques are the instruments with which the necessary organizational change is completed.

New information and communication technologies result fundamentally from various further technological developments. The immense increase in performance potential of hardware and software systems enables the transfer and processing of an ever-growing data volume, which above all can eliminate bottlenecks in cross-corporate communication relations. The design and standardization of integrative interface agreements in the economic world is spreading. Thereby, new possibilities arise for hardware and software neutral interaction between application systems of different corporations and regions. The integration of data streams and data elements is no longer limited to the internal core of the firm, but increasingly includes the cross-corporate field (see, for example, Mertens, 1985). At the same time, integration efforts can be noticed, which comprise various levels of information processing and data transfer. For example, in multi-media systems, image and sound information as well as data can be integrated in a common presentation and processing form. In turn, new forms of intercorporate communication relations ensue. Finally, the quantitative and qualitative expansion of public and private telecommunication infrastructures provides for faster and simultaneously less expensive data transfer. For example, on the basis of ISDN networks or through the realization of so-called information highways, tremendous volumes of data can be transported. To summarize, new information and communication possibilities manifest themselves in qualitatively improved, faster and less costly transfer and processing forms. As a result, a variety of individual competitive advantages arises. Figure 2.9 shows in an exemplary manner advantageous application possibilities of Electronic Data Interchange in the corporate value chain.

It is indisputable that new information and communication technologies have implications for all areas in the creation of corporate value. The effects on the efficiency of economic coordination forms can be presented in the paradigm of transaction cost theory as shown in Figure 2.10.

Activity	Partners	EDI applications
Corporate Infrastructure: Management, Planning, Finance, Accounting, Legal questions, Organization, Electronic Data Processing	Banks, customers, suppliers, trade, postal services, tax offices	Quick data and document exchange, quick decisions, changed management demands, automated handling of payments, cash-management, FEDI, JIT-information, electronic billing and payment services, tax filings, exchange of booking data, outsourcing Contract design using EDI Changes in organization structure and processes Decisions concerning standards, services, integration of internal application systems, access rights
Human Resources Management	Banks, insurance companies	Electronic transfer of salary payments and social security contributions, Electronic exchange of social security data Occupational retraining, qualification, layoffs, hiring
Research and Development	Suppliers, customers, designers	Exchange of development guidelines and design data Research and development cooperation International development projects, simultaneous engineering
Procurement	Suppliers	Electronic ordering, electronic offers Electronic supplier markets, electronic processing of procurement transactions Global procurement conceptions

Inbound Logistics	Operations	Outbound Logistics	Marketing	Customer Service
Suppliers, shipping agents logistics services	Suppliers, customers	Customers, trade, shipping agents, customs clearing services	Customers, trade, suppliers	Customers
Transfer of transport and inventory data, outsourcing of warehouse keeping, quality control, elimination of receiving inspection, electronic tracking of forwarding agents, JIT-connections	Exchange of relevant production data, reduction of production depth, lean production, concentration of strategically important tasks	Faster information about freight and location Outsourcing of warehousing quality control	Transfer of sales data, product data, prices, offers, ordering data, customer information systems, advertising, eletronic supply markets	Transfer of help desk information, miminization of defects and errors, improv-ed and expanded customer service, telediagnosis, reinforcement of the information component

Figure 2.9 *EDI-based value chain and task accomplishment. Based on Neuburger, Rahild (1994)*

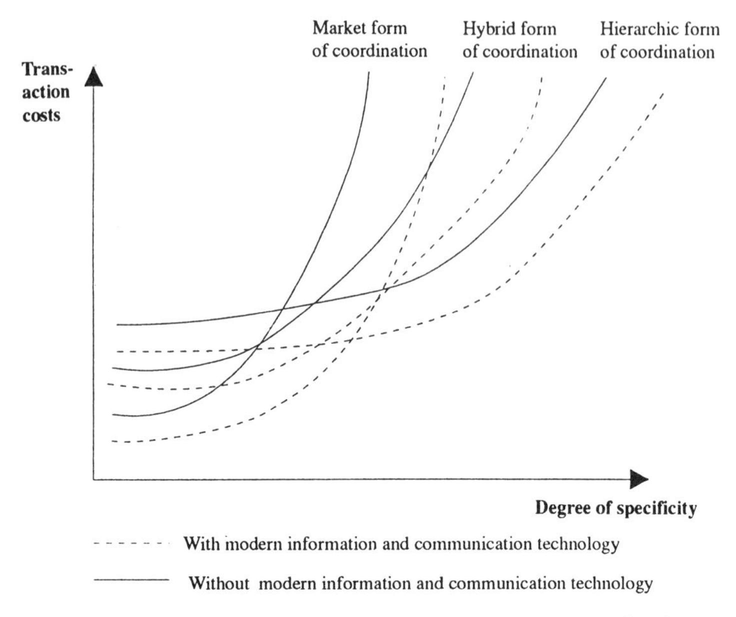

Figure 2.10 *Influence of information and communication technology on transaction costs. Source: Picot and Reichwald (1994)*

Figure 2.10 shows again, that services with a low degree of specificity can be principally more efficiently coordinated over the market, highly specific services should be coordinated by hierarchical coordination forms, and services with a medium degree of specificity by hybrid forms (see pages 37–42). The implementation of new information and communication technologies tends to lead to decreases in transaction costs. Thereby, the curves in the figure shift downwards, as the graph with the dotted line shows (see Picot, Ripperger and Wolff, 1996, p. 69). If one regards the graph of each transaction cost minimizing coordination form, one can see that the transitions to the next hierarchical coordination form have shifted to the right. In other words, the change from a market to a hybrid, and in turn respectively from a hybrid to a hierarchical coordination form only pays off with a higher degree of specificity than with the old technology.

As a tendency, these changes lead to the phenomenon that task completions previously related with high information and communication problems have to be completed less and less in the internal area of the corporation or at a common location, and that production cost and transaction cost efficient, *physically distributed solutions and coordination forms* closer to the market can be increasingly implemented. Figure 2.10 illustrates this fact. Inter-firm information and communication technologies decrease arising transaction costs with given information and communication problems. Hence, within a certain scope of coordination problems, the efficient completion of tasks shifts to more market-like, that is cross-corporate coordination, forms.

IMPLICATIONS FOR MANAGEMENT

It becomes increasingly difficult to identify corporations as relatively closed, integrated constructs (see Picot and Reichwald, 1994). The interfaces between corporations and markets, the clear separation between internal and external, disappear. Instead, coordination forms between corporations and markets, such as network organizations, cooperative ventures, virtual organizations or telecooperative undertakings, are becoming increasingly popular. They are the results of reactions to new market and competitive situations and of new information and communication technologies.

These factors lead in many cases to the *deterioration of previously typical foundations of entrepreneurial activity*. Rather stable production technologies, rather permanent organizational forms and governance structures shift towards more flexible forms, which can be quickly adapted to new situations. A global orientation replaces clear, regional business activities. With this, the institutional conditions confronting corporations change also, which as a rule presented hitherto stable and clear foundations for entrepreneurial activity (see, e.g., Wolff, 1996). Through close-knit business and communicative nets, as well as through the institutionalization of business activities, corporations are increasingly confronted with a wide variety of new institutional situations. Organizational and governmental structures no longer require adaptation to rather uniform cultural situations and behavioral patterns, but require the consideration of individual, corporation or region-specific cultural and behavioral characteristics. The close dovetailing of firms, for example within cooperative ventures, requires corresponding adaptations, and translating mechanisms for behavioral patterns and cultural properties. Changing market and competition conditions, as well as new information and communication possibilities, lead not only to basic redefinitions of corporate boundaries, but also revolutionize previously successful foundations of entrepreneurial activity.

New information and communication technologies lead to a fundamental change in the exogenous and endogenous parameters of entrepreneurial decisions. These changes, however, do not occur accidentally and arbitrarily, even if they may surprise the single individual, but follow a basic system, the theory of which has been explained in this chapter.

3
Fundamental Information and Communication Models: Insights into Communication and Information Behavior

FUNCTIONS OF INFORMATION AND COMMUNICATION MODELS

Information and communication are essential for human existence. The increasing variety of information and communication forms and media in both the business and the private world document their growing significance. In order to fully understand these advancements, it makes sense to explain the various principles of information and communication with the help of theoretical models.

Information and communication models are valuable tools for the interpretation and design of entrepreneurial behaviors and structures. An interesting fact is that information and communication behavior was modeled long after other economic phenomena. One reason for this is the relatively late acknowledgment of information as a production factor. Considering that production factors such as land, labor and capital have long been studied and their influence on economic activity has been determined, the construction of models describing information and communication phenomena is relatively new.

Information and communication can be considered in various contexts: they promote interpersonal understanding (page 57) and are associated with various behavioral options, restrictions and problems (page 73). In addition, information is a good which—similar to other goods—must be produced and nurtured (page 86). A variety of theories and models have been introduced focusing on these particular aspects. These theories identify diverse key factors which influence the quality of actions and institutions associated with information and communication and in turn, are decisive in overcoming information and communication barriers. This chapter discusses the complexity of communication barriers and the necessity for considering not only one, but several approaches in overcoming practical information and communication problems.

The final section of this chapter (page 92) demonstrates that the various approaches in modeling communication processes have very dissimilar traditions, resulting in different perspectives. These differences exist in the theoretical as well as in the practical world. As a result, a standard communication model does not exist. Specific model features, which are relevant to the particular explanation and design problem, can be singled out and then combined with aspects from other models. In this manner, communication barriers can be identified and ultimately overcome.

New information and communication technologies provide more freedom in establishing and arranging information and communication relations, and in particular creating unique alternatives for cross-corporate relations.

At the same time, certain typical communication problems may become more serious or new ones may arise. Models designed to explain communication processes can aid in identifying and reducing those barriers which hinder a firm from overcoming its own communication barriers, and in turn, its organizational boundaries. The same holds true for models for information behavior, coordination, and information production.

COMMUNICATION MODELS

It is necessary to define the *object of communication processes* and to present the prevailing description of communication. An example depicts this definition problem: When one person tells another to "go jump in the lake" and the other actually does it, then a communication process has obviously occurred between the two actors. If the second person, however, is pushed into the lake by the first, one could hardly attribute the fact that the second is sitting in the water to a communication process between the two actors. What is the difference between an induced action (being pushed) and a spoken message (being told to)?

In the former case, an unavoidable cause and effect relation exists. In the latter case, the message receiver can estimate the probability of potential reactions to his possible resistance. With communication, the receiver of a message has the freedom of choice between alternative actions, and, respectively, reactions. One needs to distinguish here between signals and other causes of actions, in that a signal must be able to cause various reactions, which themselves again may serve as signals. With this, signals bring about other signals in an endless chain of feedback. A signal not only causes a single reaction-signal, but an unlimited variety of possible reaction-signals (see Gallie, 1952). A simple push does not present a process of communication, since falling into the lake does not present a reaction signal, but is plainly the physical consequence of the push.

Levels of Semiotics

Semiotics is known as the scientific research of the objects and functions of communication processes (see, for example, Eco, 1977). Semiotics differentiates three different communication levels: *syntactic* as the analysis of individual signals and relationships among signals; *semantic* as the analysis of relations between signals and their meaning; and *pragmatic* as the analysis of effects of signals on their users, and respectively receivers.

The communication process can be illustrated through a simple example. A professor says to one of her students: "If your upcoming presentation is not significantly better than your last one, then I will have my doubts concerning your grade in this class." At the syntactic level, accurate transmission of her words must be questioned. Is the student able to hear clearly what the professor says, or is this process influenced, for example, by the professor's unclear speech or through disturbing noises? The question at the semantic level is whether or not the student correctly interprets his professor's words, for example, whether he realizes that the words "have my doubts" imply a bad grade. The pragmatic level deals with the professor's intention in saying these words as well as with the student's reaction. He may work harder, as the professor had planned, or he may become so frustrated that he gives up.

The three levels of analysis cannot be independently examined, in fact, they overlap and build upon each other. All three levels deal with signals, their relations, and rules. The pragmatic level presents the most comprehensive analysis level. At this level, all personal-psychological and constitutional factors distinguishing one communication event from another are taken into consideration. In addition, intentions and practical consequences related to the communication process are analyzed. Thus, this level presents the foundation for the description of different communication models. Figure 3.1 illustrates the different levels of analysis in a communication process.

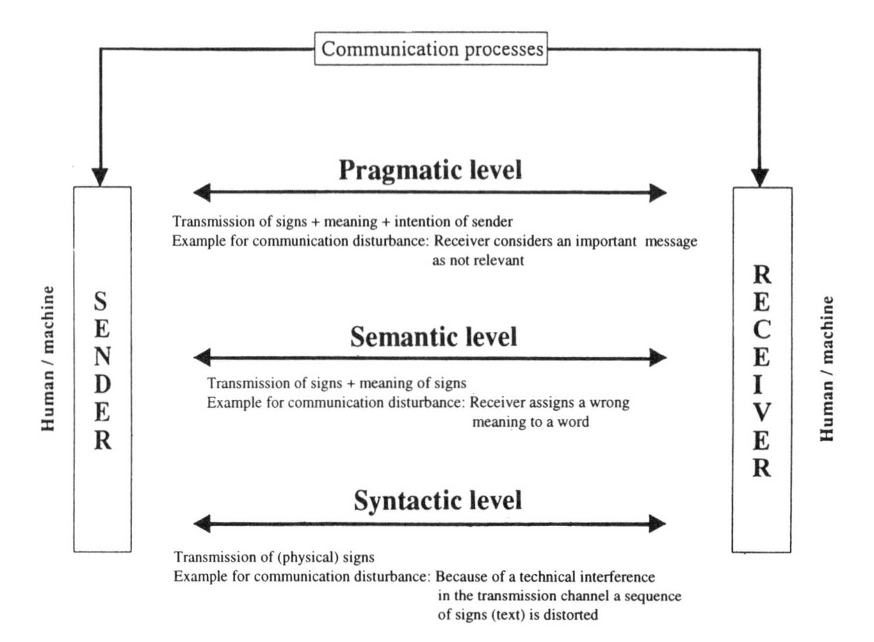

Figure 3.1 *Analysis levels of information transmission. Source: Reichwald (1993a, p. 451)*

Communication processes are often associated with various terms such as *signal*, *sign*, *message*, or *information*. In respect to the semiotic levels, these terms can be differentiated to clearly demonstrate their role within communication processes.

Signals or signs are the observed objects at the *syntactic level*. This level focuses on the relation between signs and signals, as well as on the formal rules determining their structure. These terms are not associated with meanings or interpretations. They are used only to describe problems of correct and complete transmission or to analyze the composition of sign combinations (grammar).

The relations between signs and their so-called designata are described at the *semantic level*. Signs always refer to some types of objects, events or situations. Each sign's meaning stems from the user. When both sender and receiver attribute an identical meaning to the transmitted signs, that means, if a semantic agreement exists, one can speak of a message.

The effect of messages, however, is discussed at the *pragmatic level*. This level illuminates the intended and the actual consequences and effects of a transmitted message. In linking a sign's meaning with its consequences for action, a message turns into information. In this framework, *information can be interpreted as purpose-oriented knowledge*. Using this definition it becomes clear that information triggers action.

Using this three level model, information can also be differentiated from data. The essential criteria for this distinction are their differences in relation to context and purpose. *Data* represent meanings which are not directly applicable to a purpose. *Information*, in contrast, is relevant for certain actions. Thus, data are closely related to *messages*. Yet, in comparison, the term data is more narrowly defined. Data is typically referred to in those situations when messages are generated, processed, and transmitted by electronic means. The term message is used with reference to verbal or written communication.

Communication models pertain to levels of action. They focus on information and its effects. This does not mean that messages or signs should not be considered, since signs and messages are implicitly a part of information. Focusing on them, however, poses other problems, which become apparent when taking a look at the technical communication model.

Technical Communication Model

The *technical communication model* by Shannon and Weaver presents the foundation for dealing with a variety of technical questions related to information and communication (see Shannon and Weaver, 1949). This model's object of examination is the syntactic level of the communication process. It focuses mainly on categories such as signs, sender, receiver, capacities, redundancies or encoding-decoding which are clearly defined and measured with mathematical-statistical procedures. This model depicts a message's path from a sender over a transmission channel to a receiver. Figure 3.2 shows this arrangement.

An *information source* selects or generates certain sign combinations (message). The *transmitter* codes these signals, which are then routed over a *transmission channel* to the *receiver*. There the signals are decoded and transmitted to their final *destination*. This technical communication model is especially well suited to analyze noise which might occur during transmission. Noise means that the received signals are no longer identical with the original signals. The syntactical exactness of a message transfer, however, is a prerequisite for a successful communication process, through which certain actions can be provoked. Thus, this technical modeling of a communication process is an important step towards the guarantee of successful message transfers, especially in telecommunications. For example, through the transmission of redundant signals, noise can be neutralized, or identified through discrepancies (e.g., test digits

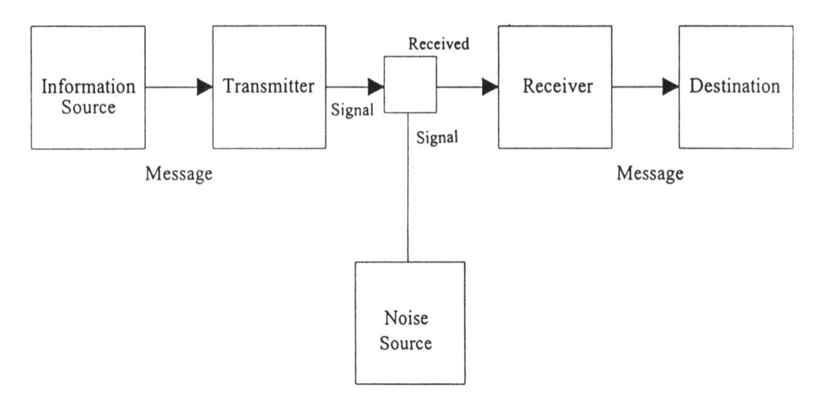

Figure 3.2 *Technical communication model by Shannon and Weaver (1949) (Copyright 1963 by the Board of Trustees of the University of Illinois. Used with permission of the University of Illinois Press)*

for electronic data transfer). Although this model deals with distinct situations, it can only serve as a starting point for the analysis of communication processes. Sender and receiver are only analyzed formally as static objects. The application of communication models dealing with the semantic and pragmatic level is necessary in order to describe the phenomenon of communication in a comprehensive manner.

Newness-confirmation Model

Ernst and Christine von Weizsäcker analyzed the action promoting effect of information based on their simple but significant *newness-confirmation model* (see von Weizsäcker, 1972). According to this model, the pragmatic effect of information is closely related to previous experiences. The prerequisite for an action-promoting effect of information is that the information implies neither a high degree of new experiences nor a high degree of past experiences. Pure newness and pure confirmation represent the extremes on a continuum, within which the pragmatic effect of information is manifested. In Figure 3.3 the continuum together with the pragmatic content of information is illustrated.

Completely new information has no pragmatic effects and cannot be used in a purposeful manner. The receiver is unable to link this information to previous experiences, i.e. to an existing contextual framework. Certain innovations do not spread because of their high degree of novelty. As an example, it would be difficult to convince a small business owner of the benefits of electronic data processing when he employs craftsmen and lives in a developing country in which the people have no

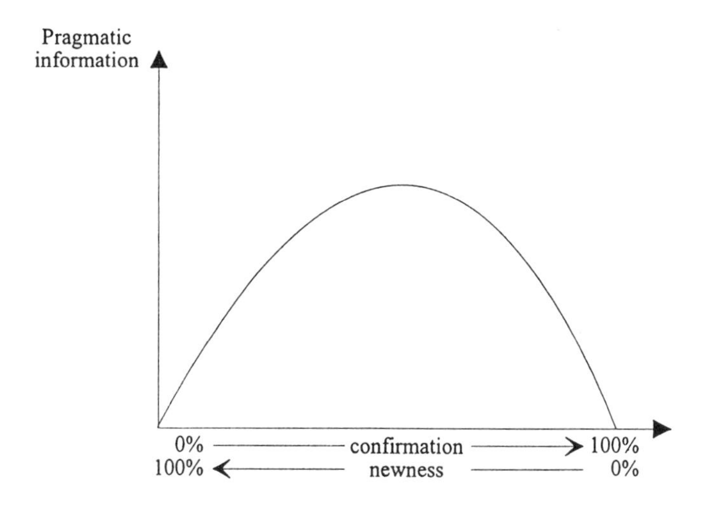

Figure 3.3 *Confirmation, newness and pragmatic information. Source: Schneider (1988, p. 220)*

experience with computer applications. Information can only develop its pragmatic effect if it contains additional confirming elements which can be linked to previous experiences. An excessive number of confirming elements, however, causes a decrease in the information's pragmatic content. The more confirming elements information contains, the less new elements exist. The action promoting percentage of information which only includes confirming elements approaches zero. Also at this end of the continuum one can no longer speak of information, but only of a message. A university graduate with a degree in mathematics, for example, who visits a high school math class will gain little relevant new knowledge.

These reflections provide useful insights for interpersonal communication. Communication is only fruitful with a healthy mixture of new and confirming elements. it is also apparent that two people from very different contextual backgrounds might have communication problems due to a high degree of newness. More serious communication problems, for example, will then be expected in international cooperations than within a regionally active firm.

Axioms of Communication According to Watzlawick, Beavin and Jackson

In contrast to the newness-confirmation model which is related to the degree of novelty, Watzlawick, Beavin and Jackson take a different approach in describing the pragmatic effect of communication. They develop a comprehensive, socio-psychologically oriented model of human communication and are mainly interested in behavioral effects. The authors describe general properties of human communication and derive five axioms which are illustrated in Figure 3.4 (see Watzlawick, Beavin and Jackson, 1967). Based on these axioms, they identify interferences in human communication processes and possibilities for their remedy. One fundamental realization is that some communication interferences are themselves caused through pragmatic communication conditions and thus paradoxical communication situations can arise. An example is the contradictory request "Be spontaneous!". Such situations can only be explained at a meta-level through metacommunication. In contrast to the rather technical sender-receiver models which usually possess a linear character, the authors stress a circular communication process. Through the alternating effects of feedback, both communication partners are able to influence each other.

In their first axiom, Watzlawick et al (1967) designate any form of behavior as communication. Every form of behavior has something to say. There is no opposite to behavior. Thus, *it is impossible for a person not to communicate.* Even when a senior employee walks past a coworker without saying a word, her behavior has a certain meaning, thus it is a form of communication. This realization paves the way for the

1. Axiom:
The impossibility of not communicating.

2. Axiom:
The content and relationship levels of communication.

3. Axiom:
The punctuation of the sequence of events.

4. Axiom:
Digital and analogic communication.

1. Axiom:
Symmetrical and complementary communication.

Figure 3.4 *Axioms of communication according to Watzlawick, Beavin and Jackson (1967). Reproduced by permission of W.W. Norton and Co. Inc.*

analysis of interpersonal interaction problems with the help of communication theory, without requiring explicit communication in the traditional sense. All human behavior is therefore open to interpretation.

The second axiom says that all communication consists of *a content aspect and a relation aspect*. The content aspect pertains to the transmission of facts. For example, the head of a department makes monthly controlling reports to her co-workers. The relation aspect refers to the interpersonal relationship between the communication partners and lays the foundation for the interpretation of the pure content. For example, the boss praises or criticizes the monthly results. Thus, communication not only conveys facts, but also has a lasting effect on the social bonds between the communication partners. The less problematic the social relations are, the easier facts can be exchanged, since less communicative effort has to be devoted to clarifying the content.

The third axiom expresses that relations between communication partners are influenced through the *type of punctuation in communication processes*. Watzlawick et al refer to punctuation as certain manners of interpretation and causal perceptions of the communication partners' statements and behaviors. A problem of punctuation exists, for example, when a boss criticizes a co-worker because of a lack of initiative, whereas the co-worker sees the constant criticism as the reason for his poor performance. Context-dependent communication interferences can arise due to different manners of punctuation, which often can only be solved through communicating about the meaning of the original communication (meta-communication). In intercultural communication relations in particular, such divergences in punctuation can often arise and lead to considerable misunderstandings or even to the failure of the communication process (see Keller, 1992).

The fourth axiom distinguishes between *digital and analog communication*. Digital communication manifests itself mostly in written or spoken language and is—due to its clear syntax—especially suited for transmitting the content aspect of a communication. Analog communication takes place mainly outside the scope of the original language, for example, through mimic, gestures, and intonation. Even though it does not possess a clear syntax, it has various semantic possibilities and serves mainly to convey the relation aspect. In the case of the previous example, the data in the controlling report (digital communication) can come across either in a critical, concerned, or in a positive tone (analog communication). Thus, with the help of analog communication, the intended message can be conveyed without explicit praise or criticism.

The fifth axiom comprises the differentiation between *symmetric and complementary communication relations*. Symmetric relations exist when all communication partners are at the same level, for example co-workers with the same job titles. In this case, both partners possess the same communicative possibilities. Complementary relations exist when communication partners differ in a mutually complementing manner. This can be the case, for example, between boss and co-worker.

With their five axioms of communication, Watzlawick, Beavin, and Jackson (1967) do not offer a complete, self-contained communication model. Their reflections, however, point out some important aspects of communication having a considerable influence on interpersonal communication relations. With this, they offer useful recommendations for the design of intra-firm and inter-firm communication relations as well as the implementation of communication media. An important consideration to be made is that different media are differently suited to convey content and relation aspects of communication. A fax machine, for example, is well-suited for the fast and clear transmission of printed data (content aspect, digital communication). When reprimanding an employee, however, where the relation aspect plays a major role, face-to-face contact would be appropriate. In this case the required analog communication will be difficult to convey through technical media.

Explanation of Communication Interference According to Schulz von Thun

A further socio-psychological perspective on interpersonal communication is taken by Schulz von Thun in reference to Watzlawick et al (see Schulz von Thun, 1993). According to Schulz von Thun *every message contains four different components*, which principally correspond with the content and relation aspect in the above described model. Schulz von Thun does not present a separate model of communication, but further develops the model of Watzlawick et al and differentiates it for a better applicability on concrete communication problems and interferences. The message itself becomes the object of the communication diagnosis. Similar to the model of Watzlawick et al (1967), each communication includes a *content* and a *relation* aspect. In addition, Schulz von Thun introduces the aspect of *appeal*, which is intended to have a certain effect on the communication partner. The fourth component presents the *self-revelation*, which means that any communication can include an intended promotion of one's public image as well as an unintended disclosure of one's self. These four aspects are analyzed in respect to their intentions and effects between sender and receiver.

Communication interferences are inevitable when the sent and received messages are interpreted differently by sender and receiver. For example, a superior's message to a co-worker "Mr Smith, you work too much", can be related to all four aspects. In reality, the boss may stress the content and simply mean that Mr Smith works ten hours instead of eight. Mr Smith, however, may interpret these words as a reproach (critical relation to his boss/request to work even harder/self-revelation of the superior's dissatisfaction) and conclude that the boss is unhappy with him and his performance. One reason fur such a misinterpretation of a message may lie in the interpretative key, which the receiver uses due to a certain self-image (punctuations according to Watzlawick et al, 1990). Such a misunderstanding can lead the receiver to respond in a manner which seems inappropriate to the sender in respect to the original message. These conflicts can be solved only when both communication partners enter some kind of meta-communication. They have to come to certain conclusions as to how a message is to be interpreted in order to agree upon its underlying meaning. This process, however, would require that both partners are willing and able to reach such an agreement at the meta-level, which—in reality—cannot always be assumed. Standardization, as well as the individuality of communication processes, plays a further important role in avoiding such misunderstandings at the relation and self-revelation level (see Koller, 1994).

Mechanisms for Coordinating Actions According to Habermas

The circumstances of communication are the main subject in the sociologist Habermas' theory of communicative action (see Habermas, 1981). Habermas describes *conditions and fundamental patterns of human interaction* to develop a comprehensive social theory. Although it is not his intention to design a communication model in a narrow sense, important factors for the understanding of human communication can be derived from his work. Habermas' concern is the description of social action. He analyzes mechanisms for coordinating activities, which enable conformance of rules and stable linkages of interactions (see Habermas, 1984). Since the coordination of actions is closely related to communication processes, important communication theoretical conclusions can be drawn from Habermas' thoughts. Within the framework of semiotics these reflections can be assigned to the pragmatic level of communication.

According to Habermas, there exist two fundamental coordination forms for the coordination of purposeful (teleological) single actions. He distinguishes whether coordination is achieved exclusively through *the actors' reciprocal intervention* or through *the creation of a rationally justified agreement between the actors*. The difference between these two forms consists in the actors' different attitudes towards each other. In the first case the attitude can be described as success oriented, whereas in the latter case finding an agreement presents the major motive for the

Action situation \ Action orientation	Success-oriented	Agreement-oriented
Non-social	Instrumental action	——
Social	Strategic action	Communicative action

Figure 3.5 *Types of action according to Habermas (1984)*

actors. According to Habermas, an actor cannot simultaneously take both attitudes: they are mutually exclusive.

Habermas confronts these two attitudes with different circumstances of action. He distinguishes between social and non-social situations. *Non-social situations of action* refer to an objective world with all its properties and circumstances. A *social situation of action* refers to a social world with certain rules for the social community. From this Habermas derives three different forms of actions (see Figure 3.5).

The classification of social situations of action is important for the understanding of communication processes. They can be classified in *success-oriented* and *agreement-oriented situations of actions*. In the first case of strategic action, the actor sees his fellow man as an object. His primary concern is to achieve his goals, even if under certain circumstances manipulation, deception or fraud is necessary (e.g., an aggressive marketing strategy). In contrast, the agreement-oriented actor treats her partners as co-subjects (Kirsch, 1992, p. 33). The actors achieve the coordination of their respective action intentions through mutual agreement. They try to reach a consensus on the common action. Manipulation between the actors does not take place, but is replaced by a search for consensus and common solutions to the problem (e.g., the search for a family vacation destination).

Habermas refers to the agreement-oriented manner of action as *communicative action*. This term illustrates the importance of communication as a guidance mechanism for the coordination of actions. Besides, there exist other media, such as money or power, through which actions can be coordinated without requiring communicative agreement. Habermas argues that these (non-communicative) media increasingly enter fields in which a communicative orientation of action should be used, such as families, friendships, or other groups.

This orientation towards actions based on agreement (communicative) resembles the previously mentioned example of telling someone to jump into the lake, in contrast to the strategic action (eventually pursued with guile) of pushing someone into the water. Communicative action leaves room for alternative courses of action which can be evaluated in communication processes until a mutual consensus is achieved with benevolent intention. The agreement achievable through communication depends upon three criticizable claims for validity, which an actor can state. When presenting facts from the objective world, the speaker *claims validity of truth*. When creating and renewing interpersonal (social) relationships (social world), the speaker *claims validity of (normative) correctness*. For expressive statements, such as personal experiences or emotional impressions, the speaker *claims validity of sincerity*. Each speaker always makes all three claims for validity, whereby one claim can dominate. If these claims are not accepted by the listener, an agreement (and thus communication) does not take place.

For the elimination of communication interferences this implies that two actors' actions must necessarily be oriented towards agreement. Through manipulation or deception, an agreement on the conditions of the underlying communication would not be possible. One of the actors would simply fake the metacommunication and would use it to pursue his own goals.

In economically relevant contexts, a variety of examples for situations can be found in which strategic and then communicative action can occur. These action orientations have a particular importance for the types of interorganizational forms described later in this book. Forms of cooperation, such as strategic partnerships, require agreement-oriented (communicative) consensus mechanisms. One could even argue that agreement-oriented forms of action present a prerequisite for such cooperation forms. Governance structures, such as quasi-vertical integration, however, entail a much wider scope for strategic actions by single actors. These contexts are interesting in respect to the voluntariness of participation in organizational forms, the development of trust, as well as the existence of imbalances in power. Cooperation forms are based on a company's voluntary decision to participate. Thereby, the existence or the creation of trust presents a necessary prerequisite. Although trusting relations may also exist in governance structures, it is easier for the more powerful partner to act strategically and thus to realize his own objectives at the cost of the weaker partner, due to the typical power imbalances between the participating corporations.

The *concept of the living world* presents a further important aspect for the understanding of communication processes in Habermas' theory. A living world is the epitome for a certain life and language form, which determines an actor's possibilities and limits of thinking and speaking. The entire background knowledge, which is tacitly presumed for communicative action to become possible, is referred to as living world. This means that statements or messages do not possess a context-independent, denotative meaning, but are always based on certain experiences and thought patterns. This can lead to considerable communication problems between actors from different living worlds. Wittgenstein speaks of *language games*, for which rules exist that a human has to apply within a certain living world in order to communicate with other members of this living world. These rules and the background knowledge are learned in the course of socialization processes. Thereby, a system of belief evolves. Thus, the meaning of a sentence has to be seen in the context of this background knowledge.

When communication partners stem from very different living worlds, then considerable communication disturbances can arise. This is especially true for corporations from different regions which belong to different cultures. Various examples can be found in contemporary business literature for culturally determined communication defects between American and European corporations and corporations from the Far East (see, for example, Keller, 1992). But culturally-caused communication defects can also arise within corporations, for example between certain groups of employees and management. This might occur for instance when people working together come from different *private living worlds*, those described as *original*. The more co-workers adapt to the *organizational* and therefore *derivative living world* of their corporation instead of their private living and language forms, the more this shared living world presents a suitable foundation for functioning communication.

Communication from the Rational Constructivism Perspective

Different insights in information and communication processes and thus in the principles of communication can be gained from the view of the so-called *rational constructivism*. Rational constructivism describes a certain view on the functioning of human cognition. According to this view, any form of comprehension does not reflect an identical image of reality, but only presents an internal construct of the external reality, which is generated through the cognitive processes of the nervous system. This perspective on cognition was considerably influenced through the neuro-biologists Maturana and Varela (see, for example, Maturana and Varela, 1987).

The basis of constructivism presents the view that the nervous system (in a narrow sense the brain) as a cognitive system is *operationally self-contained.* A system is operationally self-contained when it produces its (in the case of the brain, mental) states itself. In contrast to traditional input-transformation-output models, operationally self-contained systems are defined in such a way that they are active by themselves without requiring external impulses. When interacting with its environment, the system's structure determines the system's reactions (see Maturana and Varela, 1987). Operational self-containment refers to the informational, not to the material level (energetic openness). Thus, one can talk also about informational self-containment, which means that no information from the environment is received directly by a cognitive system. The cognitive system itself generates the information which it processes. For example, the same event can cause different mental states in different persons, depending on their respective previous mental states.

Since a cognitive system does not possess direct access to the external reality, it cannot depict this reality. All it can do is generate a *construction of this reality*, hoping that this construction is suitable for its own survival. Thus, there exist no right or wrong constructions of reality, but only more suitable and less suitable ones. None can judge the degree to which a construction of reality really corresponds to reality. All cognitive systems are equally closed. This view has important consequences for the evaluation of communication. When cognitive systems are self-contained in the above sense, then information cannot be transferred from one system to the other during communication processes. Successful communication has to be explained in a different manner.

Language psychology differentiates between the *denotative* and *connotative meaning of language symbols.* The denotative meaning expresses the relation between a sign and an object in reality. For example, the word "dog" describes a certain species of mammal which has been domesticated by humans. The connotative meaning, in contrast, comprises all emotional and appraisal associations, and therefore interpretations, which are related to a sign. This connotative meaning is specific to each individual. A person who has been bitten by a dog assigns a different connotative meaning to this word than does a successful dog breeder. From the perspective of rational constructivism, there do not—in a strict sense—exist any denotative meanings of words. Communication happens exclusively through a connotative attribution of meanings to signs. Thus, no instructive interactions can take place in a communication process; a sender cannot influence a receiver in a deterministic manner. Communication functions when the receiver's construct is similar to the sender's intended meaning of a message.

Based on common, identical or similar experiences and events, for example through similar processes of socialization, identical or similar cognitive states develop and thus identical or similar constructions of reality, so-called *consensual fields*. Communication functions when the interpretation of communication takes place within such a consensual field. Consensual fields are closely related to Habermas' living world. When two communication partners interact within consensual fields, they interpret the used signs (for example certain terms, gestures and so on) in a relatively strong corresponding manner. Communication becomes possible because similar cognitive states cause signs to trigger similar reactions. When two Americans talk about a dog, they will usually regard it as a pet, whereas in China it might be considered as dinner. The anecdote about the American couple dining in a restaurant in China illustrates the fatal misunderstanding which can arise when two people from different consensual fields communicate. The woman pointed to her poodle sitting at the table and then to the table to express that the dog needed something to eat. The waiter took the poodle into the kitchen, returning later with the dog prepared as an "appetizing" meal.

Interpretation of Communication According to Luhmann

The sociologist Luhmann takes up the discussion of rational constructivism and attempts to describe modern society's most important communication areas as operationally self-contained systems (see Luhmann, 1994). He identifies with the discussion led by Maturana and Varela, however, he develops a terminology with which social systems can be described in a more detailed manner as *autopoietic systems*. Such systems create their own interpretation patterns, independent of other systems, and refer exclusively to those (self-reference). Luhmann argues that *autopoietic social systems evolve through communication*. According to him, it is not the living elements (humans or groups of humans) which represent the system elements, but communication. Thus communication is a necessary element for the emergence of social systems, for example, forms of organization such as corporations or markets. In the sense of autopoiesis, these elements are created through the respective social system itself. Communication is characterized as decisions in such organized social systems. Corporations or markets not only consist of decisions but also produce these decisions upon which they are established (see Luhmann, 1986).

Luhmann's contribution for the understanding of communication consists of the fact that he does not attribute the results of communication processes exclusively to a single actor or to a pair of communication partners. Communication processes always possess a further reaching effect at the pragmatic level. Single communication processes, which are first attributed to single communication couples, provide a contribution to the constitution of the social system in which they occur. Luhmann stresses the independence of social processes from a methodological individualism in the context of communication processes.

The models of communication presented in this section illustrate how much the construction of models and hence their content of explanation depend on the standpoint of the respective theorist and how aspects which are irrelevant for this question are intentionally neglected. Whereas, for example, the contributions to the description and explanation of communication processes of the psychologically influenced authors such as Watzlawick, Beavin, and Jackson are based principally on the study of individual communication processes, sociologically influenced authors such as Habermas or Luhmann focus more on the effects of communication on the whole social construct. The technical communication model by Shannon and Weaver, in contrast, deals mainly with the technical explanation of communication interferences. All these models present partial approaches for the description and explanation of economically relevant communication processes. Although a self-contained, comprehensive theory of human communication does not exist, these different approaches offer various perspectives which can be used in a situational manner to describe, analyze, and finally design communication phenomena.

INFORMATION BEHAVIOR MODELS

Every kind of task completion within a corporation requires information. Communication is required to ensure that this information is provided to the person responsible for the task. This is especially true for organizations with a high degree of division of labor. Through different models, the various aspects of communication have been presented in the preceding section. This section will focus on the information behavior of those responsible for task completion. It would seem rational for an actor to adjust his information demand to the information need and to first use existing information before asking for more. He would have to find and analyze relevant information before the decision is made and actively use this information to reach a decision. Various theoretical reflections and empirical studies, however, show that the actual information and communication behavior of decision-makers does not necessarily reflect this systematic-analytical procedure.

Although relevant information is available, it is often not put to use. Sometimes the search for relevant information takes place only after the decision is already made, even though by then it is no longer necessary. The subsequent acquisition of information simply serves as justification for the decisions already made.

There are numerous models which describe the human information behavior. The wide variety of existing perspectives makes a simple classification difficult. Oppelt (1995) chooses a pragmatic division in four aspects, which integrates the most important behavioral models. Figure 3.6 presents an overview of different approaches and shows their most important advocates, their perspectives, and their respective relation to the questions of a decision-maker's information behavior. The following section presents a more detailed selection. The approaches provide starting points for the design of efficient information management in corporations.

Restrictions on Human Information Processing Capacity

Various approaches exist for the explanation of the above illustrated, seemingly irrational behaviors (see Picot and Wolff, 1994). An important explanation attempt refers to *the limitation on human information processing capacities* as well as to man's information behavior characterized through bounded rationality. These approaches refer to the depiction of a human as a "homo oeconomicus", and in turn "homo informatiens", who is constantly seeking complete information in order to make rational decisions. Due to the principal limitation of his cognitive information processing capacities, a human will not be able to absorb, evaluate, and process all relevant information and thus will usually not be completely informed. From a psychologically oriented, experimental study, G. A. Miller concluded that the simultaneous information

Function-oriented approaches	Decision process-oriented approaches	Activity-oriented approaches	Integrative, multidimensional approaches
• Fayol • Barbard • Drucker • Mahoney and more • Anthony • Other function.oriented approaches	• Works of Simon and March • The model of incrementalism • Empiric decision research • Other decision process-oriented approaches	• Carlson • Stewart • Mintzberg • Kotter • Other activity-oriented approaches	• O'Reilly 1983, 1987 • The model of Daft & Lengel • The works of Picot & Reichwald 1984 • The studies of Jones & McLeod 1986 • The works of Müller-Böling & Ramme 1990 • Other approaches and studies

Figure 3.6 *Models for the activities and information behavior of management*

processing capacity of a person is limited on average to six or seven information categories (see Miller, 1967). For example, he observed people listening to music and analyzed how many different stimuli a listener could receive simultaneously and after a certain period of time, distinguish without confusion. He came to similar conclusions under other experimental arrangements. He described this limitation with the maximal number of information units an average person could process. With the help of statistical combination theory, for example 32 distinct alternatives can be deduced from five informational units, each combination reflecting its own informational content. It is at about this number that the human information processing capacity clearly reaches its limits, resulting in an "information overload". This limit can be extended through different techniques. The general conclusion can be drawn from this study that human cognitive capacities are as a rule insufficient for fully understanding especially complex tasks, to recognize the relevant information need and to completely process all relevant information.

Human Rationality Restrictions

The limits of human information retrieval and information processing capacity, as well as the limited possibility to transmit information through language, present essential reasons why humans are assumed to have a *limited rational information behavior* (see Simon, 1955). According to Simon, a person does not behave as an optimizing actor, but only tries to reach a satisfying level of goal attainment (satisfaction). Having a given set of alternatives, he does not seek until he has found the optimal alternative, but he stops seeking as soon as he has found an acceptable alternative. The view of bounded rationality thus explains the limitedness of human information behavior. Instead of a complete search for all relevant information, the decision-maker only tries to attain a subjectively satisfying, yet incomplete level of information. This implies that in a decision situation there will always remain a certain amount of ignorance regarding any alternative actions and their consequences. In this context, selective information behavior can be observed. Only a certain portion of potential information, deemed important, is selected. In such situations, "rational search procedures" (Simon, 1978, p. 11) can at least support the *selective information behavior*. These are procedures for seeking information, such as rules of thumb or computer-based database requests, which are likely to extract relevant information. According to Simon, the bounded human rationality is supplemented by a procedural rationality (see Simon, 1978). Kirchgässner stresses in this context the dependence of bounded rationality on given institutional conditions, such as the amount of information costs, respectively the costs of suboptimal decisions or the pressure to improve the information base due to competitive pressures (see Kirchgässner, 1991).

Information and Communication Behavior According to O'Reilly

O'Reilly also examines institutional conditions of human information processing capacity, in that he relates information and communication behavior to organizational context variables (see O'Reilly, 1983). O'Reilly establishes in an integrated perspective a connection between organizational context variables, the information and communication behavior, the level of information, and the actors' resulting decision behavior. According to this view, decisions can be described as a function of existing or applied information. Relevant context variables include the organizational structure, the existing incentive and control systems, the system of norms and values as well as the qualities of the tasks to be completed. In addition, the information and communication behavior is influenced by the formal and informal power relations resulting from the respective context. O'Reilly formulates different statements which refer to the association of context variables and information behavior. According to O'Reilly, the probability that information will be considered is higher:

- the more power the informing party has over the decision-maker;
- the more relevant the information is for task completion by the decision-maker (whereby difference may exist between subjective and objective task definition);
- the stronger and clearer the information is related with the planning, control, and evaluation systems relevant for the decision-maker, since these are the criteria for incentive and punishment systems;
- the stronger the information contributes to actions which are positively sanctioned through the control system (conformity);
- the more the information favors the decision-maker's personal goals;
- the less conflict it generates with cooperation partners;
- the more accessible it is (organizationally, physically, intellectually);
- the more compact and easier it is to understand (for example a graphic with a short verbal summary);
- the more personal the contact to the informing party is (advantage of oral communication); and
- the deeper the trust is in the information source.

Ultimately each of these factors can be traced back to a cost-benefit calculation of information utility. Information is more likely to be used when the costs for its acquisition are low and the expected gains from its use are high, respectively, the eventual sanctions for not using the information are serious.

Information as a Signal and a Symbol

O'Reilly assumes that the quality of a decision increases with the decision-maker's information level. If the quality of information itself or of resulting decisions, however, can rarely or not at all be evaluated, then serious evaluation problems arise. According to Feldman and March, in such situations *a decision-maker's visible information behavior is often used as an evaluation substitute* for the quality of information and therefore decisions (see Feldman and March, 1981). They emphasize that information behavior can have important signaling effects on observers. A decision-maker can influence the belief in the quality of his decisions through signaling his information-seeking activities to his external environment. Thus, the original substance of information is substituted through visible signals about informational behavior. In such a case, the evaluation of the decision is influenced through the transmission of metainformation. This, however, implies a change in the evaluation and incentive criteria with a related change of individual steering possibilities.

Decision-related information behavior may thus be substituted through signaling information activities. Although the real quality of a decision might not be considered enough, the implementation of a decision can be positively influenced through the signaling of a respective information behavior. Thereby, the credibility of a decision can be increased, even if the decision itself cannot be evaluated. Such signaling measures can be essential for decisions whose implementation is expected to cause considerable problems. Here, information does not serve as a basis for the objective evaluation of a decision, but fulfills the function to refute existing or expected criticism. This behavior can foster the tendency that too much information is consciously demanded and thus the costs of procuring information are unnecessarily increased. This is possible especially when a decision-maker has to bear the consequences of his decision but not the costs for his information-seeking activities. A decision-maker is more likely to hear the reproach that he made a wrong decision due to a lack of information, than that he collected too much information for a decision. Thus, there is an incentive to demand too much and sometimes unnecessary information.

A person who relates an increase in prestige or power to the possession of information will seek and provide information, even if it is not required for the original task completion. It results in an overactivity in the information search due to rational cost-benefit calculations.

Subjectively preferred decision results as well as signaling effects of information behavior play—compared to professional information need—a weighty role in the solution of objective problems. This kind of effect of information also influences the type of information transfer and thus the choice of communication media, as well as the communication behavior of decision-makers. A multitude of theoretical and empirical studies about communication behavior and the choice and effects of communication media have been undertaken. Although these studies differ in their proceedings and their detailed results, collectively they paint a relatively clear picture of a decision-maker's information and communication behavior, which is that of the *individual* utility maximizer.

Communication Media and Purpose

As discussed on pages 58–73, in context with the Watzlawick, Beavin, and Jackson's communication theory, the practicality of a communication media depends upon which aspects of a communication process come to the forefront (for Watzlawick et al, the content and/or relation aspect). Which aspect should be emphasized is determined through the task to be completed. Thus when choosing a communication medium its *task relation* always has to be considered. Depending upon the task and the resulting communication requirements, the use of suitable communication media can be planned (see Figure 3.7).

These four, empirically verified, basic problems of organizational communication are classified according to the degree of structure of the respective communication problem. The consequences for the choice of the communication media and for the choice of the communication partners' locations are also mentioned according to their tendency. The oral form of communication with its various possibilities of expression and dialogue is better suited for the solution of low structured communication problems, and thereby tasks, but requires—especially in the form of face-to-face communication—the local proximity of the communication partners. For example, the negotiation of a long-term cooperation contract. In contrast, highly structured, invariant tasks foster the use of indirect, documented communication, because writing enables a high degree of exactness. For example, the transmission of large volumes of accounting data.

Empirical Analysis of Communication Behavior by Picot and Reichwald

In an empirical research project, Picot and Reichwald studied the communication behavior of middle and upper management (see Picot and Reichwald, 1987). They found out that this group spent almost two-

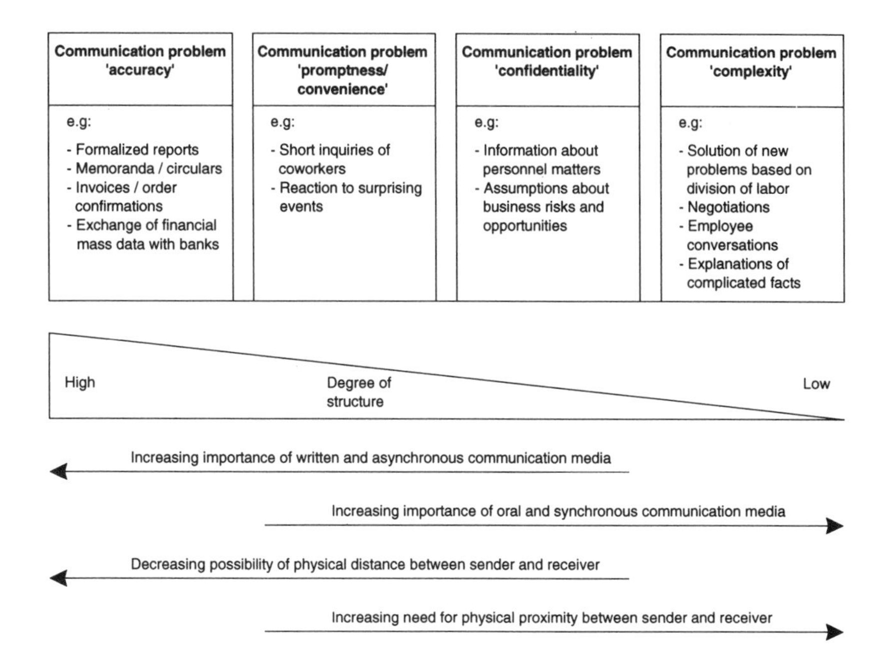

Figure 3.7 *Basic problems of organizational communication and the choice of communication media. Source: Picot (1993a, p. 151)*

thirds of their working time on information and communication activities. The remaining work time is used for task related activities through the manager alone and for administrative activities. It is apparent that information and communication related activities clearly dominate management activities at all levels. In addition, the study of the connection between communication channels and communication partners provides important insights into the communication behavior of managers. From this it is clear that managers' choices of communication channels depend on the communication partner. Figure 3.8 illustrates this relationship.

Altogether, the proportion of oral communication forms (84%) clearly dominates over written communication (16%). The personal contacts between managers and their communication partners are especially strong within their own departments, whereas for external partners this form of communication makes up the lowest portion on the total volume of communication. This communication behavior leads to the assumption that the choice of information behavior also depends on the physical distance to the communication partner. From this, important conclusions can be drawn for the management of a "boundary-less" corporation. When the proportion of traditionally corporate internal and even department-internal tasks will decrease and more tasks,

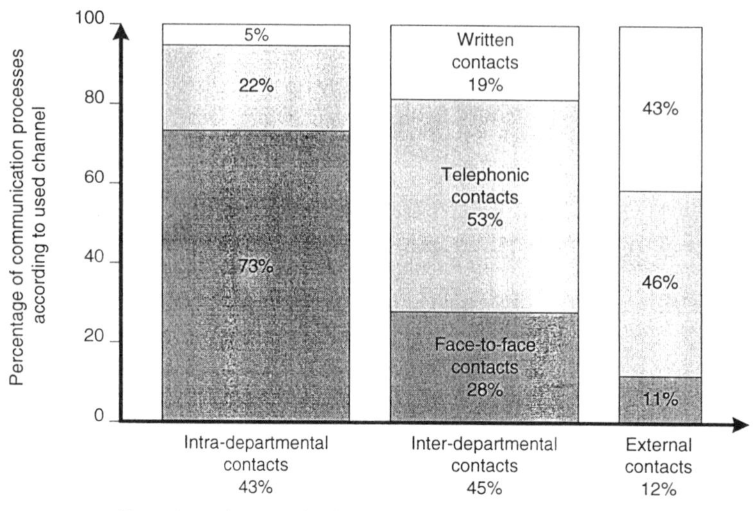

Figure 3.8 *Communication partners and channels. Source: see Picot and Reichwald (1987, p. 36)*

together with the related information and communication processes, will be completed externally, then this generally implies an increase in the physical distances between the communication partners. Thus, face-to-face communication can no longer present the dominant form of communication without being connected with considerable cost increases. With this development, various advantages of personal contacts, such as maintaining the relation aspect between the communication partners and the possibility to discuss complex and poorly structured problems, can no longer be realized. Picot and Reichwald's study shows that management has primarily to deal with non-standardized, situational, and complex problems which are poorly structured. Such activities and their complexity will increase in interorganizational task completions. It becomes necessary to evaluate the various new possibilities of new communication systems (for example video conferencing, CSCW, or systems to support telework) in order to offer management a suitable communication platform for their tasks and to ensure the stability of the "boundless" corporation.

Empirical Analysis of Communication Behavior by Müller-Böling and Ramme

The dominance of oral communication is also confirmed by a study from Müller-Böling and Ramme (see Müller-Böling and Ramme, 1990). In addition they found out that the respective communication behavior of managers differs with branch and size of the corporation. For example, management of service corporations clearly prefer oral communication in comparison with management of commercial (trade) corporations. Compared with smaller enterprises, managers of corporations which employ more than 1000 people clearly prefer written communication channels. The authors discovered various factors which determine the choice of certain communication channels. For example, the more communication partners get to know each other and develop closer relationships, the more they substitute oral for written communication channels. Similar to Picot and Reichwald, Müller-Böling and Ramme discovered that oral forms of communication are especially used for the generation of ideas, for negotiations, and for decision-making processes, thus always when, in individual situations, specific personal contact is required between the communication partners. Personal contact takes place mainly when complex problems have to be solved with known partners, or between persons who have a certain trusting relationship with each other. For unknown partners or for the transmission of information which is voluminous or difficult to define, written communication is preferred.

Management's Choice of Suitable Communication Channels

Daft and Lengel advocate a theoretical approach towards management's choice of suitable communication channels (see Daft and Lengel, 1984). They introduce the term *media richness* into their analysis. Daft and Lengel refer to media richness as the potential information transmitting capacity of communication media. The content of this term is closely related to a communication's relation aspect described by Watzlawick, Beavin, and Jackson. The higher the media richness of a communication channel, the more it offers the possibility to transmit the relation aspect as well as the content aspect. Daft and Lengel implicitly assume that managers have to deal more with "atmospheric" or unclear communication tasks than with the exchange of clear content-oriented problems. The dimensions used to describe media richness also include factors such as feedback possibilities, number of used channels, personal and impersonal contacts as well as type of language (including body language). They attribute to face-to-face communication the highest degree of media richness, which decreases for telephone, personal correspondence, formalized documents, and formalized data communication. Founded on the concept of media richness, Daft and Lengel develop a model for the information and communication behavior of managers (Figure 3.9).

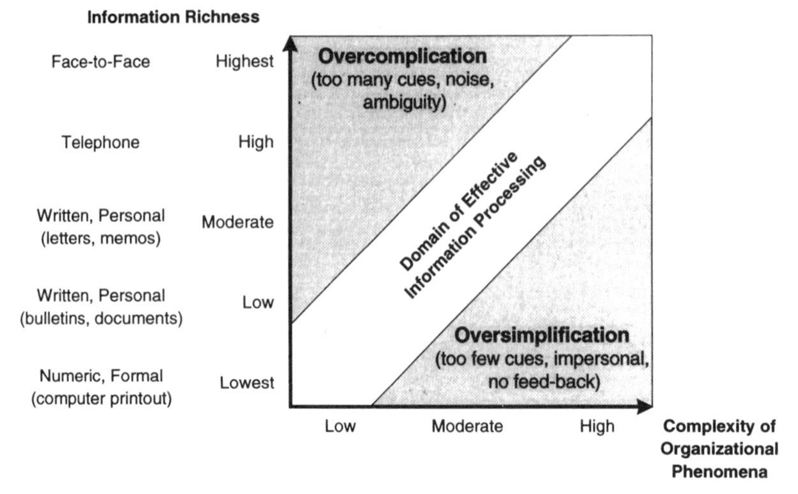

Figure 3.9 *Information processing by managers. Source: Daft and Lengel (1984, p. 199). Reproduced by permission from JAI Press Inc., Connecticut.*

The organizational problems and phenomena confronting managers range from simple to complex. Simple problems can be solved in a programmable and routine manner. Complex problems, however, require innovative solutions and the search for information outside of daily routines. Communication media have to be adapted to the problem's degree of complexity. A too high degree of media richness can lead to unnecessary complications; a too low degree can lead to unjustified problem simplifications. As a rule of thumb, one can conclude that the right combination lies on the diagonal. This contradicts the possible assumption that the most valuable information for managers is plain and precise information.

Information Pathologies

Besides the proper choice of communication media, potential malfunctions in organizational knowledge processing have to be considered for the guarantee of functioning information supply and successful communication processes. They too influence the success level of production, transmittal, and application of information. Such malfunctions can be described as *information pathologies* (see Wilensky, 1967; Scholl, 1992). They include

> "avoidable mistakes, that means producable information which will not be produced, procurable information which will not be procured, existing information which will not be (correctly) transmitted and . . . transmitted

> information which is misunderstood or not put to use." (*Scholl, 1992, p. 901, translation by authors*)

Following Wilensky's example, Scholl describes three dimensions in which information pathologies may arise: actor-related, interaction-related, and knowledge-based information pathologies. His first assumption is that actors do not consciously misuse or distort information.

Actor-related Information Pathologies

These are the result of certain inadequacies in individual human qualities. The acquisition of knowledge takes place through the gradual assimilation of new information and experiences with existing knowledge, as well as through the accommodation of existing knowledge to new facts, which could not be assimilated due to lack of comprehension. Thus, new information can only be assimilated if there exists some kind of linkage to existing knowledge. If these links are missing, however, new potential information cannot be understood. Increasing the level of confirmation of new information, for example through systematic continuous education, decreases these kinds of information pathologies. These thoughts correspond to a high degree to the newness-confirmation model of von Weizsäcker (see pages 62–63).

An insufficient information demand has similar grounds. Often, it results from a lack of aggregate knowledge or the inability to see the whole picture. The longer a person completes the same tasks, always requiring the same information, the stronger this effect may be observed. The acquisition of new knowledge is inhibited.

Individuals with one-sided knowledge and low general knowledge are confronted with the additional danger of information overload. On the other hand, those with a comprehensive knowledge base are more likely to possess the capacity to identify patterns in a large volume of information and thus to structure information in such a manner that it can better be arranged in the existing base of experiences.

A further source of actor-related information pathologies is a person's inclination to perceive only things which fit into his own personal structure. This attitude, previously displayed as a constructivist view of the perception process, can lead to a distortion of one's own perceptual abilities. An example of this phenomenon is the "not-invented-here syndrome", meaning the denial of unfamiliar ideas, or the adherence to a visibly weak standpoint in order to protect one's own self-esteem.

Interaction-related Information Pathologies

Interaction-related information pathologies arise from faulty communication processes. An exchange of information and opinions leads to a potential increase in knowledge, however, the exchange of opinions takes place mainly between like-minded persons. The relatively low degree of novelty within such communication processes leads to a limited information exchange. Often, however, a controversial discussion with persons who have a different knowledge and different views proves to be more fertile for both partners. Nonetheless, a confirmation of one's own opinion is evaluated higher than a contradiction, due to the human pursuit of consistence. When experts from different areas communicate, there often exist communication barriers caused by different fundamental knowledge and technical terminology.

Besides semantic problems within communication processes leading to classical misunderstandings, there also exist conscious and structural distortions of communication contents. In distortions caused by hierarchy, negative information which flows bottom-up from lower to higher hierarchy levels is glossed over or kept silent, in order to avoid expected sanctions or to maintain current power structures. The same phenomenon can be observed for persons at the same hierarchy level, where sectoral and competitive thinking leads to information distortion and restraint. Especially in bureaucratic organizations non-transparent structures can exist, through which information over long communication channels is distorted. Thereby, adaptations and innovations are hindered. Conscious distortions of information are described in economic theory as *influence activities* (see Milgrom and Roberts, 1992, p. 271).

Knowledge-based Information Pathologies

These are based on people's assumptions as to which characteristics, in general, valid knowledge should possess. Many people, for example, have a rather simple view of knowledge, according to which knowledge has to be clear and must be provable by reality. Such a reality-oriented view leads to black-and-white thinking, leaving no room for other opinions. This naive realism often manifests itself in exaggerated facts and in preference for quantitative "hard facts" to qualitative information ("soft facts"). Moreover, there often exist organizations in which insights (declarative knowledge) are overstressed compared to experiences and vice versa. Knowledge-based information pathologies depend on each individual's attitude, however, through the characteristic of the organizational environment they can turn into an essential and stable element of the corporate culture (see Habermas' concept of the living world and Luhmann's concept of autopoietic social system on pages 67 and 72). The disassembly of such culturally based information pathologies is difficult and generally takes place over time.

Problems in Interorganizational Information Transfer

Distinct problems arise in an interorganizational information transfer. As mentioned above, the exchange of information—which has a pragmatic value—has the consequence that the receiver gets an additional value, whereas the value of the information tends to decrease for the sender, due to a reduction in the information's exclusiveness. Following von Hippel, Schrader describes, with the help of the theoretical model of the *prisoner's dilemma situation*, the conditions under which an information transfer between competitors occurs despite this phenomenon (see Schrader, 1990; von Hippel, 1988).

The prisoner's dilemma, known from game theory, has the following basic structure (see also pages 31–50). Two players have an option to act cooperatively or non-cooperatively. The non-cooperative behavior presents the dominant strategy for both players, because however the other player behaves, this strategy leads to a higher utility than the cooperative option. Should both players choose the non-cooperative strategy, however, then their pay-offs are lower than if both of them chose to cooperate. In a one period game both players will choose to act in the non-cooperative manner. In games with more than one period, however, cooperative behavior may occur. The so-called *tit-for-tat strategy* was proved to be the most successful in computer simulations (see Axelrod, 1984). Tit-for-tat presents a heuristic, which recommends cooperation in the first round and in the following rounds copies the partner's previous behavior. A cooperation lasts between two players until one partner acts in a non-cooperative manner. In the following round the partner copies this behavior and the cooperation is terminated.

This prisoner's dilemma situation can be applied to interorganizational information transfer (see von Hippel, 1988; Schrader, 1990). Two corporations, A and B, each possess information unknown by the other. It is assumed that the information is equally valued in both corporations. The information's value comprises two different components, the basic value r and the additional value Δr. This additional value reflects the advantage which stems from one corporation's information lead over the other. This information lead, however, vanishes as the information is exchanged. Then, only the basic value is maintained. An information transfer dilemma can be modeled from this (see Figure 3.10).

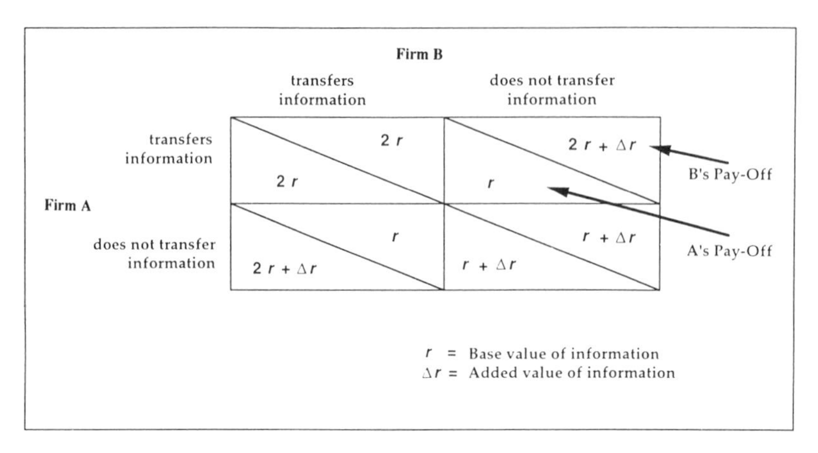

Figure 3.10 *Structure of the information transfer dilemma. Source: Schrader (1990, p. 27)*

If the assumption of a one-period game is given up, then cooperative behavior between the two corporations becomes possible. Whereas not transferring information may be advantageous from a short-term perspective, from a long-term perspective it can be useful to encourage the partner to a lasting, mutually beneficial cooperation through its own cooperative behavior. From the model it can be deduced that inter-organizational information transfer proves to be economically beneficial for both partners, if the information has a high basic value and a low additional value. Competitive behavior occurs in situations in which information possesses a low basic value and a high additional value.

The model further shows that such an information transfer can only take place when a *certain amount of trust* exists and when there is a long-term perspective for the cooperation. From an empirical study, Schrader concludes that informal interorganizational information exchange in particular can positively contribute to success. He further states, that the asynchronous exchange of services, as well as a certain blindness to beneficial cooperative relations together with a prevalent competitive manner of thinking often present the reason for the refusal of such information transfer. It should be remembered, however, that there exists no insoluble contradiction between cooperation and competition.

INFORMATION PRODUCTION MODELS

A systematic planning of information as a corporate resource is as important as the planning of human, financial, or material resources. Due to the different qualities of information as a production factor, traditional planning systems cannot be applied. Information possesses various typical qualities which have to be considered (see Picot and Franck, 1988). Examples are:

- Information is an immaterial good which is not destroyed even through multiple usage.
- When evaluating information, the so-called *information paradox* arises (see page 91, "Evaluation of information").
- Information expands through its usage.
- Information can be condensed.
- Information can substitute other economic resources.
- In the extreme, information can be transported at the speed of light.
- Buyers of information have to be satisfied with copies.
- Information is inclined towards diffusion.
- Information initiates relationships.

Information Production

These properties require special models and procedures for the analysis of the production and use of information. Nevertheless, in reference to information, one can talk about "production" in the traditional sense. *Original information* presents the foundation for the production of further or derivative information. Original information consists of either practical messages which a firm receives, for example, about markets, economic trends or competitive situations, or information about the corporate situation, which has not yet been processed, such as figures related to usage, inventory, or running time. *Derivative information* is gained through processing original information. The production of derivative information can include three different components, which can be distinguished by their different requirements on information processing systems.

Information production generally consists of a *transmission* of information, which is simply the transfer of input information from a sender to a receiver. In a *translation*, the form of the information is altered, but not the content. Information is encoded in different forms of presentation, for example displaying figures through graphs or entering written information into an electronic application system. The real production of new information takes place in a *transformation* of original information. Thereby, the form of input information, as well as the content, is altered into derivative information.

In addition, one can distinguish between analytical and synthetic information production. In the case of *analytical information production*, many resources and products are gained from one source. In the *synthetic form*, in contrast, one product originates from many sources. As an example of the former, the accounting system from Riebel is one in which a basic calculation presents the foundation for further analysis. An example for the synthetic information production is the calculation of financial figures such as cash flow.

Efficiently handling information as a production factor is an inevitable responsibility of a corporation's management. This task has to be planned, organized and controlled in an economic manner. The purpose of information management is the effective and efficient use of information. For this purpose, not only technical, but also organizational and human resources conditions which influence information as a production factor have to be designed. Besides the implementation of suitable information and communication technical infrastructures and systems, the *design of the information use* presents an important responsibility of information management (see Wollnik, 1988). The information need has to be planned and controlled to ensure that it meets the essential corporate requirements. *All in all, the systematically provided planning, steering and controlling information for decision-makers has to be prioritized.*

Information Need and Supply

The *information need* is defined by the type, quantity and quality of information which a person requires within a certain period of time to complete her tasks. In many cases, the information need can only be vaguely defined and depends above all on the underlying task, the objectives and the psychological properties of the decision-maker. An information oriented analysis of the task to be completed determines the so-called *objective information need*. It defines which type and quantity of information a decision-maker should use to fulfill her task. The *subjective information need*, in contrast, takes the subjective view of the decision-maker and indicates which information the decision-maker considers as relevant for completing her tasks. As a rule, the subjectively expressed information need deviates from the objective one. It should be the goal of information management to match the subjective information need with the objective infomation need. This will be even more difficult for those underlying tasks which are unstructured, complex, and unstable. The amount of information which is finally demanded, presents again only a portion of the originally expressed information need. Only in the area in which information demand and information supply overlap, does this lead to an actual information supply (see Picot and Wolff, 1994). The part of the information supply which is objectively required for the completion of tasks indicates the level of information.

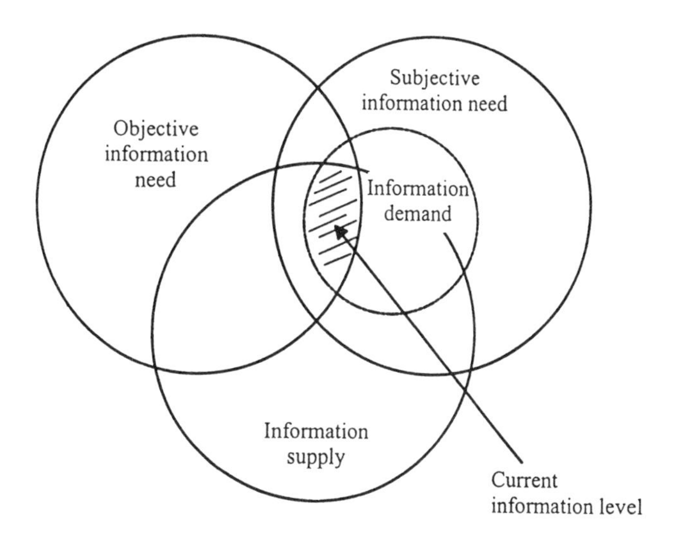

Figure 3.11 *Information need and information supply. Source: Heinen (1991, p. 276)*

Figure 3.11 illustrates this situation. It should be considered that the definition of the task itself depends on the given level of information.

In order to match both the objective and subjective information need, it makes sense to use methods which allow the one responsible for the task to express his information needs. At the same time, further aspects regarding content should be considered. This process is offered by the *method of critical success factors (CSF)*. With this method, those factors and parameters are identified and analyzed which are of special relevance for task completion. This happens in a meeting in which the decision-makers themselves as well as experts in this method participate. Among other things, the advantage of such a method is that the decision-makers become conscious of those factors which require most attention. Besides interviewing the decision-makers, those tasks for which the information need has to be identified are theoretically analyzed. The information needs analysis and the task analysis complement each other.

Life Cycle Model for Information Production

Based on the information need, the *information supply* has to be planned, organized, and controlled. Thereby, the focus is on how the person completing a task actually receives the identified information. Levitan's so-called *life cycle model* for information production is

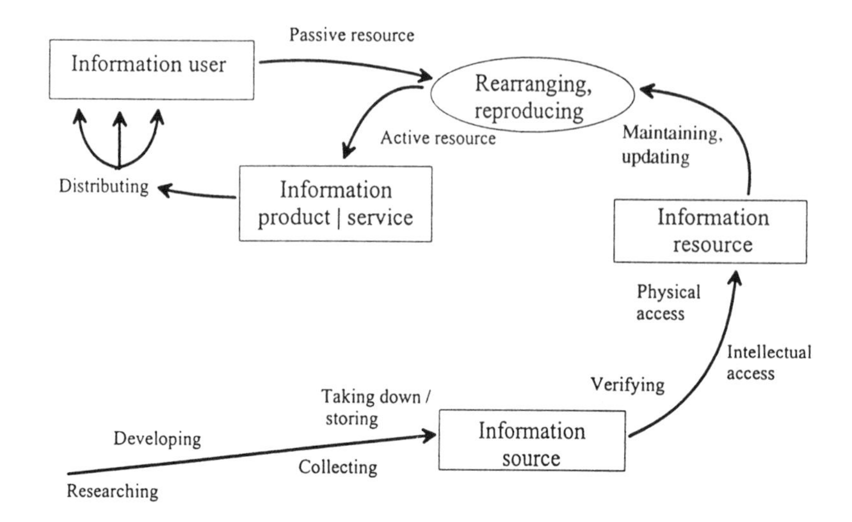

Figure 3.12 *Life cycle model for information production (following Levitan). Source: Heinen (1991, p. 283)*

suitable for analyzing the satisfaction of information needs (see Levitan, 1982). Figure 3.12 shows this life cycle model.

The *life cycle for information production* begins with the identification of potential information within a batch of data. The collected relevant data present the so-called *information source*. Several steps are necessary in order to transform an information source into an *information resource*: verification of information source, establishment of mechanisms for the physical as well as intellectual access, provision of storage possibilities, and consideration of various legal, organizational, and economical conditions. The information resource serves for satisfaction of the user's information need. Thereby, it can have an active or passive status. A resource is passive when it is used only through the user's initiative. It can then be referred to as a user-active information resource. In the active state, the resource is transformed into information products and services, which are transferred to the information user, for example in the form of either regular reports or messages triggered by over-, or underpassed threshold values (see Szyperski, 1980).

The advantage of such a life cycle model is that the various "production phases" of information can be identified and developed. These phases of production can be used as a starting point to answer questions related to the planning of information resources. At the same time, the different phases of the life cycle model offer an important starting point to determine potential supports through information and communication systems. Information management should identify and implement these starting points.

Evaluation of Information

A further, very important task of information management presents the *economic evaluation of information*. The economic value of information is determined through information's utility for problem solving and decision-making processes and the activities necessary for procuring and producing this information. Due to the previously named typical information properties, however, the evaluation of information causes several problems.

Theoretically, the *optimal degree of information* is reached when the additional costs of information activities equal the utility gained from this information. The practical identification of this optimum, however, fails due to the inability to sufficiently quantify costs and the utility of information. Furthermore it is assumed that all relevant information can be either procured or produced.

The previously mentioned *information paradox* is a typical problem of information evaluation. An evaluation of information presupposes that the information to be procured is already known. For what is not known, and thus not testable, cannot be evaluated. However, if information can be evaluated, then the buyer has already grasped the information and no longer has to buy it. In this ironic situation an evaluation can only occur *ex post*. In order to assess an economic advantage of procuring and thus producing information, however, its value would have to be known *ex ante* (see Arrow, 1974; Williamson, 1985). This triggers far-reaching consequences for the transfer of information within and between organizations. Instead of an explicit evaluation of information, *trust in the information source often serves as an evaluation substitute*. When searching and evaluating information it further has to be considered that temporal and financial restrictions are often given. Therefore, in practical situations, information production is stopped as soon as alternatives are recognized, with which at least a satisfying solution can be expected (see pages 75–76).

In conclusion, procuring and producing information presents a very important task of a corporate information management. Due to the differences between the production factor information and other corporate resources, traditional models for an economic use of resources can hardly be applied to information. The analysis of the economical advantage of information causes serious problems due to the information paradox and the difficulties in identifying and quantifying costs and benefits. This has to be considered when assessing the importance of information in interorganizational information and communication relations.

IMPLICATIONS FOR THE MANAGEMENT OF INFORMATION AND COMMUNICATION

The discussions in this chapter have identified problems of information behavior, information production, and information evaluation. Various theoretical information and communication models show how such problems may have an inhibiting effect on tasks based on the division of labor within and between organizations. It became clear that defects in communication processes between actors can occur on different levels:

- syntactic, semantic, or pragmatic defects in communication between actors (levels of semiotics, von Weizsäcker);
- technical intereferences of information transfer (Shannon, Weaver);
- psychological-sociologically related defects in human communication processes (Watzlawick et al);
- behavior of economic subjects deviating from the ideal of efficient and effective information use (O'Reilly);
- bounded rationality and limited information processing capacity of actors (Simon);
- existence of information pathologies (Wilensky, Scholl);
- failures in the interorganizational information transfer due to prisoner dilemma situations (Schrader, von Hippel).

Successful communication between actors within and between organizations depends greatly on how certain typical behaviors in dealing with information are considered in the design of information and communication systems: bounded human rationality and limited information processing capacity; the characteristic communication behavior of decision-makers, such as the preferred use of oral communication forms; as well as organizational factors such as not passing on information for egoistic motives or influence activities, all influence the efficiency and effectiveness of communication.

Whatever causes may exist for communication problems, they have to be identified through the *management of information and communication* and neutralized through a suitable design of information and communication systems. This is especially true for interorganizational information and communication relations. The problems illustrated are supported in two ways: first, certain communication problems become even more serious in the interorganizational context, for example through the physical and/or temporal distance or technical problems; second, the solution of problems becomes more difficult, because the management of information and communication crosses organizational boundaries. System design is no longer the responsibility of a single corporate management, but requires the coordination of a variety of corporate interests. This causes a cross-corporate dilution of responsibilities regarding system design, complex coordination mechanisms, and a wider scope for self-interest seeking, opportunistic behavior.

The described models of information and communication possess a considerable application potential for the explanation of different communication defects within and between organizations. In addition, they contribute important insights to the discussion of interorganizational cooperation forms. Compared to the traditional, highly integrated firms, in *symbiotic organizational forms* or in *telework* (more on virtual corporations in Chapter 8) the above-mentioned problems can be intensified, possibly even multiplied, because larger distances have to be overcome when communicating. With increasing distances, transmission mistakes at the syntactic, semantic, and especially the pragmatic level of communication, as well as defects in human communication processes, become more likely because of the relational aspect. With increasing distances, also the dependence on a reliable technical transmission of information increases.

Thus, the potential disadvantages regarding communication in symbiotic arrangements or virtual corporations need to be compensated via a higher efficiency of these new organizational forms or have to be mastered through the use of modern information and communication technology (video conferencing, picture phone, fiber optic networks and so on). In contrast, when modularizing a corporation, these communication problems are rather diminished if tasks which have been previously completed in different departments and by physically separated task responsibilities are organized in autonomously acting entrepreneurial subunits.

Regarding the question whether the *emergence of hybrid organizational forms* generally increases or decreases these problems of information behavior, compared with the traditional organization, no general conclusion is possible. However, two major starting points for the solution or alleviation of these problems can be identified:

1 Although the *use of modern information and communication technologies* (for example electronic archive systems and document administration, databases, artificial intelligence systems) cannot eliminate the limits imposed by bounded rationality and restricted information processing capacity, it can extend them. Through the use of information and communication technologies, the information behavior of co-workers can be improved, in order to promote efficient and effective information behavior. For example, the use of distributed data bases or the possibility to search for information at any

PC can smoothen problems of insufficient information procurement due to great distances from information sources.

2 Next to and together with information and communication techniques, problems regarding information behavior can be solved in many cases through the *implementation of institutional conditions favorable for human information processing*. For example, the non-realization of information transfer in a prisoner dilemma situation cannot be solved through the most modern information and communication technology, yet can be overcome through cooperation based on long-term contracts and mutual trust. Also, positive incentive structures for sufficient information procurement and the efficient use of information can be created through institutional rules, for example through systems in which the department asking for information is also charged with the costs in gathering the information.

In addition, *problems of information production and evaluation* are of equal importance to the discussed phenomenon of fading organizational boundaries. Information production generates problems if it is too much effort, if it is not oriented towards actual needs, and if it is encumbered with evaluation problems. These problems of information production are especially present in symbiotic arrangements with other corporations, where the objective is the production of new or the transfer of existing information (e.g., information partnerships, development cooperations, cooperative research projects). In these types of symbiotic arrangements, problems related to information production appear in a cumulative manner, since not only the specialties of the production factor information, but also the relation with the cooperation partner have to be considered. On the other hand, in the case of a modularization of corporations as well as for the virtual organization there generally arise no specific problems of information production, which fundamentally differ from those of traditional, highly integrated corporations.

The problems of information production can be partially controlled or lessened through *information and communication systems*. Due to the progress in recent years in information and communication techniques (artificial intelligence, neuronal networks, fuzzy logic), today all phases of information production can be supported; in some phases humans can be even replaced through information and communication systems. But also institutional factors can contribute to the dismantling of inefficiencies in information production. For example, one could think about the possibility of overcoming the information paradox through hostage exchange or through building the information seller's reputation. Also through long-term contracts, which create and maintain mutual trust between the transaction partners, the problems resulting from the information paradox can be more effectively controlled.

The fundamental thoughts presented in this chapter will be further developed in the following chapters and combined with other theoretical approaches. Thereby it will be shown which driving forces foster the disintegration of firms, which possible forms of disintegration exist, what role information and communication technology plays, and how the emerging organizational forms can be managed. This book's fundamental concept is that organization and information and communication technologies have to interact in order to allow a corporation to enter into new forms of symbiotic arrangements without losing its internal cohesion.

4
The Potential of Information Technology in Developing the Market-driven Organization

In the previous chapter we discussed basic models of information and communication. Subsequently, the reader was presented with models of understanding, communication, as well as information behavior. It was then possible to discuss models of coordination, a most basic and omnipresent task in all organizations brought about through the division of labor. We concluded with models of information production and addressed the consequences for management.

Throughout this chapter the authors address various potentials and limits of information technology and how they extend organizational boundaries. On the one hand, we are aware of certain limits in the sense of knowledge, capacity, time, geography and speed. All of these can be addressed in terms of information technology itself, but also in terms of people. For example, information technology has capacity limits within each device conceivable. Analogously, human beings using information technology sooner or later will experience such capacity limits and usually people are served well when using information technology to expand their human capacity limits. Very often information technology serves as an impressive device to overcome time limits, as such technology may work well continuously 24 hours per day (Wigand, 1996, 1985b, 1984). Similarly, information can be processed and transmitted today at speeds inconceivable just a few years ago. Such technology may establish geographical boundaries or may do away with them entirely. For example, a customer service telephone line can be managed and run today from almost any location in the United States and the employees answering the phone could be dispersed throughout the nation. With that, however, come opportunities also to extend market boundaries.

Rather than operating just on a state-wide basis, information technology may allow us to offer the same service on a national basis through the appropriate use of information technology. Several information technologies open boundaries, expand markets, as well as enable the market-driven firm and previously unthought of and impossible processes.

As organizations we may have reached our collective performance limit that, in turn, may be extended through information technology. Moreover, it appears that information technology can dissolve many other traditional boundaries such as geographical limitations, distances, speed and also work time (Wigand, 1996). With the help of groupware software such as Lotus Notes it is possible for a software company with subsidiaries throughout the world to work around the clock via differing shifts in several locations. It can develop software, for example, during an eight-hour working day in country A, the team in country B continues when that eight-hour working day is over in country A. Lastly, country C in yet another time zone carries on with the software project when the team in country B finishes its work schedule. Next morning the team in country A continues and the cycle repeats itself. With information technology, software and networks certain types of tasks can be worked on continuously, regardless of time differences and geographical location. Information, when viewed as a resource and commodity, brings along peculiar characteristics: In contrast to physical goods, information may be shared and we (or even more people) both have a copy (e.g., Wigand, 1988a). With physical products only one person can have that product. With this unique characteristic come also unique ownership rights for information. Information technology and the information resources managed by organizations make possible the potential dissolution of various traditional organizational aspects: different structural arrangements are conceivable within organizations, as divisions and departmentalizations may no longer be the most advantageous organizational form. We may also rethink traditional forms of the division of labor, as information technology may suggest different arrangements. The recently gained knowledge from trends in modularization (see Chapter 5) and decentralization, as well as telework (see Chapter 8), all can be viewed as outcomes of recognizing new potential in information technology and in developing the market-driven organization. In doing so, new extended boundaries and opportunities are emerging that were previously inconceivable without the advent of newer information technology. Chapter 3 addressed basic models and understanding of communication and how communication is a fundamental entity in any coordination effort. This chapter shows how information technology can be seen within a theoretical framework, how this technology becomes a tool in various coordination efforts and how the potential of information technology enables the market-driven organization to achieve its goals.

BASIC POSSIBILITIES AND LIMITS OF INFORMATION AND COMMUNICATION TECHNOLOGY

Human information processing capacity is limited. Information and communication technologies offer the possibility to overcome this limitation of human information reception, storage and processing. In turn, these technologies make possible the expansion of human performance limits with regard to space, time and speed. It is this most fundamental potential of technological media that make them so attractive; on the other hand, we recognize also limits of these media that are just as fundamental. Here we are not so much concerned with the technological limits typically encountered by the user in the daily use of information and communication technologies, but we would like to focus on the restrictions of processing speeds, the storage capacities or the transmission speeds and capacities. As processors, storage chips and transmission channels continue to enjoy ever-increasing capacities, speed and capacity concerns gradually lose their importance (see pages 114–130). Of much more fundamental importance are the *theoretical* limits of computer-supported information processing. These limits are equally applicable for hypothetical computer models with unlimited processing and storage capacity. Specifically, these are the limits of *formalization* and *computability*, the central research focus of theoretical computer science.

For the present purposes merely some aspects of *formalization* can be discussed. They are sufficient in that they assist the reader in understanding fundamental information and communication technology performance boundaries. The interested reader may review the much more detailed and relevant literature on this topic (e.g., Cohen, 1986; Engeler and Läuchli, 1988; Sander, Stucky and Herschel, 1996; Schöning, 1992; Stetter, 1988; Hopcroft and Ullman, 1979; Börger, 1992).

Formalization as a Precondition of Information and Communication Technology Configuration

Computer systems are being developed to help people in solving information processing problems. In the final analysis, however, computer-supported information processing always implies carrying out specific processing instructions and procedures over this information.

Computer-supported problem solving is always preceded by the formalization of problem-solving rules, in addition to the formalization of the needed information. More specifically, this implies a formal description of the problem to be solved: *Without formalization there will be no implementation, without implementation there can be no information system.*

Of central importance, therefore, is the question for what kind of problems it is even possible to find formalizations and what such formalizations appropriately ought to look like. Closely linked to these questions is a multitude of additional questions: What descriptive techniques are available for the specification of problems or problem solving instructions? Which modes of expression may be attributed to certain descriptive techniques? May we point the finger at a chosen descriptive technique (e.g., a programming language) when certain problems do not lend themselves for formalization? In addition, which attributes characterize universal descriptive techniques, i.e. techniques suitable to describe formally *all* problems that are principally formalizable?

Within the context of information processing precise and finite processing instructions are labeled *algorithms*. The term algorithm is one of the oldest roots of information processing and still is an essential and important building block today. This term goes back 1200 years to the mathematician and teaching master Al Chwârismî, who taught at the court of the Caliph of Baghdad. His focus was originally exclusively on the mechanical rules for the calculation of written numbers. Leibniz generalized this algorithm and developed fixed rules for the processing of general symbols and symbol sequences that may have any arbitrary meaning (Bauer and Wössner, 1981; Bauer, Brauer and Jessen, 1992). Vivid examples for algorithms are computer programs, although one should note that in order to formalize such programs the type of computer language utilized is by itself not essential. Essential is solely the *unequivocally and finitely specified sequence of elementary processing steps*. These are needed in order to understand the stepwise transformation of input data into output data. Increasingly today formal problem specifications in descriptive languages are also viewed as algorithms. Although these do not offer precise processing steps, they enable computer-based interpretation and problem solving. Informal hints and instructions, cooking recipes or craft work instructions typically do not meet this demand for computer-based interpretation and execution. Consequently, they do not fall into the category of algorithms.

Basic algorithms find application in a number of differing areas. Among them are search and sorting algorithms, algorithms for the processing of symbol sequences or algorithms for solving graph and network problems (see, for example, Knuth, 1973a; Knuth, 1973b; Knuth, 1981; Sedgewick, 1988; Ottman and Widmayer, 1990). Each mathematical formula, in its capacity as a processing rule for its respective input parameters, is an algorithm. The field of management utilizes a multitude of useful algorithms for special application areas, e.g. production industries use algorithms for the determination of optimal lot sizes, cycle times and capacities, for machine and job scheduling, or for minimizing traffic and routing problems.

Computer programs in popular programming languages are merely a special case in the formulation of algorithms. Generally, an algorithmic description may occur through the aid of mathematical constructs, on the basis of so-called *formal languages* or through the use of abstract computer models such as Turing machines. The latter devices are abstract, symbol-processing machines that are merely *theoretically* capable of executing a specific algorithm. A few basic models of formal description are briefly presented in the following sections. Before doing so, it is important to point again to the already mentioned theoretical limits of formalization: not all problems can be solved with algorithms. One of the more interesting aspects of theoretical informatics is the sheer existence of proofs that for certain problem settings *no* solution-generating algorithm is possible. Indeed, we may point to many examples in the past when sizeable research and development projects failed and in which the search for algorithms failed because of their provable unsolvability.

Alternative Models of Formalization

Communication, as a prerequisite for task accomplishment through the division of labor and via one or another form of coordination, always utilizes a carrier *language*. As long as a single individual autonomously faces problems of the real world, it may be sufficient when this actor carries in his/her head an implicit picture of the goal's direction or a path to solve a problem. For a transmission of tasks and partial problems onto other actors, however, it is necessary to formulate problem solving paths or a goal direction in a language that occurs through the specification of a mental model representative of the real world situation. People in organizations who need to carry out tasks usually deem it sufficient to communicate with others through a rather informal or semi-formal description, in other words: a natural language. In order to translate tasks in the sense of the above discussed computer-based algorithms, a highly *formal* task description is required. Such a description is characterized by stringent and precise formation rules and they are specified in *formal languages*.

Formal languages, programming languages belong to this category, are of an artificial nature. They are determined just like their less formal counterparts through a certain basic vocabulary, the *alphabet*, and a number of rules, the *grammar*, that specify how words and sentences of that language are built with the elements of the basic vocabulary. The syntax of a formal language is thus clearly specified and its semantics are well defined, i.e. the correctness and the meaning of a sentence in this language is always unambiguously determinable. It is, for example, always possible to determine whether a given program text represents a formally correct program, and which semantic meaning is to be assigned to the program.

The determination of syntactic rules within a formal language may occur in a number of ways, e.g., via the use for formal *grammars* or through the use of so-called *automata*, i.e. abstract machines capable of understanding sentences in a respective formal language. Both of these formalization models are briefly highlighted here.

Grammars. These are quantities of rules that determine the syntax of a language. The rule stating that a declarative sentence in the English language consists of subject, predicate and object is part of English grammar. Analogously within the realm of formal languages, e.g., the structure of a Pascal program is defined as *program reader*, *declarations* and *statements*. Although natural languages typically offer only very incomplete grammatical rules due to their volume and constant change, formal languages are highly and precisely describable by formal grammars. Such precision, however, comes with a price: the more correctly the structure of a language is specified, the more limited are the possibilities to express oneself. In other words, the *power* of a language is dependent on the degree to which it can be described in detail. Given the degree to which a formal language can express itself makes possible a differentiation of language classes. This classification is based on the work of the language theoretician Noam Chomsky. In 1959 he created a central and basic scaffolding, the so-called *Chomsky Hierarchy*, making possible the classification of formal languages (see Figure 4.1). Each language class can be characterized through a certain type of formal grammar.

A *regular* grammar, the rule system for the so-called Chomsky-3-languages, is distinguished in that the formation of sentences in this language has to occur strictly from left to right or vice versa. Variable labels in Pascal programs, for example, are defined as a letter, followed by any quantity of numbers and letters, a formation rule that can be applied stringently from left to right. Other application areas for such

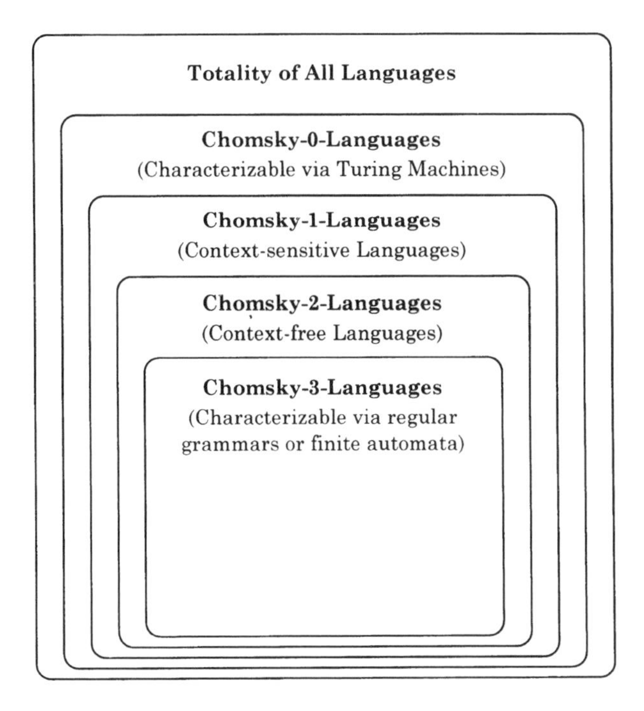

Figure 4.1 *The Chomsky Hierarchy. Source: adapted from Schöning (1992, p. 20. Reproduced by permission from Spektrum Akademischer Verlag, Heidelberg/Berlin/Oxford.)*

grammars are the specification of logical switches in the electronics industry. On the other hand, if that grammar permits a sentence formation in a mixed sequence, without the context of the respective sentence exerting any influence on its meaning, this is a *context-free* grammar, represented in Chomsky-2 as a language class. The grammatical basis of an entire Pascal program, consisting of variable labels, commands and other structural elements, is context-free.

Formal Automata Models. These are abstract descriptions of machines that are capable of transforming input into certain output. A chewing gum vending machine, for example, demonstrates well the "transformation" of a coin into chewing gum. The individual processing steps are: acceptance of money, checking of each individual coin, checking of number of coins, return of coins when overpaid and release of chewing gum. The execution of these processing steps brings about each time a change of conditions within the vending machine: the quantity of coins present, the number of chewing gum packets available, etc. These conditions and processing steps together define the formal automaton.

Within the context of formal languages abstract machines can be utilized to accept sentences of a formal language as either correct or to refuse them as incorrect. In this way the above-mentioned Chomsky language classes can be distinguished clearly via the machines that are necessary in order to *accept* all sentences of their respective language class. Sentences of a Chomsky-3 language, for example, can be determined by machines with only a finite memory, i.e. by machines that, casually speaking, do not have the facility to store an infinite amount of data somewhere for a later work step. Such automata are called *finite automata*. They accept sentences from classes fitting the Chomsky-3-grammatics. A compiler uses such a finite automaton in order to partition the individual letters of source code into meaningful words. The entire program, on the other hand, belonging to the class of *context-free* languages, is recognized by a so-called pushdown automaton, an abstract machine that for its work occupies (theoretically) an infinitely large, last in-first out storage area, the so-called stack.

What do these language-theoretical deliberations have to do with management? A decisive factor is that such automata models, e.g. in graphical notations, represent *actions*. A single action describes the transformation of inputs into outputs, a fact that is of highest importance for the formalization of organizational processes. Approaches to workflow modeling, i.e. the description of organizational events supported by information technology, often utilize formal automata for descriptive reasons. Figure 4.2 depicts a conversation network structure modeled via an automaton (state chart) based on action workflow theory (see pages 67–70). The network describes a possible conversation discourse for the conversation type "order", as it was presented in *Coordinator*, the first and probably best known computer system for explicit conversational support. The nodes of the diagram specify the potential circumstances during the course of the conversation process; the edges represent the occurring speech acts. This kind of modeling forms the basis for a large class of newer systems for communication and decision support in organizations compare with the basics of Action Workflow Theory—Winograd, 1986; Winograd and Flores, 1986; Medina-Mora et al, 1992).

The depicted conversation network is an example for a *finite automaton*. The earlier mentioned automata with only finite memory are capable to recognize sentences in a Chomsky-3-language. This most limited automata class, due to its simple way to implement, is most important for practical descriptive purposes.

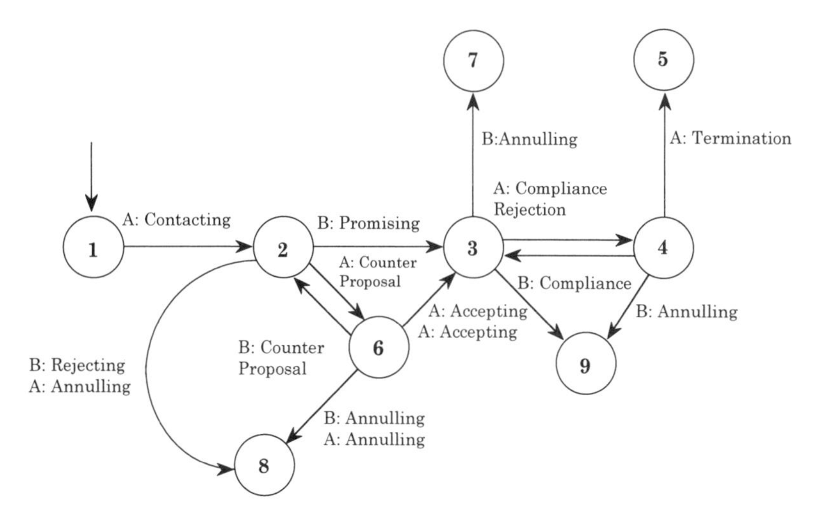

Figure 4.2 *Example of a conversation network structure modeled as an automaton. Source: based on Borghoff and Schlichter (1995, p. 187)*

The most comprehensive automata model suitable for the classification of Chomsky-0-languages is the so-called Turing machine. It was proposed in 1936 by the mathematician Allan M. Turing as a formal model. Above all it is important for its theoretical significance as a basis for making assertions about the fundamental limits of fomalizability. An important prerequisite in this effort is not the provable, yet generally accepted supposition, that the power of Turing machines is principally equivalent to the power of algorithms. In other words, *each and every* by intuition formalizable problem can always be described via a Turing machine. This statement is known as Church's Hypothesis.

Originally Turing wanted to model systematically how people handle problem solving, inferences and judgments. He came to the conclusion that notepads, pencil and eraser, as well as the knowledge of a few symbols together with a few elementary moves are quite sufficient. In Turing's modeling conception, a systematically thinking person does nothing else but record symbols within boxes on a notepad following simple rules, or erase them. Each problem that is somehow formalizable can be handled using these tools, except that depending on the circumstance a considerable amount of time and paper may be required (and in some cases it may require an infinite amount of time and an infinite amount of paper). The Turing machine reflects the conception of the systematically calculating individual: the paper becomes an endless work band, pencil and eraser converge into a read and write-head whose actions are determined by a regulator following simple rules. In accordance with Church's hypothesis, everything that can be managed via the use of computers can also be described via this simple model. Problems for which we cannot find a solution using this Turing model, however, can never be solved via a computer-supported solution.

The above mentioned automata models have two aspects in common: the control through a *central* authority and the sequencing of processing steps. This corresponds with the classical perspective of information processing and communication processes. It is evident in organizations today that the classical, largely centralized, view of organization structures is merely a special case along the dimension of *centralization* and *decentralization.* This perspective also carries over into the realm of information and communication systems and allows us to place the concept of central control onto a continuum of varying degrees of "distributedness". Analogously, the classical view of the largely sequential perspective of organizational processes, as well as technical processes, merely allows us to view this situation as a special case along the dimension of *sequencing* and *parallelizing.*

The need for a discussion concerning the degree of freedom of *distribution* and *concurrency* is well recognized. For several decades experts have been working on improving the understanding of cooperative processes; the existing knowledge about the organization of distributed systems and concurrent processes is still limited.

An important approach for the description of distributed, concurrent and also indeterminate systems is the so-called *Petri Net Model* (see, for example, Baumgarten, 1990; Reisig, 1990; Starke, 1990). Carl Adam Petri built the foundation for this approach with his thesis in 1962, making possible the depiction of time-based relationships. Petri nets are used today in a multitude of areas, e.g., in the description of human interaction processes, technical communication processes, but also in businesses processes. Page 144–147 on "Enterprise Modeling", describe this in greater detail.

An important application area of Petri nets is the modeling of communication protocols. Such protocols are needed in order to ascertain in computer networks (see pages 114–130) a regulated information exchange and to exclude undesirable network behavior such that a modicum of error tolerance is achieved. Nationally and internationally normed communication protocols (e.g., the ISO/OSI Reference Model, see pages referred to above) are typically too complex today in order to be tested comprehensively in applied situations. Network models offer here the opportunity to bring about a graphically pleasing description, formal analysis or the simulation of extensive test runs. Within the context of business applications Petri nets are enjoying increasing popularity for the analysis, description and simulation of office and general business processes. They permit the description of structured processes within and among organizations when such processes are to be accomplished through the division of labor. Petri nets are not limited to the depiction of solely sequential processing steps, but they make possible also the description of processing alternatives and simultaneous processes.

Limits of Formalizability

Information processing requires communication; communication requires language. While interpersonal communication can take advantage of informal language means, the utilization of computer systems and the technical communication between computer systems always requires formalized communication. The possibilities for formalized communication are always limited based on the degree to which formal languages and their characterization models (mathematical constructs, logical calculations, grammars and automata) can express themselves. Computational theory addresses the question which problems can be described through which language classes and where the limits of 'computability' are. These questions, however, are of a lesser importance when looking at the field of computer supported information processing (see, for example, Bauer, Brauer and Jessen, 1992), as computers, strictly speaking, must always be merely finite automata. The reason therefore lies within the *finite-ness* of the available storage space. Beginning with the problem classes characterizable via the Chomsky-2-languages a theoretically infinite storage area is required for the implementation of the respective formal automata model. No matter how large the available storage area, regardless of how high the processor's performance or how much time is available, under real applied conditions space and time are always finite. It follows then that the model assumptions of the unlimited storage capacity or unlimited time beyond the Chomsky-3-language classes are unreal.

But what can computers deliver under these real restrictive conditions? This is a question addressed by *complexity theory*. It also addresses questions of resource demands for the processing of principally solvable problems and attempts to classify problem approaches according to the volume of resource demands. Answers to these questions, in turn, make possible the ascertainment—a necessary prerequisite—for fundamental cost estimates in the area of computer-supported information processing. On the basis of resource consumption one may easily demonstrate that even for many fully formalizable or, respectively, algorithm-based problems a precise computer-supported problem solution is not possible. Numerous business problems fall into this complexity class, e.g., the problem of the traveling salesperson who is concerned with determining the travel route of any given number of travel destinations while trying to minimize the transportation costs. Another example falling into this class is the problem of the maximal utilization of machines within a given factory. All of these problems are generally more meaningfully manageable when applying heuristic principles.

Limits of computation already exist with relatively well describable problem situations in a static problem domain. In addition the conditions of business reality "complicate" the situation: the business problem domain is subject to permanent, more or less strong changes. Formal descriptions, however, are of a static nature. Moreover, real problem situations change also precisely due to our attempt to describe them. Nevertheless intensive efforts are made in conducting research on new and continued development of descriptive techniques for system specification. Correctness, unequivocality, completeness, verifiability and consistency are priority qualitative characteristics of an "ideal" system description. Little doubt exists that comprehensive modeling of the social system "firm" is realizable and appropriate, i.e. it is generally agreed that this goal is potentially achievable. When attempting to apply economic theory, however, the achievement of this goal becomes questionable. Already in 1987 Ciborra (with a view toward the development of comprehensive data models of the firm) pointed to this fundamental problem of realizability of formal models of the firm: "Now, if this were all possible, the enterprise would not have any reason to exist according to the transaction cost view: its dissolution would be warranted on efficiency grounds (reduction of overhead costs)" (Ciborra, 1987, p. 31). Consequently, the theory of transaction costs is not comprehensively describable (see Ciborra, 1987; Picot, 1989b).

The complete description of information architecture of a firm would immediately negate the raison d'être for the coordination mechanisms within that firm. The highly simplified consequence is: Either the firm is to be reorganized, i.e. the hitherto existing (e.g., hierarchical) organizational form is to be changed or the chosen approach to describe the problem was inappropriate. Under the influence of ever-increasing expansion of information and communication technology infrastructures, the predicted consequences manifest themselves already today in the applied world. Monolithic enterprise structures are dissolving in favor of decentralized, distributed and network-like organization architectures. Today's information models, however, cannot support the change capabilities of firms toward modular or virtual structures; they hinder the change process. Modular, network-like or virtual organizations (see Chapter 8) do not emerge out of the blue: they emerge through organization change from within existing organization structures. Actual descriptive techniques so far have not been able to support this change process.

FOUNDATIONS OF INFORMATION AND COMMUNICATION TECHNOLOGY AND INFORMATION MANAGEMENT

Are organizational or also societal changes a product of technological progress? Or do social processes determine technological development? For a long time social science research focused rather one-sidedly on the influence of new technologies on society as a whole, concentrated on groups or organizations, as well as on the individual as both the afflicted and user. Questions of technology assessment, as well as of effects and user research occurred largely from a perspective of technological determinism. On the other hand, social conditions and practices are not without influence on the nature and speed of technological progress. Questions pertaining to the nature, degree and effect trends of reciprocal influence factors are everything but settled (Wigand, 1995d). Some fundamental viewpoints and perspectives may be identified. Knowing about them is a necessary prerequisite for the critical appraisal of the role of modern information and communication technologies for the development of the firm.

Information and Communication Technology and Society

In a very broad interpretation technology is described as the applied science directed toward an industrial problem. While science is merely concerned with the understanding of facts, technology manifests itself in the concrete *application* of this knowledge. Technology in general, and information and communication technologies specifically, may be viewed from varying perspectives pertaining to its utility for society. At least with regard to such well-known literary works as Aldous Huxley's *Brave New World* and George Orwell's *1984* it is clear that an exclusively positive relationship between technology and society is by no means intended. The potential nature of these relationships can be differentiated from a utopian, dystopian, neutral and contingency perspective.

The *utopian perspective* associates principally positive effects for individual and society. Representatives of this view are Daniel Bell and Buckminster Fuller who are strong believers in the supportive power of technology and they view technology as a problem solver. Consequently, these proponents demand rapid technological development and expect policy support. In exact contrast to this position is the *dystopian perspective*, described for example by Jacques Ellul and John McDermott. Here, technology is viewed as a problem generator and no supportive function is attributed. Representatives of this view fight technological progress and attempt to stop it. The position of David Sarnoff, however, may be described as a *neutral view*. Here, technology is said to have no correlation with societal problems. In other words, an evaluation and assessment of technology is unnecessary. A fourth perspective, the *contingency perspective*, considers the context within which a technology is being introduced. This situational argumentation, as manifested in the work by Ithiel de Sola Pool and Rob Kling, reflects the dual nature of technology as a problem solver and a problem generator. Innovations in this area therefore demand an individual and selective judgment and progress underlies social, as well as technological limitations.

The basic problem-solving capabilities of technology cannot be contested in light of recent spectacular economic growth. The standard of living in the United States of America, Japan and Western Europe during the last 50 years has risen enormously and incomparably. On the other hand, the phenomenon of worldwide global pollution or the increasing dependence of individuals upon certain technological achievements demonstrates clearly how the introduction of technologies, in turn, may trigger new problems. In order to solve these problems, one is again dependent on new technologies.

Information and Communication Technologies and Organization

Information processing belongs to the fundamental activities in all organizations. Organizational information processing reduces risks through the collection, change, aggregation, prioritization and moving of information within organizational limits and beyond these. Information and communication technology forms in this an essential foundation, even though opinions pertaining to the question which elements of information and communication systems belong under the rubric of technology diverge considerably (see Orlikowski, 1992). Some authors refer here solely to the underlying hardware (Hickson et al, 1969; Blau et al, 1976; Barley, 1986; Bjørn-Andersen, Eason and Robey, 1986; Davis, 1989), while within broader definitions immaterial factors are included also, such as activities, methods and knowledge of technology (Perrow, 1967; Thompson, 1967; Eveland, 1986). The more general the use of the term technology, however, the more difficult it becomes to find concrete answers to the question of the interplay between man and technology.

Looking at the role of information processing within organizations more carefully one may also delineate among varying perspectives. Robbins (1990), as well as Orlikowski (1992) offer three important currents within technology research. The so-called *Technology Imperative Model*, originated and developed further by Hickson et al (1969), Aldrich (1972), as well as Blau et al (1976), posits a direct causal context between technology and various organizational dimensions such as structure, size, performance or degree of centralization. Moreover, within this framework technology effects manifest themselves in the individual such as in the form of lack of work satisfaction, task complexity, qualification, communication behavior and productivity (see Orlikowski, 1992). The fundamental assumption of this perspective is that all of these dimensions, including the technology itself, can be measured and predicted.

While technology may be viewed as an independent variable from this imperative perspective, the *Strategic Choice Model* views technology in the role of a dependent variable brought about through various organizational forces. Proponents of this position (e.g., Child, 1972; Davis and Taylor, 1986; Kling and Iacono, 1984; Markus, 1983; Perrow, 1983; Trist et al, 1963; Zuboff, 1988) emphasize that on the one hand technology is being influenced by the context in which it is introduced, and, on the other hand, by the strategies pursued by affected actors and decision-makers. The goal of these socio-technical studies is the attempt to demonstrate how worker satisfaction and productivity may be manipulated through the optimization of social and technical working conditions.

A third perspective can be found with Barley (1986, 1990), i.e. his *model of technology as a trigger of structural change*. In a study focusing on the introduction of computer tomography within two radiology centers Barley discovered a change in the institutionalized roles of the employees, as well as in the interaction patterns among themselves. Barley sees technology as the trigger for certain social processes that may lead to expected and also unexpected structural changes. Technology here is being characterized as a variable that enters the relationship between actors and the organization structure.

Orlikowski (1992) criticizes in Barley's perspective the lack of attention to the *change in the technology during the course of its deployment*. Especially with regard to information technology, however, one can observe that the very same technology when deployed by different users may take on varying forms and functionalities even over a longer period of time. Orlikowski developed for this purpose the *Structurational Model of Technology*, a model based on the earlier work of Giddens (1979, 1984) (see Rosenbaum, 1996). Giddens attributed institutional structures a dual character: (a) the way in which structural characteristics exert influence on human behavior, and (b) how human behavior may enforce or change a given structure. This thought is developed by Orlikowski with the perspective that technology is in constant interaction with the organization. The dual influence of technology on the institutional context on the one hand and the deliberate behavior of human actors on the other hand is to be understood here in a reciprocal fashion. It should be noted though that this perspective does not make any directly causal model claims, but places its major emphasis on the *interaction* of the components.

All four perspectives presented here, i.e. technology as an independent, dependent, dependently-influencing or independently-influencing variable, are relevant for the comprehensive understanding of the relationship between technology and organization. The way in which technology can be positioned within the spectrum ranging from determinism to unpredictability is in the final analysis reflected in the way of thinking by researchers, those responsible for technology or information managers. In turn, this way of thinking will be reflected in the assessment of the potential of information and communication technologies.

The Three-levels Model of Information Management

It is the role of information management to make sure that information in the organization is deployed effectively (goal-directed) and efficiently (economical). In order to achieve this goal, information management needs to be accomplished on three interrelated levels as shown in Figure 4.3 (see Picot and Reichwald, 1991).

The Level of Information Deployment. On this level all information demand and supply is being planned, organized and controlled for all essential organizational purposes (internal and external). The management of information deployment is especially the role of the firm's leadership. In the final analysis we are concerned here with the setting of priorities for planning and controlling information, as well as document requirements, all of which need to be made accessible in a systematic fashion. This level defines the demands and receives the support services from the level of information and communication systems.

The Level of Information and Communication Systems. Information and communication systems are synchronized arrangements of personnel-based, organizational and technical elements that meet the needs of

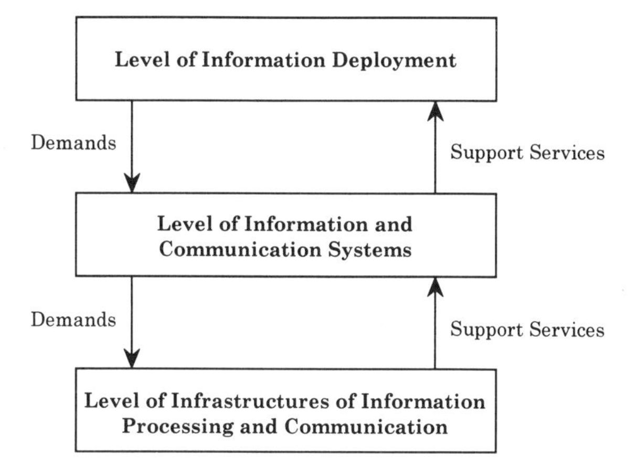

Figure 4.3 *The three-levels model of information management. Source: Wollnik (1988)*

information demand. Here we are thinking, for example, of standardized systems of accounting, production planning and controlling systems, as well as enterprise-specific systems of product and customer information. It is the role of the information and communication systems management to determine the structure of these systems through the appropriate combination of their elements. In these efforts one needs to consider the demands and requirements established in the first level. This second level simultaneously defines the demands and receives support services from the third level.

The Level of Information and Communication Technology Infrastructures. Components of the technology infrastructure may be seen (initially at least) as utility-neutral or utility-free service deliverers (Wollnik, 1988), i.e. their utility for the organization yields only from the goal-directed combination of single infrastructure components, as well as their deployment in the context of task accomplishment. Infrastructure-related decisions include decisions pertaining to computer configurations, system architecture or network solutions.

The discussion of infrastructure components and their concrete potentials is the focus of the next section. The structure and implementation of information and communication systems on the basis of the above described infrastructure components can be found on pages 131–147. Pages 147–158 address questions of deployment and productivity of information and communication in organizations.

DEVELOPMENT TRENDS OF INFORMATION AND COMMUNICATION INFRASTRUCTURES

The construction and administration of information and communication technology infrastructures encompasses the combination of appropriate computer architectures, operating systems, networks, as well as appropriate software. In such efforts it becomes essential to understand the fundamental workings of information and communication technology and the resulting potential such that professional decisions may be made.

Information technology as the classical "enabler" for new and innovative organization structures offers much potential in a number of ways. In general it is rather difficult to offer concrete suggestions for efficient deployment, due to the mass and multitude of technical details. It is much more essential to gain an understanding of information technology (IT) derived from strategic deliberations and following the Three-levels-model such that an appropriate potential can be achieved. Some fundamental IT development trends will be addressed below and an attempt is made to highlight some known potentials. In this context, gains in capacity improvement, improved mobility, cooperative work, integration, openness, distribution and globalization are addressed.

Gains in Capacity Improvement

One important potential for market-driven organization development may be derived from the increased performance capacities of computers and networks along such factors as processing and transmission speeds or the capacity potential of accompanying storage media. Figure 4.4 demonstrates an example of the technological development of processor speed and the storage improvement of personal computers. An examination of all aspects in Figure 4.4 shows an exponential improvement. In order to strengthen this impression, below we address more specifically the capacity improvements in the areas of computer architecture, networks, as well as the special case of miniaturization.

Modern *computer architectures* have long ago overcome in many areas the classical deficits of the "von Neumann Architecture," the program-controlled computer whose instructions are stored together with the appropriate data in a common storage location (see Hennessy and Patterson, 1994). In this, for then revolutionary and open architecture, the main storage area was connected via a *bus* with other specialized components such as the central processing unit (CPU) and the input/output units. In doing so a program-independent architecture was created that stood out because of its high degree of flexibility, at least

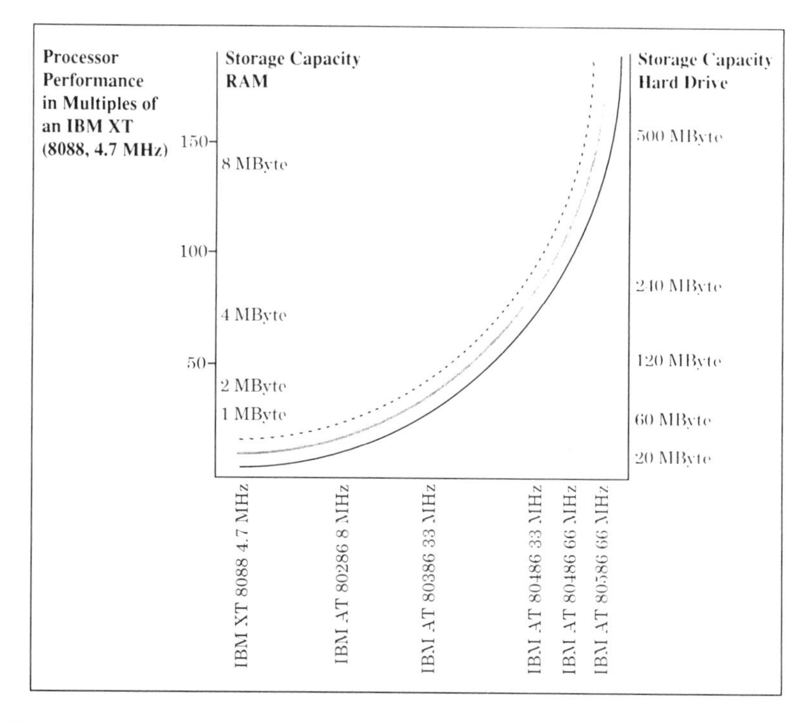

Figure 4.4 *The development of processor speed and storage capacity of micro-computers. Source: Kyas (1993, p. 26. Reproduced by permission from DATACOM-Verlag.)*

when compared to hard-wired architectures at the time. The bus plays an extremely important role in that it may be viewed generally as a transmission route that is open and connected to both sides and to which all transmission carriers are connected equally. This concept may be visualized by imagining the shape of a comb where each tooth could be used to connect bus participants. This structure then can be viewed in contrast to star or ring-like architecture concepts. During the course of technology development one encountered quickly capacity limits of a pure "von Neumann Architecture" due to natural and technical miniaturization. The bus as the sole connector of computer parts turned out to be a bottleneck with regard to processing speed which, in turn, led to the development of new, innovative computer architectures (Hwang and Briggs, 1985; Bode, 1990). RISC, superscalar, vector computers and massive parallel computers are merely some of the key proponents of new computer generations that are currently considered at the leading edge of processing speed.

With regard to modern downsizing strategies, however, the sole consideration of computer hardware is no longer sufficient for the assessment of system performance. With the migration of mainframe-oriented data processing to distributed processing on networked workstations one recognizes the necessity of adequate *network performance.* High performance networks gain prominence, fiber optic cable and new techniques increase transmission speed while reducing the error rate at the same time. In the area of local networks one should mention *Fiber Distributed Data Interface* (FDDI), *100VG* (IEEE 802.12) or *Fast Ethernet* (IEEE 802.3u) as representatives of current state-of-the-art technology. Transmission speed, labeled *bandwidth* in the terminology of digital transmission, is typically being reported in the neighborhood of 100 Mbit/s while the classical Ethernet in comparison functions at speeds up to 10 Mbit/s.

With regard to the types of communication connections one distinguishes basically two types. One such connection, known to everyone through the daily used telephone, is the *line connection*, a synchronization between sender and receiver through the construction of a line that can be used exclusively for the duration of the connection. The other connection reflects the concept of *packet switching*, i.e. the data to be transmitted can be partitioned into little blocks, so-called packets, that are then sent from sender to receiver. The lines needed for the transmission of an individual packet are activated step by step only from one node to the next. At each receiving node the next node has to be determined such that overall the entire transmission sequence is *a priori* somewhat unpredictable. The advantage with line connections is clearly with a higher rate of actual transmissions, while the packet-switched variant distinguishes itself more through its robustness. If a network node within the packet-switched network is defunct or unavailable, the packets can simply be rerouted via an alternate route.

Especially with regard to worldwide networks, the so-called *Wide Area Networks* (WAN), the demand for bandwidth plays an important role. Through the simultaneous use of a large number of worldwide distributed communication participants unusually high load demands exist. Generally, it is not possible at this level to somehow equalize potential high peak load periods. The architecture of city-linking network technologies, for example, is analogous to the situation of highway, traffic: important network nodes are connected worldwide via a dedicated data highway with sufficient capacity. Analogous to the highway, on and off ramps enable access to this *Information Highway* only at certain locations.

Three techniques feature prominently in the discussion of planning and implementation of worldwide networks: Frame Relay, DQDB and

ATM. The most widely available technology is *Frame Relay*, an optimized, packet-switching technology with transmission speeds up to 2 Mbit/s. Frame Relay, however, is not very suitable for the realization of the high-speed Information Highway in that it has too little bandwidth. A considerably higher transmission rate is available with the *Distributed Queue Dual Bus* (DQDB) technology, functioning via two unidirectional buses. Just as with a conveyor belt, empty or filled cells are sent continuously via this bus reaching the recipient with a speed of up to 140 Mbit/s.

Bandwidths of presently 155 Mbit/s and eventually up to 2.5 Gbit/s are promised with the *Asynchronous Transfer Mode* (ATM). This technology—already utilized when implementing broadband ISDN networks—is based on the packet-switching concept and uses a specific packet size. Through the construction of a so-called *virtual channel*, i.e. a virtual connection between sender and receiver at the individual network nodes, a path is made available through which very small packets may be routed. The *a priori* decision about the course of the actual transmission reduces the need for initial checking and correct distribution of individual packets during the transmission. The high speed of ATM technology is made possible through the use of *ATM switches*, network access components that no longer require the actual execution of algorithms through the participants. The sender merely has to submit the individual packets with the ATM switch and does not, as is common with many LANs, have to communicate with other network participants in various ways about the intended utilization of the transmission medium.

Figure 4.5 captures these and other communication technologies as an overview based on the transmission speeds and their time of emergence. One should note that the ordinate reflects a logarithmic scaling that also emphasizes the impressive increase in transmission speed for each respective technology.

A capacity increase of a very particular kind is *miniaturization*. This refers to the manufacture of ever smaller integrated circuits with an increasing *integration density*, i.e. the number of components on a chip are advancing more and more toward physically-determined limits based on their increased heat generation, operability and external conditions. For example, the size of a printer is determined by the paper format (8.5″ by 11″, DIN A4, 8.5″ × 11.75″) or the size of a notebook keyboard needs to offer dimensions suitable for human fingers. A telephone must be able to bridge the distance between mouth and ear and its number key pad has to offer sufficient space for appropriate use.

While factors of usability and other external conditions may be solved via clever design such as foldable key pads, the high amount of heat

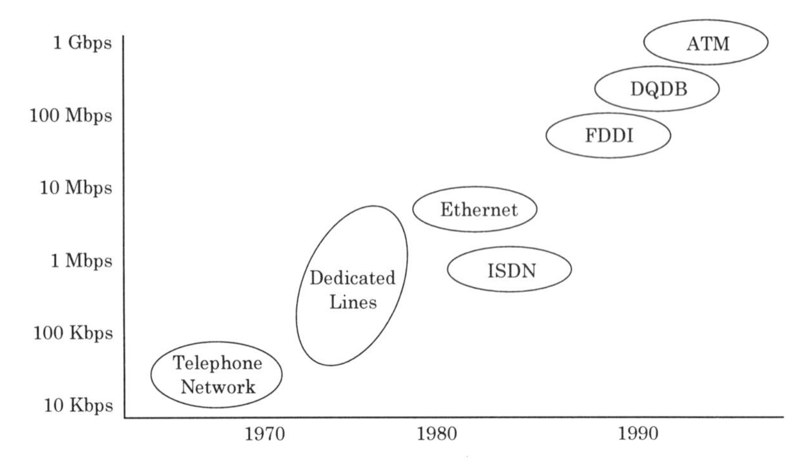

Figure 4.5 *Development of communication technology. Source: Geihs (1995, p. 4)*

generation of highly integrated circuits pose a considerably larger problem. Overheating of microprocessors is today largely addressed through the reduction of integration density. This is accomplished through the *reduced instruction set computer* (RISC) that needs to activate fewer instruction sets which, in turn, utilize fewer circuits. The coupling of this hardware technology with an optimized compiler may bring about a performance increase while keeping the physical component's size the same.

While miniaturization on the processor level advances increasingly, other potentials emerge that are based on the miniaturization of entire component groups. Accordingly, it is possible to achieve a storage capacity expansion, the functionality of a modem or even the functionality of a hard drive the size of a credit card through so-called *PCMCIA cards*. This technology is used in conjunction with notebooks and laptop computers and is based on a standardization of insertable cards whose respective function is directly recognized by the interface logic such that a reciprocal exchange of the respective cards becomes possible.

Mobility

An important trend in information and communication technology is derived from the possibility to support the change in location when using hardware and software, i.e. *mobility*. Language, pictures, as well as general data can be transmitted today from almost any location worldwide. Integrated solutions such as an attaché case equipped with a PC, printer, fax and telephone utilize these capabilities when combining *mobile computing* and *mobile radio.*

These developments become increasingly important due to advanced miniaturization and lower costs. The gradual dissolution of telecommunication monopolies and increased competition worldwide have contributed significantly to these developments.

Cooperative Work

Cooperative work, when applied to information and communication technology, demonstrates its justification in that it enables cooperative support and group work. The development leading toward computer supported and labor-divided task accomplishment found its origin with the deployment of mainframe machines at the organizational level. In subsequent years, initially individuals were supported through workstations in their work (Grudin, 1991; see Figure 4.6). First attempts to support cooperative work through appropriate hard and software is said to be 1984 (Grudin, 1991), although earlier efforts may be found under the label *office automation* even though the focus here was less with information technology.

The many labels assigned to computer supported group work are confusing. One way to introduce some clarification is to decide whether or not information and communication technology support in group work the *content* of cooperation or concerns the *process.* As depicted in Figure 4.7, Picot and Reichwald (1991, p. 298) distinguish between

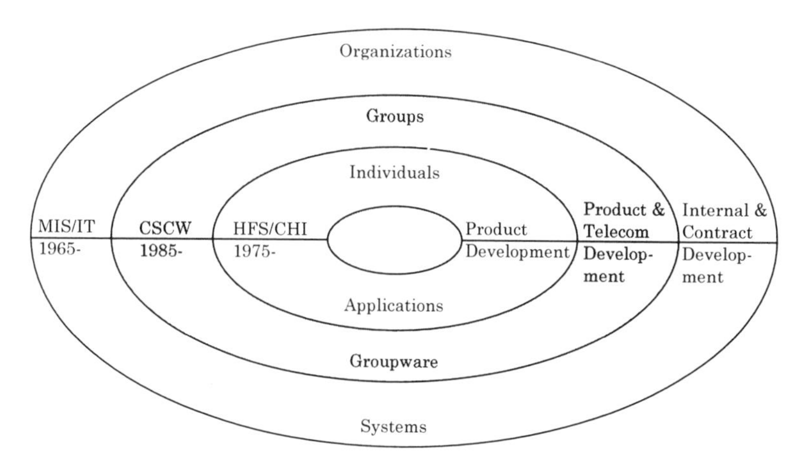

Figure 4.6 *CSCW and groupware in the research and development context. Source: Grudin (1991, p. 92. Figure adaptation courtesy of ACM, © 1991 Association for Computing Machinery, Inc.)*

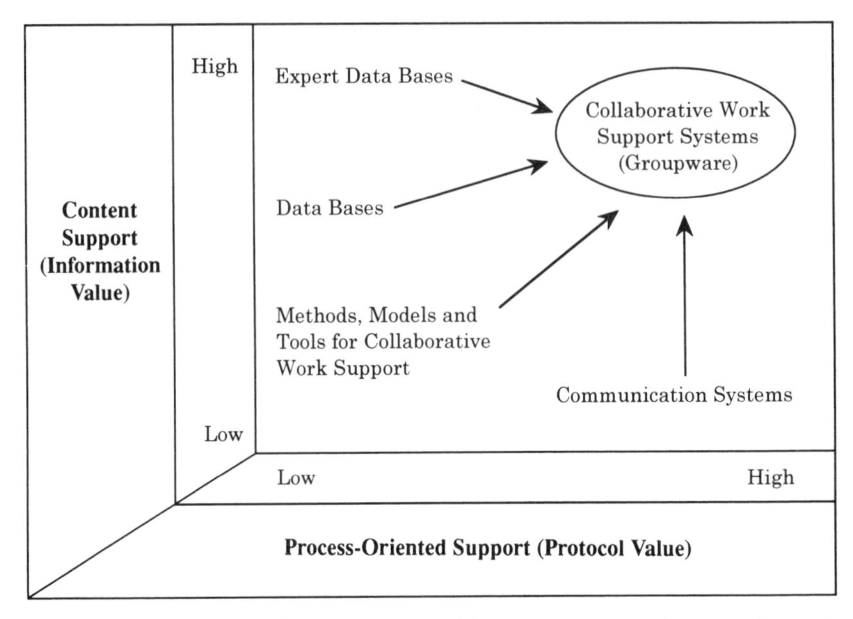

Figure 4.7 Content- and process-oriented forms in support of cooperative task accomplishment. Source: Picot and Reichwald (1991, p. 299)

information and *process support*. When data bases, for example, are deployed during group work, they serve primarily in their support of information. The telephone, on the other hand, just as most other communication technologies, typically supports the very process it is connected to. Independent of the type of support, *Computer Supported Cooperative Work* (CSCW) is the all-encompassing term for all partial aspects of computer-supported cooperation.

The basis for sufficient information support is, among others, the *database system*, consisting of a data base as well as software for its administration, i.e. the *database management system* (Schlageter and Stucky, 1983; Date, 1990). In 1975 the US-American study group for standardization ANSI/SPARC developed the three-level architecture for the design of data base systems (see ANSI/SPARC, 1975). This concept enabled for the first time an independent design of the physical aspects of data storage, optimization and security, as well as aspects concerning applications running on the actual database. The conceptual database model remains unchanged, no matter if the underlying character is reflective of a hierarchical, network or relational nature, since this character remains unchanged toward modifications occurring at the lower and higher levels. This level-oriented design (physical level, conceptual level and external level) can be illustrated in the following example. Two users, one from the Financial Planning Department and the other from the Production Department, access stored organization data in a database management system. In doing so, both users gain access merely to those data that are essential in the accomplishment of their respective tasks. Concrete interaction with the users occurs on the *external* level of the database system, where each user is availed of an individual perspective of data. If a third user is now to receive access to a relevant portion of the data base, this is then possible without modification of the lower levels. The central unit in charge of the data base may decide that—due to the higher data volume—it may be appropriate to optimize the physical storage of data through the introduction of an additional index. Also this operation is executed on the *internal* level and is possible without influencing the other levels; typically it occurs completely unnoticed by the users involved.

A higher degree of information support is offered by *expert systems.* These systems offer information support by providing access to a knowledge base, a vast amount of facts and rules that can be accessed by the user through queries. A key difference from data bases is the very existence of these rules and constructs that make possible an *intensional* definition of subject matters (Oldenburg, 1991). Via this special form of knowledge representation the expert system draws conclusions through which new information may be generated based on already existing information.

Such interaction with the user is further enhanced through the expert system components *inference mechanism* and *user interface* (Liebowitz, 1988). The inference mechanism serves first of all to *prove* the user's query on the basis of the available knowledge. This occurs in the form that knowledge formulated by the questions is checked for its presence in the available knowledge data base. Expert systems are built upon this basic philosophy and then, almost as a by-product, the delivery of a set of facts from the knowledge data base is possible as well. This occurs through the specification of *free variables* in the query, i.e. variables which are not assigned any values until inference processes decide such value attribution. The results are then listed on the monitor via the user interface component.

We will now take a look at process-supporting aspects of cooperation. Due to the temporal and geographical distribution of group members one may distinguish four differing communication types (Figure 4.8) that may be supported by groupware (Krcmar, 1992; DeSanctis and Gallupe, 1985).

Such groupware systems may be identified as *Group Decision Support Systems* (GDSS), *Joint Editing* and *Electronic Mail* and are discussed below.

Presence of Participants	**at the same time**	**at different times**
in the same location	Comprehensive computer-supported session Computer-supported moderated session Group decision support system Presentation software	Calendar management for groups Project management software Text filtering software
in different locations	Audio and video conference Screen sharing Spontaneous interaction through information exchange within computer network	Electronic conferencing and bulletin boards Tools enabling the structuring of conversions Multiple author software

Figure 4.8 *Synchronous/asynchronous and distributed/not distributed communication. Source: Krcmar (1992, p. 7)*

An example of synchronous communication support in the same location is the Group Decision Support System (GDSS) (Krcmar, 1992; Maaß, 1991). As a subclass of *Decision Support Systems* (DSS), researched by Keen and Scott Morton (1978), GDSS may provide support through such computer-supported methods as brainstorming, determination of preferences or idea-structuration techniques to a group of decision-makers while attempting to find a solution when poorly structured problems exist. In order to bring about an ideal discussion atmosphere one considers often group dynamics aspects and ergonomic considerations in the conceptualization of such systems (see Lewe and Krcmar, 1991).

A distributed, both asynchronously and synchronously staged situation is the basis for Joint Editing, the editorial work conducted on the same text through different users. When texts are edited by just one person and are then sent asynchronously to other individuals, one refers to Electronic Mail.

Computer-supported group work of a particular kind is the *videoconference*. This is audio- and video-enabled synchronous telecommunication, a technology that approximates most closely classical face-to-face contact. Minimal bandwidth demands for transmission channels amount to 64 kbit/s. A multimedia conference via high-performance workstations poses considerably higher demands on bandwidth: transmission speeds in the neighborhood of 100 Mbits/s are not uncommon.

The highest degree for process support for a group is offered by the *Workflow System*. With the assistance of such a process control system it is possible to coordinate the tasks of individual workers during which even existing application programs and tools can be integrated. The system automates the *process*, i.e. individual steps are made available to the users in a stepwise fashion. Since the execution of these steps does not necessarily need to occur on the same computer, *distributed processing*, i.e. the *client-server concept*, lends itself as an attractive foundation for the handling of this type of software (see pages 126–129).

Demands for a workflow system in the administrative area are, for example, the integration of text processing systems when producing documents, the determination of workflow paths, the simple regulation of problems and user availability. Factory workflow may highlight the transmission of data from one application program to another so that the system should be capable of communicating with *application programming interfaces* (APIs).

Integration

Not only hard- and software, but even system and application programs, all show increasingly a trend leading to *integration*, i.e. the confluence of specific functional characteristics. Varying computer architectures and system technologies are synchronized to enhance their *compatibility* and they are built into heterogeneous networks and systems based on their degree of *interoperability*. An additional level of integration is the confluence of application programs under a unified user interface. Below, integration tendencies are addressed at varying levels and attention in this area focuses on computer networks, data, as well as the forms of data, i.e. how they may surface within the utilized media.

An integration in terms of existing local networks occurs typically when connecting the network to a *backbone network*. Such a network is capable of connecting several existing local networks via special links without any extensive new configurations. The network component at the interface of the two technologies is labeled *gateway*. It is the gateway's job to translate between varying standards. High-speed technology, ATM for example, was conceived for its suitability as a backbone technology. An ATM gateway can translate and transmit data efficiently through the so-called *ATM Adaptation Layer*.

On a far different level of integration we find the collection of all data needed in an organization as a prerequisite for the integration of information. The incorporation of data from various organizational functions, including the vertical direction, as well as data external to the organization is labeled data integration. Data integration incorporates the advantages of a central administration of organization-relevant data and forms also the prerequisite for the suitable configuration of entrepreneurial processes. Very obvious is the need for the multiple capturing of the same data. For example, order information needed in the finance department as well as in production, only needs to be captured once and is then subsequently available to all departments needing such information. Such freedom from redundancy ensures consistency, as data that are available in only one location cannot be contradictory.

Integration can be observed as well with the communication media. *Multimedia* is the term used to denote such communication media as language, graphics and video. One typically identifies five media that are linked in a given platform: text, vector graphics and bitmaps, audio and video. Sizable differences in terms of technical demands can be recognized with audio and video since the presentation has to occur in *real time*. In order to receive a satisfactory reproduction of picture and sound sequences these need to be sampled fast enough to exceed human information processing capabilities, i.e. they need to be *sampled*, although for text and graphics only a one-time digitalization is needed. Figure 4.9 offers a comparison of the individual storage needs of various media.

Storage Requirements of Digitized Information	
1 Page of Typewritten Text	2 KB
1 Page Graphic Picture	50 KB
Video Freeze Frame Picture	200-700 KB
1 Minute Audio in Stereo	5.3 KB
- Compressed	1.3 KB
1 Minute Video Moving Pictures	>1 GB
- Compresed	9MB
1 Page Color Print	200 MB
Movie (color, 90 min.)	1 TB

Figure 4.9 *Storage requirements of digitized information. Source: Wolff (1993, p. 12. Reproduced by permission from HUTHIG GmbH, Heildelberg.)*

The transmission of multimedia data causes, in spite of ingenious compression algorithms, unusually high demands on the capacity of the various media. Video, for example, necessitates a bandwidth of at least 140 Mbit/s. Such a transmission speed can presently only be achieved via such technologies as DQDB or ATM (see pages 114–118). The capacity problem is also an issue with the storage of multimedia data. Traditional storage media such as the diskette are being replaced quickly in the read-only realm of the CD-ROM and the optical disk.

In spite of all technical difficulties with the integration of media, their organizational importance in the area of office work is presently under considerable discussion.

Openness

Integration and openness are related terms. An *open system* is a system that can be utilized while following generally accepted and openly accessible rules in conjunction with other systems. The official definition of open systems from the Technical Committee on Open Systems within the series of IEEE publications refers to

> "... the complete and consistent number of international technology standards and functional standards for the specification of interfaces, services and formats for the assurance of interoperability and portability of applications, data and people." (*Bues, 1994, p. 22*).

Accordingly, openness may be viewed as a prerequisite for integration, especially with regard to integration-determining factors such as interoperability and portability. *Interoperability*, i.e. the cooperation of different components, and *portability*, i.e. the transferability onto other systems, are two important aspects on the road to integration of information and communication technology infrastructures.

A few of the most important standards deserve attention in the present context. A first step in the direction of openness is the standardization at the *network level*. The OSI Seven-Layers Reference Model for the structuring of computer networks of the *International Organization for Standards* (ISO) depicted in Figure 4.10 may be viewed at least as the basic concept for interoperability of network architectures. The individual layers of this model are assigned specific tasks (Tanenbaum, 1989, pp. 18 ff.). Communication between layers is based on a standardized language, the *protocol*. The physical layer, for example, handles all functions with regard to the transmission and error handling for a single transmission path, while the network layer is responsible for data transmission within the network.

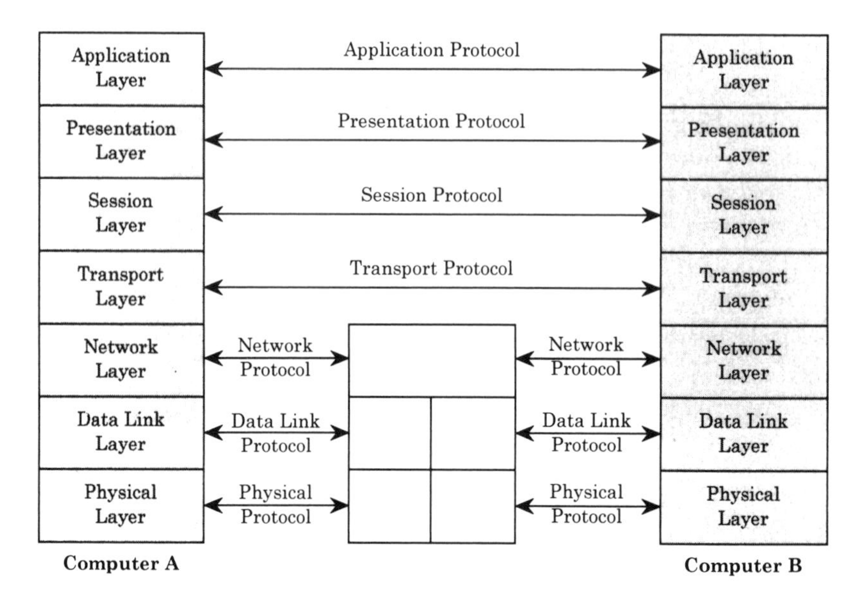

Figure 4.10 *The ISO/OSI seven-layer reference model. Source: Scheller et al (1994, p. 20. Reproduced by permission from Springer-Verlag GmbH and Co. KG.)*

Such official norms and standards are always in competition with industry standards such as TCP/IP, IPX/SPX and others. Typically such praxis-developed variants are often more convincing than their counterparts developed at the joint design table. In any case, these efforts toward standardization reflect the desire for openness and integration.

Standards such as those for the electronic data interchange among organizations need to be incorporated at the Presentation and Application Layers, respectively (Niggl, 1994; Neuburger, 1994). With the goal being a seamless processing of transmitted data, *electronic data interchange* (EDI) (cf., Chapter 6) may be viewed as a foundation for efficient organizational communication, an effort in which standards are an important prequisite. In part due to the varying demands for data exchange within different industries it becomes extremely difficult to address comprehensive EDI standards. This, in turn, results in many industry-specific standards (Wigand, 1994). One way to differentiate this setting is to classify the data to be transmitted as trade, product and text data.

Distribution

The aspect of data integration extending beyond organizational boundaries deserves special consideration. The related demands of the so-called *distributed database* were expressed rather elegantly by C. J. Date in one sentence: "A distributed system should appear to the user just like a non-distributed system." (Date, 1990, p. 620) Based on this fundamental rule, the so-called *transparency demand*, twelve demands may be derived that offer a useful means for the evaluation of distributed data bases, even though no commercially available software has yet been accomplished to follow all of them. Twelve broad rules for distributed data bases can be identified:

1. Local Autonomy
2. No reliance on central site
3. Continuous operation
4. Location independence
5. Fragmentation independence
6. Replication independence
7. Distributed query processing
8. Distributed transaction management
9. Hardware independence
10. Operating system independence
11. Network independence
12. DBMS independence

The most essential components of this listing, local autonomy, location independence, fragmentation independence, replication independence, distributed query processing and distributed transaction management are now briefly addressed.

Local Autonomy. The demand for local autonomy refers to the necessity for complete independence of the individual locations. Function-determining dependencies may not exist between the individual locations nor may there be dependence upon a single authority since otherwise, for example, in the case of the malfunctioning of a partial system, other locations may be negatively impacted as well. Conversely, however, the expectation exists that for each user the impression is created as if all data were stored centrally in one local, i.e. the user's own, focal location. Date refers to this demand as *location independence.*

Fragmentation Independence. This belongs to the aspects of physical storage of data. Based on efficiency reasons data should be stored at the location of their highest demand, even when they originate from the same group. For example, personnel data of interest to the business branch in London should be stored there and, accordingly, Chicago personnel data should be stored in Chicago. In spite of these locational differences *all* data are available to the user no matter where he or she is located. Similarly controlled redundancy should be available beyond a given location, i.e. the demand for *replication independence*. The keeping of data copies should be equally transparent for users and system administrators at different locations.

Also for efficiency reasons the need for a *distributed query processing* is important. This need implies the simultaneous processing of a query to the data base at *all* locations in which fragments of a relevant data set are maintained. This possibility requires a similarly *distributed transaction management* through which the malfunctioning of one node, for example, should not be able to trigger any consistent damage to the entire data base. Newer approaches attempt to exceed the goal for optimal but static placement possibilities for a dynamic and location-independent distribution of database sets and fragments. Under the label of *object migration* it is conceivable to permit data objects to travel dynamically within a worldwide-distributed airline reservation system to those locations where they are needed on a priority basis.

In a distributed system the transparent distribution of internal functionality is the basis for the integration of internally controllable functionality. Accordingly, the linking of different users in different locations is usually only possible through the externally not visible duplication of single location systems and similarly hidden coordination. In the closed system of information and communication the concepts of distribution and integration are always coupled in one form or another. In the following section we discuss the Client/Server Concept as a method for distribution of internal functionality and how it enables the optimal placement of tasks onto the most suitable authority and, consequently, the integration of computer performance of all computers.

The term client/server must first be viewed in its completely abstract meaning (Geihs, 1995). It is implied here that a request submitted by an applicant, the client, is being processed by a service provider, the server. With regard to information technology the participating parties may take on different forms; it is even possible that they might exchange entirely their respective roles as client and server.

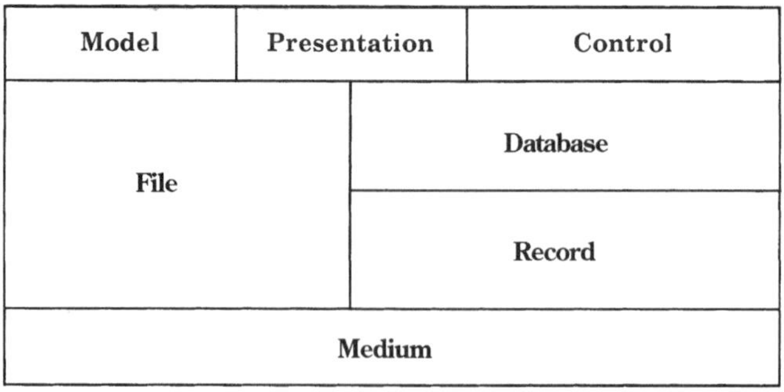

<table>
<tr><td>Model</td><td colspan="2">Presentation</td><td>Control</td></tr>
<tr><td colspan="2" rowspan="2">File</td><td colspan="2">Database</td></tr>
<tr><td colspan="2">Record</td></tr>
<tr><td colspan="4">Medium</td></tr>
</table>

Figure 4.11 *Application system architecture from a client/server perspective*

Figure 4.11 shows the possible depiction of the fundamental architecture of application systems. The actual application, consisting of model and presentation components, as well as *control* component connecting the former two components, utilizes a hierarchy of abstraction levels. For example, a PPS system uses particular algorithms for the calculation of delivery dates and processing times that can be assigned to the model component. For the visualization on the monitor various routines are available in the presentation component. The linking of the information windows with the calculated values occurs via the routines of the control component. The lower levels refer to the storage of data. Here it is possible on the one hand to access via data bases individual data segments or, on the other hand, to gain access directly to files. On the levels medium, files, data base and presentation it is presently already possible to enact the client/server concept, although the application of this concept onto the other modules is also conceivable.

Globalization

The last aspect of an examination of the potential of information and communication infrastructures refers to their distribution crossing national boundaries, in other words, their *globalization*. Making information available in more and more locations worldwide is the goal from purely technical, as well as from the development of international standards perspectives (Wigand, 1984). Such mobile communication efforts can be observed worldwide in numerous quarters. Much is expected from the presently developing *Personal Communication Networks* (PCN). Similarly, several worldwide large-scale satellite-based communication systems have been conceived and some are being built (e.g., Motorola's Iridium system). In the long run it appears almost inconceivable that PCNs and satellite systems would not be linked in some fashion.

Much attention has been paid to the formation of a *Global Information Infrastructure* (GII), the global data highway (see, for example, Wigand, 1996, 1995c). A first impression of this vision of the future is offered by the *Internet*, the largest computer network in the world. This network was first supported and financed by the United States Department of Defense to prepare for a secure network that would also continue to function when some network components were destroyed. The structure of the Internet is extremely heterogeneous and no central authority exists through which a coordination of individual participants nor the control of individual services is possible. Right from the beginning the Internet was conceived as a network with a completely decentralized administration.

The basis for communication on the Internet is the *Transport Control Protocol/Internet Protocol* (TCP/IP). The only common ground of the TCP/IP and the ISO/OSI standard is that both have a layered structure, but the individual layers cannot be compared. In spite of all the international standards setting efforts of the ISO, TCP/IP as a part of the BSD UNIX operating system has developed into a most-applied protocol standard. This is certainly in part due to the support of open operating systems environments encouraged by the United States government.

Broadly speaking one identifies a number of important basic Internet services:

- bulletin board services;
- directory services;
- file-oriented systems; and
- information retrieval systems.

Uncountable applications may be utilized on the Internet and due to its open character new services may be offered and implemented at any time in a decentralized fashion. For example it is possible to implement a communication system on the basis of TCP/IP linking two firms in an EDI cooperative effort. This service then can be used exclusively by these two firms and may be offered to newly joining partner firms. Numerous firms have been using the Internet for strictly internal purposes, i.e. the so-called *Intranet*, while protecting such firm-internal use through firewalls.

Telnet service enables the user to link from one location via the Internet to the computer system of another location, i.e. the monitor and keyboard are in essence being connected with the distant system. In principle work on distant computer systems is possible from any location on earth. FTP refers to the *File Transfer Protocol* service for the transmission of files between two computer systems. The transmission of text between two individuals typically occurs through the use of an electronic mail system.

Of particular interest as an application of information retrieval is the *World Wide Web* (WWW). This system is based on the hypertext concept, i.e. a network-like information distribution that the user may follow via optional paths. At every node within this information network the possibility exists to connect to other nodes such that the order of the individual information to a certain extent may be determined by the user. To conduct such searches WWW browsers are available. Embedded within such tools are often additional basic services of the Internet such that a combination of search, security and data-related activities becomes possible.

INFORMATION AND COMMUNICATION SYSTEMS

In the previous section many foundation cornerstones and singular elements of information and communication technology infrastructures were presented and discussed in light of developmental trends. For a firm and its development within the market these technical cornerstones will not have significant meaning until they are linked to the organizational information and communication system. It is important to note that "technology is to serve the firm, not vice-versa" (Picot and Reichwald, 1991; Picot, 1993b; Wigand, 1996, 1995d).

Information and communication systems unite personnel (qualification, motivation), organizational (assembly and process organization) and technical (hardware, software) components. The combination of these components determines the structure of information and communication systems and influences their efficacy in view of organizational task accomplishment. Differing tasks pose always specific demands upon organization structures; differing organization structures, however, demand specific support through information and communication systems.

Information and Communication Systems and Coordination Forms

In order to discuss the organizational application of information technology and its broader role within the enterprise, it is helpful to develop abstract models. Moreover, many organizational activities today go beyond traditional structures and boundaries. We can observe numerous forms of cooperation and strategic alliances among firms that blur the conventional boundaries of firms. Many of these developments have come about and are made possible with newer information and communication technology. Here we will explore four abstract models representing varying forms of coordination.

The information technology requirements of an organization have to be seen within the larger context of the firm's tasks, the market-based interconnections and linkages among firms, as well as resulting enterprise structures. Consequently, data-based and function-oriented approaches of systems development need to be illuminated with an organization theory or economics background.

Transaction cost theory (see Chapters 3 and 7) demonstrates that organizational or coordination forms are dependent on the characteristics of each task and exchange relationship. These respective characteristics influence in the final analysis the information and communication problems to be mastered together with the tasks to be

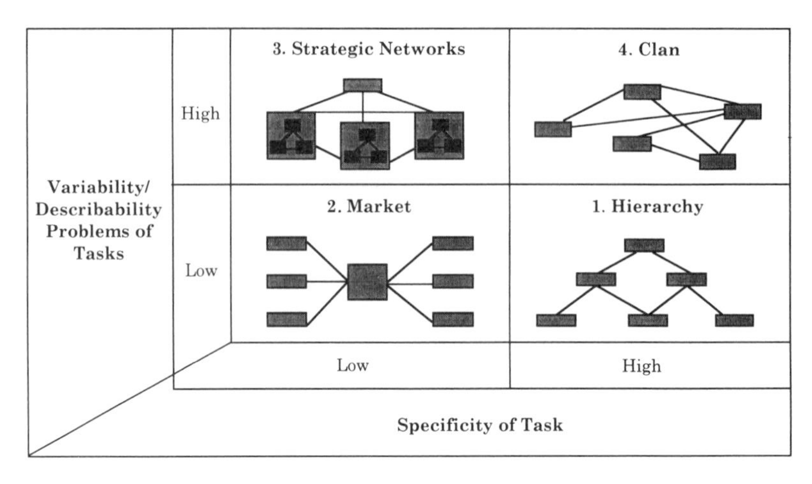

Figure 4.12 *Organizational forms and macro-structures of information and communication systems*

accomplished through the division of labor. It follows then that that form of coordination is chosen which minimizes the information and communication problems within the performance exchange among firms and the resulting transaction costs.

Following this line of thinking, Figure 4.12 depicts four types of exchange relationships. These are dependent on the task characteristics *specificity* (i.e. degree of uniqueness) and *variability/describability* (i.e. uncertainty or, respectively, dynamics and definability). Next, these can be grouped broadly and rather simplified into four *efficient* coordination forms: hierarchy, market, strategic network and clan.

Based on the nature of the observed performance relationships, demands placed on the information technology support may vary. Accordingly, the resulting information and communication problems together with the peculiarity of task accomplishment and the division of labor must determine the configuration of organizational structures and processes, including information and communication systems. Based on the exchange relationships derived from transaction cost theory, one can describe differing macrostructures of information and communication systems (see Figure 4.12).

Information and Communication Systems in the Hierarchical Form of Task Accomplishment (Domain 1: Hierarchy)

A (more or less bureaucratic) hierarchy as a model for organizational information processing lends itself suitably for highly specific, stabile tasks. Internal control structures will have to be developed accordingly. Assuming that the hierarchical structure of the organization is desirable, information and communication systems can be developed based on the hierarchical range (vertical), as well as on functional criteria (horizontal).

If one differentiates information and communication systems based on the criterion of hierarchical range, an orientation based on the structure of formal planning and control systems may occur. Frequently one differentiates then between strategic planning and control, as well as operative planning (Anthony, 1988). These three levels can be differentiated based on their respective planning horizon and planning content.

The basic structure of a hierarchical coordination can be fine-tuned in conjunction with information and communication systems. Frequently a distinction is being made among: (1) quantitatively-oriented operative systems; (2) value-oriented accounting systems; (3) analysis, report and control systems; and (4) planning and decision support systems (see Mertens and Griese, 1991; Mertens, 1988; Scheer, 1990). These then serve directly the basic tasks of the information economy. For instance, quantitatively-oriented operative systems and value-oriented accounting systems support documentation efforts. For controlling support services one mainly utilizes analysis, report and control systems. Planning and decision support is based primarily on planning and decision support systems.

Quantitatively-oriented Operative Systems. At the operative level, information and communication systems serve in support of individual value-added activities, as well as the interconnection of different value-added stages. It is the task of these systems to steer transaction processes and to deliver information about the status and course of quantitatively-oriented value-added processes.

These systems are deployed in all functional areas. In industrial manufacturing, for example, transaction processes are increasingly supported by computer-based production planning systems (PPS), as well as through data processing systems serving product descriptions and the steering of manufacturing facilities. Jointly these systems constitute the basis for Computer Integrated Manufacturing (CIM). With CIM systems an integration of production planning and control for organizational and technical tasks is attempted. In the human resources area we must refer in this context, for example, to systems in support of work time management; in sales we think of systems in support of shipping logistics.

Value-oriented Accounting Systems. Technically-oriented, product-based basic functions, as well as the organizational functions for the immediate realization of basic processes, are overlaid by planning and transaction functions. On the side of organizational planning functions quantitatively-oriented processes are accompanied by value-oriented transaction systems (e.g., warehouse accounting, facilities accounting, accounts receivables) that, in turn, make organizational consequences of quantitatively-oriented processes visible.

Analysis, Report and Control Systems. Based on data derived at the operative level and by compressing such data, information is generated for use by analysis, reporting and controlling systems in support of coordination and controlling efforts. Analysis, reporting and controlling functions are carried out mainly with the methods cost accounting and performance measures. Moreover, on this level analysis and reporting systems are deployed in which, aside from the already mentioned compressed data of internal processes, also data and information from external sources are being utilized.

Planning and Decision Support Systems. At the top level we encounter planning and decision support systems for strategic planning and business policy decisions of upper management. Decision support systems are interactive, computer-supported systems through which decision-makers seek support in poorly structured decision-making situations. Decision support systems contain a collection of methods and decision models and they make possible the access to suitable data bases. Often such systems bring along also specific computer languages or programs in support of model construction or data preparation. All decision support systems are expected to support interactively various business functions in the widely varying decision processes throughout the firm.

Decision support systems can be designed in principle for differing management levels and functions. Decision support systems at the upper levels of information processing activities are not only fed by compressed data and information from lower levels, but also by external data and information (e.g., market share and competitor data).

Computer supported quantitative operative systems and value-oriented accounting systems are used extensively throughout industry. Computer supported analysis, reporting and control systems are, on the other hand, not deployed as widely, whereas planning and decision support systems are in even less frequent use. Information technology and management research is concerned with all system types and of particular interest in recent years are planning and decision support systems.

Interorganizational Information Processing and Electronic Data Exchange (Domain 3: Strategic Networks)

Given that the systems of intra-organizational data processing have achieved a relatively high level of development in most firms, considerable discussion concerning the appropriate deployment and utilization of interorganizational information processing can be reported. Systems designed for interorganizational processing of information lend themselves especially to the coordination of performances and tasks characterized by relatively small specificity, but high variability (e.g., the linking of parts, components and services).

Interorganizational information processing refers to system applications occurring between two or more independent firms and where these applications connect these firms. It is characteristic for such systems that information for specific partners in the market are made available and that other partners in that market are excluded from this information. Electronic data interchange (EDI) takes on a central role in this interorganizational information processing effort (Picot et al, 1994; Wigand, 1994). EDI aims to realize an immediate interorganizational linkage on the level of application systems (e.g., the direct coupling of ordering systems between supplier and buyer).

Expressions, Application Forms and Utilization of Interorganizational Information Processing.

- *Support of administrative tasks.* Interorganizational information processing, as well as overlapping processes of product and service delivery together with administrative activities and secondary value-added activities, can support industrial firms. The support of administrative tasks may occur through the electronic exchange of accounting data and the computer-supported transmission of payment orders (e.g., the payment of supplier/customer invoices, payroll payments, payment of tax contributions).
- *Ordering systems.* In product and service delivery efforts, as well as in primary value-added activities, interorganizational information processing serves primarily within the functional areas of purchasing, sales, marketing and customer service. With ordering systems, as they are well known with automobile manufacturers, part orders from suppliers can be activated based on demand at the assembly line such that just-in-time (JIT) production becomes possible. Typically, larger order quantities are agreed upon via a contract or other stabilizing mechanisms (e.g., EDI contractual framework, cooperative agreements). With the introduction of interorganizational

ordering systems one can frequently encounter the need to change existing organizational forms within participating firms. Through electronic ordering systems coordination efforts and processes can be minimized. Various information-intensive preliminary order specification efforts can be streamlined and will require less time, as well as warehoused supplies can be reduced, if not eliminated.

- *Marketing and sales systems.* In the marketing and sales area purchasing data can be exchanged with trading partners or customers. Also in the shipping logistics area electronic connections to shipping agents or trading firms can be established. The utilization of electronic marketing and sales systems may lead to the situation in which distribution channels are occupied and with that market entry barriers are created for potential competitors. Through strong interorganizational information processing systems in the sales area it is often possible to offer new or improved service delivery such as the tele-diagnosing of problems and management of maintenance systems for technical facilities (e.g., elevators) becomes possible from afar.
- *Systems for product development.* Interorganizational information exchange may also lead to interorganizational cooperation when developing products such as with the exchange of technical specifications or construction data. Aside from the possibility of improved product development one may also be able to realize shortened product development cycles.

Frequently specific investments in the technological infrastructure are necessary in order to take advantage of interorganizational information and communication systems (e.g., special standards for communication purposes). In this way entry as well as exit costs will result for the various partners. With this a stronger commitment to the designed and constructed purchasing and distribution channels result. If the application exchange relationships are based on generally accepted standards or services, it is then possible to realize the potential for cost savings and flexibility advantages embedded in the electronic exchange of data. Here we need to recognize the extensive efforts of the United Nations Organization and the European Union, among other organizations, to develop international standards for interorganizational exchanges of business documents (e.g., EDIFACT) such that efficient economies can be enjoyed from industry to industry and nation to nation.

Interorganizational Information Processing in Support of Value-added Partnerships. Value-added partnerships, also called strategic networks (see Jarillo, 1988, 1993), form institutional coordination patterns, all of which contain elements of market-based and hierarchical coordination. Strategic networks consist of independent and specialized small and medium-sized firms carrying out jointly executable tasks within close exchange relationships that are also characterized by a focused division of labor. The coordination of network enterprises is usually carried out by a lead firm.

Network enterprises are connected with the lead firm through long-term and largely open contracts. In order to carry out the individual partial tasks each network enterprise is afforded a considerable range within which to operate and make decisions. Through this arrangement it is possible for individual firms to develop entrepreneurial interests in the efficient and effective task accomplishment with such a cooperative setting. With this cooperative relationship it is also possible to carry out complex and specific exchange relationships in a similar flexible manner as with the hierarchical form of coordination. It should be noted that it is largely through the entrepreneurial independence of the partners that it becomes possible to lower coordination costs. Examples of such strategic network organizations, strongly supported by electronic communication systems, can be found within the textile industry and large-scale construction projects. One refers to such organizational forms also as "virtual hierarchies".

Information and Communication Systems for Market Coordination (Domain 2: Market)

Electronic markets are characterized mainly by the fact that firms offer and exchange largely standardized products and services by utilizing communication and information transmissions systems and data bases (see, among others, Benjamin and Wigand, 1995; Hubmann, 1989). Market transactions are being "mediatized" through information and communication systems. With market-processed transactions one recognizes typically frequently recurring, clearly describable and assessable, standardized and rarely variable barter and service relationships. The services are procured based on few, but unequivocal information pieces about quality, quantity and market price. Well-established electronic markets can be found in the area of trade with standardized financial products. It is the task of information technology to support short-notice contractual agreements between independent commercial agents. When this is accomplished electronic brokering and pooling effects can be brought about. Supply and demand relationships will become concentrated and focused through the use of electronic media and joint data bases. This, in turn, makes possible business deals through the use of electronic systems, triggering the so-called electronic brokerage effect. Information and communication systems support then market-based transactions through an improvement of the market transparency, as well as through the automation of processing of market-based transactions, e.g., ordering, accounting and payment procedures. Thus a lowering of transaction costs among the market partners is enabled. A "mediatization" of markets can be achieved with the help of data bases and public communication systems and the services offered within such systems.

Aside from the brokerage or pooling effect it is also possible to achieve an integration or interlinking effect between organization-overlapping value-based activities. Such integration effects are especially then achievable when the market, as well as interorganizational and the intra-organizational communication occurs through uniform and standardized data formats and transmission protocols. Electronic markets constitute an expansion of interorganizational information and communications systems and in this sense they extend traditional organizational boundaries. For a more detailed discussion on electronic markets see Chapter 7.

Information and Communication Systems for Group-oriented Task Accomplishment (Domain 4: Clan)

Tasks, as an outcome of the division of labor, with high specificity and variability cannot be directly depicted through formal systems. Above all they are in need of well functioning social communication within the group.

With group-oriented forms of task accomplishment coordination usually occurs less through structured coordination systems, but more frequently via the orientation of organization members at commonly held values, perceptions of quality, norms and attitudes. In reference to Ouchi (1980), such forms of task accomplishment can be labeled "clan organizations".

Especially for uncertain, highly complex and specific task relationships such as research and development, as well as leadership and consulting tasks and project work, such a coordination form can enable a transaction environment characterized by a lack of bureaucracy, adaptability and low transaction costs. It must be the outstanding characteristic of the information and communication system to bring about the professional capabilities of the participants in the best possible way such that a creative problem solving process is enabled (see Picot, 1989b). First of all, free and open face-to-face communication (e.g., group work) is necessary such that through idea and information exchange novel solutions are explored, developed and implemented. Information and communication technology has a secondary function in this process, i.e. to augment and support participants in the preparation and actual group communication in the best possible fashion. This, for example, may occur through the ease with which access to internal and external information and data can be achieved through the use of communication technology and data bases. Similarly, computer-supported tools for individual information processing (spreadsheet calculations, text and graphics generation), the creation and management of presentation materials and personal archives can be facilitated. For the support of these activities the user needs especially user-friendly and individualizable technology with performance and flexible characteristics which, in turn, will also support the work in groups.

When viewing exchange relationships from a transaction cost theory approach, a number of important options for the utilization of new information technology can be recognized. In doing this one needs to realize that the basic coordination forms can also be established within organizations. With "internal markets" one can open market as well as hierarchy coordination elements in firms (e.g., internal labor market) and they can be processed favorably in terms of transaction costs through information and communication systems.

From these deliberations it became clear that the planning of information and communication systems has to be suitable for the differing task types and coordination forms. It has to consider internal and organization-overlapping coordination and cooperation and needs to ensure appropriate organizational, personnel and technical configurations.

System Development

Software engineering, the development of application systems, typically views the software product in the form of the *software development life cycle*. Two fundamental directions were first differentiated (McDermid and Rook, 1991): (a) the perspective of project management, differentiating along phases that belong together based on temporal considerations, as well as a more technical approach in which development stages of software are differentiated. The classical example for the management approach is the *Water Fall Model*, receiving its name because of the association brought about by its step-like or cascading depiction of sequences of individual project steps (see Figure 4.13). The individual phases of this model envision a strict delineation between problem-specific and implementation-specific tasks, manifesting itself with separation between analysis and design. The system model derived from the

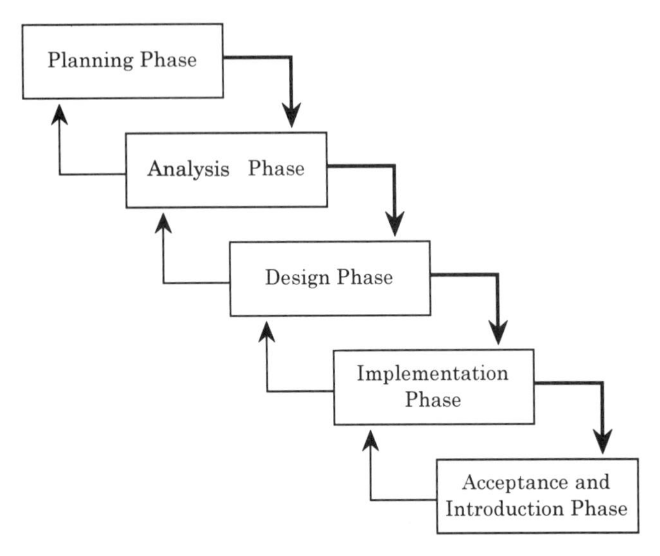

Figure 4.13 *The Water Fall Model of software development. Source: Royce (1970)*

analysis phase can be characterized by the absence of any sort of implementation-orientation, suggesting that appropriate competence and responsibility lies with the subject matter specialists or their respective department. In contrast the system model created in the design phase suggests a predominant participation of the responsible information systems department. In the meantime the Water Fall Model, originally conceived by W.W. Royce (1970), has been expanded through the introduction of validation steps and feedback loops within specific phases with the aim of ensuring better quality in the development process.

Prototyping is one representation of the technology-oriented approach. This is the developmental process of a model of the final software, the *prototype*. This method permits the early linking of users and thus may avoid the consequences of imprecise specifications. Prototyping can be classified into three forms; explorative, experimental and evolutionary, and takes on an important role, especially *vis-à-vis* object-oriented system development to be discussed later. The differences between the individual types of prototyping are explained by their respective goals (Pomberger and Blaschek, 1993). The *explorative* prototype serves as an illustrative object as a means of ensuring the completeness of the system specifications. The *experimental* prototype reflects an approach allowing for a test of the software's usefulness while relying on partial specifications, i.e. an attempt to test the feasibility of specific goals. Of most interest for software development is *evolutionary* prototyping in which the prototype is being developed in a stepwise fashion up to the final end product.

A linking of the two differing development methodologies was accomplished by Barry Boehm (1988) via his Spiral Model (Figure 4.14). Here the project phases Analysis, Design, Implementation and Testing are embedded within an iterative framework such that after each phase an improved prototype becomes available. For each of these prototypes a Planning Phase, Risk Analysis, as well as the already referred to project phases for the actual software generation together with an Evaluation by the customers are considered.

With regard to the high level of complexity of modern software systems such methodologies gain increasing importance for software development, especially since the classical, phase-oriented procedures as an exclusive structuration concept fail. Recognizing this shortcoming, various expansions of the phase-model were undertaken. Among these

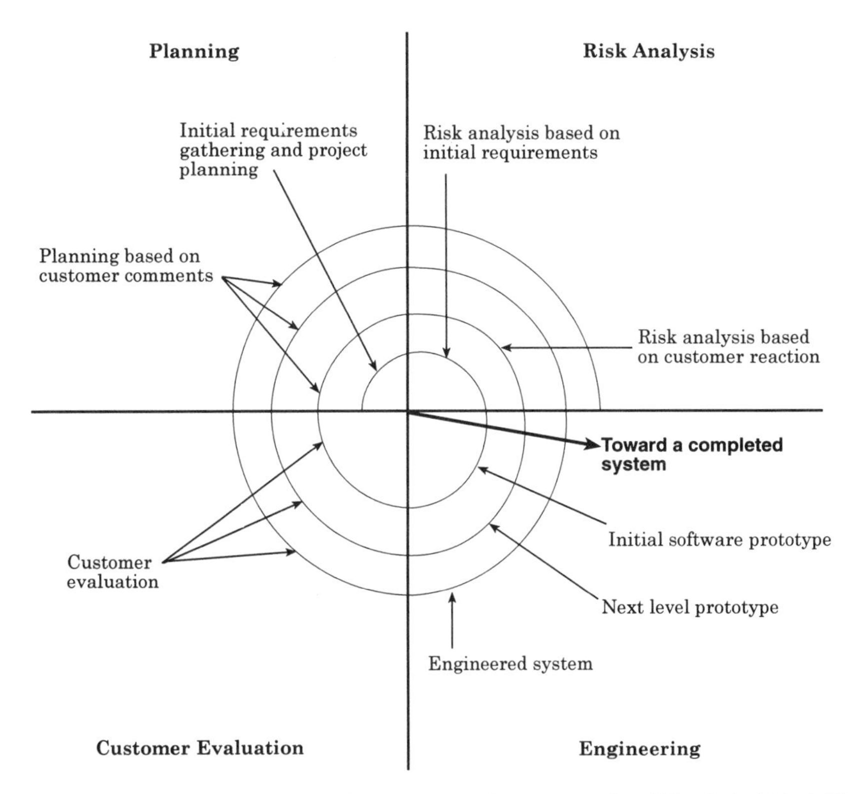

Figure 4.14 *The Spiral Model. Source: Boehm (1988) after "The Spiral Model"*

efforts one should note especially two models contributing toward object-oriented software development; the Cluster Model by Meyer (1989) and the Fountain Model by Henderson-Sellers and Edwards (1990).

Modeling of Information Systems

The model as an abstraction of reality is the focal point of the project phases Analysis and Design. Software is here usually *a priori* specified through graphical notations that, in turn, make possible a basis for comprehensive planning of peripheral conditions such as project duration or occurring costs. The modeling of software usually relates to two aspects: the dynamic *functionality* and the static *structures* of the system. In accordance with this dichotomous partitioning one typically differentiates between *functional modeling* and *data modeling*.

One well-known representative of functional modeling methods is the data flow diagram developed by Tom DeMarco (1978) within the framework of Structured Analysis (SA). The essence of this notation method is limited to three key elements: the *tasks* depicted as "bubbles"; *conditions* labeled through the use of arrows; as well as *data sources* labeled via two parallel lines. It is the challenge for the analyst to link tasks with the help of condition-arrows in order to capture the functional aspects of the software to be specified. The notation is embedded in a hierarchical concept, the *Structured Analysis*, which is a simple and comprehensive method for the top-down specification of dynamic relationships.

The second aspect of a system description refers to static relationships. Six years after the first publication of the relational model by E. Codd (1970), Peter Pin-Shan Chen (1976) presented his modeling method of data and their relationships. This so-called entity/relationship approach has become the standard method for data modeling and is viewed as a mature concept. It again unifies three different elements and in doing so takes advantage of structural simplicity. Through the aid of the constitutive elements *entity*, *property* and *relationship*, it is possible to depict objects, object characteristics and relationships between objects. The following example should simplify the understanding and usage of these terms: Using the terminology of the entity/relationship approach the term *entity* may refer to a customer, a product or an order. The characteristics of these entities, the *properties*, manifest themselves in the names and the address of the customer, the price of the product or the order number. A possible *relationship* between the three mentioned entities might be, for example, the "placing of an order", linking the customer, the product that was ordered and specific data pertaining to the order.

Since the method's invention considerable improvements have occurred (e.g., Date, 1990). Among the most important improvements is the introduction of the specialization and decomposition relationships. The first variant, also known as *IS-A-Relation* may be explained as a relation between the entities, e.g., BMW, Mercedes, Audi, etc. and the entity automobile. All available automobile models are types of the entity automobile, whereas a decomposition or *HAS-A-Relation* concerns the *components* of automobiles. In this latter relationship the entity automobile is viewed vis-à-vis to the entity's body, wheels and so on.

Software systems unify always static, as well as dynamic elements. For this reason there is usually a need for a combined use of methods for data and function modeling. In doing this one needs to be aware of the difficulty in combining both perspectives. The parallel development of both methods demands very intensive coordination among the relevant employees, especially since the interdependencies between static and dynamic perspectives are typically very high. The separated treatment of data and functions is therefore somewhat inappropriate, although this depends no doubt on differing histories of software development on the one hand and of data base systems on the other hand.

A possibility for improvement is offered through *object orientation*. In this world view the delineation between data and function is dissolved and partitioning occurs along modular boundaries. The term *encapsulation* denotes the integration of the components of an object, together with its executable operations and thus forming the basis for modern system development considering such concepts as reusability, dynamic data exchange, compatibility, client/server, etc.

The basic idea of object orientation originated from the creators of the programming language SIMULA (Dahl, Myrhaug and Nygaard, 1970) and was later integrated into the programming language Smalltalk by Goldberg and Robson (1989). Within this paradigm a program is viewed as a number of *objects*, individual data and functional units, all of which are capable of communicating among each other through the use of messages. This modular approach toward a software system enables better program planning and coordination, as well as more flexible and lucid adaptability and maintenance.

Representatives of the object-oriented modeling approach are Rumbaugh et al (1991), as well as Coad and Yourdon (1991). Rumbaugh's method, the *Object Modeling Technique* (OMT), utilizes essentially already known concepts and can be grouped in the category of so-called *evolutionary* methods, while the procedures used by Coad and Yourdon may better be described as *revolutionary*. The constituent elements of Rumbaugh's object modeling technique are a sophisticated entity/

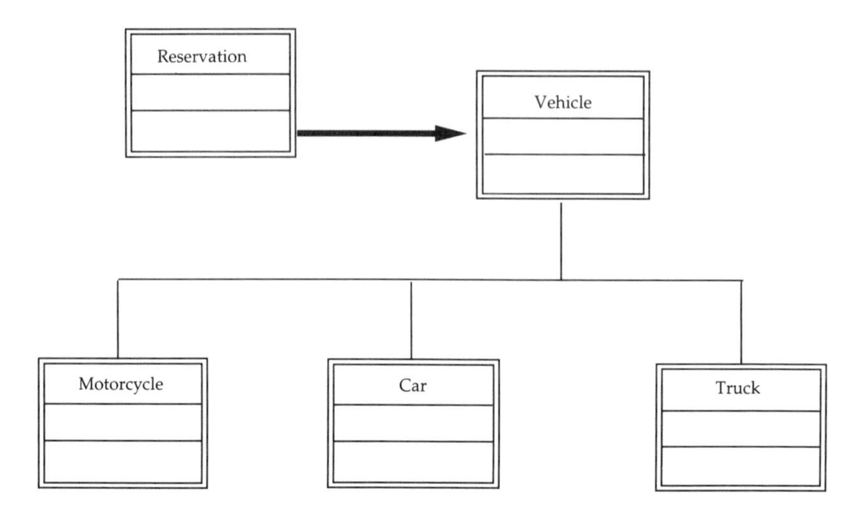

Figure 4.15 *An example of an OAA Diagram*

relationship diagram, a data flow diagram, as well as a transition diagram that depicts events occurring within the system. In contrast, Coad and Yourdon use a single integrated notation.

Figure 4.15 shows an example of an Object Oriented Analysis (OOA) diagram according to Coad and Yourdon. The functionality, for instance, is represented by arrows (so-called *message connections*). This notation is, most obviously, less powerful as the already referred to three separate models of OMT. Nevertheless they offer an advantage in the integrated perspective of data and functions early during the analysis phase. An additional advantage is the seamless continuation of the work in the subsequent design phase using exactly the same notations.

Enterprise Modeling

When model building is being applied to real-world objects such as the enterprise itself it may become necessary to incorporate actors into the model. Above that, the relative sequence of events can become important and might need to be depicted as well. One refers to the *organization and event models.* With regard to the enterprise the organization model essentially includes the organizational units, i.e. the structure of the enterprise. In the events model one models the temporal relationships of the system, i.e. information about which action triggers which event and which additional events are caused in a given sequence. Planning software for workflow systems such as the *ARIS Toolset* by Scheer (see Figure 4.16) or the product *Bonapart* (see, for example, Krallmann and Klotz, 1994) offer these possibilities in order to assign certain activities to individual actors.

Even though the four levels of modeling (data, functions, organization and events) are not always explicitly considered in all known methods and models, all four dimensions are always existent. Important approaches to enterprise modeling are the Architecture for Integrated Information Systems (ARIS) by Scheer and the Semantic Object Model (SOM) by Ferstl and Sinz.

The ARIS concept according to Scheer (1994) approximates the above-mentioned four-dimensional perspective most closely (see Figure 4.16). Here all four perspectives toward the information system within the overall framework of enterprise modeling are described: data, function, organization and control perspectives. Events are introduced into the model from a control perspective and serve as the basis for linking the function and data perspectives. The result of such a linkage is the so-called *event-controlled process chain*. A linkage to the organization perspective occurs through the assignment of the individual functions to organizational units.

The *Semantic Object Model* (Ferstl and Sinz, 1990, 1991) is an attempt to minimize the structural misfits among the various perspectives to the enterprise. Embedded within a comprehensive procedural model using a top-down approach, data, functions, organizational units and events are developed in a combined fashion. At each level of refinement a complete model becomes available reflective of all dimensions such that a structurally continuous collaboration is always assured. The final specified result, the so-called *conceptual object scheme* is then the point of departure for actual software development. The consideration of organizational aspects in the model give the design process a holistic perspective.

A basis for the modeling of the event-controlled dynamic system *enterprise* in ARIS and SOM is, even though in a deviating form, the *Petri net*. This modeling method referred to earlier (see pages 106–107) permits a description of temporal relationships through the use of two different types of network nodes.

A Petri net describes on the one hand a set of conditions and they are typically depicted as circles. Within these conditions one may encounter symbolic tags called *markers*. The second type of network nodes refers to events. Events and conditions are reciprocally interconnected, i.e. an event leads to a condition, and, in turn, from a condition an event may occur, and so on. Events, noted by rectangular symbols, have the potential to bring about changes in the conditions through a rearrangement of

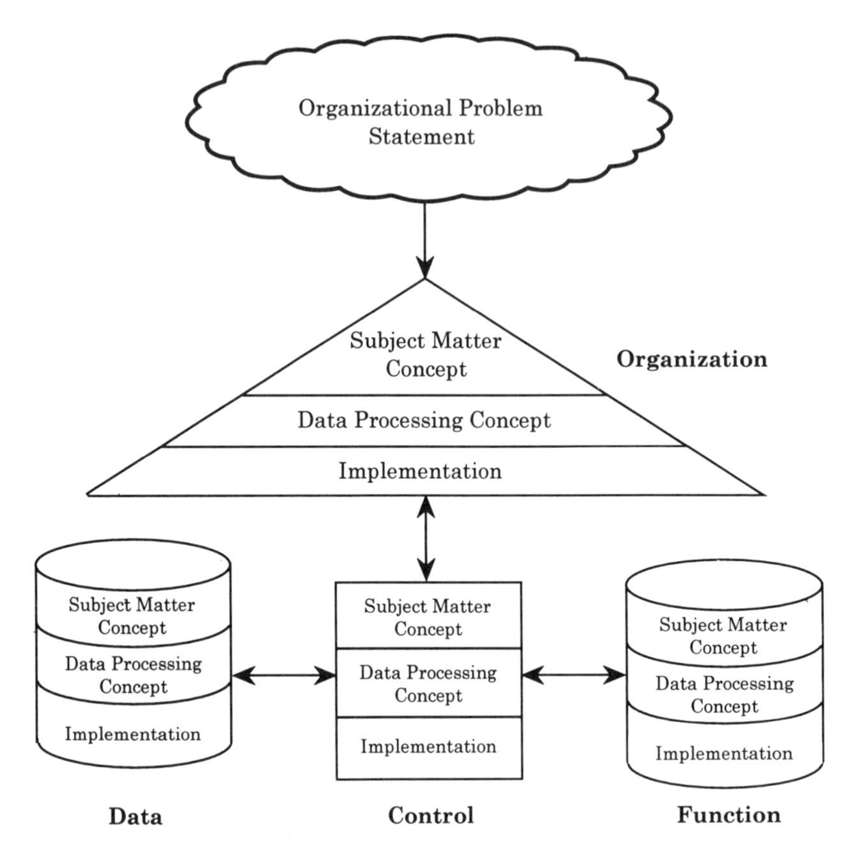

Figure 4.16 *The ARIS concept, Scheer (1994, p. 17. Reproduced by permission from Springer-Verlag GmbH and Co. KG.)*

the markers. These changes may be described mathematically such that control and analysis of the quantity of the relative time intervals and sequences of events become possible within the net.

In the example of the event *screwing together* of sheet metal and screws one needs in each case a screw, a nut, a punch tape and a punch plate. In addition, a wrench and a screwdriver have to be readily available and the container for the completed screw objects must have sufficient room for new objects. All of the necessary resources for this event are symbolized as tags (markers) inside some condition bubbles. The activity of screwing together may be simulated within a Petri net by removing markers from some containers and depositing them in other containers.

INFORMATION DEPLOYMENT

As already mentioned above, planning for information deployment poses a special challenge for organizations and management: The management of information and communication systems, together with their respective technical infrastructures, is in part driven by demands and has to be directed into goal-oriented paths. In the final analysis the question "Which information at which point in time needs to be available in which location?" needs to be answered.

Strategic Deployment of Information and Communication in the Firm

Vis-à-vis the potential opportunities to influence entrepreneurial success through information and communication technologies, a framework or matrix assisting in the systematic search for promising application areas is highly desirable. Such an attempt was made by Porter and Millar (1985) in the form of the information intensity portfolio.

The portfolio concept is based on the following fundamental idea: just as there are capital or material-intensive business areas, a business area may also be information intensive. It is precisely these information-intensive business areas of a firm that need to be identified, because not only is this where the opportunities are greater for the firm's competitors, but also the focal firm can contribute in special ways to business success through targeted information management activities. Porter and Millar suggest two dimensions for the operationalization of information intensity (see Figure 4.17). The *information intensity in the value chain* on the one hand describes the role of information processing in purchasing, logistics, product and sales. On the other hand, *information intensity in performance* refers to the need to explain products and services. This can be seen, for example, in the high degree of information intensity of documentation and product information, as well as consulting or training settings. Individual business areas or partial functions may be positioned within a portfolio matrix using these criteria.

Additional investigation of the information intensity is warranted when considering the firm's respective competitive position and general attractiveness of the business area in question. The strategic competitive position influences the urgency for the deployment of information and communication systems. If a firm possesses a strong competitive position in successful and future-oriented markets, the deployment of information and communication systems has high importance. For business areas with relatively weak competitive positions and relatively low future-oriented markets a strategic reorientation is of greater

Information Intensity in the Value Chain			
	High	Field 1 Example: Multi-stage, complex assembly processes	Field 3 Example: Systems Business
	Low	Field 2 Example: Simple Telework Processing	Field 4 Example: Simple Consulting
		Low	High
		Information Intensity in Performance	

Figure 4.17 *Information intensity portfolio. Source: Picot and Reichwald (1991, p. 273, based on Porter and Millar, 1985) (Adapted and reprinted by permisson of* Harvard Business Review. *An exhibit from* How Information Gives You Competitive Advantage *by Porter and Millar. Copyright © 1985 by the President and Fellows of Harvard College, all rights reserved.)*

importance. The target building of information and communication systems from a competitiveness perspective becomes more meaningful after an assessment of the strategic competitiveness of a firm in specific business areas has been conducted.

Strategic directions and priorities for information management may be derived from the combined examination of information intensity and competitive position of business areas (Krüger and Pfeiffer, 1988; Figure 4.18). Strong success positions and high information intensity of business areas demand aggressive development strategies and the consequent deployment of information and communication systems. When a shift occurs in the position held within a given business area in the direction of decreasing success or information intensity, respectively, information and communication systems, however, take on a lesser role of importance. It would behove the firm then to pursue moderate development strategies, momentum strategies, and maybe even defensive strategies.

With regard to achieving strategic advantages the above described procedure, however, still has a weak point (see Ciborra, 1994). If one

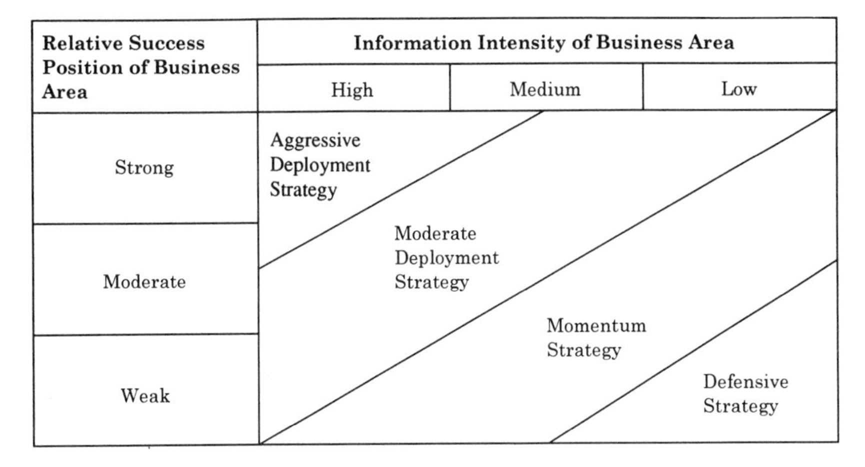

Figure 4.18 *Strategy-oriented development and deployment of information and communciation systems. Source: Picot and Reichwald (1991) based on Krüger and Pfeiffer (1988)*

expects from a strategy-oriented information and communication systems, i.e. a *strategic information systems* (SIS), that it is actually capable of creating a strategic advantage for the firm, it has to fulfill at least three demands:

1 the SIS has to generate added value for the firm;
2 it should be largely of a proprietary nature;
3 it may not be readily imitatable by competitors.

The approach described above as a widely used methodology is precisely suited to generate *non-proprietary* solutions, i.e. solutions that basically are available to all competitors. Only a new comprehension of the information systems planning process as an innovation process seems to promise a way out of this dilemma (Ciborra, 1994, p. 15). Just as product and process innovation strategies may form the foundation for achieving lasting competitive advantage, the information management area may just as likely conceive innovation-oriented approaches triggering lasting advantages. Later in this chapter we will address again this aspect in the discussion of management perspectives for the deployment of information and communication technology within the firm.

Once the business areas are identified for which deployment of the production factor information is important, the next step is to determine concretely information demand that is to be supported by information and communication systems.

Information and Communication-oriented Design of Organizational Processes

Looking abstractly at organizational processes one realizes quickly that a large number of activities transform a specific input into a specific output. This perspective is not just accidentally comparable to the automaton on pages 103–105, as the automaton may actually be understood as the formalization of processes. The differences between both terms is to be found in the characteristics of the *activities*. The basic activities of an automaton are exactly describable, something that generally cannot be said for processes. With regard to organizations one may think of many other important parameters such as the amount of time needed or the technology platform deployed. These processes may be manual ones (e.g., the manual sorting of mail) or they may be automated (e.g., the sorting of account statements through the use of a special machine designed for this purpose).

In order to describe a process the above-mentioned activities are arranged such that they depict the flow of activities. From a more formal perspective one may utilize here the notations of function and process modeling already described on pages 119–120. For present purposes, a much broader and general, i.e. non-technical, perspective is pursued here. In accordance with Davenport's (1993) deliberations on the necessity of *process innovation*, i.e. the fusion of information technology with the human factor, the term process here is understood in a broader sense than the mere chaining of elementary transformations. The concept of process innovation is assisted by new information technologies, but an essential factor that makes the process successful in the first place depends upon the motivation of the employee and the engagement of the upper management with regard to strategic vision. Information technology is the cornerstone of this paradigm and presents itself thusly in the role of the enabler (or the *impeder*).

This new process orientation implies also customer orientation. Within the realm of an implemented process-cost accounting, one could also mention a cost orientation as an additional aspect. Within all of these concepts it is important to design processes that do not become consolidated strongly and thus might create barriers *vis-à-vis* the dynamics in the rest of the organization. An example of this is the introduction of workflow systems and the imperative of immediately and deliberately working against any sort of cementing of organization structures.

Value Added Through Information and Communication

The actual goal in the design of organization structures and entrepreneurial processes and their respective synchronization with information technology is in the generation or increase of *value*. If such added value cannot be generated, one must question the entire effort in the first place (Wigand, 1995a, 1995d).

In the past many managers assumed that the desired added value was brought about through the introduction or the actual application of information technology (Wigand, 1995d, 1985a). Today, however, we may reflect on a number of projects that broadly speaking resemble nothing more than the sheer automation of already existing bureaucratic processes. The expected high productivity improvements did not come about through such efforts. This discrepancy is explained by the false assumption that information technology directly causes added value and that, consequently, a number of results are brought about on the side of efficiency (e.g., return on investment), effectiveness (e.g., quality of management information), but also with regard to transformations within the firm (e.g., innovations, competitive advantage) (Wigand, 1995d). The assumption that the deployment of information technology and value added function in such a trivial relationship is, as we know today, fundamentally incorrect.

The Productivity Paradox

The impossibility of discovering a direct causal relationship between information technology and value added can be demonstrated in the results of many studies, as well as the first-hand experiences within many organizations. This may be reported, for example, from the service industry offering extensive experience and many examples. This phenomenon known as the productivity paradox (e.g., Picot and Gründler, 1995; Wigand, 1995a, 1995d; Brynjolfsson, 1993; Morrow and Thurow, 1992; Strassmann, 1990; Weitzendorf and Wigand, 1991), i.e. the missing positive correlation between investment in information technology on the one hand and productivity on the other hand, is described by Roach (1991) as the overinvestment in computer technology. This is especially relevant for the service sector encompassing 85% of all installed information technology in the United States.

Morrow and Thurow (1992) reach essentially the same conclusion: output in the United States between 1980 and 1990 rose 30%, the total number of hourly workers increased 2% and the number of salaried employees rose by a total of 33%. At the same time the productivity of hourly workers rose 28%, whereas the productivity of salaried employees fell 3% during the same time period. New technologies, hardware and software moved into the American office, yet the result is negative productivity.

Analogous results were found by Brynjolfsson (1993) who also addresses this much discussed but difficult to explain contradictory relationship between information technology deployment and productivity. The various explanatory approaches for the paradox were grouped into seven categories by Picot and Gründler (1995):

1 Reinvestment of employee-related savings
2 Redistribution of gains among the firms within a business area
3 Delay in realizing gains
4 Inadequate measurability of inputs and outputs
5 Political obstacles
6 Mismanagement of information and technology
7 Insufficient reorganization of organizational processes.

Through *reinvestments of employee-related savings*, gains do not manifest themselves outside of the organization. Especially within the administrative realm savings in the form of lower labor costs are typically not noticeable; an increase in the quality of work delivered is rather more likely.

An additional explanatory approach may be found in the *redistribution of gains among the firms in a business area.* Such productivity gains, i.e. those that extend to several business areas, have to be viewed here from the perspective that potential productivity improvements of *individual* firms will always become a burden to other firms. Consequently, this will not be noticed generally.

Delay in realizing gains may be explained in a two-fold fashion: on the one hand the industry branch offering the new information technologies to the market has to be developed first with regard to product quality and service structures. On the other hand, learning and adaptation difficulties surface on the side of the users that, in turn, trigger a delayed pay back of the acquired information technology.

The *inadequate measurability of inputs and outputs* is at the same time the most frequent and also most plausible explanation of the paradox. Utility in the form of better quality, speed, variety, customer service or flexibility typically is not considered in productivity statistics of the firms studied. Because of the delayed occurrence of input and output one must also struggle with the problem of accounting for the effects of inflation.

An additional plausible explanation can be found in *political obstacles*. Here one needs to consider the potential resistance of employees with regard to reorganization and the deployment of information and communication technologies.

The argument of *mismanagement of information and communication technologies* refers to the wanting assessment of benefits by the responsible decision-makers. Information technology in this context is often not introduced in the interest of the firm, but for reasons that are much more based upon personal motives.

Insufficient reorganization of organizational processes pertains to the incorrect deployment of information technology. Such deployment often refers merely to the electrification of existing processes without any adaptation to the organization structure. Consequences are inefficiencies and a potential unwanted solidification of the organization structure.

It is especially this latter point, the insufficient reorganization of organization processes, that deserves additional detailed discussion. Here we encounter the problem of an insufficient adaptation of organization, personnel and technology. On pages 158–160 the importance of an appropriate adaptation of information technology, organizational goals, strategies and processes and the human factor in the sense of *organizational fit* will be addressed.

Information Deployment and Efficiency

Problems with regard to the assessment of productivity have intensified in the organizational practice in conjunction with increasing economic importance of information as a factor of production. Goal directed deployment of information and communication technology, systems and technical infrastructures in the firm has made classical efficiency calculations largely useless (see Reichwald, Höfer and Weichselbaumer, 1996; Weitzendorf and Wigand, 1991; Wigand, 1995d). But why is efficiency evaluation of the deployment of networked information and communication technology in the firm so difficult? The classical pattern of investment calculations for an isolatable investment object do not apply, since aside from the traditional investment costs for technology we encounter always intensive associated costs for measures to change and adjust the organization and human work. Our focus can therefore no longer be on the isolated project alone, but we need to consider an entire range of factors, partially with even temporally delayed and geographically displaced efficiency effects.

The assessment of efficiency of new information and communication technologies therefore encounters problems in theory and actual practice. Essentially these problems may be grouped into six problem categories (see Picot, 1979a; Picot and Reichwald, 1987; Reichwald, 1993b; Wigand, 1995d):

- *The Measurement Indicators Problem:* Which measurement or indicators reflect the effort and cost-benefit effects best?
- *The Situational Problem:* To what extent are the efficiency effects influenced by the respective and specific situational conditions?
- *The Networking Problem:* In which part of the performance based on the division of labor of the firm do relevant effects surface that are important for an efficiency evaluation?
- *The Attribution Problem:* How can one account for temporally delayed or geographically dispersed cost and performance effects?
- *The Innovation Problem*: How can one evaluate innovative applications of new technologies that exceed simple substitution of traditional work processes?
- *The Holistic Assessment Problem:* How can one consider complex recursive relationships within the organizational, technical and human resources total system in efficiency evaluations?

These problem areas define the demands that need to be addressed in an adequate efficiency evaluation (see Figure 4.19). An ideal evaluation method needs to consider the following:

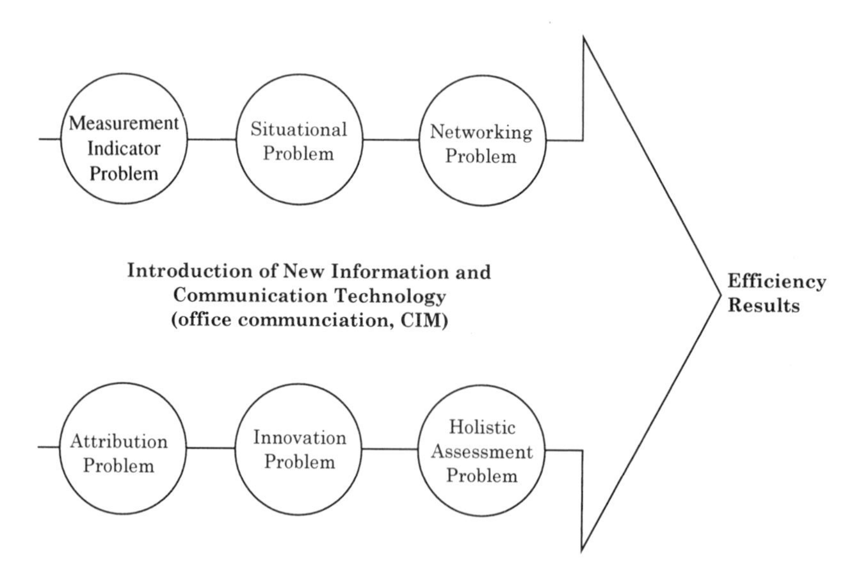

Figure 4.19 *Evaluation problems with networked information and communication technology. Source: Reichwald, Höfer and Weichselbaumer (1996. Reproduced by permission from Schäffer-Poeschel Verlag, Stuttgart.)*

- Relevant cost and performance criteria in monetary and non-monetary form must be generated (*measurement indicators aspect*).
- Those cost and performance criteria need to be emphasized that identify weak spots and that during deployment already were identified as needing change (*situational aspect*).
- It has to be assured that dependent relationships between participating sub-systems will become transparent and that networking effects will be considered (*networking aspect*).
- No restrictions may exist for the consideration of temporally or geographically dispersed cause-effect relationships (*attribution aspect*).
- Innovative effects in the efficiency approach need to be accepted that pertain, for example, to market supply (*innovation aspect*).
- Aside from purely technology-related cost and performance measures, comprehensive effects (organization effects, qualification effects, human effects, external effects) need to find consideration. An evaluation of information and communication technologies can meaningfully only occur in the context of information and communication systems and while considering the importance of the goal-directed deployment of information and communication in the organization (*holistic assessment aspect*).

Classical investment calculations (e.g., Blohm and Lühder, 1991; Perridon and Steiner, 1991) cannot meet these demands. Based on their ease of use and understanding in business they are being used widely. There are numerous more recent suggestions about how one might address appropriately the efficiency evaluation problem in the deployment of information and communication technologies. In order to gain a better understanding of such a new evaluation approach one needs to look for the following (see Schumann, 1993):

- *the type of procedure:* Are we concerned about a purely quantitative, purely qualitative or a combined evaluation approach?
- *the type and number of goal measurements to be addressed:* Are we concerned about a one-way, multiple-way or multi-dimensional evaluation approach?
- *the deployment area of the procedure:* Is it to be understood as a decision aid *prior* to the introduction of an information and communication technology solution, as a companion instrument *during* the introduction or as a control instrument *after* the completed introduction of the solution?
- *the extent of the procedure:* Are we concerned about an isolated auxiliary tool or a comprehensive evaluation methodology?
- *the object of evaluation:* Are characteristics of singular

technologies, isolated effects of singular technologies or integration effects of integrated information and communication systems being evaluated or is a holistic concept for strategic information and communication technology planning being delivered?

An overview of existing new procedures for efficiency evaluations of information and communication technologies are, for example, presented by Kredel (1988), Nagel (1991), Schumann (1992, 1993), Reichwald, Höfer and Weichselbaumer (1996), Weitzendorf and Wigand, 1991; as well as Wigand (1995d). An approach of *networked efficiency thinking* (Reichwald, Höfer and Weichselbaumer, 1996) is now presented briefly to serve as an example of an expanded efficiency approach.

The approach of networked efficiency thinking. Expanded efficiency approaches that also consider qualitative criteria in the cost, as well as performance areas offer opportunities to point out advantages of networked objects to be evaluated. The basis of evaluation in the final analysis is the extent of effectiveness. An organizational or technical change in the firm is, from this perspective, effective when the pursued goals are better accomplished due to this change. Change is therefore to be evaluated and to be compared from several perspectives (multilevel evaluation). The efficiency evaluation is to encompass all direct and indirect cost and performance consequences from the view of the employees, the firm, as well as from a societal perspective. Figure 4.20 depicts an overview of the basic concept of the evaluation approach of networked efficiency.

Central to the approach of networked efficiency evaluation is (1) the active participation of the organization's interest groups in the evaluation process and (2) the equally high ranked consideration of human criteria within the framework of the efficiency evaluation. Why is the participation of interest groups so important? There are at least two reasons:

1. Investments in information and communication technologies typically bring along a high degree of complexity and uncertainty. Only through the incorporation of the employees from the affected areas of the firm is it possible to utilize their experiences and know-how.
2. Each efficiency result may basically be manipulated, i.e. all evaluation methods are based on subjective assumptions. Even in the traditional investment calculation methods based on monetary measures—often touted as being objective—estimates about future monetary in- and outflows, interest forecasts, and so on must be made. Marginal changes of these assumptions may lead to the considerable shifting of relative advantages of the evaluated alternatives. Essentially, the evaluation results may be highly questionable.

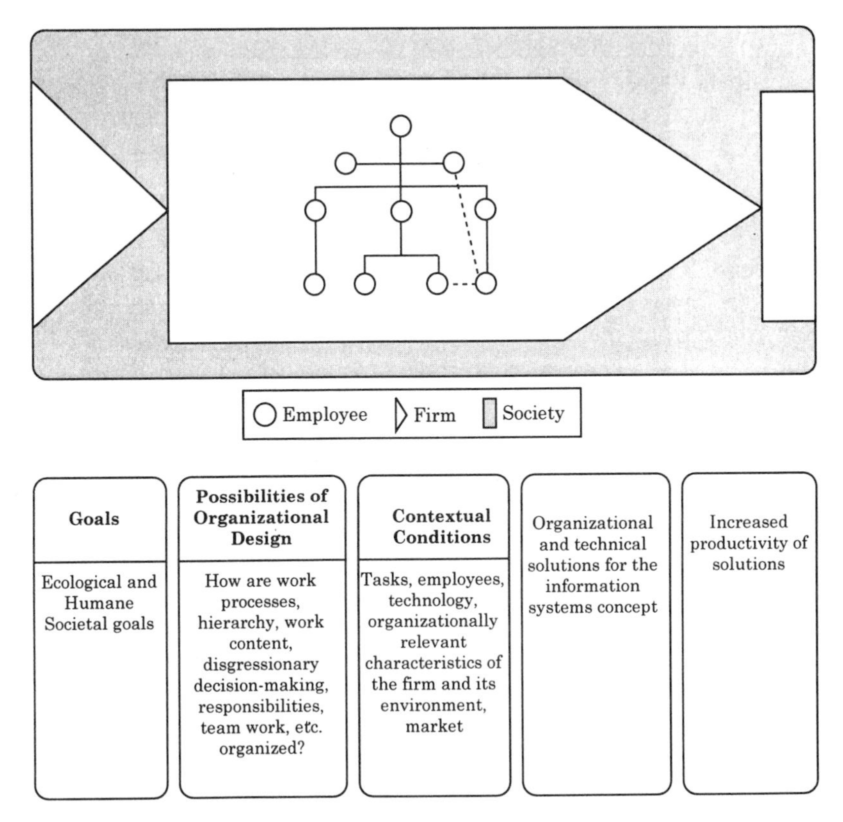

Figure 4.20 *Fundamental concept of the evaluation approach of networked efficiency. Source: Reichwald, Höfer and Weichselbaumer (1996. Reproduced by permission from Schäffer-Poeschel Verlag, Stuttgart.)*

Each evaluation result is, in the final analysis, subjectively shaped through each respective evaluator. The danger that another evaluator may reach quite different conclusions under the same conditions suggests that demands for a better form of objectivity is highly desirable. This may occur in that all interest groups affected by the change participate in the evaluation process, offer their anticipated goals and jointly pursue a consensus. In this way numerous aspects of concern to all parties will be considered from an entrepreneurial and societal perspective and a comprehensive and holistic view of decisions will be formed. It is especially the evaluation of the deployment consequences of newer information and communication technologies in the firm, as well as their potential for the firm's development in the market, that create such a complex problem set for efficiency evaluation.

MANAGEMENT PERSPECTIVES FOR INFORMATION AND COMMUNICATION TECHNOLOGY DEPLOYMENT IN THE FIRM

In the often trendy striving toward the development of ever newer and better approaches for the management of organizations, firms are driven from one fashionable concept to another. Movements of the not all-too-distant past such as Total Quality Management, Empowerment, Quality Circles or Reengineering were viewed as the all-round cure for the problems of the firm. Within such trendy developments it is becoming more and more difficult to recognize a truly rich idea with value for the future (Wigand, 1995d). Recent developments seem to suggest that ideal organizational forms are gaining shape along the concept of the *horizontal organization* (Wigand, 1995d). This concept is based among other factors on the strategic determination of core processes, the redesign of work processes, as well as alignment of information and communication technology with organizational goals, strategies and core processes (Wigand, 1995d). All of these activities require that the understanding of the firm's own competitive position and its knowledge about possibilities to achieve necessary competitive advantage is a fact.

The change affects essentially the model for organization design, i.e. the functional hierarchy, that was so dominant during the last half century. Moreover, core processes need to be found that are not only central to the entire firm, but they also must incorporate suppliers and customers. The process stands here in the foreground, i.e. focal attention should be not *what* firms produce, but rather *how* they produce. But even when firms have identified the right processes, to build them or to change them becomes difficult and is a task not to be underestimated. Information and communication technologies play here a decisive role. Their potential can only be exploited when their deployment is *appropriate.* The right alignment of processes overlaid with information and communication technologies is the basic premise for successful transformation to the horizontal organization (Wigand, 1995d).

The discussion on page 151 points out the missing direct correlation of information and communication technology deployment and value added. Of greater importance is to pay focused attention to the business strategy or the firm's goals. These derived demands placed on the information technology have to be seen in conjunction with demands resulting from the concrete organization of business processes. Adequate means in this context that the relationship is reciprocal: on the one hand business strategy and processes define their demands on information technology, on the other hand information technology is the enabler for new strategies and processes. The trick is to identify the optimal point

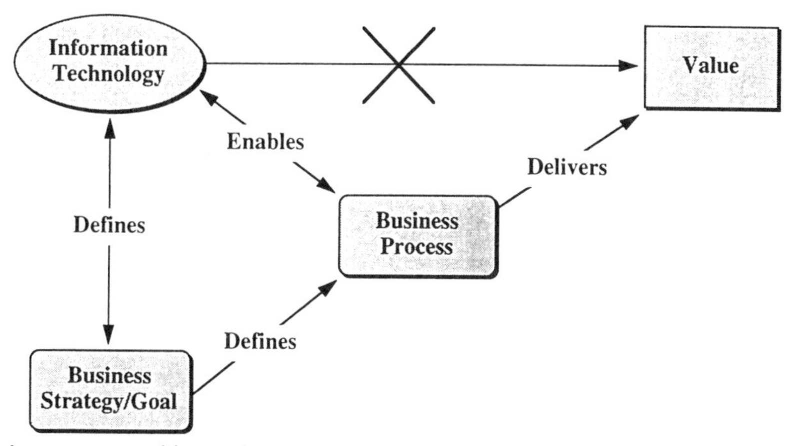

Figure 4.21 Adding value within the organizational fit of information technology, processes and goals/strategies. Source: Wigand (1995d)

for the deployment of information and communication technologies, i.e. the optimal *organizational fit and alignment* (Wigand, 1995d).

In order to achieve the appropriate organizational and strategic fit several iterations of implementation efforts may be necessary, each followed by improvements and adaptation processes and analogous to the self-regulatory mechanisms of a cybernetic system. Only when the optimal relationships among information technology, business strategies, goals and processes have been developed, all mistakes have been corrected and the organization has adapted to the changes, may one then expect the anticipated improvements in efficiency and effectiveness, i.e. the *adding of value* occurs (Wigand, 1995d). These relationships are depicted in Figure 4.21.

Aside from adequacy the principle of *innovative* deployment of information and communication technology counts. Especially with regard to international competition the deployment of information as a production factor must occur in novel and unique ways as much as possible. Ciborra (1994, p. 19) recommends for this a deliberately paradox procedure, i.e. by considering the following often contradictory guidelines; existing work processes, thinking patterns and behaviors may be softened or may even be dissolved entirely:

- *Strategic evaluation of "tinkering".* Ideas, improvements and experiments in various operations of the firm must be considered in strategic deliberations. Especially in this area the possibility to generate creative, innovative ideas based on local knowledge and experiences from day-to-day activities exist. These, in turn, need to be evaluated by management during the planning of information and communication technology deployment.

- *Planning for experiments.* Through the deliberate introduction of organizational measures in support of experimental and prototyping activities by the end user, local innovations may be recognized and enabled.
- *Systematization of accidents.* The simultaneous linking of experimental activities, the concrete realization and consideration of improvement suggestions support the emergence of accidental solutions.
- *Striving toward gradual breakthrough.* New ideas and solutions may not be impeded by deadlocked organizational structures. Management must be prepared for the emergence of detours, incongruencies and inconsistencies and may not cultivate a desire for control and the continuation of present conditions.
- *Incompetent learning.* This is the lack of prejudice toward learning processes that question the very existence of cognitive and organizational learning structures. Here, too, management ought to avoid clinging to standardize perceptions about such things as competence or behavior.
- *Striving toward failure.* Striving toward success implies that attempts are made to complete already well-known tasks even better. This enabled potential for efficiency improvement may, however, be overshadowed by the danger of eventually emerging routines. The underlying processes loose their flexibility and the firm finds itself in the so-called *competency trap*.
- *Joint striving toward non-imitatability.* Also in cooperation with competitors it is possible to gain suggestions for the generation of innovative and difficult to copy solutions.

Ciborra (1994, p. 20) argues that these seven paradoxes describe a new "systematic" organizational approach in order to control the development of innovative information systems. They are suited to enhance learning processes and creativity and to place the need for control into the background.

The striving toward innovative information technology solutions on the one hand and the appropriate organizational fit on the other hand are the key for overcoming performance boundaries of the organization. Not only are the traditional boundaries of the firm affected with regard to geographic limitations, distances, speed and working time, but also awareness limitations of the employees in the organization. Through the continual balancing of information technology, business goals, strategies and entrepreneurial processes on the one hand and the awareness about the expansion of entrepreneurial boundaries and limits on the other hand it becomes possible to realize the vision of the horizontal firm. This is supported and encouraged by the steadily growing potential of information and communication technologies.

5
Dissolution of Hierarchies: Modularization of Corporations

FUNDAMENTAL PRINCIPLES OF MODULARIZATION

In recent years, an increasing number of theoretical and practical contributions have been made which, in reference to changing competitive conditions, demand a reorganization of corporations. In particular, large corporations with mostly hierarchic and functionally divided organizational structures come under fire from all sides. In a pithy manner, the end of the "dinosaurs" is proclaimed, being replaced by modular, highly flexible "flotilla" organizations (see Drucker, 1990). According to many authors, the restructuring of the corporate organization should be accompanied by a dissolution, respectively a flattening of hierarchies (see for example Davidow and Malone, 1992; 1993). In the following sections, these theses will be discussed.

Before further analyzing the causes and economic explanatory approaches for this development, it is necessary to first define modularization as an independent organizational principle. In the analysis of value chain reorganization recommendations which call for a formation of "modules", "segments" or "fractals" (see for example Wildemann, 1994; Warnecke, 1992), clear similarities can be seen between these concepts (see Frese, 1993). The common principle of these related approaches can be summarized in the following manner:

> Modularization is the *restructuring of corporate organization* based on *integrated, customer-oriented processes* in relatively *small, manageable units (modules)*. These units are characterized by *a decentralized decision-making competence and results-oriented responsibility*, while the coordination among the modules is increasingly achieved through *non-hierarchical forms of coordination.*

The common principle of modularization concepts is applied at different corporate levels: from the modularization at the level of the work organization through the formation of autonomous groups to the restructuring of the entire corporation into relatively independent profit centers (see also page 187). The arrangement of the corporation in modules is meant to reduce the complexity of production and to increase the proximity to the market. As a result, the modular corporation should be more flexible and react faster to market changes, customer needs, and competitors' activities. Here we discuss the fundamental characteristics of modularization concepts according to the above definition.

Restructuring of the Corporate Organization

Modularization is viewed here as an *intra-organizational form of reorganization* (see Schwarzer and Krcmar, 1994). This distinguishes it from the new organizational forms discussed in Chapter 6 and partially in Chapter 8 (networks and virtual organizations) focusing on relatively long-term, respectively situational cooperations between different organizational units, and offering an interorganizational perspective.

The assumption is made that the value-creating processes which are completed in modules are highly specific and thus, are to be sensibly established in permanent organizational structures, but not in the market (see the transaction cost theoretical perspective in Chapter 2). The "classical" firm, characterized by long-term contracts and ownership rights, therefore presents the object of reorganization in the sense of the modularization concept. However, this does not exclude the displacement of entire modules to be permanently managed as independent firms or to be integrated in other firms, for example in the process of focusing on core competencies and the optimization of the vertical degree of integration.

Process Orientation

In addition to the modularization concepts, the arrangement of organizational units based on processes, meaning chains of interconnected activities for the production of a good or a service (see Fromm, 1992), is propagated by many recent contributions to corporate organization (see for example Striening, 1988; Gaitanides, 1983; Harrington, 1991; Davenport, 1993). Thereby, the emphasis is on the contrast with the mainly functional organizational concepts, which focus primarily on optimizing productivity of single corporate areas through functional division of work and specialization. The priority of process-oriented approaches, however, is the reduction of organizational interfaces in the production process. In recent years these interface problems, such as communication barriers, goal conflicts and delays at the borders between functional departments, have been identified as one of the major organizational causes of low competitiveness of corporations (see for example Gaiser, 1993). They lead to long processing times for development projects and order processing, high modification costs due.to late identification of quality defects, and a low flexibility in reacting to new market demands (see page 168).

With respect to organization theory, modularization can be classified as an object-oriented structuring approach, due to this alignment towards processes instead of functions. Thus, modularization concepts principally resemble the well-known divisional organization. In contrast, however, modularization concepts emphasize the consequent implementation of object-oriented structures at all corporate levels. Likewise, the objects which serve as an orientation for the modules are not limited to marketable end products (respectively the process chains for their production), but also include internal semi-products and services.

Customer Orientation

The consistent alignment of modules towards the objects of corporate activities—internal as well as external products and services—inevitably emphasizes customer orientation. This is based on the customer's primary role in defining the requirements of a product or service and thus, for the process. Due to the above-described extension of object-orientation to internal products and processes, the term customer then also includes internal buyers of semi-products and services. Thus, the modularization approaches also comply with the requirements of current total quality management (TQM) approaches, which generally focus on the quality of services along the entire value chain (see for example Mizuno, 1988; Oess, 1989; Weaver, 1991).

This identical customer-orientation emphasis for market and internal exchange processes produces an interesting side effect: the reorganization of corporate areas which are further away from the market, for example R&D, finance and human resources, can be based on the same customer-oriented principles as the restructuring of those value chain elements which are directly tied to the market. Prerequisite, however, is the precise definition of the relevant internal customer and his specific requirements.

Degree of Task Integration

Directly related to the process orientation and customer orientation is the call for an extensive integration and self-containment of a module's distinct tasks (see also Frese, 1993). This requirement results directly from the process-orientation approach, which is to integrate all correlated activities for the fabrication of a (semi-)product in one organizational unit. This is founded on the general rule of organization theory, which is to avoid organizational interfaces for strongly interdependent tasks as much as possible. A module's minimum size is thus determined by the process steps between two clearly definable semi-products. The problem arises in that the optimal degree of task integration can no longer be managed by a "small unit" (in the sense of the above definition of modularization). This dilemma will be examined in the next section.

Creation of Small Units

Whereas process orientation presents a quality which the modularization approaches have in common with almost all current reorganization approaches, the creation of small organizational units can be described as the basic principle of modularization. The goal is to adapt the organizational structure to an individual's or a small group's problem-solving capacity, in order to avoid mistakes, costs and time losses caused by complexity (see Chapter 9).

Since these limits on human capacities to manage are extremely task specific, there is a fluctuation in the appropriate size of "small units". For this reason, Frese correctly refers to a "relatively small number of people" (Frese, 1993, translation by authors). Empirical results, however, conclude that practical upper limits exist. Peters and Waterman, for example, determined that labor conflicts, fluctuation and dissatisfaction increase disproportionately at the corporate level with more than 500 employees at one location (see Peters and Waterman, 1984). For semi-autonomous groups, which present the basic form of modular organizational units at the labor level, the proposed number for an efficient maximum unit size is about 15 people.

Thus, aside from the demand for the self-containment of a module's tasks, a second fundamental requirement for the building of modules can be determined: the volume and complexity of the module's tasks have to correspond with the human or group capabilities as a managerial and executive factor. Here a serious conflict can arise, when even the minimum on task integration—when viewed from a process perspective—exceeds the limits of control through a "small unit". However, through the use of new information and communication technologies which help to break down the constraints on human capacities for control, this conflict can be often avoided. Thus, similar to re-engineering approaches (see for example Davenport, 1993), new information and communication technologies play an important role as "enabler" of reorganization in the context of modularization.

Decentralized Decision Competence and Responsibility for Results

A further common characteristic of modularization concepts is the transfer of decision competence and responsibility for results to the modules. The concrete extent of this reintegration of managerial and administrative tasks depends upon the level of perspective and the task. Basically, the subsidiary principle (see Picot, 1991c) is used as a directive for the decentralization of management functions: decision competence and responsibility for results should be placed as low as possible in the hierarchy and thus as close as possible to the actual value creating process. The goal is to improve process efficiency with respect to current market demands. A decision competence close to the process, for example, means a corporation's increased flexibility through many decentralized feedback systems which are close to the customer (see also Beuermann, 1992) and the omission of long decision channels which are susceptible to mistakes. Simultaneously, this should increase the employee motivation through complete task fulfillment and strengthen the incentive for market-oriented action. Along with this, the manager's role is changing. In the framework of these new concepts, a change from supervisor to "coach" takes place (see, for example, Hammer and Champy, 1993, as well as Chapter 9). In this sense, Hammer and Champy refer to a dissolution of hierarchies in connection with the new organizational forms.

Non-hierarchical Coordination Forms between Modules

As mentioned in Chapter 2, the representatives of classical economics favored the market form of coordination through the market's "invisible hand". The focus is on the price mechanism, which coordinates the activities of the single market participants, concentrates market information, signals possibilities for exchange, and enables an optimal resource allocation.

As a countermove, Alfred Chandler, the well-known economic historian at Harvard, refers to the "visible hand" of management and signifies the hierarchical coordination of economic activities through managers within a corporation (see Chandler, 1977). The "self-regulating" mechanisms of the market are replaced by the "third-party-regulation" of organizational members through the management. Recently, the observation has been made that large corporations in particular are making the effort to introduce market-like mechanisms to coordinate relatively autonomous organizational units, in addition to the "visible hand" of management (see Frese, 1995). The purpose of these instruments, such as internal transfer prices, is to allow the "invisible hand" of the market to guide the internal exchange of products and services. "Softer" measures, such as the development of a strong corporate culture, are discussed as further alternatives to hierarchical coordination (see, for example, Wilkens and Ouchi, 1983). The problem of coordinating modular organizational units with respect to corporate goals triggers many questions which will be discussed later (see page 200). Also in this case, new possibilities to master the task of coordination will be brought about by new information and communication technologies (see page 203).

DRIVING FORCES BEHIND THE DEVELOPMENT OF THE MODULAR CORPORATION

Changing Competitive Conditions

In connection with the actual discussion on corporate restructuring concepts, distinct changes in competitive conditions are always emphasized which justify the need for reorganization. The globalization and intensification of competition, the advancing innovation dynamic, the potentials of new information and communication technologies, as well as the changes in social value systems are named as a few of the most important developments (see Chapter 1).

Using the basic hypothesis of the contingency approach from organization theory, which claims that an organization's efficiency is determined essentially through its adaptation to relevant environmental circumstances (see Staehle, 1973; Kieser and Kubicek, 1992), then the necessity for reorganization can essentially be derived from a change in these fundamental frame conditions. The changed competitive conditions pose new requirements on the corporate organization. Organizational structure should enable the corporation to simultaneously:

- be globally present, yet act locally;
- react quickly to market changes;
- promote employee creativity and thus, secure a high rate of innovation;
- reach short processing-times in product development as well as in order processing;
- demonstrate a general orientation towards the customer and his demands on quality; and
- meet employee expectations.

Within the framework of these requirements, the observable deficits in classical organizational principles—hierarchy, bureaucracy, and Taylorism—will be presented, in order to examine subsequently the awaited competitive advantages of the modularization concepts in the light of different organization theoretical models.

Dysfunctionalities of the Classical Organization Principles—Hierarchy, Bureaucracy, and Taylorism

In the literature on new modularization concepts, the hierarchy and the bureaucracy are often referred to as organizational models which are to be replaced (see, for example, Peters, 1993; Bennis, 1993). Generally in these contributions, the terms hierarchy and bureaucracy are relatively interchangeable, whereby they imply an organizational concept which contrasts with modularization. Further, the contrast between modularization and Taylorism is emphasized. In many publications, inadequacies attributed to these classical organizational principles advocate the legitimization of modular organizations. A few examples are *Beyond Bureaucracy* (Bennis 1993) and *Beyond Hierarchies* (Peters 1993, German title), *The End of Bureaucracy and the Rise of the Intelligent Organization* (Pinchot and Pinchot, 1993) and *The Overcoming of Hierarchies Through Human Networks* (Fuchs, 1994). These prognoses will be analyzed and discussed in the following pages. In order to do this, a definition is necessary of the three organizational principles—hierarchy, bureaucracy and Taylorism, whereby each of their dysfunctionalities and their relation to modularization will be presented.

Hierarchy and Modularization

Hierarchy generally means the structure of supraordinated and subordinated positions in an organization (see Heinen, 1991, p. 98). Positions present the smallest organizational units, to which partial tasks are assigned, independent of the person occupying this position. The first considerations are given to the structural relations between them (position hierarchy). Characteristic for hierarchic relations between positions is the one-sided allocation of executive and decision rights to the higher position (authority) over the subordinate (operative) position. Even though more than one person can fill a position of authority (committees, boards), single managers generally are responsible for the authority's tasks. Thus, the position hierarchy actually corresponds to a person hierarchy, which is accompanied by a power and status hierarchy. As a consequence, organization theoretical studies of the hierarchy and its alternatives cannot be examined without considering the related sociological questions, for example, the acceptance of power structures in corporations.

In the organization theory literature on vertical integration, the term hierarchy has an additional meaning (see, for example, Picot, 1991b). Here, "hierarchy" describes the extreme form of organizational integration of parts of the value chain, in contrast to coordinating transactions over the market or hybrid organizational forms (see Chapter 2).

In this context long-term employment contracts as the basis for service exchanges are emphasized as a hierarchy's most important characteristic. The direct relation to the above described basic conception of hierarchy results from the fact that long-term contractual relations enable extended powers of instruction and control in comparison to exchanges on the market.

Dysfunctionalities of hierarchical forms of organization. These are (see, for example, Bennis, 1993; Peters, 1993):

- long decision channels on the "official channel" and thus, inflexibility in responding to market changes, as well as high coordination costs caused by turbulent market conditions;
- decision-makers which are distant from processes and markets;
- problems of filtered and distorted information;
- concentration on departmental goals and objectives, since only the highest level in the hierarchy has a process overview;
- lack of acceptance of hierarchical coordination through commands, especially in the context of an authoritative management style.

This short consideration of the different interpretations of hierarchy and its dysfunctionalities shows that many aspects have to be analyzed separately when judging the relation between hierarchy and modularization. The titles cited above have to be questioned. For example, in respect to modularization, the "Dissolution of hierarchies in corporations" thesis can be interpreted in different manners:

1 as a dismantling, respectively flattening of the position hierarchy;
2 as a change from a person hierarchy into a working party hierarchy; and
3 as a reduction of the degree of vertical integration in the value chain.

So, although the thesis can be generally confirmed, a complete dissolution of hierarchies, as suggested, cannot be expected (see also Kühl, 1995).

Thus, a differentiated view is necessary when comparing hierarchy and modularization. In the context of the theoretical discussion of modularization, selected aspects will be discussed in more detail.

A similar situation exists for the relationship between bureaucracy and modularization.

Bureaucracy and Modularization

For a general characterization of bureaucracies, the work of Max Weber provides a good starting point (see Weber, 1972). He determined the following characteristics of bureaucratic organizations (see Derlien, 1992 for a summary):

- full-time personnel
- separation of (private) households and businesses
- hierarchical supraordination and subordination of positions
- graduated scales of instruction and control powers
- duties of obedience and reporting
- formally defined physical and technical distribution of competencies
- dependency on rules and thus impersonality of processes
- written documents on record to guarantee their later verification.

Although Weber's bureaucracy model relates in detail to public administration, most of these characteristics can also be applied to classical administrative structures of private corporations. One talks of "bureaucratization" when these qualities are strengthened within an organization and of "debureaucratization" when these qualities fade away. For example, Frese attributes a positive debureaucratizing effect to modularization concepts for large corporations (see Frese, 1993, p. 1015).

Although Weber's model was constructed (only) to describe ideal types, his characterization of bureaucracies presented the foundation for a wide spectrum of approaches criticizing bureaucracy (see Derlien, 1992). These approaches deal with various dysfunctionalities of bureaucracies, beginning with the danger of self-sufficiency of bureaucratic structures, over the dehumanization of their processes ("without respect of person"), through to critical statements about its efficiency.

Criticism of bureaucracies focuses on its hierarchical characteristics (see, for example, Bennis, 1993). Thus, the most commonly named dysfunctionalities of bureaucratic organizations correspond with the ones listed above for hierarchy. Correspondingly, the relatively poorly differentiated use of the terms hierarchy and bureaucracy in the literature of new organizational concepts is understandable.

With regards to the relation between bureaucracy and modularization, however, one should note that the characteristics of Weber's bureaucracy model comprise significantly more discussion than those of a hierarchy. This is especially true for the conformance to rules in bureaucratic processes. In this context, the organization theorists Kieser and Kubicek stress that the widespread assertion of a debureaucratization, meaning a dismantling of rules when building teams (and, accordingly, when forming small organizational units), is barely verified (see Kieser and Kubicek, 1992). These authors even suggest that general rules for the coordination of teams may gain in importance (similar: Reichwald and Koller, 1995). They do not refer to the inflexible rules which stand in the center of the bureaucracy, but rather the determination of behavioral guidelines, norms and values as suggested in many new organizational concepts (see Chapter 9).

Similarly, the comparison between bureaucracy and modularization with respect to the characteristic of limited distribution of competencies must be differentiated. Specifically, though modularization concepts propagate the expansion of the autonomous units' competencies in the frame of a stronger process and customer orientation, the necessities of task division will simultaneously entail a limitation of competencies in functional respects. Thus, the previously suggested hypothesis of a diametrical comparison between a "bureaucratic" and a "modular" organization cannot be maintained in this respect as well.

Taylorism and Modularization

The dominating design principles of the Tayloristic production concept present (see Taylor, 1913, pp. 37–42 and Figure 5.1):

- the personnel separation of managerial and operative work
- the concentration of work methods on task division
- the physical separation of all planning, steering and controlling activities from the field of production.

The industrial organizational model of assembly-line production, which has dominated for a long time for example in the automobile industry, presents this principle. In the German and American management literature, these organizational models are connected with the names Taylor and Fayol. Until today, their organizational philosophies have influenced large industrial organizations significantly through methods and principles of scientific management.

The unsatiated demand for mass products, traditional production technologies as well as a low innovation frequency for industrial

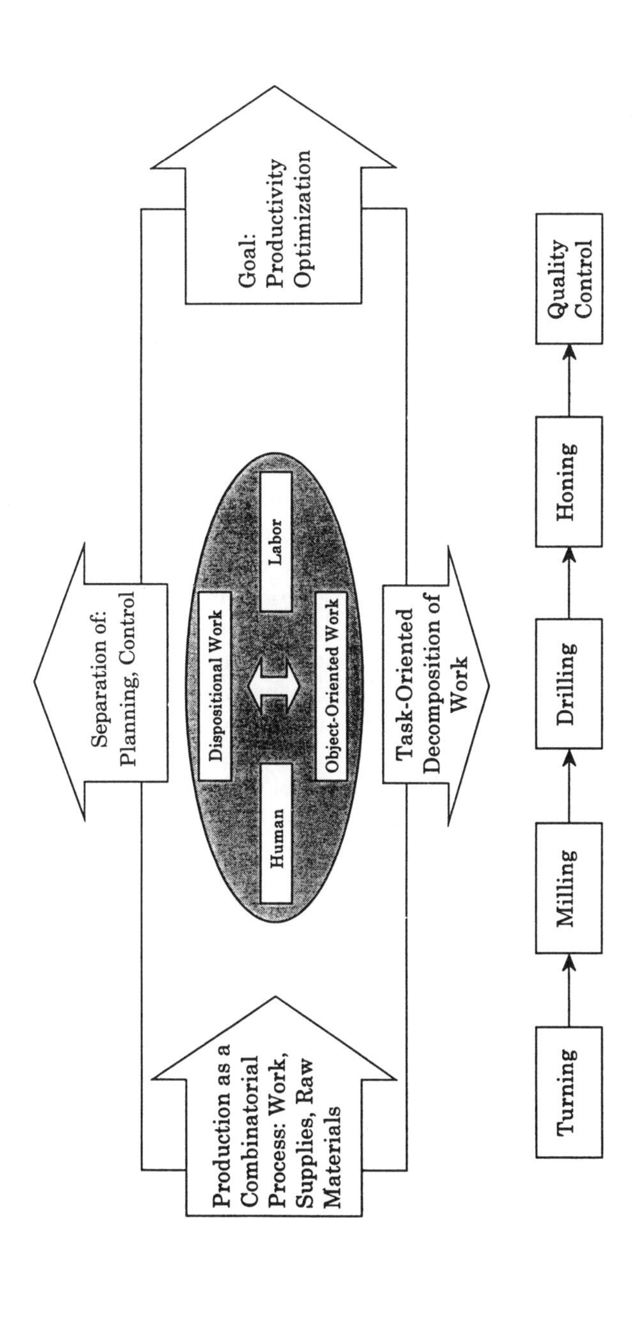

Figure 5.1 *Model of a Tayloristic work organization. Source: Reichwald (1993. Reproduced by permission from Lehrstuhl für Allgemeine und Industrielle BWL.)*

products were the essential characteristics of classical industrial markets. In this competitive situation, the dominant corporate objective was reaching a high degree of productivity, meaning output per unit of time. The design of organizational processes—especially in manufacturing—was marked through a permanent increase of production volume (see Reichwald, 1992a).

This resulted in the division of the industrial corporation into two parts, the shop and the administration areas, and thus the division of the workforce into workers and employees, in blue-collar and white-collar labor worlds, in those earning wages and those receiving salaries. The Tayloristic labor organization did not only typify the workshop area of industrial corporations, but also the corporate administration. Thus, the whole corporation was affected. The production based on division of labor required a strictly hierarchically organized corporate administration which had bureaucratic characteristics and qualities.

This concept's primary rationalization effect resulted from a cost lowering, meaning a decrease in unit costs of production with an increasing degree of division of labor. After all, the dissection of the production process in simple steps also formed the basis for later automatization, resulting in the far-reaching substitution of human labor through technology.

The declared goal of dissecting and standardizing work processes was a reduction of demands on the single individual. In this way, the individual in his entire complexity could be turned into a "functionable production factor", and with this could be made predictable. Narrowing human labor to clearly definable and quantifiable performances also presented the prerequisite for production- and cost-theoretical reflections for determining the optimal degree of division of labor (see, for example, Reichwald, 1977). For long-term adaptation processes with unchanged products and stable markets, classical production and cost theory assumes a decreasing course of unit costs of production due to the extension of production capacities and the increase in the degree of specialization.

Yet in the long-term analysis of corporate growth, this cost lowering effect can be overcompensated through the over-proportional increase in administrative expenses, meaning the costs of the managerial factor. Coordination costs, which were already discussed by Gutenberg (see Gutenberg, 1958, p. 318) and Heinen (see Heinen, 1965, p. 453), are today the dominating cost factors in many branches. With the growing influence of new market and competition situations the internal costs of adaptation and coordination of a Tayloristic, performance-oriented division of labor increase. The stronger the new influence factors of today's market and competition situation are, the steeper is the curve of internal

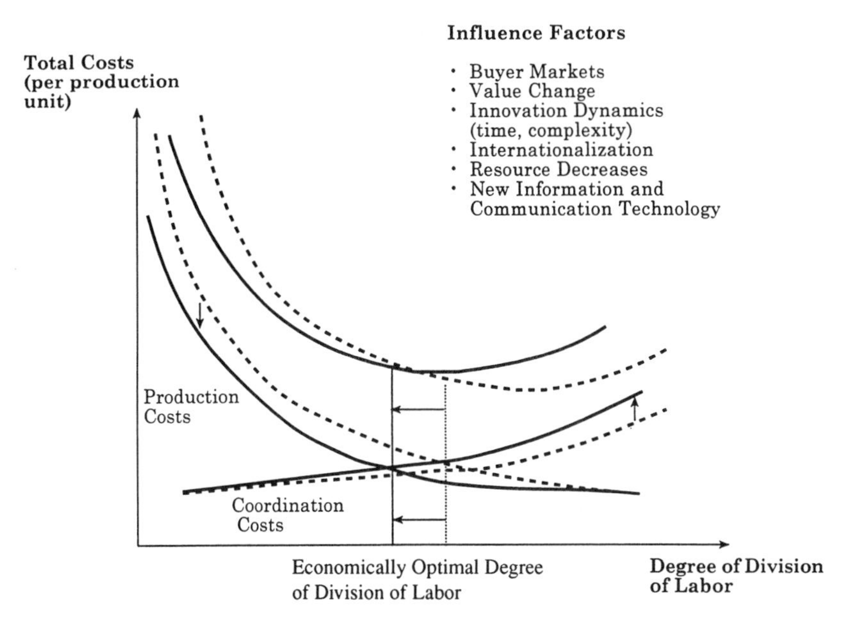

Figure 5.2 *Cost optimal degree of division of labor. Source: Reichwald (1993c. Reproduced by permission from Lehrstuhl für Allgemeine und Industrielle BWL.)*

coordination and adaptation costs and as a tendency, the optimal degree of division of labor decreases. Figure 5.2 clarifies this correlation.

In order to meet the new market requirements, many corporations have started under the motto of "de-Taylorization" to develop and implement new organization and work structures for the production area (see, for example, Reichwald and Dietel, 1991; Martin, 1992) which places people as the most important corporate resource in the center of attention. Warnecke and Hüser refer to "the renaissance of the human role" (translation by authors) within complex production systems (Warnecke and Hüser, 1992, see also Chapter 9). Under the key phrase "task integration", this was discovered early on as an important organizational potential of integrated information and communication technologies (see, for example, Picot and Reichwald, 1987).

In summary one can see that the labor-divided, bureaucratic organization principles of hierarchy, bureaucracy and Taylorism have recently been confronted with a lot of criticism (see also Chapter 9). Nevertheless, it should not be forgotten that they still present, especially for mostly standardized goods (e.g., mass consumer products) and stable market conditions, the most efficient and least expensive organizational forms. Further, the discussion so far should have shown that a diametrical comparison of the modularization concepts with these classical organization principles generally presents an inadmissable simplification. Thus, the effects of modularization cannot simply be deduced through inversion of the defects of hierarchy, bureaucracy and Taylorism. Rather it is necessary to derive the prognosticative effects of modularization from the above described characteristics of modular organizational units. These will now be studied from the perspectives of different theoretical organization models.

Competitive Advantages of Modularization from the Perspective of Theoretical Explanatory Models

Explanatory Approaches Based on Competitive Strategy

In the contributions to business process reengineering as well as to modularization concepts, new competition requirements frequently serve as an argument to justify the advantage of these measures. Here, depictions on the basis of single case studies are dominating, generally based on plausibility considerations (see, for example, Hammer and Champy, 1993, as well as von Koerber, 1993). Theoretical models are rarely applied in the literature.

An exception is presented by Frese's reflections on the "model function of medium-sized business structures for large corporations" (see Frese, 1993). Frese distinguishes as essential efficiency goals of organizations:

- *resource efficiency*, meaning the avoidance of unused capacities and uneconomical allocation of scarce resources;
- *market efficiency*, meaning the use of synergies through coordinated appearance on sales and supplier markets; as well as
- *process efficiency*, meaning the optimization of the total process, for example in respect to cycle time, quality, service or flexibility.

The mostly functional organization of large corporations is here seen as an expression of the primary aspiration for resource and market efficiency. In the face of increasing dynamic and uncertainty in markets, however, the growing importance of process efficiency is stressed.

Hence, the competitive strategy has a decisive influence on coordination requirements and thus on the organizational structure (see also Chandler, 1962). Starting from this assumption, Frese develops a competitive strategic model to discuss the advantage of "small units". This model is based on Porter's classification of competitive strategies (see Porter, 1988), which are then modified under consideration of different production types (see Figure 5.3):

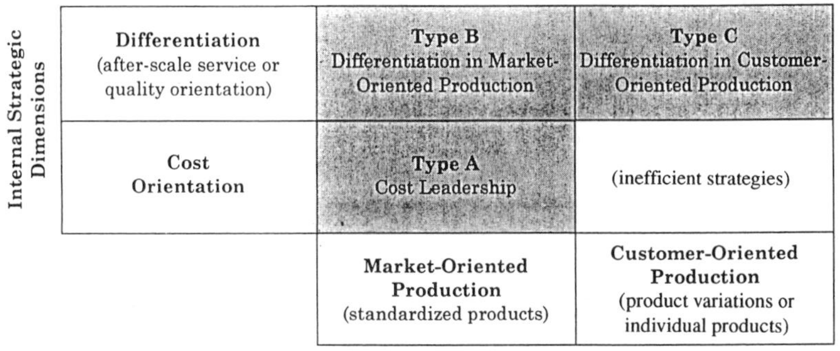

Figure 5.3 *Classification of strategies. Source: Frese (1993. Reproduced by permission from Verlagsgruppe Handelsblatt. Copyright © 1993 absatz wirtschaft.)*

- Type A: cost leadership for market production
- Type B: differentiation for market production
- Type C: differentiation for commission production.

The essential result of Frese's contemplations is that the importance of process efficiency increases from strategy type A to strategy type C. The competitive advantages which can be expected through the formation of small organizational units depend on the respective corporate strategy and the corresponding importance of process efficiency. The general development of markets (see pages 166–167), however, forces more and more corporations to adapt the strategy types B and C.

Task-oriented Explanatory Approaches

Every division of labor requires coordination and agreement, generally requiring a certain amount of effort. Through alternative organizational structures (structure and process rules), the attempt is made to minimize these coordination costs. It is one of the most important insights of contingency organizational research that one optimal way (the one optimal organizational structure) cannot exist. Rather the answer to the question "which organizational structure minimizes coordination and communication costs?" depends on the respective qualities of the task to be organized. When these tasks' characteristics change, then new solutions for the organizational problem are required (see, for example, Picot, 1993a).

Typologies classifying tasks have been successful numerous times when studying the relationship between task and appropriate organizational form and when deducing respective norm strategies (see, for example,

Picot and Reichwald, 1987; Nippa and Reichwald, 1990). Accordingly, today's need for reorganization in favor of modular organizational units can be well justified. The relationship between the modified characteristics of contemporary corporate tasks and the trend towards modularization will be illustrated using the example of production. These arguments can be analogously transferred to other corporate fields.

The characteristics of the task determine extensively the concrete design of organizational processes and structures (see Perrow, 1970; Picot, 1990). This general insight is successfully applied for the design of the production economical decision field. Typical qualities describing the task situation present the starting point for the production economical decisions (see Frese, 1989; Frese and Noetel, 1990; Picot, Reichwald and Nippa, 1988; Schomburg, 1980; Zäpfel, 1989a). These production-economic task characteristics are derived especially from the peculiarities of the performance offered and from the type of market supply. Task complexity (the number of elements to be considered and their linkages) and variability (the extent and predictability of changes) are considered the dominating characteristics for the determination of the production task (see Reichwald and Dietel, 1991). Their properties determine the essential requirements for a situation conform design of the production economy. The complexity of the production task is decisively influenced through the production program, the variability through the market supply of the industrial corporation. Figure 5.4 depicts the situation-dependent view which will be further discussed on the following pages (see also Picot, 1990a; Reichwald, 1984; Reichwald and Schmelzer, 1990).

The combination of the features' complexity and variability into a simplified production-economic description results in four fields with different characteristic manifestations (see Figure 5.5). Whereas field 2 shows a production situation which, for example, is typical for plant construction in the investment good field (high complexity and high variability of the performance program), field 3 represents a production situation of the consumer goods industry with mass products (low complexity and low variability of the performance program). Fields 1 and 4 show combined forms.

Depending on the task field, different requirements on information and organization structures as well as on the methods of production planning, steering and control can be derived. This results from the different information need, the communication and coordination requirements and thus from the differences in the planning situations (Zäpfel, 1989; Reichwald, 1990a).

In a simplified manner, three production types are created from the four fundamental situations of Figure 5.5, as well as from the reflections underlying Figure 5.4, whose requirements on the planning situation and

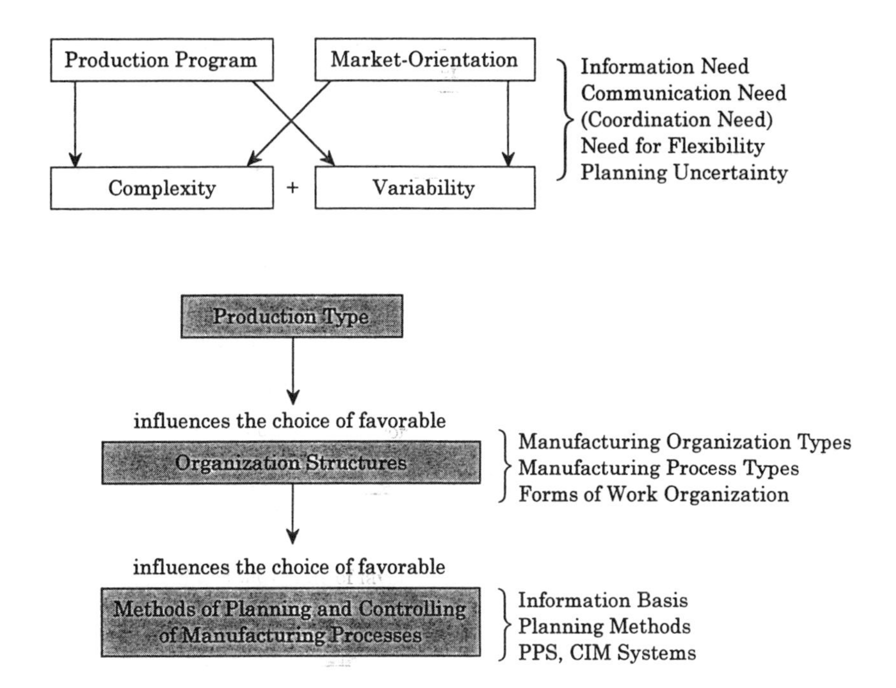

Figure 5.4 *Relationships among production-economic task, production type and decision field. Source: Reichwald and Dietel (1991, p. 406. Reproduced by permission from Gabler Verlag GmbH.)*

organizational solution are illustrated in Figure 5.6 (see Picot and Reichwald, 1987; Nippa and Reichwald, 1990).

Order-based, customized production (Type 1) distinguishes itself by the production of individual units. The customer defines the product features. Industrial corporations with order-based, customized production are confronted with an uncertain planning situation. Their competitive position is determined by their ability to adapt as comprehensively and quickly as possible to customer requirements.

The *market-oriented, mass production type* (Type 3) is marked by a stable planning situation. Production programs and production processes are tied to a low degree of flexibility and coordination between production and market, thus cost-efficient standardization processes can be used for production. Aspects of differentiation only play a subordinate role. The definition of product features derives from the general needs of an anonymous market.

The *mixed serial production type* (Type 2) can be seen as a hybrid form of the two production types described above, and hence is characterized through a medium degree of planning uncertainty.

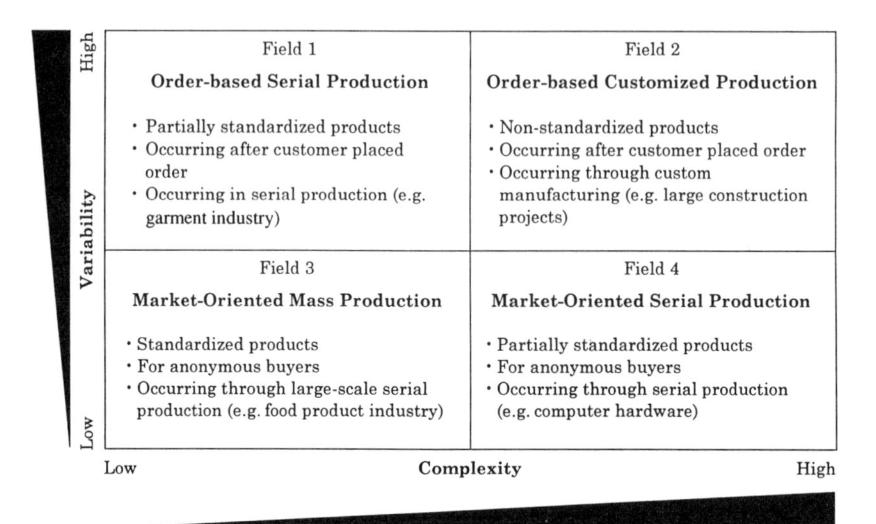

Figure 5.5 *Production-economic task fields. Source: Reichwald and Dietel (1991, p. 405. Reproduced by permission from Gabler Verlag GmbH.)*

Characteristics \ Production Type	Type I Order-Based Customized Production	Type II Mixed Serial Production	Type III Market-Oriented Mass Production
Information Needs	Very High	Medium	Low
Need for Flexibility	Very High	Medium	Low
Need for Coordination	Very High	Medium	Low
Planning Uncertainty	Very High	Medium	Low

Figure 5.6 *Three production types and their characteristics. Source: Reichwald and Dietel (1991, p. 407. Reproduced by permission from Gabler Verlag GmbH.)*

These three production types have to be interpreted as ideal types, meaning they simplify reality as necessary for models. The reduction to three types does not do justice to the variety of forms encountered in the real business world. Nevertheless, this typological simplification increases the awareness for the necessity of task-related solution designs for structure-oriented decisions and production planning and control (process decisions).

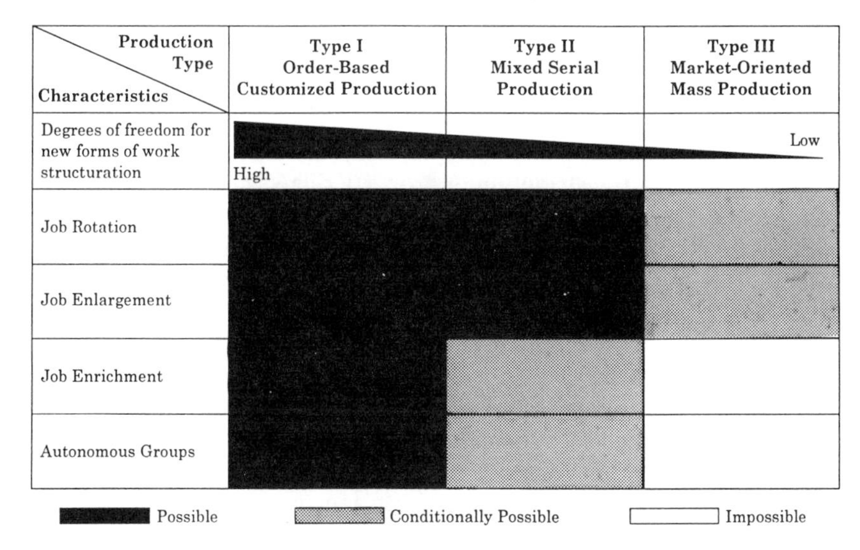

Figure 5.7 *Production types and organization design. Source: Reichwald and Dietel (1991, p. 442. Reproduced by permission from Gabler Verlag GmbH.)*

For each task-oriented production type classified here, a suitable variant of organizational design can be attributed (see Figure 5.7).

As long as the industrial production was predominantly aligned with products of low, at best medium complexity and specificity (for example, mass products) and as long as the quantities of these goods grew over a long period of time, meaning stable markets and uniform customer needs (seller markets), hierarchical organizations based on division of labor presented the optimal organizational form which could not be outperformed through any other mode of organization.

In industrial practice, however, a growing trend towards customer oriented and individual production can be recognized, especially in the automotive industry or machine building industry. The intense interaction between industrial corporations and the market demands a high flexibility in all fields of industrial performance.

The previously described new competitive conditions call for this observable tendency to production tasks of Type 1 (commission-based job production). The current prognosis is that this development will be amplified in the future.

The changes in performance features, in task characteristics as well as in the market towards higher complexity and variability let a development be expected towards autonomous team structures in production and accordingly in other corporate fields. Thus the trend toward modularization is confirmed from the perspective of task-oriented explanatory approaches of organization theory.

Modularization as Adjustment of Property Rights

From a property rights viewpoint (see Chapter 2), modularization can be interpreted as a redistribution of property rights within the organization. Rights of action, respectively competencies of execution, which are horizontally· distributed in functionally and hierarchically organized corporations, are combined in the modules related to processes. Rights of disposal, respectively decision competencies, are simultaneously transferred vertically from management to lower levels which are closer to the process.

This aspect of modularization concepts corresponds with the fundamental organizational recommendation of property rights theory, i.e. to assign property rights to the actors as far as possible. Through this an incentive to act in a responsible and efficient manner is expected. In addition, high transaction costs are avoided, which are related to the transfer of property rights from case to case in instruction oriented, hierarchical coordination forms.

However, the transfer of property rights to the modules refers primarily to the rights to use the available resources in the sense of the prescribed task (*usus*). Concerning the extent to which further property rights are transferred, there exist considerable differences between modularization concepts for different corporate levels. Partly, the concepts are not completely developed with respect to the property rights distribution.

The rights to keep the profits from business activities, as well as the duty to carry one's own losses (*usus fructus*), are increasingly transferred the higher the level of modularization (modules as cost centers or profit centers). However, it is unusual for corporate management to abandon these property rights completely, for example, the right to carry out strategically relevant shifts of capital resources between the modular units. Even in modularization, however, the further reaching property rights of alienated use, respectively, alteration of goods (*abusus*), as well as disposal to a third party remain essentially in the hands of the owners, respectively their directly authorized representatives.

Due to this incomplete attribution of property rights to the direct actors, the danger of external effects principally exists. These could be limited only by measures in which the employees would hold a share from the corporate capital, a topic which is rarely discussed in the context of modularization concepts.

Modularization from the Perspective of Transaction Cost Theory

Although transaction cost theory was originally developed to explain the emergence of corporations as centralized, hierarchically coordinated forms of production (see Coase, 1937; Williamson, 1975), it also proved to be a valuable instrument in analyzing the efficiency of organizational structures (see, for example, Picot, 1982b). In this generalized application form, it is very helpful to study and explain observable centralization and decentralization tendencies, such as modularization efforts. Transaction costs stand in the center of attention, which vary with the organizational structure and which can be interpreted in this context as the costs of information and communication to coordinate tasks in organizations based on the division of labor (see Chapter 2).

According to the assumptions of transaction cost theory, efficient organizational forms are characterized through low transaction costs compared to alternative forms of organization. Hence, it has to be studied to which degree and under which conditions the modularization of a corporation is tied to a transaction cost reduction and thus presents an advantageous organizational approach from a transaction cost perspective.

As previously determined when analyzing the essential features of current modularization concepts, modularization basically means to create object-oriented organizational units around processes, whereby these organizational units act in a rather autonomous and profit-responsible manner and thus, present quasi-enterprises within the corporation. Hence, transaction cost theoretical reflections on the economically useful degree of vertical integration (see Picot, 1991b) can be analogously transferred from the corporate level to the level of modular organizational units. An integration of production processes in a modular organizational unit would be recommended for those cases in which high specificity and strategic importance present major performance features (see Picot, 1991b). Frequency of transactions as well as high environmental uncertainty would support this tendency.

By taking a look at today's competitive situation, one can see that process qualities such as order processing time or flexibility in respect to customer needs have gained as much importance from the customer's perspective as physical product features. Consequently, processes are then a strategic factor. Furthermore, processes are less prone to imitation, in contrast to products in the market which can be analyzed and eventually copied by others. Therefore, a strategic differentiation through processes presents itself and is successfully practiced by many corporations (see, for example, Stalk, Evans and Shulman, 1992). The above described environmental uncertainty triggered by market turbulence and pace of innovation supports this basic argument.

However, the trend towards process-oriented modularization can also be justified when directly contemplating the coordination requirements for today's value creating processes. The frequency of cross-functional and cross-departmental transactions increases with the growing competitive relevance of processes. Thereby, the arising transaction costs, meaning the costs of initiating, agreeing upon, processing, adapting and controlling the single transactions, are especially high for classical, functionally structured organizations. The reasons lie in the often deplored interface problems between functional fields due to different departmental goals, different organizational cultures and different terminologies. Only when considering the additional opportunity costs in the market (for example through late market entry) next to the actual coordination costs, does the economic importance of these transaction hindrances become obvious to the full extent.

Interface problems can be successfully reduced through organizational integration of those partial processes with the most frequent transactions. Transaction costs decrease drastically. Here, communication in a common language as well as an atmosphere of trust which evolves through the close collaboration play an important role in lowering transaction costs (see Ouchi, 1980). In this context, especially the property of modules as small, supervisable units has a trust-building effect. In addition, due to social control in small groups, there is a decrease in the danger of opportunistic behavior, which normally causes high transaction costs (for example through costly control measures).

Small, process-oriented units, however, imply an increased demarcation, meaning a decentralization, in a functional respect. Thus, from a transaction cost theoretical perspective it has to be exactly examined, whether the improved coordination at the process level may be related in some cases for coordination problems and thus with a significant loss of synergy potential in the functional respect. Thereby it has to be analyzed, for example, which type of specificity is more important in the individual case: technical specificity (here: along the process) or infrastructural specificity (see Picot, 1990; Picot and Reichwald, 1991). This differentiation will be taken up again when discussing modularization concepts at different corporate levels and their conflict potentials (see page 192).

A further characteristic of new modularization concepts which is likewise relevant under transaction cost considerations concerns a comparably high degree of control necessary in hierarchical organizational forms, which—due to the observable change in social values—gains less and less acceptance and therefore increases transaction costs. Moreover, the tendency towards turning away from hierarchical coordination instruments in favor of self organization and market-like incentive structures in modular organizations adds additional support to these concerns. Thus, also in this respect modularization concepts present an approach for transaction costs reduction. This aspect plays an important role in the subsequently discussed principal-agent problems.

Modularization and Principal-agent Problems

The principal-agent theory (see Chapter 2) also provides valuable hints for the theoretical justification of current modularization concepts. In the center of this theory stands the danger existing for buyer/contractor relationships that the contractor (agent), given a behavioral scope of action, may not act according to the agreement with his buyer (principal). As decisive factors for the occurrence of such principal-agent problems, the theory names incomplete information on the principal's side (asymmetric information distribution) as well as deviations between the principal's and the agent's goals which cause the latter to behave in an opportunistic manner.

Economically relevant (negative) consequences of these principal-agent problems are welfare losses caused by the agent's behavioral deviations as well as the principal's non-value-creating expenses for control and the costs of trust-building measures (guarantee costs) on the agent's side. These so-called agency costs present the efficiency criteria when evaluating modularization concepts from the perspective of principal-agent theory.

Principal-agent relationships occur in almost any kind of corporate structure, since the emergence of organization is usually related to a delegation of the owner's property rights. These buyer/contractor relations in a corporation, however, turn only then into a problem in the case of substantial information asymmetries as well as goal deviations between principal and agent. This is especially relevant for hierarchical, functionally structured organizations in two aspects: between corporate management and functional areas in particular as well as between authorities and operative positions in general. In the following sections we will take a closer look at the extent to which modularization concepts counteract these principal-agent problems.

The first problematic principal-agent constellation in functionally structured hierarchies concerns the buyer/contractor relationship between general management and managers in functional areas. In the center stand the observable deviations between the market requirements and, thus, the objectives that general management has to pay attention to these matters and the actual behavior of managers in the functional areas. In practical life, a tendency towards departmental optimization can be observed which leads to suboptimal results in respect of major goals such as total cycle time, total costs or total quality.

Thus, special attention has to be paid to those objectives which are actually relevant to the managers in functional areas as well as to their available scopes of action. The managers' goals can primarily be derived from the respective result indicators which are used to measure their performance. In practice, departmental key figures are still dominating, whose isolated pursuit eventually leads to suboptimal total results. Further individual goals of area managers, such as striving for as many employees as possible for status purposes, even increase the divergence from corporate goals.

In the analysis of an area manager's scope of action, a paradoxical situation can be recognized. Although managers principally have significant scopes of action, these are often substantially limited through area-oriented controlling figures. This finally contradicts the process orientation required by the market.

Through modularization and appropriate process-oriented alignment of the management structure, corporate management as principal can change the agents' objectives in a manner suitable for the market. Nonetheless, a simultaneous alignment of the controlling system is required, for which only few conceptual reflections exist.

The other manifestation of principal-agent problems in hierarchical organizations which is interesting in this context concerns the general buyer/contractor relationship between authorities and operative units. The principal-agent problem manifests itself in the business-damaging exploitation of opportunistic scopes of action through employees at all levels. Typical manifestations of this "moral hazard" (see Chapter 2) are, for example, high absenteeism, inattentiveness at work or lacking engagement for productivity improvements.

Even when such statements are not empirically proven, theoretical reflections based on principle-agent theory suggest a current increase of moral hazard in hierarchical forms of organization. On the one hand the tendency towards increasing qualification and improved information about employee rights enable a better identification of behavioral scopes. On the other hand, the observable changes in social values (see Chapter 1) lead to a growing discrepancy between corporate objectives and personal goals as well as to a low acceptance level of hierarchical management and control systems. Therefore, it can be expected that qualified employees in operative positions in strictly hierarchical organizations will increasingly take advantage of the identified behavioral scopes for their own interests.

Studying the measures suggested by these modularization concepts, reveals that these are to a high degree identical with the general recommendations of principle-agent theory restricting moral hazard (see Chapter 2). An important aspect certainly is the fact that small, supervisable units entail better information and control possibilities. Their transparency supports the dismantling of information asymmetries. "Blind spots" from the view of the controlling authority are substantially reduced. The social control observed in team structures amplifies the effect of considerably reducing behavioral scopes of individual employees and thus the pursuit of "private" goals. These improved possibilities of control, however, cannot be seen as the main advantage of modularization in respect of principle-agent problems. After all one has to assume that resourceful employees with a corresponding (de-)motivation will always discover and exploit new behavioral scopes.

Therefore, the reduction of the discrepancy between employee objectives and the organizational unit's economic goals has a much greater impact on the decrease of principal-agent problems through modularization. The suggestions of modularization concepts to delegate decision competencies into the modules as well as to organize in teams correspond in this respect to the recommendations of principal-agent theory. Admittedly, new principal-agent problems can arise during modularization, when goal discrepancies between the module's interests and those of the entire corporation are not prevented through appropriate coordination measures (see page 200).

One solution to reduce principle-agent problems has scarcely been taken up in modularization concepts: the theoretical recommendation of profit sharing for employees to increase the incentives to act on behalf of the corporation (see Chapters 2 and 9). Starting from the often stated prognosis that business organizations will increasingly develop into "open systems of shareholders" (see, for example, Laske and Weiskopf, 1992), this aspect will gain in importance in the future.

Modularization and Motivation

Insights from labor science substantiate that human motivation is generated through comprehensive tasks, scope of action, and a transparent environment as well as through a quick feedback of work results. The results of studies conducted through Hackman, for example, support the predicted advantages of modular organizational structures in respect with employee motivation (see Hackman, 1969, 1977). The possibilities to integrate tasks, together with higher responsibility and a larger scope of action (Ulich et al, 1973), offer opportunities for work enrichment and self-realization.

The results of Herzberg (see Herzberg et al, 1959 and Chapter 9) point toward the same direction. In his two-factor approach, he distinguishes between hygiene factors and motivators. Hygiene factors are those conditions whose insufficiency creates employee dissatisfaction, without their existence creating performance motivation (according to Herzberg, for example, the salary level, external working conditions or relations to colleagues). The motivation to perform is only caused through the motivators which are also responsible for employees' satisfaction at work. Noteworthy is that especially the four most important motivational factors according to Herzberg (performance, recognition, work content and responsibility) can be positively influenced through the creation of small, self-contained and mostly self-organized units in the sense of modularization concepts. In this manner, an impression of individual performance and thus the basis for personal recognition and recognition from others can only develop through integral work. The formation of modules based on relatively self-contained process chains delivers the necessary organizational prerequisites.

The principles of self-organization and self-responsibility within modular units are more interesting, more versatile and responsible activities and thus positive effects on motivation can be anticipated. Nevertheless, the principle of (horizontal and vertical) task integration underlying these measures presumes a much higher employee qualification. Therefore a lack of appropriate qualifying measures can hinder the acceptance of the new organization concepts through substantial fractions of the staff, as shown for example through the case studies of Frieling (see Frieling, 1992).

These insights to the advantages of small units and team structures are not new. They were previously proclaimed in the discussion on the humanization of the labor world in the 70s (see, for example, Picot, Reichwald and Berbohm, 1985; Reichwald, 1989), but could not assert themselves in practical life. From today's perspective one has to realize that these concepts partly came too early. Only the radical change in competitive conditions described in Chapter 1 fully brings out the economic benefits of modularization concepts. These benefits are based mostly on motivated and thus more flexible and more creative employees thinking more in a process-oriented manner.

Meanwhile, this competition-oriented evaluation of new organizational concepts and their motivational effects has gained widespread acceptance. Today even leading representatives of the theory of business organization stress the motivational effects of modular, respective segmented structures (see, for example, Frese, 1993, p. 1003). Thereby, however, a shift in the interpretation of the term "motivation" has occurred: whereas motivation was interpreted as an expression of work satisfaction in the discussions of the 1970s, contemporary organization theoretical publications primarily consider motivation effects for market-conforming behavior. In this sense, for example, Frese stresses the motivating effect of creating market pressure within the corporation, for example through the introduction of profit centers (see Frese, 1993, p. 1017).

The following statement from Bennis can be considered characteristic for the new, economically shaped perspective of rediscovered modularization concepts:

> "While various proponents of 'good human relations' have been fighting bureaucracy on humanistic grounds and for Christian values, bureaucracy seems most likely to founder on its inability to adapt to rapid change in the environment." (*Bennis, 1992, p. 10*).

FORMS OF MODULARIZATION

The Spectrum of Modularization Concepts

Reorganization concepts which correspond to the previously described fundamentals of modularization were recommended for all levels of the corporate organization: for the macro-area (entire corporation), for the micro-area (work place design and labor organization) as well as for the intermediate levels in between (departments, respectively processes). Although similar in their fundamentals, the modularization approaches on each level are characterized by different focal points. At the corporate level, the formation of modules is oriented on the supraordinated goals relevant for competitiveness, such as market proximity or technology leadership. At the process level, the emphasis is on connected task chains. At the level of labor organization, the orientation is on the employees and the available information and communication technologies for their support.

The modularization concepts within a particular level also often exhibit different focal points, placing them in competition with each other and inducing conflict situations. Also the potential for conflict between the modularization attempts on different levels can be identified. In the following, an overview is provided of the currently discussed modularization approaches, whereby special attention is given to the potential conflict situations.

Modularization Concepts at the Corporate Level

Profit Center Structures with Centralized and Decentralized Modules

A common characteristic of those corporations which are normally presented as examples for modularized corporate structures (e.g., ABB, see von Koerber, 1993) is their arrangement in numerous, legally

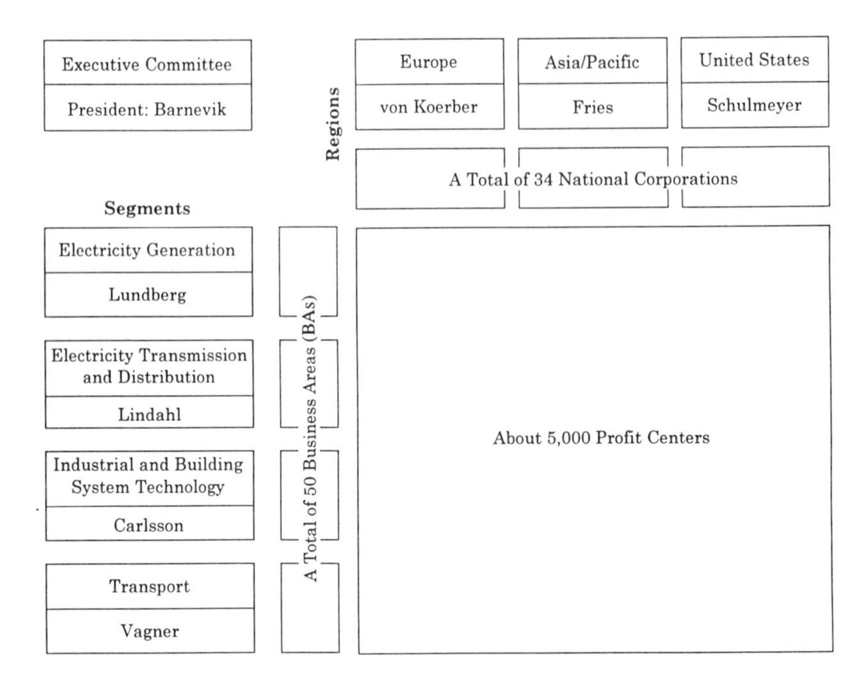

Figure 5.8 *Modularization at the corporate level, using ABB as an example. Source: von Koerber (1993, p. 1061. Reproduced by permission from absatz wirtschaft, Düsseldorf.)*

independent profit centers (see also Frese, 1995). These profit centers are then combined at a higher modularization or segmentation level according to distinct criteria, for example divisions and products, core competencies respectively regions and markets (see Figure 5.8). As a rule, a relatively small coordinating central authority leads this corporate federation. In the case of ABB, this is a management group in Zurich made up of only about 100 employees.

In the analysis of profit center organizations, the focus is once again on the classical tension between the centralization and decentralization of task completion which must be dissolved again for each organizational form. There is no pat solution for this problem. It is necessary to determine the appropriate balance between decentralization and centralization, meaning the mix which is tailored to the task attributes. Extreme positions are often dangerous. A complete centralization can possibly fail due to an overtaxing of the central authority. In a similar way, a decentralized solution can not function, when suitable central conditions, respectively a suitable infrastructure, is missing. To a certain degree, decentralized corporate organizations also require a unified arrangement of corporate-wide tasks such as strategic development, accounting, controlling, finance, personnel and technological research.

The organizational form of the management-holding company is increasingly propagated in the practical business world as a solution for this conflict (see Bühner, 1987, 1993). The management holding is a decentralized form of the divisionalized organization (see Bühner, 1993, p. 9). This is a corporate federation, in which several entrepreneurial and legally independent divisions act as profit centers, carrying the responsibility for the actual business activity. The principal company leading the combine, which is often accountable for only a small part of the entire personnel (like at ABB), is responsible for the long-term coordination of its subsidiaries, especially in the areas of global strategy, allocation of finances in the sense of an internal capital market, corporate-wide personnel management and accounting systems, as well as the coordination of further corporate-wide tasks (see Figure 5.9).

The holding is then responsible for the realization of financial, technological and managerial synergy effects. Operative synergies (e.g. the common use of distribution systems) are realized through the divisions. This broader operative responsibility of the divisions leads to an increased employee motivation. Shorter channels make the divisions more agile, allowing them to react faster to market changes. A further advantage lies in the structural and strategic flexibility, as in the linking or

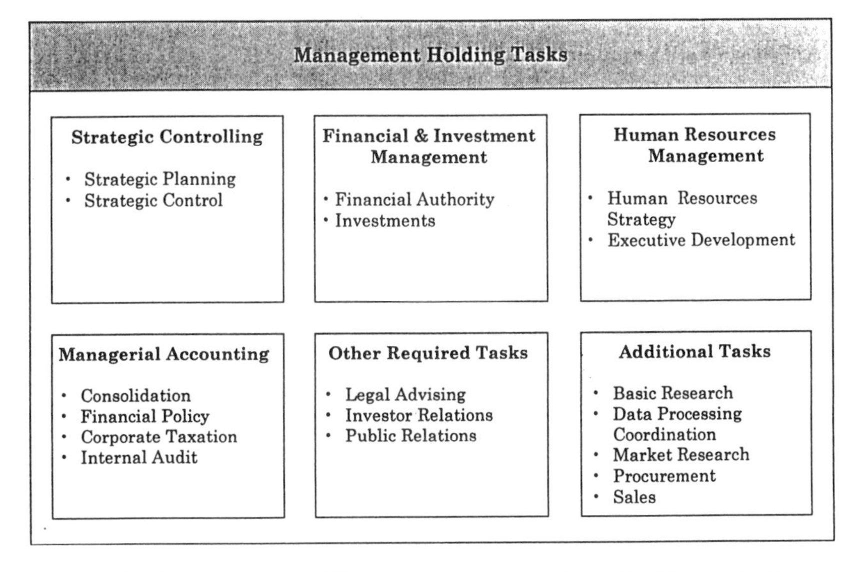

Figure 5.9 *Management-holding tasks. Source: Bühner (1993, p. 13. Reproduced by permission from FBO-Verlag.)*

partitioning of divisions respectively in the participation of external partners in existing divisions.

Modularization Based on Divisions and Products

The divisional organization, first introduced by Alfred Sloan at General Motors in the 1920s, is the prototype of the breaking down of the corporate structure based on market-oriented lines of business. As a rule, the corporation is split up at the second hierarchy level (directly under the level of corporate management) according to product groups, in the sense of an object-oriented centralization. The resulting divisions are internally arranged primarily according to functional criteria.

Modern modularization concepts refine the object-oriented arrangement of the divisions through the formation of individual market-oriented (and often legally independent) modules for smaller lines of business all the way to single products. For example, the average number of personnel at ABB's approximately 5000 profit centers is less than 50 (see von Koerber, 1993). The reason behind this is the previously mentioned increasing differentiation on the markets which requires a corresponding arrangement within the corporation.

Simultaneously with this growing product-oriented differentiation in the formation of modules, corresponding coordination facilities are being created at higher levels, for example in the form of groups within the central principal company which are responsible for a division. The goal here is to promote the exchange of know-how between related profit centers and to take advantage of the potential technological synergies in the corporate federation.

Modularization Based on Core Competencies

A further type of module formation at the corporate level is the arrangement of long-term organizational units for the subsequent development of core competencies (see Prahalad and Hamel, 1990) and capabilities (see Stalk, Evans and Shulman, 1992).

The concept of core competencies based on Prahalad and Hamel stresses above all the importance of building and mastering key technologies that can be applied to a variety of products. Canon Corporation, whose broad spectrum of products actually stems from three core competencies, i.e. precision mechanics, fine optics and microelectronics, provides an exceptional example for the targeted development and combination of core competencies. These three core compentencies have, individually and mutually, enabled the production of 23 key products, ranging from basic cameras to laser beam color printers and copiers (Prahalad and Hamel, 1990, p. 90).

In addition to core competencies in the sense of key technologies, Stalk, Evans, and Shulman stress the mastery of fundamental value-creating processes as decisive for ongoing competitiveness. Using one of Prahalad and Hamel's examples, Honda, they state that Honda's core competencies in the areas of engine and power drive technology have always been and still are an important reason for the continual expansion in the business fields of motorcycles, lawnmowers, generators and automobiles. Although less noticeable, Honda's extraordinary core capabilities in the areas of dealer management and product development are just as crucial (see Stalk, Evans and Shulman, 1992, p. 66).

These examples show that in contrast to the classical portfolio of divisions, business lines and market segments, the building and further development of a portfolio of core competencies and core capabilities which are specific for the corporation are gaining in importance. Accordingly, supraordinated coordinating modules must be established for this task also in a modularized corporation (see Prahalad and Hamel, 1990). There is currently a distinct tendency toward centralization in this area. In order for core competencies to create customer value, decentralized units which are closely linked to the market must serve as information efficient interfaces between customers and the corporation.

Modularization Based on Regional and Local Markets

The increasing necessity for corporations to participate in local markets in order to guarantee success on international markets leads to a further type of module formation: the establishment of regionally specific organizational units (see, for example, von Koerber, 1993, ABB example). Reasons for this are, on the one hand, that corporations attempt to site specific organizational units as close as possible to the individual markets. This is, for example, of great importance in highly developed regions with innovation-friendly customers, because these markets often play the role as forerunner for global mass markets. On the other hand, this regional differentiation of the corporations can be considered an answer to the clear preference for domestic products and employers in local markets.

Analogous to the modularization based on divisions and products, practices in the regional modules, and given today's finely-tuned structuration the market activities must also be coordinated to take advantage of synergy effects. Also in this case, the establishment of supraordinated modules for regional areas on the upper level of the corporate structure is a sensible measure.

Potential for Conflict at the Corporate Level

The formation of modular organizational units for each of a corporation's different lines of business, core competencies and regional markets can naturally not take place without some degree of overlap. Modular corporations are therefore often structured at their highest structural level in (sometimes multiple) matrix forms.

Conflicts of interest are practically unavoidable in such organizational structures, even when disciplinary channels for employees generally run along only one axis of the matrix (e.g. at ABB, responsibility to regional headquarters). Corporations, however, consider these conflicts as the fundamental essence of their activities, which have to be dealt with and solved. The individual profit center managers play a particularly meaningful role, in that they are as "servants of several masters", responsible for the direct maintenance of a balance between clashing interests within the matrix structure (see von Koerber, 1993). The requirements on managers filling these interface positions in modular structured corporations are accordingly very demanding.

A further significant conflict field at the corporate level deals with the division of labor between centralized and decentralized modules. Here the synergy advantages from centralization must be carefully weighed against the disadvantages of a centralization of tasks. Thereby, for example, the differentiation between technically specific and infrastructure specific tasks discussed on page 182 can offer methodical assistance (see Picot, 1990). Tasks with high technical specificity, meaning those for which knowledge about specific business processes is decisive for the solution of problems (see Picot, 1993a, p. 140), should be solved decentrally in the technical departments or modules. In contrast, tasks with a high infrastructure specificity, meaning those having significant overlapping methodical and technical aspects for the solution of problems, should be completed in centralized forms (see Figure 5.10).

Presently, the attempt is made to reduce central staffs and services, as the new forms of information and communication technologies facilitate the outsourcing of these tasks or the reintegration of these staff tasks in the divisions. Nevertheless, the above discussions on the influence of core competencies and core capabilities on the lasting competitiveness demonstrate that there must at least be a coordination of R&D efforts in the strategically oriented development of technology.

Modularization Concepts at the Level of Process Chains

Institutionalization of Business Processes

Associated with task expansion and object orientation, a function and department overlapping process orientation is gaining in importance. With this process chain orientation, considerable reductions can be achieved in information transmission and waiting times, thus lowering

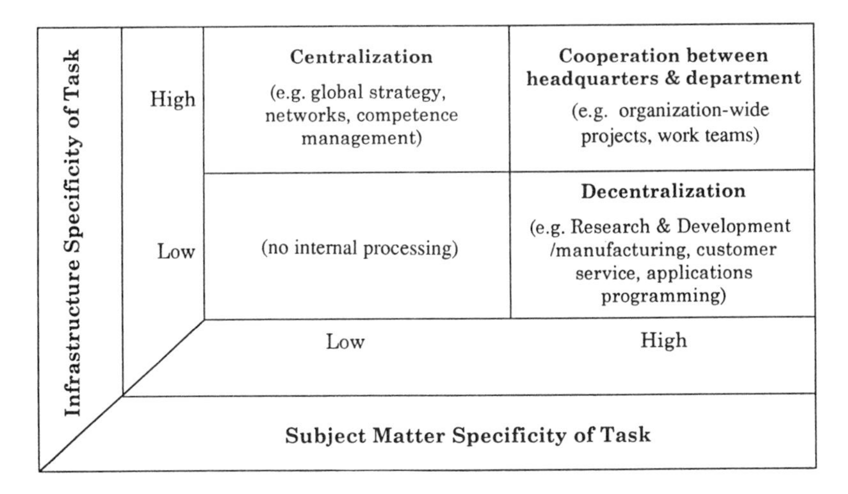

Figure 5.10 *Standard strategies for the (de-)centralization of functions. Source: Picot (1990, p. 302. Reproduced by permission from C.H. Beck'sche Verlagsbuchhandlung, München.)*

the total processing time (see, for example, the case study on re-engineering from Hammer and Champy, 1993).

Concepts for process-oriented restructuring of corporations have been an issue of discussion for quite a long time (see, for example, Gaitanides, 1983). The ideal objective is to completely substitute the traditional functional organizational structure through process-oriented organizational units. This restructuring process is not yet advanced in the practical world. But a few progressive corporations have institutionalized business processes and have appointed certain employees as so-called "process owners" (e.g., IBM, see Striening, 1988). Typical examples for such business processes are order processing, procurement, or product development (see Fromm, 1992, p. 7). As a rule, business processes span substantial portions of the value chain.

Segmentation and Island Concepts

Concepts for the process-oriented formation of smaller organizational units were first developed for the area of manufacturing (e.g., the "focused factory" model from Skinner 1974). In the meantime, several fully matured approaches exist for this area which have successfully been put into practice. Examples are the concept of the "product islands" (see Wagner and Schumann, 1991; Figure 5.11) and the concept of the "manufacturing segments" (see Wildemann, 1994; Figure 5.12).

Production Island (according to Wagner & Schumann, 1991)	Production Segment (according to Wildemann, 1994)
• Combined Assembly of a Product Group – Spatially, and – Organizationally	• Market and Goal Orientation – Formation of delineated Production-Market-Production Combination – Strategic success factors
• Holistic Work Content –Planning –Executing, and –Controlling tasks	• Product Orientation –Coordination costs –Degree of interlocked performance –Production specificity and strength
• Largely Self-Controlling of the Production Island within the Organizational Framework	• Multiple Steps of the Logistics Chain –Integration of several organization-internal value steps
	• Delegation of Indirect Functions –Controlling –Material supply, transportation –Preparation –Quality Control –Maintenance
	• Cost and Results Accountability

Figure 5.11 *The concept of production islands. Source: Wagner and Schumann, 1991 and Wildemann, 1994. (Reproduced by permission from Verlag TÜV Rheinland.)*

The basic characteristics of these organizational concepts correspond to a high degree with the principles of modularization which were described at the beginning of this chapter: formation of smaller, process- and customer-oriented units, self-contained task areas, and decentralized responsibility for decisions and results (see page 161).

In the meantime, segmentation and island concepts have also been applied to other areas. Well-known examples are the sales islands, in which order processing and design adaptation are combined in a product specific manner (see Bullinger, 1991). Additionally, this expansion is recommended all the way to the corporate level in the form of "corporate segments" (see Bullinger and Seidel, 1992; Figure 5.13).

It is noteworthy that the spectrum of modularization approaches at the process level develops bottom-up to further integration of value

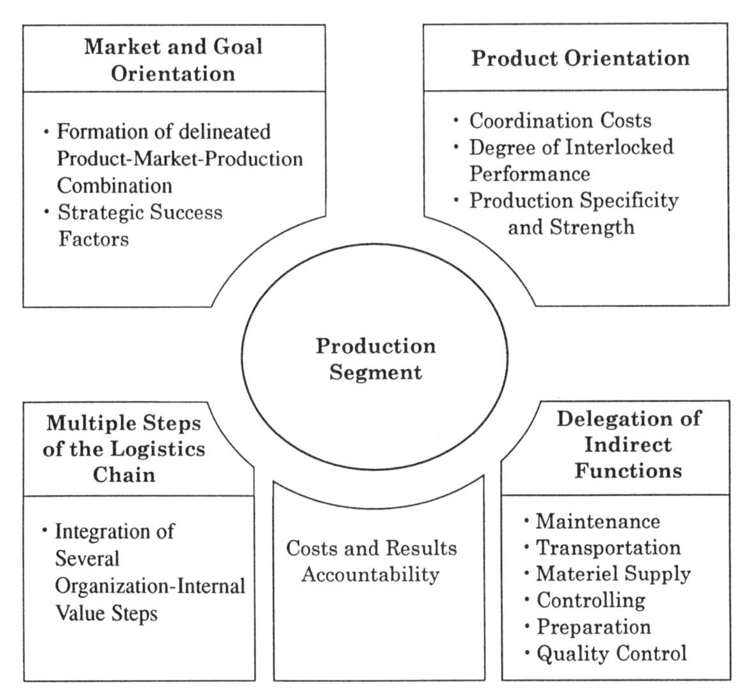

Figure 5.12 *Fundamental characteristics of manufacturing segments. Source: Wildemann (1994, p. 48. Reproduced by permission from FBO-Verlag.)*

creating steps, and thus converges with the modularization approaches at the corporate level, which develop top-down from the original divisionalized organization.

Potential for Conflict at the Process Level

In the establishment of modular organizational units at the process level, conflicts can arise in multiple respects. One example is that the number of tasks belonging to a process chain can make their completion through small organizational units impossible, even when taking advantage of modern information and communication technologies. For process chains of this type, hierarchical intermediate structures will be unavoidable.

Conflicts can also arise at the interfaces between modular units, for example between sales islands and manufacturing segments (see Figure 5.13). The attempt must be made to avoid goal discrepancies between the cooperating modules.

Likewise, conflicts of interest can ensue between similar modules, for example between manufacturing segments for related product lines,

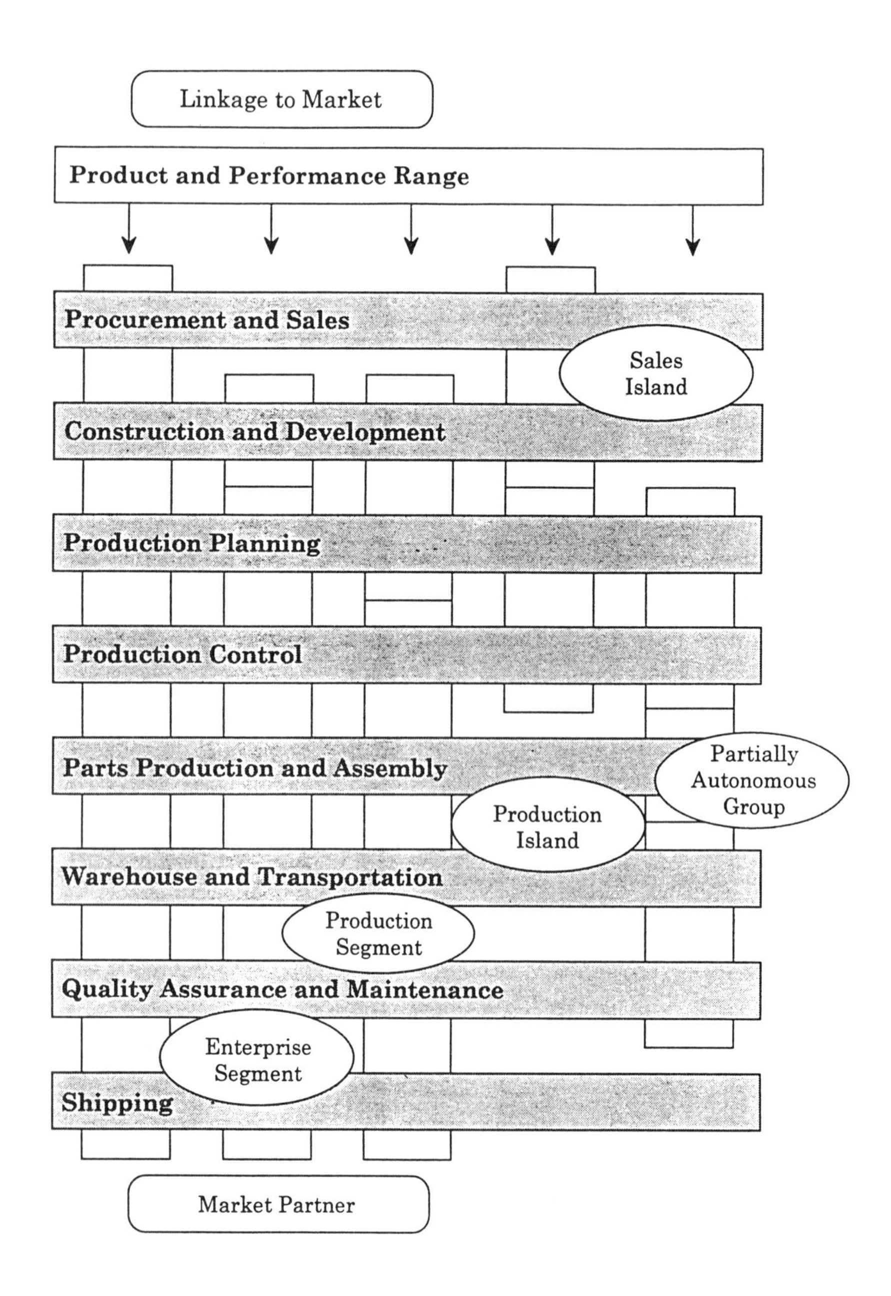

Figure 5.13 *Modularized concepts along the value chain. Source: Bullinger and Seidel (1992, p. 153. Reproduced by permission from REFA, Darmstadt.)*

when indivisible resources have to be shared, for example expensive production machinery. It can be seen that the tension between centralized and decentralized allocation of resources also presents a serious issue at the process level, for which only tailored solutions are appropriate.

General conflict potential at the process level particularly arises through the reorganization of corporate processes being planned and implemented top-down by corporate management and their advisors. Such a procedure can possibly bring about a timely implementation of reorganization plans. Moreover, it can provoke considerable resistance from the affected employees. These types of acceptance problems can be lessened and possibly overcome through the adoption of participative elements in the planning and implementation phases of reorganizational measures (see Picot and Franck, 1995).

Also barriers to personnel changes, such as employees clinging onto old habits and attitudes, can eventually cause labor organization and modularization to fail. Resulting dilemmas can be avoided when management makes early announcements of the motivations, goals and consequences of the imminent organizational changes and ties qualification concepts into the reorganization plans which can prepare the employees for more complex and demanding tasks (see Nippa, 1995).

Modularization Concepts at the Level of Labor Organization

Autarky Model Versus Cooperation Model

With respect to the application of new information and communication technologies, there are principally two design possibilities in the formation of autonomous units at the level of labor organization (see Picot and Reichwald, 1987, p. 125):

1 The attempt can be made to integrate tasks in such a way that an entire process can be essentially completed by one employee. In this case, the emphasis is placed on the self-sufficient processing of the corresponding technical respectively managerial tasks (*autarky model*).
2 It might prove necessary or sensible to assign the entire task or process, from the beginning, to a team. Because the focus in this organizational design must be given to the coordination and cooperation among group members, this form is known as the *cooperation model.*

Realization forms of autarky models respectively cooperation models at the level of labor organization are fully integrated single work places on the one hand, and semi-autonomous groups on the other. Hammer and Champy make an analogous differentiation, in that they make reference to both "case worker" and "case team" (see Hammer and Champy, 1993). Both forms of modularization at the lowest organizational level have their individual strengths and weaknesses, which will be discussed separately in the following sections. Impressive examples for successful modularization at the level of labor organization can be found for both concepts (see, for example, Hammer and Champy, 1993; Davenport, 1993).

Fully Integrated Single Workplaces

Organizational concepts at the level of labor organization which correspond with the autarky model, are also known under expressions such as "integrated all-round office worker" or "integrated single work places". Although they describe the smallest form of modular organizational units, they can be exceptionally productive. Numerous examples of the successful implementation of this concept can be found particularly in those service areas which are close to customers. Hammer and Champy report, for example, noteworthy breakthroughs with respect to cycle time and quality of service, which credit institutes and insurance companies achieve through EDP-supported complete processing of customer applications "from one hand" (see Hammer and Champy, 1993). These authors name the increased personal contact to customers as a further advantage of the integrated task processing. Apart from this, the recurrent practical problem can be avoided, that the present status of a current specific order (e.g., customer inquiries or alterations) cannot be determined because nobody is directly responsible.

Recommendations for an extensively self-sufficient task processing have also been worked out for the industrial R&D area (see, for example, Ehrlenspiel, Ambrosy and Aßmann, 1995). Here, for example, integrated construction and production planning work places are recommended, at which one employee can directly complete correlated partial tasks from both areas. Thereby, iteration loops in the product development process can be run through more quickly.

Especially in the R&D area, however, the deficiencies of the autarky model can be clearly seen: whereas the relatively standardized construction and planning tasks in the area of the detailing and finishing of product designs can be handled independently, the innovative development tasks often require the creative potential of teams.

A further constraint in the application of the self-sufficient organizational concepts stems from the maximum number of tasks to be completed. Independently working specialists and managers can without doubt be supported through expert advisors or assistants; but with increasing magnitude of a task, the actual work situation develops towards a cooperation model.

Semi-autonomous Groups

The typical organizational form for the implementation of the cooperation model at the level of labor organization is the semi-autonomous group (see also Chapter 9). Through the most extensive backward integration of managerial tasks into the primary area, groups made up of eight to ten widely qualified people can accomplish the entire value-creating process for less comprehensive task areas, or at least a large section of the value chain. In the ideal case, this spans from the procurement all the way to final assembly of a distinct customer order (see, for example, Frieling, 1992; Martin, 1992).

In the development towards the stronger use of semi-autonomous groups, the human is the focal point (see Heinen, 1986). The organizational model of the autonomous group was propagated in the 1970s as the labor model which corresponds highest with human needs. This model possesses all the requirements which aid the development of human creativity and productivity potential and in the promotion of motivation and economic utility, as long as it is sensibly placed in the value-creating process. The insights of the labor structure debate substantiates (see page 185, as well as Chapter 9), that humans will be given a better opportunity for self-development through sensible job responsibilities, through a healthy work environment, through timely feedback of results, as well as through sufficient qualifications, scope of action and responsibility. At the same time, personal willingness to perform and the respect from others increases. In turn, individual goals can be more easily brought in agreement with corporate goals (see Womack, Jones and Roos, 1990; Reichwald and Hesch, 1993).

Conflict Potential at the Level of Labor Organization

As mentioned at the beginning of this chapter, the modularization approaches at the direct level of labor organization are based on the resources available for task completion, especially on employee potential, as well as on the new possibilities for their support through information and communication technologies. Accordingly, the most visible conflict potential at this level is to be expected in the acceptance of new organizational forms and the new information and communication technologies. Some examples for possible causes of conflicts at this level are:

- insufficient technical qualifications for the completion of the expanded task areas (especially for the application of the relevant information and communication technologies);
- lack of social competencies for self-organization and conflict management in the group;
- group internal tension stemming from disparities in abilities and levels of willingness to perform (especially in evaluations based on group performance) etc.

Potential for Conflict Between the Modularization Concepts at Different Corporate Levels

The debate on centralization and decentralization of direct or indirect functions at the different levels of the corporation has a tradition and is often the focus of controversial discussions. Certainly, the current spectrum of decentralization approaches is wider than ever before. Therefore a main issue is, to what extent are decentralized organizational structures at the level of labor organization compatible with decentralized organizational structures at the intermediate and macrolevels. Although numerous questions are still unanswered, there are already a few promising approaches for important partial aspects.

One main inter-level problem deals with the coordination and synchronization of the modules at the different levels. As discussed previously, there is an inherent danger in the establishment of autonomous organizational units in that individual interests will be pursued through these autonomous modules at the cost of corporate interests. For this reason, hierarchic coordination structures will be generally maintained for the coordination of the operative modular units at the level of labor organization, as well as process and corporate levels (see Reichwald and Koller, 1995, p. 21). In these hierarchies, the manager's role undergoes a distinct change: from supervisor to moderator, respectively coach (see Chapter 9).

Corporations with such "hybrid" organizational forms increasingly realize that the classical hierarchic coordination by goal setting through a central authority and reporting of results through the operative levels contradicts self-organization and self control in the modules. To lessen such interference, these corporations often make the transition to setting goals in a participative manner, with the employees of the modular units, thus attaining a more effective coordination as well as a motivational effect (see Reichwald and Koller, 1995, p. 23).

Likert's system of overlapping groups (see Likert, 1961), which has been apparently rediscovered in respect to the modularization attempts, goes one step further. This approach suggests a coordination of a corporation's activities through a system of hierarchic, but overlapping

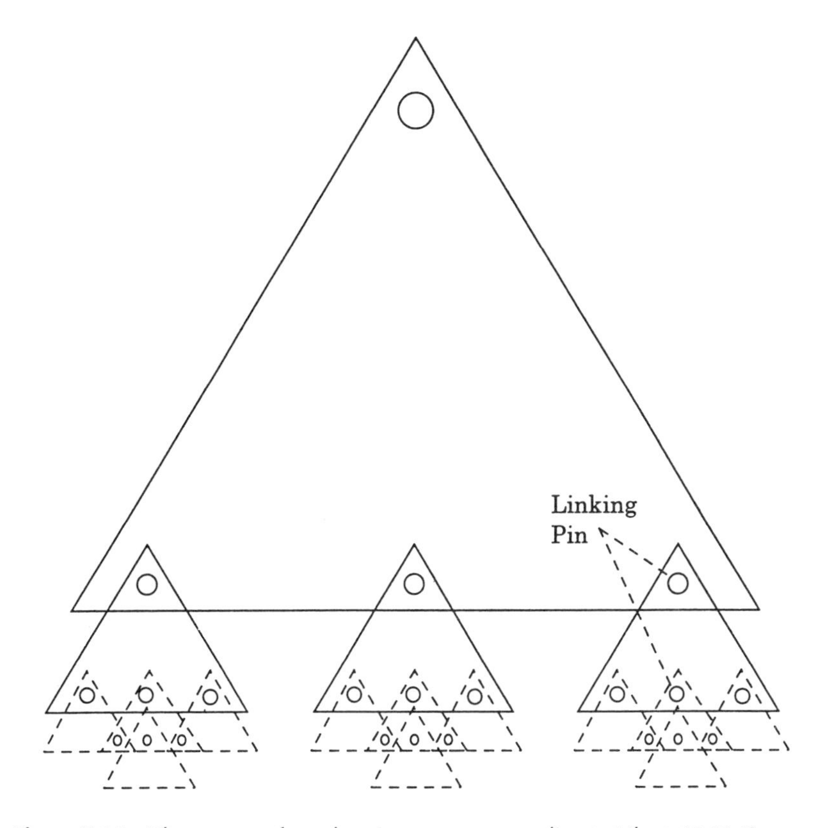

Figure 5.14 *The system of overlapping groups according to Likert, 1961 (Source: Bendixen, 1980, c. 2230. Reproduced by permission from Schäffer-Poeschel Verlag, Stuttgart.)*

groups (see Figure 5.14). One employee from each of the subordinate groups functions as the "linking pin" between the levels through his membership in the next higher group.

This overlapping group approach provides an outstanding possibility to link the modular units at the different corporate levels. Simultaneously it enables the realization of group specific advantages with respect to mutual loyalty and cooperation. This increases the acceptance of the commonly agreed upon goals and guarantees their implementation.

This coordination approach (in a slightly modified form) was recently used by so-called "Sociocratie" model (see Pfefferkorn, 1991; Endenburg, 1994), which has been put into practice in the Dutch corporation *Endenburg Elektrotechniek*.

Further conflict potential between the modules at different levels stems from the centralization or decentralization of functions in corporations, respectively. Certainly, the tenet formulated by Bühner for the management holding can be applied (see Bühner, 1993, p. 12), that nothing is to be centralized which is essential for the success of the modules (Bühner: "the divisions"). In this respect, module interests often contradict with supraordinate interests. In turn, the decision concerning decentralization of functions (mainly in large corporations) is a complex, multiple-step process, which once again is to be mutually agreed upon and implemented with participation of employees.

The basis for coordination between centralized and decentralized modules as well as between modules on the macro-, intermediate-, and micro-level is lastly the availability of efficient coordination methods and instruments. New information and communication technologies, which will be discussed in the following section, play a decisive role.

THE ROLES OF INFORMATION AND COMMUNICATION TECHNOLOGIES FOR MODULARIZATION

Requirements for Information and Communication Technologies in Modular Organizational Forms

The holistic integration of tasks along the value chain of modularized corporations requires corporate-wide coordinated information and communication systems. The most important assignment is to supply the decentralized modules with the necessary quality information in a timely manner. In order to guarantee the access to the required data and information and their individual decentralized processing, all business information systems must be integrated and linked through networks. This is the only way possible that, for example, production-related customer inquiries can be reliably managed and controlled in order processing. Figure 5.15 provides an overview of the process-related requirements on the information and communication technologies, which will be discussed in more detail in the following sections.

In order to meet these requirements, the entire diversity of objects, resources and functions in a corporation, as well as their interlacing, would have to be reflected in information and communication systems. Such highly complex information and communication systems (for example integrated PPS) are still difficult to control in the practical corporate world and require a considerable commitment of capital and know-how.

Instead of attempting to exhibit the corporation in its complexity, modularization leads to a development in another direction. The

Process Related Requirements	Technical Support Through Information and Communication
Decentralized access and exchange of information, timely availability of required information for different employees	Communication technical linkage of processing capacities, integrated respectively via distributed application architecture with distributed databases
Support decision-making	Decision support system
Support of self-sufficient generalists instead of several specialists	Workplace systems, expert systems
Tools for the support of group work	Work group systems
Process-oriented support of structured workflows	Workflow systems
Cross-corporate data exchange	Use of telecommunications infrastructure, electronic data interchange (EDI)

Figure 5.15 *Requirements of modular, process-oriented organizations for information and communication technologies*

apparent trend is towards self-organization, which is especially supported through the individualized application possibilities of modern information and communication systems.

With the process-oriented arrangement of the modular organization, self-organizing wholes (modules) are created at all levels of the corporation. When totally integrated in the corporate value chain, all modules at each of these levels autonomously complete their own tasks. This results in simple, clearly defined structures. The process simplification goes hand in hand with the simplification and reduction in complexity of information and communication systems. This insight leads to another basic understanding of the use of information and communication technologies. Modern information and communication systems must no longer cover all eventualities of complexly structured processes, but must be tailored only to a lean core process and its specific task requirements and information needs. It is obvious that such individualization of information and communication systems cannot be united with centralized information processing solutions. Thus, modern information and communication systems which are tailored to lean core processes can be realized and supported above all through distributed, decentralized information processing solutions. Thereby it must be assured that first, the functional task support within the modules is given, and second, that the links between the modules are reflected through the information and communication system.

This leads to the fundamental question as to what degree standard software can fulfill the business requirements on modern information and communication technologies. Core competencies and highly specific tasks are the requirements for a corporation's sustained competitiveness. They differentiate the corporation from its competition and are necessary for long-term survival on the market. Particularly technical support of the relative unique core processes is of special value for the corporation. Commercial standard software, however, supports mostly standardized processes, which are less specific to the corporation. Whereas until now this only presented a minor problem, because traditional complex process structures always contained a high degree of standardized processes, modularization and concentration on core processes requires specific functionalities. Therefore, modern software tools must meet new requirements, such as the possibility for quick and comfortable provision of customized solutions.

More decisive than the information technical support of the core processes is their corporate-wide coordination and integration. The grounds for this are first, the (passive) provision of an information and communication infrastructure in the form of networks and integrated data bases and second, the (active) process coordination, for example, through workflow systems.

The Task-oriented Use of Information and Communication Technology as Prerequisite for the Efficiency of Modular Forms of Organization

Basic Considerations of the Task-efficient Use of Information and Communication Technology

Concerning the organizational consequences of the use of technology for the division of labor, the underlying organizational model is decisive. With the autarky concept (see page 197, as well as Picot and Reichwald, 1987), the use of technology in management and in office work is intended to make those responsible for the task independent of other positions and assistance. The goal is to provide those responsible for a task (manager, developer, designer, office worker) with multifunctional technology at the work place, so that they accomplish for example their text generation, graphics and image processing, as well as communication processes, information filing and information retrieval on their own. The cooperation model, in contrast, is based upon the retention of the division of labor. Team related processes for task completion are promoted. All participants in a cooperation should be able to complete their tasks more efficiently through the use of information and communication technology. To summarize, the autarky model promotes a productivity increase through reducing the division of labor, whereas the cooperation model concentrates on the efficiency increases in teamwork through improving communication relationships.

At this point, a differentiation of the discussed business processes according to the underlying process and task characteristics would be appropriate (see Picot and Reichwald, 1987; Nippa, 1995, p. 54), in order to evaluate the advantages of the autarky and the cooperation models, from case to case. The following design recommendations stem from such a task-oriented perspective. In more structured task fields with low variability and complexity, the autarky model proves to be advantageous (e.g., in the deterministic claim processing in the insurance industry). In contrast, the cooperation model is superior especially in less structured task fields with high variability and complexity (for example in R&D or project management). Both models present the natural extreme points on a continuum of interesting hybrid forms.

Remarkably, a closer study of the available reengineering examples in present literature shows that the recommendations relate extensively to well-structured, repetitive processes. Nippa, for example, (see Nippa, 1995, p. 53) states this for the work of Hammer and Champy (1993). A corresponding analysis of Davenport's (1993) work provides similar results. For poorly structured, highly complex and variable processes (for example R&D, strategic planning), few approaches can be found in the publications dealing with reengineering. At this point, the illustrated task typological approach and the resulting design recommendations present a good starting point for suitable reorganization concepts.

MANAGEMENT PERSPECTIVES FOR THE MODULAR CORPORATION

The above discussions have explained in detail that the modularization of organizations is tied in closely with process thinking, which itself has once again received attention in organization theory and practice. The holistic, market-oriented production process stands in the center of all modularization concepts. This process has first to be divided into interwoven partial processes for which it is to be decided, on the basis of appropriate efficiency criteria (e.g., level of production and transaction costs), whether they should be completed within the corporation, outsourced to the market, or completed in symbioses with selected external partners (see Chapter 6). For those (highly specific) business processes which should be completed within the organization, suitable modularization concepts subsequently have to be found. The guiding principle is to form small, easily describable and mostly self-organizing organizational units (modules), in order to establish holistic customer-oriented processes and thus, to take advantage of synergy and motivation effects resulting from the integration.

The modularization as an organizational approach can be applied at all levels of the corporate organization. Corporate-wide (macro-level) modules can be established which are responsible for entire divisions or regional markets, for core competencies or for even strategic planning and coordination of the whole corporation (see page 187). At the business process level (meso-level), sensible process boundaries and thus modules can extend from simple production segments all the way to entire corporate segments (with the full responsibility for a product). At the micro-level of labor organization, the same fundamentals of the modularization lead to the formation of semi-autonomous groups and fully integrated single work places. In modularized corporations one recognizes—in accordance with the fractal factory propagated by Warnecke (see Warnecke, 1992)—homogenous and compact structures at all levels.

Information and communication technologies play a leading role in modularization. They are justifiably designated by many authors and experts as the true "enablers" of the process-oriented reorganization (see, for example, Davenport, 1993), as they break the previous limits of control of interwoven processes through humans and pave the way for present modularization concepts. As a rule, the combination of advantages from small organizational units respectively teams (flat hierarchies, self-organization, stronger motivation, social controls etc.) and the advantages of an integration of connected processes can only be achieved through the use of new information and communication technologies.

Modularization is a holistic approach, which must also include those people who work in the corporation. Employees as well as corporate management in modularized organizational units must face new challenges and thereby develop a new understanding for the roles they play (see Chapter 9).

The role of the employees as trigger and key factor for radical organizational changes has recently received increased attention. The generally higher qualification levels as well as the increasing demands on the quality of work are considered as opportunities, in order to—with information technical support—do away with the traditional, no longer justified, separation between performing and management tasks. New demands on the social and technical competencies of the employees arise especially during transition- to team-oriented labor forms, which are generally connected to modularization concepts.

More importantly, new challenges also arise for management in a modularized corporation. The transition to self-organizing, that is self-regulating and self-controlling, forms of group work reshapes the role of management, which must see itself as more of a coach or coordinator. The traditional hierarchic relationship patterns between supervisors and subordinates must be forgotten.

The modularization of corporations also has its limits: these limits come up quickly, and stem from simply practical implementation problems, such as through an insufficient qualification of the employees for the teamwork, underdeveloped electronic data processing support, or until recently, through nonexistent methods and instruments for the efficient coordination of modules among one another. The most significant modularization constraints are based on the inherent danger that through the formation of mainly autonomous, self-organized modules which will inevitably pursue individual interests, a shattering of the corporation will follow. The appropriate balance, distinct for each corporation, must be found between centralization and decentralization from competencies, which preserves the long-term advantages of the corporate internal task completion in the area of core competencies.

Limits and Dangers of Modularization

This chapter's discussion on modularization has indicated various limits and dangers of this organizational concept, which are highlighted and discussed here.

Principal limits of modularization can be derived from the general realization of contingency theory, that no universally valid design principles for organizations exist. Rather, the efficiency of a certain form of organization depends on the respective task. The reflections on competitive strategy presented on page 175 show that modular corporate structures are especially suited for market- and customer-oriented differentiation strategies. For stable mass markets, hierarchic, functionally structured organizations are still more efficient, even though such markets become rare due to the observable differentiation and market segmentation. The task-oriented considerations on page 175 have further shown, that differing modularization concepts have to be chosen dependent on the respective task characteristics. This topic was also addressed and analyzed on pages 198–199.

Practical limits of modularization result primarily from the high qualification requirements which these organizational forms pose on their employees. Many employees are inhibited by the necessity of comprehensive qualifying measures and management often shuns the accompanying costs. In addition, managers often have objections to the flattening of hierarchies through a modularization, since—according to popular opinion—this would substantially restrict advancement possibilities (see Chapter 9). This topic shows a general problem of modularization concepts which have been realized so far: the omission of suitable accompanying measures. Examples include the lack of alternative career ladders and personnel development possibilities or the need for new team-oriented controlling instruments. The low number of published empirical reports addressing first the results of modularization efforts presents an additional hindrance for a quicker practical implementation.

In the literature, the possible loss of important synergy effects in the area of the corporate infrastructure, in the wider sense, is further stressed as an important danger of modularizing a corporation into small, process-oriented units. The danger of a shattering of the corporation exists (see Picot and Reichwald, 1994). In this context, it is important to build a common basis for action with respect to the development of new strategies, management and control instruments, EDP-infrastructure, personnel, and so on. Finally, the well-known tension between centralization and decentralization becomes visible in the new, modular organization concepts.

Finally, modularization entails the danger that those carrying responsibility for the modules concentrate too much on module-related, operative objectives, eventually neglecting the interests of the entire corporation. The strong shift of property rights which has already been mentioned earlier in the chapter, amplifies this danger even more.

6
Dissolution of Corporate Boundaries: Symbioses and Networks

THE FUNDAMENTAL IDEA BEHIND SYMBIOTIC ORGANIZATIONAL STRUCTURES

In the business world there is a growing trend towards the dissolution of traditional organizational structures and boundaries in favor of the establishment of *symbiotic arrangements* with external partners. The fundamental idea behind these symbiotic arrangements can be described as follows.

An organization establishes strong relations by integrating legally and economically other independent corporations as part of the accomplishment of its own tasks. This integration creates reciprocal dependencies providing mutual advantage. In order to avoid or at least to limit the opportunistic exploitation of these dependencies by one partner, symbiotic arrangements are usually planned as long-term relationships. They focus on establishing close networking relations and are based on mutual trust. Symbiotic arrangements such as networks or joint ventures induce change in corporate boundaries: traditional corporate boundaries are blurred, meaning they can no longer be sufficiently described by the intersection between hierarchy and market. Whereas corporations have historically turned to markets only for the completion of standardized tasks, today an increasing tendency towards integration of external market partners into the corporation's core activities prevails. This blurs the traditional differentiation between firms and markets (specific vs. standardized tasks) and simultaneously leads to a dissolution of the corporation.

The expression "dissolution of the corporation" can be used in the following cases:

1 When a corporation fosters *vertical disintegration* and begins acquiring standardized products and services from the market.
2 When a corporation utilizes information and communication technology to overcome site restrictions by shifting office jobs to the employees' homes (see Chapter 8 for more on virtual corporations and telework).
3 When either internal factors (e.g., lacking know-how or capital) or external factors (e.g., EDI, see page 216) force a corporation to *integrate an external third party into original, meaning specific and/or uncertain, corporate activities*. This outsourcing of core competencies and core activities leads to a scattering of the corporation's activities and in turn, increasingly unclear boundaries. The corporation enters a symbiotic arrangement with other companies. Bridging the gap between resource markets and consumer markets in order to provide customer services (see Chapter 2, pages 25–31) is achieved less often within the corporation and more frequently as a virtual organization in variable symbiotic arrangements with third parties. This third form of dissolution presents the focal point of this chapter.

DRIVING FORCES FOR THE DEVELOPMENT OF SYMBIOTIC ORGANIZATIONAL FORMS

In the following section, the theory of core competencies, transaction cost theory, contract theory, and the theory of the firm are presented as approaches in defining and/or explaining the dissolution of corporate boundaries and the establishment of symbiotic arrangements with third parties, i.e. external partners.

Explanation of Symbiotic Arrangements Through the Theory of Core Competencies

Growing competition forces management to dedicate increased attention to the optimal balance of corporate mission, degree of vertical integration, and competitive environment. A high degree of vertical integration excessively ties up management capacity, know-how, and capital. These resources are then no longer available for strategically relevant tasks, resulting in a lower degree of flexibility. In the past few years, corporations have increasingly met the challenge of concentrating on their *core competencies*. According to Prahalad and Hamel (1990, p. 92) core competencies present "the essential technical, technological, distributional, and organizational capacities of a corporation", hence, they are capacities which are specific to a corporation. These core competencies have to be accompanied and supported by *complementary competencies*. Complementary competencies present economies of scale and economies of scope, as well as integration advantages for core competencies. However, since they are not as relevant for the corporation's strategic success as core competencies, they are not necessarily controlled by the corporation, but are often held by third parties.

In order to create a healthy balance between core and complementary competencies for the realization of competitive strategy, the corporation often depends on strategic alliances with other organizations. Thereby a corporation can acquire supporting complementary competencies (see Reve, 1990) without developing them on its own. In contrast, *peripheral competencies* have so little influence on a corporation's competitive position that they are neither produced internally nor acquired externally through cooperation. Peripheral competencies can simply be obtained from the market based on short-term buying or service contracts.

Based on competency theory, only the possession and internal maintenance of core competencies are required. That means, the corporation should concentrate on its strategic core, its actual mission. Products and services not belonging to its own core competencies can be obtained more efficiently from a third party, either by buying them directly on the open market or by establishing cooperative and strategic alliances with external partners (see Jarillo, 1993).

The theory of core competencies suggests that *efficient corporate boundaries* seem determinable. In the business world however, a variety of reasons exist for the apparent trend towards integration of third parties in the development and expansion of a corporation's core competencies. One reason is that necessary competencies can be obtained quickly and cost efficiently. Philips AG, for example, was dependent on Sony Corporation when developing the compact disk and related optical storage technology, because development costs and efforts to create a standard could be better managed by two large corporations instead of one. Today, optical storage technology is considered a core competency of Philips AG (see Prahalad and Hamel, 1990, p. 70).

However, the theory of core competencies and its theoretical instruments are not yet refined enough to explain the creation of symbiotic arrangements. In addition, a clear distinction can hardly be made between core and complementary competencies simply on the basis of this theory. For this reason, the concept of core competencies is currently being criticized for its high level of analytical abstraction, leading to a demand for more concrete theoretical terms and analysis.

Extension of the Theory of Core Competencies Through Transaction Cost Arguments

Reve (1990) shows an approach for a more precise definition of the theory's central terms—core and complementary competencies. He suggests a *transaction cost theoretical interpretation* of these terms (see also Strautmann, 1993). According to Reve, core competencies manifest themselves in stationary investments or highly specific assets and human capital. Core competencies can also be generated through transaction-specific investments, meaning investments in an exchange relationship with a certain client.

On the contrary, complementary competencies are characterized by a medium specificity of tangible fixed assets, human capital, transaction related investments, and stationary investments. The use of transaction cost theoretical arguments makes it easier to determine a healthy balance of core and complementary competencies and, in turn, efficient corporate boundaries. The transaction cost theoretical approach for the determination of a corporation's core and complementary competencies, as well as for the explanation of symbiotic arrangements, is presented in the following section. More attention will be given to transaction cost theoretical arguments, whereas reference to the parallel content of the core competencies approach will remain in the background.

The Dissolution of the Corporation Through Symbiotic Arrangements Based on a Transaction Cost Theoretical Perspective

Symbiotic Arrangements and the Optimal Degree of Vertical Integration. Initially, the analysis requires a differentiation between the dissolution of a corporation through the creation of symbiotic arrangements on the one side and the problem of vertical integration/disintegration on the other side. The market-hierarchy paradigm described in Chapter 2 discusses alternative coordination mechanisms for the fulfillment of labor-divided tasks, namely market, hierarchy, and hybrid organizational forms. With the help of transaction cost theory, the boundaries of a business can be determined based on its internal sphere of responsibility for production and utilization of outputs. These organizational boundaries have to be re-determined based on changes in the organizationally relevant factors (strategic importance, specificity, and uncertainty), the behavioral assumptions (bounded rationality, opportunism), the information impactedness, the transaction atmosphere, the transaction frequency, or the entry barriers to know-how and capital. The re-determination of corporate boundaries leads to the integration of those tasks whose degree of specificity has significantly increased, and to the disintegration of those tasks whose degree of specificity has significantly decreased. This leads to a new definition of the intersection between the corporation and the market, whereby particularly the production of standardized goods and services is left to the market. This presents a permanent optimizing process which is inevitable in a dynamic economy with changing performance and task characteristics.

As well as this re-determination of corporate boundaries, the previously mentioned creation of symbiotic arrangements represents an important aspect of corporate development. In contrast to the new determination of corporate boundaries, the establishment of symbiotic arrangements requires the integration of external partners in the production of original, and thus specific and highly uncertain, activities. In the establishment of symbiotic arrangements, which usually takes place after the corporation has defined its borders with the market, the attempt is made to establish close and long-term cooperations with external third parties, who are expected to support the corporation in the fulfillment of its main tasks. When this type of integration takes place, it is difficult to determine where one corporation ends and the other begins. Symbiotic arrangements blur corporate boundaries and spheres of responsibility. Boundaries of individual corporations can no longer be clearly defined.

It is apparent that the dissolution of corporations through symbiotic arrangements is closely linked with the problem of vertical integration, but should not be placed on the same level with decisions related to inhouse production and outsourcing. Both concepts, the new determination of corporate boundaries and the dissolution of the corporation through symbiotic arrangements, are related to each other, yet they describe different phenomena within the life cycle of a corporation.

Symbiotic partnerships take a variety of forms: cooperations, strategic alliances, joint ventures, networks, franchising and licensing agreements, Keiretsus or interorganizational clans, and so on (see page 220). Under which circumstances, to what extent, and into which form a corporation dissolves through the establishment of symbiotic arrangements, are all questions requiring consideration. In addition, the economical advantages and disadvantages related to the dissolution of a corporation and the blurring of corporate boundaries must be determined.

Four factors influencing this dissolution can be identified:

- medium task specificity
- high environmental uncertainty

- changes in the transaction atmosphere (technological progress, for example in information and telecommunication technologies, trust and shared values among transaction partners)
- market entry barriers due to lack of capital or know-how.

Classical Transaction Cost Theoretical Explanation: Medium Task Specificity as the Reason for Cooperation

Transaction cost theory recommends a *hybrid form of integration* (e.g. long-term cooperation agreement) as the appropriate coordination form for partial tasks of medium specificity (i.e. for complementary competencies) and medium uncertainty. Since tasks of medium specificity, in contrast to standardized goods have to be adapted to the highly specific core of corporate activity, they cannot simply be acquired over the market. However, it does not make sense to complete tasks of medium specificity within the corporation, because their characteristics do not justify the implementation of expensive hierarchical incentive, control, and sanction mechanisms.

Transaction cost theory therefore recommends supply through third parties as an efficient integration form for tasks of medium specificity. This integration should be secured against opportunistic exploitation through *long-term skeleton agreements* and *cooperation agreements*. Hence, the first reason for the establishment of symbiotic arrangements is identified: the coordination of partial tasks of medium specificity through markets as well as hierarchies entails excessive transaction costs. Many single-sourcing agreements and interorganizational simultaneous-engineering approaches can be characterized as symbiotic arrangements.

High Task Uncertainty as a Reason for Symbiotic Arrangements

Until now, the discussion has concentrated on partial tasks of medium specificity for which the dissolution of the corporation and the establishment of symbiotic arrangements are appropriate. We have assumed a "normal" degree of environmental uncertainty in the completion of transactions. In reality, however, an increasing environmental uncertainty can be observed (see Chapter 1).

A high degree of uncertainty manifests itself in unpredictable, frequent changes of qualitative, quantitative, timely, or technical parameters of output-relations. When environmental uncertainty considerably increases and remains at a high level, it might even be necessary that highly specific partial tasks (core competencies and core products) be accomplished in collaboration with external partners. In a dynamic market environment, specific investments are especially prone to devaluation. These investments carry considerably more risk in an environment characterized by a high degree of uncertainty than under normal uncertainty. For this reason, corporations operating under such environmental conditions will make a greater effort to *divide risk* related to highly specific investments and will even complete risky core activities together with external partners. Besides this division of risk, a symbiotic partnership helps to achieve economies of scale and/or economies of scope during the relatively short life cycles of such investments, which could not have been realized by one corporation alone.

In the case of highly specific and highly uncertain investments, the need to establish a symbiotic arrangement is even greater than for tasks of medium specificity. Under such conditions, external partners have to be involved even in the very proprietary core areas of a corporation. R&D cooperation, as well as production and distribution alliances with legally and economically independent partners can be used as examples for such cooperations and networks stretching into the entrepreneurial core area.

Promotion of Symbiotic Arrangements Through Changes in the Transaction Atmosphere

Information and Communication Technologies. Transaction costs can be considerably influenced through the use of information and communication technologies, making the replacement of hierarchical solutions through symbiotic arrangements with external partners or even through market coordination economically feasible. According to transaction cost theory, the use of information and communication technologies can reduce transaction costs. The original break-even points for the transition from one coordination form to the other shift to the right (see "Transaction Cost Theory", pages 37–42). This means that market and hybrid coordination forms are now able to process transaction cost intense outputs, i.e. those specific core competencies characterized by high uncertainty. The importance of hierarchical coordination mechanisms decreases, whereas the application potential of market and symbiotic arrangements increases. Hence, information and communication technologies promote the organizational orientation towards markets and symbioses. They strengthen and encourage the tendency toward dissolution of the corporation through symbiotic arrangements such as networks and joint ventures. Efficient cross-corporate information and communication systems present an essential requisite for the implementation of these symbiotic arrangements. Technical compatibility, meaning the degree of standardization of interorganizational information and communication systems, plays a crucial role.

Interorganizational information and communication technologies can *support cross-corporate cooperation* and coordination in many functional areas, such as planning, product development, production, and marketing. When appropriate information and communication technologies are available, especially modern telecommunication infrastructures, contacts between potential transaction partners can be more easily established, negotiations better supported, and agreements more efficiently met over long distances. These transaction phases can be supported, accelerated, and simplified, for example, by videoconferencing services, data transfer services such as Datex-P, value-added services or electronic data interchange (EDI). EDI (see Picot, Neuburger, and Niggl, 1994) in particular presents a great potential: EDI is a form of interorganizational electronic communication, in which data and documents in standardized form are exchanged between the electronic data processing systems of different corporations. Media ruptures are avoided and the cross-corporate communication process is automated and accelerated. On the one hand, EDI can support tasks in existing cooperative networks and strategic alliances, and on the other, EDI can assist in the establishment of new symbiotic arrangements (see Neuburger, 1994).

The main requirement for the implementation of cross-corporate information and communication systems such as EDI is the existence of efficient telecommunication networks and attractive prices for data transfer, as well as a wide variety of value-added services. In the practical world, many symbiotic arrangements such as networks could hardly be realized without technical support from modern information and communication systems. Information and communication technologies also facilitate the cooperation with third parties in specific task areas. However, there are immanent limits to the use of information and communication technologies in supporting market or cooperative symbiotic processes. These limits are reached especially in those situations in which personal contact and interpersonal face-to-face communication are required in solving information and communication problems (see pages 238–239). Interpersonal communication fosters trust and facilitates interactive and creative solutions for unstructured problems. In these cases, telecommunication plays at most a supporting role in the preparation and evaluation phases, as well as in the interaction process itself.

Trust and Common Values. Trust and common values are also important elements of the transaction atmosphere. Similar to information and communication technologies, trust and common values help to reduce transaction costs in that they speed up and facilitate the agreement and execution of transactions. In a trusting atmosphere, symbiotic arrangements for the interorganizational performance of even highly specific core activities become possible and economically feasible (Ripperger, 1997). The risk of opportunistic exploitation of existing dependencies is lower than in anonymous market transactions. Trust and common value systems promote and strengthen existing tendencies to establish symbiotic arrangements. Trust between transaction partners reduces the need for exact contractual specification of future events or for explicit rules for sharing cooperation profits. With mutual trust, costly protection mechanisms for the deterrence of opportunistic behavior are superfluous.

Long-term transaction relations are advantageous for the creation of a trusting atmosphere. It is quite possible under these circumstances to overcome the prisoner's dilemma which results from a lack of trust (see page 31). In long-term transaction exchanges, opportunistic behavior in order to gain short-term advantages at the cost of the transaction partners makes little sense, since this would imply the surrender of future expected gains resulting from the continuance of the exchange relationship.

Entry Barriers to New Know-how and Capital Markets as Reasons for Symbiotic Arrangements

Entry barriers to new know-how and capital markets are additional factors which promote blurring of organizational boundaries through symbiotic arrangements. In an uncertain and competitive environment, a corporation's core competencies which were used to build its competitive position can quickly lose value. Therefore, the corporation has to build up new core competencies constantly to ensure its long-term entrepreneurial success (see page 22). Here, the corporation must decide to either build up the necessary know-how and capacities internally (for example through further education and training) or to purchase the required know-how from the market. Under certain circumstances, however, neither option seems feasible. This is most often the case because the internal creation of new core competencies can cause prohibitively high transaction costs and hence, can only be realized after a long period of time.

It is the *information paradox* which speaks against purchasing the required know-how externally from the market (see page 86). This is the phenomenon that until a buyer has the information, he is unable to judge the quality of the desired information. As soon as he has access to and understanding of the information well enough to judge its value, the knowledge is already in his possession and no longer needs to be purchased. In addition, transfer problems related to tacit knowledge are often factors prohibiting the exclusive purchase of know-how from the market. In order to build new core competencies, it proves critical to acquire practical knowledge resulting from past experiences. But due to its tacit character, this knowledge can hardly be transferred by written text, figures, or blueprints. The information paradox as well as the phenomenon of tacit knowledge constitute prohibiting factors for acquiring new knowledge through the market. Even if these barriers could be overcome, the danger of a corporation becoming highly dependent on external specialists would still remain.

These three entry barriers to know-how can be easily overcome through long-term symbiotic relationships based on mutual trust with the external knowledge supplier (e.g., franchising contracts). Long-term cooperations considerably reduce the information supplier's risk of not receiving a service in return for having provided his knowledge. Within a symbiosis between information supplier and information buyer it is possible to transfer tacit knowledge through solving mutual problems on the job (e.g., common projects). In long-term exchange relationships based on mutual trust, exchange partners less often take advantage of existing dependencies than in short-term market contracts. In addition, through such information partnerships, the risk involved in the internal creation of new core competencies and activities can be carried by a number of partners.

Limited access to capital together with high and risky capital investment for the development of core competencies further increases the need for symbiotic arrangements. Future capital-intense strategies, which should have been realized internally, can more easily become a reality. The limited access to capital frequently forces even large corporations to enter into such cooperations in their central activities with external third parties.

In conclusion, it is apparent that lack of capital and know-how render entrepreneurial solo attempts more difficult and can force the corporation to enter symbiotic arrangements with external partners. In order to build new core competencies, it often becomes necessary to loosen corporate boundaries in acquiring knowledge and capital from cooperation partners.

The Dissolution of the Corporation as a Nexus of Internal, External and Symbiotic Contracts

According to the theory of core competencies, organizational boundaries are loosened when an organization is forced to include an external partner in the building and improvement of core competencies. Transaction cost theory explains that organizational boundaries are blurred when external partners are brought in for the accomplishment of highly specific or uncertain tasks which are actually original tasks of the organization. As a follow up, it is necessary to examine which contribution contract theory provides for the explanation of symbiotic arrangements (see pages 45–50).

According to contract theory, the dissolution of a corporation through symbiotic arrangements can be described as a model in which the organization is presented as a nexus of internal and external contracts which extend through organizational boundaries (see Williamson, 1990). The hierarchical structure of an organization is composed of *internal contracts* with its members. Only highly specific tasks will be completed internally. Symbiotic arrangements such as joint ventures, franchising, and licensing arrangements, which serve in the accomplishment of tasks of medium specificity, will be controlled through *external contracts* (cooperation contracts, franchising agreements). Bilateral relationships with external partners which serve to accomplish less specific, i.e. standardized tasks, will also be organized through external contracts (*spot-market contracts*). Internal contracts and the latter kind of external contracts define the efficient organizational boundaries, which are blurred by the first category of external contracts (cooperation contracts, franchising agreements).

Symbiotic arrangements are also established when external contracts with independent third parties replace internal work contracts. The advantage is that the corporation can extend its organizational boundaries, and in turn, overcome its resource and performance limits. Support and resources can be secured from its current market environment and new expansion possibilities can be created. Efficiency gains can not only be realized through an adequate definition of boundaries between hierarchy and market-related to make-or-buy decisions, but also through symbiotic arrangements. There is a risk that the external partner will be more involved in the accomplishment of the organizational assignments than originally planned. As a consequence, the partner could gain too much knowledge of the organization's internal affairs and unwanted dependencies upon the external partner could develop.

The overcoming of traditional organizational boundaries through symbiotic arrangements can not only provide exceptional opportunities for the organization, but also generate aggravating contractual and management problems (see Reve 1990, p. 149). The realization of these opportunities and, simultaneously, the avoidance of opportunistic behavior of transaction partners, must be secured through *efficient contracts*. The fact that these long-term cross-corporate networks are often based on incomplete relational contracts renders this task more difficult. They require special contractual (hard) and non-contractual (soft) protection mechanisms, such as exchange of hostages and trust. Contracts with such mechanisms often have the character of symbiotic contracts (see Schanze, 1991).

Comments on the Theory of the Firm

The question arises as to which effects the above described tendencies in the dissolution of the organization through symbiotic arrangements have on the theory of the firm. The "theory of the firm" is a branch of economic research which focuses on explaining the creation of a corporation. The works of Coase (1937), Williamson (1975, 1985), and also Alchian and Woodward (1987) were essential contributions to this field of research. Until now, the theory of the firm, which is inspired by institutional economics, has mainly provided insight into the creation of the corporation, but very little into the fading of or the loosening of its boundaries. Approaches for further research in this area have already been addressed.

In considering network, franchising, licensing and cooperation agreements, the question arises as to how such networks of incomplete contracts and bundles of diluted property rights are to be held together: considerations in regard to corporate identity, corporate culture, and corporate constitution (see Wagner, 1994) will gain in theoretical and practical importance. In consideration of the above mentioned tendencies, this leads to the question of whether or not corporations can still be explained through the existence of property rights and control rights (see Moore and Hart, 1990; Riordan, 1990, p. 96). Can organizations be classified by their range of influence or that of their members and by the common corporate values and cultural basis of their market affiliates? In any case, the determination of where a corporation begins and where it actually ends will become more complex in the future. Considerable effects can be expected especially on the competition and cartel controls, and also on empirical research.

APPLYING ORGANIZATIONAL FORMS

Overview

A *unified systematization* of hybrid coordination forms and their placement on the continuum between market and hierarchy has until now not been found. The common characteristic of the various models is the description of the degree of vertical integration and the distinction between market and hierarchy coordination forms. Imai and Itami, for example, use the *type of decision-making* as well as the *duration of a relationship* to describe hybrid completion mechanisms (see Imai and Itami, 1984; an overview is offered by Baur, 1990). Accordingly, the degree of vertical integration increases with extending duration of a relationship and the possibility to coordinate through instructions. Kappich names the *type and necessary degree to secure against opportunistic behavior* as a criterion for vertical integration which grows with an increase in scope for opportunistic behavior (see Kappich, 1989). Benjamin, Malone, and Yates use the *degree of ad-hoc choice of business partners* as a criterion for the degree of integration (see Benjamin, Malone and Yates, 1986). To the degree to which future purchasing activities from certain suppliers—who no longer stand in competition with one another—are predetermined, a degree of vertical integration exists. Schneider concentrates on the *form of influence from business partners.* In coordination forms similar to markets, the results of actions will be influenced in growing measure by the price mechanism, whereas in forms similar to hierarchies, actions will be more directly influenced through the scope of instructions (see Schneider, 1988). Figure 6.1 provides an overview of these criteria.

The dependency relation between exchange partners depends greatly upon the degree of specificity of a performance relationship. The majority of descriptive approaches are targeted at characterizing the *degree of integration* based on the dependency level between business partners. Coordination forms close to the hierarchy are marked by a higher

Imai/Itami (1984)	• Nature of decision making • Duration of relationship
Kappich (1989)	• Sort and extent of need for safeguarding against opportunistic behaviour
Benjamin/Melone/Yates (1986)	• Degree of ad hoc selection of business partners
Schneider (1988)	• Form of influence on business partners

Figure 6.1 *Criteria for assessing the degree of integration*

degree of both one-sided, and two-sided dependency relations between business partners than forms close to the market. One-sided dependencies enable the usage of power potentials. These forms are known as vertical *governance structures* and are characterized by a comparatively high degree of vertical integration which brings about a coordination form similar to the hierarchy. In governance structures, middle- to long-term relationships exist between legally independent, although one-sided economically dependent partners. Governance structures are appropriate for assignments which require completion mechanisms similar to the hierarchy, but not necessarily the corresponding control mechanisms. Examples of this are tasks with comparatively high specificity, but of less strategic importance or less frequency. On the other hand, the term *cooperation* characterizes the collaboration between legally and economically independent organizations at the same level.

In the following section, various governance structures and cooperation forms will be presented together with relating characteristics and manifestations. A multitude of terms exist in the literature and in the practical business world characterizing distinct forms of coordination mechanisms between market and hierarchy. Expressions such as strategic alliances, strategic (value-adding) partnerships, strategic cooperations, operative cooperations, and joint ventures can be found.

All of these can be summarized under the term "cooperation", although they display differing forms of cooperation. Similarly, one talks about vertical, horizontal, or diagonal cooperation forms (see, for example, Sydow, 1992a). The various forms of cooperation are the main topic of the following section. A broad terminology describing governance structures can also be found. The spectrum reaches from quasi-vertical integration or vertical quasi-integration all the way to *de facto* integration or capital investment. These governance structures will be examined closely on pages 228–230. Following this is a discussion of the conditions under which the described symbiotic coordination forms will be chosen.

In addition, various forms of appearance and special characteristics of multilateral coordination forms will be described. Such interorganizational networks consist of a variety of legally independent corporations whose ties are more or less loosened. The term network is not necessarily tied to a certain proximity to market or hierarchy, but can be described as a hybrid organizational form, which can be realized in different manners depending on the kind of relationship. Also the discussion of networks lacks a unified terminology. Expressions such as strategic networks, dynamic networks, or also value-added networks can be found. Although these terms are often used as synonyms, they sometimes indicate different types of networks. These topics are discussed later in this chapter.

Cooperative Forms

The Term "Cooperation"

Cooperation forms characterize a middle- to long-term planned contractual collaboration between legally independent corporations for the common accomplishment of tasks (see, for example, Rotering, 1990). They are most suitable when various advantages can be realized that otherwise would not materialize. Common examples are time and cost advantages, know-how advantages, economies of scale, gain in competencies, reduction of risk, and ease of market entry (see, for example, Bronder, 1993; Vizjak, 1990; Porter and Fuller, 1989). Nothing in this definition explains how this accomplishment of tasks takes place or which relationships the cooperation partners have with one another.

Tröndle describes the essence of cooperation (see Tröndle, 1987; see also Rotering, 1993) using as criteria the *degree of autonomy* and *degree of interdependence*. Corporations participating in a cooperation are autonomous to the degree in which they make their own decisions about entering or leaving the cooperation, without having to follow instructions from a higher level. They find themselves on the same level with their cooperation partners. An organization is also autonomous when it does not experience direct pressure from other participating partners relating to the beginning or the ending of a long-term collaboration. This is the point in which cooperations distinguish themselves from the governance structures which are described in the following section.

At the same time, *dependencies between cooperation partners* arise after the origination of a cooperation, which relate to matters of collective decision-making. Interdependencies arise in that many decisions are made collectively which must be negotiated within decision committees and which will be binding for both cooperating partners. Cooperations present a form of resource pooling (see Vanberg, 1982) in which agreement and negotiation processes take place concerning not only the type and the quantity of the resources to be brought into a cooperation, but also the distribution of the targeted output. In these processes, the respective bargaining potential is principally equal. Otherwise, the weaker partner would not join a cooperation.

Further frequently named characteristics are the *voluntary attribute of cooperation formation* as well as the existence of *explicit contractual agreements*. The voluntary attribute means that cooperations are only joined when both partners expect the relationship to be beneficial. This is not found in governance structures. A further characteristic is the existence of explicit contractual agreements. Governance structures can arise on the basis of implicit contracts. Frequently, the use of explicit agreements in establishing a collaboration will be considered as a defining attribute of cooperations (see Rotering, 1993 and listed literature). Rotering defines a cooperation as a long-term, explicitly agreed upon, and one-sided terminable collaboration between organizations (see Rotering, 1993).

Cooperations are frequently affiliated with a strategic component. One talks of strategic alliances or strategic partnerships, or in the context of networks, also of strategic networks. Through these additional remarks, the strategic purpose of such cooperations should be clear: to create competitive advantages for all cooperating partners.

Classification of Cooperations

The most popular classification approach differentiates cooperations with respect to the direction of collaboration, that is, whether organizations work together horizontally, vertically, or laterally (see Büchs, 1991; Bronder, 1993). *Vertical cooperations* relate to corporations on the same level of the value chain, for example customer and supplier. Such cooperations are often called value-adding partnerships (for example, a manufacturer and a retailer cooperate closely in the sales promotion for an innovative product). In *horizontal cooperations*, businesses in the same branch as well as at the same level on the value chain collaborate (for example, R&D cooperation among microelectronics firms). In *diagonal cooperations*, businesses stemming from different branches work together.

Cooperations also can be related to the entire corporation or to single functional areas. When the collaboration relates to individual functional areas, several functional cooperations can be differentiated. *Logistic cooperations* describe a form of joint effort in which the businesses agree upon a close and long-term contractual agreement on the logistic processes entering and leaving the businesses. *Marketing cooperations* relate to the joint effort of businesses with respect to sales, marketing, or customer service. *Technology cooperations* exist when businesses collaborate in the research and development of new technologies.

Examples of Cooperation

There are numerous examples for the above-mentioned cooperation forms between corporations in differing branches and industries. Especially strong cooperative activity can be found in the microelectronics industry. Two motives for the foundation of strategic partnerships are apparent. On the one hand, the development and production of a new microchip generation requires high investment costs which cannot be carried by one business alone and the market risk increases as competition increases. On the other hand, a successful market activity in this industry requires, to a high measure, technical standards which provide a very important utility factor for consumers. For the establishment of *de facto* standards, considerable market shares are necessary, which frequently can no longer be attained or held through an individual corporation. With this thought in mind, the corporations Apple, IBM, and Motorola established a strategic alliance for the development of a standard for the RISC processor. This collaboration resulted in a common technology center. In a further strategic alliance, the same corporations have joined together and founded the common firm Kaleida, with the purpose of creating a future multi-media standard. Apple brings considerable technological know-how into this cooperation, while IBM possesses fundamental experience in creating *de facto* standards as well as established access to markets. A marketing partnership has been founded by Siemens Nixdorf and the software company SAP. The computer manufacturer possesses market access to medium-sized businesses, while the software firm offers competitive software. In this case, suppliers of different components of a system technology (hardware and software as complementary goods) work together. Through close collaboration, the goal is to continually find solutions, especially for compatibility problems. The variety of cooperative relationships and the resulting "cooperation networks" can also be illustrated in the following example for cooperation networks in the semiconductor and the automotive industry (see Figures 6.2 and 6.3).

The Organization of Cooperations

Dependent upon the concrete attributes and goals of the underlying cooperation, a variety of possibilities exist for the organization of cooperations. This does not imply that every cooperation must have its own unique organizational form. For example, if a cooperation is based on the completion of a contract or on a functional area, it would not be necessary to arrange the cooperation in a unique organizational form. When, however, this uniqueness seems necessary, there are principally two possibilities: joint ventures and consortia.

Joint Ventures. In a joint venture, cooperating businesses form a legally independent association solely for this purpose, into which each

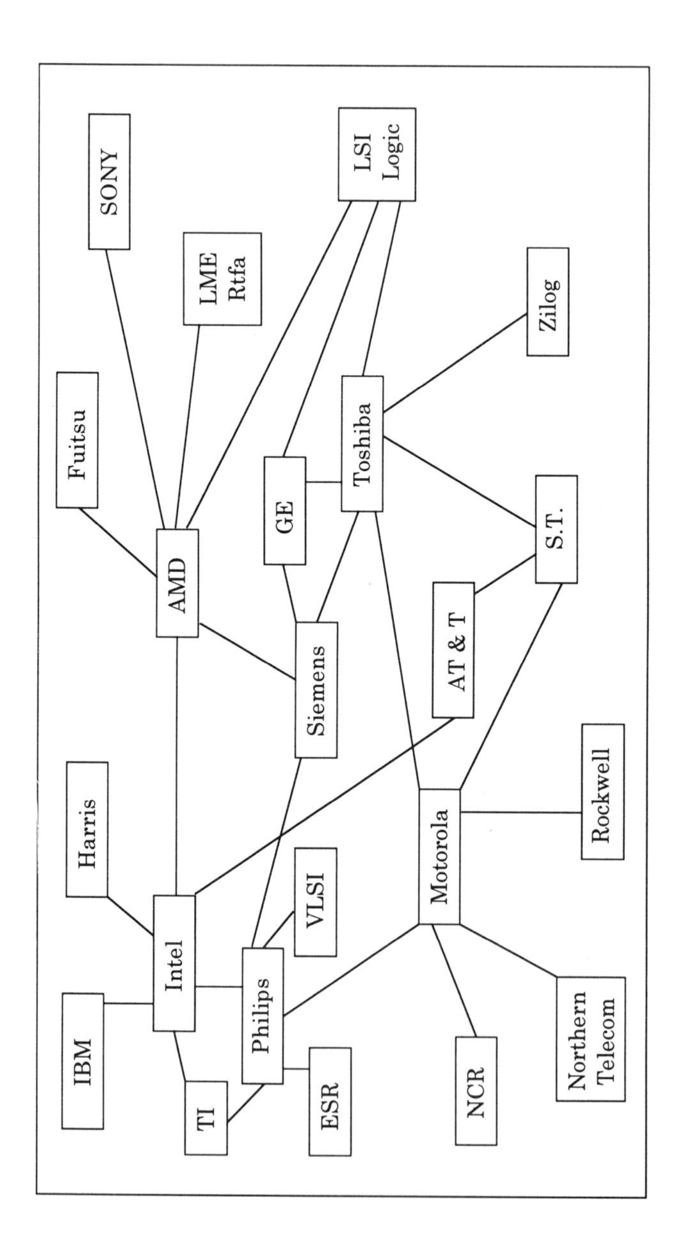

Figure 6.2 *Cooperation networks in the semiconductor industry. Source: Backhaus and Plinke (1990, p. 22. Reproduced by permission of Verlagsgruppe Handelsblatt.)*

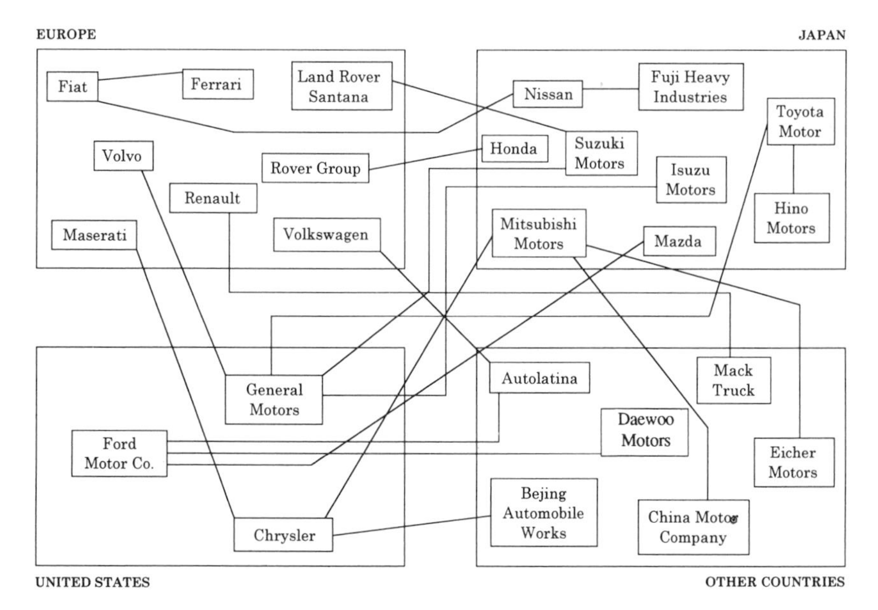

Figure 6.3 *Cooperation networks in the automotive industry. Source: Devlin and Bleakley, "Strategic Alliances—Guidelines for Success", p. 20, 1988, with kind permission from Elsevier Science Ltd, The Boulevard, Langford Lane, Kidlington, OX5 1GB, UK.)*

cooperation partner brings distinct resources. The cooperating businesses are generally equal participants (see Liessmann, 1990). Joint ventures are established especially in situations where highly complex tasks of a technological nature cannot be managed by a single corporation. For example, joint ventures are often found in the aeronautics industry and in the microelectronics industry. In an attempt to share the high R&D risks and financial burdens and to increase the sales opportunities in the protectionary markets, major projects will be undertaken in the form of international joint ventures. They entail the development, production, and the sale of such goods. Many practical examples can be found, for example, the development of the airplanes Concorde and Airbus, the carrier rocket Ariane, and the military fighter Tornado. An example of a joint venture from the microelectronics field is the mutual development of a 4-megabyte chip by Siemens and Philips, or the previously mentioned alliance between Apple, IBM, and Motorola.

The formation of joint ventures between corporations in the former East Bloc states and western countries or between corporations in the First and Third World countries is based on other reasons. Typical for the establishment of this kind of joint venture is the sharing of risk which stems from legal or economic factual restraints (see Liessmann, 1990). Since the opening of the former communist states, the number of joint ventures between western and eastern businesses has multiplied. In 1990, for example, 1200 such associations existed in the area of the former USSR. At the end of 1993, there were already 25 000. In the People's Republic of China the number of joint ventures increased from 188 in 1979 to over 30 000 towards the end of 1993 (see Raffée and Eisele, 1994).

Consortia. A second possibility for the organization of cooperations is in the formation of a project community. In this form of organization called consortium, the participating corporations oblige themselves to collaborate for the common completion of one or more precisely specified projects, without founding a firm with its own legal status. As a rule, consortia are formed for a limited period of time, lacking the intention of a permanent association. Aside from the realization of synergy advantages created by resource pooling, consortia help to decrease the risk involved with major projects for the individual cooperation partners. The economic and legal independence of each consortium member is maintained. Working associations for major construction projects are typical examples. Banks frequently form consortia for the extension of large credit or the issuing of bonds. Further noteworthy examples of joint effort within the bounds of a consortium are diverse standardization attempts in the information and communication sector. Although they still possess the typical characteristics, such mutual activities are seldom called consortia. An example for this is presented by a project group known as X/OPEN which follows the goal to standardize the different versions of the operating system UNIX. The development of a unified operating system standard is realized by a variety of corporations, which are actually in competition with their proprietary UNIX designs. However, the competitive chances over other operating systems can only be realized when a unified UNIX operating system can be offered to customers. This common standardization activity possesses all characteristics of a strategically significant consortium between the participating corporations.

Governance Structures

In contrast with cooperative forms of interorganizational collaboration, joint effort under a governance structure entails one-sided dependencies between participating corporations (see the overview from Baur, 1990).

The limited economic independence of the participating organizations causes governance structures to possess characteristics more similar to the hierarchy than the above described forms of cooperation. Such tendencies towards vertical integration are then efficient when tasks to be coordinated display a relatively high degree of specificity, but, on account of their comparatively less strategic importance or frequency, do not necessarily require completion within the corporation. Hence, the necessity for complete integration falls away for these tasks. The contract design allows the dominant organization to more or less influence the partners' business activities. This can be apparent in the fact that decisions influencing the level of utility of all participants are not made in a decision committee with equal power relations. The governing corporation has the power to implement even those decisions which imply economic disadvantages for the other business partner. Various contractual agreements exist between the parties, causing the shift of power in favor of one partner. Figure 6.4 provides an overview of possible vertical governance structures as well as their causes for unequal distribution of power (see Baur, 1990).

Important Vertical Governance Structures

The different governance structures are distinguished through the underlying dependency relationships. When, for example, a buyer of a certain good owns the resources necessary for the production of the supplier's goal, a *quasi-vertical integration* exists. Although the supplier is freed from the risk involved with investing in specific assets, he has little negotiating power against the buyer for realizing his own

Vertical governance structures	Reason for the power-position
Quasi-vertical integration	Ordering party maintains ownership in specific production factors (for example presses)
Vertical quasi-integration	Size of the orderer's turnover share in the suppliers total turnover (important customer)
Implicit contracts	Orderers threat to break off the tacit prolongation of the contract
De facto vertical integration	Geographical location of the supplier (specific site proximity)
Licensing agreements	Possibility to withdraw know-how
Partial integration	(Credible) threat to completely integrate the stage of production
Capital investment	Ownership position

Figure 6.4 *Important vertical governance structures. Source: (Baur, 1990, p. 101. Reproduced by permission from VVF. Verlag.)*

advantages. When supply conditions are renegotiated, the supplier hardly has the chance to exhaust the range of prices, despite a possibly high specificity of his performance. The buyer can threaten to withdraw the production factors and to either carry out the production order himself or to offer the order for new bids. The supplier, who is only the holder of the production resources, has little chance for opportunistic behavior. In turn, the quasi-vertical integration can provide an appropriate alternative to a fully integrated (hierarchic) production of specific goods and services. Hence, within the frame of outsourcing activities, the supplier can be provided with technological know-how without having to fear the related costs of opportunistic behavior. Examples for a quasi-vertical integration of goods can often be found in the automobile industry, when automobile manufacturers construct presses at the supplier's facilities, but maintain ownership.

In a *vertical quasi-integration*, a large percentage of a supplier's sales volume is earned through one main customer. The dominating customer can threaten the weaker organization with the termination of the business relationship. When this threatens the weaker partner's existence he will be principally willing to make concessions. The dominating buyer can apply control measures in the supplier's processes and as a result, exercise considerable influence on the production of the goods. For example, the buyer can demand the gearing of production process and merchandise logistics exactly to his needs, in order to optimize the just-in-time supplier relationship. Regardless of these advantages, similar to that of a hierarchic coordination, the buyer does not have to carry all the risk involved in production. The risks stay with the legally independent supplier. The only remaining counter-measure for the supplier is to change the one-sided dependency relationship into a mutually dependent one. One possibility lies in the development of specific know-how. For example, a supplier in the automobile industry can attempt to build up a specific negotiating position over the buyer through an innovation such as the anti-lock braking system. Aside from the typical examples in the automobile industry, tendencies towards vertical quasi-integration can be found everywhere, where considerable size discrepancies between business partners exist, resulting in a notable concentration of market power.

Implicit contracts, which are closely related to vertical quasi-integration, have a similar effect. These are based on the dominating partner's threat to cancel contract extensions which have been formerly granted on a tacit basis. The weaker organization has no chance to enforce or to sue for the adherence to components of implicit contracts. In turn, the weaker partners can be forced to behave in the dominating partner's best, i.e., actually preferred, interest. Thereby, between business partners with unequal distribution of power, implicit contracts foster the realization of an important advantage of a fully integrated hierarchic coordination, without carrying the disadvantages related to the latter.

A further vertical governance structure is the *de facto vertical integration.* This form becomes apparent in a site specific investment by the supplier. Such a site specific investment exists, for example, when a supplier settles in close proximity to the buyer in order to optimize just-in-time delivery. The more this supplier restricts his possibilities for the supplying of alternative buyers, the more he brings himself into a location specific dependency upon a single customer. For this customer, the same power potentials are created as with the previously described governance structures. An example for a *de facto* vertical integration is the settlement of Recaro, a manufacturer of automobile seats, directly next to the automobile manufacturer, Mercedes Benz, in Bremen. Although Recaro is still legally independent, a very close economic dependency of this production facility on the dominating automobile manufacturer is apparant.

A *partial integration* exists when a buyer threatens to integrate a supplier's production phase into his own process. The requirement for such a threat is that the buyer owns the appropriate technical assets and capacities for internal production or when he can create or develop them relative quickly. However, this form of restricting opportunistic behavior presupposes that the buyer has no significant production disadvantages, for example, due to lack of digression effects. Further it should be taken into account, that the realization of a partial integration—not considering unused capacities—takes a certain period of time, which allows the supplier to take countermeasures. Therefore, partial integration presents the weakest form of vertical governance.

Further possibilities to implement vertical governance lie in the award of licenses as well as equity participation. Presupposed for the award of licenses is that the licenser owns a patent or specific experience with a certain technology (for more on licensing, see von der Osten, 1989). The patent holder has the option to either use this technology for internal production or to grant the use of this technology to others in the form of a license. As an alternative to the personal use of know-how, the award of licenses offers several advantages. The licenser can dictate the utilization of the licensed technology by the licensee within the framework of a licensing contract. As a rule, only certain uses are allowed, for example, the licensee does not have the right to share the technology with a third party. With this, the diffusion of know-how remains under the licenser's control, although the utilization takes place externally. For example, the licenser can avoid competition with his own technologies or other licenses through the use of regional restrictions. Often the licenser stipulates the observance of certain quality standards as well as the adherence to production limits, or retains influence on pricing. Through the licensing of this know-how, the licenser increases his entrepreneurial flexibility in that he is not forced to develop his own production capacities. On the whole, the licenser can gain a considerable influence on his licensee's business politics. Depending on the extent to which the licensee renounces the development of his own know-how foundation, he leads himself into an economic dependency upon the licenser. Should the licensee behave in an opportunistic manner, the licenser can threaten to cancel the contract, to not extend a limited license, or to not provide him with new licensed know-how in the future. The licensee can attempt to change a one-sided dependency relationship into a mutual dependency through the awarding of counter-licenses. Such awarding of licenses often provides for quick entrance into markets. Especially in foreign markets with unfamiliar conditions, customer needs or trading hindrances, the awarding of licenses provides a way for a licenser to bring quickly his own know-how into a market.

Equity participation presents another way to restrain opportunistic behavior. Depending on the nature of the relationship, either one-sided or mutual equity participation are appropriate means. When, for example, a buyer's desired product improvements require specific investments on the supplier's side, the latter finds himself in danger of a one-sided dependency relationship. As soon as he has completed the necessary investments, the buyer can refuse to pay the agreed upon price for the products. When the supplier anticipates this risk, he will renounce the specific investment. This would also lead to a disadvantage for the buyer. In order to avoid the disadvantages, the buyer can offer his supplier an equity participation, which would provide security against the exploitation attempts on the buyer's part. When specific investments are necessary for both parties, monitoring and control possibilities can be created through mutual capital participation, reducing the motivation for opportunistic behavior.

The Choice of a Symbiotic Coordination Form

The question of which concrete organizational characteristics a symbiotic coordination form should have has not yet been answered. One wonders whether an answer should contain more or less integration elements, for example, in the form of capital participation, awarding of license (joint venture), or a consortium.

The analysis of resource interdependencies existing between the participating corporations can assist in finding the correct form of hybrid organization. Important insight into this type of relationship has been gained through Teece (1986), Wigand and Franckwick (1989), as well as Dietl (1995). (See also Picot, 1993; Picot, Dietl and Franck, 1995.) An economically advantageous symbiotic relationship between corporations requires that at least one of them provides resources through which, as a whole, higher utility can be realized than could be through the resources of just one organization. These kinds of resources which are relevant for symbiotic relationships can be described as interdependent. Resource interdependencies provide for valuable recommendations for the design of symbiotic relationships. There are three different resource characteristics which must be considered: dependency, potency, and plasticity.

Resource dependency is given, when a resource brings a higher utility in combination with resources from another corporation in comparison to an isolated utilization. *The combined knowledge in a team in comparison with the individual knowledge of each team serves as an example.* A resource possesses a high *potency* when other resources are dependent upon this resource, but not vice versa. As an example, the continuation of a business could be dependent upon the further extension of credit from a bank. When a resource is dependent but not potent, a one-sided dependency exists. The *plasticity* of a resource describes the predictability of the type of resource utilization. The more difficult the prediction of a resource's final uses, the higher its plasticity. Employees with an extensive knowledge reservoir can be considered as plastic resources.

When two organizations plan to establish a symbiotic relationship, then several typical design situations can be differentiated on the basis of the classification of these resource characteristics. In order to create an efficient symbiotic relationship, each situation requires a special type of design (see Dietl, 1995). Initially, the type of resource dependency will be determined through the resource characteristics above (dependency, potency, plasticity). Depending on the combination of these three resource characteristics, as well as on the distribution of resources among the competing partners, different organizational design recommendations will result (see Figure 6.5).

When the resources of organization A are dependent upon potent and very plastic resources held by organization B, then the dangers of hold up and of moral hazard exist in this one-sided dependency (see Chapter 2, page 42). Such a case exists when corporation A owns production facilities whose economic utility very strongly depends upon the technical know-how held by corporation B. Thereby, corporation A encounters considerable difficulties in the observation and judgment of the use of B's know-how. In this case, the only efficient solution entails a unified

		Resources of corporation A		
		dependent	**potent and of low plasticity**	**potent and of high plasticity**
Resources of corporation B	**potent and of high plasticity**	Majority holding (eventually acquisition or fusion) Case 1	Capital investment from B in A Case 3	Joint venture Case 5
	potent and of low plasticity	Licensing Case 2	Consortium Case 4	Capital investment from A in B Case 6

Figure 6.5 *Choice matrix. Source: Dietl (1995, p. 580. Reproduced by permission from Verlagsgruppe Handelsblatt.)*

resource management which can be reached through a higher degree of integration through, for example, a buy-out or majority interest (Case 1).

When corporation A's resources are dependent and the potent resources of corporation B have little plasticity, a different design recommendation results (Case 2). In this case, the necessary resources from B can be appropriately described within the framework of a less complex contract, for example, a licensing contract. Such contracts, however, cannot be completely formulated and require support through trust-promoting measures. The adherence to contractual agreements can be controlled, for example, through checking whether certain goods or information have been delivered or not. Examples are licensing contracts with organizations in the Third World for the production of steel, chemical products, or trucks.

When both sides have potent resources at their disposal, a mutual dependency exists (Cases 3 and 6). The organization holding the more plastic resources, has an advantage over the other because its contribution for the mutual completion of the task is more difficult to control. The intrinsic possibility of moral hazard behavior must be limited through appropriate measures. One suitable possibility exists in that *the corporation with higher resource plasticity holds minority interest in the other corporation*. The capital investment serves as a security for the party with less resource plasticity, since the party with the higher resource plasticity would not take advantage of the other. An example for such a form of symbiotic relationship is the cooperation between airlines, hotel and car rental chains. Airlines frequently hold minority interests in these corporations.

In the case of mutual dependency between corporations with equally low resource plasticity, the formation of a consortium proves to be the most efficient organizational structure (Case 4). Both parties commit themselves to the completion of mutual, relatively clearly defined projects, in which utility advantages through synergy effects and distribution of risk can be realized for both sides. Examples of this are associations from construction companies for the completion of large construction projects or the joint effort from banks for issuance of securities.

When both parties bring potent and very plastic resources into the collaboration, the possibility for moral hazard behavior exists on both sides (Case 5). Because one partner is not able to sufficiently control the other partner's contribution to the mutual project, each party has a chance to perform less than is agreed upon. A party which behaves in this manner can realize significant cost advantages for itself while the forfeit of utility will be shared by both parties. This problem can be overcome in an efficient manner through each party bringing its resources into a joint venture. A common association eases the mutual control, lessens the possibilities for opportunistic behavior, promotes the development of a common culture, and contributes to the attainment of common goals by building trust. Examples of joint ventures can be found in shared R&D projects in which qualified personnel and technological resources are brought in from both sides.

Organizational Networks

The discussion up to this point has concentrated on bilateral cooperations and governance structures. Interorganizational cooperation, however, must not be limited to bilateral relationships. Cross-corporate tasks can also be organized through several contractual relationships between legally independent corporations. This leads to a *network* of cross-corporate collaborations. Until now, a unified terminology has not been developed for this form of cooperation. Some expressions found in current literature are *dynamic networks* (see Jarillo, 1988, 1993), *strategic networks* (see Sydow, 1992a), *value-adding networks* (see Pfeiffer and Weiß, 1992) or *cooperative networks* (see Thorelli, 1986; Wigand and Franckwick, 1989).

In general, such networks can possess a character either more similar to a hierarchy or to a market. Likewise, they belong either more to the cooperative form or to the governance form of cross-corporate collaboration. When cooperative relationships form the foundation for a joint effort, the term *cooperative networks* can be used (see Thorelli, 1986; Wigand and Franckwick, 1989). R&D alliances, point-of-sale systems in which several organizations take part, or rationalization associations between suppliers, buyers and transportation companies for an efficient conveyance present examples of cooperative networks (see Neuburger and Wolff, 1994). Other networks are characterized through one or several organizations taking a leading role. These so-called *focal corporations* coordinate the process of the cross-corporate task completion (see Sydow, 1992a). Long-term contractual relationships with requirements similar to hierarchies exist between these and the other participating organizations. Typical examples for such interorganizational, hierarchy-like networks are the Benetton network or the *Keiretsu* found in Japan (see page 237). There are also attempts in the German automobile industry to establish such networks.

The Italian clothing company Benetton, which offers high quality fashion collections, procures textiles from approximately 350 legally independent but economically dependent suppliers (see Sydow, 1992b, as well as the indicated literature). Some of the suppliers are settled close to the few Benetton owned production plants. In Benetton-owned facilities, only sophisticated tasks are performed whereas labor intense activities are outsourced to generally small suppliers. By carrying out the competitively relevant activities, such as design and quality control, Benetton controls the production process which is characterized by strong division of labor. The coordination of suppliers' activities takes place centrally through Benetton. The suppliers are economically dependent, because they are not able to produce a finished product which could be sold directly to the consumer. In turn, Benetton guarantees the suppliers an agreed upon percentage of the profits. The sale of the textiles takes place through approximately 4,200 stores which are bound to Benetton through franchising contracts. The stores are furnished and managed in compliance with exact Benetton standards. In addition, 75 independent sales agencies which are paid on provisions provide the link between Benetton and the stores. These sales agencies assist store management and coordinate regional competitive activities. Benetton itself exercises significant influence on sales channels. This form of intense division of labor practiced by Benetton, with a variety of autonomous businesses, is only made possible through the use of well-suited information and communication technologies.

Various advantages for Benetton result from this strategic network. Because the need for investment on their part is comparably low and the possibility exists for a more flexible reaction to fluctuations in demand, their own entrepreneurial risks are considerably reduced. The risks do not vanish, but are passed on to the governed business partner. On the whole, Benetton has realized a concept for collaboration between corporations which is is often used as a model for other reorganization projects.

A further example for a multilateral network is the so-called *Keiretsu*. The Keiretsu is a typical Japanese form of cross-industry cooperation. The heart of a Keiretsu group is usually made up of a bank, a trading company and an industrial company. These corporations, together with 20 to 30 other business partners from various branches, form the inner circle of the Keiretsu group. Those corporations belonging to the inner circle meet on a regular basis for information exchange and coordination of business politics. In addition, suppliers of those corporations forming the inner circle belong to the extended circle, resulting in a network of up to 100 organizations.

Apart from personal relationships, a Keiretsu is interwoven through financial and economic ties. Although such bilateral capital investments seem rather trivial, they add up to a considerable amount in the Keiretsu group as a whole. As an example, the aggregate capital share in the Mitsubishi group which is held by the companies in the inner circle amounts to more than 20%. When the capital shares held by members of the extended circle are considered in the calculation, the numbers are even higher. Despite this fact, the organizations taking part in the Keiretsu retain their decision autonomy; there is no central leadership. Also, the competitive forces are kept alive. Although each corporation in a Keiretsu would prefer to choose a fellow member as a transaction partner, there are no obligations to do so. For this reason, business relationships also exist between corporations belonging to different Keiretsu groups.

A central position within a Keiretsu is filled by the Keiretsu bank. The bank provides the Keiretsu members with the necessary financial means and services and provides for the follow through of necessary adjustment and restructuring measures. When a member experiences economic difficulties, the Keiretsu bank provides the guarantee for necessary credit. When the management of the affected corporation is not able to solve the economic problems, it is then replaced, through pressure from the Keiretsu bank, by a crisis management group which is organized solely for this purpose.

The general trading house also fills a central position in most of the Keiretsus. Through its sales activities, it retains direct contact with customers and directly receives important market information. With such information, the trading house can efficiently and effectively steer product development. In addition, the trading house often coordinates the Keiretsu's internal transfer of know-how, the creation of new companies, or the completion of large projects.

This illustrates that within a Keiretsu, size advantages in the areas of finance and strategic planning can be gained without hindering market and competitive powers as in a complete integration. The Japanese capital market which is weak in comparison to that in the US presents an important influence factor on the efficiency of a Keiretsu form of cooperation. The disciplining effect stemming from the Japanese capital market on the management of joint stock companies is relatively low. The Keiretsu is an alternative form of organization which replaces important functions of the capital market. It also limits the problems associated with the personal separation of ownership and management.

THE ROLE OF INFORMATION AND COMMUNICATION TECHNOLOGY

Demands on Information and Communication Technology

The *formation of symbiotic coordination forms* places particular demands on the design of information and communication relationships between the participating organizations. As well as organizational and personnel design problems, various technical requirements have to be considered for the application of appropriate information and communication systems. The technical demands for symbiotic coordination forms principally do not differ from those of the organization's internal task completion. However, in the case of interorganizational communication relationships, the successful implementation of information and communication technologies is considerably hindered by various additional factors. This includes the bridging of generally longer distances and differing time zones with necessary public telecommunication infrastructures and possibilities for temporal data storage, as well as the handling of deviating organizational structures and processes and the partly considerable heterogeneity of the applied information and communications technology in the participating organizations.

Between the organizations in a symbiotic organizational relationship, differing types of information can be exchanged. *Verbal communication* dominates especially in the initiation of symbiotic organizational relationships as well as in the solution process of poorly structured problems, where interactive and creative information must be generated.

The telephone is a quick and comfortable form of telecommunication which makes interactive agreement and problem solving possible, even for difficult assignments, without offering direct personal contact between the communication partners. *Face-to-face communication* has a more complete character, which cannot be attained through technical communication media. Where personal contact between the communication partners is absolutely necessary, information and communication technology can at the most play a subsidiary role. For example, documents can be exchanged in the preparation phase of a personal meeting, or important information can be requested *ad hoc* even over great distances in the course of a negotiation. Video conferencing, with the help of multi-media, comes close to the entirety of personal communication. Video conferencing attempts to reproduce the typical communication situation in a meeting without requiring the participants to gather at the same location. Therefore, information and communication technologies must be able to integrate video, voice, and data. Without these capabilities, the intense knowledge exchange and the discussion of complex problems necessary for successful R&D cooperations could not take place.

The *exchange of information through written documents* dominates the coordination of administrative assignments. Written documents include letters, contracts, protocols, notes, and similar documents. The important advantage of the written form is its acceptance as evidence in legal disputes. The signature following a text documents the correctness of its contents and therefore plays an important role in the judgment of the sender's professed intention. As well as this evidence function, documents also often have a certain representative function, for example, through the letterhead or the design. These functions limit the possibility to substitute the transmission of written documents through telecommunication media.

However, this substitution would be desirable for two reasons. First, the transmission times are considerably shortened through telecommunication in comparison to the postal system. Second, paper-based communication requires once again the expensive and time intense input into the receiver's application system. The use of fax reduces the transmission time, but does not replace the eventually necessary renewed data input. Therefore, it makes sense to realize rupture-free processing of text documents into the receiver's application system through the electronic transmission of text files. The same applies for the transmission of technical drawings or graphics. The quick and inexpensive conveyance of construction drawings is of considerable importance in interorganizational R&D projects. Under certain circumstances, this is even a necessary requirement for profitable cooperations in this field.

The completion of similar and recurring tasks is one domain in the data communication and processing which can be supported through EDI. Examples for this are the transmission of inquiries, order confirmation, delivery requests, invoices, transfer orders, and so on. An invoice always includes components such as customer number, invoice number, invoice position as well as invoice amount. Such messages are especially suitable for generation as well as transmission through information and communication systems. Similar to the application of information and communication technologies for the transfer of text documents, special requirements are also necessary for the sender's and receiver's application system's compatibility. Such data communication is often required for logistic partnerships and vertical governance structures, in which large quantities of information accompanying transactions must be exchanged between the participating organizations as inexpensively and time-efficiently as possible.

All forms of information which are suitable for transmission through information and communication technology within symbiotic organizational relationships place certain demands on compatibility. *Compatibility* in the interorganizational transmission of information generally means that sender and receiver application system configuration allows the communication process to be completed successfully. Therefore, this requires the exact specification of the application systems' interfaces, through which compatibility between the systems of sender and receiver can be achieved.

Diverse forms of interfaces are to be taken into consideration. *Hardware interfaces* relate to the physical transmission possibilities of data between two application systems. They require pin-compatibility (see Kleinaltenkamp, 1993). *Software interfaces* relate to the procedures with which information is transmitted through the hardware interfaces. They comprise the rules of data transport. *Data interfaces* are of considerable relevance for interorganizational communication processes. In data interfaces, the formats are to be determined which enable further processing of transferred data in the receiver's application system without media ruptures and with a minimum of human interference. With that, similar to a data integration within an organization, an interorganizational data integration is pursued (see Mertens, 1991).

Data interface compatibility requires *agreements between communication partners* about the data formats to be used, for example, for the exchange of information accompanying transactions through the introduction of EDI. Thereby, various design problems arise.

The *creation of proprietary formats*, meaning the development of an individual standard for data exchange between two or more organizations, prolongs design time, increases design costs, and hinders the flexible admittance of new members into the network due to the individual character of the agreed upon format (see Niggl, 1994). Especially in networks, problems can arise in the integration of new partners using other formats. These factors have, as a rule, less influence in governance structures on account of the partners' differing power positions. However, their influence is especially strong in cooperative organizational relationships. The individual agreement upon common formats for non-recurring *ad hoc* communication, such as short-term market transactions, as a rule does not make economic sense. The use of a format agreement between a large (expected) number of users, therefore (possibly) creating a standard, is generally more cost and time efficient, and increases the flexibility of creating and modifying symbiotic organizational forms. This holds true especially for the arrangement and expansion of corporate networks.

The foregoing integration aspects present a consequential factor for the efficient design of interorganizational information and communication relationships. Over and above that, certain symbiotic organizational relationships require *a coordination of organizational structures and processes as well as planning and control processes*. This coordination, called *business integration* (see Kleinaltenkamp, 1993), is of special importance in value-added partnerships. For example, to optimize just-in-time supplier relationships or to lead rationalization groups to success, it is necessary to closely coordinate the structures and processes of the interconnected corporate value-adding chains. Thereby, the applied information and communication systems are a further important design field.

Corporate networks are necessary for the transmission of data between organizations, on which varying demands are to be placed. Considerable data quantities are to be transmitted in diverse types of information or communication forms. In common R&D projects, for example, frequent and quick transmissions of large data quantities are necessary. Considerable transmission speed and capacity are also required, for example, for multi-media applications or video conferencing. On one hand, integrative transmission of data, text, graphics, and video require noticeable transmission capacities. On the other hand, especially for the transmission of moving pictures, there is no time flexibility, because they are exchanged simultaneously. A further example for the necessity of large transmission capacities is in the exchange of technical data such as construction drawings. As soon as a large number of diverse organizational cooperations with intensive exchange of technical data exist, there is always the danger of public transmission capacities creating a bottleneck.

The general *availability of public telecommunications infrastructure* can prove to be a tangible barrier for interorganizational communication relationships. Without transmission networks, traditional means of communication must be used, for example, the shipment of documents through the postal service. This can considerably hinder the establishment of symbiotic organizational relationships. For example, the frequent opinion in a recent survey conducted within an empirical research project was that the lack of infrastructure in the former East German states made it in some cases impossible to initiate closer communication and intense organizational relationships after the unification of Germany (see Kilian et al, 1994). Not all regions in the world are equally equipped with appropriate telecommunication infrastructures. In the former East Bloc states or in Third World countries, for example, obsolete or lack of public networks limit the realization of efficient communication relationships between local, western, and Far East organizations. A central assignment for the economic development in these countries is the construction of appropriate telecommunication infrastructures, for example, mobile radio networks and satellite networks which could provide a relatively inexpensive widespread use.

Further, *security aspects* in data transmission place important requirements on the functional ability of interorganizational communication relationships. Several reasons exist for this. Technical problems can arise during transmission which will possibly not be discovered by security controls or by plausibility tests on the receiver's end. Further, the risk of intentional data manipulation increases during the transmission from sender to receiver, because, apart from actual communication partners, at least one additional actor such as the operator of the public transmission networks or the value-added services being used comes into contact with the transmitted files. The causes for errors are practically indeterminable.

Legal questions arise concerning the liability for damages on account of faulty data transmission (see Kilian et al, 1994). The solution is made more difficult by the fact that with an electronic data transmission, *authenticity forms* analogous to a signature on a document have up until now received little legal acknowledgement.

The risks of voluntarily or involuntarily modified transmission data are difficult to estimate. For example, one can imagine a situation in which a faulty transmission of a certain order quantity is followed by a delivery shortfall. Under certain conditions, this can lead to production bottlenecks or even to production fall-out on the buyer's end, with corresponding economic losses. Hence, until now the question remains unsolved as to which party would carry the liability when, for example, an automobile manufacturer experiences a production fall-out because of a shortage of required goods based on a faulty data transmission.

The pure data transport is often not enough guarantee for a fully functioning and efficient interorganizational communication. For example, it can be more cost efficient for a corporation to outsource the management of interfaces or of other communication tasks to specialized corporations. The outsourcing of such services can be especially beneficial when communication partners use differing transmission networks, protocols or technologies, so that considerable interface problems are to be solved. For this reason, it is often necessary to establish bridges between different networks or to achieve compatibility between differing transmission processes through gateways. Organizations which specialize in these services are called *value-added network services.*

Practical Potential of Information and Communication Technology

The potential of information and communication technologies was described in Chapter 4. It was demonstrated that a variety of technical developments raise expectations for a considerable performance increase through these technologies. As an approach for increasing potential, new architectural concepts, capacity increasing technological developments, as well as clear trends to open communication have been discussed. Following the technical information and communication requirements for the establishment of symbiotic coordination forms described in the last section, important development trends shall be identified and discussed at this point. On page 238, it was explained that the basic demands on information and communication technologies can be seen in overcoming spatial and temporal distances and in standardizing formats, structures and processes. Various patterns and tendencies exist which point to the corresponding potential of information and communication technology.

The application potential of information and communication technologies are also influenced through the development of hardware and data transfer technologies. The *further development of hardware technology* is especially triggered by the increasing performance capacity of processors and microchips. For example, the current maximum storage capacity of microchips is approximately 64 megabytes. In the future, considerably higher storage capacities can be expected. The development of a 256 megabyte chip has been predicted for the year 2000.

At the same time, *decentralized processing systems* enable a specialization of data processing tasks, for example in the context of client server architectures. Hence, in a so-called front-end mode, specialized communication computers are able to process all tasks connected to communication processes. This also influences the performance of communication devices.

Three basic trends can be observed in public data transfer facilities. Initially, a considerable increase in transfer capacity due to the *use of new transfer media and protocols* can be expected. Whereas currently, for example, slim-band ISDN achieves a transfer rate of 64 kbps, broadband ISDN reaches up to 155 mbps and will reach up to 622 mbps in the near future. SONET (Synchronous Optical Network) is a high speed network promising a capacity up to 13 gbps. Such efficient transfer media form the foundation for the realization of so-called *information highways*, on which enormous data transfer capacities will be made available over long and communication intense distances (see, for example, Frazier/Herbst 1994). They possess considerable significance for the unlimited realization of data intensive relationships between corporations, such as R&D cooperations. Further, the trend is towards a growing number of services being integrated into one transfer network, such as ISDN. It seems probable that the telecommunication network of the future will include all possible services, such as telephone, data exchange, broadcasting and so on. The worldwide diffusion of telecommunication infrastructures is advancing rapidly. In turn, transfer media and corresponding protocols will be globally available in the future.

Value-added network services (VANS) offer a variety of telecommunication services (see Stoetzer, 1991). Besides support services for basic data transfer, these include compatibility, distribution, temporary storage, supervision or maintenance services, as well as general management functions related to data transfer. Value-added network services often rent transfer capacities from infrastructure suppliers in order to run their own networks on these transfer channels. With the help of these networks, a variety of services such as electronic mail, conference services, information services, point-of-sale systems, or multimedia communication are offered (see Schrader, 1993).

Value-added network services enable a temporal, organizational, and technical decoupling of communication partners through autonomously controlled communication processes, whose requirements would otherwise have been agreed upon by the communication partners. This includes the provision of network and service bridges through gateways or temporal data storage, which is required, for example, in the communication between corporations in different time zones. In less than ten years, the entire market for international value-added network services has expanded dramatically with respect to geographical expansion as well as with the variety of services offered. Various studies foresee a considerable growth in the market volume for value-added services (see Schrader, 1993). More exactly, an increase from $3.7 billion in 1991 up to more than $11.5 billion in 1996 is expected within the European market for suppliers of value-added network services.

Since the first postal service reform in Germany, the monopolies of the Bundespost Telekom have been loosened. Due to the pressure from the European Union, the telephone monopoly will be abolished in 1998. In 1993, the first steps to end the exclusive control of the Bundespost Telekom were taken. Since then, voice transfer over data channels is allowed within closed user groups, for example, between headquarters and dependent companies. A growing availability of video and voice services, as well as multi-media services can thus be expected. Due to liberalization tendencies and a broad variety of specialized offers of communication services, considerable quality improvements and cost reductions for interorganizational communication processes will follow.

Another significant factor for the growth in application potential of information and communication technologies appears in the various *standardization attempts*. The importance of standardized interfaces for an efficient communication between corporations has already been discussed. Besides various activities to establish common rules, for example, for multi-media applications (strategic alliance between Apple, IBM, Motorola) or for the unification of operating systems (X/Open Group), intensive activities to standardize business and technical documents exist. Corresponding standardization serves in the implementation of *Electronic Data Interchange* (EDI).

EDI is a certain form of communication in which business and technical data, as well as general business documents such as text, pictures and graphics, are structured according to standardized formats and are exchanged between computers of different corporations using open electronic communication processes which enable rupture free follow-up processing (see Picot, Neuburger and Niggl, 1991). This communication concept stems from the multitude of incompatible hardware and software in the business world. In order to achieve compatibility between different organizational applications and to have positive integration effects, syntactic and semantic rules are designed and standardized so that a hardware and software neutral interoperability between dissimilar applications can be realized. Due to their high transaction volume, communication processes containing recurring, similar message blocks and structures are especially suitable for these applications, since standardization would set a considerable potential free for rationalization and competition. Hence, numerous efforts exist to standardize syntax and semantic of messages accompanying transactions such as invoices, orders, reservations, or delivery inquiries. Currently there are several regulations for these applications, yet their design and reach are limited to regional and/or industry specific user groups: for example, the nationwide standard ANSI X.12 in the United States, or the TRADACOMS-standard in the United Kingdom. In comparison, the number of industry-specific standards is clearly higher (for an exemplary overview see Neuburger, 1994; Niggl, 1994). Parallel to these standardization activities is an attempt to promote a worldwide and industry-independent standard. The *regulation EDIFACT* was developed to support the realization of open communication instead of group-specific specialized standards. Similar developments can be observed in the standardization of technical data and open text documents. With the help of a regulation called *STEP*, technical information such as blue prints which have been designed with CAD systems are intended to be exchanged and processed between R&D departments, using any type of hardware and software. The ODA/ODIF regulation serves in the worldwide and industry independent standardization of open text documents, such as business letters. Here, multiple formatting rules are documented which allow for further processing of received files by any word processing program, without having to enter new formatting information (see Niggl, 1994).

The direct result of these standardization efforts is the achievement of interface compatibility between application systems of different corporations, guaranteeing a hardware and software independent follow-up processing of received messages. This kind of linkage between application systems has considerable *integrative effects* similar to those resulting from integration efforts within an organization. Figure 6.6 shows examples of possible electronic linkages between different corporations.

A necessity for this kind of integration exists especially in networks or in the Japanese Keiretsu. The use of a common standard is a major key in minimizing friction. These standardization attempts also have indirect consequences. The full potential of an EDI application can only be realized through a comprehensive adaptation of organizational structures and processes (see Neuburger, 1994). Therefore, EDI can be used as a mean for the alignment of organizational structures and processes between communication partners. By linking application systems, tendencies to integrate organizational structures and processes, and as a consequence, planning and control processes, are supported (business integration). Hence, a notable potential for information and communication technologies to homogenize symbiotic organizational forms is shown. The empirical relevance of this development has been illustrated in a recent study, in which the organizational effects of EDI have been analyzed (see Kilian et al, 1994). The development of industry-wide network structures between customers, suppliers, banks, shipping companies, public administration as well as service companies can clearly be seen.

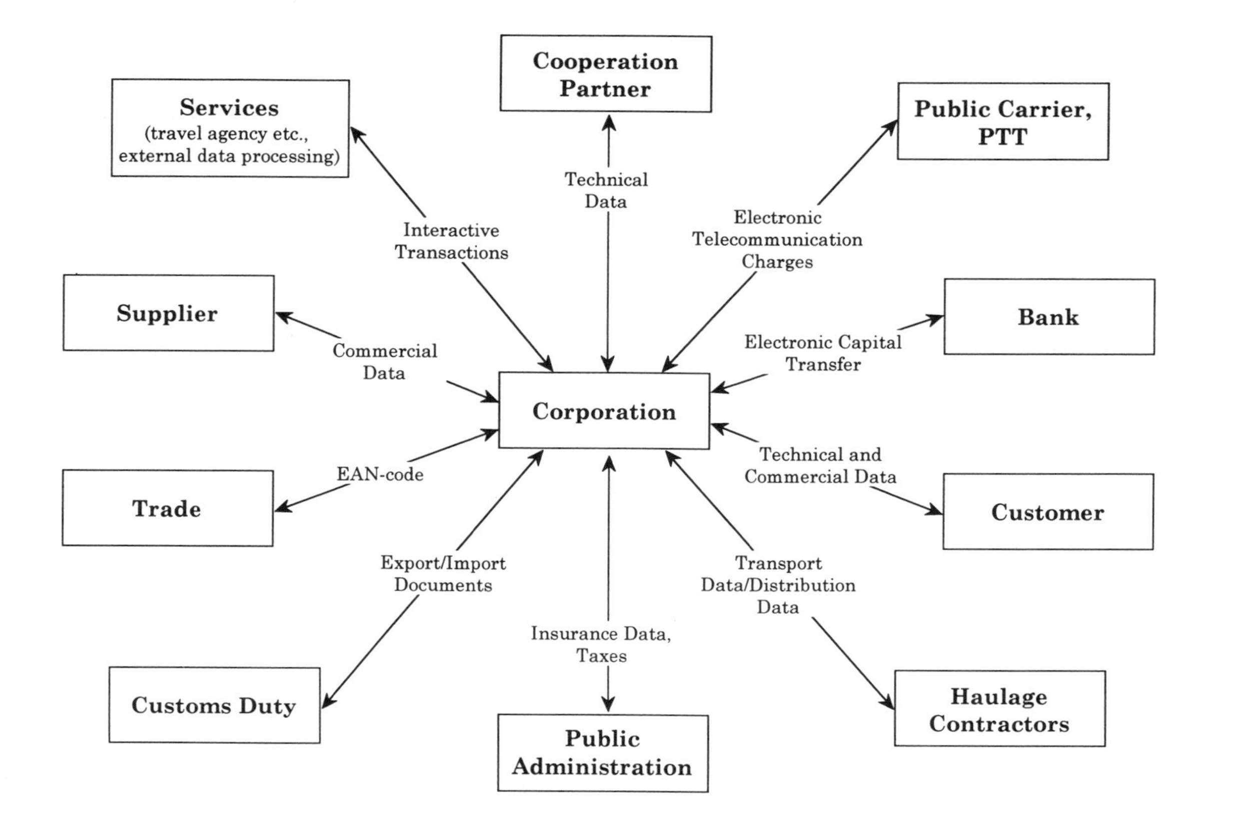

Figure 6.6 *Electronic communication relationships. Source: Kilian et al (1994, p. 44. Reproduced by permission from Nomos Verlagsgesellschaft.)*

Tight technical communication links, together with the related networking tendencies, can lead to the *establishment of interorganizational electronic groups or hierarchies.* Interorganizational electronic groups are formed when several corporations have established a close communication link with a common standard, on the basis of a cooperative relationship. This enables an open communication between the members of that group. When communication relations change, new agreements are not necessary. In addition, tendencies to assimilate organizational structures and processes, as well as planning and control processes can evolve, without the force of a dominating corporation. These interorganizational electronic groups strongly resemble the coordination form of an electronic market (see Chapter 7). However, they differ from electronic markets with respect to their limited, rather small number of members, as well as a common goal orientation. Examples are the previously mentioned point-of-sale systems, rationalization associations, or R&D alliances between several corporations.

An interorganizational electronic hierarchy is a long-term, electronic integration of the information processing systems of two or more legally independent, although economically dependent, corporations. A dominating corporation can, for example, force the installation of an EDI network and, in turn, influence the assimilation of the governed corporations' organizational and business processes. In this type of electronic hierarchy, other companies cannot participate directly. The implementation of proprietary application systems and standards reinforces the hierarchic character. Through this form of electronic integration, governance structures cannot orignally be established; the control intensity, however, can be increased. In turn, they gain in resemblance to a hierarchy. It is likely that the differences between the properties of exclusive, internal information and communication systems and those within a governance structure will disappear over time. One example is the information and communication system between the automobile producer Ford and its suppliers, which is described in one of the following sections.

Muli-media offers interesting application potential for many business areas through the integration of various communication channels. This will change the conventional ways in which tasks are completed or new forms of services are provided. In the medical field, for example, the number of diagnoses can be reduced through the use of multi-media. Through the exchange of patient information, X-rays, computer tomographies or correspondence between hospitals and doctors with the help of multi-media, multiple examinations can be avoided. Through the use of multi-media in corporations, desktop video conferences can be carried out offering advantages over the use of simple video phones.

They allow for an integrated communication of voice, video, and other data, which can be seen simultaneously and processed in an interactive way. Such possibilities change traditional forms of collaboration (see Chapter 8).

Problems and Risks

Besides the above described potential, the use of information and communication technology entails a variety of *problems and risks*. Under certain conditions, these negative factors can inhibit the potential of information and communication technology, so that the advantages, which are usually related to the emergence of symbiotic organizational structures, cannot be fully realized.

Problems can arise when information and communication systems are specifically tailored to the interests of established symbiotic corporate relations. This can result in a *limited or even lacking of openness in the communication system* and as a consequence, to a considerable reduction of future design options. This means that certain technological conditions can limit the flexibility to create symbiotic relations on the basis of already existing information and communication technology, or to realize future combinations of corporate networks. The danger exists that entry barriers into existing symbiotic relationships are created which, to overcome, can possibly outweigh expected gains. In the extreme case many of these technologies are so specifically tailored to the information and communication requirements of the network corporations that they can hardly be used for communication purposes with corporations outside the network.

In governance structures, it can even be the controlling corporation's strategy to establish or to reinforce a *dependency relationship* through the implementation of specific information and communication technology. The communication strategy of Ford Europe might serve as an example. To communicate with suppliers, the automobile manufacturer uses a proprietary communication system, its own data transfer network (Fordnet), and its individual EDI-standard, which is especially fitted to its own information and communication needs (see Hartzheim, 1990). However, this strategy can hinder relationships with potential business partners which refuse the use of such a proprietary system.

The possibilities for the establishment of symbiotic arrangements grow with the *diffusion of uniform transfer and messaging standards*. Through these standards, principally open communication conditions can be created, under which the initiation of new business contacts can take place without expensive agreements about transfer and formatting rules. However, this is only true for those standards which have found universal acceptance. Yet, the establishment of widely accepted standards entails a characteristic problem of standardization which has to be overcome. This problem can best be illustrated through the EDIFACT standard, which has been designed for the exchange of EDI messages accompanying transactions (see Niggl, 1994).

EDIFACT was developed under the control of the International Standardization Organization (ISO) as a worldwide and industry independent regulation. For achievement of this goal, a multitude of different information and communication requirements had to be considered. The regulation is extremely comprehensive, requiring a rather long development time, and making maintenance and further improvement difficult. It can only be used efficiently when certain subsets, suited for specific information and communication requirements, are selected from the entire repertoire of the EDIFACT regulation and are agreed upon for use in bilateral communication. This has two consequences which again limit the possibilities for open communication. The use of specific, group related subsets leads to the tendency towards closed user groups, which to avoid was the original purpose of EDIFACT. Indeed, these group-specific EDIFACT subsets are based on a common syntax, which principally facilitates the coordination between users of different subsets. Nevertheless, due to the need to negotiate expensive agreements concerning the message modules to be used, the EDIFACT regulation approaches proprietary special standards. Hence, there is no real open communication possible without a considerable need for coordination. Entry barriers for user groups of EDIFACT subsets remain. Figure 6.7 shows the suitability of diverse EDI-standards for open communication.

A comprehensive *diffusion* is a necessary requirement for the realization of a relatively open communication. Similar to any other standard, an application's utility depends on the total number of its users (*net effect*). Yet this is exactly what is causing diffusion problems, since most potential adopters wait until a sufficient number of users has been reached. This diffusion problem is additionally complicated by the fact that EDIFACT has to compete with a variety of earlier developed standards which fulfill the information and communication requirements of specific groups. Potential adopters of EDIFACT have to question the gains of switching when, aside from other switching costs, communication barriers with partners outside the group still have to be overcome. This might undermine a comprehensive diffusion of the EDIFACT regulation. Similar mechanisms hindering the realization of open communication also exist for other types of formatting rules.

The use of information and communication technology can involve *risks* which, when anticipated, might set limits on the establishment of

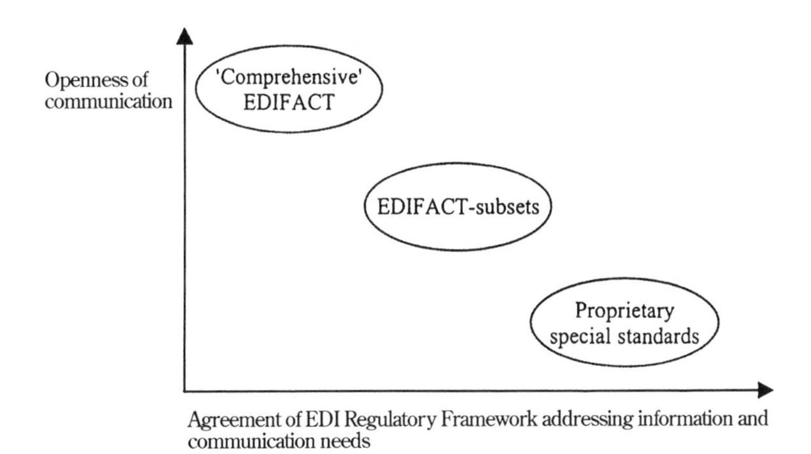

Figure 6.7 *Suitability of diverse EDI standards for open communication. Source: Niggl, (1994, p. 52. Reproduced by permission from Betriebswirtschaftlicher Verlag.)*

symbiotic coordination forms. This increases the *vulnerability of information and communication systems*. Through the close informational linkage of legally independent communication partners, as well as through the increased importance and complexity of information and communication technologies, serious dangers arise. Intentional or unintentional mistakes cropping up in information and communication systems can cause far-reaching and extensive damage. In a closely-knit network of communication relationships, errors can possibly multiply without being recognized soon enough. Thereby, damages can be magnified. Often, the causes as well as the origin of potential mistakes cannot be identified. Under certain circumstances, considerable difficulties can arise in assessing the liability for mistakes. Marshaling of evidence is hardly possible in court. Written documents, normally carrying a signature with probative weight, do not exist. For these reasons, security mechanisms are necessary, so that potential damages can be turned into a calculable risk. For example, the replacement of *encumbering liability* through *endangering liability* is being discussed (see Kilian et al, 1994). This means that an encumbering for appearing mistakes no longer has to be proved, but that risks can be covered through insurance. Legislation must adopt respective laws for these new communication conditions. Moreover, in international communication relationships, problems can occur with differing national laws.

IMPLICATIONS FOR THE MANAGEMENT OF INFORMATION AND COMMUNICATION

Symbiotic arrangements with other companies require planning, and organization just like any other economic activity. Management of symbiotic arrangements demands that requirements for the symbiosis with other corporations be met, that the risks of such blurring of organizational boundaries be controlled, and that the entrepreneurial chances linked with symbiotic arrangements be taken. In the following sections, recommendations for the management of symbiotic relationships will be derived from various theories.

Transaction cost theory emphasizes the importance of transaction atmosphere for the coordination of labor divided tasks. The transaction atmosphere is especially important in symbiotic arrangements between corporations. In this context, the presence of stable and viable infrastructures on the one hand, and the existence of trust and common values between cooperating partners on the other, are essential *prerequisites* for symbiotic arrangements.

Availability of Infrastructure

The main requirement for the creation of symbiotic arrangements is the *presence of stable, viable, and inexpensive infrastructures*. As an essential element of the transaction atmosphere, these infrastructures contribute to the lowering of transaction costs in interorganizational cooperations. Infrastructures here include mainly those publicly (not necessarily meaning governmentally) provided infrastructures. These, in turn, are used by symbiotically-related corporations. These infrastructures can be:

- technical (public telecommunication networks on slim-band or broad-band ISDN basis, transmission ways, supply and disposal systems, research institutions;
- institutional (e.g. corporate law, trade law, labor law, property law), and
- personnel-related (e.g. public schools and universities, dual professional training).

The term infrastructure, in a wider sense, also includes *private infrastructure* existing in corporations, such as common corporate networks, EDP systems, and computer networks exclusively used by the linked corporations. Public and private infrastructures form together the business infrastructure, which is an essential foundation upon which symbiotic arrangements, such as networks, franchising systems, and strategic alliances, can be built. In comparison to markets and hierarchies, symbiotic arrangements generally place different, usually stricter requirements on the available technical infrastructure, as well as on information and communication systems. Symbiotic arrangements are often supported, intensified or only made possible through the use of information and communication technologies. Conversely, the implementation of new information and communication technologies considerably changes the possibilities for collaboration between organizations. Completely new, previously unknown forms of symbiotic arrangements can become possible and economically efficient through innovative information and communication technology. Today, the spectrum of known and new symbiotic organizational forms, which has evolved and is still growing due to the expansion of new technologies, can only be seen in its initial stage of evolution. The development leans towards *cross-corporate and cross-location network structures* placing enhanced requirements on basic infrastructures.

However, the above-mentioned infrastructures can only effectively and efficiently support symbiotic arrangements when they are individually stable and viable enough, and can be used at a reasonable *rate*. When these infrastructures are completely lacking (as is often the case in Third World countries or in the former USSR), or are underdeveloped, the corporation cannot dissolve through the establishment of symbiotic arrangements, but has to further integrate. In continental Europe, excessive fees for the use of high performance telecommunication networks (information highways, based on fiber optics) inhibit the development of symbiotic arrangements. The same development is imaginable when stable legal infrastructures are lacking. At present, this can be seen especially in Russia, where the extensive lack of a stable legal framework hinders, if not even impedes, the establishment of strategic alliances between domestic and foreign corporations and, as a consequence, forces them to a higher degree of vertical integration. Also in Germany, e.g., the establishment of symbiotic arrangements is afflicted with legal risks. In particular, the fair trade laws, anti-trust laws, the labor and liability laws are rudimentary with respect to the new requirements imposed by symbiotic forms of task performance. From a legal perspective, symbiotic arrangements are confronted with many open questions. One question not yet fully regulated is that of retro-liability of the mother company, for example, when a joint venture managed by several corporations goes into bankruptcy or is charged with a claim for indemnification. Also, the anti-trust treatment of symbioses between corporations, such as strategic alliances and joint ventures, can lead in some cases to considerable decision insecurity and risks, since no clear guidelines for fair trade politics have until now been developed.

The original management task is to build up the internal infrastructures required for symbiotic arrangements as much as possible and to secure the access to the public infrastructures required for symbiotic arrangements. In addition, management should seek new organizational forms suitable for symbiotic task completion in cooperation with other corporations.

Trust, Common Norms and Values

Common norms and values, as well as mutual trust, are further elements of the transaction atmosphere which facilitate cooperation and lower transaction costs (see Ripperger, 1997). Hence, the corporation can and should build up the capability for interorganizational collaboration as a strategic potential, nourishing and securing competitive advantages. The establishment of trust, common norms and values is promoted, but not guaranteed, by mostly long-term cooperations prevailing in symbiotic arrangements. For this purpose it is necessary that both partners are committed to written or unwritten rules of cooperation, which might be interpreted as a corporate constitution for the symbiotic arrangement (a kind of network or cooperation constitution). One example is found in Mathews (1994): TCG (Technical and Computer Graphics) is a cluster of 24 medium-sized Australian corporations in the EDP service sector. The group as a whole has 200 employees and realizes sales of $43 million per year. Each corporation belonging to the group is specialized in a certain EDP application or in a certain field in the area of information technology. The corporations, to a large extent, are legally and economically independent; TCG is organized in the form of a network. The individual companies acquire contracts from outside the network and fulfill them mostly by subcontracting to other members of the network (sister corporations). To external groups, TCG appears as one homogenous entrepreneurial unit, meaning the subcontracting relationships are not visible to the outside business world. This corporate group has been especially successful in the past because it successfully developed efficient *governance structures* for the management of interorganizational network relations. Essential elements of this "interorganizational governance structure" (Mathews, 1994, p. 16) are:

1 *Autonomy of network corporations coordinated through bilateral contracts.* This does not exclude the possibility of crossed capital investments between network members.

2 *Mutual preference of sister corporations when completing contracts.* This behavioral rule gives the corporate group its identity. However, the completion of contracts with corporations not belonging to TCG group remains possible.
3 *Exclusion of competition between network corporations.* This rule forms a basis for trust between network corporations.
4 *No mutual exploitation.* Network companies do not realize profits from transactions with sister corporations. Mutual performance relationships are managed on the basis of cost-plus contracts. This rule promotes trust to a high degree between network members and avoids the formation of a hierarchy between economically powerful and weak corporations of the network.
5 *Flexibility and preservation of the group members' economic autonomy.* Group members do not have to receive permission from other members in closing contracts with external partners or in building up new business fields.
6 *Democratic constitution of the network.* There is no owner of the whole network group, no holding company, and no central planning committee. The network is only held together by the business relations existing between network members.
7 *Non-observance of rules leads to exclusion from the network.* This potential sanction ensures that member corporations follow the rules.
8 *Entry of new corporations in the network.* The entry of new corporations in the network is generally welcome and even desired. This rule allows the network to expand and to constantly renew itself.
9 *Withdrawal of corporations from the network.* No member is held in the network against its will, but can leave at any time.
10 *Relationships of individual network members to external third parties.* Every corporation can offer its products and services to the outside market, hence no member is dependent on subcontracting within the network.

These ten rules form the TCG constitution and give the network its cohesion and development dynamic. According to Mathews, these rules have never been explicitly documented, but have evolved over time in an evolutionary manner, simply being put into practice. Mathews concludes:

> "Above all, the study of the governance structure of networks brings the issue of trust back to the center of attention. Trust is not a natural but a social construct. It is produced from the norms that govern people's behavior and their commercial interactions." *(Mathews, 1994, p. 19)*

This example clearly demonstrates that a common corporate constitution can increase the capability for interorganizational cooperation through the promotion of fairness and openness, enabling the creation of trust, as well as of common norms and values. The development and enforcement of rules for the performance relations between symbiotically linked corporations, as well as the cultivation of a network culture, present fundamental assignments for the management core.

In conclusion, it can be stated that the transaction atmosphere, which essentially includes the infrastructure of the transaction and mutual trust between the transaction partners, is of special importance for symbiotic arrangements and constitutes a major determinant for their success.

Besides the creation of technical requirements for symbiotic arrangements, a further management assignment is to control the *risks* associated with symbiotic arrangements. These risks can entail the loss of identity or of market advantages. The risk of identity loss is especially high when corporations with dissimilar cultures or traditions enter a symbiotic arrangement. In this situation, there is an inherent danger that the linked parts of the corporations either do not develop a corporate culture at all, or that the culture of the dominant network partner supersedes those of the other network members. The termination of the symbiosis is inevitable in both cases as sooner or later differing norms and values make coordination between partners too strenuous and transaction cost intense. Often in such situations, the interwoven parts of the corporations are either dissolved or are absorbed entirely by one partner. In the latter case, the corporation selling its shares can lose significant core competencies. This leads to the second danger related to the creation of symbiotic arrangements, namely, the possible loss of market advantages and the emergence of asymmetrical dependencies.

The theory of core competencies and transaction cost theory give valuable design recommendations aimed at controlling these risks. Both theories indicate that core competencies and specific activities should be carried out internally by a corporation and only in exceptional cases in cooperation with external partners. Furthermore, transaction cost theory recommends that, if lack of capital and know-how requires a cooperation with an external third party, this symbiotic interweaving should be secured by trust and common values or by long-term contracts between partners. If corporations neglect these recommendations, they are in danger of losing their core competencies, which requires an immense effort to build up again. They may also be threatened by asymmetric dependencies, which requires many resources to overcome. For its first personal computer in 1983, IBM made the decision to buy the operating system from Microsoft and the chips from Intel, instead of producing internally these core elements of a PC. As a consequence, IBM has almost entirely lost its core competencies in these areas and has fallen into an asymmetric dependence upon Intel and Microsoft. The recent attempts to rebuild these core competencies (development of the operating system OS/2 and the microprocessor Power PC), in order to decrease these dependencies, required considerable expenditures on the part of IBM. In addition, in the case of the Power PC project, this goal could only be reached by entering new symbiotic arrangements with Apple and Motorola. This development could have been prevented by IBM, if in 1983 it had analyzed more closely the activities to be externally acquired with respect to their relevance to IBM's core competencies; if it had been more careful in choosing its partners; if it had paid more attention to the very different corporate cultures of Microsoft, Intel and IBM; and if it had protected the cooperation through long-term exclusive contracts. These critical points represent the focus of analysis of the theory of core competencies and transaction cost theory. Hence, both theories indicate possible limits for the use of symbiotic networks in the organization of labor-divided activities.

The chances of these arrangements can be seen in additional resources (especially know-how and capital), which partners provide and access to a cooperation. In this respect, symbiotic arrangements help to multiply the resources available to a corporation. Since symbiotic arrangements between corporations are not restricted by national boundaries, but can be established globally, they provide participating corporations with the opportunity to use regional and global potentials in a flexible manner and take advantage of international division of labor. International symbiotic arrangements often pursue competitive advantages resulting from international wage disparities, know-how differences, and contrasts in national legal systems (for example internationally differing regulation standards in environmental regulation and social law). Hence, symbiotic arrangements at an international level do not only blur organizational boundaries, but have the additional effect that national borders become less important for the global activities of corporations.

In conclusion, the management of symbiotic arrangements between a variety of corporations requires above all to:

1 assess whether the technical, legal, and personnel requirements for a symbiotic arrangement with another corporation are fulfilled;
2 evaluate the opportunities resulting from the symbiosis; and
3 weigh them against the risks.

The above discourse has made clear that the management of the borderless corporation, compared to that of the traditional, highly integrated corporation, has to give special attention to the management of technical information and communication infrastructures, to the management of interorganizational contracts, and to the management of cross-corporate culture.

7
New Forms of Market Coordination: Electronic Markets

OVERVIEW OF ELECTRONIC MARKETS

Modern communication and information technologies can enable change in organization structures and business processes (see Chapters 4, 5, and 6). They influence also the competitive advantage of organizations (Chapter 2). Under their influences markets gain importance increasingly as a coordination form. But also events within the market and market structures are experiencing changes due to the increasing utilization of modern telecommunication media. Drivers, nature and magnitudes of these changes are the focal points in this chapter.

Markets within our economic system are places of exchange. It is here where supply and demand meet. Basic characteristics, tasks and forms of markets when viewed as processes were already discussed in detail in Chapter 2: the market is viewed aside from the hierarchy as the second basic form of coordination (Coase, 1937; Williamson, 1975; Williamson, 1985). Between the two poles of "market" and "hierarchy" one can recognize a continuum of hybrid forms that offer—depending on differing task situations—varying degrees of efficiency and, in turn, advantages. Based on efficiency reasons, the coordination form of the market lends itself well for standardized transactions of performance relationships that have little variability and are easily describable.

Electronic commerce is a relatively new concept and has crept into the business vocabulary no sooner than the 1970s. We encounter many economic activities that find electronic support. The literature and trade press refer to "Electronic Business", "Electronic Commerce", "Electronic Markets", and similar terms. A clear delineation is not offered and maybe we should not be surprised as the field of electronically-supported markets and organizational processes is subject to fast and often dramatic, and externally induced technological changes. The widespread use of personal computers coupled with the proliferation of telecommunication networks, as well as their joint integration, has made paper-free trading a real possibility even for common citizens.

Within the framework of this book the term *electronic commerce* denotes any form of economic activity conducted via electronic connections. The bandwidth of "Electronic Commerce" spans from electronic markets to electronic hierarchies and incorporates as well electronically supported entrepreneurial networks and cooperative arrangements (electronic networks). Electronic markets therefore are *one* selected institutional and technical platform for electronic commerce. The market coordination mechanism is their common characteristic. Services within the tourism, finance or insurance industries, but also product distribution services are typical fields of application. Delineating between differing forms of electronic markets becomes even more difficult, as:

- organizational boundaries change or disappear and, as market coordination forms, may also find a place within organizations themselves;
- value added chains change and as value added activities are newly distributed;
- customers become part of the value added chain and as private citizens become entrepreneurs on their own.

Many of the concepts and ideas presented in this chapter are based on the work of numerous authors, including Benjamin and Wigand (1995), Ciborra (1993), Coase (1937), Malone, Yates and Benjamin (1987, 1989), Kirchner and Picot (1987), Picot (1982a and b, 1986, 1991a, b and c), Schmid (1993), Wigand (1995a, b and c) and Williamson (1975, 1979, 1985). Electronic data interchange (EDI) and electronic mail, for example, are central business tools underlying the operation of electronic commerce (Kilian et al, 1994). Yet it is impossible to trade over EDI without a contractual agreement. Both EDI and electronic mail today may be viewed as value-added network services and they allow the user to substitute electronic forms for their paper-based counterparts. Over 45 000 firms in the United States alone exchange data electronically (Stewart, 1994, p. 78; Wigand, 1994) and more than 60% of all US firms utilize some form of EDI.

Development of the Internet, as well as the World Wide Web (WWW) demonstrates business' and industry's increasing interest in and recognition of importance of electronic commerce (Wigand, 1996, 1995a). Solutions to buying and selling in these environments, how to handle electronic cash transactions, various security issues and other topics are emerging.

The time seems to be approaching, however, when organizations will engage in multinational non-contractual EDI trading in an environment called *Open EDI*. In this model the user will be able to search a directory and locate, for example, all the pencil makers worldwide and, subsequently, send out a request for a price quotation. Parallel developments allow EDI service for companies to send and receive EDI transactions using the World Wide Web (WWW). In time and with similar services, electronic markets will form where participants connected to electronic networks and value-added networks will advertise their products just as in any other market place. Standard universal product codes embedded in catalogues, as well as standardized formats for business transactions (e.g., purchase orders, requests for proposals, invoices) will evolve. Proprietary or open standards being developed for such transactions will in part determine the reach within the market place. Once developed, electronic markets will offer an efficiency that can only be dreamed of in conventional markets. Retailers, wholesalers and manufacturers worldwide have considerable incentives to embrace the new media making electronic commerce possible, as it will restructure traditional markets as we know them (Benjamin and Wigand, 1995; Wigand, 1996).

Although electronic commerce has been around for some time in the form of EDI and financial transactions among banks, financial institutions and certain other industries, when viewing this setting as a potential market, one must realize that it is not understood well. One must also make a distinction between markets for information and a market for ordinary commodities on at least two counts (Ciborra, 1993, p. 103): on the surface, information can be considered a factor of production. This notion will also be discussed below in the context of transaction costs in that buyers and sellers depend heavily on the efficient transmission of information about scarcities and needs in the economy. Another perspective enters the picture when information itself becomes the commodity and when private markets have formed, in which information can be bought and sold as a commodity. Information then takes on a more complex role as it has peculiar characteristics in that it is easily copied, transmitted, sold without being destroyed, that it is expandable, diffusive, compressible, difficult to establish property rights at times, and sometimes it is a public good (see, for example, Chapter 3, Ciborra, 1993; Wigand, 1988a).

In some settings, for example, too much transparency within electronic commerce may be undesirable and potentially dysfunctional. An example will demonstrate this situation: American Express Company used caller identification as an information technology that would allow the immediate electronic linkage directly to the customer's account. In essence, when the customer's call rang in the call service center, the American Express employee receiving this call had the customer's account on the computer screen immediately and was able to welcome the customer with: "American Express. Hello Mr Smith, how can I help you today?" The caller was immediately identified. On the one hand, this may be interpreted as an extremely forward-thinking form of customer-orientation; on the other hand, many customers regarded this almost as an invasion of their privacy. In this setting, caller identification, i.e. information transparency, was too much of a good thing. American Express stopped the practice of immediately identifying the customer, continued with the caller identification technology, but then waited for the caller to provide some identification (e.g., account number) as if this information then triggered the pulling up of the customer's account statement. Numerous other companies went through similar experiences.

Many applications can be thought of in which business is taken care of, partially at least, on an electronic basis such as in current forms of teleshopping or electronic banking. These two applications usually cannot fully be carried out by the consumer in a seamless and complete electronic framework. Benjamin and Wigand (1995) have provided a vision how such a fully electronic cycle may evolve in time and it is addressed later in this chapter.

Business transaction patterns may include the following: inquiry about products, price formation inquiries, support services, transactions (logistical, financial), research, placing of orders, confirming purchases and others. Most, if not all, of these could be done electronically if the firms and customers within a market are linked electronically and when such linkages reflect a critical mass among potential participants. Electronic markets can then be envisioned that serve just in the electronic support of some of these business transactions, but one can also envision electronic markets within which—and that may be their primary purpose—prices are shaped and formed. This, in turn, may trigger new markets entirely as it may reach buyers that previously were difficult or impossible to reach. Moreover, this setting may result in new forms of market behavior that are different from traditional, i.e. non-electronic, markets. Lastly, new forms of market mechanisms may emerge that are still unclear at present.

Electronic linkages among firms may help these firms to reduce their transaction costs. This in itself is a desirable effect of an electronic market. It demonstrates that electronic markets can link firms in a tighter fashion than previously thought possible. Only one needs to think about the 24-hour stock trading cycle and recognize potential market effects. This, however, may also have in part led to the market crash in 1987. We can recognize that certain traditional actors and agents in a market, for example, retailers of certain products, may be substituted or may lose their role entirely. This is indeed, at least given past practices, a revolutionary development (Benjamin and Wigand, 1995).

Definitions of Market and Electronic Market

Before discussing electronic commerce in more detail, it is imperative to define two key terms: market and electronic market. The term *market* is indeed a multidimensional concept (see Chapter 2). A market is conceived to consist of all goal-seeking firms, government agencies or individuals producing some commodity, as well as all firms, government agencies or individuals purchasing the commodity. Within this market, the exchange of goods and services takes place. In a competitive situation, a competitive market is characterized by:

1 many buyers and sellers;
2 homogeneous products; and
3 easy entrance to and departure from the market.

The first characteristic suggests also that no individual producer or consumer is sufficiently large enough to influence the price of the commodity. Consequently, each market participant accepts the price of the commodity and behaves as if this price is beyond his/her control. Information is an essential ingredient for the functioning of any market and is exchanged frequently between buyer and seller such as when price information is exchanged (e.g., Hirschleifer, 1980). The second characteristic denotes, in addition to what is already stated in (2) above, that consumers do not have strong preferences about which producers they buy from and that they will seek out sellers with the lowest price. The third characteristic suggests that supply and demand adjustments can and do come about easily and occur quickly.

The concept of electronic markets has been discussed since the 1970s, and more formal discussions occurred in the literature at least since 1987. Although several authors have reviewed this topic (e.g., Schmid, 1993), a uniform usage of terms does not exist. The term *electronic market* denotes a market place in which business transactions within a given market are carried out or supported, at least partially, electronically utlilizing information technology and telecommunication networks. An electronic market can also be characterized as one in which a prevailing market intensity requires a certain volume of activities that, in turn, becomes attractive to be carried out electronically. Consequently, electronic markets emerge through the mediation of market transactions.

An electronic market may not be viewed in an absolute sense, i.e. not necessarily all activities will be carried out electronically in a given market. In essence one may view an electronic market as a very wide or narrow concept and one should realize that there are steps in between: one may envision hierarchies that can function electronically, but also as an electronic market, as well as hybrid electronic forms in between hierarchies and market are conceivable (see Figure 2.10 and related discussion, as well as Picot, Bortenlänger and Röhrl, 1995). Moreover, such an electronic market makes available the electronic inquiry by firms about products and services offered by other firms within a particular industry branch and where such inquiry makes possible the comparison of offers, as well as the eventual electronic purchase of such products and services. The often idealized, optimum electronic market that is fully automatized, operating around the clock without imperfect human interference and still be understood as a market is not possible. It is important to distinguish here, as mentioned by Schmid (1993), Wigand (1995c) and others, that such an electronic setup through networks is not envisioned as a market, as this would constitute merely an automated processing system of some sort. A market in this sense, and an electronic market as well, necessitates that (at least minimally) human actors are engaged, trigger an action, make a decision or choice, express a preferred behavior or maybe avoid doing something, but it is essentially this human involvement that characterizes a market rather than a fully automatized process (Wigand, 1995c). Very often past experiences, typically *joint* past experiences, play an important role, but also such essential features as trust, faith, confidence and credibility characterize an actor's behavior in a market (Schmid, 1993; Wigand, 1995c). All of these attributes would be most difficult to capture by an automated processing system in order to make crucial decisions. An electronic market then is not different.

There are other limitations or forms of boundaries within electronic markets. People will *meet* in an electronic market with certain expectations. One expects that the price rises; another expects that the price decreases. Both, however, agree that they can talk and do business. It may be that only certain people are attracted to electronic markets or would consider doing business there. It is clear, however, that information technology can support and help in this process, but, in the final analysis, the very essence of the electronic market will always be the human being, i.e. man as actor.

Malone, Yates and Benjamin (1987, 1989), and Benjamin and Yates (1991), Benjamin and Wigand (1995), Wigand (1995b), as well as Wigand and Benjamin (1995) argue that organizations increasingly coordinate their activities electronically and that this coordination takes the form of single source electronic sales channels (one supplier and many purchasers coordinated through hierarchical transactions) or electronic markets. Moreover, they argue that electronic markets are a more efficient form of coordination for certain classes of product transactions, especially those where asset specificity is low and where products are easily describable. An example is the issuance of electronic requests for proposals (RFPs) by firms that can be retrieved or inspected electronically. Similarly, it may be possible to submit a full-fledged proposal electronically. Thus one can argue that with cheap coordination costs or transaction costs, interconnected networks and easily accessible data bases, a proportional shift of economic activity from single source sales channels to market is likely to occur.

An electronic market is a coordination system that is characterized by the following features (Schmid, 1993):

- Coordination mechanisms in electronic markets are supported electronically in varying degrees: the spectrum ranges from simply coordination support (e.g., price information) to complete electronic coordination of the market participants (e.g., price fixing).
- The development of communication and information systems simplifies above all the activities of information acquisition and evaluation for the market participants. Typically, though, this market transparency can be increased and thus information asymmetry between market partners can be reduced. In addition it is especially during the information and decision phase that transaction costs can be reduced.
- Communication and information technologies reduce increasingly the importance of temporal and spatial distances. In principle this enables a location-independent participation in markets for connected market partners.
- Aside from the equalizing of market partners and the freedom of choice in their market participation one needs to emphasize the openness to enter the market. This is an elementary demand for an electronic market.
- A fundamental characteristic of electronic markets is the participation of human actors and thus the market processes are being influenced by their expectations, experiences and the interpretation of market information. Fully automatized processes are therefore not viewed as electronic markets.

Underlying Principles of Electronic Markets

It is becoming increasingly difficult to accurately delineate the boundaries of today's organizations. As already discussed, does the boundary simply encircle the actual internal organization structure or does it extend to include the tightly linked and strategic relationships with suppliers and customers, as we know them from the Japanese Keiretsu? Does it extend to include other organizations where cooperative relationships are enjoyed? Do these boundaries cross national boundaries as well? It appears that many of these boundary-spanning developments have become possible through various advances in computing and telecommunications, especially as these two technologies have been merging in the form of networks. Networks, in turn, have enabled various forms of electronic commerce (see, for example, Picot, Ripperger and Wolf, 1996).

Developments leading to ever-increasing applications of electronic commerce must be considered and a number of underlying principles need to be emphasized. Electronic commerce has been enabled by four main factors:

1 Coordination costs when conducting business via electronic networks (e.g., EDI) have been lowered over time. Consequently, it has become attractive to explore the conduct of business electronically.
2 Computing costs have been decreasing steadily (McKenny et al, 1995; Arinze, 1994; Weiser et al, 1991) in terms of hardware acquisition and processing costs (e.g., millions of instruction per second), thus making electronic commerce attractive.
3 Single-source sales channels have been emerging providing market access that due to their efficiencies make electronic commerce a desirable means to conduct business (e.g., Benjamin and Wigand, 1995).
4 It is reasonable to assume that firms in their desire to conduct business will prefer entrepreneurial settings and competition. These, as will be shown, do indeed exist when conducting commerce electronically.

Driven by information technology's ability to produce even cheaper unit costs for coordination activities, organizations are, at an increasingly rapid rate, implementing new linkages for the ways they relate to each other. These linkages take on many forms, among them: electronic data integration, just-in-time manufacturing, electronic hierarchies and markets, strategic alliances, network organizations, teleworking, and others. Such new organizational settings indicate an on-going transformation of value chains, largely due to technological change and resulting capabilities (see, for example, Wigand, 1996).

The concept of the national information infrastructure (NII) or the information highway under construction in many countries reflects an idealized model of anyone connecting to almost anyone else (including organizations), at a very high capacity communication bandwidth at a relatively low user cost and that most services can be called upon on demand. This underlying concept permits analysis and to some extent observations about what will happen to the organization of industry value chains. *Value chains* in this context refer to the collection of firms involved in producing, distributing and selling a related set of products from raw materials to the ultimate consumer.

The Market Transaction Process and Transaction Costs

Classic market transactions can be classified ideally into two phases (see Langenohl, 1994; Neuburger, 1994):

- *The Information and Decision Phase.* Central to this phase is the search for potential market partners: this search is focused on the search for information about potential suppliers and customers, the comparison of such information, as well as the decision concerning the submission of an offer. This phase—in terms of transaction cost theory—is subject to certain initiation and preparation costs.
- *The Agreement and Execution Phase.* Following the information and decision phase is the agreement and execution phase. In transaction cost theory terms, this phase will incur agreement and execution costs. Within the framework of the agreement the participating market partners make contact, negotiate on the basis of the offer over the conditions of the proposed transaction (e.g., delivery and payment conditions) and then close the contract. This contract becomes the basis for the execution. Aside from primary transactions focusing on the performance transfer, we can recognize here also indirect and supportive secondary transactions (e.g., financial transactions, insurance, logistics) (see Himberger, 1994).

The information described above — decision, agreement and execution steps, are the essential elements of market transaction processes. The phases of performance coordination are depicted in Figure 7.1 (Langenhohl, 1994).

The analysis of *transactions* provides a framework for examining the potential changes in organizational and industry value chains. Chandler and Daems (1979) noted that: "every coordinative activity that improves

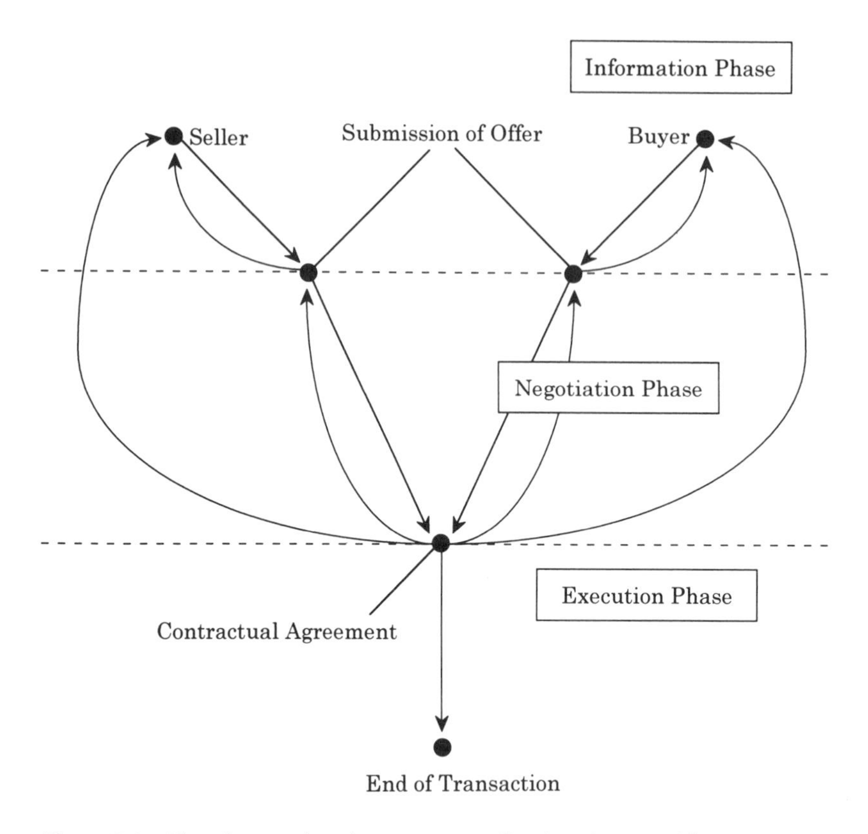

Figure 7.1 *The phases of performance coordination (Langenohl, 1994). Reproduced by permission of Dr. Th. Langenoh)*

organizational efficiency speeds up flow through the system, or permits a more insensitive use of the factors of production, is likely to improve the performance of the economic system." Williamson (1981, p. 1538) similarly pointed out that "the modern corporation is to be understood as the product of a series of organizational innovations that have had the purpose and effect of economizing on transaction costs." What was said about the corporation seems equally true for the industry value chain. If it is true that the NII dramatically economizes costs of information and communication, i.e. costs of coordination, then this is the result of a fundamental restructuring of entrepreneurial opportunities and roles in various value chains. Within a given value chain, each business organization will search for transactions that provide an advantage over its competitors and grant a viable entrepreneurial position, i.e. taking advantage of the new NII or electronic commerce potentials. The reader may want to review the related discussion on this topic in Chapter 2.

As we study patterns of transactions in terms of the idealized model of the NII we must ask if certain transactions can be simplified or avoided entirely. For example, one or more of the organizations in the industry value chain can be by-passed, when the NII or electronic commerce capabilities provide the facilitating electronic linkages for a new pattern of transactions (Wigand, 1995b; Benjamin and Wigand, 1995).

It is appropriate to review transactions, coordination costs and electronic market and hierarchies within a larger context (Benjamin and Wigand, 1995; Ciborra, 1993; Malone, Yates and Benjamin, 1987, 1989; Kirchner and Picot, 1987; Picot, 1986) and then make some observations about growth patterns in electronic markets and hierarchies. It is precisely the coordination of the entire enterprise, including the design and manufacturing, parts delivery and assembly, sales, etc., that determines the ultimate competitiveness of each individual company (see, for example, Jarillo, 1993). This organization of the entire enterprise from raw materials to the end consumer became known as vertical integration. In exploring these areas our thinking is guided by the writings of Ciborra (1993), Picot (1982, 1991), Williamson (1975, 1979, 1985), and Coase (1937).

The total cost of any economic activity can be divided into two interacting subclasses: production costs and transaction costs. *Production costs* are the producer's or provider's costs of producing a product or delivering a service, respectively. *Transaction costs* imply all the resources that have to be sacrificed in order to arrive at a mutually acceptable agreement of the exchange of goods and services between two or more parties. They comprise, for example, four different types of costs:

1 contact costs (such as searching for information);
2 contracting costs (such as negotiation, formulation of contract);
3 monitoring costs (such as checking of quality, quantity, prices, deadlines, secrecy);
4 adaptation costs (such as changes during the validity of the agreement).

Given the character of transaction costs as opportunity costs, the level of some of them may vary depending on the economic actors involved. The reader is encouraged to review the discussion on transaction costs in Chapter 2.

In the case of direct distribution from producer to consumer, the following cost structure emerges. It is assumed that the unit costs can be adequately calculated, that profit can be neglected and that no relevant production costs arise on the consumer's side. Thus, total costs impinging on a consumer consist of production costs, producer's transaction costs and consumer's transaction costs.

An Office of Technology Assessment study (US Congress, 1994, pp. 30–31) describes a consumer purchase from a transaction cost perspective:

> "Consider markets in the context of a consumer buying a high-end stereo system. The buyer mulls over the features that are most important—wattage, audio performance, appearance, size, speakers, CD player, tape deck, and cost. There may be hundreds of dealers to choose from. The consumer reads catalogs, compares specifications, consults *Consumer Reports*, calls for price information and visits dealers to compare models and prices. The search can take hours, days or weeks. The time spent in research, comparative shopping, and making the deal are the transaction costs, as are the expenses for fuel, wear and tear on the automobile, magazine and catalog purchases, and telephone charges."

It appears obvious that the level of transaction costs offers an incentive to create entrepreneurial activity, especially if that level becomes prohibitive. In addition to other measures (e.g., information and advertising, internal sales organization, consumer associations) trade is one possible and frequently observed way to reduce transaction costs in distribution.

In an efficient trade channel, the total of transaction costs of producers, traders, and consumers and of production costs of traders does not exceed the total of transaction costs of producers and consumers without trade.

Thus traders may be defined as specialized agents selling services which reduce the transaction costs of producers and/or consumers. They substitute for activities which previously had to be carried out by producers or consumers. Both producers and consumers are willing to engage in trade if the opportunity costs of their own activities are greater than the price of the traders' services. Transaction costs, of course, can only be identified for particular types of mutual agreements (for example, depending on the products involved). According to the special characteristics of transaction type and technology support, different forms of distribution and trade will emerge.

Figure 7.2 depicts how the above considerations need further deliberations when considering traditional market hierarchies and levels progressing from manufacturer, to wholesaler, then retailer and, finally, consumer (Wigand, 1995c). An additional step or level could be possible if a distributor is involved. Moreover, it is conceivable to recognize antecedent steps to the initial stage, i.e. manufacturer level, as recognized in an example with the production and sale of a shirt later on in this chapter. More specifically, under the rubric of manufacturer one could envision an entire chain of sub-manufacturers of a product, e.g.,

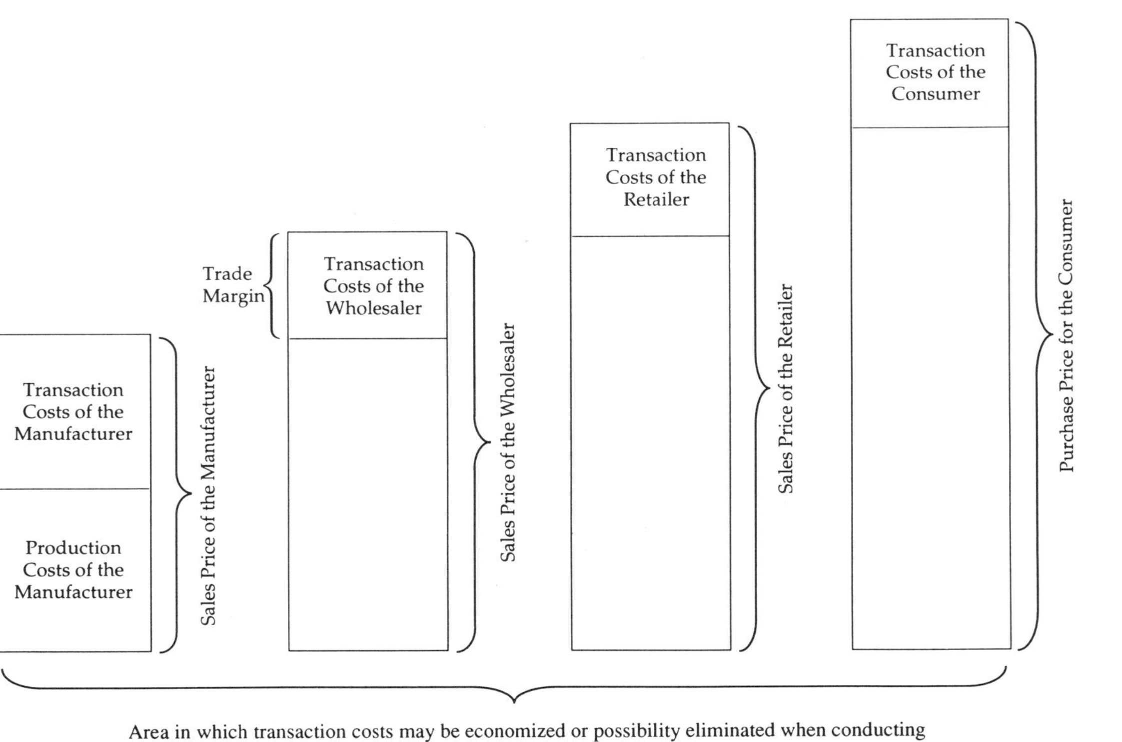

Figure 7.2 *Market hierarchy and transaction costs in a stepwise fashion. Source: Wigand (1995c)*

the yarn maker, a firm that dies the yarn, a trader, the cloth manufacturer, another trader, etc. It is clear that transaction costs may be economized at the wholesaler and retailer levels—potentially at the distributor level as well—when conducting business electronically.

Figure 7.2 demonstrates that the sale price of the manufacturer comprises the manufacturer's production costs plus transaction costs. These costs when combined become the acquisition costs for the wholesaler to which the wholesaler adds his/her own transaction costs and so on until the consumer purchases the product.

Underlying Principles for a Shift Toward Electronic Markets. Arguments for a proportional shift of activity toward electronic markets can be advanced as follows:

1 *Lower coordination costs favor electronic markets.* This claim was already advanced earlier and is briefly reiterated here. Organizational forms are a balance of production and coordination costs. Organizational forms that increase economic performance will be evolutionary survivors. Markets have been characterized by low production costs and high coordination costs and hierarchies with high production costs and low coordination costs (Benjamin and Wigand, 1995; Malone, Yates and Benjamin, 1987). Information technology has continued and will continue to lower overall costs of coordination. Thus the lowering of coordination costs will favor markets (see also Picot, 1989b; Wigand, 1995b).
2 *Low computing costs can expand products favoring market transactions.* Products that are easy to describe favor electronic markets. Low cost computation can simplify complex product descriptions. For example, stock index funds which in the case of the New York Stock Exchange require averaging several thousand securities daily into one easily described product are just one example. Asset-specific transactions (Malone, Yates and Benjamin, 1987), i.e. those favoring hierarchies, can be narrowed by the use of electronic technology. For example, the personal computer, on the surface a highly asset-specific device, has been successfully sold by mail order companies such as Dell, Gateway and Compac. They are able to ameliorate product specificity with help desks, installation configurations, etc. Thus core product transactions over time will favor electronic markets, and over time proportionately more purchasers will choose to purchase through electronic market makers rather than through hierarchical arrangements.
3 *An evolution from single-source sales channel to market can be anticipated.* Benjamin and Wigand (1995), Wigand (1995c), as well as

Malone, Yates and Benjamin (1987, 1989) suggest revolutionary paths for electronic single source sales channels and markets. Electronic single source channels will evolve from separate data bases within the firm to linked data bases between/among firms (e.g., EDI), to shared data bases between/among firms. Electronic markets are likely to evolve from electronic single source sales channels to biased markets where the market maker is one of the providers and uses the market transaction mechanisms in his/her favor, to unbiased markets and finally to personalized markets, where customers can take advantage of personalized decision aids in making their choices.

4 *Trade-offs in market participation.* An organization with a successful sales channel will consider setting up an electronic market for itself and like competitors, when the potential profit from an increased volume of market transactions is greater than the potential loss of profit from having to sell at a lower competitive market-based price. Similarly, a single source sales channel will enter an electronic market only when convinced that the total share of market transactions available to them at the market's price range is greater than the profits generated by the channel at its higher price margins.

Expansion of Traditional Market Limits

Electronic markets potentially can function worldwide, although one must recognize the potential limitations of national boundaries in the form of import and export restrictions, tariffs, customs and other concerns. These concerns have been well stated in the past within the context of transborder data flow (TDF) (e.g., Shipley et al, 1985; Wigand, 1984, 1985b; Wigand et al, 1984). Very often these restrictions to commerce were precisely imitated to establish boundaries for a traditional market. One example will suffice here (Wigand et al, 1984): A multinational company with its headquarters in New York has subsidiaries and factories worldwide. This company chooses to centralize many of its transaction activities in New York. For example, when the payroll for its employees at its Caracas, Venezuela factory is processed the following transactions occur:

> The raw payroll data for the employees are transmitted at 2 a.m. from the Caracas-based computer to a satellite uplink facility on its premises and they are transmitted via two-satellite hops to its downlink facility at headquarters in New York. The data transfer occurs at this hour as transmission costs and satellite transponder time are the cheapest. From the downlink facility the data are transmitted to a computer at its headquarters that processes all payroll data for the firm on a worldwide basis. The data are quickly processed and the results are formatted such that payroll

> checks can be printed in Caracas for the net amount with a stub indicating remaining amounts of vacation time, sick time, taxes, various other deductions, etc. These processed data now travel back in reverse order to Caracas. At the end of this trip the data are sent to a printer where paychecks and payroll data stubs are printed which in turn are handed to the employees.

This sounds like a straightforward process, except that the Venezuelan government gets involved. The subsidiary in Caracas is told that it exported *information* and *data* to be processed abroad and that it needs to pay an export duty on these exported data. Similarly, when the processed payroll data return a few seconds later via satellite, the Venezuelan government will come forward and request the payment of an import duty on the value-added portion of the received data, i.e. the value differential between the raw payroll data and the processed payroll data. The Venezuelan government justifies such taxation as it is this firm's decision to process data abroad, even though a Venezuelan data processing industry and infrastructure exists. In essence this example illustrates how the Venezuelan government has established a market boundary through its tariffs and import and export controls. We are not going to make any value judgments here or offer any justifications for any party's actions. One must realize, however, that it appears that the firm in question should have a right to process its data wherever it pleases. On the other hand, the Venezuelan government, a sovereign entity, has the right to protect its citizens and industries. Conducting such business electronically as described demonstrates nicely how the world is shrinking, is intricately linked, integrated and interdependent. Electronic commerce can provide a worldwide unifying umbrella to conduct business effectively and efficiently. As always with newer information technologies, it is people and governments that tend to be slow in developing appropriate laws, policies and regulations. This may also be viewed as a potentially vulnerable area for businesses in that this lack of boundaries may compel governments to find new revenue sources.

Through electronic commerce it is possible, technically at least, to overcome some of the barriers mentioned above, but we need to recognize that at times new barriers may be created by the information technologies themselves, at least temporary ones. In time, however, maybe we can see the increased emergence of worldwide electronic commerce as a key driver to reduce, if not eradicate, such barriers.

Nevertheless, through the ubiquity of computers and communication networks and services, it is easily possible to navigate these networks and conduct business on them on a global basis. Recent developments on the Internet and the WWW only strengthen this argument (Wigand, 1996, 1995a and 1995c).

DRIVERS FOR THE DEVELOPMENT OF ELECTRONIC MARKETS

Nearly all firms in the industrialized world compete among each other today, often also at the local level. This has brought about a highly competitive global economy in which multinational firms play a greater role than previously. Within this setting one can recognize the growing importance of information as an economic resource just like other resources (e.g., land, labor, capital, energy) (Wigand, 1988a). These information technologies then enable firms to be quick, highly responsive to market conditions, flexible, and, in turn, just-in-time delivery, flexible production and mass customization become possible. At the same time information serves as the primary resource, and as an entity and commodity by itself, but also as a key factor in production. In that sense, then, information is a resource and a commodity that can be bought, traded and bartered for in the market place. Often information can become a substitute for labor and can enhance the efficiency of production processes (Wigand, 1988a and 1988c). Several drivers for the development of electronic markets can be identified. These are discussed in the following sections.

The Internationalization of Electronic Markets

With increased competition on a global scale and the ease with which electronic markets can be internationally expandable one can quickly appreciate how electronic markets are attractive on a worldwide basis. A key role in this scenario is played by the electronic market maker and how he/she may take advantage of consumers and suppliers. Electronic networks, once established and a critical mass of users exists, are convenient devices to reach customers quickly and easily. Such information technology plays of course a central role in the emergence of every National Information Infrastructure (NII) in almost every nation, but also on a worldwide scale with the emergence of a Global Information Infrastructure (GII) (Wigand, 1996). Consequently, it appears that a nearly unlimited expansion capability for electronic markets exists. Their success will be determined by supply and demand for electronic commerce, varying from market to market and product to product.

The Electronic Market Maker

If the market maker owns or has a substantial interest in any suppliers, it can bias the market in their favor, and both the consumer and other suppliers will be disadvantaged. In the airline reservation system business, e.g., SABRE, the airline market maker was legally stopped from continuing this tactic (Copeland and McKenny, 1988). If the owner of a physical communication channel also becomes a market maker, this too may severely bias a market in his favor. Similarly, if the owner of a physical communication channel such as a long distance carrier or a telephone company restricts access to any market channel because of interest in a particular product market or another market channel, it limits a consumer's free access. The potential, but dissolved, TCI-Bell Atlantic merger posed such a threat, since both firms own electronic channels into the home. TCI has substantial interest in market suppliers of entertainment programming and home shopping. Thus, it could have restricted access to producers, retailers and market makers to suit its own economic interests. In addition, the channel owner—also having a monopoly on supplying information to the consumer—can keep access costs unnaturally high and curtail the rate of technology advancement, as when AT&T maintained a total monopoly in telecommunications (Benjamin and Wigand, 1995).

Regardless of how many channels are connected to consumers' homes, for the electronic market effect to occur, those channels must not limit or control access to the product or service providers who want to reach the home.

Quick and Easy Reach of Consumers

The consumer who purchases traditionally through market-oriented mechanisms such as retailers is a prime candidate for the growth of electronic markets. Electronic markets or sales channels, however, will be unable to make significant inroads with the consumer until technology opens the door. Electronic market activity to the consumer will be highly constrained until the capabilities assumed for the NII are actualized, e.g., the wiring of the home with sufficient communications capabilities to allow interactive presentation of high quality video pictures and, at the same time, the consumer has a user-friendly and flexible market access device available. Until then the retailer remains the traditional consumer market, buying and displaying merchandise from multiple suppliers for the consumer to choose. The technologies required for the consumer are evolving rapidly and the NII represents the organizing mechanism for reaching the consumer with these technologies. An absolute imperative of any future developments along these lines is that the technologies utilized must be truly interactive and user-friendly. Although the current cable television shopping is successful, the consumer still has to watch the cable channels (medium A) and needs to utilize the telephone (medium B) to place an order. For one, the buyer has to switch the medium to place the order and consequently no interactivity, or at best an indirect interactivity, exists. Experience with catalogues and cable television shopping channels indicates that (1) there is a vast amount of product available that meets the criteria for electronic markets described earlier, namely asset specificity and ease of description, and (2) consumers are willing to buy these products without a traditional retail transaction.

In summary, expansion of electronic single source sales channels is proceeding rapidly and electronic markets are growing at a much less rapid rate. There is little likelihood of this situation changing significantly until the consumer and the industry value chain are interconnected with interactive capabilities such as those anticipated with the NII. Recent video-on-demand and interactive cable television trials have shown, however, that consumers perceive such services as too expensive to subscribe to or may not yet be ready and willing to subscribe to such services. Families in such studies would have to spend about $50 per month more on their entertainment budget or displace some other entertainment activity, which they were not willing to do. Maybe the service is ahead of its time.

The Role of Information Technology in the Development of the National Information Infrastructure

The National Information Infrastructure (NII) is an ambitious program in the United States to guide industry's development of the national information superhighways (Hollings, 1990). The White House Administration perceives this superhighway as the seamless web of communication networks, computers, data bases and consumer electronics (Gore, 1993). The intent is that these technologies are built largely by the private sector, putting vast amounts of information at citizens' fingertips. A belief dominates that this superhighway, if it can emerge without the constraints of a rigid regulatory environment, can fundamentally change the way we work, learn, receive health care and public services, shop, do business, communicate and entertain ourselves. Some initial version of this infrastructure already exists, although this occurs at relatively high cost, relatively slow transmission speeds and there are concerns with regard to equal access, universal access, privacy, security, interoperability and reliability. Among those already existing services is, for example, the Internet, various on-line information services, and thousands of electronic bulletin boards. Many of these services are not necessarily secure, ubiquitous or user-friendly. Building this information highway will deploy and integrate various advanced communications technologies with existing communication networks and will require the investment of many billions of dollars to build various *on ramps* to connect residential, institutional and business users in cities and rural areas.

Most industrialized nations are building their respective national information infrastructures. This development is not seen in isolation for a given nation, but is often envisioned within a regional or worldwide context. A national information infrastructure depends on its information highways, i.e. information technology in the form of networks such as fiber optic cable, coaxial cable, microwave or satellite transmissions. The degree to which these highways are attractive and affordable to those engaged in electronic commerce, these respective technologies and networks will thrive. This varies greatly around the globe. For example, the present fee structure of networks available for potential electronic commerce in Germany is rather prohibitive. As a consequence, the emergence of broad-scale electronic commerce via existing networks is slow until—it appears—additional deregulation has occurred and competition is established.

Although Europe may have lost the computer wars over the years to the United States, many European firms are moving ahead to land a secure position on the information highway. When coupled with strong interests in the multi-media business, this industry is estimated to generate revenues of $39 billion in Europe by the year 2000. In Germany, Mercedes-Benz and BMW tested a Deutsche Telekom system to design cars faster via computer links with suppliers in order to reduce automobile development cycle time. Hundreds of small firms are producing interactive CD-ROM titles in such areas as art and business. Deutsche Telekom is working with Microsoft and IBM to replace its text-driven online service with a new service using graphics, sound and video images. British Telecommunications PLC is developing software for airlines to run interactive in-flight entertainment systems offering everything from stock quotes to catalogue shopping. The French software company CAP Gemini Sogeti developed a multi-media package allowing travel agents and their clients to take virtual reality tours of cities and hotels. France's Thomson Multimedia allied with Sun Microsystems in interactive services such as video-on-demand and home shopping. All of these examples demonstrate how businesses are enabled by new means and information technologies. All of them have in common the means to carry out processes electronically and several are suggestive for potentially emerging electronic markets.

These firms are pressuring their respective governments trying to make sure that these markets develop as quickly as possible. They are pressuring policy makers to set international standards and to accelerate telecommunication deregulation throughout Europe, especially in Germany.

On the consumer side, cable companies, water utilities and telephone operators are investing sizable funds into interactive television tests. One such effort is the British Telecom video-on-demand trials using fiber-optic wires reaching 2500 homes. This $30 million trial will find out to what extent British consumers are interested in video-on-demand, banking at home, home shopping, fashion videos and more. The German city of Stuttgart is testing 65 interactive programs to 4000 homes, businesses, hospitals and schools. Infogrames Entertainment, a 12-year-old French company that started out designing services for Minitel, the world's first online service, is launching its own online product called Infonie. Infonie has aligned itself with 50 content providers and with its colorful, slick interactive format may supersede the aging Minitel system.

In Europe, as well as in the United States, it is well known that any anticipated payoff is many years away. In the past European firms have been slow in bringing information technologies to market. Often promising technologies never made it past the laboratory or testing stage or they were commercialized by others. Now European firms are innovating faster and racing the new technologies to market; this is especially the case with multimedia technologies. If this new attitude becomes institutionalized, European firms will be joining the winner's circle.

The Expansion of Electronic Commerce is Nearly Unlimited

Once the information technology and respective networks are in place, the expansion of electronic commerce is nearly unlimited. Limitations might include the cost of information technology, joining networks, transaction costs and the like. Another limitation might be that a critical mass of users, both customers and suppliers, has not yet materialized. It is relatively easy to link networks to other networks. Consequently, national boundaries do not constitute a technological limit necessarily, but nations may be slow in bringing about changes in tariffs, as well as customs, import and export laws and other requirements when goods and services cross national boundaries. This may be especially true when physical goods, as a result of electronic commerce, cross national borders.

An example *par excellence* is the rivalry among AT&T, Deutsche Telekom, France Télécom and Sprint: Germany's Deutsche Telekom and France Télécom have proposed to buy a 20% stake in Sprint for $4.2 billion. AT&T, the US giant, is furious that the German and French government-owned monopolies may soon own a 20% stake in the third largest US long-distance carrier while non-German and non-French investors are locked out of the two biggest markets in Europe. Even though

Germany and France talk about competition in the telecommunication business, their markets are still closed to AT&T. AT&T has been pressuring Germany and France to open their respective telecommunication markets prior to the 1998 deadline set by the European Union. Moreover, AT&T has approached the Federal Communications Commission to make equal market access mandatory for foreign carriers seeking to get into the US market. It has requested that the Sprint deal be placed on hold until Germany and France meet this standard. Germany has agreed in principle to open its market sooner; the French market, however, remains resolutely closed. Simultaneously, Germany is organizing a European Union counterattack: This nation wants the US to end its current limit of up to 25% on foreign ownership of media and telephone companies. These developments on the global information highway seem to have found a temporary parking lot with a global boxing ring.

Electronic Supply and Demand in Competition with Traditional Supply and Demand: Limits for the Consumer

Although some of the electronic network services such as America-On-Line, CompuServe and Prodigy, as well as other on-line shopping services or electronic shopping malls offer some opportunities for making electronic purchases, their choices and capabilities for comparative shopping are limited. Especially the graphic depiction of products is limited and the interaction with the consumer is interactive to an extent, but is far too slow. Better experiences, at least in economic terms, can be reported so far with consumers' buying practices via traditional catalogues and cable television shopping networks.

Catalogues. Both the rapid growth in catalogue businesses and television home shopping networks provide evidence of a readiness of consumers to shop electronically. Both of these related trends are causing retail market erosion and illustrate how electronic markets will affect consumer markets. Catalogue marketers such as Land's End cumulatively sell an enormous amount of merchandise. Ten thousand mail order companies sold $51 billion worth of goods through catalogues in 1992 (Brubach, 1993, p. 55). According to the Direct Marketing Association (personal interview, 1995), Americans spent $60 billion in 1994 through catalogues, television shopping channels and other direct marketing alternatives. This, however, is merely 2.8% of the nation's $2.1 trillion-a-year retail market place, including supermarkets, mall outlets, car dealerships, department stores, etc. Economists, merchants and technologists predict that conventional retailing will hold steady or increase slightly, while technology-driven direct marketing is predicted to surge and capture some 15% of total sales. If these predictions are correct that would make this new business one of the world's biggest with annual revenues of well over $300 billion.

Obviously, mail ordering economizes on transaction costs. Because catalogue sales must have the same characteristics as electronic markets, they must be easy to describe and not very asset-specific and they indicate the wide product varieties amenable to electronic markets.

Cable Television Shopping Networks. Home shopping through cable television is a rapidly growing business, accounting for several billion dollars of sales annually. It represents a very limited form of market where the consumer is shown choices of different kinds of merchandise, but has no ability to compare merchandise within a class, thus preserving high profit margins for the channel owner. This limited market form is dictated by the current capabilities (limited choice, interactivity and display quality) of the cable television systems. Home shopping, however, demonstrates the consumer's willingness to buy products that meet the electronic market test previously described. The successful shopping channel QVC—also available in Europe—is said to have moved goods in 1994 at the rate of $39 per second by broadcasting product pitches around the clock.

Limitations for the consumer come in to play in that one will have to be a subscriber to a cable television service reaching his home. There is obviously a connection fee associated with such a service and there will be population segments that are not willing or cannot afford to subscribe to these services. In addition, a rather sophisticated device needs to assist the consumer through the myriads of choices that will be offered. A market choice box is needed with considerable built-in intelligence, otherwise the consumer will lose interest or give up in frustration. Lastly, the distribution of such services appears to be without any bounds. They can be transmitted worldwide via satellites into cable or fiber optic network services and thus be distributed into the home. Limitations exist, of course, with regard to import and export requirements and restrictions from one country to another.

THE EMERGENCE OF ELECTRONIC MARKETS AND THE ROLE OF THE MARKET MAKER

Various business processes focusing on information inquiries, seeking agreements, making payments among others lend themselves nicely for computer support. Until just a few years ago such computer support found application merely for a few types of transactions. The emergence of electronic markets brings about the computer support for significant portions of market transactions (Ritz, 1991).

The coordination of exchange relationships among firms with the support of communication and information technology may occur on the one hand in the form of single-source sales channels or via electronic hierarchies. Within this coordination mechanism the firm is electronically connected with several buyers in the form of a hierarchy. On the other hand, electronic markets are efficient forms of coordination of the exchange of deliverables with which the specificity is low and the deliverables can easily be described (see Chapter 2). It is conceivable that when coordination costs are low, the widespread use of interconnected networks is common, and easily accessible data bases prevails, a shift from single-source sales channels to electronic markets may occur. The following developments favor such an expansion of electronic markets:

- lower coordination costs through new communication and information technology;
- standardization of deliverables and products;
- increasing expansion of efficient communication and information technology.

Firms have to achieve a balance between production and coordination costs. Markets tend to achieve low production costs with high accompanying coordination costs; hierarchies, however, tend to achieve low coordination costs, but with high production costs (Picot, 1991a). Together with the lowering of intra-organizational production and coordination costs, the deployment of communication and information technology has led to lower coordination costs at the interorganizational or inter-firm level. Consequently, higher coordination costs lose in importance as a decisive disadvantage in the coordination of markets, i.e. the importance of the electronic market for the exchange of goods and services increases. An example demonstrating these developments is the standardized depiction of several thousands of differing securities traded at electronic stock exchanges. Consequently, it is becoming increasingly attractive for more and more firms to offer products in electronic markets.

The increasing use of information technology leads more and more to a unified depiction and simplified handling of service and product descriptions. These developments give rise to an evolution from electronic hierarchies to electronic markets (see Malone et al, 1989) at least for suitable products and services. Electronic hierarchies may emerge through the so far intra-organizational connections to data bases that may evolve into inter-firm (interorganizational) connections such as EDI. Electronic markets, in turn, develop electronic hierarchies further. During this evolution, dominating markets may develop in which the market maker is also a market participant and, at the same time, is capable of influencing the market in his/her favor. On the other hand, markets may evolve that are entirely open and in which all participants are equal. A firm will give up a single-source sales channel only then in favor of an electronic market if the potential profits resulting from the increased number of potential sales relationships exceed those experienced within an electronic hierarchy with its higher price range. Many forms are conceivable in such developments. These are described in the following section.

Patterns of Emergence for Electronic Markets

The formation of electronic markets comes about especially due to the evolution of existing information systems. How does such a development occur? When an electronic market first forms, electronically supported or conducted market transactions are initially often complementary, i.e. they surface in addition to traditional market transactions. Moreover, electronic markets may surface as a substitute, i.e. as a replacement for the so far prevailing transaction forms: new services are being offered and traditional services are substituted. In conjunction with the introduction of electronic services innovative applications emerge and entirely new services may be offered for which specifically a new market may come about. Based on existing communication and information systems, according to Ritz (1991) four elementary patterns may be observed:

1 the opening of electronic hierarchies
2 the creation of common distribution channels/market information systems
3 closed electronic trading systems
4 the expansion of the services offered by value-added service providers.

It is the goal of an electronic hierarchy or of a single-source sales channel to achieve competitive advantages through a technological head start. This goal is achieved through the electronic tying-in of buyers. Such a monopolization of the distribution channels leads to a dependence of the tied-in buyers on the operator of the system. Examples can be found in the travel industry or hospital supply industry in the form of order and reservation systems. These information systems were first developed for the firm's internal use and over time customers and buyers were tied into this system electronically. This buyer dependence offered the airline companies operating these order and reservation systems a definite competitive advantage (Porter and Millar, 1985). The opening of these systems in the form of also including competitive systems was only brought about when the matter was settled in the courts. Such a forced opening in an electronic hierarchy and its expansion into an electronic market necessitates too the suitability of a market-based coordination form for the respective exchange relationships (see Neuburger, 1994). However, one should note here that electronic markets lend themselves well for the processing of standardized tasks, while for specific tasks controlled relationships are more suitable and preferable. It therefore follows that market-based tasks and resulting challenges must move into the direction of standardized performance relationships.

Joint distribution channels or a joint market information system may also serve as the starting points for the creation of an electronic market. In addition to the already existing market information such systems may be developed in support of the conclusion of an agreement. All participating firms hope that they will achieve a joint competitive advantage and they do not pursue their own individual competitive advantage. This continued development of distribution channels is often fostered by professional, trade or industry associations.

Participating firms expect, with the creation of closed trading systems, a more efficient coordination of the exchange relationships among themselves. The total number of participating firms is usually low. In closed trading systems firms often act as buyer and seller. An example of this form of electronic market is the stock exchange with its limited membership. At a securities exchange an exchange occurs only between the relatively small circle of admitted participants who act as buyer and seller at the same time. Closed trading systems usually operate via a central clearing office through which demand and supply are equalized.

An essential foundation for the existence of electronic markets are the technical prerequisites such as communication networks, as well as the value-added services available on them. These necessary (for an electronic market) data bases are accessed via these networks and services and transactions are carried out. Operators of communication systems and the suppliers of value-added services do not only possess the technical know-how to operate these systems, but in contrast to potential market makers from a specific line of business they are unbiased. These two advantages can be utilized by network operators in that they no longer just focus on the technical side of their business, but that they offer or expand their mediating function as a business. In addition to the various technical communication services they offer, they now also take on a coordination role.

In the above described formation patterns the points of departure are existing systems and institutions. When additional functions are taken on and when systems and institutions open for greater participation they will expand to electronic markets. In such formed electronic markets information can be exchanged that only reflects the business traded within that market, thus one may also speak of information markets (see Ernst, 1990 (in Neuburger, 1994, p. 105)).

Aside from the obvious gains in efficiencies, new opportunities for the processing of transactions among market partners, as well as entirely new applications and services, may be enabled.

Mediation Effects

In the stock exchange business the tasks and roles of the players are changed by new technical information and communication applications. In the business of the tourism and travel industry one can observe an enterprise-wide integration of booking processes. In traditional commodity markets one can realize quicker, more flexible and transparent coordination processes, even when considering the final buyer. All of the changes outlined can be put down to the effect of the markets operating with the help of technical communication and information infrastructures.

When observing these effects within the above described developments, Malone, Yates and Benjamin (1987) state that there are three main effects of information technology on markets:

1 the *electronic communication effect*, whereby technology allows more information to be communicated in the same amount of time, at a much lower cost;
2 the *electronic brokerage effect*, whereby computers and communication technologies allow many potential buyers and sellers of a given good to be matched in an intelligent way, that is, by increasing for each party to the transaction the number of alternatives, filtering them and selecting the best one;
3 the *electronic integration effect*, that is, coupling more tightly (coordinating) value-adding stages of production and distribution across different organizations.

Overall these three effects assist in the reduction of information asymmetries and thus improve and expand the functioning of the electronic market.

The electronic communication effect pertains to two aspects of the technical communication and information influence: (1) the ability of a quicker and wider distribution of larger amounts of information, as well as (2) the simultaneous lowering of costs of this information distribution. The *electronic brokerage effect* denotes the possibility to connect buyer and supplier to common information and data bases. Thus the classical function of the broker as an information mediator or agent is being substituted at least partially by electronic media. The *electronic integration effect* enters this picture when originally separately functioning partial processes of market events are bundled into integrated, electronically supported processes.

All three types of effects can be documented through examples in business. The *communication effect* can be illustrated through the example of online shopping. Via the Internet, online services or via home shopping cable channels on television can reach worldwide a potentially unlimited number of buyers directly. For comparatively extremely low costs and with almost no time loss products can be presented, offered and traded worldwide.

The example of the stock exchange demonstrates the *brokerage effect* especially well. Electronic exchanges offer today considerable support functions for the classic information broker activities. At the same time, though, electronic trading systems ensure today also various functions of market control and market regulation for exchanges and clearing activities.

The *integration effect* through booking systems in the tourism industry is self-evident: previously separate booking processes (e.g., airline flight booking, car rental and hotel bookings) can be handled today in ways that link multiple enterprises. Analogous effects of an enterprise-surpassing and industry-surpassing integration of market transactions can be observed in the field of logistics (e.g., shipping agent, customs and transport insurance) and financial services (e.g., payment systems and warehousing administration).

Electronic markets, at least when they first emerge, are largely substitutes and complementary to traditional markets. Due to lower transaction costs, greater speed of conducting business or due to access to new market segments or distribution channels, electronic markets may generate new business. This scenario also suggests that old business may discontinue and sometimes traditional ways of doing business may be replaced by electronic means. Often, such change appears almost radical as it may alter drastically rather institutionalized business practices penetrating as far as the local level.

A necessary precondition for conducting business electronically is of course the total number of businesses and customers connected to widespread and nationally well distributed networks. The network structure itself may or may not enable the desired level of electronic commerce. A critical mass of connected users is essential for the creation and flourishing of an electronic market.

Once a critical mass has been achieved, vertical network services must be available to create seamless connections to other networks and their services. Various network management services are likely to follow. Once electronic markets are established, it is then possible and common that new services will be offered; often these are services that previously did not exist. Consequently, completely new markets may form offering new and added values that were not available in the past.

Expansion in Electronic Single-source Channels

Before electronic markets can manifest themselves and be realized, a critical mass of users with the appropriate electronic devices and with access to a reliable network must exist. Vertical network services as well as network management services must be available for the user. Without such a critical mass, market forces will not materialize. As an electronic market manifests itself, one must realize that initially at least such electronic transaction activities will probably serve as complementary transactions, i.e. transactions occurring in conjunction with traditional transaction practices. Moreover, one must realize, too, that electronic markets eventually become substitutive services, i.e. they become replacements for traditional transaction services and practices. In doing so, they tend to generate new business and services. Eventually old ways of doing business will fall by the wayside. Very often, in conjunction with the introduction of electronic services, new applications and entirely new services, i.e. previously unthought of services may surface as well, and, in turn, may emerge as new markets themselves.

Some growth of electronic markets, sometime just segments of markets, and hierarchies can be observed. The trade press and the academic literature cover reports and research studies frequently describing a rapid expansion in electronic single source sales channel activities. Relatively little has been reported on the expansion of electronic markets. Several explanations are advanced why this may be so:

1 *Impact of interorganizational value chains.* Organizations readily see the opportunities afforded through electronic interorganizational value chains in improving their competitiveness, especially as they focus on higher quality, increased customer satisfaction and business reengineering. Thus they choose hierarchical arrangements rather than lower cost of market transactions with less control of the

variables noted above. In this context the reader may want to review Chapters 5 and 6.

One such example is electronic supply chain integration. Buyer-supplier linkages such as electronic data integration transactions produce inventory and coordination savings for large purchasers and providers are forced to accommodate. Such arrangements often make just-in-time (JIT) delivery possible, but frequently the burden of warehousing is shifted from the buyer to the seller. Retailers such as WAL-MART and the relationships among auto manufacturers and their suppliers (Benjamin and Scott Morton, 1988) are illustrative of this trend. Numerous examples of maximized JIT production and delivery also abound (e.g., WAL-MART Stores), demonstrating that "warehousing" has been eliminated, i.e. it occurs in the form of goods or parts on trucks in transit delivery to the store or assembly line, respectively, without any storage occurring at all.

Another example is *lean production*. Processes that are highly coordinated to drive process and inventory time to a minimum (Womack, Jones and Roos, 1990) require tight electronic linkages between firms where asset-specific relationships based on assured delivery and very high quality bias firms away from electronic market transactions and push them into a direction of a small number of *partner-like* suppliers. For example, as Xerox moved to its high-quality JIT processes, it also moved its supplier base down from several thousand to several hundred.

Another example fitting the present context is *strategic alliances*. Single source sales channels such as Rosenbluth Travel have been able to expand their business through partnerships with country travel agencies where they share a common process and data base for tracking their own and each other's customers as they wind their way around the world. At the same time, Rosenbluth Travel is providing the customer with the best costs and emergency services needed in each country (Miller, Clemons and Row, 1993). This example is a clear illustration of the last evolutionary stage, i.e. shared data among partners, predicted for electronic single source sales channels (Malone, Yates and Benjamin, 1987).

2 *Fear of profit margin deterioration.* Firms are very cautious in giving up their single sales channel profit margins until it is clear that a virtual market has been created with enough participants to force their entry. This is particularly true when a market is controlled by a very small number of large corporations. In that situation each must risk sizeable segment of market share and profit margin in an electronic market. There is evidence, as in the case of the travel reservation system electronic market (APOLLO, SABRE) that the profits

of the former sales channels, i.e. the airlines themselves, are drastically reduced and the profits of the market maker remain high. Even the market maker owners, American Airlines and United Airlines, have given little evidence of being able to price tickets for their own airlines at a satisfactory margin. Bakos (1991) offers theoretical insights that the electronic market effect drives profit margin from the supplier. Additional evidence is needed to further validate this phenomenon, i.e. the consumer does very well and companies providing the production function have much of their profit margin stripped from them. Whatever profits there are accrue to the market makers. This *market maker effect* suggests a world where producers will find it hard to generate sustainable profits. It appears then that rather than forward integration into market making, innovation and differentiation of products seem to be an adequate remedy for the producer.

Despite these developments, electronic markets continue to expand in financial markets. For example, Charles Schwab's ONESOURCE mutual fund market should be mentioned here. Electronic markets expand in commodities (e.g., TELCOT) and in the travel industry from airline reservations to all travel-related reservations. Electronic markets have also expanded into niche markets where there are no large single source sales channel suppliers with high market share to protect such as spare parts for airplanes (Inventory Locator Service) (Malone, Yates and Benjamin, 1989).

Schwab's ONESOURCE mutual fund market is further evidence of the market maker effect. ONESOURCE ("The Next Giant . . .," 1994) is rapidly growing its equity in mutual funds within its market amounting to $10 billion as of February, 1994. The same source states that "For the industry as a whole, Schwab's action threatens to push down fees across the board." The mutual fund industry sees itself threatened by a market maker, i.e. Schwab, growing too large and is concerned about a significant share of its operating margin of $0.25, about half of the industry's average service charge for equity under their management, for each dollar of equity under Schwab's control, going to Schwab. The four largest no-load funds have currently in the range of $700 billion in assets under their control. Movement of only $10 billion accounts for a $25 million shift in operating margin to Schwab. To protect themselves, Fidelity, the largest of the no-load providers, has set up an equivalent market and there are several smaller markets that no-load purchasers can buy from. Schwab has introduced its own software to transfer one's own funds via a personal computer hooked to the telephone network. An additional 10% reduction in transaction fees is paid to those customers who do their own computer-based transactions. Thus the market maker effect may in fact threaten the profit position of the mutual fund industry similarly to what occurred in the airline reservation system market. Time will tell whether the pattern of profits moving to the market maker will take place in the mutual fund industry, but the financial stakes are clearly enormous.

Criteria for a Typology of Electronic Markets

Electronic markets and commerce exist in various forms. A distinction needs to be made between these two terms. Electronic commerce may include the processing of various—often *a priori* agreed upon—business activities. The notion of the electronic market, as previously emphasized, requires the at least minimal, direct involvement of human beings in making, buying, selling or preference choices or decisions. As already indicated, an electronic market that would be fully automatized would not be defined as an electronic market, but would probably better be labeled as a highly sophisticated processing system (e.g. Wigand, 1995c). As argued above, the notion of market entails also inherently human traits and values such as trust, past experiences (often *joint* past experiences), faith, confidence and credibility, all attributes that would be most difficult to capture by an automated processing system in order to make crucial decisions. It is fully acknowledged that this makes for grayish definitional areas and boundaries, yet the present attempt sheds light on this quickly emerging form of market and commerce.

When analyzing recent developments in electronic commerce, typically the access to the market is first electronic, followed by the human being. This is manifested in a number of applications that should be highlighted briefly. The highly successful QVC Shopping Network broadcasts its programs via cable and satellite television subscribers. This is largely a broadcast mode and whoever chooses to watch this channel will be exposed to the product being offered at a particular time. The consumer who is interested in purchasing the product will then have to make a phone call, place an order and pay by a credit card.

In contrast it is possible for me to place an order for a suit to be manufactured in Hong Kong electronically, i.e. I submit my precise specifications electronically or maybe they are on file already with the Hong Kong tailor. The suit can be shipped to me within a couple of days.

With the advent of the cellular telephone industry, intelligent networks and personal communication services (PCS), certain industry branches may thrive on this technology and may conduct business electronically rather than in delayed fashion via the telephone. For example, it is quite common in the construction industry that subcontractors are late, do not show up or that it is difficult to get hold of them. If a critical mass of contractors and subcontractors has, for example, a cellular phone, it is relatively easy for them to contact each other during the day, discuss the situation and make alternative plans. The traditional practice—as most subcontractors are small or medium-sized firms—was to call the subcontractor's home phone and leave a message on the answering machine or leave a message with a secretary. Then telephone tag started.

One may also view the semi-successful MINITEL project in France as an interesting form of electronic commerce. A vast number of information-related services emerged over the years, became profitable and many still prosper today. Obviously, the French government in the form of the PTT played an important role in bringing this application about by making massive initial investments assuring the formation of a critical mass and infrastructure.

Some electronic commerce is highly automated such as EDI which is a special variant of an electronic market. An initial inspection of the EDI setting might suggest that merely a very sophisticated processing system among numerous firms is at work. After all, the International Data Exchange Association defines EDI as "transfer of structured data, by agreed message standards from one computer system to another, by electronic means". On the surface, then, EDI may be viewed as a concept of interorganizational communication, yet it may also be conceived as a basis for an electronic market. When studying the initial EDI setup, one realizes quickly that numerous agreements and contracts do exist describing the conditions in considerable detail under which this form of electronic commerce is to take place. Lawyers, for example, have spent a considerable amount of time agreeing on precise conditions specifying the buying and selling of goods and services. Moreover, often these arrangements are long-term, yet allow for the adjustments and changes necessitated by prevailing market conditions. With such developments as Open EDI described above, however, EDI may take on a new role as the features of an open market enter that setting.

Electronic banking services (home banking as it is known in the US) should be recognized as they make possible the transfer of funds, bill payment, etc., but this setting is not reflective of market behavior *per se*. Home banking in this form is merely a transaction processing system made possible via third party vendors. It is still highly limited as not that many firms and banks participate, i.e. a critical mass is at best still emerging. It is by no means the electronic banking system available to every bank customer in European countries allowing with considerable ease for the transmission of funds from the customer's bank account via a central bank to the recipient's bank elsewhere.

In this context one needs to mention also SWIFT (Society for Worldwide Interbank Financial Telecommunication) as an electronic system offering efficient electronic funds transfer exclusively among banks at a national and international level. Among the exchange are also message texts describing financial transactions. SWIFT is a hierarchical communication network. At the highest level System Control Centers manage the network. Below these are a number of Slice Processors that control, store and transmit messages as network nodes and they also generate account statements and various statistical reports. Access to the entire system is offered by Regional Processors to which bank terminals are connected and they also transmit received messages and transaction data.

A typical example of an electronic market is the computer-assisted processing of stock certificates. Mertens and Griese (1991, pp. 133–135) describe the electronic functioning of the German futures market. For example, with the purchase of options or futures the following market participants can be recognized in the business process:

Customer: The buyer places a purchase with Bank A, e.g., by phone, telex or electronic mail. The seller transmits the purchase order to Bank C.

Bank A: After the customer has specified an option, Bank A can then transmit the order via a terminal to the electronic exchange.

Bank B: If Bank A is not directly connected with the clearing network, the possibility exists to place the order via a general-clearing member bank (Bank B) and to place the order on behalf of Bank A.

Bank C: For the sale of the option the purchase offer is distributed via Bank C within the electronic stock exchange.

Electronic Stock Exchange: With the help of the on-line connection to the electronic stock exchange it is possible to carry out the purchase order between both banks (Bank A and Bank B) simultaneously and bindingly.

With the aid of the data network of the electronic stock exchange a relationship exists among participating banks. The sales process occurs on-line and is stored within the electronic exchange. The actual buyer or seller does not participate directly, but is represented by Bank A or Bank C, respectively.

Consequently, there is only an indirect legal relationship between the buyer and the seller. The purchasing contract is completed via Bank A and possibly also via Bank B with the electronic exchange. The latter, in turn, completes its contract via Bank C with the seller.

The payments move from the customer via Bank A and Bank B to the clearing house of the German Stock Exchange. There a credit is issued and accounted for in conjunction with other transactions of Bank C. Any remaining balance will be transferred to Bank C which, in turn, credits the sale proceeds to the account of the seller.

Another example is presented demonstrating anticipated changes in the traditional retail market due to the forthcoming introduction of electronic interactive shopping. The example shows also how transaction patterns may change when the NII or highly sophisticated cable television shopping networks (among 500 or so cable channels) are implemented and what effects this may have on the selling price to the consumer.

Figures 7.3A and B describe the industry value chains that terminate with the consumer, as contrasted with intermediate goods value chains. Figure 7.3A illustrates three variants of an industry value chain and the Figure 7.3B shows the growth in value added and selling price for the first value chain. The actual prices presented in the figure for high-quality shirts originate from an article in *Fortune* magazine (Thornton, 1994) unrelated to electronic commerce and serve to advance arguments presented here.

- *Value chain 1.* The first value chain in Figure 7.3A describes the traditional pattern of producer, wholesaler, retailer, and consumer. When the *value added's* are summed, the consumer pays $52.72, plus the consumer's transaction costs (not figured here).
- *Value chain 2.* An alternative value chain bypasses the wholesaler and results in a price to the consumer of $41.34, again the consumer's transaction costs are not calculated here. The savings to the consumer are substantial, about 28%. In reality, because the wholesaler's costs are eliminated, the retailer can eliminate some of his margin, further reducing the selling price and the cost to the consumer.
- *Value chain 3.* Further opportunities exist when appropriate information technology can reach the consumer directly (e.g., the NII, interactive cable television shopping as described above). The manufacturer can now use the NII to leap over all intermediaries. The consumer's purchase price for the shirt will be $20.45, not including his transaction costs. The net savings amount now to about 62%. The manufacturer will surely try to retain a significant part of these savings, unless market forces make this impossible.

An alternative scenario exists when a market maker provides the consumer with direct access to a number of shirt manufacturers. In this case the electronic market effect should drive costs down to those of the lowest cost producer thus reducing the manufacturer's ability to

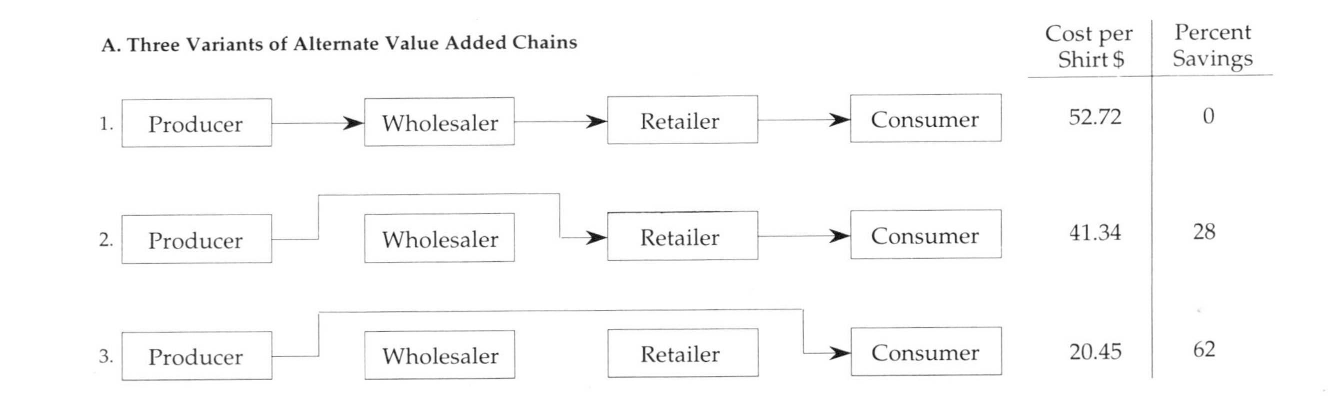

B. Growth in Value Added and Selling Price

	Producer	Wholesaler	Retailer	Consumer*
Value Added $	20.45	11.36	20.91	
Selling Price $	20.45	31.81	52.72	52.72

* Consumer transaction costs are not considered

Figure 7.3 *Value added chains in the shirt industry. Source: Reprinted from* 'Electronic Markets and Virtual Value Chains on the Information Super-highway' *by Benjamin and Wigand,* Sloan Management Review, *1995,* ***36****(2), p. 67, by permission of publisher. Copyright 1995 by the* Sloan Management Review Associated. *All rights reserved.)*

appropriate a share of the value system savings. A likely outcome is a potential shrinkage in profit margins for each of the manufacturers, as discussed already. This reduction in price will be balanced by the small profit that the market maker will make on each transaction. A final alternative may occur when:

1 the consumer, connected to the network by interacting through what is described later as the *market choice box* or set-top box, can easily access a sufficient number of single source sales channels to purchase the shirt; or
2 can accomplish the equivalent by making use of interactive agents ('Hopes and fears . . .,' 1994) to search the shirt manufacturers to come up with a shirt that satisfies the consumer's requirements. In each case the market maker effect may provide the consumer with a minimum price without a significant market maker transaction profit.

Figure 7.4 depicts an attempt to identify some criteria that may lead toward a *typology of electronic commerce* (Wigand, 1995c). The various types of electronic commerce range from one-way teleshopping broadcasts via cable and satellite channels, via automated electronic markets to electronic shopping on the Internet and the World Wide Web, to full-fledged electronic commerce utilizing an electronic market maker with a market choice box in the consumer's home. This latter stage, i.e. the probably poorest form of electronic commerce, will not be very meaningful without the application of a well-working *intelligent agent*, greatly assisting the consumer in searches, comparisons and evaluations. It appears that in all conditions the buyer's deliberate choice or decision at the time of the transaction is assumed or required. Some transactions may be automatized buying transactions.

The degree of *interactivity* is high in most electronic commerce settings. It appears also that the higher the degree of interactivity, the more perfected the electronic market might be, although one needs to realize people's limits in their willingness and desire to be interactive in some settings (Dittlea, 1995). During the last decade there has been an explosion of interactive services ranging from online networks to two-way television to telephone-based banking and investment services. They all are changing the way we inform, educate, work, play and manage our resources. Interactive services are fast changing how businesses connect with customers and suppliers. Moreover, interactive services can personalize the information people need and use it in a manner that suits them best. Interactive services are easy to use telecommunications-based services designed for information exchange, communication, transactions and entertainment. More than five million Americans subscribe to

Increasing electronic interactive capabilities →

Type of electronic commerce	Buyers' deliberate choice/decision at time of transaction	Automatized buying transactions	Degree of interactivity	Buying choice/ decision made by computer/software on behalf of buyer	Direct buying choice/decision made by human	Potential for full-fledged electronic market	Role of market maker
Teleshopping via television (e.g. QVC)	Yes	One-way only	Limited, one -way	No	Yes	High and successful, but only partially electronic	High
Automated Market (A): simple, largely automated transactions (e.g. EFT, EDI, SWIFT, Value-Added Services)	Yes and No	Largely Yes	High	Largely Yes	No	Limited, only transaction and processing system	Small
Automated Market (B): simple transactions with some human choices/ decisions required (e.g., SABRE, APPOLO, stock market transactions)	Yes	One-way only	High	Generally No	Yes	High and successful	Medium
Mobile and Wireless Cellular Phone/PCS-based applications (e.g. construction industry)	Yes	No	High	No	Yes	High	Small
Electronic Shopping (e.g. via Internet, WWW)	Yes	No	High	No	Yes	High	High
Full-Fledged Electronic Commerce utilizing electronic market maker with market-choice box (e.g. available in the future via 500 cable television systems, phone, maybe wireless, etc.)	Yes	Mainly one-way only	High	No	Yes	High	Very high

Figure 7.4 *An electronic commerce typology. Source: Wigand (1995c)*

PC-based commercial consumer online services generating annual revenues of $750 million. Voice-based telephone information services generate more than $600 million per year. Hardly a day passes in which the business page headlines do not announce another alliance or merger between telephone companies, cable companies, online service and financial service companies, and entertainment businesses. Interactive services, it appears, needs to feature four essential features in order to ensure their acceptance:

1 The device or service must replace a process that is inefficient, costly or boring.
2 Consumers must not be asked to choose between competing technologies.
3 Consumers must not feel *tracked* or that privacy is threatened.
4 Consumers must perceive that the use of the service (and information technology) is relatively easy and user-friendly.

Figure 7.4 suggests also that the more perfected the electronic commerce and as an electronic market, the less the buying choice or decision is automated or made by a computer or software on behalf of the buyer. In most forms of electronic commerce, a direct buying choice or decision is made by a human being and ultimately, such as with standard EDI, this is of course always a human decision. The role of the market maker varies considerably in the various forms of electronic commerce. The market maker's most prominent form is evident when the market maker is the driver of the electronic market and can offer single-source channels as is the case in teleshopping, electronic shopping or in the full-fledged electronic commerce situation through the use of a market choice box.

Lowering of Profit Margin Due to Electronic Markets

As more and more electronic markets emerge, competition for certain consumer products will become more competitive. It appears that certain segments of the retailing business as we know it, in the form of traditional shops and stores will be restructured and some may close entirely. The drastic reduction in transaction costs and the reduction if not elimination of market hierarchies suggest that the profit margin is likely to become smaller. At least initially when an electronic market would manifest itself as the dominant market form for a product, the market maker's profits are likely to be very high. He is not likely to pass these profits along to the consumer in the form of lower prices. When competition, however, enters the picture, the market maker is likely to lower the profit margin and prices.

New Customer Relations

Relations to customers in electronic markets are likely to be less personal and more remote. The local retailer is able to offer advice, help in customization efforts, offer delivery and installation of products and the like. These services will be difficult to replicate for market makers and manufacturers within an electronic market situation. On the other hand, entire industries might segment themselves based on the nature of products and services and the end consumer's need to have local service and support. The consumer, however, may be very willing to make sacrifices if he is able to buy the product at substantial savings electronically. Initial attempts in electronic commerce (e.g., shopping on the Internet and WWW), however, have not brought about such envisioned drastic cost savings for the consumer. The prevailing price structure so far is equivalent to catalogue shopping prices. In order to establish strong customer relationships and loyalty, new means need to be invented to foster such loyalty. Real and perceived advantages must be created before such buying behavior is likely to develop a critical mass. Security and privacy must be ensured and perceived as such by potential buyers. Incentives need to be created that would encourage a buyer to become a regular electronic buyer.

THE ROLE OF INFORMATION AND COMMUNICATION TECHNOLOGIES AND CHANNELS

An Emerging Information Infrastructure

Numerous information technologies and their applications are converging and the previously clear delineations among computing, telephony, television and publishing are blurring. This convergence is permitting the development of an information infrastructure, often called the National Information Infrastructure or the *information superhighway.* This is the seamless web of communication networks, computers, databases and consumer electronics, largely built, owned and operated by the private sector in the United States.

The development of this superhighway is generally agreed to be slow and arduous. Its evolution is described as being analogous to an increasingly steep slope that society has been climbing since the early communication networks were established. Although a complex web of fiber optics, wires, cables, satellites and other communication technologies already connect existing telephones, televisions, radios, computers and facsimile machines, the information superhighway is expected to integrate these services into an advanced, high-speed, interactive, broadband and digital communication system. While industry is beginning to build this information superhighway, little is known about how it will be structured and what services it will provide. On the other hand, a common vision of its capabilities seems to be emerging among industry experts, policy makers and public interest groups.

Changes with Distribution Channels

Traditional distribution channels such as retail stores will change and even their very existence may be questioned. New electronic sales channels are being conceived via bank-owned electronic transmission systems. Banks are exploring radically new ways of selling their products. An increasing range of transactions can be carried out entirely via electronic media. For cost reasons, European and US banks, and especially their customers may prefer to dispense with personal service altogether for certain types of business. Nonetheless, for the present time nationwide branch networks will remain one of the strengths of most banks everywhere. Discount brokers started to set up shop in 1994 or sooner in most European countries while concentrating on securities business or financial investment in the broader sense. Since then commercial banks are planning to broaden the range of banking products that are offered by telephone and electronic media. Branch networks vary considerably internationally when comparing the number of inhabitants per branch office. The United States reports the number of inhabitants in a city area per bank office as averaging 2419; Italy as 3030; the United Kingdom as 2958; followed by France with 2212 and Canada with 2045; Germany reports 1633 and Switzerland 1631, followed by Belgium with 954. It is desirable, on the one hand, for banks to reduce their total number of branches if it is possible to offer electronic services and if the customer is willing to shift to such services, as transaction costs are bound to be cheaper. Direct banking then, in the form of home banking mentioned above, is bound to have far-reaching consequences. If direct banking is to take root, further technological improvements are needed. Above all, a larger clientele has to be willing to accept the new approach and services. This is no small accomplishment, as often electronically envisioned services (when offered) may be ahead of their time or customers simply do not perceive them as more convenient. Commerzbank AG, for example, estimate that in 1995 only about one-tenth of its banking customers in Germany to be potential users of direct banking products. Such telephone and home-banking services call for sizable expenditures in information technology by banks which are naturally wary about investing in technologies that may not yet have been perfected. All of these deliberations about new electronic sales channels suggest that the size of banks' branch networks will remain an important competitive advantage for several years to come. The new sales channels for bank products will thus complement rather than supplant the traditional branches for the time being.

When analyzing this situation in terms of competitive advantage, it appears that in the case of Germany, for example, these large branch networks maintained by banks currently constitute a competitive advantage *vis-à-vis* the electronic sales channels. Even though banking regulations in Germany have been fairly liberal, new market entrants in the form of foreign banks have merely attained a market share of 5%, the lowest in any major industrial country with the exception of Japan. In view of these large branch networks maintained by local banks and the high quality of service they provide, foreign banks have traditionally been fairly reluctant to enter the retail banking market in Germany. This may change of course once more banking business can be taken care of electronically and directly from business premises or from customers' homes.

Electronic distribution channels are also undergoing drastic changes in the form of competition and mergers. These electronic channels struggle with the demands and whims of the customers, with concerns in offering their services *universally* (universal access), and other issues. Featuring prominently among these distribution channels are cable and telephone companies who seem to pay more attention trying to invade each other's markets than forming joint ventures in order to conquer new markets jointly.

These firms still do not know what level of interactivity is appropriate for today's consumers, nor does one generally know what consumers are willing to pay for services and how to deliver them at an attractive price. Several research efforts and actual trials have demonstrated that in order to connect the consumer such that video-on-demand would be possible, shopping via their cable system or to be able to retrieve and play video games a very high investment of up to $1700 per user is required. Moreover, some market researchers have found that consumers are not willing to pay more than about $10 per month in addition to their existing cable television fees for such services. Once truly interactive information and entertainment networks come about, merchants are likely to find a place in an electronic shopping mall or information mall where advertisers may pay for commercials. Several major firms have just stepped forward and made considerable investments in this area.

Clearly a digital signal is needed and a set-top box (market choice box) in each home to process these signals. Making a present cable network one-way digital is said to cost around $250 per home, plus some additional costs for the set-top box. Such one-way digital networks are said to be pseudo-interactive, meaning that the end receiver can send some limited digital information to a designated place via the cable system. Industry experts estimate, however, that for a truly interactive digital network, more than twice these costs need to be calculated. A true digital network can offer up to 500 channels and most US cable networks are gradually upgrading their systems in this fashion. Fully interactive networks, then, still have to prove their true commercial worth.

On the telephone system side, companies face a different problem. Most of the telephone networks are built of fiber optic cable with more capacity than the cable companies can dream of, but the last few meters to the home are all copper wire that some have compared to a mere sipping straw. Telephone companies then have a difficult choice: they can either replace these copper wires at an estimated cost of about $1000 per home or make the best of what they have. Several telephone companies are building digital factories (e.g., Bell Atlantic at $200 million) to produce multi-media content for future networks; some companies (e.g., USWest at $10 billion) are planning on rewiring their customers for interactive television.

Local telephone companies in the United States are deregulated through the 1996 Telecommunications Act and are open for competition. Telephone companies are allowed to enter new territory such as mobile telephony and cable television, but these are relatively smaller markets. If US cable television firms were to take over 30% of the local telephone market, they would capture a $20 billion market. Conversely, if the telephone companies were to take over 30% of the cable market, they would have gained a mere $8 billion market. One big unknown factor in these deliberations is, as already mentioned, the open question what ordinary homeowners will be willing to pay for new interactive services. The Time-Warner video-on-demand trials in Florida showed very quickly that families must be willing to spend $50 extra in addition to their current monthly entertainment budget before video-on-demand could ever become economically viable. The trials were broken off prematurely, as it became quickly obvious that people in Florida were unwilling to spend this additional amount per month or to shift $50 from other entertainment services.

New Demands on Information Technology and Markets: Requirements and Possibilities for Electronic Commerce

These new demands are numerous and multifaceted. A few deserve to be highlighted. We have already addressed the notion of interactivity with newer information technologies and how consumers related to it. We can recognize very formidable demands such as video-on-demand bringing along a challenging bandwidth and switching problem. This begs the question whether or not video-on-demand, for example, should be available nationwide to every citizen, no matter if the person resides in a major metropolitan area or lives in a remote rural area. Should there be a universal service? Will our policies create an information-rich (and with that maybe an information-poor) segment of society? In addition, one could mention numerous standards problems and questions that need to be solved nationally and internationally (e.g., Wigand, 1988c). The list of demands on information and communication technologies seems to be endless and we are likely to build the technology before we will fully understand how to use, manage and regulate it.

To describe these new demands on information technology and markets, many of which have yet to emerge, a likely scenario can be envisioned, especially in conjunction with the building of the NII, that incorporates electronic commerce. The scenario presented below addresses specifically the likely emergence of the electronic marketing and electronic consumer purchasing process. Figure 7.5 depicts the stakeholders of this process and their connections to the NII. Because much of electronic commerce requires both physical and information goods transport, the existence of the physical transportation infrastructure (rail, road and air) is assumed but not depicted.

Figure 7.5 demonstrates an information highway infrastructure connecting the following:

- *Producers of information goods,* including computer software, books, movies, music and the like. All of these are or have the potential to be maintained in digital form and transmitted over the NII on demand with little or no requirement for physical inventory movement.
- *Producers of physical goods,* including minimally all manufactured good categories now sold through catalogues and additionally those where computer technology can simplify product complexity and reduce asset-specificity.
- *Electronic retailers,* taking numerous forms, e.g., catalog merchandisers such as Land's End, specialty retailers such as Blockbuster or multi-product retailers such as Sears, Macy's, etc.
- *Electronic markets.* Market makers would build on existing electronic markets in the travel and financial industries and expand into specialty niches such as shirts, personal computer software or baseball cards.

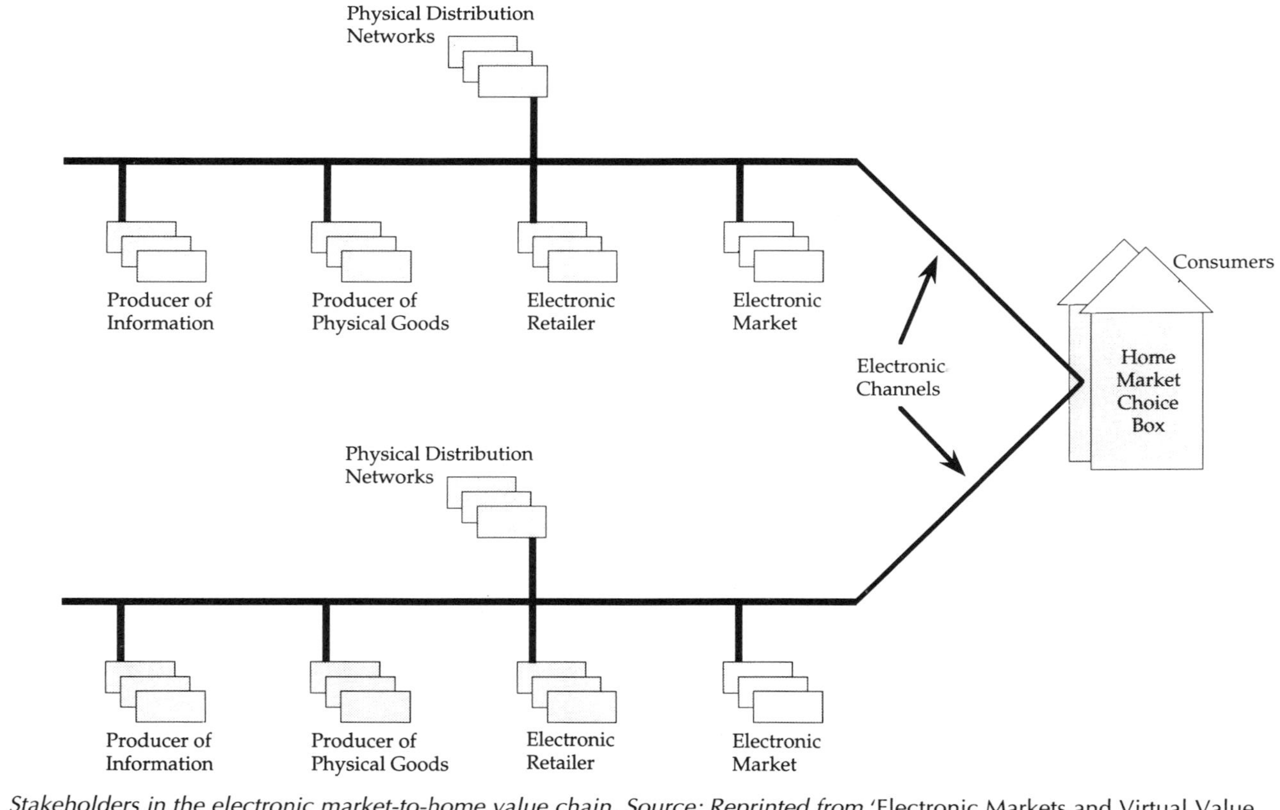

Figure 7.5 *Stakeholders in the electronic market-to-home value chain. Source: Reprinted from* 'Electronic Markets and Virtual Value Chains on the Information Superhighway', *Benjamin and Wigand,* Sloan Management Review, *1995,* **36**(2), *p. 68, by permission of publisher.*

- *Physical distribution networks.* Today's complex physical distribution between the components of the industry value chain and consumer may well be simplified to the movement from manufacturer to the consumer directly or coordinated by electronic retailer or market maker transactions. If this were to occur, the physical distribution system of the future may well resemble the process by which the catalogue vendors move their goods to the consumer, mostly through such companies as Federal Express and United Parcel Service. Where delivery times greater than same day are satisfactory, such companies are capable of providing the desired service. Within the US any parcel can be shipped anywhere within five working days. Next-day and in some circumstances same-day delivery is possible. Where time-based asset-specificity requires faster movement of goods to the consumer, variants such as the ability to order the week's supermarket purchase and then drive to the supermarket depot to pick up one's order will potentially emerge and have been tested already.
- *Electronic channels.* Electronic channels are the cable, fiber optic, telephone and wireless and electric/gas utility companies. All are capable of providing electronic access to the home.
- *The market choice box at home.* The market choice box or set-top box, the device through which the consumer will be able to select information via an intelligent agent, is located at the receiving end in the home and it is from here that the vast amount of electronic commerce is channeled and controlled. The market choice box provides interactive access to the many markets the consumer may be interested in: entertainment, sports, shopping, libraries, education, medicine, government information, etc. The market choice box will evolve from the current cable television selection box through a series of incremental implementation, each designed to serve a transition stage of the NII's evolution. Moreover, the market choice box will feature considerable built-in intelligence making consumer preferences, profile and customization of services possible.

Figure 7.6 suggests that the market choice box is a server managing the configuration of workstations, telephones and televisions in the home (Benjamin and Wigand, 1995, p. 69). It provides the telecommunications interface to those channels that reach the home directly. We may presume that the market choice box will present the consumer with a choice of markets and other activities such as entertainment, shopping, surfing on the Internet or getting health information. How the primary graphical user interface (GUI) will be designed is anyone's guess at the moment, but what is important is not to bias the consumer to one choice

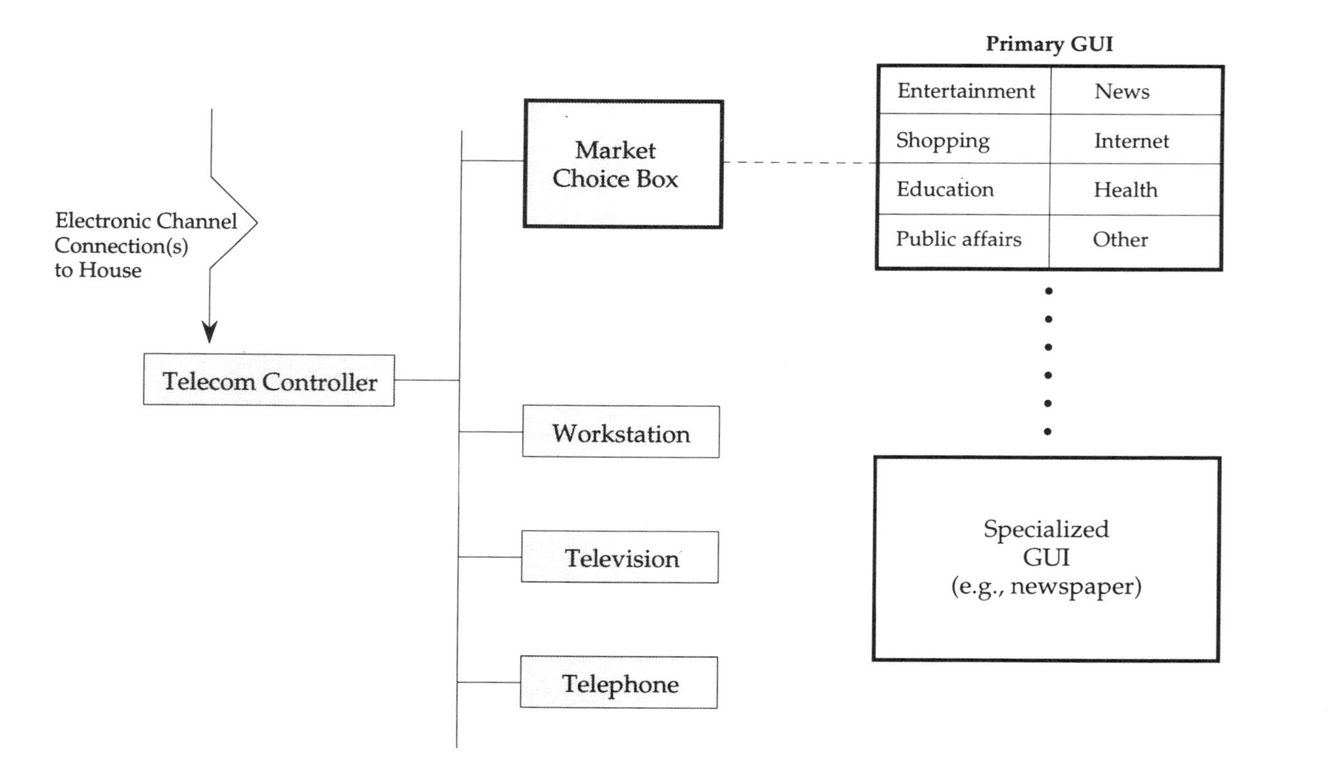

Figure 7.6 *Interfaces of the market choice box. Source: Reprinted from* 'Electronic Markets and Virtual Value Chains on the Information Superhighway', *Benjamin and Wigand*, Sloan Management Review, *1995, (**36)(2), p. 69, by permission of publisher. Copyright 1995 by the*** Sloan Management Review Associated. *All rights reserved.*

over another, as did the initial airline reservation systems in terms of flight choice. Gilder (1993) suggests that the ideal GUI may be the newspaper format, as it is an interface designed for human interaction having served the test of time. Analogously, we read the headline, skip to sports, back to the financial page, in between advertisements catch our attention and we would like to go deeper into them and get more information about products. The primary GUI may also be personalizable or customizable depending on how we configure our priorities, needs for information and lifestyles. The figure also suggests that each class of market choice may require a GUI ideally set up to help each explore its potential.

One potential metaphor for the market choice box is General Magic's TELESCRIPT user interface (Levy, 1994, p. 107):

> "The interface has evolved to a geographical depiction of a portion of cyberspace . . . a virtual world where one can conduct all sorts of transactions, gather objects, and above all, maintain a sense of place. To buy things go *Downtown* and into the *Electronic Shopping Mall*. To scan newspapers go to the *Newsstand*. Eventually the local pizza shop will show up on your personal *Main Street* . . ."

Such an intelligent interface would, for example, let the consumer send out an interactive agent into the *Travel Store* on *Main Street* that would make flight reservations and purchase flight tickets. In this scenario the interactive agent would act as a pseudo-electronic market potentially by-passing APOLLO, SABRE and travel agents. One might speculate that a user interface owner, such as General Magic, would like to appropriate a portion of the resultant value system and market maker savings rather than share them with the consumer.

Thus the market choice box and the standards associated with choice (e.g., labeling of catalog items, the marketing of client and server software for products such as TELESCRIPT) can all affect openness of information and market access.

The consumer is the wildcard in this scenario and analysis. Transaction cost theory requires that an economizing transaction takes place satisfying both parties. There is some evidence, as discussed above in conjunction with catalogue and television shopping networks, that the consumer will choose alternate forms of transactions to retail store-based transactions in favor of price, high quality, selection choice, convenience and savings.

The potential changes in consumer behavior as they take advantage of transaction cost opportunities made possible by the NII are on such a large scale and the current electronic transaction capabilities afforded to the consumer are in such a rudimentary form that our understanding of the consumer's future behavior is at best cloudy (Benjamin and Wigand, 1995).

This suggests a three-tiered evolution of the NII to a model consisting of multiple electronic channel connections to the home, connections to electronic switch and brokerage services and connections to application and products available on the NII. Such a model is consistent with the evolution of the electronic market and it interconnects with the consumer as described above.

MANAGEMENT PERSPECTIVES OF BORDERLESS AND BOUNDARY-LESS ELECTRONIC COMMERCE

Much attention has been paid to the unfolding Global Information Infrastructure (GII) in terms of structure, how it will take shape, who will be its drivers and the impact it is likely to have on society and the way commerce is done in a global market place, all of this, maybe, in a borderless electronic world. This envisioned GII is to provide us with unlimited amounts of information via data, voice, image and video anywhere and any time. This new world undoubtedly will have profound impacts on our social, economic and political life. The development of the GII, however, will be closely linked to the market forces of rather routine economic laws of supply and demand. This boils down to the economic interplay among three factors: consumers, services and an encouraging regulatory framework (Wigand, 1996, 1995a). Consumers must exist in the market who are willing to buy services they need. Moreover, these consumers who must have the services still need to come to grips with how the information available will fit their needs and what they are willing to pay for these. There is also the question of high bandwidth networks as in the video-on-demand situation: Should farmer Jones in Nebraska, living 100 miles from any sizable city, have the same access to video-on-demand as citizens and businesses in downtown Chicago? At the present time one could argue that there is little that cannot be delivered over copper or coaxial cable while using traditional technologies. Network and service providers then would engage in a risky gamble if they were to build high bandwidth information highways to homes at the present time. Supply and demand, as was suggested above, are not sufficient alone to encourage development, but government too must contribute here in the form of a favorable regulatory environment encouraging investment. In that sense regulators worldwide need to cooperate and work together to shape an appropriate global framework making global commerce, ideally in a borderless world, possible (Wigand, 1996). This implies that we need to do away with patchwork quilt-like national regulatory practices with often regional and trading block controls. Building the GII implies free competition with a bare minimum of regulatory controls. This vision has been stated well by the National Telecommunications and Information Administration (NTIA), a branch of the US Department of Commerce. In essence, this agency has argued that these issues apply just as much for the development of the NII in the United States, as well as for an emerging GII. The NTIA has developed five essential principles: a flexible regulatory framework, competition, open access, private investment and universal service.

It may take time and considerable investments but most observers agree that there is no doubt that our computer, television and some machines not yet dreamed of will one day be a two-way window to the world through which we can tweak our bank accounts, order groceries or broadcast our own views to anyone who is willing to listen. Many of these things are already possible today, but maybe not yet in a user-friendly fashion.

The effects of these developments will be modest at first, probably more modest than has been predicted, as is usually the case with newer information technologies. Most newer information technology is used initially to replace familiar tasks, i.e. they may perform familiar tasks better and cheaper (Wigand, 1985a). Thus the $4–$5 billion home-shopping market which McKinsey and other consulting firms have predicted in the United States in 2003 will involve not new retail spending, but a switch of customers from shops and catalogues to computers and interactive television (Wigand, 1996). An additional built-in dilemma here is that these new services not only need to cover their basic costs in terms of actual service provision, they also need to be priced such that they can recover the cost of building the network that delivers them in the first place. In essence, the entertainment that many expect to be beamed into people's homes some day must not only replace the trip to the local video store, but it must persuade customers to spend more on those pleasures than they are now. It appears that his behavioral change will come with time, especially when completely new services are being offered and applications are possible that we still have not dreamed of, and when users realize the added value to be gained via these services and new applications. Historically the same was true with other technologies such as the steam engine.

The perspectives presented and the implications for management here are the realization that the world of economics is essentially borderless, as well as boundary-less and those who do not see this will create more difficulties for themselves and their organizations than otherwise. Kenichi Ohmae (1995, 1991) has eloquently argued this perspective and has expressed the need to work toward a global economy and a global logic. Those organizations wishing to remain competitive and use strategy to their advantage will seek a balance among the strategic triangle, according to Ohmae, the triad region including the United States, Europe and Japan.

Almost all aspects of human existence come down to an issue of economics; whether this is good or bad is uncertain. The fact remains that if human existence is held in the power of economy, then the national and international organizations of the world must turn their focus outward rather than remain internally focused (Wigand, 1996). Many of today's organizations focus only on those improvements that are internal and are not creating a management perspective seeking a globally united economy. A novel way of thinking must be established focusing not only on the internal, but one lending itself to a better understanding of the external environment as well. In a borderless world the key is a balanced combination of both perspectives. Only those organizations that alter their outlook of management to combine both environments shall remain competitive in the global market of tomorrow's world. Electronic commerce, it seems, will be one major contributor toward shaping this borderless and boundary-less world of economics.

8

Overcoming the Boundaries of Location: Telecooperation and Virtual Enterprises

THE BASIC CONCEPT OF ORGANIZATIONS WITH DISPERSED WORK LOCATIONS

Business textbooks tend to depict organizations as integrated, systematically organized and relatively solid structures. In reality rigid hierarchies are changing into flat and modular structures (see Chapter 5). Traditional organizational boundaries are dissolving, creating symbiotic and interconnected enterprises with a network structure (Chapter 6). Through the gradual dissolution of temporal and spatial constraints, technical infrastructures are revolutionizing market places (Chapter 7) and enterprises (Chapter 8). This chapter examines various possibilities of changing organization structures. The appropriate deployment of specific information technology makes these changes possible. The dissolution of spatial constraints and the accompanying requirements and implications for organizations in order to achieve task and performance outcomes are addressed.

Location Problems in Organization Theory: An Appropriate Approach?

Organization theory traditionally interprets the choice of a location as a constitutive decision usually made when a firm is first established. Decisions concerning location, legal forms, organization structures, and the eventual growth of an enterprise influence organizational processes of performance and commercialization (see Kappler and Rehkugler, 1991; Steiner, 1993). Since Alfred Weber (1909), known as the founder of classic location theory, numerous location theories have been developed. Essentially, these theories analyze and systematize the factors influencing location decisions, i.e. location factors. In addition, they look into the development of decision models for making location determinations. Regardless of the nature of the location problem, the main goal is usually "optimizing" the location among a set of relevant location factors. Minimizing transportation costs still plays a major role in these theoretical deliberations, often in contrast to actual business practices.

Once the best possible location has been identified, organization theory simply considers spatial arrangements as part of the organizational framework. As a consequence, traditional organization and management theories placed little emphasis on spatial arrangements. These organization theories do not solve specifics on how to coordinate the coordination problems related to distributed or mobile task accomplishment. Likewise, management theories typically ignore the management of "invisible" employees, those who are not at the same time at the same place as their superiors.

This treatment of the time/space aspects in the division of labor should not only be noticeable in the discussion of new developments. Problem solving has always taken place in the context of spatial distribution and mobility. Also, organizations have always used special technologies and mechanisms to coordinate the division of labor in such settings. Nevertheless, we are challenged by fundamentally new phenomena: new developments in information technology, especially in the areas of distributed applications, Computer Supported Cooperative Work (CSCW), mobile information technology systems and multimedia applications. These developments not only improve the possibilities for cooperative work and coordination, *in spite of* the spatial and temporal dispersion of the individuals involved, but also provide more opportunities for spatial and temporal independence *in spite of* joint task accomplishment.

Based on these deliberations, we can no longer be concerned primarily with the search for the "one best place" for the production of goods and services. It is much more important to know and critically discuss the acute and future possibilities for the dispersed and location-independent work place.

"The Worldwide Group": A Scenario for the Future of Work

In order to understand these developments we have to envision an ordinary working day for Tara Rodgers by shifting 10–15 years into the future. Rodgers works for the "Worldwide Group" (management consultants) and is jointly responsible for a marketing campaign, which has to be accomplished in less than eighteen hours. This scenario (according to Jarvenpaa and Ives, 1994) illustrates one aspect of the future employment world. It gives us an idea about how dealing with information could be within changed technical, organizational, legal and social settings. Information activity will change radically, unlike the physical transport of goods and people: a transatlantic flight will still take at least five hours. On-board food and drinks will be served in the usual manner. Communication systems support and partially replace transport systems, without hindering mobility.

"As the pilot retracted the 787's landing gear, passenger Tara Rodgers linked her personal assistant to the onboard computer built into the armrest. Although this plane's systems were no longer state of the art, the display screen was larger and of higher resolution than that available on her assistant system. It also provided access to the airline's electronic amenities. She chose to tune into the airline's audio system, which provided capabilities similar to those engineered into her personal assistant—connection to the in-flight entertainment, the ability to listen to ground control, as well as the special circuitry required to eliminate the plane's background noise. She touched an icon on the screen in front of her and called up the in-flight service menu. She cancelled dinner, and eliminated such non-essential messages from the flight personnel as the pilot's sightseeing instructions. She requested a glass of port for two hours later. She did not expect her electronic documents to attract the attention of the European Community's customs and immigration systems, but she authorized the system to wake her if an onboard interview with immigration officials was requested. By speaking softly into a microphone plugged into the armrest, she completed her custom's declaration electronic forms. The flight number, date and trip duration had already been completed by the airline's computers. She wondered if the customs people knew, or even cared, about the massive knowledge base and expert systems that were contained in her personal assistant system or the wealth of information and tools that were immediately accessible using the worldwide data network to which her firm subscribed.

Rodgers barely noticed the selection of soft classical music that served as background to her audio system. Her personal profile, stored in her assistant—or was it the airline's frequent flier database—had chosen the type of music and preset the volume based on her personal preferences. The personal profile would also suggest that her morning coffee be served with cream but not sugar. With the touch of another icon, Rodgers began to make arrangements for her brief stay in Oxford. This was a spur of the moment transatlantic crossing, so she had left with no hotel reservation. The electronic reservation agent her firm subscribed to had meanwhile booked her into the charming guest house she had been so delighted with during her last visit to Oxford. Using her travel agent's virtual reality simulator, she wandered into the rooms with open doors (i.e. available to be rented this evening) and selected one with lovely pink wallpaper, a canopied bed, and a view of one of the colleges. She then booked a car to pick her up at Heathrow and transport her to Oxford. She could have looked at a short video segment showing where to meet the cab. Closer to the time of arrival, she could even look at a prerecorded introduction to her driver or talk to him or her directly. Assuming on-time-arrival, which the onboard computer informed her was 95% likely, and normal early morning traffic, she would arrive in Oxford five hours before her meeting with Professor Fearl and the prospective customer. For the first two hours of the flight there was a great deal of work that needed to be completed. But first she called home to talk to her husband and proudly watched her littlest one take a few more faltering steps around the living room. (. . .)

With a touch she activated her electronic messaging system and listened again to the message from a senior partner of her consulting firm that had prompted this sudden trip to London. 'Tara, this morning I was forwarded from our London office a message that had come in from Professor Frank Fearl at Templeton College at Oxford. Fearl is a well known B-School academician with the ear of many of Europe's CEOs. Apparently over the years Fearl has worked closely with our UK and European offices on a number of projects that have proven mutually beneficial to us, Fearl, and clients. London believes that Fearl may have the inside track on a most promising opportunity, but we need to move quickly and decisively.'

'The prospective customer is Empire Software, a UK-headquartered firm that specializes in the production of integrated software systems for the international freight business. Sir Thomas Baker-Knight, CEO of Empire, is in residence at Templeton College for three days attending a Managing Directors' forum. Over coffee, Baker-Knight expressed a concern to Professor Fearl that his firm is not embracing the tumultuous advances in software engineering and that his management team is poorly prepared to respond to competitive threats from a variety of unexpected quarters. In an informal discussion, Baker-Knight expressed considerable interest in a tailor-made educational offering for the firm's top 100 employees. Fearl has set up a follow-up meeting with Baker-Knight for tomorrow afternoon at Templeton to explore this further. He thinks that with quick action, we might be able to land this without an arms-length call-for-proposal process. Fearl suggests a joint effort between Templeton and Worldwide, where we would use our contracts to supply expertise not available to Templeton. (. . .) I've checked your availability over the next two days and it appears that we can reassign most of your responsibilities to other associates. Hopefully, you can pick up the remainder from your airplane seat or hotel room. Your contact person in the UK is Jeremy Wainright, a partner in our London office.' (. . .)

Rodgers then listened to the forwarded messages from Professor Fearl and from Jeremy Wainwright in the London office. (. . .)

While she waited, Rodgers prompted the assistant to identify an initial list of individuals who might add value to the program. Using just her firm's data base, she checked on availability over the next six months and watched video clips of several professors working with an executive audience. She called one in Oregon who had worked with her and Baker-Knight years before. His enthusiasm for the planned program and obvious respect and fondness for Baker-Knight were so great that she asked him if she could use his automatically recorded remarks, and contagious smile, during her presentation tomorrow. Rodgers then contacted Cinko Kolors, a multi-media services company to which her firm often outsourced graphics work. Cinko Kolors front-ended for a variety of small, often one-person, graphics consultants that tended to work out of small towns, artists' colonies, resort locations. These graphic artists provided multi-media artistic talent while Cinko Kolors marketed services, kept the artists' technology up to date, took care of the bookkeeping, and provided technical expertise and training. Inducements from the Singapore government, coupled with that island nation's superior information technology infrastructure, had led Cinko Kolors to establish their legal headquarters there.

Cinko Kolors ensured that the customers received worldwide presentation consistency, copyright clearances, a standard of quality, and onsite presentations equipment for the end user. Because of the lateness of the hour and short time horizon, Cinko Kolors first offered Rodgers an artist on Kuai. Rodgers viewed several short segments of the artist's work and then, using Cinko Kolor's data base, gained assurance of his ability to deliver in a timely fashion. From her own firm's files Rodgers retrieved and reviewed a previous project for which this same artist had received high marks. Satisfied, Rodgers forwarded logos from her own firm, as well as that of Empire along with names, titles, pictures of Templeton, pictures of Empire's corporate headquarters, and the information that would permit the artist to access the previous multi-media presentation. Cinko Kolors would collect, and share with the original multi-media design consultant, a standard fee if that presentation were modified for reuse. Through the next hour Rodgers and the multi-media artist discussed the initial story board for the ten-minute marketing presentation. Site venues, talent presentation clips, and segments from her would be forwarded to a companion multimedia artist in London who would complete the work. The final rough cut of the promotional piece would be available for Rodger's review upon arrival in Oxford. Cinko Kolors would ensure that presentation equipment was available both at her guest house and at Templeton. That would still leave several hours for final edits and perhaps even inputs from Fearl, Wainwright, the firm's European managing director, or the Japanese partner who had supervised the Tokyo project and was now cruising the Caribbean.

Rodgers wrote up a summary of her activities thus far and forwarded it and the various working documents and contact people to Wainright and The Worldwide Group's data base. She also took the liberty of recording a 5.30 a.m. wake up call for him. If the human resource profile on him was accurate, she could trust him to pick up the ball and move it forward while she caught a little sleep. She set a relative wake up call for herself for 45 minutes before the plane touched down in London. Her personal profiler would ensure that a gentle voice would awake her with some sweet words of encouragement.

As the flight attendant arrived with the port wine, Rodgers reviewed the personal assistant's profile of Tom Baker-Knight. When she came to work for The Worldwide Group, the information in her old portable had been transferred to the assistant and, for all she knew, to the Group's central data banks. Although she had been far less experienced in those days, she had the sense to record the wine Baker-Knight had ordered and so much enjoyed five years before. She forwarded the name and year to Wainwright, who with his alleged penchant for detail, perhaps might be motivated to get an Oxford wine merchant to embellish the Templeton College wine cellar before tomorrow's meeting. Sipping her port with some satisfaction, she downloaded a short story into the audio system and reclined the seat.

Tara Rodgers airplane 'office', and the other nodes she interacts with illustrate the essence of a dynamic network: a globally dispersed and dynamic web of knowledge nodes drawn together on a one-time basis to address a unique problem. A knowledge node can be an individual knowledge worker, a team of knowledge workers, and/or an independent organization. Among the knowledge nodes making up the web in our scenario are Tara Rodgers, Jeremy Wainright, Cinko Kolors, their graphic artists, a graduate student at Irvine, and the Japanese partner aboard the cruise ship in the Caribbean. Knowledge nodes have their own distinctive competency. For instance, the Cinko Kolors' knowledge node adds value that cannot easily be provided by the various artists the firm represents." (*Jarvenpaa and Ives, 1994*, "The Global Network Organization", *in* Journal of Management Information Systems, *1994, Vol. 4, pp. 30–34. Reprinted by permission from M.E. Sharpe, Inc., Armonk, NY 10504.)*

This scenario gives us an idea of what new types of problem solving and task accomplishments may arise based on new and future technology. Perhaps some of them (e.g., technological) will be achieved more quickly than others, some of them (e.g., organizational) more slowly, and others will be accomplished quite differently than depicted here. Nevertheless, the example of the "Worldwide Group" gives us some indication of future organizational forms such as the "Global Web" (Reich, 1991) or *virtual organizations* (Davidow and Malone, 1992).

This organizational form explodes the classical boundaries of the firm, not only with respect to space and time, but also from a legal perspective. The coordination of tasks no longer takes place in static or predefined structures. A problem-specific and dynamic linking of actual resources occurs for the accomplishment of specific tasks. This is an organizational form that in part, and also in its entirety, may be shortlived and transitory, e.g., it may entirely dissolve after the problem is solved or is capable of adapting itself through a dynamic reconfiguration to meet highly variable task demands.

Thus, virtual organizations are considered to be more "spider webs" rather than networks. They are counterparts to organizations with relatively well-defined contractual and ownership boundaries, stable locations, relatively permanent resource assignments, and controlled process structures. According to Aristotelian philosophy, the virtual organization can be understood as the idealized goal of a boundary-less organization (Legrand, 1972, p. 269). It may also be understood as an organizational form that considers virtuality in the same sense as information systems researchers might, i.e. as a concept of performance improvement. Moreover, this perspective recognizes a systematic and dynamic attribution to concrete locations where the actual work takes place (see Mowshowitz, 1991; Szyperski and Klein, 1993).

Following we will first address the fundamental aspects of the dissolution of work location, as well as questions pertaining to the motivation for and organizational manifestations of dispersed work locations. The virtual organization as a specific result of telecooperative work forms is presented later (see page 337).

"Anytime/Anyplace": Improving Organizational Adaptability

The "Worldwide Group" scenario depicted only a few examples of potential work situations. In the future, we will still work not only on airplanes, but at desks, in shops and on construction sites. Human beings, not data bases, will continue to carry relevant, personal and confidential information. It is not necessarily a given that this organizational form of task accomplishment will provide the most suitable environment for human beings and the most economically efficient organizational form. The choice of the most efficient organizational models always depends on the characteristics and the context of the assignment. We need, therefore, a systematic conceptualization of spatial and temporal options as a basis for their organizational use. A particularly simple and graphically pleasing conceptualization is the "Anytime/Anyplace Matrix" (see Figure 8.1).

This four-square map describes a two-dimensional differentiation between time and space, depending on whether the interaction takes place at the same location or at different locations, at the same time (*synchronous*) or at different times (*asynchronous*). These settings can be grouped into four situation types. Accordingly, current technologies which support cooperation (e.g., groupware) can be assigned to each square in Figure 8.1. Considering today's developments one needs to expand this model by the dimension "mobility." A number of information technologies have evolved that enable and support location-independent, mobile work forms, i.e. going beyond the dispersed work location, yet stationary cooperation.

What does "Anytime/Anyplace" mean for the future organization of production processes based on the division of labor? It means that when accomplishming tasks we will still need to consider time- and place-related work configurations. Organization design rules will not be replaced by the new technological developments, but the flexibility of organizational design will be extended. This extended freedom confronts organization theory with new questions: These are questions of

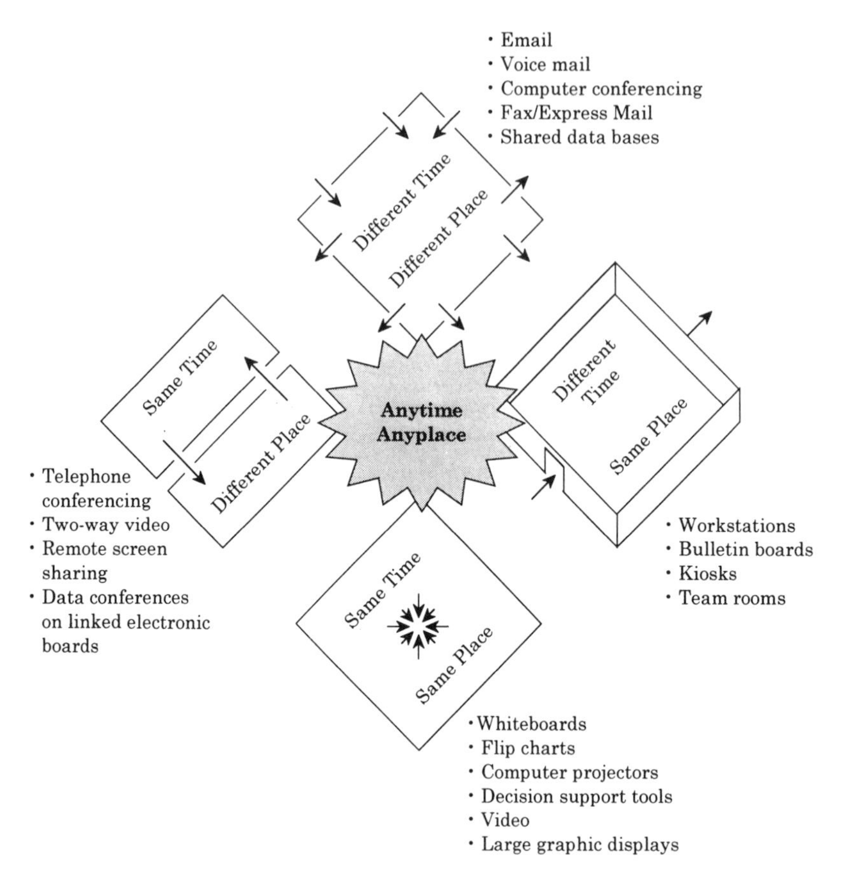

Figure 8.1 *Anytime/Anyplace matrix. Source: O'Hara-Devereaux and Johansen (1994, p. 199. Reproduced by permission from Jossey-Bass Inc., San Francisco.)*

allocation of tasks and coordination as far as distribution and independence of location is concerned.

As discussed before, organization is always then necessary whenever an assigned task cannot be accomplished by one person in a single step. In this context, organization has three aspects:

1 dividing tasks appropriately
2 coordinating the execution of the individual activities and
3 providing motivation during task accomplishment.

It follows that organization is the reciprocal interplay among division of task, coordination and motivation. *The accomplishment of an assigned task requires the accomplishment of coordination tasks and motivation tasks*. New information technologies assist in accomplishing assigned tasks (IT as *production technology*, see Malone, 1988), in overcoming coordination tasks (IT as *coordination technology*, Malone, 1988), as well as in designing motivation systems (see Picot, Ripperger and Wolff, 1996). They are increasingly emerging as a platform for the accomplishment of tasks (IT as *mediating technology*, Ciborra, 1993). In this case, the spectrum of organization design alternatives cannot be discussed without explicitly addressing the issues of time and space.

The Necessity of Spatial Proximity as an Obstacle of Dispersed Work Situations

Spatial proximity is the decisive characteristic of "same time/same place" organizations for people involved in accomplishing tasks under the division of labor, in contrast to organizations with dispersed work locations or those that are location-independent. Today, not enough is known about the actual *meaning* of spatial proximity and its non-existence, as well as about the *possibilities of its substitution* in the context of organizational task accomplishment. Obviously, spatial distance is foremost a communication problem when accomplishing these tasks.

Chapter 3 demonstrated the importance of the spatial setting of the communication partners, task-specific communication requirements, and the choice of appropriate communication means (see page 78). Task-specific requirements of communication channels need to be considered and specified from a user's perspective. This is where the problem of organizations with dispersed work locations becomes obvious: certain types of problems, especially those which lack focus and are complex, generally demand synchronous, verbal communication and spatial proximity of the communication partners. With increasing capacity of exchanging information effectively and for conveying social presence—in spite of the use of media during communication processes—the problem of spatial distance for task accomplishment in work-dispersed locations will become less relevant.

In a survey of 500 scientists and engineers in the area of industrial research and development (R&D) it was shown that even when a large number of employees share one location, social presence and face-to-face communication occurs only on a relatively small scale (Kraut and Egido, 1988). Communication among employees whose offices were in the same story, but in different hallways, is merely one-fifth of the personal communication processes which could be observed among colleagues sharing a hallway. Communication is even less among co-workers on different floors. Thus, the accumulation of people at central locations, i.e. those responsible for achieving tasks, does not guarantee comprehensive social presence (see Kraut and Egido, 1988).

New solutions are especially necessary for work situations with a large number of or frequently changing cooperation partners requiring personal, problem-related meetings among cooperating partners, requiring increased mobility from all participants, and competing with media-supported cooperation processes. An improved spectrum of technical channels with regard to *information richness* is a prerequisite for the improved accomplishment of task-related communication needs (see pages 81–82, as well as the overview on information richness theory by Markus, 1994, p. 503 ff.) In this way media-supported forms of task accomplishment (telecooperative work forms) may make gradual progress into task areas that previously were only handled by direct forms of interaction.

Today's multi-media communication enables us to express ourselves in virtual realities. Multi-media communication makes virtual conferencing possible and product development is supported by virtual prototypes before the physical products are manufactured. The creation of virtual environments within the conventional accomplishment of tasks makes the partial substitution of real spatial proximity possible. In the near future, less effort will be placed on virtual environments and more effort on media-supported connections among real work spaces, but with dispersed work locations, in the sense of a *joint reality* (see, for example, Grenier and Metes, 1992; Harasim, 1993; Barnatt, 1995).

DRIVING FORCES BEHIND THE DISSOLUTION OF WORK LOCATIONS

In order to understand organizations with dispersed work locations, we must first address the driving forces behind the dissolution of work locations. The role of information and communication technologies as a force behind these developments has been referred to on several previous occasions. The creation of new technology alone, however, by no means guarantees its actual use. Examples abound in which technology applications failed due to a lack of market or societal acceptance or were not utilized due to a lack of inadequate quantifiability of its benefits. A combination of a number of factors influence structural development. Even though we may not yet be able to fully explain their influences, it makes sense to consider them from three different perspectives:

- the "market and environmental context" level (see page 321)
- the "business process and value-creation" level (page 321)
- the "work place" level (page 322).

Driving Forces for the Dissolution of Work Places on the "Market and Environmental Context" Level

New technological possibilities are usually considered as the trigger for dispersed and location-independent work models and organization forms (e.g., Grenier and Metes, 1992; Allen and Scott Morton, 1994; O'Hara-Devereaux and Johansen, 1994).

The following four trends are most influential as driving forces:

1 Miniaturization of information technology through progressive integration of microprocessor components
2 Decreasing processing costs
3 Decreasing information storage costs
4 Expansion of electronic connectivity, increased transmission capacity of telecommunication networks, as well as reduced user costs for telecommunication networks.

The new information and communication technologies pave the way for the dissolution of work places. The dissolution of work places is also a requirement for a number of current environmental protection activities, social trends and political developments.

Driving Forces for the Dissolution of Work Places on the "Business Process and Value-creation" Level

Economic forces of work place dissolution are expectations on improved resource productivity and the related increased competitiveness, as well as the opening of new markets.

A firm's *increased resource dependence*, especially with regard to know-how and capital, increasingly supports the dissolution of work locations. The accomplishment of increasingly complex tasks within a competitive global setting, for example, requires an optimal combination of knowledge workers. Knowledge, capabilities and skills, however, are not homogeneously distributed throughout the world. They have developed under prevailing historical, cultural and structural conditions. As a simple example, it is unlikely that the best aerodynamic scientist, the most innovative airbag developer, and the most creative chassis designer will work at a central location (such as Detroit or Chicago), and receive optimal management support. Although *global sourcing* has become today a fully accepted strategy in the area of supplier selection, personnel selection typically still occurs locally. Human resources managers will generally follow the motto: people work where the company is. The combination and utilization of heterogeneous human resources for the support of supraregional or international activities becomes only possible in a location-dispersed or location-independent organization (see, for example, Simon, Bauer and Jägeler, 1993).

A firm's competitiveness depends to a large extent on how economically beneficial its processes are designed. Economic benefits can be influenced by concentrating on the dimensions *costs, time, quality,* and *flexibility* (see Reichwald, Höfer and Weichselbaumer, 1993). New organization designs and technical concepts promising clear positive effects on these dimensions have realistic chances for their implementation. If new technologies additionally have a positive influence on human work situations and also consider external entrepreneurial effects, the prospects are promising.

Numerous arguments speak for the economic benefits of organizational concepts for workplace dissolution. They are the driving forces for an introduction and implementation of telecooperative work forms. For illustrative purposes, a few are presented here.

Cost Factors. Regional and national differences often in salaries and wages and, therefore, personnel costs, are often the motivation for a shift in work location of business activities. Moreover, high real estate costs in densely populated areas often account for a spatial decentralization of organizational units.

Time Factors. The streamlining of organizational processes is made possible by taking advantage of differing time zones or internationally differing work patterns and holiday regulations.

Quality Factors. The targeted use of national strengths provides the improved achievement of quality standards. For example, the adaptation of software for international applications and the translation of user handbooks can best be accomplished by experienced native speakers.

Flexibility Factors. The increasing need for flexibility in reacting to changing demands makes it necessary to adapt company capacity and performance limits to problem-specific demands. On page 337, the virtual organization resulting from telecooperative work forms will be introduced. To a considerable degree, this organizational form meets this demand for flexibility.

Driving Forces for the Dissolution of Work Places on the "Work Place" Level

There are a number of indications that western industrial nations have experienced a far-reaching change in values since the early 1960s (see

Klages, 1984; Rosenstiel, Djarrahzadeh, Einsiedler and Streich, 1993; for an overview see Rosenstiel, 1987). This shift in fundamental values and social preferences results in different demands and expectations in the working world. Jobs and working conditions are in demand that enable employees to harmonize their profession and private lives, as well as jobs that provide a high degree of self-sufficiency and flexibility. Praise, appreciation and personal development are the most salient motivational factors, especially for highly qualified younger employees with high expectations.

In the future, it will be important for firms to design their organizations in a way which reflects these shifts in values and new structural requirements. It will become more difficult to reach entrepreneurial goals without considering co-workers' personal goals. In the end, enterprises will maintain their competitiveness and secure their chances for survival through the consistent development and utilization of human capabilities and potential creativity. Firms will take advantage of their human resources by providing practical organizational and technical conditions to foster their development.

Telecooperative work models and organizational forms are well suited for this shift in values and social preferences. They allow for personal goals, for example, self-determination, mobility and independence, to be fundamental components of organizational concepts. Resistance at the management level is considered the main barrier in implementing telework, and demonstrates how far away firms are from fully integrating entrepreneurial and employee aspirations (Reichwald and Hermens, 1994; see also below). In addition, empirical surveys show that public interest in telecooperative arrangements is much higher than that of firms (see Korte, 1994).

SUCCESSFUL MODELS OF ORGANIZATIONS WITH DISPERSED WORK LOCATIONS

Telecooperation: Media-supported Work in Units with Dispersed Work Locations

Figure 8.2 provides an overview of the dimensions of media-supported work, definitions used and aspects examined in this chapter. *Telecooperation* is viewed as a generic term for media-supported, distributed cooperation in the following section from three perspectives (Reichwald and Möslein, 1996b; Reichwald, Möslein and Oldenburg, 1997). Each of them provides answers to one of three central questions.

- The *telework* perspective pursues the question how human work is influenced under the condition of spatial distribution.
- The *telemanagement* perspective examines how such distributed task accomplishment can be coordinated.
- *The teleservices* perspective asks questions about the products delivered by distributed work arrangements.

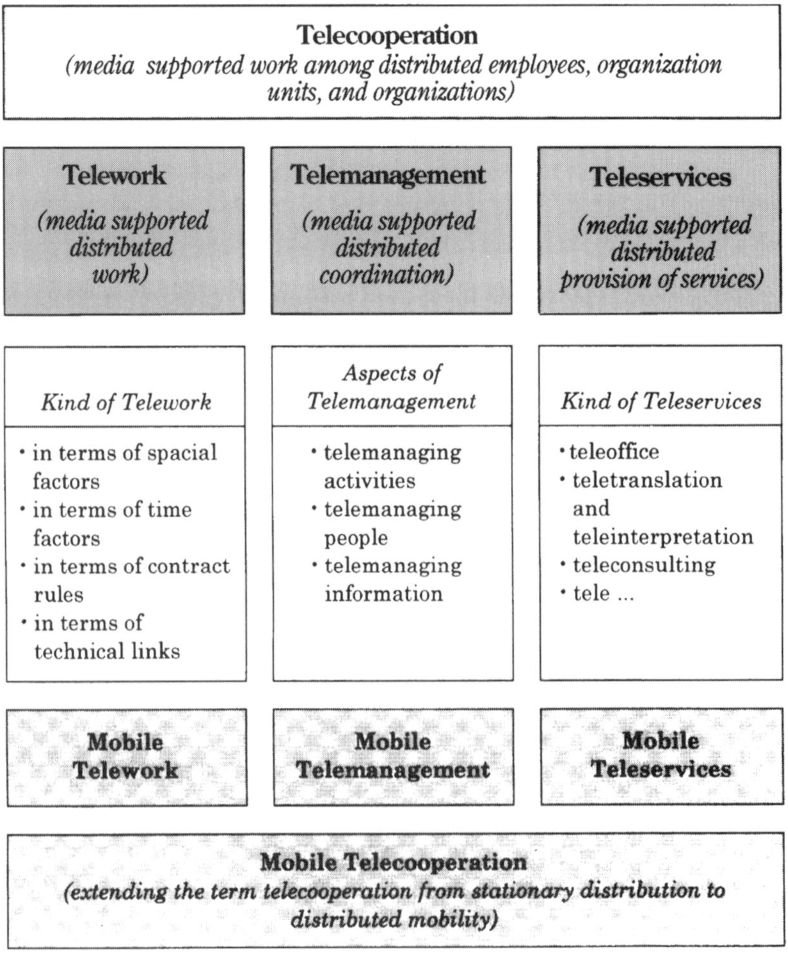

Telecooperation
(media supported work among distributed employees, organization units, and organizations)

Telework *(media supported distributed work)*	**Telemanagement** *(media supported distributed coordination)*	**Teleservices** *(media supported distributed provision of services)*
Kind of Telework	*Aspects of Telemanagement*	*Kind of Teleservices*
• in terms of spacial factors • in terms of time factors • in terms of contract rules • in terms of technical links	• telemanaging activities • telemanaging people • telemanaging information	• teleoffice • teletranslation and teleinterpretation • teleconsulting • tele ...
Mobile Telework	**Mobile Telemanagement**	**Mobile Teleservices**

Mobile Telecooperation
(extending the term telecooperation from stationary distribution to distributed mobility)

Figure 8.2 *Dimensions of Telecooperation. Source: Reichwald and Möslein (1996a, 1996b)*

Telecooperation: from the Fixed Work Location to the Dispersed Work Location

In a time of change in structures and values future telecooperation forms are the object of much speculation. A number of designs envision new opportunities for entrepreneurial action and individual goals, for supplying markets, for cooperation and inventive ideas for the marketing of services and products. There are also designs which provide a novel image of man and his future working world. The work place in familiar surroundings, such as a nearby telecenter or a mobile work place in a customer's firm, in a hotel or at a vacation resort, creates new opportunities and challenges for employees. An employee will not only be able to take advantage of flexible working hours and to carry the responsibility of self-organization and motivation, but also, unfortunately, may risk exclusion and isolation from other employees.

Information technologies enable the rearrangement of traditional business value chains, the restructuring of organizational location, and the decentralization of work places, even into private homes. These restructuring trends are observable today; the predicted final stage will be the location-dispersed organization, i.e. the "enterprise délocalisée" or the "de-localized enterprise" (Benchimol, 1994), the "global work space" (O'Hara-Devereaux and Johansen, 1994) or the distributed organization (Grenier and Metes, 1992). With the vision of "Any Time/Any Place", we have gained a first impression of the consequences for the future world of employment. We also discussed some of the driving forces which may trigger and support these trends. We have yet to discuss the actual structures which these organization designs will have in the future. Moreover, we have not yet drawn the line between various successful designs, many of which are the topic of current discussions in the literature and have been put to use in actual business settings, in order to systematize them. For this purpose, we will use the classifications presented in Figure 8.2.

Entrepreneurial organizations can be differentiated with regard to their location as follows:

- location-bound organizations
- location-dispersed organizations
- location-independent organizations.

While participants in location-bound organizations primarily cooperate directly in the production of goods and services, location-dispersed and location-independent (mobile) task accomplishment occurs through media support. The term *telecooperation* denotes the entire spectrum of media-supported production of goods and services based on the division of labor.

It was made clear earlier in this chapter that accomplishing goals always implies the coordination of tasks. This reflects the difference between *telework* as media-supported, distributed work processes and *telemanagement* as a media-supported, distributed coordination of work processes. Since telecooperation can only be applied to information-related tasks, the resulting product is always information. The product of telecooperation is the provision of services and is labelled *teleservice*.

The differentiation in telework, telemanagement and teleservice suggests three perspectives of telecooperation:

1 the design of distributed work processes and conditions (*telework*)
2 the management of distributed work processes (*telemanagement*)
3 results of the cooperation processes, relevant markets and customers (*teleservice*).

The following section examines these three perspectives.

Telework: Media-Supported Distributed Work Processes

The History of Telework. Telework is a recent, but not an entirely new phenomenon. The English FI Group, founded in 1962, is attributed with being the first in explicitly implementing the concept of telework by having female programmers work at home. Today, this project is known as a precursor of current telework projects (see, for example, Godehardt, 1994). The academic discussion of telework finds its roots in the publications of J.M. Nilles (Nilles et al, 1976) who, during the 1973 oil crisis, analyzed the possibility of alleviating commuter traffic by increasing data transmission. In this study, he coined the term "telecommuting", which is still predominant in the US and is almost synonymous with the English term "telework". These first steps in the 1970s were followed by intensive academic examinations and euphoric predictions during the 1980s. Surprisingly few practical advances were made in the 80s. Today's popularity of telework is due to the wider perspective, new information technologies, and recent economic and political concepts. These developments were supported by numerous national and international initiatives and congresses (e.g., the conferences: *Telearbeit* (1994), *Telework* (1994), *Telecommute* (1994). The term "Telework" is preferred here as it places emphasis on work being done at a distance rather than placing emphasis on commuting, especially since much telework is done that has little to do with commuting aspects *per se*. The term includes notions of independent, alternating, mobile and generally telecooperative forms of work and denotes media-supported, dispersed task accomplishment utilizing a multitude of expressive forms and types of work places.

Types of Telework Arrangements. From the beginning, comprehensive attempts were made to systematize applications and organizational forms of telework. These efforts were complicated, however, due to continuous modifications of telework patterns and features. Today it is no longer sufficient to approach classification attempts from an exclusively spatial-decentralization perspective. Wollnik (1992) suggests the development of a general catalogue of universal criteria with which existing telework can be compared, typified and differentiated (see Figure 8.3). Accordingly, telework is carried out by a producer for a consumer. The producer or consumer may be individuals, organization units or entire enterprises. They are interconnected by cooperative regulations, legal contracts or authorities empowered to issue directives. Furthermore, these interrelationships may be equal relationships (e.g., divisions of enterprises) or they may be unequal (e.g., enterprise and freelance contractors). The work place where the producer provides telework (*organizational unit*) is located (as long as it is not mobile) in a specific work place or room (*spatial unit*). The geographical location of these particular work places marks the location of labor (*geographic unit*). (Wollnik, 1992, cls. 2405–2406).

Based on selected criteria, a few essential forms of telework are examined:

- In terms of *spatial factors*, we can distinguish among four relevant organization types of telework: (1) *Home-based Telework* as a work model of achieving tasks at home; (2) *Centre-based Telework* may occur in *satellite offices* (decentralized transfer of groups of employees or organization units from headquarters) or *neighborhood offices* (collection of decentralized work places on corporate premises, often occupied by several firms in common facilities); (3) *Mobile telework* takes place mainly at the management level, but can also be found in field service and the construction industry; and (4) *On-site Telework* takes place at the location of the customer, supplier or cooperation partner.
- In terms of *time factors*, we can classify (1) full-time telework and (2) alternating models of telework (while considering the application of various location models).
- *Contractual rules* differentiate whether telework is based on an employment contract or freelance contracts for work. Between these two extremes is a sizable spectrum of conceivable contract models. Worch (1994) refers to contract models based on their frequency of today's actually observed contract terms: (1) telework within an employer-employee-relationship, regulated by an employment

Criteria	Workplaces			
1. Degree of centralization of the actual work location when viewed as a workplace	Employees at a workplace support the location of use, which holds a central status	Employees at a workplace support a location of use, which does not hold a central status (e.g., organization units at the actual location of use and the work location interface as business partners)		
2. Decentralizing workplaces from a location of use's point of view	Supraordinate unit encompassing the actual location of use within a spatially decentralized workplace	Locations of use and workplaces are integrated into a supraordinate unit		
3. Number of teleworkplaces at the place of work	Single workplace (individual place of work)	Workplaces in a collective place of work		
4. Provider of workroom and workspace	Workplace in facilities provided by the producer	Workplace in facilities provided by a third party. The rooms are available for telework on long- or short-term basis	Workplace in facilities provided by the consumer	
4a. If workplaces provided by consumer: Number of bodies responsible	Workplace within a place of work with only a single consumer	Workplace within a place of work with multiple participating consumers		
5. Person or institution fitting out and maintaining the workplace	Producer fits out and maintains the workplace	Consumer fits out and maintains the workplace		
6. Functional specialization of workplace/workplaces in the place of work	Specific activities in specialized single workplaces/workplaces in a collective place of work, in which workplaces with functionally specialized tasks are integrated	Single workplace where different activities (telework) are being accomplished/workplace in a collective place of work with functionally differentiated workplaces		
7. Number of potential consumers	Workplace where tasks are being accomplished for only one consumer	Workplace where tasks are being accomplished for numerous consumers		
8. Geographical connection between residences and the place of work of producers	Workplaces which are outfitted by producers	Workplaces which are integrated into the living environment of producers	Workplaces which are mobile, i.e. not related to a headquarters of producers	
9. Geographical connection between residences and the headquarters of consumer	Workplaces are integrated into headquarters of consumer	Workplaces are spread out into decentralized units of consumer (e.g. places of business)	Workplaces are spread out narrowly into decentralized units of consumer (e.g. offices)	Workplaces are not related to headquarters of consumer
10. Availability of workplaces for the producer	Workplaces are available permanently	Workplaces are available occasionally		
11. Planning the task accomplishment for consumers	Workplaces which accomplish tasks on consumer's call	Workplaces which accomplish tasks according to producer's arrangements		
12. Degree of timing accuracy	Workplaces which accomplish tasks with fixed deadlines	Workplaces with no time-regulated activities		
13. Intensity of telework at a workplace	Workplaces with exclusive and/or permanent telework/workplaces which are outfitted for telework specifically	Workplaces with partly and/or sporadic telework/workplaces which are capable of telework		
14. Mobility	Stationary workplace	Mobile workplace		
15. Considering legal issues when designing workplaces	Employee's workplace	Residential workplace	Workplace where the producer is a freelance or a self-employed person	
15a. Working hours, if an employer-employee relationship exists	Full-time workplace	Part-time workplace		

Figure 8.3 *List of criteria to typify telework settings. Source: Wollnik (1992, cls. 2403-2404. Translated by the authors. Reproduced by permission from Schäffer-Poeschel Verlag, Stuttgart.)*

contract; (2) telework by an independent entrepreneur; or (3) telework by an employee, but not necessarily completely fulfilling (1) and (2) above.

- In terms of *technical links* we can distinguish between asynchronous off-line-work with more or less synchronized points of information exchange, and synchronous on-line-work, including a permanent synchronous interaction.

Problematic Contradictions and Unanswered Questions. Even though the supply-side problem of telework (i.e., how to implement telework) seems to be almost solved, demand-side issues (i.e., how to address business challenges by implementing telework) remain still an open question (see Gray, Markus and PonTell, 1996; PonTell et al, 1996).

It is still unclear which form of telework is best suited to particular circumstances and applications. In the early stages of these new work models, telework was put into practice designated for basic, supportive tasks with well-defined structures, lines of demarcation and, above all, limited communication requirements (e.g., text and data collection). The German Trade Union (Deutscher Gewerkschaftsbund or DGB) presented in its latest survey, that relocating work places from firms to domestic areas are appropriate for results-oriented, managerial and creative positions exhibiting a high degree of autonomy. These characteristics are found in professions requiring relatively high qualification levels (Fischer, Späker and Weißbach, 1993). Although both recommendations are based on the same form, tele-homework, contradictions and unanswered questions arise which need to be recognized and addressed.

A paradoxical situation is encountered in these design recommendations in several ways. At first glance, the required division of labor in telecooperative work models clashes with the organizational suggestions for the integration of tasks (Picot and Reichwald, 1987). Recent trends promoting the comprehensive implementation of teamwork concepts seem to collide with autonomy-oriented individual work in telecooperative work arrangements (Ulich, 1991; 1994). Similarly controversial are the latest proposed solutions that try to solve these contradictions and to realize predicted advantages of teamwork (e.g., Ulich, 1994, p. 188) in spite of spatial decentralization tendencies: The concept of *teamwork in satellite offices* (Ulich, 1994; Godehardt, 1994) implies the organization of team members in decentralized units whereby the maintenance of direct personal interactions between parties is of major importance. On the other hand, the *concept of virtual teams* (e.g., Savage, 1990) accepts the spatial distance among team members supporting cooperative relationships by electronic networks (see Oberquelle, 1991).

When addressing these contradictions and considering solutions, we must differentiate between the design models of telework and their incorporation into the surrounding work systems. Choosing a suitable cooperative telework configuration can only be accomplished by taking a closer look at work-related conditions and circumstances (Reichwald, 1990b).

Telemanagement: Media-Supported Distributed Coordination of Work Processes

Telecooperative work models pose new demands on the coordination of task accomplishments. They substantially change management and work processes and also require inventive forms of self-organization and self-coordination of dispersed employees. Telemanagement, the collective term for *all media-supported forms of dispersed coordination of tasks*, comprises patterns of both self- and extraneous coordination. The following discussion focuses on management processes. For more information concerning aspects of self-organization and self-management see Probst (1992).

Interorganizational linkages, decentralization and the globalization of companies place new demands on management strategies. Empirical surveys of transnational enterprises illustrate (Bartlett and Goshal, 1992; Pribilla, Reichwald and Goecke, 1996) that linking, decentralizing and internationalizing goes hand-in-hand with increased travel activities and the intensified use of telecommunication media among management. Presumably in the future, travel activities of executive personnel will increase, despite the increasing availability of telecommunication media (see Reichwald, 1994), a phenomenon that Pribilla, Reichwald and Goecke (1996) label the "Media Paradox".

Managing "invisible workers" represents a new challenge for managers. If possibilities of personal supervision wane because of telecooperative arrangements, behavior-oriented management models inevitably will fail as well. This, however, need not necessarily be a disadvantage: If managers learn to supervise without constantly observing employees at their work place, they will gain the freedom to focus on and observe actual performance (Collins, 1986, p. 25). Thus, with dispersed task accomplishment results-oriented supervision of the *Management by Objectives* (Di Martino and Wirth, 1990) replaces behavior-oriented management. Management by setting goals, as well as organizational management measures such as frequent talks between managers and employees, personal qualification, career and development processes, can partly substitute the need for direct management. The feasibility of management without personal supervision depends above all on the bond of trust between employees and managers, the motivation and qualification of employees, as well as the methods of planning and structuring of tasks (Godehardt, 1994).

Empirical research on the influence of telemedia on management processes demonstrates (Grote, 1994) that there is no technical

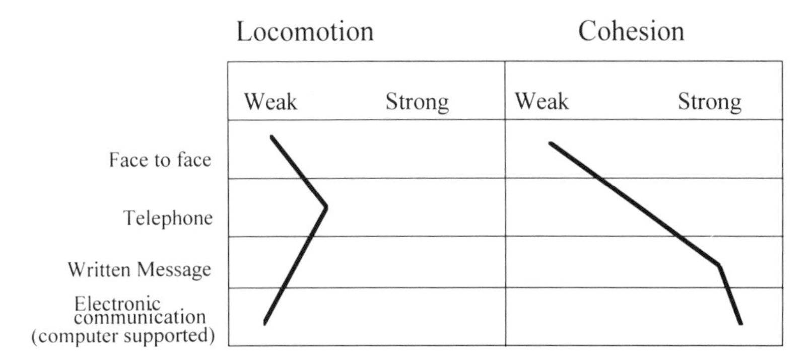

Figure 8.4 *Effects of electronic communication on management processes. Source: Grote (1994. Reproduced by permisson from Hogrefe Verlag GmbH and Co. KG.)*

communication form that entirely substitutes the confidence- and motivation-building of face-to-face communication. Taking this into account, the supervision of employees in dispersed work locations has restrictions. These restrictions have far-reaching consequences on organizational conditions under which telecooperative work models are effective and efficient. The support of specific management tasks through electronic media is of particular importance.

Apart from influencing task-oriented group activities (*locomotion function*) an essential element of management is personal interaction, i.e. the building and care of individual relationships (*cohesion function*). Depending on the chosen communication form, social presence may be more or less experienced (Kiesler, Siegel and McGuire, 1984). Restrictions of electronic communication-media to provide social presence encourage functional communication styles (Sorg and Zangl, 1986). Electronic communication media are not considered as appropriate for all management tasks (Grote, 1993): *The use of telecommunication media for communication purposes between managers and employees is considered appropriate for supporting team tasks and goals (locomotion).* On the other hand, computer supported communication forms like electronic mail (e-mail) are—based on empirical studies—less useful in promoting social relationships (cohesion) between employees and managers (see Figure 8.4). Accordingly, the choice of technical communication form may influence content, responsibilities and social relationships among communication partners. Research demonstrates that locomotion-oriented management correlates positively with team performance and cohesion-oriented management patterns are associated positively with team member satisfaction.

New ways of accomplishing telecooperative tasks may perhaps require a new understanding of the relationship between manager and employee (see Chapter 9). This is important since the development of the management of organizations and the role of managers in organizations is directly connected to the development and improvement of the organization itself. Management as a profession emerged during the course of industrialization. Classic management theory by Fayol (1916) and the POSDCORB-classification of fundamental management functions (POSDCORB = Planning, Organizing, Staffing, Directing, COordinating, Reporting, Budgeting) by Gulick and Urwick (1937) suggested that the manager's role was reduced to purely rudimentary administrative functions. Today, Mintzberg (1994) tries to integrate different aspects of successful management in a comprehensive approach with his "think-link-lead-do"- model. He describes three levels of management: *Managing action, managing people* and *managing information.* These three different levels are distinguished by their relative degree of immediate influence: A manager may be able to directly influence the progression of events; he may also be able to indirectly control events by influencing people and may have an influence on individuals' actions by means of managing information. If telemanagement is reduced to managing information, management as a whole is at stake, since: "To manage by information is to sit two steps removed from the purpose of managerial work." (Mintzberg, 1994, p. 16)

Teleservices: Media-Supported Provision of Services

New organization forms enable new services. The manufacturing organization inspired by Taylor (1913) enabled the cost-effective production of mass-produced goods. Today's modular manufacturing concepts based on flexible manufacturing systems enable the individualization of these industrial mass-produced goods ("Mass Customization", see Pine, 1993). Analogously, telecooperative organization designs based on a productive information infrastructure ("Infostructure", see Diebold, 1994) offer the key to a new product class: *teleservices* (see Reichwald and Möslein, 1995).

This teleservices field, i.e. the *media-supported dispersed provision of services*, opens the door for a wide range of innovative information products. Until now, public, political and scientific discussion focused on the design of a fundamental technical infrastructure, i.e. the National Information Infrastructure (NII), as well as the Global Information Infrastructure (GII) (e.g., Benjamin and Wigand, 1995; Wigand, 1996). However, very few issues concerning the potential products themselves, their markets, and necessary organization forms to enable such products have been satisfactorily researched. An extensive survey conducted for the French government (Breton, 1994b) analyzed the applicability of teleservices, as well as supply and demand structures for France and in international comparison. To familiarize the reader with the field of teleservice, selected extracts are presented providing an overview and introduction.

The product range of teleservices can be divided into seven segments. Figure 8.5 depicts selected applications and their respective teleservices.

Application Segment	Teleservices
Functional Teleservices	• Tele-Consulting • Tele-Secretarial Services • Tele-Translation • Tele-Interpretation
Computer-related Teleservices	• Tele-Programming • Tele-Installation • Tele-Engineering • Tele-Systems Support • Tele-Data Security and Archiving
Teleservices in Information Processing and Information Transmission	• Travel and Airline Bookings • Electronic Banking • Electronic Brokerage • Electronic Catalogues • Electronic Ordering and Delivery Systems
Tele-Learning	All forms of media-supported education and qualifications: • Tele-Instruction • Tele-Lecture • Tele-Education
Tele-Medicine	General medical and expert medical tele-consulting, -treatment and -care • Tele-Diagnosis • Tele-Office Hours • Medical image processing and transmission • ...
Tele-Surveillance of Sites, Infrastructure Installations and Processes	Telesurveillance of, e.g., buildings, elevators, alarm installations, air conditioning plants, supply sites, transport routes, production processes ...
Teleservices for Private End-Users	• Pay TV • Video-on-demand • Teleshopping • ...

Figure 8.5 *The product range of teleservices. Source: Breton (1994b, p. 20. Translated by the authors. Reproduced by permission from La documentation Française.)*

These application segments provide only a one-dimensional and rough classification. Positioning the identified teleservices qualitatively in relevant assessment criteria of supply and demand provides a detailed depiction of potential use. Figures 8.6 and 8.7 display the resulting portfolios systematizing teleservices into:

- capital and qualification intensity of service delivery for the provider (supplier);
- Performance depth (single step, partial process, total process) of the supply of services and specificity of service customers (buyers).

The spectrum of useful teleservices illustrated in these figures shows clearly that the potential of telecooperative task accomplishment reaches far beyond spatial decentralization opportunities of work places. Basically, telecooperation allows for the contribution of all sorts of information products in the form of professional services. This has far-reaching consequences pertaining to the *make* or *buy* decision of information services, centralization vs. decentralization of service delivery, as well as the international division of labor within the area of information production.

Breton's study considers teleservices as services that are exchanged among firms. Intra-organizational services as a form of work relationships are not considered. This restriction referring to the legal status of

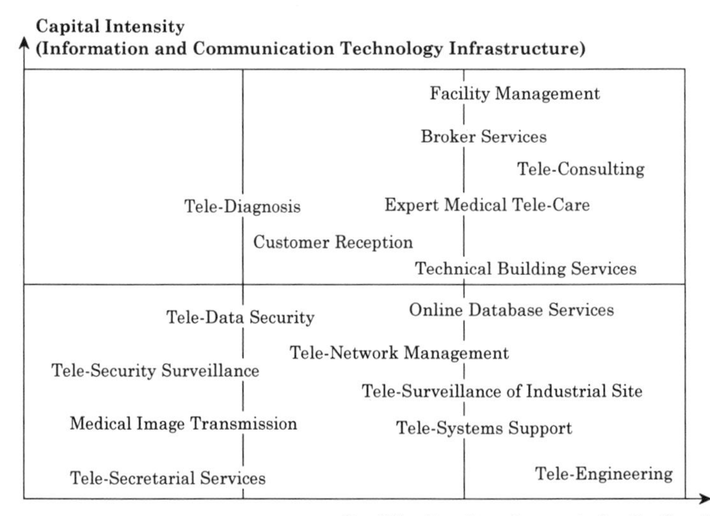

Figure 8.6 *Capital intensity and qualification requirements in the supply of services. Source: Breton (1994b, p. 26. Translated by the authors. Reproduced by permission from La documentation Française.)*

Performance Quality of External Service

	Standard (Industry-wide)	Standard (Industry Group)	Industry Specific
Total Process	Online-Database Services Tele-Security Surveillance	Technical Building Services	Facility Management Broker Services Expert Medical Tele-Care
Partial Task	Tele-Consulting	Customer Reception Tele-Surveillance of Industrial Sites	Tele-Engineering
Partial Step	Tele-Systems Support Tele-Secretarial Services		Tele-Network Management Medical Image Transmission Tele-Diagnosis

Specificity of Service Customers

Figure 8.7 *Depth of performance quality of service providers and specificity of service recipients. Source: Breton (1994b, p. 28. Translated by the authors. Reproduced by permisson from La documentation Française.)*

the service provider seems to be unnecessarily narrow and is reminiscent of the former restrictions applicable to conventional employees. However, we can assume that in many cases dispersed services are appropriate to replace traditionally internal office and administrative tasks.

Addressing the risks and potentials of teleworking, the study (based on the restricted terminological definition) concludes that:

- the willingness to outsource on the one hand and the openness for advanced information technology on the other, influence the degree of development potential for teleservices;
- the willingness to outsource on the one hand and the degree of internationalizing on the other, influence the potential for work relocation of service delivery to a foreign country.

Mobile Telecooperation: From the Dispersion of Work Location to the Independence of Work Location

Today's most popular and widespread form of telecooperative task accomplishment worldwide is mobile location-independent work (see Gray, Hodson and Gordon, 1993, p. 3). A Cornell University study concludes: nearly half of all employees are assigned with desk work. On each working day, however, an average of 40% of all desks are not occupied. Even if we only take 25% as the basis for unoccupied desks, that means 13.68 million desks in the United States and three million desks in the United Kingdom are vacant (Gray, Hodson and Gordon 1993, p. 16). Using the 40% as a basis, if we also suppose a rate of 5% as sick days and an additional 5.8% as vacation days, there is still an "unreported case" rate of about 29%. This percentage of "unreported cases" can be ascribed to *nomadic (tele)workers* (persons with alternating telework relationships), *hidden (tele)workers* (persons without official telework programs, who carry out part of their job at home), and *mobile (tele)workers* (e.g., sales people, service technicians, but also managers). In addition, there are other mobile employees who traditionally carry out their work in a mobile fashion and never occupy a desk within an office. Gray, Hodson, and Gordon estimate that there are 3.6 million automobile-based teleworkers in the United States and 480 000 of the same in the United Kingdom (1993, p. 16).

Important fields with a high degree of mobility, for example, are (Niemeier et al, 1994):

- Management
- Product configuration and technical support
- Insurance claim assessment
- Transportation services and shipping logistics
- Press, publishing and broadcasting
- Financial services
- Manufacturing, construction and planning offices
- Health care.

Mobile communication systems (such as mobile phones, fax machines, notebooks, printers and modems) provide potential for support of different methods of task accomplishments at independent locations. They enable access to information from any location possible, and support from distant secretaries, co-workers and colleagues. The location of a mobile office is the customer's place of business, the building site, the car, the hotel room or vacation destination. Office-hotels ("hotelling"), which provide mobile managers with a stationary, entirely equipped office environment for the duration of hours or a few days, fit in well with today's ideas of mobility and independence (e.g., Eurotechnopolis Institut, 1994).

A short case study exemplifying telecooperation on the basis of mobile communication technology is summarized here: The project

"Mobile Telecommunication in the Construction Industry" is a pilot project in telecooperation based on mobile communication technologies (Reichwald and Huber, 1996, pp. 10–13). It has been financed by the BMFT (German Federal Ministry for Research and Technology) and includes the development of a mobile office for the construction industry. Organizations supporting this effort are: Heilit+Woerner Bau AG, Siemens Nixdorf AG, BPU GmbH, Munich and the DeTeBerkom, Berlin. This project addresses internal coordination tasks in large construction firms with decentralized building sites, as well as information exchange among organizations with medium-sized suppliers via mobile communication technologies.

The reason to develop a mobile work place in the construction business is to support the project leader in his/her coordination tasks among the head office, distributed building sites, suppliers, and building authorities. This work place enables the site manager to perform tasks within a network and to coordinate the involved partners in a flexible and efficient way. In order to increase productivity and to improve punctuality in construction companies, it becomes more important to reach cooperation partners quickly and without undergoing the common delays (e.g., telephone tags) and to have access to documents irrespectively of location (e.g., construction plans, calculation reports). The site manager will be supported in the following activities:

- synchronous and asynchronous communication
- accessing necessary documents
- calculating, drawing up forms, collecting data
- scheduling with cooperation partners.

In summary, the use of mobile information and communication technologies extends possibilities of telecooperative work models from dispersed work locations to a dimension of location-independence. Telework, telemanagement and teleservice are all equally influenced by these steps toward mobility. These concepts pose new challenges for management research and business practice, and also provide new opportunities.

Virtual Enterprises as a Result of Telecooperative Work Models

Advanced information technologies enable the dissolution of time and spatial dependence as constraints on organizational arrangements. What are the advantages of the dissolution of such organizational boundaries for various institutions? Are classical hierarchies with fixed locations going to be replaced by location-independent "electronic hierarchies"

(Benjamin and Wigand, 1995; Malone, 1990; Malone, Yates and Benjamin, 1986)? Will the opportunities of dispersed locations promote a trend of partially dissolved hierarchies and encourage the establishment of cooperative structures between markets and hierarchies? Or do hybrid cooperative structures only represent a temporary transition between the two ideal types, market and hierarchy? From an institutional-economic point of view (see Chapter 2), it is always that division of labor-based accomplishment of tasks that succeeds which, as a coordination form in the spectrum between market and hierarchy, minimizes total cost of performance (as a sum of production and coordination costs). Media support fundamentally provides new approaches for all coordination forms by enabling (telecooperative) solutions for division of labor-based work. It is still uncertain how increased efforts in establishing telecooperative work models will influence the relative advantages of institutional arrangements in the long run and only initial approaches can be reported so far (e.g., Ciborra, 1993; Krüger, 1993; Picot, 1993a; Benjamin and Wigand, 1995; Picot, Ripperger and Wolff, 1996).

One organization form inspired increasingly by information and communication networks, is gaining in both theoretical and practical importance: *the virtual organization* (see particularly Davidow and Malone, 1992; Ettighofer, 1992; Szyperski and Klein 1993; Bleicher, 1996; Reichwald and Möslein, 1996a). We have already examined the "as-if-organization" form (Klein, 1994) earlier in this chapter. It turned out to be the result of targeted deployment of new telecooperation possibilities and describes the clever meshing of different organization design strategies, thus simultaneously enabling efficiency and flexibility.

If we understand the term "virtual" in the sense of "not real," the raison d'être of this organizational form remains unclear from an economic standpoint. The virtual enterprise, interpreted as an internally and externally "shapeless structure" (Davidow and Malone, 1992; Mertens, 1994), is at best different from the classical form of an enterprise. This difference, however, does not necessarily improve the enterprise. It is certainly not a universal remedy.

> "*The virtual corporation* will, we believe, for the first time tie all of these diverse innovations together into a single cohesive vision of the corporation of the twenty-first century. (. . .) the virtual corporation, that results from integrating these components is so extraordinarily adaptable and fast moving as to almost overnight leave traditionally organized competitors far behind." (*Davidow and Malone 1992, p. 17; emphasis in the original*)

Exaggerated euphoria does not apply: Contingency theory demonstrates clearly that there cannot be "one best way" of organization design (e.g.,

Hill, Fehlbaum and Ulrich, 1989; Kieser and Kubicek, 1992; Kieser, 1993; Picot, 1993a). Numerous attempts to deduce universal design principles out of early organization-theoretical approaches have failed in the past. Accordingly, today's progress in organization theory focuses on the question concerning the conditions under which forms of organization design are observable (*descriptive approach*) or can be recommended (*normative design approach*). This design aspect becomes the focus of attention with regard to our discussion of the virtual organization.

Virtual organizations may be viewed as a further development of hybrid coordination forms in the spectrum between market and hierarchy on the basis of changed legal and technological conditions (see Chapter 2). They constitute division of labor-based linkages among firms. The fundamental idea of a symbiosis is of vital importance for their existence. Chapter 6 views symbiotic organizational networks as long-term entrepreneurial linkages. But where are the differences of the entrepreneurial networks when compared to a virtual organization? Even if a clear-cut boundary is unlikely to be delineated, a virtual organization may be characterized on the basis of unique features and characteristics. Accordingly, four main questions can be addressed (see Reichwald, Möslein and Oldenburg, 1997; Reichwald and Möslein, 1996a):

1 What is the theoretical basis of the concept of virtual organization? (see below)
2 What are typical characteristics and design principles of virtual organizations? (page 341)
3 Which design goals are pursued utilizing these design principles and under which conditions is their deployment meaningful? (page 344)
4 What are the boundaries of the "boundary-less" organization? (page 347)

Virtuality as a Concept for Performance Improvement

The virtuality concept is important for architectural principles in information systems and science in several ways (e.g., Jessen and Valk, 1986; Siegert, 1991). Through conceptual differentiation between physical and logical computer components it is possible to overcome capacity and flexibility limitations of the hardware architecture. The concept of virtual system components enables, for example, numerous "clients" of only one system to be given the impression of exclusive use. The "client" is only aware of the logical system, but is not familiar with the dynamic transfer of requirements from logical to real system components.

The concept of virtuality in the area of memory architecture in computer systems is probably the best suitable and most cited example for the architecture of virtual organizations. The creation of virtual memory is based on the trade-off between speed, cost, and capacity of storage media. High speed memory is expensive and, consequently, can be stocked only sparingly. In contrast, low speed memory is comparatively cheap. Theoretically it is at one's disposal almost without limits. If an order has to be fulfilled that needs to be carried out quickly, in spite a great demand of capacity, the logical overall memory assigns it to a small, but fast real memory.

Through a clever combination of heterogeneous components with varying performance characteristics (e.g., speed, high capacity, low cost) inside the system an impression can be created that the system is "almost as fast, as the fastest—as big, as the biggest—as cheap, as the cheapest." With the help of virtual concepts, it is possible to fulfill even contradictory goals, without requiring that each particular system component accomplishes all demands optimally and simultaneously. The function of this concept goes back to the "idea of sampling extraction" from the 1950s and means: Only if a particular snap-shot of the world (i.e. the overall memory), is in use at a specific time (or period of time) in order to accomplish an assignment, can we optimize the whole system by creating an appropriate extraction of the world. The allocation of resources is influenced by dynamic storage processes.

It is obvious that this technical concept, created to increase the performance of computer architecture, cannot be directly applied to social systems and the organizational architecture. However, there are several analogies identifiable today, which represent virtual units within enterprises. Translation agencies, collaborating with other independent translation agencies (and/or freelance translators) on an international basis, are a concrete example for this concept representing a worldwide network. Correspondingly, these agencies establish a virtual organization operating worldwide. It is able to perform translations in (almost) every language and in (almost) any field through qualified professional translators. Each assignment uses only particular extracts of the entire system and no longer exists after the assignment has been completed. Each actor contributes his/her specific performance and qualification profiles to the virtual enterprise. Each can be a member of different, entirely independent, as well as supplementary "organizations." Task accomplishment does not take place in static, predefined structures, but as a problem-oriented, dynamic networking of real resources to tackle concrete tasks.

A virtual enterprise is equipped—analogous to the virtual concept of computer memory architecture—with much more capacity than a classical, legal organization unit with its limited human, technical, infrastructural or financial resources available in its core areas. In a virtual organization, company performance conditions and in turn traditional organizational boundaries lose their importance. Telecommunication technologies make it possible to perform tasks largely independent of time and space. Consequently, spatial limits can be extended by creating communication networks with business partners in all functional areas. Linkages with suppliers or customers can extend the development potential; linkages with market partners can extend the range of products and services. Even linkages with competitors are at times inevitable, if perhaps a temporarily extended production capacity becomes necessary (e.g., to accomplish large-scale orders, such as the construction of a major airport that cannot be handled by one company alone). Overcoming time limits occurs then, when an enterprise has dispersed its work locations over numerous time zones. Thus, a global company can provide services such as consulting, remote diagnosis, maintenance or provide order status information around the clock through the use of telecommunications technologies (Wigand, 1996). In this case, the customer inquiry will be forwarded to the work location on duty, independent of the time zone. The inquirer or customer is not even aware of the actual location providing the information. Overcoming time limits is normal for today's internationally operating airlines, security services, software development firms and customer service in high-tech fields.

Virtual enterprises develop through a network of physically dispersed organization units, participating in a coordinated division of labor-based value-added process. A multitude of diversely organized people work in professional core areas. These people accomplish their assignments internally or externally and, in addition, they themselves are associated with others through several cooperative arrangements. Even the professional core may consist of organization units that are either physically dispersed or in a fixed location. Virtual organizations are considered a counterbalance to organizational forms with long-term internal and external boundaries, a fixed location, and relatively permanent resources. Such an enterprise is able to improve its performance through the dissolution of classical time and space limits and structures beyond the point possible through its traditionally available resources. In reality, however, the concept of the virtual organization can only be enacted when the necessary resources, especially the qualification of human resources, are available in a real time fashion. Chapter 9 discusses these possibilities, as well as the conditions and limits of access to qualified human resources.

Characteristics and Design Principles of Virtual Organizations

The virtual organization as an architectural concept of information systems and science was discussed generally in the previous section. Some analogies to entrepreneurial organizations were presented. Apparently this organizational concept of virtuality, created to increase performance, can be part of organizational architecture. However, the implementation of a concept always requires tangible applicability. Multiple strategies have been developed in order to design computer memory architecture in recent history. The advantage of these strategies depends upon the purpose of the task and the related requirements. However, it is too soon, i.e. fundamentally we know too little, to discuss design strategies and their particular advantages as they may pertain to virtual enterprises. Therefore, it appears to be more meaningful to highlight characteristics and fundamental design principles of virtual enterprises.

Virtual enterprises manifest themselves as dynamic networks of organizational units. Single network nodes can be set up either by authorized individuals, by organization units or by entire organizations. The connections among single nodes are established dynamically and in a problem-oriented fashion. Therefore, task-oriented assignments determine the structure of a virtual enterprise at any point in time. In spite of its transitory nature, this organizational structure is not shapeless, as performance increases by means of virtuality within systems are only attainable if fundamental components are able to meet the demands of specific basic tasks. Accordingly, we can isolate three characteristics that are essential for virtual enterprises and their goal attainment.

Modularity. Fundamental fragments of a virtual enterprise constitute modular units, i.e. relatively small but manageable units with decentralized decision-making competence and responsibilities (see Chapter 5). While Chapter 5 interpreted the creation of modules as an internal structural concept, virtual enterprises demand, however, "virtual modules". These are units, consisting of assignees, which can belong to different legal institutions. Without a high degree of modularity among its components, as well as internal unity and external openness, the efficient dynamic reconfiguration of a system is not possible.

Heterogeneity. Basic components of virtual enterprises have different performance profiles with regard to their strengths and competencies. The targeted focus on core competence creates the necessary prerequisite for the formation of a symbiotic relationship (see Chapter 6). Without the qualitative differentiation of the components the dynamic reconfiguration of the system is limited to a purely quantitative adaptability. It follows that the expected realization of performance goals, for example, with regard to quality and flexibility, would be lost. Moreover, advantages gained over other organizational forms may be doubtful.

Time and Spatial Distribution. Basic components of virtual enterprises are spatially distributed and depend on dynamic reconfiguration. The possibilities of telecooperative task accomplishment constitute therefore the emergence of virtual enterprises. Information and communication infrastructures, however, define the boundaries and limitations of the system.

The three characteristic features of virtual enterprises illustrated above are directly connected to three fundamental design principles, constituting the very essence of virtual enterprises.

1. The Open-Closed-Principle. The open-closed-principle is based on the *modularity* of virtual enterprises. Because of their modular construction, virtual organizations give the impression of an integrated system while, at the same time, internally manifesting open and dynamic structures. A customer places an order with a company which he trusts and which seems to be tailored to his needs. The visible "envelope" of such an enterprise presents itself to the customer as a cohesive whole. However, the actual custom-built organization which carries out the order constructs itself *after* the process of task accomplishment has been initiated. The internal structure (the content of the envelope) forms the open system.

2. Complementarity Principle. This principle is based on *heterogeneity* of the nodes within the network of virtual enterprises. Modular units with heterogeneous performance profiles supplement one another with complementary competence in the sense of symbiotic organization configurations.

3. Transparency Principle. The transparency principle refers to the *time* and *spatial distribution* of virtual enterprises. System transparency means in computer science terminology that a system can be considered a "black box". Consequently, a virtual enterprise appears to the user as a black box in that he/she only recognizes the envelope, but is not concerned with the exact location of performance. In spite of, and especially because of this, the permanent reconfiguration of the enterprise appears to be tailored especially to the users' needs at any given time.

The illustrated characteristics and design principles seem at first to be very abstract. The example of the translation agency puts them, however, into more concrete terms and in addition, the scenario of the "Worldwide Group" (see page 312) demonstrated a visionary form of virtual enterprises containing the features just discussed. These fundamental characteristics and basic principles help us to judge to what extent virtual enterprises may indeed be able to increase their performance based on virtuality as an organizational concept. The design of virtual enterprises is additionally enabled by already known, common organization design strategies. Moreover, the demarcation of organizational characteristics of virtual enterprises enables the scope of their applications. The following section focuses on the goals that can be pursued by these design principles and under which task-oriented conditions and settings their application is appropriate.

Perspectives of Organization Design

Flexibility is the main goal when forming virtual organizations. It describes the capability of an organization to dynamically adapt to environmental changes. While stabilizing strategies maintain internal stability of organizations *vis-à-vis* outside forces, flexibility strategies try to achieve adaptability and the capability to process change actively (Klimecki, Probst and Gmür, 1993). As a rule, stabilizing strategies are more efficient if there are only few environmental changes or little variability in demands. However, the more turbulent the environmental conditions and the higher the variability of demands, the more successful a flexibility strategy will be. Flexibility strategies were long considered a waste of resources and efficiency in organization theory, e.g., the formation of organizational slack, the development of redundant structures, or the creation of loose couplings (see Staehle, 1991b). However, these strategies represent mainly an intra-organizational application to increase flexibility (see Reichwald and Behrbohm, 1993). The organization itself continues to exist, but its internal potential to cope with and process environmental change is increased.

The flexibility approach by virtual enterprises, however, is perceived differently. It questions the very existence of permanent organization structures. Virtual organizations configure themselves along a task orientation. They use the flexibility potential of information and communication technologies. For many years the entrepreneurial use of technology was determined by efficiency perspectives. In fact, advanced technologies increased the productivity, but always at the expense of flexibility. Competing goals developed and an incompatible trade-off remained between the concepts of productivity and flexibility (Wigand, 1995d). More recently, modern information technology allowed the partial recovery of lost flexibility (Klimecki, Probst and Gmür, 1993).

Modern information and communication technology has an enormous influence on organizational flexibility. However, this influence does not always appear to be completely beneficial. Lucas and Olson (1994) emphasize the immense flexibility potential made possible by utilizing information technologies. They address improvements of flexibility in three primary areas:

- Changing the time and spatial dimensions of performance
- Increasing the speed of performance
- Improving the response time of enterprise to market changes.

Moreover, they point out that when deploying information technology the *flexibility paradox* exists, the latter being based on the differences between organizational and technical flexibility. Basically, information technology may augment the degree of organizational flexibility. Flexibility can change over time triggering an opposite effect, i.e. resulting in infrastructural rigidity and inflexibility. This phenomenon is based on an inherent inflexibility often embedded in an aging technical infrastructure.

How can a virtual organization go about becoming flexible? It would be wrong to focus only on the flexibility potential provided by the technical infrastructure. The infrastructure simply provides a foundation for the possible reduction of organizational problems. Therefore, virtual organizations aim at:

- achieving "virtual largeness" in spite of "actual smallness";
- taking advantage of centralization within a decentralized structure;
- abolishing the contradiction between generalization and specialization.

"Virtual largeness" in spite of "actual smallness". Today's global trade and investments in technology and innovation demand largeness. Growth and largeness, as well as consistency on the market and in competition are relevant factors for a company's success. Largeness, however, is also considered a synonym for heaviness or clumsiness. Inflexibility and inefficiency as a concomitant of largeness has to be avoided. Until today, economic goals, like value linking (economies of scale, economies of scope), could only be achieved by steady economic growth. In today's world, however, not only small companies are favored by information and communication technology (see Scott Morton, 1992; Brynjolfsson, Malone, Gurbaxani and Kambil, 1993; Wigand, 1995d), but they gain the potential to grow to virtual largeness (Gurbaxani and Whang, 1991). The open-closed-principle of virtual

organizations and their distribution lead to an impression of largeness on the market. Largeness as a result of symbiotic cooperational structures ends in the shared use of resources and/or financial means. Strategies of vertical integration are very often associated with disadvantages of competition. Consequently the considerable shift toward outsourcing and downsizing leads to disintegration. On the contrary, virtual organizations take advantage of virtual integration concepts, because of the multiple linkages between independent units (e.g., Voskamp and Wittke, 1994). This concept results in an "insiderization of outsiders" (Peters, 1994), indicating the breakdown of formal organizational boundaries either from the inside or the outside.

Centralization in spite of Decentralization. When deciding between centralization and decentralization, organizations have to question which instruments they want to use from the market-hierarchy-continuum in order to coordinate economic activities (see Picot, 1994; Reichwald and Koller, 1996). Complete centralization ends in self-sufficiency; complete decentralization implies the transfer of all tasks to independent entrepreneurs. To what extent should firms take advantage of centralized (i.e. hierarchic) or decentralized (i.e. market) organizational forms to accomplish their tasks? Unfortunately, neither ready-made solutions nor either/or answers exist. In this case, it is essential to find an intermediate solution, combining an appropriate mixture of centralization and decentralization. Taking an extreme position can prove to be dangerous. Complete centralization could trigger a breakdown because of high demands imposed on the central authority. On the other hand, a decentralized solution cannot work if no appropriate centralized framework, infrastructures, etc. exist.

Generalization in Spite of Specialization. Generalization requires existing redundant resources both for entrepreneurial organizations, as well as for organizational units or individuals (Staehle, 1991b). In accomplishing a single, specific task, generalists cause inevitably higher costs and lower efficiency than a specialist who is assigned specifically for this task. This advantage of a specialist disappears instantly, however, if the accomplishment of task bundles takes place in a dynamic and uncertain environment. Figure 8.8 illustrates this. The advantages (degree of fit) of a specialist (B) are placed in the interval of low environmental variability (n, m), while we can recognize the advantages of external generalization of this interval. Through their modularity and heterogeneity, virtual organizations can simultaneously achieve a generalized external appearance (e.g., performance offer) and to make use of cost advantages

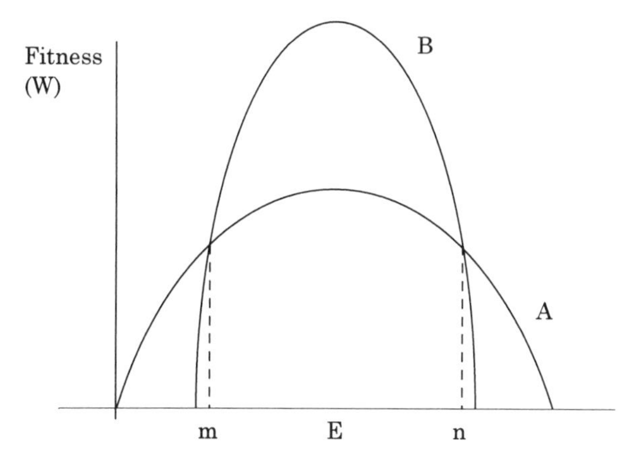

Figure 8.8 *Generalizing versus specializing. Source: Hannan and Freeman (1977, p. 947)*

through a specialization of single components internally (Reiß, 1992b). Again, we remind the reader of the example of the translation agency illustrating the strategy of generalizing in spite of specializing. Every single translator is a specialist for a specific combination of languages and particular field. The virtual enterprise "translation agency" is able to offer a whole range of languages and fields on the market by means of combining skills of individuals into a symbiotic network.

There is still a question as to under which circumstances a virtual organization can take advantage of its potential flexibility. A virtual organization is the appropriate organizational form, if there is a need for a high degree of flexibility. If a task is characterized by a high degree of product complexity and high market uncertainty, this situation requires the formation of temporary task-related cooperative structures (to control uncertainty) in which competencies complement each other well (to control complexity). Accordingly, this virtual organization lends itself as an organizational innovation strategy for accomplishing complex, highly variable problems or for tasks reflecting a high degree of novelty in an uncertain environment.

Boundaries of Virtual Organizations

Virtual organizations manifest themselves across many boundaries: across defined boundaries of time and space, across boundaries of a legally defined internal and external sphere of the organization or extending beyond long-range contractual boundaries concerning the membership or non-membership of organizational participants. However, this organizational form also has its limits which may stem, e.g., from the technical infrastructure. This infrastructure is considered to be the nerve center of an enterprise and determines the possibilities for participation (see Jarvenpaa and Ives, 1994). There are also boundaries and limitations imposed on institutions by human behavioral patterns (see Chapter 2; e.g., bounded rationality or opportunism). The theoretical bases of the role of information for markets and firms developed in Chapters 2 and 3, as well as the insights gained in communication and information behavior enable us, however, to discover initial problem areas with regard to the "boundarylessness" of virtual organizations. Two such problem areas are addressed briefly here.

- Improved support of economic activities via modern information systems are a promising strategy for the expansion of human performance limits. Human beings have only limited capacity to process information (see Chapter 3, page 73). We try to compensate for this through the use of information systems. It is possible, for example, to disseminate requests for proposals with low costs and almost no waste of time, as well as to make worldwide online offers (see Benjamin and Wigand, 1995). Therefore, costs for economic transactions are reduced. The limits of appropriate dynamic technical arrangements are no longer generated by the costs for such arrangements, but by the quality of the electronically available information. The practicality of virtual organizations depends on the willingness to provide information and also on the readiness to use available information. Nevertheless, "No technology has yet been invented that can convince unwilling managers to share information or even to use it" (Davenport et al, 1992, p. 56; cited by Jarvenpaa and Ives, 1994). What are the consequences for a virtual organization as an institution for the processing of economic activities?
- Trust counts as a decisive coordination mechanism for virtual organizations (see Handy, 1995). Opportunistic human behavior, in the sense of pursuing self-interests at another person's expense, causes risks. Principle-agent-theory might be helpful to describe how opportunistic usage of asymmetrical information influences the relationship between buyer and seller (see Chapter 2, page 42 "Principal Agent Theory". Asymmetrical information can cause a risk of delegation. The higher the uncertainty of behavior and the higher the risk of sustaining a loss, the more someone wants to safeguard his/her actions. Likewise, the more complex and strategically important a performance, the higher the interest for contractual guarantees (see Chapter 7). Contracts are traditionally used to provide for performance guarantees. However, virtual organizations mostly renounce

contractual guarantees in order to ensure their dynamic features. Contracts in this case are based on *trust* (Luhmann, 1989; Luhmann, 1994). Nevertheless, blind trust is definitely not recommendable. Short-lived and dynamic virtual organizations based on trust require therefore a long-term relationship including stable and informal confidence, generally accepted reputations, and reliable certifications or "rules of the game." Only the long-range stability of the rules of the game assures the necessary flexibility of organizations (see Bonus, 1994).

Conditions for a Global Organization with Dispersed Work Locations

Information and communication technologies are generating a new industrial revolution on a global basis. Technological progress enables us to exchange information with high speed and retrieve information in various forms from data bases. Numerous advanced work forms already collide with legal norms and current policies in many ways. These policies and laws have been established under differing circumstances and require further development and specific supplementation. The information-based revolution demands an adjustable legal framework which allows for further technological developments. The intercontinental shipment of books, for example, requires an adherence to customs regulations. The transfer of exactly the same information (i.e. the content of these books) via electronic data exchange can be carried out with no delay or any supplemental formalities. The resources of information and knowledge, as well as available human resources, are becoming more important for companies, still the balance sheets of enterprises focus on fixed and current assets. Financial accounting enters transfers of goods and money in the books, but the exchange of information within or between organizations is not considered. Above all, information is considered to be the key ingredient in the service sector, yet we are not able to measure the quality, determine the value, or guarantee the protection of information. Organization theory and business practice still ignore the importance of information as a valuable resource (e.g., Wigand, 1988a). If information truly is to play such an important role for firms in the future, as it is ascribed today, what role do organization theory and business practice play in this setting?

The outcome of the 1995 G7-meeting, including the most powerful western industrialized countries, underlined the urge for a global liberalization of telecommunication markets. Since then, the creation of a *global information infrastructure* (GII) as a prerequisite of the predicted information society, is no longer considered solely a vision. However, there are numerous barriers hindering the transition towards an information age: strengthening existing network infrastructures and accelerating the construction of new ones; creating a clear and stable regulatory, as well as a legal, framework; discussing different international priority programs. Stimulating an awareness, reducing fears and coping with risks are decisive efforts for development and advancement. It should be noted that similar and often parallel initiatives can be observed worldwide. In order to illustrate these efforts, the European initiative is highlighted here as an example.

Europe has taken the first steps to become an information society (see Bangemann, 1995): The "White Paper on Growth, Competitiveness and Employment: Present Challenges and Steps into the 21st Century" from December, 1993 lays out future perspectives. Information and communication technologies, services and applications are to stimulate and ensure a steady economic growth, augment competitiveness, as well as create new jobs, leading to an improvement in the quality of life.

In June, 1994 a group of information society experts presented the so-called Bangemann Report, "Europe and the Global Information Society—Recommendations to the European Council". The Council adopted an operational program defining precise procedures for actions and necessary means (European Commission, 1994a; Vertretung der Europäischen Komission in Deutschland, 1995). The legislature is charged *to create an appropriate regulatory and legal framework*. Above all, the Council recommends to accelerate the on-going liberalizations of the telecommunication sector by means of:

- opening infrastructures and services to competition;
- removing non-commercial, political burdens and budgetary constraints imposed on telecommunication operators;
- setting clear timetables and deadlines for the implementation of practical measures for achieving these goals.

The report outlines essential features of the deployment of the information infrastructure: one is a seamless interconnection of networks and the other that the service and applications which build on them should be able to work together (*interoperability*). This is a prerequisite demanded by internationally delivered services. The report identified primarily five points:

1 Protection of intellectual property rights
2 Protection of privacy
3 Information security
4 Media ownership
5 The role of competitive policy.

The follow-up paper "Europe's Way into the Information Society: An Action Plan" from July 19, 1994 (Europäische Kommission, 1995) responds to the recommendations of the European Council (Bangemann Report) and offers conclusions in the form of a work program. Although these initiatives in Europe, and similar ones in the US and Japan have begun relatively independently, since the G-7 conference in Brussels in February, 1995 one can observe a trend toward intensified cooperation within this triad. Trade policy aspects must be formulated in a global and consistent approach, necessitating an intensified dialogue among Europe, the United States and Japan in the context of an information society. The importance of integrating economically less developed regions in a global infrastructure is known. The following eight principles will help to ensure the openness of a global information society (see EU-Informationen, 1995, p. 11):

- Fair competition
- Stimulating private investments
- Establishing an adjustable legal framework
- Equal access to networks
- Universal provision and unrestrained access to offered services
- Equal opportunities and access rights to information by all citizens
- Improving the diversity of information, also with regard to culture and language
- Acknowledging the necessity of global cooperation (especially the inclusion of developing countries).

A number of basic requirements can be derived from the principles above, which have to be taken into account when building a global information and communication infrastructure (EU-Informationen, 1995, p. 11):

- Promoting compatibility and interoperability
- Developing global market places for networks, services and applications
- Protecting privacy, as well as ensuring data security
- Protecting intellectual property rights
- Collaborating in the development of applications
- Observing social effects of the information society.

The industrial age brought about a new framework. Similarly, the world of work in the information age has to be viewed within a new framework. Today, we find many legal constraints which have to be updated, such as labor law, tax law, and laws pertaining to competition. Also, adjustments and extensions in economic policies require deliberation. These adjustments are no longer limited to individual nations. To a large degree, the diversity of legal systems influences questions pertaining to the distribution of work places and cooperation among firms. Currently, Europe is in the process of harmonizing its differences. It is still uncertain whether the diversity of national legal systems is, in the final analysis, a facilitator or barrier for firms, customers, workers, as well as society and the environment.

THE ROLE OF INFORMATION AND COMMUNICATION TECHNOLOGY

Application Types and Fields of Efficient Network Infrastructures

Cooperative work surpassing locational boundaries demands suitable information and communication infrastructures, especially since overcoming the boundaries of space and time is primarily a communication problem. Recent technological developments assist in many applied areas to defuse this communication problem and improve, in turn, the cooperative work of spatially distant partners. If, for example, the advice of specialists is needed who are not locally available (teleconsulting), the possibilities to express oneself and to demonstrate one's points by phone are relatively limited. In this setting, additional video channels or the integration of different media (text, data, voice, freeze-frame or moving pictures) within multi-media applications offer in this setting clear improvements. Realizing such possibilities, however, is directly tied to the availability of effective communication infrastructures. This direct connection between efficiency of the network infrastructure and meaningful application possibilities becomes clearly visible in the following examples (see Bayer, 1994, p. 303):

- Network connections with a capacity of 64 Kbit/s make possible, for example, the simple transmission of text. Interactive text processing, however, is severely limited at this bandwidth.
- Network connections with a capacity of 2 Mbit/s allow the transmission of black and white freeze-frame pictures with acceptable transmission times (ca. 5s), assuming a middle-level of network load. This network capacity, however, is insufficient for color freeze-frame pictures, video sequences or moving pictures.
- Network capacities of more than 100 Mbit/s (FDDI, DQDB, ATM; see Chapter 4, Figure 4.5) permit the use of interactive multi-media applications in support of telecooperative work.

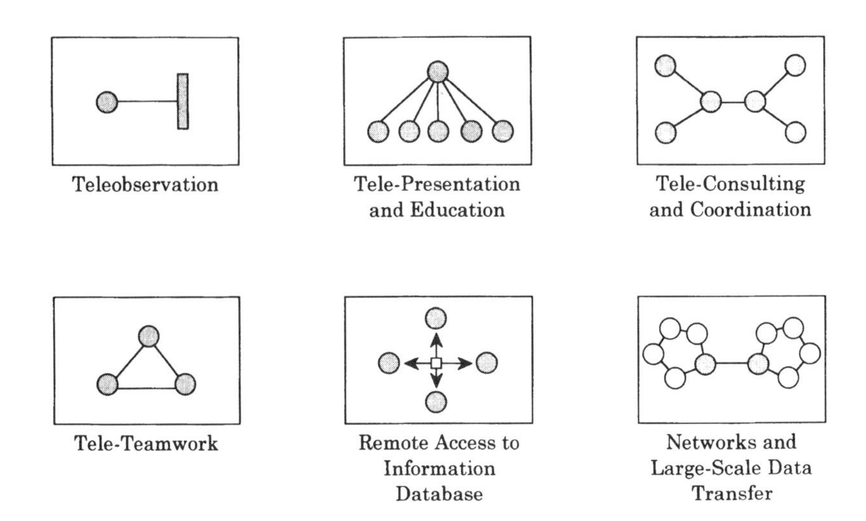

Figure 8.9 *Basic deployment types of broadband applications. Source: adapted from Bierhals, Nippa and Seetzen (1991) Reichwald (1991a. Reproduced by permission of Schäffer-Poeschel Verlag)*

In conjunction with the German BERKOM Project (1986–1991), numerous empirical studies were undertaken that estimated the market potential of the future use of digital broadband networks (see Kanzow, 1991; Bierhals, Nippa and Seetzen, 1991; Reichwald, 1991a). On the basis of about 1000 applied cases, eight general application types for communication and information infrastructures emerged. These, in turn, evolved into six basic structural types based on communication theoretical considerations. Figure 8.9 depicts these six basic types.

For the identification of deployment types, the BERKOM market analysis identified the following potential and application focal points (see Reichwald, 1991a):

Teleobservation. Teleobservation allows the control and regulation of procedures and processes without a physical presence at the actual location of the event. Certain problems, therefore, can be analyzed and solved on a 24-hour basis, independent of location. The following applications suggest themselves for teleobservation:

- For after-sales service applications, the quality of customer service may increase dramatically through the rapid, uncomplicated analysis of problem situations while using broadband-transmitted freeze-frame and moving pictures (e.g., capturing and transmission of the actual trouble and trouble spot). This is of particular interest in the areas of assembly and start-up of machines and facilities, their maintenance, and problem identification.

- Remote observations of controlling systems in factories, hazardous processes in scientific experiments, as well as the observation of precious cultural treasures permit location and time-independent and, simultaneously, risk-free tele-presence while using relatively low-cost resources.
- Application potential can be found, too, at the interface between Research & Development and sales/distribution, especially in conjunction with the development of customer-specific products within the chemical and synthetic materials processing industry. Here we can think of the controlling function of the proficiency of special machines during the manufacture of synthetic materials testing phase as a realistic applied example.

Tele-presentation and Tele-education. Tele-presentation and tele-education implies multi-media-based information processing from an information center to many participants in the communication process. Through the support of network infrastructures, interactivity between communication participants, for example, in the form of joint processing of documents with parallel voice and video communication in such situations. This provides new opportunities for seminars and continuing education sessions and makes it possible to transfer existing knowledge, independent of time and location, to employees and customers. The following applications suggest themselves for tele-presentation and tele-education:

- Knowledge-intensive businesses (e.g., air and space travel) and certain functional areas within firms (e.g., Research & Development) may benefit from the interactive yet remote participation in continuing education events or university-based lectures.
- For product presentations as a central information activity in the sales and distribution effort within industry, trade and service organizations, telemedia support promises a goal-specific deployment, an increased sphere of activity, as well as improved quality in consulting, advice-based and information services.

Tele-consulting and Tele-coordination. Tele-consulting and tele-coordination include the location-independent communication between two or among a small number of individuals. This can be supported through the use of multi-media documents and simple contact initiation with organization-internal information carriers. The location-independent utilization of documents, as well as the possibilities for feedback and information retrieval, are unquestionably critical application features needing support on the level of communication and information infrastructures. The following applications are highlighted for tele-consulting and tele-coordination:

- An unusually high application potential can be identified for teleconsulting and tele-coordination in the area of technical advising/consulting and case worker tasks within the financial services sector. Customer service support through the quick utilization of case-specific information (e.g., investment and financing forms, model calculations, customer data) at the time and point of interaction brings time advantages, creating time for a more intensive problem- and customer-specific analysis.
- Computer-supported case work as a central activity within banks and insurance companies encompasses voluminous data communications within which contracts, procedural and investment documents (e.g., plans, drawings, designs, photographs) will have to be exchanged beyond locational boundaries. More efficient infrastructures promise here immediate improvements with regard to the quality of the data to be transferred and the duration of such transfers. Performance volume, as well as the speed with which the firm is able to react, should profit from such deployments.
- Additional application focal points for tele-consulting and coordination can be envisioned especially in the realm of distribution support, as well as the production of printed materials within industry and trade.

Tele-teamwork. Tele-teamwork explores new forms of cooperation among work groups at geographically dispersed locations. In contrast to tele-consulting and coordination, tele-teamwork usually involves multiple participants. The possibility of interactive multi-media communication increases the potential for spontaneous reactions and the direct utilization of new ideas. Tele-teamwork promises therefore increased flexibility, a quicker response capability and improved efficiency, especially in conjunction with the formation of technical and enterprise-wide cooperative efforts and alliances. Within tele-teamwork we can identify the following areas as application focal points:

- In the manufacturing of industrial goods, especially during the planning and acquisition phases, the support of locationally dispersed cooperation among customers, suppliers and internal units within the manufacturing enterprise are areas ripe for the fruitful application of tele-teamwork concepts.

- Efficient cooperation within interdisciplinary developer teams requires an infrastructure that, in turn, enables the group to mutually design, work on, and manage CAD drawings. At the same time, there is also a need to support project management with suitable groupware tools.

Remote Access to Information Data Bases. A central role among the trends toward the globalization of business relationships (e.g., worldwide research and development, international financial markets), mass customization of products and product-related services, as well as the qualification demands within employee training and development, is played by jointly-used data bases. Infrastructures with sufficient bandwidth are required that enable the archiving of multi-media documents in an integrated fashion such that they can be retrieved on demand from distant locations. Such knowledge pools constitute the starting point for the emergence of self-reliant information markets (see Chapter 7). Multimedia information may then be offered as an independent service and is likely to develop based on supply and demand while continuously developing quantitatively and qualitatively. The following initial focal points can be identified during the remote information retrieval from data bases:

- In the area of scientific basic research, as well as in the area of research and development in large firms within the chemical industry, there is an unusually high application potential for internal and external online data bases.
- In an effort to maintain certain levels of competitiveness among small and medium-sized firms, as well as to intensify technology transfer between the scientific community and industry, we often encounter government supported efforts in the building of voluminous data bases. The utilization of such data bases may be stimulated in these areas, especially through wide-reaching information supply and qualitatively improved content.

Networks and Large-scale Data Transfer. The formation of computer connections and linkages with other computers enables the use of distant computing capacities (e.g., high performance or specialized computers). Such a utilization of distant capacities is always then important when extreme performance demands are at stake which cannot be delivered locally. The following application fields can be identified:

- High performance demands are encountered typically during applications with real-time conditions, large-scale simulation runs, forecasting calculations or the visualization of large-scale processes. Already today, research facilities within the areas of environmental protection, energy and medicine utilize the computer capacities for large-scale computing centers for the evaluation of experiments, event analysis, and process simulations.

- Computer linkages also need to be mentioned in conjunction with the trend toward performance optimization and the resulting outsourcing efforts of data processing services. Especially the areas of chemistry and machine building utilize the capabilities of external computing centers to a large extent, for example, for data security and actualization.

However, these innovative areas of application for efficient communication and information infrastructures may not overlook the following. On the one hand, the newest technologies are perceived as drivers of development. Video conferencing systems, groupware and work-flow technologies, multi-media applications on the basis of efficient traffic networks; mobile communication and mobile computing form the foundation for innovative telecooperative concepts. On the other hand, successful, practical deployment of such systems so far is limited. Areas of application are found typically within the realm of high technology business (e.g., the multi-media industry) or in highly technical applications of research and development. Actual applications of telecooperation within manufacturing and service industries are still limited to individual applications, as well as to communication via telephone, fax and electronic mail, simple data transmissions and terminal emulation (see IDATE, 1994). These so far isolated *technology building blocks*, however, are gradually growing together into an integrated support system. How these connections between the telecommunication and the information system world are being shaped and the resulting utilization potential is discussed in the following section.

The Integration of Computer Systems, Telecommunications and Telecooperative Work Forms

Even today, telephone and computer systems are mainly used independent of one another. The goal now is to explore the integration of varying functionalities of telecommunications and information system infrastructures within firms. This integration of computer applications and telephony may be seen as the formation of a strategic alliance that may enable a multitude of innovative problem-solving possibilities. Only a few aspects pertaining to this interplay can be addressed here. For a detailed depiction of innovative integration developments and their applications, we refer to the research work by Pribilla, Reichwald and Goecke (1996).

Through the example of the call-center concept, it is possible to demonstrate elements, functions and application possibilities of computer-telephone-integration (CTI) (see Gable, 1993). Call Centers are CTI applications attempting to process large volumes of calls as quickly and as efficiently as possible. Information and hotline services, reservation offices, customer service and telephone sales are typical application areas in which a large number of inbound calls and/or outbound calls have to be processed. In this context, problems arise in reaching a communications partner and determining a suitable load for the employee. Classical telephone practices offer little support for these problems. Newer possibilities enabling automatic phone call distribution (Automatic Call Distribution (ACD)), Voice Response Unit (VRU) or computer-supported telephony and the telephone information teaming (PBX and Computer Teaming (PaCT)) promise assistance in such a setting.

The main job of an inbound Call Center is the acceptance and answering of incoming phone calls through the Call Center agents. In order to reach a maximum percentage of reached communication partners for the caller and, at the same time, in order to maximize the Call Center capacities, telephone equipment needs to offer suitable features for call routing and distribution. Essentially, one can differentiate between three system classes among call distribution features:

1 *Automatic Call Sequencers (ACSs):* ACS units form today an essential and widely available component of telephone equipment. They allow the automatic reception of calls with standard announcement features ("Please wait for the next available customer service representative!", or music). Received calls are placed in a queue behind other calls. Call Center representatives are then informed about the status of the call waiting queue, but handle the processing of these calls themselves.
2 *Uniform Call Distributors (UCDs):* UCDs are simple software blocks allowing the equal distribution of calls to Call Center agents. Typically, the basic distribution algorithms only take the number of calls processed by an individual agent into account, not the duration of the calls. In the case of an unusually long call, this may lead to extremely uneven call distribution to agents. ACSs and also UCDs are, consequently, not sufficient to meet the demands of efficient Call Center concepts.
3 *Automatic Call Distributors (ACDs):* ACDs offer so far the most efficient support for Call Centers. As a basic function, ACD systems

offer the automatic reception of inbound calls and their placement into a queue behind other calls, as well as their subsequent distribution to free agents. During this distribution process, this system monitors the number of available lines, as well as the appropriate utilization of agents in terms of frequency and duration of calls made. In addition, the system generates reports on call distribution. ACD systems increase the employee's productivity, making it easier to process more calls given the same capacity. Fewer phone calls are "lost" and important customers can be served through the use of automatic number identification (ANI) on a priority basis. The actual utilization of potential advantages through the deployment of automatic call distribution is dependent upon two conditions: (1) The caller wants to use a service (e.g., information) and does not need to reach a specific individual, and (2) the requested service may be provided by every agent within the Call Center.

In addition to the above, new opportunities of voice recognition and voice commands expand the functions of modern telephone equipment. *Voice Response Units (VRUs)* offer two basic functional features. On the one hand, they allow the voice recognition, which can be used in data base queries through prestructured dialogues over the phone. On the other hand, through the use of the multiple frequency procedures instead of the older impulse procedures via the telephone buttons, multiple frequency tones can be generated that may be used for the distribution and routing of prestructured questions. Through the translation of the spoken words, or rather multiple frequency tones into computer commands, it is thus possible to query, for example, account balances or product information, or to make reservations. In Call Center applications voice-response technologies are frequently used in combination with forms of automatic call routing (see Figure 8.10).

When using the mechanisms of call distribution and structured dialogues with a targeted combination of the capabilities of the telephone equipment together with the functions of a firm's information systems, one then refers to *PBX and Computer Teaming (PaCT)*. This type of telephone-based infrastructure (see Figure 8.11) enjoys multiple deployment possibilities. Depending on whether or not the system reacts to incoming queries or whether it becomes externally active, two basic application situations can be identified (see Pribilla, Reichwald and Goecke, 1996):

1 *Basic schema in the interplay of PBX and computer systems in inbound applications:*
   - Incoming calls are identified through automatic caller identification.

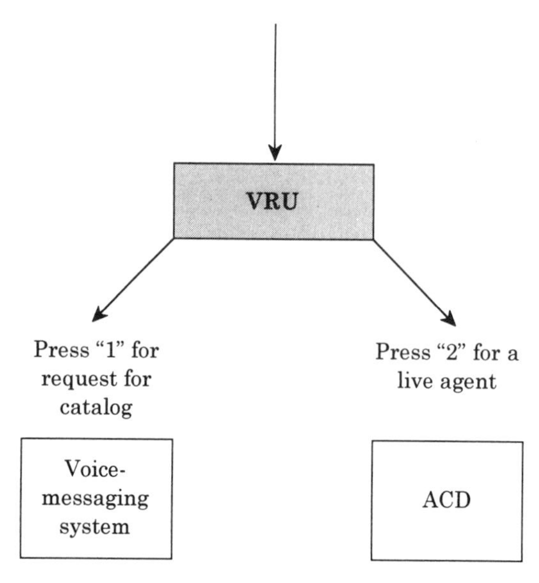

Figure 8.10 *Call prompting for voice messaging*

- The call number is transferred from the telephone to the computer system and the corresponding customer data are selected from the data base.
- From the customer profile it is possible, for example, to identify the appropriate case worker and his/her telephone number that the caller can be linked with *his/her* customer representative.
- At the same time when the phone rings with the appropriate case worker, the relevant customer data appear on his/her computer screen.
- In certain circumstances, for example, when answering highly specialized questions, the call and the appropriate data may be routed to another case worker. At the same time the phone call is received, the accompanying data are received as well. During such intelligent transfers, the customer does not need to repeat his/her question(s).

2 *Basic schema in the interplay between PBX and computer systems in outbound applications:*
   - Within a computer application a data base generates a listing of calls to be made.
   - The telephone numbers from the call listing are transmitted from the computer system to the telephone system.
   - The telephone system automatically dials the numbers to be called and then connects the call only when a connection has

been made and a case worker is available. The application with the appropriate data and functions to handle the case appear on the case worker's computer screen simultaneously with the delivery of the call (see Figure 8.11).

The demonstrated functions evolving from the stepwise growing-together of telephony and computer applications are predominantly utilized today in the processing of large call volumes in Call Center applications. With increasing availability and decreasing operating costs for these functionalities, it is also evident that definite improvements in the communication between participants and their efforts to overcome location and firm-specific limitations through cooperative work arrangements are forthcoming. For customers it is then irrelevant whether *their* case worker receives the call in the office, in the telework center near the employee's home, or at the employee's work place at home. In achieving a 24-hour availability, a firm can take advantage of differing time zones. For virtual enterprises that configure themselves into legally independent, but spatially distributed units, it is becoming easier to present a uniform appearance. For small and medium-sized firms, it is possible to assist each other during certain times of high demands or, for example, during vacation times, without this being obvious to the customer.

CONCLUSIONS FOR MANAGEMENT

New developments in information and communication technologies help in overcoming traditional boundaries of time and space. They allow, simplify, and promote the dispersion of locations. The mere distribution of locations, however, does not result in a competitive advantage for the company. Dispersion and/or independence of locations, (1) as a result of a particular time/space management in order to take advantage of specific locations, and (2) as a reaction to new demands in an environment whose complexity and dynamics obviously increases, leads to the realization of lasting advantages in global competition.

Both aspects will be examined in the following sections. First we look at the benefits of distributed locations, taking a global disintegration of the value chain into account. Then we inspect the profound changes within the division of labor as expressed, for example, in the establishment of virtual organizations. For significant changes, however, a gradual adaptation of mental models will not suffice. Significant changes, as argued later in this chapter, demand a fundamental reconceptualization of basic business principles.

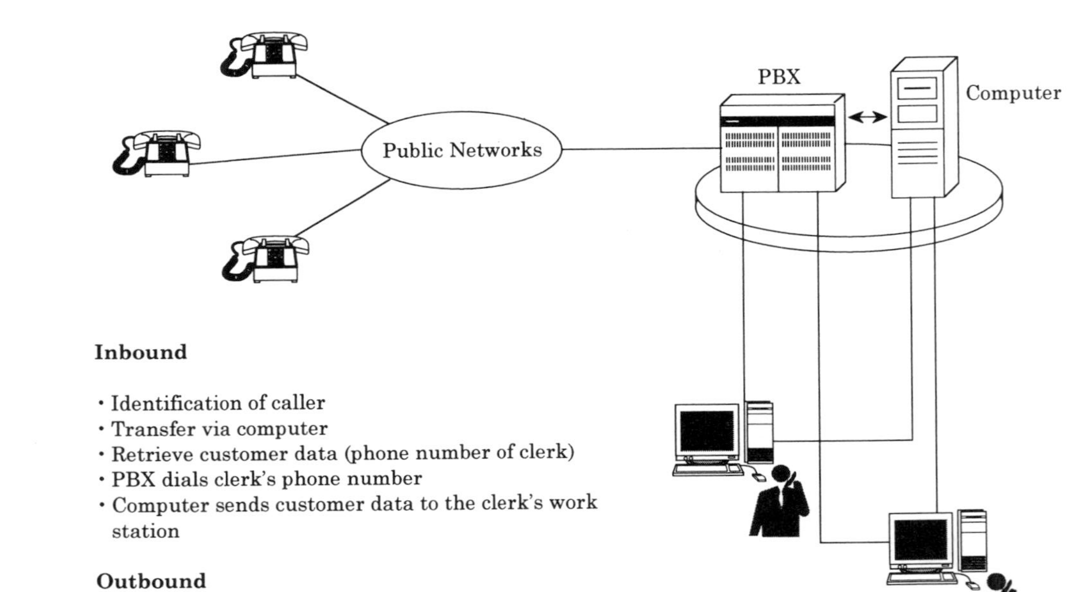

igure 8.11 *The workings of PBX and Computer Teaming (PaCT). Source: Pribilla, Reichwald and Goecke (1996. Reproduced by permission from Schäffer-Poeschel Verlag, Stuttgart.)*

Disintegration of the Value Chain and Dispersion of Locations

Value linking and competence advantages can be realized through the dispersion of a company's location. As mentioned above, knowledge, skills and abilities are heterogeneously distributed on a global basis. Through a targeted combination of varying regional and national strengths, the performance capacity of the entire organization may be improved. Griese (1992) refers to opportunities for the organization which arise from global information and communication systems for networks and firms operating on a worldwide basis. For him the transition from a "real" to a "virtual" enterprise is linked to the systematic dissolution of the value chain: "In reality, the value chain is not fully present in each country, however, within the firm, as well as from the perspective of the customer and supplier, the firm enjoys a 'virtual' presence within the entire value chain." (Griese, 1992, p. 170, translation by authors) (Griese 1993; Mertens, 1994). According to Griese, Figure 8.12 depicts a schematic interpretation of disintegrating the value chain.

Correspondingly, Simon, Bauer, and Jägeler (1993) state that European management advantages can be realized in the targeted use of heterogeneity. Not in the search for commonness, but in working out the differences and their utilization, they see advantages for European firms:

> "For example, a trouble-free combination of French communication capabilities, German organizational talent, and Italian flexibility and improvisational talent opens a European perspective which may create an

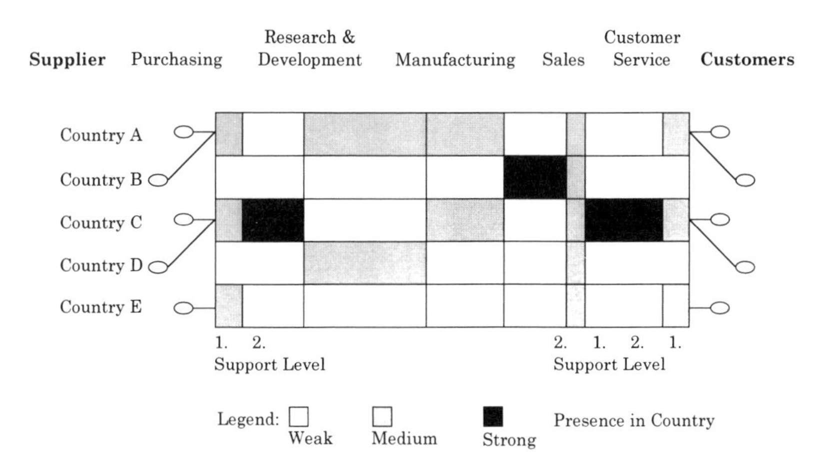

Figure 8.12 Schematic interpretation of disintegrating the value chain. Source: Griese, (1992, p. 171. Reproduced by permission from Walter de Gruyter Verlag, Berlin.)

almost unbeatable competitive advantage in a global market. A condition for this, however, would not only be mutual understanding and tolerance, but also a high sensibility for cultural and structural change, as well as for their own strengths and weaknesses." (*Simon, Bauer and Jägeler, 1993, p. 119; translation by authors).*

In their analysis of management cultures, structures and success factors in Germany, England, France, Italy and Spain the authors present a model of a European-wide, distributed firm in which "all functions and positions are filled corresponding to country-specific strengths". Figure 8.13 depicts the working model of such an idealized "European enterprise".

The Virtual Organization: Toward a Cognitive Division of Labor

Previously illustrated working models take selective use of competitive advantage into account in order to cope with increasing demands and complexity of tasks. Virtual organizations represent a task- and competence-oriented approach in the design of an organization. Static and long-term boundaries of responsibility will be transformed into dynamic and specific allocations of competence, specific for task accomplishment. In this case, abstract assignments transfer into concrete combinations of problem-solving competence.

Moati and Mouhoud (1994) interpret this scenario as a fundamental change from traditional forms of division of labor to competence and quality-oriented forms of a division of labor. Division of labor seems to be increasingly dominated by cognitive rather than by technical aspects (Moati and Mouhoud, 1994, p. 52).

Their arguments can be summarized as follows: Information as a production factor has no intrinsic value. The value originates through the transformation of information into knowledge and its application in the company. Nevertheless, the transformation and application of knowledge requires competence. The extraordinary expansion and growth of data, information and knowledge has led to a constant increase of specialization, and therefore triggered an organizational dilemma. On the one hand, these circumstances require rather holistic approaches to the accomplishment of tasks; on the other, mastering complex tasks necessitates increased specialization ("hyperspecialization"). Consequently, the entire enterprise transfers from a classic location of production to a location of allocating competence: production is no longer divided into numerous sequences, following Taylor's model; the division of labor depends on knowledge and competence of employees. Moati and Mouhoud refer to this as a *cognitive division of labor*. This form of

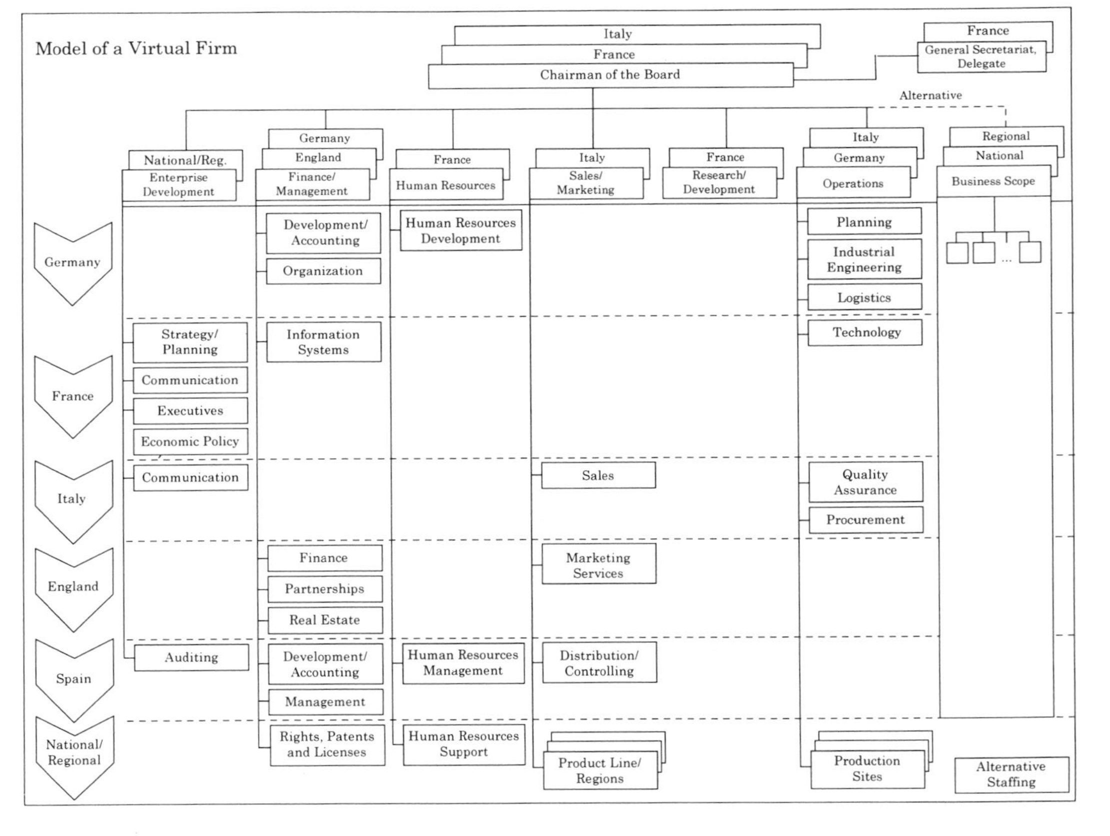

Figure 8.13 *Working model of an idealized "European Enterprise". Source: Simon, Bauer, Jägeler (1993, p. 262. Translation by the authors. Reproduced by permission from Verlag Moderne Industrie, Landsberg, Germany.)*

division of labor is similar to the pre-industrial division of labor in handcraft-based production structures.

The range of performance is restricted by the attainable range of competence and knowledge that an enterprise is able to provide. Know-how barriers, found in the model of optimizing the range of performance (Picot, 1991b) increasingly restrict internal accomplishment of specific or strategic important tasks. If specialization of performance is more often accompanied by specialization of knowledge (with highly variable requirements), the internal accomplishment of tasks is increasingly restricted by the prohibitive cost of internalizing knowledge:

> "Often the problem does not really exist in finding out whether or not it is more economical to accomplish tasks oneself or to letting someone else do the work. One has to let the work be done by someone else because one is unable to do the work oneself." (*Moati and Mouhoud, 1994, p. 60; translation by authors*)

Reflections on the cognitive division of labor are naturally fitting for the approach of distributing tasks in virtual organizations: distribution of tasks occurs as a dynamic separation, division, and distribution (Reiß, 1992a) of problems to highly specialized people. Reflections referring to the range of knowledge within enterprises makes it clear which tasks virtual organizations are responsible for: highly specific tasks and those of strategic importance, whose internalizing fails by lack of know-how, are suitable for the concept of virtual organizations (see page 337).

Once more, we will use the example of the translation agency in order to clarify this subject. Consider the adaptation and translation of software and additional documentation for targeted markets. An American software firm has to decide whether to produce a product for the European market by itself or to give away the order to another company. The software product should be available on the European market shortly after the release in the US market. The high degree of interdependence between different sub-tasks points to an internal processing. Additionally, highly specific knowledge is necessary, as well as the strategic relevance of a software product. Nevertheless, internalizing fails, based on know-how barriers. Only specialists who are native speakers in the particular market, are aware of product details, and who have the necessary background knowledge, are able to sufficiently accomplish the task. The higher the complexity and the volume of the product, the more of these problems come into the picture (e.g., producing a multi-media encyclopedia). In this case, a virtual integration of the necessary competencies is the only acceptable procedure.

Realistic Premises for Realistic Design Strategies

The way "business thinks" is still influenced by premises which emerged in an earlier time and held true under previous circumstances. These premises are only valid today, if the particular task is embedded in a stable environment with a low degree of variability and a high degree of repetition, i.e. the characteristic conditions of mass production are recognizable. Lutz (1995) considers six design principles (Principles of Common Wisdom) for this environment (see also Reichwald and Möslein, 1995):

- The principle of maximized planning of organizational processes
- The principle of drawing a clear dividing line among responsibilities
- The principle of the preference for organization-internal solutions
- The principle of maximized utilization of serial effects
- The principle of market control through incremental product innovation
- The primacy of labor-saving investments.

Unfortunately, the premises underlying these principles cease to be valid in large parts of business today, as they emerged from a different time under different conditions. Changing conditions require new premises. However, new premises question the current principles and demand a verification of working models established on these principles. It is still unclear which further steps have to be taken in order to cope in a turbulent and variable environment. Moreover, it is uncertain how changed premises for economic explanation and design approaches have an effect on future working models. Today, we are in an experimental state. Grenier's and Metes' (1992) approach "Simultaneous Distributed Work (SDW)" stimulates new concepts and experimentation. Four (unconventional) assumptions of the reality of distributed collaboration ("Working Together Apart") are the foundation of this approach:

- Change is constant
- All work is distributed
- Knowledge is the critical resource
- There will never be enough time.

Virtual organizations might be an attempt to accept these assumptions and to use them in restructuring organizations.

9
Rediscovering People as Resources: Improving Human Performance in Organizations

DRIVERS FOR THE EXPANSION OF HUMAN PERFORMANCE LIMITS IN ORGANIZATIONS

It is becoming difficult to delineate the borders and boundaries of today's organizations. Organizational, spatial and technical boundaries of enterprises are expanded and some are removed, while hierarchical structures are being reconfigured. It becomes necessary, on the one hand, to improve abilities, knowledge and qualifications. On the other hand, employees enjoy opportunities to develop their responsibility, personality and performance. Consequently, it is important to know what the particular role of employees is within new entrepreneurial concepts in order to achieve maximal performance. These new entrepreneurial concepts, i.e. borderlessness, virtual, modular, as well as telework structures influence the role, leadership as well as value added processes carried out by workers and managers. It becomes obvious that achieving new entrepreneurial structures implies different role behaviors and, therefore, distinctive patterns of qualification and motivation need to be followed. Knowledge about human motivation, job satisfaction, as well as the connection between employee, work and performance will become essential components to successfully integrate and lead human resources. A brief historical excursion leading to today's developments is appropriate.

The Mechanistic View of Human Work

Early in this century organization theories were strongly influenced by scientific management, whose founder was Frederick W. Taylor (Taylor,

1913). Taylor was of the opinion that enterprises focus on financial prosperity of both employees and employers. He assumed that employees strive for the highest possible wages, while employers have the cheapest possible production costs in mind. Taylor implied that employees always try to maximize their income. Already by the 18th century, the image of man was viewed as a *homo oeconomicus* (Smith, 1776). Accordingly, achieving the highest possible wage is said to be the highest incentive for employees. Taylor suggests supporting a worker's motivation, because a desired higher standard of living is a result of increased income to workers. Moreover, Taylor suggested the introduction of a new, scientific factory management whose aim would be to achieve productivity improvements through the optimization of manufacturing processes (e.g., Reichwald and Hesch, 1993, as well as page 167). In order to stimulate workers to higher performance, a program of high wages for the individual as a reward for high production had to be established benefiting both employees and employers.

Taylor basically advocated three principles (Taylor, 1913, p. 37):

1 Delineation between manager and worker
2 Work segmentation and division of labor applied to the work to be executed
3 Separation of all planning and controlling activities from the production process.

Taylor's interpretation of human work caused the integration of human resources into the process of manufacturing like no other factor enabling performance increase. Analogously, the worker is considered to be a mechanism who functions in a way very similar to machines and thus it was argued that workers can be controlled and planned for just like other components of manufacturing and production processes. This perception of the worker was manifested in functionally structured industrial work.

This mechanized image of man described in Taylorism also influenced the economic production and cost theory by Gutenberg. This theory refers to the human work force as the third key factor besides tools and materials (Gutenberg, 1951). Industrial performance is often expressed with formalized mathematical production and cost functions.

Gutenberg points out that human beings, influenced by their economic environment, do not exclusively show a rational behavior. Human beings reveal numerous irrational characteristics and behaviors which cannot be grasped quantitatively. Thus, the evolution of an enterprise depends additionally on numerous psychological elements (Gutenberg, 1929, p. 40).

Gutenberg stresses though that economic *man* with his/her quantitatively immeasurable irrational characteristics and behavior does not follow a rationality principle *per se*. It follows, therefore, that the development of an organization is dependent on a number of social and personal factors (Gutenberg, 1929, p. 40). Accordingly, it was deemed appropriate, following the *zeitgeist*, prevailing social conditions and stable market situation, to reduce the actual multiplicity of the human being and behavior to the image of *homo oeconomicus* (Werhahn, 1989, p. 77).

The Human Relations Movement

The human relations movement emerged from American industrial psychology and sociology, because the concept of Taylorism had been criticized increasingly during the 1920s and 1930s. Mayo and his co-workers examined human behavior in the Hawthorne plants (*Hawthorne Experiments*) of the Western Electric Company in Chicago (Roethlisberger and Dickson, 1939; Mayo, 1949). These experiments had been conducted in order to analyze the influence of technical working conditions on internal productivity. It had been examined, for example, how illumination and ventilation affects the performance of industrial workers. Interestingly, it turned out that it is not sufficient only to examine the connection between technical working conditions and productivity in order to explain human working behavior entirely. The importance of social relationships among workers were recognized, as well as the phenomenon of internal teams and their relevance for organizations. Informal teams emerged in addition to formally defined group structures; such informal teams have their own rules and norms, which can stimulate individual performance to a higher degree than holding out the prospect of wage increases. The results contradict Taylor's theory, who claimed that workers are maximizers of wages. Accordingly, social and psychological conditions under which human being work became the focus of attention. The Hawthorne studies were reanalyzed during the 1980s, although the considerably disparate findings have not penetrated the management literature.

The key thrusts of the Human Relations movement were taken into account when revising the image of man. The working human being was no longer considered a rational individual acting in isolation, who can only be motivated by monetary incentives, but as a social entity whose behavior is mostly influenced by the affiliation to groups and its specific rules and norms (Wunderer and Grunwald, 1980, p. 96). Roethlisberger and Dickson (1939) and Mayo (1949) made attempts to design and improve internal and interpersonal relationships by supporting teamwork and interpersonal communication among employees.

Eventually criticism of the human relations movement followed (e.g., Miles, 1975, p. 39). It is based on overestimating the influence of interpersonal relationships within organizations, while content and structure of actual tasks, as well as the principles of scientific management (increasing productivity through division of labor) remained unchanged.

Consequently, the distinction between the human relations movement and scientific management is based solely on the choice of methods that increase productivity. The theory of a monocausal connection between job satisfaction and performance is as problematic as the theory of Taylor, arguing for a direct connection between wages and performance. Nonetheless, explaining human working behavior by exclusively taking social relationships with organizations into account is surely not sufficient. This line of thinking has to be embellished by taking individual needs and values into consideration (e.g., Kupsch and Marr, 1991, p. 734).

Satisfying interpersonal relationships, required by the human relations approach, will not automatically lead to higher performance. Accordingly, motivation, i.e. the perceived period of time between a current and an attainable future event, is decisive in order to achieve performance as well as satisfaction. Correspondingly, McGregor (1960) points out that motivation rather than satisfaction is of paramount importance, because satisfied needs are not the source of maintaining motivation. Therefore, it became obvious that human needs and their linkages to motivation, frustration, satisfaction and performance had to be acknowledged and researched (Hill, Fehlbaum and Ulrich, 1992, p. 424). This recognition is also of importance for the evaluation of today's related developments.

The Theory of Job Satisfaction

Several factors affecting a worker's attitude towards his/her job were increasingly investigated by numerous psychologists. These approaches deal with workers' individual needs and attitudes and develop a more comprehensive model of man than does the human relations movement. According the Maslow (1954), a range of motivations can be divided into levels in which different needs are dominant. The concept of a "need hierarchy", in which the various needs of an individual can be placed on a hierarchy of prepotency, laid the foundation for the dynamic structure of human needs. According to this theory, when a need is satisfied, the next prepotent (higher) need emerges. His hierarchy starts with physiological needs, followed by safety, then social and esteem needs, culminating at the top level with self-actualization needs. In Maslow's system the hierarchy begins with the motivation of the organism and extends through a variety of psychological needs as initially less prepotent, but ready to become more prepotent when the physiological needs are satisfied (Maslow, 1954). Maslow's needs hierarchy is a conceptually systematic paradigm, yet Maslow did not claim empirical validity for his model.

According to his theory, Herzberg developed Maslow's theory of motivation further and detected that there are two sources of employees' motivation: job environment and job content. Herzberg factors distinguishes between two major categories: influencing job satisfaction and job dissatisfaction (see Herzberg, Mausner and Snyderman, 1959; Herzberg, 1968):

- motivators pertaining to work content itself such as performance, acknowledgement, work content, responsibility and promotion;
- hygiene factors pertaining mainly to peripheral work conditions such as organizational politics, working conditions, remuneration and social conditions.

Motivators serve to bring about job satisfaction and factors of hygiene are primarily the cause of job dissatisfaction. In Herzberg's opinion, the job content has a major influence on job satisfaction and, therefore, on motivation. He emphasizes as did Maslow, that humans strive for self-actualization.

German economic literature and decision-theory-based organization theories described by Heinen (1968) were influenced by psychological and sociological approaches to a large extent while proposing a differentiated view of man. At the end of the 60s, Heinen's approach postulated a synthesis between logical result-oriented assumptions, psychological and behavioral perceptions. He further developed the concept of rationality (March and Simon, 1958), which was founded in American sociology, as well as the theory of decision making (Siegel, 1957). In this case the image of man is explicated as an economical human being with bounded rationality whose information storage and processing capacity are limited. Instead of searching for the optimal solution, human beings accept suggestions which fulfil certain levels of expectations. The so-called *descriptive decision theory* tries to incorporate non-economic and social psychological factors. Further development and use requires an interdisciplinary collaboration among economics, psychology and sociology (Heinen, 1968; Kirsch, 1970; Kirsch, 1971). Business administration, which is predominantly technically or quantitatively-oriented, will be replaced by a more socioeconomic orientation (cf., Reichwald and Hesch, 1993).

Approaches Toward the Humanization of Work

In the early 1970s a value change in the nature of work could be observed first in Scandinavia that then moved on to other countries. This value change was an essential influence factor fostering the debate about the humanization of work. Part of this change was an overall desire for better living conditions and quality of work (see Kreikebaum and Herbert, 1988, p. 22).

Much of this discussion was derived from Herzberg's two-factory theory and the emphasis on work content, as well as work structures, as the most important sources for motivation. Through the application of new work structuration principles such as job rotation, job enlargement, job enrichment or the formation of partially autonomous work groups (see page 409), the worker's degree of autonomy and flexibility would be expanded. It follows that a Tayloristic specialization would be curtailed and personality development and qualification of employees would be enhanced (see, for example, Ulich, Groskurth and Bruggemann, 1973; Gaugler, Kolb and Ling, 1977; Ulich, 1994).

Shaped by the findings of industrial psychologists an image of man emerges which depicts an individual characterized by a desire to learn, capable of development, striving toward self-determination and self-actualization (see Kreikebaum, 1977). In praxis, however, these developments are slow to come about.

Information and Communication Technology and its Role in Changing the World of Work

Already in the early 1980s one could recognize a shift in the reorganization of work. Information and communication technology enables new forms in the division of labor. Partial processes can now be integrated and processed as objects through the use of multi-functional information and communication systems. Task integration may occur horizontally (the integration of different types of tasks on a given level), as well as vertically (incorporation of planning, decision and control tasks) (see Picot and Reichwald, 1991, p. 300; Wigand, 1985a).

Data integration enables the capturing of those partial tasks and processes that utilize the same data and, like task integration, may occur horizontally and also vertically. While horizontal integration links different subsystems of the organizational value-added chain, vertical integration enables the coordination and linking of information systems to varying degrees and details (see Picot and Reichwald, 1991, p. 288 ff.)

Organizational concepts can be supported through data integration leading from a functional division of labor to a procedure and process integration. In such efforts all systems rely on a uniform, integrated data base whose data can be utilized jointly (see Picot and Reichwald, 1991, pp. 286. 301). Process-oriented linkages of tasks via common data demands a comprehensive cooperation of various functional areas leading to an integrated perspective of business functions. Moreover, vertical task integration is closely linked to organizational decentralization in the sense of increasing the privilege in making decisions, contributing to and accessing information. Consequently, vertical task integration is likely to lead to flatter organizational structures (see Picot and Reichwald, 1991, p. 302).

This option-enabling character of information and communication technology in support of the creation of new forms of work organization, however, was by itself not sufficient for a fundamental change in work. The principle of the functional division of labor essentially continued to exist until today (see Martin, 1992, p. 180; Blum, 1992, p. 319 ff.). These described developments had relatively minor impact in Europe and North America where a predominantly Tayloristic industrial culture underwent little change (see, for example, Ulrich, 1986, p. 107 ff.).

THE REDISCOVERY OF HUMAN WORK AS A PRIMARY ORGANIZATIONAL RESOURCE

New Competitive Conditions

The competitive environment of firms has changed drastically in recent years due to such developments as internationalization, globalization and societal value change, as well as an increasing complexity of technical knowledge and information flows. Employees tend to expect more from their work than merely a sufficient income as means of survival. Such factors force organizations to find new ways for a more effective deployment of human capital (see, for example, von Rosenstiel, 1992a; Macharzina, 1993; Manz and Sims, 1993). As a consequence, increasing pressure is posed upon Tayloristic and highly hierarchically segmented organizations and production concepts.

The strategic potential to achieve competitive advantage (see Schreyögg, 1993) is shifting away from the traditional factors such as product and process technology, economies of scale, financial resources or protected and regulated markets. Such shifts occur increasingly in the direction of the adequate deployment and management of the resource *man* (see Pfeffer, 1994, p. 6). Consequently, firms view their employees increasingly as an investment needing careful attention rather than a cost factor that needs to be lowered (see Manz and Sims, 1993, p. 9;

Reichwald, 1992b, p. 4). The individual in this context is being viewed, so-to-speak, as an "entrepreneur within the enterprise" and thus finds him- or herself positioned within the center of business events. Qualifications, capacities, experiences and the creative potential of employees become primary success factors in the competition for business.

What are the implications, however, for the future development of work?

New Models of Work Structuration

Team Concepts

The definition of the term *team* varies considerably in the literature (see, for example, Boyett and Conn, 1992; Lawler, 1992; Manz and Sims, 1993; Parker, 1994). The various definitions may be deduced to a few essential core characteristics that are captured well in the Katzenbach and Smith definition. They understand the term *team* means a small number of persons with varying and complementary capabilities who are linked to a common task, common performance goals and common progress who are responsible to each other (Katzenbach and Smith, 1994, p. 45). Teams, accordingly, have the following essential characteristics (see Boyett and Conn, 1992; Katzenbach and Smith, 1994, p. 45 ff.):

- Common tasks and goals are the basis for the formation of team spirit leading to top performances of the individual team members.
- Varying capabilities to solve problems and to make decisions, as well as the professional, character and social qualifications of team members complement each other.
- Team members have a sense of responsibility that is reciprocal. Each team member supports and defends other team members and the group as a whole.
- Motivation plays the decisive role for team success. The ability to influence each team member, joint decisions and common group results increase motivation.
- Each team is equipped with the resources and the responsibility to produce complete product or services or essential components thereof.
- Instead of clearly defined performance goals, teams have a "mission" to serve customers or customer categories either internally (e.g., other teams) or externally (users, buyers).
- Team leaders are elected by the team and they take on this role on a rotation basis. They coordinate the teams, moderate team meetings and take care of team members.

The most commonly encountered teams are according to Parker (1994, p. 35 ff.):

- *Functional teams:* These consist of a superior and direct subordinates. They are the classic team form in the modern business world. All development engineers within a firm may thus be linked within a functional team. Functional teams are more likely to be found in hierarchical organizational forms within relatively stable markets.
- *Cross-functional teams:* Such teams utilize the knowledge of various employees from different departments and knowledge areas. A classic example is the product development team that acts quickly within rapidly changing markets such as the computer or telecommunications markets.
- *Self-directed teams:* In this category we see that teams are essentially responsible for a complete business process which, in turn, delivers a product or service to a company-internal or company-external customer. Team members work together to improve their work processes, to solve and to control occurring problems themselves and to plan their work themselves. Self-directed teams are suitable mainly for firms that do business in young, dynamic areas and, consequently, incorporate their employees strongly into entrepreneurial processes.

The introduction of teams and the subsequent linking of employees in decision-making and responsibility processes offer opportunities for the firm to increase the productivity and quality of value-added processes. Moreover such efforts may also increase the overall productivity of the firm and its competitiveness by better utilizing the creative potential of employees. Team concepts therefore enhance the flexibility and autonomy of employees at their work place, both of which are essential features of new entrepreneurial structures (Pinchot and Pinchot, 1993, p. 228 ff.).

In contrast to the Tayloristic division of labor and highly hierarchically structured organizations, teams plan and control work processes themselves (job enrichment) and take on indirect functions such as maintenance or quality control (job enlargement). Moreover, job rotation occurs. The classical methods of work structuration (see Ulich, 1994) lead to settings characterized by a decrease in monotony and that among employees a sense of responsibility for entire processes increases (see Gottschall, 1994, p. 236). This occurs, for example, through teams offering their members the opportunity to allocate their time responsibly and to meet, at the same time, cooperative needs of the organization (see, for example, Manz and Sims, 1993, p. 9; Katzenbach and Smith, 1994, p. 11 ff.; Parker, 1994, p. 3 ff.). Increasingly the team concept is extended from the production area to other areas of the business value-added chain as well. In such efforts, just as in the simultaneous engineering approach, also knowledge workers (e.g., researchers and developers, highly specialized information and communication technology experts) are incorporated (see, for example, Manz and Sims, 1993, p. 212; Lawler, 1992, pp. 51–144; Reichwald and Conrat, 1994, p. 235 ff.).

The success of team concepts depends on a variety of conditions. These highlight the complexity underlying the introduction of team organizations. As examples we would like to mention the following (see, for example, Manz and Sims, 1993, p. 213; Parker, 1994, p. 181 ff.; Katzenbach and Smith, 1994, pp. 173, ff., 263 ff.):

- an emphasis on and setting an example for a team culture by management-level employees;
- optimistic disposition of managers toward the capabilities and potential of employees;
- team-oriented information systems;
- constant training of team capabilities;
- increased remuneration for team-like behavior;
- external support for teams to overcome critical points;
- patience and realistic expectations during the introduction phase of teams.

The business world, however, demonstrates that the successful introduction of teams has opposition, including (see Manz and Sims, 1993, p. 17 ff.; Katzenbach and Smith, 1994, p. 149 ff.):

- the aversion of employees toward sudden and radical change;
- impeding group-dynamic processes such as mutual performance controls or internal team competition;
- difficulties of employees with self-reliance;
- expectations from employees are set too high;
- the area of business or capabilities prerequisites are too broad;
- management resistance based on, for example, prejudice.

Overcoming such resistance depends on each situation and circumstances in a given organization. Generally these efforts take much time and patience. Consequently, the necessary changes needed in conjunction with the introduction of team concepts tend to occur within the framework of "change management processes" (see, for example, Doppler and Lauterburg, 1994) in an evolutionary fashion and not suddenly and radically. Time frames extending to ten years for such efforts are not considered unusual (see Manz and Sims, 1993, p. 244 ff.).

Networking and Telework

With regard to Chapters 6, 7 and 8 one may refer to a dissolution of the organization especially in the following cases:

- Through organization-internal factors (e.g., missing know-how or capital) or organization-external factors (e.g., information highways) the outsourcing of core tasks to external organizations occurs.
- The organization decides within its efforts to optimize performance strength to pursue a vertical disintegration and buys standardized services from the market.
- Based on improved coordination of autonomous jobs through information and communication technology a shift of office jobs to work-at-home jobs is enabled.

The first two cases are seen under the topic of networking since in each case we are concerned with interorganizational linkages and placing specific demands on management. Moreover, under networking we understand also all coordination aspects of autonomous groups of a firm (see Chapter 5). These, too, work essentially in the form of a network and need considerable coordination. The model of autonomous case work lends itself to describe such networks on a theoretical basis. It enables the maintenance or improvement of open cooperation structures and support individual, as well as flexible, processes. The needed accomplishment of especially relative complex individual cases and project tasks demands quick access to voluminous amounts of information and the uninterrupted, targeted communication with frequently changing and often highly qualified communication partners (see Bellmann and Wittmann, 1991, p. 501 f.).

The third case of outsourcing of autonomous work places is seen under the topic of telework or telecommuting. In the business world this can be found in the form of work at home, mobile offices or tele-centers, all areas that have already been addressed in Chapter 8 (see Picot and Reichwald, 1994, p. 558; Reichwald and Hermens, 1994, p. 26). Telework lends itself especially for the kind of work that (see Picot and Reichwald, 1994, p. 558):

- has a high degree of autonomy
- is found in the managerial, as well as creative areas
- can be evaluated from a results-oriented perspective
- is more likely to be found in professions with a higher level of qualification.

If the social relations among the communication partners are relatively unproblematic, information needs can be planned for well and if, based on task-integration, largely individual task accomplishment is possible, the advantages of geographically dispersed locations can flexibly be utilized (see Bellmann and Wittmann, 1991, p. 505).

In the following sections we address the new roles of employees and managers and related demands in the present context.

NEW DEMANDS ON EMPLOYEES AND MANAGERS IN THE BOUNDARY-LESS FIRM

The New Role of Employees

The Role of Employees and Team Concepts

Fundamentally team concepts—as already demonstrated—distinguish themselves through the increasing integration of management-related work and task accomplishment (see, for example, Boyett and Conn, 1992, p. 83 f.). When management assigns to a team the responsibility for a complete entrepreneurial process, then team members must be authorized to make decisions to implement the necessary tasks such that the assignment can be accomplished (see Hammer and Champy, 1994, p. 96). From such holistic task accomplishment new demands are placed on employees that also shape their new understanding of roles. Essentially, one should in this context refer here to (see Boyett and Conn, 1992, p. 84; Manz and Sims, 1993, p. 210; Katzenbach and Smith, 1994, p. 45 ff.):

- the capacity to take on management and leadership responsibilities with regard to problem solving, planning, budgeting, personnel placement, team discipline, assessment and performance control;
- responsibility for the quality of task accomplishment;
- the capacity to set goals for oneself;
- the capacity for self-control; and
- being a self-starter for solving problems and conflicts.

The complete development of employees within the realm of team concepts requires their deliberate involvement in decision-making processes. In doing so decision-making competencies and responsibilities are being shifted from managers to employees. For firms one may recognize an advantage in doing so as employees generally know better how to optimize work processes and how to address customer demands and expectations (see Hoffman, 1994, p. 30).

While in such efforts the importance of authoritarian and direction-giving management is reduced, it follows that traditional management control may be substituted by the self-control of employees (see Büssing, 1988). Such efforts have the consequence that employees are given greater power, i.e. they are empowered. Empowerment is also an essential part of business reengineering, since processes cannot be radically re-designed such that they are customer-oriented without giving the involved employees the appropriate perspective of the market and granting far-reaching authority. Members of a process team are expected to have a market orientation, exchange ideas among themselves, utilize their judgment capacities and make decisions on their own (see Hammer and Champy, 1994, p. 97 f.). As a part of empowerment employees are offered trust and the understanding is conveyed that their effort, their competence and creativity are essential for the success of the firm (see Boyett and Conn, 1992, p. 109 ff.; Pinchot and Pinchot, 1993, p. 220 ff.).

The empowerment of employees in accordance with these team concepts requires qualifications and capabilities from these employees that surpass considerably traditional qualification patterns. Following we summarize the essential capabilities and know-how that such employees should possess (see Boyett and Conn, 1992, p. 83 f., p. 278 ff; Reichwald and Nippa, 1989, p. 440 f.; Katzenbach and Smith, 1994, p. 47 f.):

- *Learning to learn:* Each employee should know by him- or herself, how and where to learn best.
- *Basic competencies:* These refer to the subject matter competence, as well as the capability to utilize new information processing technologies and to be able to acquire, interpret and filter information quickly.
- *Communicative competence:* The employee should have the capability to express him- or herself and to be able and willing to listen to others.
- *Capability for self-management:* This requires above all self-motivation and self-discipline together with the capability of self-control.
- *Flexibility:* The employee must be capable to think creatively and to solve problems him- or herself.
- *Social competence and team capabilities:* Employees require capabilities to negotiate effectively within groups, to solve problems, to handle stress and the unanticipated behavior of others, as well as share task accomplishments.
- *Decision and problem-solving capabilities:* Problems and chances must be identified, alternatives need to be evaluated and necessary decisions must be made.

- *Autonomy:* The employee has to remove him- or herself from the role of the mere order recipient and must identify with the enterprise. Moreover, the employee must know his/her contributions to market success without guidance or instruction.
- *Innovation qualification:* The employee must be willing to act innovatively and to carry through improvements in the work process. This includes also the broader business context, as well as the knowledge of what makes organizations effective and how internal and external factors influence organizational performance.

These qualifications and capabilities reflect a clear trend toward higher qualification expectations of employees. The demand for uneducated and lowly qualified employees should not be high in light of the realization of newer entrepreneurial concepts. This implies that the degree to which work is being *empowered*, simple work, simultaneously, becomes superfluous.

The Role of Employees and Networking

If one understands under networking the management of interorganizational linkages among firms, as well as the coordination of autonomous teams within a firm, this undoubtedly poses a challenge to team members who have to work together within such a network framework.

An essential characteristic of these networks is that employees of a firm work together with employees of supplier firms or other market partners in the form of virtual teams (see Davidow and Malone, 1992, p. 194; Johansen and Swigart, 1994, p. 19). These virtual teams functionally interface in a customer-supplier relationship with other virtual teams. Within these relations demands and wishes need to be communicated, performance feedback needs to be sought out and acceptable quality standards for respective performances need to be negotiated for both parties (see Orsburn et al, 1990, p. 83). In this context such qualification demands as social competence and communication capabilities of employees step into the foreground. These extend too to the use and mastery of newer information and communication technologies (e.g., CSCW). The role of the employee within the network framework may, accordingly, be characterized as (see Boyett and Conn, 1992, p. 84; Manz and Sims, 1993, p. 210):

- generation of team contacts with the outside
- acquisition of external information
- cooperation with other teams and business areas, especially in light of the recognition of customer expectations.

The Role of Employees and Telework

Telework, when viewed as media-supported and *remotely located* task accomplishment (see Chapter 8), poses a number of new demands on employees due to its characteristics. The essential demands are presented here based on the original conception. Accordingly, teleworkers either carry out their work in the home and are therefore "invisible" within the firm or they work location-independent at a "mobile" place of work (see Reichwald and Hermens, 1994, p. 26 f.). The latter case can be observed, for example, with sales or mobile maintenance units (see Reichwald, Oldenburg and Schulte, 1995).

Based on the geographic distance from the firm it is not possible to have direct control over work performance of employees by their superior. In addition the teleworker is largely working alone because of his/her relatively isolated position and the reduced possibility for personal communication. The goal-oriented accomplishment of the employee's tasks requires therefore a high degree of self-discipline, motivation and mastery of the available information and communication technologies (see Godehart, 1994; Glaser and Glaser, 1995). Essential requirements for telework employees are the following:

- Open-mindedness toward telework
- High performance capability
- Good subject-matter knowledge
- Capability for self-motivation
- Capability for independent work
- Capability for self-discipline and self-control
- Capability to allocate one's work time responsibly
- Planning and organizational capabilities in order to achieve clear goals
- Capability in handling the distance to the firm
- Mastery of new information and communication technologies.

Conclusion

The new role of the employee is characterized largely by the increase in requirements of decision-making and responsibility capacities for complete, customer-oriented processes, as well as team, communication and innovation capacities (see, for example, Murphy and O'Leary, 1994, p. 110 f.). The changed role perception will vary considerably in the expression and specification of required tasks and behaviors in traditionally organized firms vs. firms following new enterprise concepts (see Katzenbach and Smith, 1994, p. 211).

The business world, however, demonstrates that so far many employees were not incorporated fully into decision-making and responsibility processes with regard to their work, i.e. that "empowerment" is practised only preliminarily. This can be substantiated, for example, in that between 1993 and 1994 US and German firms merely incorporated between 7 and 10% of all of their employees in team concept work settings as espoused here (see Gottschall, 1994, p. 235). The potential of many employees is not fully utilized. A considerable gap is observable between the theoretically achievable ideal and reality (see Lawler, 1992, p. 3 ff.).

The New Role of Managers

The Role of Managers and Team Concepts

Flatter organizations and team concept-based task integration leads to, as already indicated, a shifting of responsibility, as well as acting and decision-making responsibility. To a similar degree executives and managers have reduced responsibilities for traditional management tasks. This leads to a new task and therefore new spectrum of requirements for managers (see, for example, Bleicher, 1995; Wigand, 1985a).

Traditionally acting managers shape work and assign it to individual employees. Just the same they supervise, control and examine the work that is passed along from one employee to the next. Teams are potentially able to do this themselves. This implies that managers within the team concept framework can promote employees who are, in turn, enabled to carry out value-added processes with their own responsibility and authority. Consequently, the task spectrum of managers is likely to shift from the dominating task-orientation in the direction of increased employee-orientation.

Management is responsible for the results of the newly-formed entrepreneurial processes without exerting direct control over employees to whom these processes were entrusted. The process teams work largely autonomously under the direction of their "coach" (see page 401). Moreover, management is responsible for ensuring that the processes are conceptually designed such that employees can accomplish the requisite tasks and that they are sufficiently motivated by the incentive systems of the firm (see Hammer and Champy, 1994, p. 105 f., p. 108). The new demands placed on managers in team-oriented and relatively flat organizations extend essentially to the following areas (see Davidow and Malone, 1993, p. 180 ff.; Johansen and Swigart, 1994, p. 19; Manz and Sims, 1993, p. 210; Byett and Conn, 1992, p. 158, p. 167 f.; Kanter, 1989, p. 89):

- *Communication capabilities:* The capacity to comprehend compressed information quickly, as well as being able to write clearly, speak convincingly and to listen effectively.
- *Political capabilities:* Possessing the capacities of negotiation, conflict resolution and consensus building.
- *Motivational capacities:* Possessing knowledge about the cognitive and behavioral aspects of motivation and their utilization for enacting behavioral change among employees.
- *Capacity to shape change processes:* Manager function within change processes as change agents. In order to work effectively they need to understand human reaction to change and possess the capacity to enact change and that potential resistance is removed or minimized.
- *Capacity for trust building:* The capacity to demonstrate self-confidence, share values, giving confirmation and to show empathy and sensitivity.
- *Capacities to empower employees:* The capacity to delegate responsibility and performance control to employees, as well as the capacity to put together effective teams and to support employees in problem-solving processes.
- *The capacity to develop visions* and to communicate those effectively to employees.
- *Continued education and training* of employees.
- *Advising and coaching of employees*, i.e. the manager does not control employees, does not give them instructions and does not leave them alone and isolated, but instead offers them opportunities to make their own decisions and gain experiences that are based on their own decisions.

An essential task of managers will be the coordination of employees and teams, to advise them in a supportive fashion and to enable them to manage themselves (see Manz and Sims, 1993, p. 210; Boyett and Conn, 1992; Katzenbach and Smith, 1994, p. 45 ff.). In this way the seamless flow of value-added processes is enabled and the environment for creative entrepreneurship is to be brought about (see, for example, Kanter, 1989, p. 88 f.; Davidow and Malone, 1993, p. 180; Pfeffer, 1992). The role of the manager changes in this increasingly from the traditional order-giver and work controller to adviser and coach who encourages the creativity of his/her employees.

Based upon task integration and the shift in responsibility and decision-making competencies, as well as the extensive delegation of the planning, control and managerial functions to process-responsible teams, the level of middle management becomes largely superfluous.

This process is enabled through the new information and communication technologies that take on the information mediator functions between employees and top management under much more favorable conditions with regard to transaction costs and transparency than middle management was able to in the past (see, for example, Boyett and Conn, 1992, p. 18 ff; Davidow and Malone, 1993, p. 181).

The Role of the Manager and Networking

New demands pertaining to the role of management *vis-à-vis* networks can be seen especially based on the following developments (see Sydow, 1992b, p. 307 f.):

- the trend toward minimizing the degree of hierarchies in network organizations;
- complementing intra-organizational information systems through interorganizational information systems;
- the necessary redesign of controlling systems;
- reorientation of incentive and career systems to horizontal mobility within the network.

Boundary-spanning roles of management are of central importance within the overall management of network structures. These serve above all the linking of complementary competencies of network enterprises or differing teams. The main tasks of managers within these boundary-spanning roles are (see Sydow, 1992b, p. 309):

- search and transmission of information within and external to the network;
- the representation of network enterprises;
- the negotiation of contracts and their control;
- the coordination of network teams and enterprises;
- the management of employees who are entrusted with boundary-spanning tasks.

The observance of these and other activities occurs mainly through the development and maintenance of personal networks that surpass the boundaries of the individual, institutionalized network enterprises (see Sydow, 1992b, p. 309). In contrast to the rather formal relationships within hierarchical organizations, the appropriate employees in these personal networks take care of these relationships themselves. If the latter does not occur, the networks disappear again (see Pinchot and Pinchot, 1993, p. 282).

Another important role of management is derived from the importance of indirect, informal coordination that—when seen as part of networking—substitutes partially formal management systems. In doing so, the following aspects acquire particular significance (see Sydow, 1992b, p. 311):

- generation and enactment of strategic visions
- formation of *ad hoc* teams
- linking of experts
- network-wide access to information
- employee transfer
- integration of organizational cultures.

The stabilization of interorganizational relations by balancing divergent, frequently changing interests in networks and the creation of a trust basis poses additional demands on management. In such efforts negotiations pertaining to the definition of boundaries of the network enterprise, as well as to the work to be conducted internally need to be considered (see Sydow, 1992b, p. 312).

In summary one may state that managers within networks require the following capabilities:

- social capabilities
- communicative capabilities
- capabilities to integrate
- talent to negotiate
- cognitive capabilities such as, for example, quick comprehension and perception of essential matters.

These demands can also be substantiated with the results of newer management research (see, for example, Mintzberg, 1994; Reichwald and Goecke, 1995).

The Role of the Manager and Telework

The management of teleworkers poses a new challenge for managers since the teleworker is physically not present within the firm (see Chapter 8). Consequently, personal communication between manager and employees and, analogously, the possibility for direct management and control of the employees by the manager is limited. In this context it is meaningful to divide the total of all tasks into individual and smaller subtasks and to determine precise goal direction and timetables. It is essential to shift toward a results-oriented performance evaluation. The need for direct management can be substituted partially through the formation of appropriate management measures (see Godehardt, 1994, p. 72 ff., as well as Chapter 8).

Moreover, managers need to be concerned with the maintenance of the teleworker's feeling of belonging to the firm. This may be accomplished, for example, through the scheduling of regular meetings, agreements for regular office hours at the work place within the firm, as well as through the involvement of the teleworker in informal social activities (see Reichwald and Hermens, 1994, p. 27 f.; Godehardt, 1994, p. 72 ff.).

In this telework context it is difficult for the manager to develop trust relationships with employees, as well as the handling of problem-solving processes. This is explained in part that employees can be informed electronically about goals and norms on a limited basis only and that social needs of employees can barely be recognized and satisfied in this fashion (see, for example, Kämpf and Wilhelm, 1994, as well as Chapter 8). In contrast, the necessity for motivating the employee by the manager is deemed to be of lesser importance. This is explained in that the teleworker already brings along the capability of self-motivation which is an important prerequisite for any telework (see Godehardt, 1994, p. 75 f.). These new challenges pose the following essential demands on the manager:

- open-mindedness
- mastery of newer information and communication technologies
- fully developed social, communicative and integrating capabilities
- distinct organizational capabilities
- the capability to formulate clear goal achievements
- the capability to establish clear measures for performance evaluation.

Conclusion

Capturing full worker potential while achieving the competitive goals of the firm and operating within newer organization structures requires that the new role of the manager reflects the efficient and effective leadership of employees. This shift in roles of the manager is furthermore clarified through the juxtaposition of essential tasks and behaviors in traditionally organized firms vs. firms following newer entrepreneurial concepts.

The new roles of managers and employees are essentially determined by the operating conditions of newer organizational forms (such as self-managing teams, networks, etc.) on the one hand and through the necessary autonomy and flexibility of the employees on the other hand.

So far we have described the new forms of work organization and the related new roles of managers and employees. We now pose the question how performance limits of the employee may be expanded within such organizational concepts. The envisioned *prescription* for this is the "learning organization". We now examine the fundamental ideas of organizational learning, as well as address the necessity of reorganizing organizational incentive systems.

MANAGERS, EMPLOYEES AND ORGANIZATIONAL LEARNING

The Concept of Organizational Learning

Survival in a competitive world is the most basic goal of any organization. Any type of organization must react appropriately to each permanent change among the perceived environmental factors. This may occur, for example, as a change within or reorganization of structures, as an intra-organizational value change or as an integration process necessitated by an acquisition. Permanent and cumulative learning becomes an important success factor. Essential is not only that individual members of the organization learn, but that the organization as a whole is enabled to learn and anticipate the new environmental conditions. Organizational learning is a way to break up inherited organizational structures and to develop these as newer organization forms. Moreover, organizational learning means to continually adapt these new organization forms to changing environmental conditions.

The Relationship between Individual and Organizational Learning

In order to thrive within a market economy, firms must make organizational learning possible. The implementation of this demand, however, harbors some problems. One major reason most certainly lies with the multitude of definitions and interpretation of the term organizational learning. Psychologists have long studied learning, even though the focus here is on individual learning, while systems theory (see page 396) views systems (such as organizations) in their totality.

How is organizational learning different from individual learning? No one doubts that individuals can learn. Matters become much more complicated when we are concerned with the learning capability of organizations as a whole, as organizations act (and learn) through their members. Total performance of an organization is therefore always dependent upon the learning capabilities of its members, as well as the nature of their organizational linkages (see Reber, 1992, p. 1240).

Probst and Büchel offer a fitting example describing this situation (1994, p. 18): When an employee in a firm processes the payroll at the end of the month and he/she follows certain procedures specified by management, it is possible through a trial and error process to achieve an optimized procedure. When this new procedure is registered and recorded, the organization achieves new knowledge that now exists independently of the individual employee.

The recording of knowledge makes the firm independent of the individual knowledge of its members. Through storage of individual knowledge within organizational knowledge systems business, or more generally action, competencies are successively abstracted and implemented within the organizational system. Although businesses do not have a brain to store knowledge, they do have storage systems such as guidelines, work directions, myths or cultures at their disposal (see Pawlowsky, 1992, p. 202).

Bower and Hilgard define individual learning as: ". . . a change in behavior or behavior potential . . . with regard to a certain situation that relates back to repeat experiences in this situation, provided that this behavior change cannot be explained by innate reaction tendencies, maturation or transitional circumstances." (1983, p. 31, translated by the authors). This definition of learning implies individual rationality, dependence upon personal experiences, linkages with individual needs and motivation, as well as interests and value positions, difficulty with the subject matter to be learned and manifestations of many behavioral changes.

In contrast, organizational learning depends on collective rationality and a collective framework. Individual motives, needs or values are not of focal concern here, but supra-personal experience worlds, collective decision-making procedures, normative order and the acceptance of majority-based decisions are of considerable interest. Not only does the organization adapt to changing environmental conditions, but changing intra-organizational conditions such as motives, needs, interests, goals, values and norms of the members may occur as well. Organizational learning, then, comprises the jointly shared reality made up of the needs, motives, values and norms of several organization members (see Probst and Büchel, 1994, p. 20). Klimecki, Probst and Eberl (1994) show how one might move from one learning level to the next while considering three transformation conditions:

1 *Communication*, since without it individual knowledge cannot be made available to the organization nor can collective argumentation and organization processes be triggered.
2 *Transparency* with regard to the course and result of communication processes that may be created through storage media for knowledge

resources and symbolic values such as the *leitmotiv* in the form of leadership principles, models, stories or other symbolic forms.

3 *Integration of collective bargaining processes* into the entire system.

Theories of Action as Explanatory Aids of Organizational Learning

Each individual can draw upon knowledge and behavioral possibilities at the personal, as well as at the organizational level. This implied *theory of action*, providing the framework for actions within the system, makes it possible for the individual to learn within a professional context. The term "theories of action" was used for the first time by Argyris (1964) to denote the reservoir of organizational knowledge. Theories of action comprise expectations about consequences of certain behavioral patterns under specific conditions. They include strategies, images, goals, cultures and structures and constitute the framework of the organization *vis-à-vis* its continuity and essential characteristics. Argyris and Schön undertook a partitioning of this organizational knowledge base (see Argyris and Schön, 1978; Probst and Büchel, 1994, p. 22 ff.). Action theories may be applied as *espoused-theories* or as *theories-in-use*:

- Espoused-theories or official theories of action form the framework of the organization that determines the jointly shared image of the firm. They find their expression in images, strategies, goal determination, values, norms and structures of the respective firm.
- *Theories-in-use* emerge through the sharing of individual and collective experiences and the resulting reciprocal effects, as well as through the juxtaposition of experiences and the institutional framework.

If differences between these two types of theories exist, learning processes are activated in order to bridge both. The following section describes the nature of these learning processes.

How Does Organizational Learning Come About?

Learning is always directed toward a change in knowledge. Argyris and Schön mention the following three possibilities how knowledge may change, i.e. learning may come about (Argyris and Schön, 1978, p. 18 ff.; Schanz, 1994, p. 433, as well as Figure 9.1).

- *Single-loop learning* occurs when deviations from prescribed standards and norms (goals) are being realized. When the sources of such deviations or errors are identified and actions are taken to correct

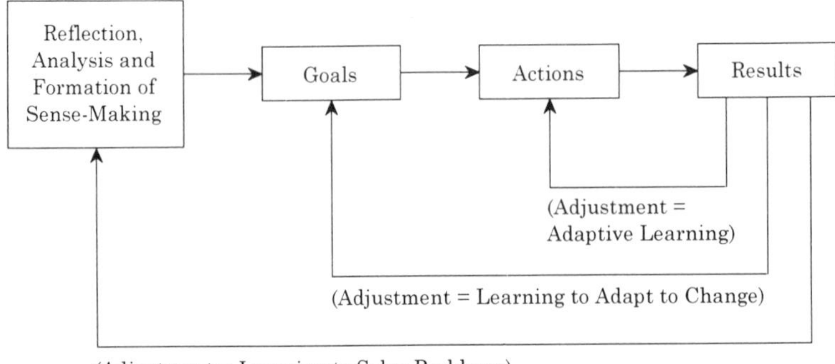

Figure 9.1 *Styles of learning. Source: Probst and Büchel (1994, p. 38. Reproduced by permission of Gabler Verlag GmbH.)*

them, single-loop learning has occurred (see Hedberg, 1981, p. 10). Changes in theories-in-use were made.

- *Double-loop learning* becomes important when environmental observations demand a modification of official action theory, i.e. a change in context. At this level of organizational learning a confrontation occurs among organizational hypotheses, norms and directions with observations of the environment and a feedback loop of these observations within the framework (knowledge system) of organizations (see Pawlowsky, 1992, p. 207). The result of such a feedback process may be, for example, the pursuit of a new strategy or the change of an organizational norm system. A prerequisite for such reorientations is the capacity of organizational "unlearning" and for the implementation of new behavioral models (see Hedberg, 1981, p. 10).
- In *problem-solving learning* (see Pawlowsky, 1992, p. 209 ff.), labelled "deutero learning" by Argyris and Schön, the improvement of the capacity to learn itself becomes subject of the learning process. This learning type is especially useful for securing creativity, innovation and change capabilities (see Müller-Stewens and Pautzke, 1991, p. 198). The process of "learning to learn" is based on the recognition of the proceedings underlying single-loop and double-loop learning.

This understanding of organizational learning is also the basis of our subsequent discussion. Organizational learning is, accordingly, a process that:

- contains a change in the organizational knowledge base;
- occurs within the interplay between individual and the organization;
- occurs through the interaction between internal and/or external environment;

- occurs with reference to existing theories of action within the organization;
- contributes to an adaptation of the internal to the external environment and/or to increased problem-solving capacity of the system (see Pawlowsky, 1992, p. 204).

The Role of Information and Communication Technology and the Concept of Organizational Learning

Information is essential for the organizational learning process. It is possible to acquire, distribute, store, rediscover or to add remarks to information in organizations (Marquardt and Reynolds, 1994, p. 42).

Successfully learning organizations know how to transform information into important know-how for the organization. One component of this transformation is the design of an appropriate technological architecture comprising user support, integrated technological networks and so-called information tools that enable access to and the exchange of information. Among such tools are various electronic tools, as well as advanced learning methods such as computer conferencing, simulations or data processing tools for computer-supported cooperative work. Marquardt and Reynolds state that the goal here is the creation of so-called "knowledge freeways" (1994, p. 63).

Information and communication technology is used in organizations for the support of learning processes. Of considerable interest is the combined set of technologies that supports individual and group learning, as well as problem-solving activities. The use of information and communication technologies for training and development activities is likely to increase considerably in years to come. An early indicator for the possible diffusion of this form of learning is the worldwide success of networked computers (see Marquardt and Reynolds, 1994).

New Demands on Employees Involved in Organizational Learning

Organizational learning may be interpreted in numerous ways and may be one reason why the concept of organizational learning has been slow in penetrating the organizational world. One other reason may be the misunderstanding of the new roles of employees and managers (see Senge, 1990b, p. 8). Briefly we would like to address here the new demands placed on employees as part of the concept of organizational learning.

The learning capacity of an organization depends largely on the individual behavior of its members. It is only when individuals learn that subsequent learning of the entire organization may follow. Senge mentions five disciplines whose combination may lead to organizational learning:

1 Personal mastery
2 Mental models
3 Shared vision
4 Team learning
5 System thinking.

System thinking as the fifth discipline integrates simultaneously the other disciplines in that it functions as a framework for the other four. At the same time, however, system thinking requires also other disciplines in order to unfold its full potential (see Senge, 1990a, p. 12, as well as page 396).

Senge views all organization members as carriers of learning-advancing processes. His approach is chosen to explain the new demands posed on employees since he conducts an analysis of the most frequent organizational disturbances at the individual level and he offers also corresponding references for training concepts (see Senge, 1994) to achieve behavior modification. The five components of a learning organization are as follows (see Senge, 1990a, p. 7 ff.).

Personal Mastery

Personal mastery does not refer to the control of or power over people or things, but to a certain type of capability of self-motivation. Individuals reflecting this trait strongly are capable of achieving expected results evenly over a period of time. They achieve this by practicing life-long learning. Personal mastery consists of the following partial capabilities:

- permanent clarifying one's own goals and scrutinizing one's achievement;
- bundling of one's own energies;
- development of patience;
- having an objective perspective of things.

Mental Models

Mental models are deeply rooted assumptions, generalizations or images that have an influence on how people view the world and how they act accordingly. Based on existing mental models within an individual, he/she anticipates certain outcomes, even though it is not clear at all that these outcomes are to occur in this form. Unreflected mental models are not to be underestimated in our professional daily life. It is possible, for example, that the opening of new markets or the introduction of newer organizational forms may fail because of the prevailing mental models of the employees. The more organization members share such mental models, the more organizational learning will be slowed, if not prevented.

How can one apply mental models to foster organizational learning? First we have to take a look into the mirror outselves, i.e., employees have to discover their own mental models, bring them to the surface and be willing to look at them critically. This requires the ability to conduct learning-conducive meetings. Employees must be able to present their own thinking and be willing to open themselves up *vis-à-vis* the influence of others. This implies that they should not continue to cling to their past mental models, but though an awareness of their existence and critical thinking be willing to revise them, if appropriate.

Shared Vision

It is a well-known fact that organizations are successful especially then when goals, values and norms exist based on which activities of the individual employees may be directed toward a common goal. Moreover, this goal is equally accepted and pursued by each employee of the organization. Senge (1990b, p. 9) sees in such equally shared goals, values and norms and the visions an essential starting point for influencing organizational learning. According to Senge, people do not learn because they were asked to learn, but because a common vision exists in the organization and through which they voluntarily align their learning. An organization-specific vision gives employees a common identity and a feeling of belonging. The difficulty in constructing such visions is the transformation of goals, values and norms of the individual organization members into a jointly shared, organization-wide vision. There are no general rules or prescriptions to accomplish this, except a set of principles and directions that need to be applied to the specific situation (see Senge, 1994, p. 295 ff.). To make sure that this vision is shared by all employees, it is important that all employees participate in its development, i.e. each employee should be invited to participate. For it is only through this participatory procedure that a shared vision can emerge that also forms a true linkage of the employee to the organization. The individual employee ought to be able to:

- recognize future developments and their relevance for the firm and the respective vision;

- incorporate the vision in group discussions;
- internalize the jointly developed vision.

Team Learning

Each organization divides into sub-groups or teams that possess internally through jointly utilized techniques or specific forms of learning their own goals, values and norms and, consequently, are differentiated from other groups or teams. A precondition for learning to occur in firms is the deliberate coordination of all sub-groups within that firm (see Schein, 1992, p. 41).

Schein (1992, p. 40 ff.) refers to the use of dialogue as a tool in support of successful learning in and between groups. He argues that organizational effectiveness is largely dependent on communication beyond the group boundaries and that dialogue is, therefore, the most suitable coordination instrument.

How is dialogue different from traditional face-to-face communication? The most common form of communication in sensitivity training and traditional group training is active listening. What is meant here is that the attentiveness of the listener is not only with the spoken word, but is also focused on other communication channels such as body language, intonation and emotional context.

System Thinking

The discipline of system thinking integrates the other four and already described components of a learning organization. Senge (1990a, p. 6 f.) uses the following example to illustrate system thinking: When clouds arise and the sky darkens we know that it will rain soon. We know also that after the thunderstorm, rain will trickle into the ground water and the sky will clear again by next day. All of these events occur with a time and spatial delay, yet all of them are connected through the same pattern. Each event has an influence on the rest, i.e. an influence that usually remains invisible. One can only understand the "thunderstorm" when observing the entire system and not just the individual parts of the model.

People are normally not used to working with complex problems and they make strategic thinking mistakes when intervening in complex systems such as firms (see Dörner et al, 1983; Vester, 1980). Probst and Gomez (1991, p. 6) infer that it is in a way a demand surpassing human capabilities in the processing of cognitive processes, as well as information overload. People no longer can recognize the system in its entirety and they correct only individual and isolated defects. They tend to focus on fragments of the supra-ordinate whole and cut or overlook important linkages. As a consequence, symptoms rather than causes are treated. The human capacity to grasp complex situations, to understand them and then to handle them adequately in a given situation is, apparently not sufficiently developed.

Figure 9.2 depicts an organization as a networked system. Based on the high complexity it is not uncommon that the results of such systems do not always correspond with the *a priori* planning. It is obviously very difficult to estimate the individual cycles and beyond that the interplay among them. For an individual firm this might imply that it may often take years until the individual structural components of the firm work together in such a fashion that recursively existing and integrated effects can be utilized fully. Since the individual employee him- or herself is also a member of the system, it is indeed difficult to recognize the system as a whole. Usually people merely take snap shots of isolated parts of the entire system. In order to work successfully in the future, however, it is imperative that each employee is capable of thinking in a networked context, i.e. be able to recognize individual elements (employee, work group, departments) and the effects among these elements of the system "firm". The individual must be able to estimate which effects his/her actions will have on the employees within the work flow before and after him/her and be able to adjust actions accordingly (see Senge, 1990a, p. 7).

The New Demands on Managers and Organizational Learning

In the past managers were focused on the individual and not on all organization members with a holistic perspective. Management did the thinking, employees did the performing. Especially the western manager was treated as a kind of hero, as he or she stepped forward particularly during times of crises. Such myths confirmed quick actions and enhanced charismatic managers with the consequence that the interplay of the individual system forces, and therefore collective i.e. organizational learning, was neglected.

In a learning organization the roles of managers are differentiated strongly from the previous, charismatic decision-makers. Leadership in learning organizations is concentrated essentially on more subtle, but therefore the more important type of activity: according to Schein leadership is inseparably linked to the shaping of the organizational culture. The construction of an organizational culture and its development is viewed as the sole and essential task of the manager (Schein, 1992). It follows that within a learning organization, a manager must function first of all as a designer, then as a teacher and as a coach (see

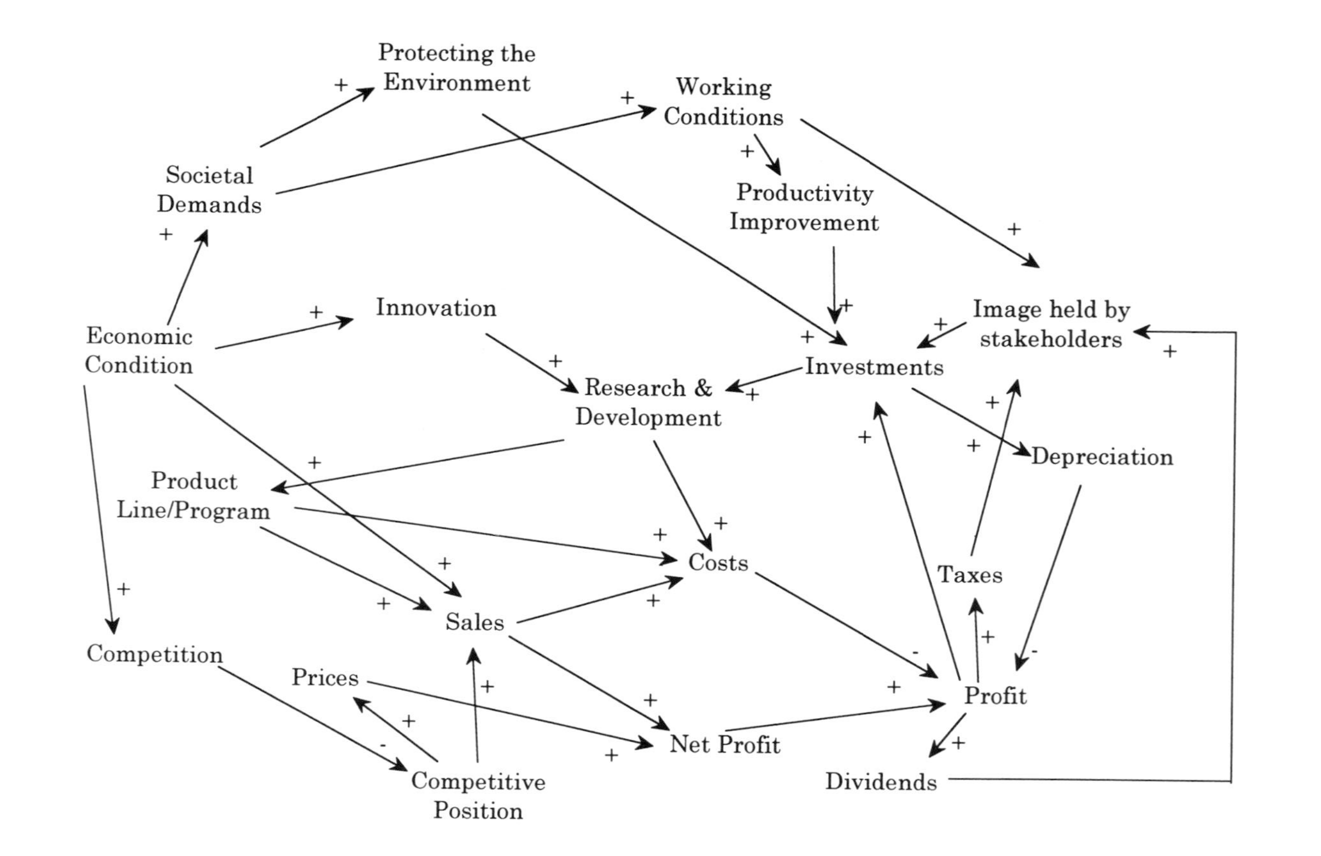

Figure 9.2 *The enterprise as a schematic network with positive and negative cycles. Source: Probst and Gomez (1992, p. 11. Reproduced by permission from Gabler Verlag GmbH.)*

Senge, 1990b). Each of these new roles requires other—different from the previously mentioned ones—specific capabilities.

The Manager as Designer

In the role as a designer Senge (1990b, p. 10) compares the manager to the designer of a ship, explicitly excluding the roles that a manger typically would have held in the past such as captain, navigator or helmsman. Senge asks what sense it would make if the captain gave an order to turn the ship 30 degrees portside if the ship's designer built in a rudder with which such a maneuver would not be possible.

This construction task of the manager—comparable to the design of a social architecture—usually occurs invisibly in the background; behind the scenes. In contrast to the previous work of managers, which was much more characterized by an emphasis on control and the struggling for short-lived fame, results of this new kind of leadership will only manifest themselves in the still distant future. Moreover, this new leadership occurs on a much more even keel and in a less spectacular fashion.

So, which tasks exactly are those that the manager as designer should pursue?

- The first task is the derivation of appropriate goals, norms and values of the organization.
- The second essential task includes the installation of a suitable business policy, as well as suitable strategies and structures that enable a transfer of the goals, norms and values into the daily lives of the organization's employees. Traditionally the derivation of a business policy and its implementation was assigned to a small and limited number of managers. This approach looks a little antiquated today in that such a perspective would no longer reflect observable realities in the dynamics of the firm's environment and the demand for participation of employees at all hierarchical levels within the concept of organizational learning. Mintzberg (1987), for example, emphasizes that a strategy is not so much of a rational plan that is implementable in an abstract fashion within an organization, but it is much more a suddenly surfacing "emergent phenomenon". The success of an organization is not so much dependent on favoring the right strategy through strategic thinking, but it is characterized much more in the achievement to gain insights into the complexity of an organization, as well as the development of concepts and perspectives such that handling this complexity becomes more feasible (Senge, 1990b, p. 11).

- The third task reflects the shaping of the learning processes underlying the business policy, as well as strategies and structures. In contrast to earlier times when managers were only responsible and had to make sure that business did have a suitable business policy and strategy, today they also need to reassure themselves whether or not learning processes are being improved on a continuous basis.

The Manager as Teacher

When referring here to the manager as a teacher, this is not meant to denote that the manager is an authoritarian expert who will force a "right" view of reality on employees. Rather, the task of the manager as teacher is that he/she helps each member of the organization to gain more insights into the presently existing reality (Senge, 1990b, p. 11).

The role of the manager as a teacher starts with the explication of the mental models of individual employees (see page 395). No one carries an organization, a market or a technology in one's head. What people do carry in their heads are assumptions. These mental pictures that are to assist in the delivery of pointers about how the world works have a strong influence on the way in which people solve problems, use opportunities, recognize the need for action and how they make decisions. Mental models are deeply rooted within human beings. A reason for this is probably that they quietly exist, i.e. no human being is conscious of his/her own mental models. Working with mental models implies that the manager needs to discover these assumptions. Since reality for most employees means pressure, i.e. pressure they endured, crises to which they reacted and coercion that they had to accept, managers in their role as teachers have to help their employees to alter their perspective of reality and to distinguish the superfluous conditions and events from basic problems. The overall goal is to enable all employees within the organization to share their respective mental models and to unify these actively such that the future can be shaped jointly The influencing of employees through the manager in this process may occur at three different levels: through individual events, through decision-making patterns or through the holistic system structure.

- Thinking of today's society is mainly *events-oriented*. The media foster such a perspective since their attention is almost exclusively focused on short-lived, dramatic events.
- It is uncommon today to find an awareness of the existence of *entire action patterns*. Action patterns explain a group of events within a long-term, historical context. Trend analysis is one example for the existence of such action patterns.

- The implementation of influencing processes within the *system structure* of organizations takes an additional step by asking which causes are responsible for the action patterns. If the employee is aware of the nature of the system within the organization he/she can meet problems through the active redesign of system parts and their connections (see page 396).

The utility of the possibilities for influence along these three levels varies. The orientation of the influencing processes with regard to events—who does what with whom—relegate the employees to a reactive encounter with the change. Action patterns help to recognize long-term trends and to evaluate their consequences. This points out how over time one may react not only on a short-term basis to changing conditions, but also how one may respond on a long-term basis in a planned fashion. An influence that is derived from the systems structure of the enterprise, however, is most powerful. Only this influence level permits the discovery of basic causes on the level upon which behavior can be changed. Presently most managers still focus too much on the first two levels, with the consequence that their respective employees behave in just the same way. This is also the reason why organizations react mainly to changing environmental conditions, but the focal case is only rarely met with truly new ideas. Based on these conditions Senge recommends that managers in learning organizations pay an equal amount of attention to all three levels in their role as teachers. Senge (1990b, p. 12) adds that it is especially the third level that needs increased attention.

The Manager as Coach (Steward)

The role of the manager as coach or steward is certainly one of the most critical and subtle roles as manager, especially since it is strongly dependent on the manager's personality and will. He/she must have the determined will to help others and to feel responsible for them.

Coaching is based on the one hand on the considerable influence that the leadership style of a manager may have on others. The importance of an appropriate leadership style exhibited by a manager must be valued very highly when one considers how much employees may suffer performance-wise and emotionally under an inappropriate leadership style. Especially the employees of a learning organization are particularly suspect, as they have strong ties to the organization and view themselves as co-owners of their organization. On the other hand, coaching manifests itself in the manager's *feel* for the goals of his employees and their relationship to the superordinate organizational goals.

The natural impulse of employees to learn is only then triggered when the thing for which they learn is also viewed as appropriate and contributing toward goal accomplishment.

Typical application areas for coaching processes are especially preparatory assistance for the acceptance of new tasks, as well as assistance in the solving of personal problems that influence professional performance (Sonntag and Schaper, 1992). The manager as coach has to develop and evolve as a kind of advisor who adapts his/her advice flexibly to the information needs of the employees (Kieser and Kubicek, 1992). In turn, the employees will be willing to offer all their powers such that the enterprise goals are achieved optimally.

DESIGNING INCENTIVES WITHIN THE NEW ORGANIZATIONAL CONCEPTS

Incentive systems play an important part when introducing new organizational forms. A brief discussion and review of motivational theories is appropriate here. Such incentive systems are based on motives that function as the driver of relatively enduring actions (see von Rosenstiel, 1977). Although actions are observable, the explanatory willingness (motive) to engage in such actions is difficult to demonstrate and one usually only makes assumptions. Moreover, an incentive must be coupled with the motive that, in turn, triggers actions. It is generally assumed that working people have a multitude of motives of which only a portion can be activated through incentives. The sum of all motives activated by incentives is called motivation (Oechsler, 1992). Within the work setting it is possible to provide guidelines on which incentives trigger motives, i.e. how one may bring about work motivation. In this process one must be aware that not only work-related motives and incentives play a role, but also those pertaining to other spheres of our lives (see Lawler, 1994).

Typically one differentiates among monetary (e.g., pay, commissions, fringe benefits) and non-monetary incentives (e.g., promotion opportunities, qualification, leadership work and break arrangements, nature of work, suggestion system). The following discussion briefly addresses incentives showing considerable potential in the work setting.

New Forms of Remuneration

Jobs are typically graded within a systematic framework through a work classification scheme making a particular job comparable to other, similar jobs within the same organization. According to Lawler (1992,

p. 145 ff.) the following four job demand types can be identified: working conditions, problem-solving capability, necessary qualifications and responsibilities. Each of these factors can be evaluated and weighted. The resulting total number of points makes possible a classification of the job within a pay or salary scale.

A disadvantage of this procedure, according to Lawler, is in the apparent objectivity applied in the form of complicated calculations: ". . . through a series of subjective decisions, an organization can translate the tasks that it asks individuals to perform into an 'objective' quantified result and a pay level. . . ." (Lawler, 1992, p. 145) Additional shortcomings can be recognized such as:

- a missing market orientation
- a reinforcement of inflexibility of the employees during future restructuring
- hierarchy-oriented career planning (see page 404)
- the emergence of fiefdoms.

One possibility of avoiding these disadvantages would be to pursue a type of benchmarking of the respective work places, i.e. in essence to compare these workplaces with similar ones in comparable industry and with comparable competitors. This procedure in turn may lead to a new pay structure but the danger exists that the effort is too work place-oriented and dependent on hierarchical considerations. For this reason, it is currently increasingly suggested that pay systems focus on the individual employee: the *qualification-based pay system* (see, for example, Orsburn et al, 1990; Boyett and Conn, 1992; Lawler, 1992). The implementation of a qualification-based pay system usually proceeds as follows (Lawler, 1992, pp. 156 ff.):

- In the first step the tasks are identified that are necessary in the firm to deliver the desired results.
- Next the qualifications of the employees are specified and who is needed for the delivery of the performance. At the same time and through the use of appropriate tests the existence of these capabilities are determined among the current employees.
- In a third step the number and the kind of capabilities are specified that an employee needs to acquire. This step is very important in that through this specification of the capabilities the structure of the future qualification-based pay system is being determined.
- Next the derived qualifications are adjusted with regard to the organizational form, business strategy and the core competencies of the organization.

- The employees are then informed which capabilities they still need to acquire in their job performance and how these acquired capabilities will alter their pay. This communication with employees is important since typically the individual worker is only paid for the qualifications which he/she momentarily possesses and needs to accomplish the task.

A major advantage with a qualification-based pay system is the possibility to motivate employees to acquire and learn differing capabilities. This is especially important in that future success of the enterprise will be increasingly dependent on the variety of work capabilities each employee possesses (see page 375). Unfortunately, also with this pay system a number of disadvantages need to be recognized:

- An organization using a qualification-based pay system must offer each employee the opportunity for permanent continuing education.
- If the employee has just completed a continuing education phase, the organization has to expect an initial subnormal performance.
- One has to consider the possibility that an individual has learned all the necessary capabilities and then may no longer have incentives which, in turn, may lead to frustration.
- The use of the pay system becomes more complicated since the application of pay scales does not occur once annually, but may occur possibly several times a year as the pay may change each time an employee learns a new qualification.

The use of a qualification-based system does not exclude the above-mentioned bonus pay. A combination of both pay forms is possible, especially if one considers that a bonus payment can be made partially dependent upon the qualification and on the delivered performance of the individual employee (see, for example, Boyett and Conn, 1992). Such an approach seems also wise in light of the recent ever-increasing focus on performance-based pay in conjunction with newer organization concepts (see Hammer and Champy, 1994). When considering bonus pay within group concepts the possibility exists to base the performance-based bonus not on the performance of the individual, but on the group's performance.

New Forms of Career Planning

Career incentives serve mainly the fulfillment of needs in accordance with the employee's esteem level and self-actualization expectations (Kupsch and Marr, 1991). In the past career path planning occurred within a generally prescribed sequence of positions to be followed by the employee. Once this sequence was completed, the employee has achieved the highest level and position within this career plan. It is important that employees were made aware that this was indeed a final position within this career path. The promotion from position to position occurred in accordance with pre-established promotion criteria. The tasks to be carried out by each position were precisely specified.

In general, as part of the new organization concepts the individual employee no longer receives specific tasks to accomplish, but the group receives a task "bundle" that is to be accomplished by the group in a holistic fashion. The group is responsible for the completion of these tasks as an entity, i.e. the individuals are jointly responsible, and the group determines the needed procedures itself (Staudt and Rehbein, 1988).

New procedures for the evaluation of performance will be necessary:

- Assuming the employee is qualified, one possible solution is the critical examination of the employee's readiness for promotion, e.g., through the use of a "qualification point system". Accordingly each employee receives a certain number of points based on his/her annual performance evaluation that will be added from year to year (see Staudt and Rehbein, 1988). When the individual has achieved over a number of years a certain point level, the individual may then expect a promotion or may apply for an examination, where passing this examination is a condition of the subsequent promotion.
- As a complement to a qualification-based promotion system, Hammer and Champy (1994) demand the complete separation of the pay system and the individual's development appraisal. In this way the possibility exists to motivate also those employees who perform very well for continued learning and education.
- In order to keep human resources in the technical areas Jamieson and O'Mara (1991) suggest as an alternative to traditional career path planning the implementation of one's own career path for technical specialists. Such technical career paths should be implemented in an organization to run in parallel with managerial career paths. In this way the organization can keep these important specialists and their know-how and in addition skills can be developed.

These above-mentioned career incentives may be utilized individually or in combination. Which solutions should actually be deployed depends of course on the prevailing conditions within the firm.

New Forms of Qualification

Qualification is an employee's totality of know-how, talents and skills suitable to current and future professional demands. There is general agreement that with the new organization concepts, new qualifications, i.e. a shift in the order of important qualification components, occur or will have to occur. The literature does not suggest a satisfactory solution, i.e. in specifying exactly which employee qualifications are needed in order to translate these new concepts (see, for example, Boyett and Conn, 1992; Hoffman, 1994; Jamieson and O'Mara, 1991; Kochan and Useem, 1992; Orsburn et al, 1990; Pfeffer, 1994).

Overall, one can recognize three common qualification components: technical competence, social skills and creativity. Although technical skills are very important, social skills and creativity take on a larger role within the present context, i.e. the implementation of these new organizational concepts in (see, for example, Lawler, 1994; Underwood, 1993).

Imparting Social Skills

It is only fairly recently that interpersonal capabilities and skills are important, indeed, essential, prerequisites (see Neuberger, 1994). The focus here is with the concept of performance in teamwork and cooperation that have been recognized as important success factors when changes occur in organization concepts such as decentralization, self-organization, flexibility, individualization, self-control (see, for example, Galbraith and Lawler, 1993; Manz and Sims, 1993; Pinchot and Pinchot, 1993; Pfeffer, 1992; Nadler and Hibino, 1990). The reasons for this necessity of increased cooperation are multi-faceted (Neuberger, 1994):

- Individual performance is no longer precisely delineatable and controllable.
- Interface problems become amplified due to increased networking, i.e. it is no longer possible to measure the best possible division of labor at one place of work, but the focus of attention is the best possible integration of work performance among differing places of work.
- The task-executing employees are the specialists who, quite possibly, may possess more expert knowledge than their supervisors.

Various methods have been utilized in the delivery of social competence. Each author uses a different scheme to systematize the effort (see,

Measures	Examples
Content-Oriented Measures	• Presentation • Video
Process-Oriented Measures	*Non-Structural Measures:* • Learning Discussions, Panel Discussions • Role Playing • Case Studies • Entrepreneurial Planning Games • Group-Dynamics Training • Team Formation *Structural Measures:* • Quality Circles • Project Work • Network Information

Figure 9.3 *Measures for the conveyance of social competence*

for example, Conradi, 1983; Thom, 1987; Neuberger, 1994). von Rosenstiel (1992b, pp. 96 ff.), in accordance with Neuberger (1991) cluster the methods for the delivery of social competence into content- and process-oriented measures.

Figure 9.3 depicts a summary of possible content- and process-oriented qualification measures together with examples to convey social competence.

Qualifications for Innovation and Creativity

The survival of most firms will depend increasingly on the degree to which they are able to (a) to supply products and services efficiently, (b) reach the market with products quicker than their competition (reducing internal research and development cycle times) (c) increase the quality of products, as well as internal processes and daily work routines and (d) react flexibly to environmental changes and customer demands through internal innovations.

As a result of these developments the capability of employees to execute existing processes carefully, with high quality and reliably loses in importance. The capacity to perceive entrepreneurial opportunities, as well as the ability to introduce new products, processes, methods, concepts or strategies (innovations) gain increasingly in importance. The ability of employees to master problem-solving processes, i.e. the application of their creativity, is going to become an important criterion for success (Schlicksupp, 1992).

How are innovation and creativity related? Innovations are qualitatively new products or procedures that a firm has introduced for the first time into a market or within its own organization (in production or administration) (Hauschildt, 1992, p. 1029; 1993). Rogers defines innovation similarly, i.e. an idea, practice or object that is perceived as new by an individual or other unit of adoption (Rogers, 1983, p. 11). Important factors for the innovation process when applied to the individual are the capacity (creativity) and the will (innovation willingness) of the employees within the innovating firm in the delivery of innovative performance. While the readiness to innovate may be influenced by an innovation-enhancing incentive system, creativity is a mix of personal and organizational measures (Corsten, 1989).

Creativity is the human capability to bring about new ideas or objects (e.g. products, problem solving, scientific knowledge) (Uebele, 1992, p. 1165).

One approach to enhance creativity was developed by Schlicksupp (1992), combining personal and organizational factors. The author views the capacity for creative behavior or creative work processes essentially as three elementary components (Schlicksupp, 1992, pp. 43 ff.):

- *Available knowledge* (including the reorganization of known knowledge elements);
- *Mechanisms of knowledge processing* (thinking principles, methods and degree of freedom in the thinking process);
- *Psychodynamic driving forces* (trigger mechanisms of creative thinking, e.g., degree of inquisitiveness).

For these reasons creativity development cannot only occur in an isolated fashion with the individual, but it concerns also the shaping of the environment within which the individual interacts.

The capture of creative reserves within the firm should therefore be directed toward three goals:

1 *Making necessary knowledge available such that creativity can flourish*, for example job rotation, the encouragement of teamwork and project management in general, organization of contacts and information exchange within the organization.

2. *The creation of working conditions that trigger creativity:* delegation, employee-oriented leadership, open-mindedness by management with regard to innovations, emphasis on team-orientation.
3. *Encouragement of creative knowledge processing:* project management through interdisciplinary teams, introduction of a suggestion system within the firm, the possibility for employees to spend a certain portion of their work time on the pursuit of individual interests.

The Special Importance of Work Structuration for Motivation

One of the most important influencing factors for working motivation is the organization of the work to be done. The structure of work is especially important: Kenneth (1987) found that in a study of 1000 employees who were asked to rank ten factors that are closely associated with their work (e.g. pay, job security), the highest ranking was reported to be 'interesting work content'.

What does motivating, i.e. interesting, work content look like? First one must identify differing factors of work design before it is possible to make statements about an "optimal" work design. One approach to this question is the freedom of action model (see Ulich, Groskurth and Bruggemann, 1973, as well as Figure 5.11, page 194) comprising a horizontal dimension (freedom of actions) and a vertical dimension (freedom for decision and control). Through these two dimensions one may derive various possibilities for motivation-enhancing tasks. While doing this one needs to distinguish among configurational options pertaining to the individual employee and those pertaining to teams and work groups (Robbins, 1994).

The following possibilities suggest themselves for the configuration of the individual work place:

Job Enlargement. This promises a motivational effect through the sequencing of structurally similar or related activities at a work place. Accordingly, freedom of actions is brought about and increased, but the freedom of decision and control is unaffected by this measure.

Job Rotation. Through this the freedom of action is increased, as previously work and task completion was limited by the division of work. Now more work variety exists and this in itself may be a motivator. Overall the individual gains a better understanding of the organization's processes with the potential effect of an increased sense of responsibility. One side benefit of job rotation may be the resulting motivation triggered by expert qualification—at least this may come about through job rotation of workers at work places with structurally differing tasks. When work processes change very quickly the possibility exists for the employee to carry out a new task (*work module*) within regular intervals. A work module is defined as a time-limited work unit that usually encompasses two hours. A 40-hour working week then would be comprised of four work modules per day for five days. The employee could then call upon a bundle of work modules, the sum of which would constitute the daily work amount. The advantage in this configuration is that the employee could divide his/her own work and thus could also determine, for example, when the most and least liked tasks will be completed. This allows an expansion of the freedom of action as well as the freedom to make decisions.

Job Enrichment. This is directed toward the structural change of work content. Through the pooling of planning, execution and controlling work content, freedom of action, as well as freedom for decision-making and control is enabled and expanded. Job enrichment is usually combined with group work in that group members, for example, can decide on their own in their work preparation about the division of labor and, consequently, they control the work outcome themselves.

CONCLUSIONS FOR MANAGEMENT

The discussions in Chapter 9 showed that *new models of work structuration such as team concepts, networking and telework* lend themselves well to meet various entrepreneurial challenges. Depending on the circumstances in such efforts a summary of task content results in a holistic and market-oriented task structure. The processing of such tasks is supported or enabled in the first place through *new forms of application of information and communication technology*.

Development and Value-adding of the Employee Potential

With the *holistic task processing* a comprehensive transmission of action autonomy and decision-making authority to the employees occurs. This becomes especially clear in conjunction with the example of the team concept. Employees enjoy greater flexibility and freedom to organize and shape things, have increased possibilities to influence their own work and carry a greater responsibility for work results. Altogether these processes lead to the so-called *empowerment* of employees. Holistic, market-oriented task development, however, leads to *new demands being imposed on employees*. These affect especially the areas of expert competence, communication competence, capacity for self-management and social competence. The new demands therefore exceed by far traditional qualification models. Accordingly, an irrevocable trend towards a *higher qualification of employees* can be recognized. This, however, implies too that the demand for uneducated and untrained or barely qualifiable employees is decreasing at an ever-increasing rate.

Based on the empowerment of employees the *task of managers* extends especially to coordinate, to advise in a supporting fashion and to enable self-management for employees and teams. Accordingly, managers have the responsibility for the seamless flow of value-added processes and for the operating conditions of creative entrepreneurship. Their role is changing increasingly from the traditional order giver and work controller to that of an *adviser and coach* who enhances the creativity of employees. *New demands for managers* are derived from such new forms of human resources management and surface essentially with such areas as social, communicative, integration and trust building capabilities, as well as the talent to negotiate.

The development and utilization of the employee potential in the final analysis is dependent upon the capabilities of management. The new forms of human resources management become therewith an essential *guiding model of new innovation strategies* (see Figure 1.2, page 12).

These new forms of work organization, specifically the targeted and holistic incorporation of the employee potential, open the opportunity for firms to increase their productivity and quality of organizational value-added processes, as well as their *innovation capability* and, ultimately, their competitive advantage. Aside from the above-mentioned *success prerequisites* such factors as an altogether optimistic demeanor, trust by managers in the capabilities and potentials of employees, team-oriented information systems and constant development of the team capabilities are also included.

Organizational Learning as a Concept to Master Change Processes

Organizational learning is a useful tool for firms when developing new organization forms. Through this *entrenched organization structures are to be broken down* and an adaptation of the organization to changing competitive conditions and changing intra-organizational conditions, such as changing needs and values, can be achieved.

Organizational learning occurs above all through the *recording of knowledge*. This makes the firm independent of individual knowledge held by the individual employee. Part of an essential *knowledge base* of the firm are, for example, joint strategies, guiding images, goals, as well as the overall organizational culture. These factors usually outlast personnel changes and provide the context for individual actions in the firm, as well as for the individual learning of the person on the job.

Ultimately, an organization learns and acts always through its employees. Only when these learn does it follow that far-reaching learning of the entire organization occurs. Within such efforts it is becoming increasingly important *to think within a networked context*, i.e. to recognize the individual elements of the system "firm" (e.g., employees, teams, networks) and their reciprocal relationships. Employees must be able to estimate which effects their actions will have on other employees within the value-chain process and they need to adapt their actions accordingly. Managers here have, above all, the challenge to enhance the development of the *corporate culture*.

Within the framework of organizational learning *information and communication processes* play an essential role. Without them neither the individual knowledge of the organization becomes accessible, nor is it possible to trigger collective argumentation or organizational processes. The *new information and communication technologies* enable and support the processes to a considerable degree. In *learning enterprises* information and communication technology is specifically utilized to generate, retrieve, encode and store knowledge and know-how relevant to the firm's competitive setting. The actual combination of the technologies that are to serve in the support of individual and group learning and problem solving is of considerable importance. Developmental trends in these areas show that *new integrated technologies* (e.g., information tools, computer conferencing, simulation programs, CSCW, multi-media technology) are being deployed increasingly that support individual, group as well as organizational learning processes.

Redesign of Incentive Systems

The new methods of work structuration require also a new design of organizational *performance evaluation and incentive systems*. Teams, for example, are jointly responsible for the accomplishment of their holistic tasks. This makes it unnecessary to assign unequivocally tasks to individual employees, and consequently also the basis for the determination of individual performance.

In the area of *monetary incentive systems* (especially pay and profit sharing) one can recognize a trend shifting from a hierarchical orientation of remuneration to a qualification-based remuneration. Its advantage is with the possibility of being able to motivate employees to learn the capabilities necessary for the acquiring of the new management concepts.

In the area of *non-monetary incentive systems* (i.e. above all career planning) a tendency toward qualification-based promotion systems depending on the respective firm's situation can be recognized.

New Forms of Qualification

The new demands imposed on employees and managers require also new forms of qualification to convey the needed capabilities. The *development of creativity* can occur only conditionally with the individual. It concerns also the shaping of entrepreneurial conditions such as making available the necessary knowledge for creative achievements and the enhancement of creative knowledge processing as part of an organizational suggestion system or through free rooms for idea generation.

Conclusion

As a conclusion we should state that the new entrepreneurial concepts presuppose a *new image of man* that takes the place of the largely Tayloristic image of man. Employees in organizations are increasingly viewed as *"entrepreneurs within the enterprise"*. Their qualifications, capabilities, experiences and their creative potential become primary success factors within the competition. People are therefore the *most important resource* of the new entrepreneurial concepts. In the hands of new forms of human resources management this resource can be developed to enhance a wide range of innovative behavior.

References

3Com (ed.) (1994) 3Com Report – The Telecommuting Phenomenon, unpublished report.
Ackerman, M.S. (1992) Answer Garden: A Tool for Growing Organizational Memory, Working Paper, Massachusetts Institute of Technology (MIT), Cambridge, Mass.
Ackerman, M.S. (1994) Answer Garden and the Organization of Expertise, Working Paper, Massachusetts Institute of Technology (MIT), Cambridge, Mass.
Albach, H. and Albach R. (1989) Das Unternehmen als Institution. Rechtlicher und gesellschaftlicher Rahmen, Gabler: Wiesbaden.
Alchian, A.A. and Demsetz, H. (1973) The Property Rights Paradigm, in *Journal of Economic History*, **33**, pp. 16–27.
Alchian, A.A. and Woodward, S. (1987) Reflections on the Theory of the Firm, in *Journal of Institutional and Theoretical Economics* – Zeitschrift für die gesamte Staatswissenschaft, **143**, pp. 110–136.
Aldrich, H.E. (1972) Technology and Organization Structure: A Reexamination of the Findings of the Aston Group, in *Administrative Science Quarterly*, **17**, pp. 26–43.
Allen, T.J. and Scott Morton, M.S. (eds) (1994) *Information Technology and the Corporation of the 1990s*, Oxford University Press, New York / Oxford.
ANSI/SPARC (1975) Study group on data base management systems: interim report, FDT 7:2, New York, NY: ACM.
Aoki, M., Gustafsson, B. and Williamson, O.E. (eds) (1990). *The Firm as a Nexus of Treaties*, Sage, London.
Apple Corp. (eds) 1994) Apple Report, unpublished report.
Argyris, C. (1957) *Personality and Organization*, Harper & Row, New York.
Argyris, C. (1960) *Understanding Organizational Behaviour*, Tavistock, London.
Argyris, C. (1964) *Integrating the Individual and the Organization*, John Wiley & Sons, New York.
Argyris, C. and Schön, D.A. (1978) *Organizational Learning: A Theory of Action Perspective*, Addison-Wesley, Reading, Mass.
Arinze, B. (1994) *Microcomputers for Managers*. Wadsworth, Belmont, Calif.
Arrow, K.J. (1974) *The Limits of Organization*, Norton, New York.
Arrow, K.J. and Hahn, F.H. (1971) *General Competitive Analysis*, Holden-Day, San Francisco.

Arrow, K.J. and Hurwicz, L. (1958) On the Stability of the Competitive Equilibrium, in *Econometrica*, pp. 522–552.

Austin, J.L. (1989) *Zur Theorie der Sprechakte*, 2nd edition., Reclam, Stuttgart.

Axelrod, R. (1984) *The Evolution of Cooperation*, Basic Books, New York.

Anthony, R.N. (1988) *The Management Control Function*, Harvard Business School Press, Boston, MA.

Backhaus, K. and Plinke, W. (1990). Strategische Allianzen als Antwort auf veränderte Wettbewerbsstrukturen, in *Zeitschrift für betriebswirtschaftliche Forschung*, Sonderheft **27**, pp. 1–10.

Bakos, Y. (1991). Electronic Marketplaces, in *MIS Quarterly*, September pp. 295–310.

Bangemann, M. (1995) Europas Weg in die Informationsgesellschaft, Opening Speech at the 13th World Congress of the International Federation for Information Processing , Hamburg, 29 August 1994, in *Informatik Spektrum*, **1**, pp. 1–3.

Barley, S. (1986) Technology as an Occasion for Structuring: Evidence from Observation of CT Scanners and the Social Order of Radiology Departments, in *Administrative Science Quarterly*, **31**, pp. 78–108.

Barley, S. (1990) The Alignment of Technology and Structure Through Roles and Networks, in *Administrative Science Quarterly*, **35**, pp. 61–103.

Barnatt, Ch. (1995) *Cyber Business. Mindsets for a Wired Age*, John Wiley & Sons, Chichester, England.

Barrett, E. (ed.) (1992). *Sociomedia*, The MIT Press, Cambridge, Mass./London.

Bartlett, C.A. and Goshal, S. (1992) What is a Global Manager?, in *Harvard Business Review*, September/October, pp. 124–132.

Bartölke, K. et al. (eds) (1978). *Arbeitsqualität in Organisationen*, Gabler, Wiesbaden.

Bauer, F.L., Brauer, W. and Jessen, E. (1992) Informatik in unserer Zeit, München: TU München, Fakultät für Informatik.

Bauer, F.L. and Wössner, H. (1981) *Algorithmische Sprache und Programmentwicklung*, Springer, Berlin.

Baumgarten, B. (1990) *Petri-Netze: Grundlagen und Anwendungen*, BI Wissenschaftsverlag, Mannheim.

Baur, C. (1990) Make-or-Buy-Entscheidungen in einem Unternehmen der Automobilindustrie: Empirische Analyse und Gestaltung der Fertigungstiefe aus transaktions-kostentheoretischer Sicht, VVF, Munich.

Bayer, R. (1994) Plädoyer für eine Nationale Informations-Infrastruktur, in *Informatik Spektrum*, **5**, pp. 302–308.

Bea, F.X., Dichtl, E. and Schweitzer, M. (1994) *Allgemeine Betriebswirtschaftslehre*, 6th edition, G. Fischer, Stuttgart/Jena, Germany.

Becker, J. (1995) Der große Kabelsalat, in *Zeitmagazin*, 3. März, **10**, pp. 20–22.

Beckurts K.H. and Reichwald, R. (1984) *Kooperation im Management mit integrierter Bürotechnik*, CW-Publikationen, Munich.

Bellmann, K. and Wittmann, E. (1991) Modelle der organisatorischen Arbeitsstrukturierung – Ökonomische und humane Effekte, in Bullinger, H.-J. (ed.), Handbuch des Informationsmanagements im Unternehmen, Beck, Munich, pp. 487–515.

Benchimol, G. (1994) *L'entreprise délocalisée*, Editions Hermès, Paris.

Bendixen, P. (1980) Teamorientierte Organisationsformen, in Grochla, E. (ed.), *Handwörterbuch der Organisation*, 2nd edition, Poeschel, Stuttgart, pp. 2227–2236.

Benjamin, R. and Scott Morton (1988) M.S. Information technology, integration and organizational change, *Interface*, **18**, pp. 86–98.

Benjamin, R. and Wigand, R. (1995) Electronic Markets and Virtual Value Chains on the Information Superhighway, in *Sloan Management Review*, **2**, pp. 62–72.

Benjamin, R. and Yates, J. (1991) The Past and Present as a Window on the Future, in Scott Morton, M.S. (ed.), *The Corporation of the 1990s*, Oxford University Press, New York, pp. 61–92.

Benjamin, R., Malone, T. and Yates, J. (1986) Electronic Markets and Electronic Hierarchies: Effects of Information Technology on Market Structures and Corporate Strategies, MIT Working Paper, April.

Bennis, W. (1993) *Beyond bureaucracy: essays on the development and evolution of human organization*, Jossey-Bass, San Francisco, CA.

Besen, S. and Saloner, G. (1988) Compatibility Standards and the Market for Telecommunication Services, Working Paper Massachusetts Institute of Technology.

Beuermann, G. (1992) Zentralisation und Dezentralisation, in Frese, E. (ed.), *Handwörterbuch der Organisation*, 3rd edition, Schäffer-Poeschel, Stuttgart, pp. 2611–2625.

Bierhals, R., Nippa, M. and Seetzen, J. (1991) Marktpotential für die zukünftige Nutzung digitaler Breitbandnetze, in Ricke, H. and Kanzow, J. (eds). *BERKOM: Breitbandkommunikation im Glasfasernetz. Übersicht und Zusammenfassung 1986–91*, R.V. Decker, Heidelberg, pp. 39–50.

Bitz, M., et al. (eds) (1993) *Vahlens Kompendium der Betriebswirtschaftslehre*, 3rd edition, Vahlen, Munich.

Bjørn-Andersen, N., Eason, K. and Robey, D. (1986) *Managing Computer Impact*, Ablex, Norwood, NJ.

Blau, J. and Schenker, J.L. (1994) Europe Prepares To Settle Issues – Infrastructure Debated, in *Communications Week International*, 17 January, p. 1.

Blau, P., McHugh-Falbe, C., McKinley, W. and Phelps, T. (1976) Technology and Organization in Manufacturing, in *Administrative Science Quarterly*, **21**, pp. 20–40.

Bleicher, K. (1992) Der Strategie-, Struktur- und Kulturfit Strategischer Allianzen als Erfolgsfaktor, in Bronder, C. and Pritzl, R. (eds), *Wegweiser für strategische Allianzen: Meilen- und Stolpersteine bei Kooperationen*, Campus, Frankfurt am Main, pp. 267–292.

Bleicher, K. (1995) *Das Konzept integriertes Management*, Campus, Frankfurt am Main/New York.

Bleicher, K. (1996) Der Weg zum virtuellen Unternehmen, in *Office Management*, **1–2**, pp. 10–15.

Blohm, H. and Lüder, K. (1991) *Investition, Schwachstellen im Investitionsbereich des Industriebetriebes und Wege zu ihrer Beseitigung*, 7th ed., Vahlen, Munich.

Blum, U. (1992) Notwendigkeiten und Möglichkeiten qualifikationsbasierter Produktionskonzepte – alternative Ansätze aus gewerkschaftlicher Sicht, in Reichwald, R. (ed.), *Marktnahe Produktion*, Gabler,Wiesbaden, pp. 315–323.

Bode, A. (ed.) (1990) *RISC-Architekturen*, 2nd ed., BI Wissenschaftsverlag, Mannheim.

Boehm, B. (1981) *Software Engineering Economics*, Prentice Hall, Englewood Cliffs, NJ.

Boehm, B. (1988) A Spiral Model for Software Development and Enhancement, in *Computer*, **21**(5), pp. 61–72.

Bohr, K., et al. (eds) (1981) *Unternehmungsverfassung als Problem der Betriebswirtschaftslehre*, Schmidt, Berlin.

Bonus, H. (1994) Die Langsamkeit von Spielregeln, in Backhaus, K. and Bonus, H. (eds) (1994), *Die Beschleunigungsfalle oder der Triumph der Schildkröte*, Schäffer-Poeschel, Stuttgart, pp. 1–18.

Börger, E. (1992) *Berechenbarkeit, Komplexität, Logik: Algorithmen, Sprachen und Kalküle unter besonderer Berücksichtigung ihrer Komplexität*, 3rd ed., Vieweg, Braunschweig/Wiesbaden.

Borghoff, U.M. and Schlichter, J.H. (1995) *Rechnergestützte Gruppenarbeit. Eine Einführung in Verteilte Anwendungen*, Springer, Berlin.

Bornschein-Grass, C. (1995) *Groupware und computergestützte Zusammenarbeit*, Gabler, Wiesbaden.

Bower, G.H. and Hilgard, E.R. (1983) Theorie des Lernens, Klettcotta, Stuttgart.

Boyett, J.H. and Conn, H.P. (1992) *Workplace 2000: The Revolution Reshaping American Business*, Penguin, New York.

Brandt, S. (1984) *Aufgabendezentralisierung durch moderne Kommunikationsmittel*, CW, Munich.

Breton, Th. (1994a) Le Télétravail en France. Situation actuelle, perspectives de développement et aspects juridiques, Collection les Rapports Officiels, La documentation Française, Paris.

Breton, Th. (1994b) Les Téléservices en France. Quels marchés pour les autoroutes de l'information? Collection les Rapports Officiels, La documentation Française, Paris.

Brockhoff, K. (1989) *Schnittstellenmanagement*, Schäffer-Poeschel, Stuttgart.

Brockhoff, K. (ed.) (1996) *Management von Innovation*, Gabler, Wiesbaden.

Bronder, C. (1993) *Kooperationsmanagement: Unternehmensdynamik durch Strategische Allianzen*, Campus, Frankfurt am Main.

Brubach, H. (1993) Mail-Order America, *New York Times Magazine*, 21 November, p. 55

Brynjolfsson, E. (1993) The Productivity Paradox of Information Technology, in *Communications of the ACM 36*, **12**, pp. 67–77.

Brynjolfsson, E. et al (1993). *Does Information Technology Lead to Smaller Firms?*, CCS WP # 123, Sloan School WP # 3142, 24 November.

Buchanan, J.M. (1984) *Die Grenzen der Freiheit*, Mohr, Tübingen.

Büchs, M.J. (1991) Zwischen Markt und Hierarchie: Kooperationen als alternative Koordinationsform, in *Zeitschrift für Betriebswirtschaft*, supplemental Volume 1, pp. 1–38.

Bues, M. (1994) *Offene Systeme. Strategien, Konzepte und Techniken für das Informationsmanagement*, Springer, Berlin.

Bühner, R. (1987) Management-Holding, in *Die Betriebswirtschaft*, **1**, pp. 40–49.

Bühner, R. (1993) Die schlanke Management-Holding, in *Zeitschrift Führung + Organisation*, **1**, p. 7.

Bullen, C.V. and Bennett, J.L. (1990) Groupware in Practice: An Interpretation of Work Experience, CISR WP No. 205, Sloan WP No. 3146–90, March 1990, Center for Information Systems Research, Sloan School of Management, Massachusetts Institute of Technology, Cambridge, Mass.

Bullen, C.V. and Johansen, R.R. (1988) Groupware: A Key to Managing Business Teams?, CISR WP No. 169, April, Center for Information Systems Research, Sloan School of Management, Massachusetts Institute of Technology, Cambridge, Mass.

Bullinger, H.-J. (ed.) (1991) *Handbuch des Informationsmanagements im Unternehmen*, (2 volumes), Beck, Munich.

Bullinger, H.-J. and Seidel, U.A. (1992) Neuorientierung im Produktionsmanagement, in *Fortschrittliche Betriebsführung und Industrial Engineering*, **4**, pp. 150–156.

Burr, W. (1995) *Netzwettbewerb in der Telekommunikation. Chancen und Risiken aus Sicht der ökonomischen Theorie*, Gabler, Wiesbaden.
Büssing, A. (1988) *Kontrollmotivation und Tätigkeit*, Osnabrück University, Osnabrück, Germany.
Chandler, A.D. (1962) *Strategy and Structure*, MIT Press, Cambridge, Mass.
Chandler, A.D. (1977) *The Visible Hand*, Belknap Press, Cambridge, Mass.
Chandler, A.D. and Daems, H. (1979). Administrative Coordination, Allocation and Monitoring: A Comparative Analysis of Accounting and Organization in the U.S.A. and Europe, *Accounting, Organizations and Society*, **4**, pp. 3–20.
Chen, P. (1976) The Entity Relationship Model – Towards A Unified View of Data, in *ACM Transactions on Database Systems*, **1**, pp. 9–36.
Cheung, S.N. (1983) The Contractual Nature of the Firm, in *Journal of Law and Economics*, **26**(1), pp. 1–21.
Child, J. (1972) Organizational Structure, Environment and Performance: The Role of Strategic Choice, in *Sociology*, **6**, pp. 1–22.
Ciborra, C.U. (1987) Reframing the Role of Computers in Organizations – The Transaction Cost Approach, in *Office Technology and People*, **3**, pp. 17–38.
Ciborra, C.U. (1993) Teams, Markets and Systems, in *Business Innovation and Information Technology*, Cambridge University Press, Cambridge, Mass.
Ciborra, C.U. (1994) The Grassroots of IT and Strategy, in Ciborra, C.U. and Jelassi, T. (eds), *Strategic Information Systems: A European Perspective*, John Wiley & Sons, Chichester, England, pp. 3–24.
Coad, P. and Yourdon, E. (1991) *Object-Oriented Analysis*, Yourdon Press, Englewood Cliffs, NJ.
Coase, R.H. (1937) The Nature of The Firm, in *Economica*, **4**, pp. 386–405.
Codd, E.F. (1970) A Relational Model of Data for Large Shared Data Banks, in *Communications of the ACM 13*, **6**, pp. 377–387.
Coenenberg, A.G. and Fischer, T.M. (1991) Prozeßkostenrechnung – Strategische Neuorientierung in der Kostenrechnung, in Die Betriebswirtschaft, **51**(1), pp. 21–38.
Cohen, D.I. (1986) *Introduction to Computer Theory*, John Wiley & Sons, New York, NY.
Collins, E.G. (1986) Eine Firma ohne Büro. Steve Shirley im Gespräch mit Eliza E.G. Collins, in *Harvard Manager*, **3**, pp. 23–26.
Conradi, W. (1983) *Personalentwicklung*, Enke, Stuttgart.
Copeland, D. and McKenny, J. (1988) Airline Reservation Systems: Lessons from History, in *MIS Quarterly*, September, pp. 362–364.
Corsten, H. (1989) Überlegungen zu einem Innovationsmanagement – organisationale und personale Aspekte, in Corsten, H. (ed.), *Die Gestaltung von Innovationsprozessen: Hindernisse und Erfolgsfaktoren im Organisations-, Finanz- und Informations-bereich*, Erich Schmidt, Berlin.
Crémer, J. (1990) Common Knowledge and the Co-ordination of Economic Activities, in Aoki, M., Gustafsson, B. and Williamson O.E. (eds) *The Firm as a Nexus of Treaties*, Sage, London, pp. 53–76.
Daft, R.L. and Lengel, R.H. (1984) Information Richness: A New Approach to Managerial Behavior and Organization Design, in Staw, B.M. and Cummings, L.L. (eds) (1984), *Research in Organizational Behavior*, **6**, pp. 191–233, JAI Press Inc, Connecticut.
Dahl, O.J., Myrhaug, B. and Nygaard, K. (1970) Simula 67: Common Base Language, in *Norsk Regnesentral*, Publication NS 22, Oslo.
Date, C.J. (1990) *An Introduction to Database Systems*, Addison-Wesley, Reading, Mass. Vol. 1, 5th ed.

Davenport, Th.H. (1993) *Process Innovation – Reengineering Work through Information Technology*, Harvard Business School Press, Boston, Mass.
Davenport, T.H., Eccles, R.G. and Prusak, L. (1992) Information Politics, in *Sloan Management Review*, Fall, pp. 53–65.
Davidow, W.H. and Malone, M.S. (1992) *The Virtual Corporation. Structuring and Re-vitalizing the Corporation for the 21st Century*, Harper Collins, New York.
Davidow, W.H. and Malone, M.S. (1993) *Das virtuelle Unternehmen*, Campus, Frankfurt am Main u.a.
Davis, F.D. (1989) Perceived Usefulness, Perceived Ease of Use, and User Acceptance of Information Technology, in *MIS Quarterly*, **3**, pp. 319–340.
Davis, L.E. and Taylor, J.C. (1986) Technology, Organization and Job Structure, in Dubin, R. (ed.), *Handbook of Work, Organization and Society*, Rand McNally, Chicago, IL., pp. 379–419.
DeMarco, T. (1978) Structured Analysis and System Specification, Prentice Hall, Englewood Cliffs, NJ.
De Pay, D. (1989) Kulturspezifische Determinanten der Organisation von Innovationsprozessen, in *Zeitschrift für Betriebswirtschaft, Ergänzungsheft 1, Innovationsmanagement – Theorie und Praxis im Kulturvergleich*, pp. 131–176.
Derlien, H.-U. (1992) Bürokratie, in Frese, E. (ed.), *Handwörterbuch der Organisation*, 3rd ed., Schäffer-Poeschel, Stuttgart, pp. 2024–2039.
DeSanctis, G. and Gallupe, B. (1985) Group Decision Support System: A New Frontier, in *Data Base*, **2**, pp. 3–10.
Devlin, G. and Bleakley, M. (1988) Strategic Alliances – Guidelines for Success, in *Long Range Planning*, **21**, pp. 18–23.
Diebold, J. (1994) Wohin führt die Informationsgesellschaft?, in *Der GMD-Spiegel*, **4**, pp. 27–35.
Dietl, H. (1993) *Institutionen und Zeit*, Mohr, Tübingen, Germany .
Dietl, H. (1995) Institutionelle Koordination spezialisierungsbedingter wirtschaftlicher Abhängigkeit, in *Zeitschrift für Betriebswirtschaft*, **6**, pp. 569–585.
Di Martino, V. and Wirth L. (1990) Telework: an overview. International Telework Report, Part I, International Labour Office, Genf.
Dittlea, S. (1995) Interactive Illusion, *Upside*, March, pp. 56–68.
Domsch, M., Regnet, E. and Rosenstiel, L. von (eds) (1992) *Führung von Mitarbeitern. Fallstudien zum Personalmanagement*, Schäffer-Poeschel, Stuttgart.
Doppler, K. and Lauterburg, C. (1994) *Change Management: Den Unternehmenswandel gestalten*, Campus, Frankfurt am Main/New York.
Dörner, D. (1989) *Die Logik des Mißlingens. Strategisches Denken in komplexen Situationen, Reinbek bei Hamburg*, Rohwolt, Germany.
Dörner, D. et al (1983) *Vom Umgang mit Unbestimmtheit und Komplexität*, Huber, Bern.
Douma, S. and Schreuder, H. (1991) *Economic Approaches To Organization*, Prentice Hall, New York.
Drucker, P. (1990) The Emerging Theory of Manufacturing, in *Harvard Business Review*, May–June, pp. 94–102.
Drumm, H.J. (1992) Personalwirtschftslehre, 2nd ed, Springer, Berlin.
Duelli, H. and Pernsteiner, P. (1992) *Alles über Mobilfunk: Dienste, Anwendungen, Kosten, Nutzen*, 2nd ed., Franzis, Munich.
Duncan, R. and Weis A. (1979) Implications for Organizational Design, in *Research in Organizational Behavior*, **1**, pp. 75–123.
Eckardstein, D. von (1989) *Betriebliche Personalpolitik. Überblick über die Grundfragen der Personalpolitik*, 4th ed., Vahlen, Munich.

Eco, U. (1977) *Einführung in die Semiotik*, Fink, Munich.
Ehrlenspiel, K., Ambrosy, S. and Aßmann, G. (1995). Integrierter Konstruktionsarbeitsplatz, in *Zeitschrift für wirtschaftliche Fertigung und Automatisierung*, **9**, pp. 410–413.
Eisenhardt, K.M. (1989) Agency Theory: An Assessment and Review, in *Academy of Management Review*, **1**, pp. 57–74.
Endenburg, G. (1994) Soziokratie – Königsweg zwischen Diktatur und Demokratie, in Fuchs, J. (ed.), Das biokybernetische Modell: Unternehmen als Organismen, 2nd ed., Gabler, Wiesbaden, pp. 135–149.
Engeler, E. and Läuchli, P. (1988) *Berechnungstheorie für Informatiker*, Teubner, Stuttgart.
Ernst, M. (1990) *Neue Informations- und Kommunikationstechnologien und marktwirtschaftliche Allokation: eine informations- und transaktionskostentheoretische Analyse*, VVF, Munich.
Ettighofer, D. (1992) L'Entreprise Virtuelle ou Les Nouveaux Modes de Travail, Editions Odile Jacob, Paris.
European Commission (ed.) (1994a). Europe and the global information society – Recommendations to the European Council, Brussels, 26 May.
European Commission (ed.) (1995). Europas Weg in die Informationsgesellschaft – ein Aktionsplan. Mitteilung der Kommission an den Rat und das Europäische Parlament sowie an den Wirtschafts- und Sozialausschuß und den Ausschuß der Regionen vom 19.07.94, 19 July.
Eurotechnopolis Institut (ed.) (1994) *Le Bureau du Futur. Les centres d'affaires et de services partagés*, Dunod, Paris.
Eveland, J.D. (1986) Diffusion, Technology, Transfer, and Implementation, in *Knowledge Creation, Diffusion, Utilization*, 1988, **2**, pp. 303–322.
Fayol, H. (1916) *Administration Industrielle et Générale*, Paris.
Feldman, M.S. and March, J.G. (1981) Information in Organizations as Signal and Symbol, in *Administrative Science Quarterly*, **26**, pp. 171–186.
Ferstl, O.K. and Sinz, E.J. (1990) Objektmodellierung betrieblicher Informationssysteme im Semantischen Objektmdell (SOM), in *Wirtschaftsinformatik*, **6**, pp. 566–581.
Ferstl, O.K. and Sinz, E.J. (1991) Ein Vorgehensmodell zur Objektmodellierung betrieblicher Informationssysteme im Semantischen Objektmodell (SOM), in *Wirtschaftsinformatik*, **6**, pp. 477–491.
Fischer, U., Späker, G. and Weißbach, H.-J. (1993) Neue Entwicklungen bei der sozialen Gestaltung von Telearbeit, in *Informationen zur Technologiepolitik und zur Humanisierung der Arbeit*, Düsseldorf, 18 August.
Flichey, P. (1994) *TELE – Geschichte der modernen Kommunikation*, Campus, Frankfurt am Main/New York.
Franck, E. (1995) *Die ökonomischen Institutionen der Teamsportindustrie: Eine Organisationsbetrachtung*, Gabler, Wiesbaden.
Frazier, D. and Herbst, K. (1994) Get ready to Profit from the InfoBahn, in *Datamation*, 15 May, pp. 50–56.
Frese, E. (1989) Organisationstheoretische Anmerkungen zur Diskussion um "CIM-fähige" Unternehmungen, in Wildemann, H. (ed.), *Gestaltung CIM-fähiger Unternehmen*, gfmt, Munich, pp. 161–184.
Frese, E. (1993) Geschäftssegmentierung als organisatorisches Konzept: Zur Leitbildfunktion mittelständischer Strukturen für Großunternehmungen, in *Zeitschrift für betriebswirtschaftliche Forschung*, **12**, pp. 999–1024.
Frese, E. (1995) Profit Center: Motivation durch internen Marktdruck, in Reichwald, R. and Wildemann, H. (hrsg.), *Kreative Unternehmen –*

Spitzenleistungen durch Produkt- und Prozeßinnovation, Schäffer-Poeschel, Stuttgart, pp. 77–93.

Frese, E. and Noetel, W. (1990) Kundenorientierte Organisationsstrukturen in Produktion und Vertrieb – Konzeption und ausgewählte Ergebnisse einer empirischen Untersuchung, in Zahn, E. (ed.), *Organisationsstrategie und Produktion*, gfmt, Munich, pp. 15–58.

Frieling, E. (1992). Veränderte Produktionskonzepte durch "Lean Production", in Reichwald, R. (ed.), *Marktnahe Produktion*, Gabler, Wiesbaden, pp. 165–177.

Fromm, H. (1992) Das Management von Zeit und Variabilität in Geschäftsprozessen, in *CIM Management*, **5**, pp. 7–14.

Gable, R.A. (1993) *Inbound Call Centers: Design, Implementation, and Management*, Artech House, Boston/London.

Gaiser, B. (1993) *Schnittstellencontrolling bei der Produktentwicklung*, Vahlen, Munich.

Gaitanides, M. (1983) *Prozeßorganisation: Entwicklung, Ansätze und Programme prozeßorientierter Organisationsgestaltung*, Vahlen, Munich.

Galbraith, J.R. and Lawler, E.E. (1993) *Organizing for the Future: The Next Logic for Managing Complex Organizations*, Jossey-Bass, San Francisco, CA.

Gallie, W.B. (1952) *Price and Pragmatism*, Penguin Books, Harmondsworth.

Garvin, D.A. (1994) Das lernende Unternehmen I: Nicht schöne Worte – Taten zählen, in *Harvard Business Manager*, **1**, pp. 74–85.

Gaugler, E., Kolb, M. and Ling, B. (1977) Humanisierung der Arbeitswelt und Produktivität, 2nd ed., Kiehl, Ludwigshafen, Germany.

Gebert, D. (1972) *Gruppendynamik in der betrieblichen Führungsschulung*, Duncker & Humblot, Berlin.

Geihs, K. (1995) *Client/Server-Systeme: Grundlagen und Architekturen*, International Thomson Publishing, Bonn.

Gemini Management Consulting (ed.) (1994) Smart Valley Telecommuting Report, Smart Valley Inc., unpublished report, June.

Gerpott, T.J. (1993) *Integrationsgestaltung und Erfolg von Unternehmensakquisitionen*, Schäffer-Poeschel, Stuttgart.

Gerybadze, A. (1995) Strategic alliances and process redesign, de Gruyter, Berlin.

Giddens, A. (1979) *Central Problems in Social Theory: Action, Structure and Contradiction in Social Analysis*, University of California Press, Berkeley, CA.

Giddens, A. (1984) *The Constitution of Society: Outline of the Theory of Structure*, University of California Press, Berkeley, CA.

Gilder, G. (1993) Telecosm "Digital Darkhorse – Newspapers", Forbes ASAP, 25 October, 1995, pp. 139–149.

Gilpin, R. (1987) *The Political Economy of International Relations*, Princeton University Press, Princeton, NJ.

Glaser, W. R. and Glaser, M. O. (1995) *Telearbeit in der Praxis*, Luchterhand, Neuwied, Germany.

Godehardt, B. (1994) *Telearbeit: Rahmenbedingungen und Potentiale*, Westdeutscher Verlag, Opladen, Germany.

Goecke, R. (1995) *Neue Arbeits- und Kooperationsformen im oberen Führungsbereich vor dem Hintergrund neuer Telekommunikationstechniken – Ergebnisse einer Fallstudienuntersuchung*, Doctoral Dissertation, Technical University Munich, Munich, Germany.

Goldberg, A. and Robson, D. (1989) *Smalltalk-80: The Language*, Addison-Wesley, Reading, Mass.

Gomez, P. and Zimmermann, T. (1992) *Unternehmensorganisation: Profile, Dynamik, Methodik*, Campus, Frankfurt am Main/New York.
Gore, A. (1993) Remarks to the National Press Club, 21 December.
Gottschall, D. (1994) Sand im Betriebe, in *Manager Magazin*, **12**, pp. 234–247.
Gray, M., Hodson, N. and Gordon, G. (1993) *Teleworking Explained*, John Wiley & Sons, Chichester, England.
Gray, P., Markus, M. L., and PonTell, S. (1996) The Role of Telecommuning in an Integrated Workplace: The Worksmart Project, Proceedings of the 1996 ACM SIGCPR/SIGMIS Conference, 11–13 April, Denver, Colorado, pp. 138–151.
Grenier, R. and Metes, G. (1992) *Enterprise Networking: Working Together Apart*, Digital Press, Bedford, Mass.
Griese, J. (1992) Auswirkungen globaler Informations- und Kommunikationssysteme auf die Organisation weltweit tätiger Unternehmen, in Staehle, W.H. v. and Conrad, P. (eds), *Managementforschung 2*, de Gruyter, Berlin/New York, pp. 163–175.
Griese, J. (1993) Informations- und Kommunikationssysteme in international tätigen Unternehmen, in *Management & Computer*, **1**, pp. 283–288.
Grote, G. (1993) *Schneller, besser, anders kommunizieren?*, Teubner, Stuttgart.
Grote, G. (1994) Auswirkungen elektronischer Kommunikation auf Führungsprozesse, in *Zeitschrift für Arbeits- und Organisationspsychologie*, **12**, pp. 71–75.
Grudin, J. (1991) The Convergence of Two Development Contexts, CH191 Conference Proceedings, New Orleans, 28 April–2 May, ACM SIGCHI, pp. 91–92.
Gulick, L.H. and Urwick, L.F. (eds) (1937). Papers on the Science of Administration, Institute of Public Administration, New York.
Gurbaxani, V. and Whang, S. (1991) The Impact of Information Systems on Organizations and Markets, in *Communications of the ACM*, **1**, pp. 59–73.
Gutenberg, E. (1929) *Die Unternehmung als Gegenstand betriebswirtschaftlicher Theorie*, Springer, Berlin.
Gutenberg, E. (1951) *Grundlagen der Betriebswirtschaftslehre, Vol. 1, Die Produktion*, Springer, Berlin.
Gutenberg, E. (1958) *Grundlagen der Betriebswirtschaftslehre, Vol. 1, Die Produktion*, 4th ed., Springer, Berlin.
Habermas, J. (1976) Was heißt Universalpragmatik? in Apel, K.-O. (ed.), *Sprachpragmatik und Philosophie*, Suhrkamp, Frankfurt am Main, pp. 174–272.
Habermas, J. (1981) *Theorie des kommunikativen Handelns, Vol. 1: Zur Kritik der funktionalistischen Vernunft*, Suhrkamp, Frankfurt am Main.
Habermas, J. (1984) *Vorstudien und Ergänzungen zur Theorie des kommunikativen Handelns*, Suhrkamp, Frankfurt am Main.
Hackman, J.R. (1969) Nature of Task as a Determiner of Job Behaviour, in *Personnel Psychology*, **22**, pp. 435–444.
Hackman, J.R. (1977) Work Design, in Hackman, J. R. and Suttle, J. L. (eds), *Impressing Life of Work*, Santa Monica, pp. 96–162.
Haddon, L. and Lewis, A. (1994) The experience of teleworking: an annotated review, in *The International Journal of Human Resource Management*, February, **5**(1), pp. 195–223.
Hahn, D. (1996) *PuK, Controllingkonzepte*, 5th ed., Gabler, Wiesbaden.
Hamel, G. and Prahalad, C.K. (1995) *Wettlauf um die Zukunft*, Ueberreuter, Vienna, Austria.

Hammer, M. and Champy, J. (1993) *Reengineering the Corporation: A Manifesto for Business Revolution*, HarperCollins, New York.
Hammer, M. and Champy, J. (1994) *Business Reengineering*, 4th ed., Campus, Frankfurt am Main/New York.
Handy, C. (1995) Trust and Virtual Organization, in *Harvard Business Review*, May/June, pp. 40–50.
Hanker, J. (1990) *Die strategische Bedeutung der Informatik für Organisationen: Industrieökonomische Grundlagen des Strategischen Informatikmanagements*, Teubner, Stuttgart.
Hannan, M.T. and Freeman, J. (1977) The population ecology of organizations, in *American Journal of Sociology*, **82**, pp. 929–964.
Harasim, L. (ed.) (1993) *Global Networks – Computers and International Communication*, MIT Press, Cambridge, Mass.
Harrington, J. (1991) *Business Process Improvement: The Breakthrough Strategy for Total Quality, Productivity and Competitiveness*, McGraw-Hill, New York.
Harris, M. and Harris, B. (eds) (1994) *Teleworking & Teleconferencing Yearbook*, NCC Blackwell, Oxford.
Hart, O. (1995) *Firms, Contracts and Financial Structure*, Clarendon Press, Oxford.
Hartzheim, H. (1990) EDI-Anwendungspraxis: Elektronischer Datenaustausch in der Automobilindustrie – EDI in einem multinationalen Konzern: Ford of Europe, in *EWI (ed.), Electronic Data Interchange*, EDI 90, Gugath, Munich.
Hasenkamp, U., Kirn, S. and Syring, M. (1994) CSCW – *Computer Supported Cooperative Work*, Addison-Wesley, Bonn.
Hauschildt, J. (1992). Innovationsmanagement, in Frese, E. (ed.), *Handwörterbuch der Organisation*, 3rd ed., Schäffer-Poeschel, Stuttgart, pp. 1029–1041.
Hauschildt, J. (1993) *Innovationsmanagement*, Vahlen, Munich.
Hax, H. (1993) *Investitionstheorie*, 5th ed., Physica, Heidelberg, Germany.
Hayek, F.A. von. (1945). The Use of Knowledge in Society, in *Economia*, **4**, pp. 33–54.
Hayek, F.A. von. (1952) *Individualismus und wirtschaftliche Ordnung*, Rentsch, Erlenbach-Zürich, Switzerland.
Hedberg, B. (1981) How Organizations Learn and Unlearn, in Nyström, P.C. and Starbuck, W.H. (ed.), *Handbook of Organizational Design Vol. 1: Adapting Organizations to their Environments*, Oxford University Press, New York, pp. 3–27.
Heinen, E. (1965).*Betriebswirtschaftliche Kostenlehre, Kostentheorie und Kostenentscheidungen* 2nd ed., Gabler,, Wiesbaden.
Heinen, E. (1968) *Einführung in die Betriebswirtschaftslehre*, Gabler, Wiesbaden.
Heinen, E. (1986) Menschliche Arbeit aus betriebswirtschaftlicher Sicht, in Schubert, V. (ed.), *Der Mensch und seine Arbeit*, EOS, St. Ottilien, Germany, pp. 307–329.
Heinen, E. (ed.) (1991) *Industriebetriebslehre: Entscheidungen im Industriebetrieb*, 9th ed., Gabler, Wiesbaden.
Henderson-Sellers, B. and Edwards, J.M. (1990) The Object-Oriented Systems Life Cycle, in *Communications of the ACM*, **9**, pp. 142–159.
Hennessy, J.L. and Patterson, D.A. (1994) *Rechnerarchitektur: Analyse, Entwurf, Implementierung, Bewertung*, Vieweg, Braunschweig/Wiesbaden, Germany.
Hentze, J. (1991) *Personwirtschaftslehre 2*, 5th ed., UTB, Bern/Stuttgart.
Herzberg, F. (1968) One more time: How Do You Motivate Employees?, in *Harvard Business Review*, **1**, pp. 53–62.

Herzberg, F., Mausner, B. and Snyderman, B. (1959) *The Motivation to Work*, 2nd ed., John Wiley & Sons, New York/London.
Hickson, D., Pugh, D.S. and Pheysey, D. (1969) Operations Technology and Organization Structure: An Empirical Reappraisal, in *Administrative Science Quarterly*, **14**, pp. 378–397.
Hill, W., Fehlbaum, R. and Ulrich, P. (1989) *Organisationslehre, Vol. 1*, 4th ed., Haupt, Bern/Stuttgart.
Hill, W., Fehlbaum, R. and Ulrich, P. (1992). *Organisationslehre Vol. 2*, 4th ed., UTB, Bern/Stuttgart.
Hilpert, W. (1993) Workflow Management im Office-Bereich mit verteilten Dokumentendatenbanken, in Nastansky, L. (ed.), *Workgroup Computing*, Steuer- und Wirtschaftsverlag, Hamburg.
Himberger, A. (1994) *Der Elektronische Markt als Koordinationssystem*, Hochschule St. Gallen.
Hippel, E. von. (1988) *The Sources of Innovation*, University Press, New York/Oxford.
Hirth, H. (1995) Market Maker, in *Wirtschaftswissenschaftliches Studium*, **8**, pp. 421–423.
Hirschleifer, J. (1980) *Price Theory and Application*, Prentice-Hall, Englewood Cliffs, NJ.
Hoffman, G. M. (1994) *Technology Payoff: How to Profit with Empowered Workers in the Information Age*, Irwin, New York.
Hollings, E. (1990) Communications competitiveness and Infrastructure Modernization Act of 1990. Washington, DC: US Government Printing Office, Report to the Senate Committee on Commerce, Science and Transportation, 12 September.
Hopcroft, J.E. and Ullman, J.D. (1979) *Introduction to Automata Theory, Languages and Computation*, Addison-Wesley, Reading, Mass.
"Hopes and Fears on New Computer Organisms" (1994) *The New York Times*, 6 January, p. D1.
Horváth, P. (1994) *Controlling*, 5th ed., Vahlen, Munich.
Hrubi, F.R. (1988) Kommunikationsmanagement, in Hofmann, M. and Rosenstiel, L. von. (eds), *Funktionale Managementlehre*, Springer, Berlin, pp. 59–94.
Hubmann, H.-E. (1989) *Elektronisierung von Beschaffungsmärkten und Beschaffungshierarchien: Informationsverarbeitung im Beschaffungsmanagement unter dem Einfluß neuer Informations- und Kommunikationstechniken*, VVF, Munich.
Hwang, K. and Briggs, F.A. (1985) *Computer Architecture and Parallel Processing*, McGraw-Hill, New York, NY.
IDATE (1994) *European Telecommunications Handbook for Teleworkers, A study for the Commission of the European Union*, ed. by ExperTeam TeleCom Dortmund, Germany and IDATE Montpellier, France, October.
Imai, K. and Itami, H. (1984) Interpenetration of Organization and Market, in *International Journal of Industrial Organization*, **2**(4), pp. 285–310.
Jablonski, S. (1991) Konzepte der verteilten Datenverwaltung, in *Handbuch der modernen Datenverarbeitung*, **157**, pp. 1–21.
Jamieson, D. and O'Mara, J. (1991) *Managing Workforce 2000: Gaining the Diversity Advantage*, Jossey-Bass, San Francisco, CA.
Jarillo, J.C. (1988) On Strategic Networks, in *Strategic Management Journal*, **9**, pp. 90–143.
Jarillo, J.C. (1993) *Strategic Networks: Creating the borderless organization*, Butterworth-Heinemann, Oxford.

Jarvenpaa, S.L. and Ives, B. (1994) The Global Network Organization of the Future: Information Management Opportunities and Challenges, in *Journal of Management Information Systems*, **4**, pp. 25–57.

Jensen, M. and Meckling, W. (1976) Theory of the Firm: Managerial Behavior, Agency Costs, and Capital Structure, in *Journal of Financial Economics*, **5**, pp. 305–360.

Jessen, E. and Valk, R. (1987) *Rechensysteme: Grundlagen der Modellbildung*, Springer, Berlin.

Johansen, R. (1991) Teams for Tomorrow, in Proceedings of the 24th Annual Hawaii International Conference on Systems Sciences, Los Alamitos, Calif, IEEE Computer Society Press, pp. 520–534.

Johansen, R. and Swigart, R. (1994) *Upsizing the Individual in the Downsized Organization: Managing in the Wake of Reengineering, Globalization, and Overwhelming Technological Change*, Addison-Wesley, Reading, Mass.

Kämpf, R. and Wilhelm, B. (1994) Vom fraktalen Unternehmen zum kooperativen Standortverbund, in *io Management Zeitschrift*, **6**, pp. 47–50.

Kanter, R. M. (1989) The New Managerial Work, in *Harvard Business Review*, **6**, pp. 85–92.

Kanzow, J. (1991) BERKOM-Breitbandkommunikation im Glasfasernetz, in Ricke, H. and Kanzow, J. (eds), *BERKOM: Breitbandkommunikation im Glasfasernetz. Übersicht und Zusammenfassung 1986–91*, R.V. Decker, Heidelberg, Germany, pp. 1–9.

Kappich, L. (1989) Theorie der internationalen Unternehmungstätigkeit, VVF, Munich.

Kappler, E. (1992) Menschenbilder, in Gaugler, E. and Weber, W. (eds), *Handwörterbuch des Personalwesens*, 2nd ed., Schäffer-Poeschel, Stuttgart, pp. 1324–1342.

Kappler, E. and Rehkugler, H. (1991) Konstitutive Entscheidungen, in Heinen, E. (ed.), *Industriebetriebslehre. Entscheidungen im Industriebetrieb*, 9th ed., Gabler, Wiesbaden, pp. 73–240.

Katz, D. (1955) *Productivity, Superversion and Morale Among Railroad Workers*, John Wiley & Sons, New York.

Katzenbach, J.R. and Smith, D.K. (1994) *The Wisdom of Teams*, Harper Business, New York.

Kaulmann, Th. (1987) *Property Rights und Unternehmungstheorie: Stand und Weiterentwicklung der empirischen Forschung*, VVF, Munich.

Keen, P.G. and Scott Morton, M.S. (1978) *Decision Support Systems: An Organizational Perspective*, Addison-Wesley, Reading, Mass.

Keller, E. (1992) *Management in fremden Kulturen*, Haupt, Stuttgart.

Kenneth, A. K. (1987) What Motivates Employees? Workers and Supervisors Give Different Answers, in *Business Horizons*, **9–10**, pp. 58–65.

Kern, W. (1992) Industrielle Produktionswirtschaft, 5th ed., Schäffer-Poeschel, Stuttgart.

Kern, H. and Schumann, M. (1986) *Das Ende der Arbeitsteilung? Rationalisierung in der industriellen Produktion*, 3rd ed., Beck, Munich.

Kieser, A. (ed.) (1993) *Organisationstheorien*, Kohlhammer, Stuttgart.

Kieser, A. and Kubicek, H. (1992) Organisation, 3rd ed., de Gruyter, Berlin/New York.

Kiesler, S., Siegel, J. and McGuire, T.W. (1984) Social psychological aspects of computer-mediated communication, in *American Psychologist*, **39**, pp. 1123–1134.

Kilian, W., et al. (1994) *Electronic Data Interchange (EDI) aus ökonomischer und juristischer Sicht*, Nomos, Baden-Baden, Germany.

Kilian-Momm, A. (1989) *Dezentralisierung von Büroarbeitsplätzen mit neuen Informations- und Kommunikationstechniken: Eine Analyse unter betriebswirtschaftlich-organisatorischen Aspekten*, VVF, Munich.
Kirchgässner, G. (1991) *Homo oeconomicus: Das ökonomische Modell individuellen Verhaltens und seine Anwendung in den Wirtschafts- und Sozialwissenschaften*, Mohr, Tübingen, Germany.
Kirchner, C. and Picot, A. (1987) Transaction Costs Analysis of Structural Changes in the Distribution System: Reflections on Institutional Developments in the Federal Republic of Germany, in *Journal of Institutional and Theoretical Economics*, **143**, pp. 62–81.
Kirsch, W. (1970) *Entscheidungsprozesse, Vol. I*, Gabler, Wiesbaden.
Kirsch, W. (1971) *Entscheidungsprozesse, Vols II/III*, Gabler, Wiesbaden.
Kirsch, W. (1992) *Kommunikatives Handeln, Autopoiese, Rationalität: Sondierungen zu einer evolutionären Führungslehre*, B. Kirsch, Herrsching, Germany.
Kirsch, W. and Klein, H.K. (1977) *Management-Informationssysteme 2. Auf dem Weg zu einem neuen Taylorismus?*, Kohlhammer, Stuttgart.
Kirzner, I.M. (1978) *Wettbewerb und Unternehmertum*, Mohr, Tübingen, Germany.
Klages, H. (1984) *Wertorientierungen im Wandel. Rückblick, Gegenwartsanalyse, Prognosen*, Campus, Frankfurt am Main.
Klein, S. (1994) Virtuelle Organisation, in *Wirtschaftswissenschaftliches Studium*, **6**, pp. 309–311.
Kleinaltenkamp, M. (1993) *Standardisierung und Marktprozeß: Entwicklungen und Auswirkungen im CIM-Bereich*, Gabler, Wiesbaden.
Klimecki, R., Probst, G.J. and Eberl, P. (1994) *Entwicklungsorientiertes Management*, Schäffer-Poeschel, Stuttgart.
Klimecki, R.G., Probst, G.J. and Gmür, M. (1993) *Flexibilisierungsmanagement, Schriftenreihe: Die Orientierung*, No 102, Schweizerische Volksbank, Bern.
Kling, R. and Iacono, S. (1984) Computing as an Occasion for Social Control, in *Journal of Social Issues*, **40**, pp. 77–96.
Knight, F.H. (1921) *Risk, Uncertainty and Profit*, Houghton-Mifflin, Boston.
Knuth, D.E. (1973a) *The Art of Computer Programming, Vol. 1: Fundamental Algorithms*, 2nd ed., Addison-Wesley, Reading, Mass.
Knuth, D.E. (1973b) *The Art of Computer Programming, Vol. 3: Sorting and Searching*, Addison-Wesley, Reading, Mass.
Knuth, D.E. (1981) *The Art of Computer Programming, Vol. 2: Seminumerical Algorithms*, 2nd ed., Addison-Wesley, Reading, Mass.
Kochan, T.A. and Useem, M. (1992) Creating the Learning Organization, in Kochan, T.A. and Useem, M. (eds), *Transforming Organizations*, Oxford Univ. Press, New York/Oxford, pp. 391–405.
Koerber, E. von. (1993) Geschäftssegmentierung und Matrixstruktur im internationalen Großunternehmen – Das Beispiel ABB, in *Zeitschrift für betriebswirtschaftliche Forschung*, **12**, pp. 1060–1077.
Koller, H. (1994) *Die Integration von Textverarbeitung und Datenverarbeitung: Analyse des Bedarfs und seiner Determinanten aus betriebswirtschaftlicher Sicht*, Gabler, Wiesbaden.
Korte, W.B. (1994) Telearbeit international und Trends für Deutschland, in *Telearbeit und virtuelle Arbeitsplätze: Neue Arbeitsformen als Chance für Unternehmen und Mitarbeiter*, Conference on 23/24 August, Frankfurt am Main, Starnberg, Germany: Management Forum, 1994.
Krähenmann, N. (1994) *Ökonomische Gestaltungsanforderungen für die Entwicklung elektronischer Märkte*, Hochschule St. Gallen.

Krallmann, H. and Klotz, M. (1994) Grafisches Organisationswerkzeug zur Unternehmensmodellierung, in *Office Management*, **5**, pp. 34–36.
Kraut, R. and Egido, C. (1988) Patterns of Contact and Communication in Scientific Research Collaboration, in *Proceedings of the Conference on Computer-Supported Cooperative Work*, ACM, New York, NY, pp. 1–12.
Krcmar, H. (1992) Computer Aided Team – Ein Überblick, in *Information Management*, **1**, pp. 6–9.
Krcmar, H. and Lewe, H. (1992) GroupSystems: Aufbau und Auswirkungen, in *Information Management*, **1**, pp. 32–41.
Kredel, L. (1988) *Wirtschaftlichkeit von Bürokommunikationssystemen. Eine vergleichende Darstellung*, Springer, Berlin.
Kreikebaum, K. (1977) Humanität in der Arbeitswelt. Eine kritische Betrachtung, in *Zeitschrift für Betriebswirtschaft*, **8**, pp. 481–508.
Kreikebaum, K. and Herbert, K.-J. (1988) Humanisierung der Arbeit, Gabler, Wiesbaden.
Kreilkamp, P. (1994) Perspektiven zur Tele-Arbeit, in *Telearbeit und virtuelle Arbeitsplätze: Neue Arbeitsformen als Chance für Unternehmen und Mitarbeiter*, Conference on 23–24 August in Frankfurt am Main, Starnberg, Germany: Management Forum, 1994.
Krüger, W. (1993) Die Transformation von Unternehmungen und ihre Konsequenzen für die Organisation der Information, in *Betriebswirtschaftliche Forschung und Praxis*, **6**, pp. 577–601.
Krüger, W. and Pfeiffer, P. (1988) Strategische Ausrichtung, organisatorische Gestaltung und Auswirkungen des Informations-Management, in *Information Management*, **3**, pp. 6–15.
Kubicek, H. (1990) *Was bringt uns die Telekommunikation? ISDN – 66 kritische Antworten*, Campus, Frankfurt am Main.
Kubicek, H. (1991) *Telekommunikation und Gesellschaft*, Müller, Karlsruhe, Germany.
Kubicek, H. (1992) Die Organisationslücke beim elektronischen Austausch von Geschäftsdokumenten (EDI) zwischen Organisationen, Unterlage zum Vortrag auf dem 16. Workshop der Wissenschaftlichen Kommission "Organisation" im Verband der Hochschullehrer für Betriebswirtschaft "Ökonomische Theorien der interorganisationalen Beziehungen," 2–4 April.
Kubicek, H. (1994) *Telekommunikation und Gesellschaft – Schwerpunkt Technikgestaltung*, Müller, Heidelberg, Germany.
Kühl, S. (1995) *Wenn die Affen den Zoo regieren: Die Tücken der flachen Hierarchie*, 2nd ed., Campus, Frankfurt am Main/New York.
Kuhlen, R. (1995) *Informationsmarkt: Chancen und Risiken der Kommerzialisierung von Wissen, Schriftenreihe zur Informationswissenschaft*, Vol. 15, UKV Universitätsverlag, Konstanz, Germany.
Kuhlmann, T. et al (1993). Concurrent Engineering in der Unikatfertigung, in *CIM Management*, **2**, pp. 10–16.
Kunz, H. (1985) *Marktsystem und Information*, Mohr, Tübingen, Germany.
Küpper, H.-U. et al (1990) Unternehmensführung und Controlling, Gabler, Wiesbaden.
Küpper, H.-U. (1995) *Controlling: Konzeption, Aufgaben und Instrumente*, Schäffer-Poeschel, Stuttgart.
Kupsch, P.U. and Marr, R. (1991) Personalwirtschaft, in Heinen, E. (ed.), *Industriebetriebslehre: Entscheidungen im Industriebetrieb*, 9th ed., Gabler, Wiesbaden, pp. 729–894.
Kyas, O. (1993) *ATM Netzwerke. Aufbau – Funktionen – Performance*, DATACOM, Bergheim, Germany.

Lange, K. (1990). Chancen und Risiken der Mobilfunktechnologien, in *Diskussionsbeitrag No. 60, Wissenschaftliches Institut für Kommunikationsdienste (WIK)*, Bad Honnef, Germany.
Langenohl, Th. (1994) *Systemarchitekturen elektronischer Märkte*, Hochschule St. Gallen.
Laske, S. and Weiskopf, R. (1992) Hierarchie, in Frese, E. (ed.), *Handwörterbuch der Organisation*, 3rd ed., Schäffer-Poeschel, Stuttgart.
Lawler, E. E. (1992) *The Ultimative Advantage: Creating the High-Involvement Organization*, Jossey-Bass, New York.
Lawler, E. E. (1994) *Motivation in Work Organizations* Jossey-Bass, San Francisco.
Legrand, G. (1972) *ictionnaire de Philosophie*, Bordas, Paris.
Lemesle, R.-M. and Marot, J.-C. (1994) Le Télétravail, Paris: Presses Universitaires de France.
Leonard-Barton, D. (1995) *Wellsprings of Knowledge: Building and Sustaining the Sources of Innovation*, Harvard Business School Press, Boston, Mass.
Levy S. (1994) *Will and Andy's Excellent Adventure II. Wired* April, p. 107.
Levitan, K.B. (1982) Information Resources as "Goods" in the Life Cycle of Information Production, in *Journal of the American Society for Information Science*, **33**, pp. 44–54.
Lewe, H. and Krcmar, H. (1991) Die CATeam-Raum-Umgebung als Mensch-Computer Schnittstelle, in Friedrich, J. and Rödiger, K.-H. (eds), *Computergestützte Gruppenarbeit (CSCW)*, Teubner, Stuttgart, pp. 171–182.
Liebowitz, J. (1988) *Introduction to Expert Systems*, Mitchell Publishing, Santa Cruz, CA.
Liessmann, K. (1990) *Joint Venture erfolgreich organisieren und managen: Neue Märkte durch strategische Kooperation*, WRS, Munich.
Likert, R. (1961) *New Patterns of Management*, McGraw-Hill, New York.
Likert, R. (1967) *The Human Organization*, McGraw-Hill, New York.
LINK Resources Corp. (1993) Telecommuting, in *USA TODAY*, 20 November.
Lucas, H.C. and Olson, M. (1994) The Impact of Information Technology on Organizational Flexibility, in *Journal of Organizational Computing*, **2**, pp. 155–176.
Luhmann, N. (1986) Organisation, in Küpper, W. and Ortmann, G. (eds), *Mikropolitik: Rationalität, Macht und Spiele in Organisationen*, Westdeutscher Verlag, Opladen, Germany, pp. 165–185.
Luhmann, N. (1989) *Vertrauen: Ein Mechanismus der Reduktion sozialer Komplexität*, 3rd ed., Enke, Stuttgart.
Luhmann, N. (1994) *Die Wirtschaft der Gesellschaft*, Suhrkamp, Frankfurt am Main.
Lütge, G. (1995) Starker Glaube, schwache Fakten, in *Die Zeit*, 24 March, No. 13, pp. 41–42.
Lutz, B. (1995) Die Notwendigkeit einer neuen Strategie industrieller Innovation, Vorlage des Expertenkreises im Rahmen der Vorbereitung des Rahmenprogramms "Produktion 2000", Munich, May.
Lutz, B. (1995) Einleitung, in Lutz, B., Hartmann, M. and Hirsch-Kreinsen, H. (eds). *Produzieren im 21. Jahrhundert. Herausforderungen für die deutsche Industrie*, Campus, Frankfurt am Main/New York, pp. 9–43.
Lutze, R. (1995) Set-Top-Boxen, in *Wirtschaftsinformatik*, **6**, pp. 609–612.
Maaß, S. (1991) Computergestützte Kommunikation und Kooperation, in Oberquelle, H. (ed.), *Kooperative Arbeit und Computerunterstützung: Stand und Perspektiven*, Verlag für allgemeine Psychologie, Göttingen, pp. 11–35.

Macharzina, K. (1993) *Unternehmensführung: Das internationale Managementwissen*, Gabler, Wiesbaden.
MacNeil, I.R. (1978) Contracts: Adjustment of Long-Term Economic Relations under Classical, Neoclassical, and Relational Contract Law, in *Northwestern University Law Review*, **72**, pp. 854–905.
Maier, M. (1990) *Theoretischer Bezugsrahmen und Methoden zur Gestaltung computergestützter Informationssysteme*, VVF, Munich.
Malone, Th. W. (1988) What is coordination theory?, CISR WP No. 182, Sloan WP No. 2051–88, MIT Press.
Malone, Th.W. (1990). Organizing Information Processing Systems: Parallels Between Human Organizations and Computer Systems, in Zachary, W., Robertson, S. and Black, J. (eds), *Cognition, Computation and Cooperation*, Ablex Publ., Norwood, NJ, pp. 56–83.
Malone, Th.W., Yates, J.A. and Benjamin, R.I. (1986) Electronic Markets and Electronic Hierarchies, CISR WP No. 137, Sloan WP No. 1770–86, 90's WP No. 86–018, MIT Press, April (Revised November 1986).
Malone, T., Yates, J. and Benjamin, R. (1987) Electronic Markets and Electronic Hierarchies, in *Communications of the ACM*, **6**, pp. 485–497.
Malone, T., Yates, J. and Benjamin, R. (1989) The Logic of Electronic Markets, in *Harvard Business Review*, **3**, pp. 166–172.
Manz, C.C., Sims, H.P. (1993) *Business without Bosses: How Self-Managing Teams Are Building High Performing Companies*, John Wiley & Sons, New York.
March, J.G. and Simon, H.A. (1958) *Organizations*, John Wiley & Sons, New York/London.
Markus, M.L. (1983) Power, Politics, and MIS Implementation, in *Communications of the ACM*, **26**, pp. 430–444.
Markus, M.L. (1994) Electronic Mail as the Medium of Managerial Choice, in *Organization Science*, November, **4**, pp. 502–527.
Marquardt, M. and Reynolds, A. (1994) *The Global Learning Organization: Gaining Competitive Advantage through Continuous Learning*, Irwin Publ., New York.
Marr, R. and Stitzel, M. (1979) *Personalwirtschaft: ein konfliktorientierter Ansatz*, Moderne Industrie, Munich.
Martin, T. (1990) Das Verhältnis von Mensch und Automatisierung in der Produktion – am Beispiel CIM, in Henning, K., Süthoff, M. and Mai, M. (eds), *Mensch und Automatisierung – Eine Bestandsaufnahme*, Westdeutscher Verlag, Opladen, Germany, pp. 91–106.
Martin, T. (1992) Das Verhältnis von Mensch und Automatisierung bei der Gestaltung der Produktion, in Reichwald, R. (ed.), *Marktnahe Produktion*, Gabler, Wiesbaden, pp. 178–187.
Maslow, A.H. (1954) *Motivation and Personality*, Harper, New York.
Mathews, R.C. (1986) The Economics of Institutions and the Sources of Economic Growth, in *Economic Journal*, **96**, pp. 903–918.
Mathews, J. (1994) The Governance of Inter-Organisational Networks, in *Corporate Governance*, **1**, pp. 14–19.
Maturana, R.H. and Varela, F.J. (1987) *Der Baum der Erkenntnis*, Scherz, Bern/Munich.
Mayo, E. (1949) *Probleme industrieller Arbeitsbedingungen*, Verlag D. Frankfurter Hefte, Frankfurt am Main.
McDermid, J. and Rook, P. (1991) Software development process models, in McDermid, J. (ed.), *Software Engineer's Reference Book*, Butterworth-Heinemann, Oxford.

McGregor, D. (1960), The Human Side of Enterprise, McGraw-Hill, New York.
McGregor, D. (1966), *Leadership and Motivation*, MIT Press, Cambridge, Mass.
McKenny, J., Copeland, D. C., and Mason, R. O. (1995) *Waves of Change: Business Evolution through Information Technology*, Harvard Business School Press, Boston, Mass.
Medina-Mora, R., et al (1992) The Action Workflow Approach to Workflow Management Technology, in *CSCW 92: Sharing Perspectives*, ACM Conference on Computer-Supported Cooperative Work, ACM Press, Toronto, pp. 281–288.
Mehrabian, A. (1971) *Silent Messages*, Wadsworth, Belmont, CA.
Menger, C. (1871) *Grundsätze der Volkswirtschaftslehre*, Braumüller, Vienna/Leipzig.
Merrifield, D. B. (1992) Global Strategic Alliances Among Firms. *International Journal of Technology Management*, Special Issue on Strenthening Corporate and National Competitiveness Through Technology, **7**, p. 77.
Mertens, P. (1985) Zwischenbetriebliche Integration der EDV, in *Informatik Spektrum*, **2**, pp. 81–90.
Mertens, P. (1988) *Industrielle Datenverarbeitung*, Vol. 1, 7th ed., Gabler, Wiesbaden.
Mertens, P. (1991) *Integrierte Informationsverarbeitung 1: Administrations- und Dispositionssysteme in der Industrie*, 8th ed., Gabler, Wiesbaden.
Mertens, P. (1994) Virtuelle Unternehmen, in *Wirtschaftsinformatik*, **2**, pp. 169–172.
Mertens, P. and Griese, J. (1991) *Integrierte Informationsverarbeitung*, Vol. 2, Gabler, Wiesbaden.
Mertens, P., (1995) *Grundzüge der Wirtschaftsinformatik*, 3rd ed., Springer, Berlin.
Meyer, W.B. (1989) Reusability: The Case For Object-Oriented Design: The Road To Eiffel, in *Structured Programming*, **1**, pp. 19–39.
Meyer, W.B. (1990) *Objektorientierte Softwareentwicklung*, Hanser, Munich/Vienna, 1990.
Michaelis, E. (1985) *Organisation unternehmerischer Aufgaben – Transaktionskosten als Beurteilungskriterium*, Lang, Frankfurt am Main.
Miles, R.I. (1975) *Theories of Management*, Implications for Organizational Behavior and Development, McGraw-Hill, New York.
Milgrom, P. and Roberts, J. (1992) *Economics, Organization and Management*, Prentice Hall, Englewood Cliffs, NJ.
Miller, G.A. (1967) The Magical Number Seven, Plus or minus Two: Some Limits on our Capacity for Processing Information, in Alexis, M. and Wilson, C.Z. (eds), *Organizational Decision Making*, Prentice Hall, Englewood Cliffs, NJ.
Miller, D. B., Clemons, E. K. and Row, M.C. (1993) Information Technology and the Global Virtual Corporation, in S.P. Bradley, J. A. Hausman, and R.L. Nolan (eds), *Globalization, Technology and Competition*, Harvard Business School Press, Boston, Mass, pp. 283–307.
Mintzberg, H. (1973) *The Nature of Managerial Work*, Prentice Hall, Englewood Cliffs, NJ.
Mintzberg, H. (1987) Crafting Strategies, in *Harvard Business Review*, **7–8**, pp. 66–75.
Mintzberg, H. (1994) Rounding out the Manager's Job, in *Sloan Management Review*, **1**, pp. 11–26.
Mizuno, S. (1988) *Company Wide Total Quality Control*, Asian Productivity Organisation, Tokyo.

Moati, P. and Mouhoud, E.M. (1994) Information et organisation de la production: vers une division cognitive du travail, in *Economie Appliquée*, **1**, pp. 47–73.

Moore, J. and Hart, O. (1990) Property Rights and the Nature of the Firm, in *Journal of Political Economy*, **6**, pp. 1119–1158.

Morrison, J. and Schmid, G. (1994) *Future Tense. The Business Realities of the Next Ten Years*, William Morrow, New York.

Morrow, W. and Thurow, L. (1994) *Head to Head: The Coming Economic Battle Between Japan, Europe and America*, Morrow, New York.

Mowshowitz, A. (1991) *Virtual Feudalism: A Vision of Political Organization in the Information Age*, Deelstudie in het kader van NOTA- Project Democratie en Informatiesamenleving, Amsterdam.

Müller-Böling, D. and Ramme I. (1990) *Informations- und Kommunikationstechniken für Führungskräfte: Top Manager zwischen Technikeuphorie und Tastaturphobie*, Oldenbourg, Munich/Vienna.

Müller-Stewens, G. and Pautzke, G. (1991) Führungskräfteentwicklung und organisatorisches Lernen, in Sattelberger, T. (Hrsg.), *Die lernende Organisation, Konzepte für eine neue Qualität der Unternehmensentwicklung*, Gabler, Wiesbaden, pp. 183–205.

Murphy, C. and O'Leary, T. (1994) Review Essay: Empowered Selves, in *Accounting Management and Information Technologies*, **2**, pp. 107–115.

Nadler, G. and Hibino, S. (1990) *Breakthrough Thinking: Why We Must Change The Way We Solve Problems, and the Seven Principles to Achieve This*, Prince Publishing, Rocklin.

Nagel, K. (1991) *Nutzen der Informationsverarbeitung. Methoden zur Bewertung von strategischen Wettbewerbsvorteilen, Produktivitätsverbesserungen und Kosteneinsparungen*, 2nd ed., Oldenbourg, Munich/Vienna.

Nastansky, L. (ed.) (1992) *Workgroup Computing*, Steuer- und Wirtschaftsverlag, Hamburg.

"The Next Giant in Mutual Funds" (1994) *The New York Times*, 20 March, Section 3, p. 1.

Neuberger, O. (1991) *Personalentwicklung*, Enke, Stuttgart.

Neuberger, O. (1994) *Personalentwicklung*, 2nd ed., Enke, Stuttgart.

Neuburger, R. (1994) Electronic Data Interchange – Einsatzmöglichkeiten und ökonomische Auswirkungen, Gabler, Wiesbaden.

Niemeier, J. et al (1994) *Mobile Computing: Informationstechnologie ortsungebunden nutzen. Technik, Einsatz, Wirtschaftlichkeit*, Computerwoche, Munich.

Niggl, J. (1994) *Die Entstehung von Electronic Data Interchange Standards*, Gabler, Wiesbaden.

Nilles, J.M. et al (1976) *The Telecommunications – Transportation Trade off*, John Wiley & Sons, New York.

Nippa, M. (1995) Anforderungen an das Management prozeßorientierter Unternehmen, in Nippa, M. and Picot, A. (eds). *Prozeßmanagement und Reengineering. Die Praxis im deutschsprachingen Raum*, Campus, Frankfurt am Main/New York, pp. 39–77.

Nippa, M. and Reichwald, R. (1990) Theoretische Grundüberlegungen zur Verkürzung der Durchlaufzeit in der industriellen Entwicklung, in Reichwald, R. and Schmelzer, H.J. (eds), *Durchlaufzeiten in der Entwicklung*, Oldenbourg, Munich/Vienna, pp. 65–114.

Nozick, R. (1974) *Anarchie, Staat, Utopia*, Moderne Verlagsgesellschaft, München.

Oberquelle, H. (ed.) (1991) *Kooperative Arbeit und Computerunterstützung. Stand und Perspektiven*, Verlag für Angewandte Psychologie, Stuttgart.

Ochsenbauer, C. (1989) *Organisatorische Alternativen zur Hierarchie*, GBI-Verlag, Munich.
Oechsler, W.A. (1992) *Personal und Arbeit: Einführung in die Personalwirtschaftslehre*, 4th ed., Oldenbourg, Munich/Vienna.
Oess, A. (1989) *Total Quality Management*, Gabler, Wiesbaden.
O'Hara-Devereaux, M. and Johansen, R. (1994) *Global Work. Bridging Distance, Culture and Time*, Jossey-Bass, San Francisco, CA.
Ohmae, K. (1991) *The Borderless World*. Harper Perennial, New York.
Ohmae, K. (1995) *The End of the Nation State–The Rise of Regional Economics: How New Engines of Prosperity Are Reshaping Global Markets*, Free Press, New York.
Oldenburg, S. (1991) *Expertendatenbanksysteme. Eine Analyse des Einsatzpotentials von Expertendatenbanksystemen für betriebswirtschaftliche Anwendungen*, VVF, Munich.
OMG (1992) The Common Object Request Broker: Architecture and Specification, OMG Document Number 91.12.1, OMG, Framingham, Mass.
Oppelt, R.U. (1995) *Computerunterstützung für das Management: Neue Möglichkeiten der computerbasierten Informationsunterstützung oberster Führungskräfte auf dem Weg von MIS zu EIS?*, Oldenbourg, Munich/Vienna.
O'Reilly, Ch.A. (1983) The Use of Information in Organizational Decision Making: A Model and some Propositions, in *Research in Organizational Behavior*, **5**, pp. 103–139.
Orlikowski, W.J. (1992) The Duality of Technology: Rethinking the Concept of Technology in Organizations, in *Organization Science*, **3**, pp. 398–427.
Orsburn, J.D. et al (1990) *Self-Directed Work Teams: The New American Challenge*, Irwin, New York.
Osten, H. von d. (1989) *Technologie-Transaktionen: Die Akquisition von technologischer Kompetenz durch Unternehmen*, Vandenhoeck & Ruprecht, Göttingen, Germany.
Österle, H. (1995a) *Business Engineering. Prozeß- und Systementwicklung, Vol. 1: Entwurfsmethoden*, Springer, Berlin.
Österle, H. (1995b) *Business in the Information Age. Heading for New Processes*, Springer, Berlin.
Österle, H., Brenner, W. and Hilbers, K. (1992) *Unternehmensführung und Informationssystem: Der Ansatz des St. Galler Informationssystem-Managements*, 2nd ed., Teubner, Stuttgart.
Ottmann, T. and Widmayer, P. (1990) *Algorithmen und Datenstrukturen*, BI Wissenschaftsverlag, Mannheim, Germany.
Ouchi, W.G. (1980) Markets, Bureaucracies and Clans, in *Administrative Science Quarterly*, **25**, pp. 129–141.
Palermo, A. and McCready, S. (1992) Workflow Software: A Primer, in Coleman, D. (ed.), *Groupware '92*, Morgan Kaufmann, San Mateo, CA.
Parker, G.M. (1994) *Cross-Functional Teams*, Jossey-Bass, San Francisco, CA.
Pawlowsky, P. (1992) Betriebliche Qualifikationsstrategien und organisationales Lernen, in Staehle, W.H. and Conrad, P. (eds), *Managementforschung 2*, de Gruyter, Berlin/New York, pp. 177–237.
Perridon, L. and Steiner, M. (1991) *Finanzwirtschaft der Unternehmung*, 6th ed., Vahlen, Munich.
Perrow, C. (1967) A Framework for the Comparative Analysis of Organizations, in *American Sociological Review*, **32**, pp. 194–208.
Perrow, Ch.B. (1970) *Organizational analysis: a sociological view*, Tavistock, London.

Perrow, C. (1983) The Organizational Context of Human Factors Engineering, in *Administrative Science Quarterly*, **28**, pp. 521–541.
Personal Interview (1995) Direct Marketing Association, 23 June.
Peters, T. (1993) *Jenseits der Hierachien – Liberation Management*, Econ, Düsseldorf.
Peters, T. (1994) *Liberation Management*, Fawcett Columbine, New York.
Peters, T. J. and Waterman, R.H. (1984) *Auf der Suche nach Spitzenleistungen: Was man von den bestgeführten US-Unternehmen lernen kann*, Moderne Industrie, Landsberg am Lech, Germany.
Pfeffer, J. (1992) Managing with Power Politics and Influence in Organizations, Harvard Business School Press, Boston, Mass.
Pfeffer, J. (1994). *Competitive Advantage Through People: Unleashing the Power of the Workforce*, Harvard Business School Press, Boston, Mass.
Pfefferkorn, P. (1991) Das "Soziokratie-Modell" – Eine Renaissance des "Linking Pin-Modells?", Soziokratisch Centrum, Rotterdam.
Pfeiffer, W. and Weiß, E. (1992) *Lean Management: Grundlagen der Führung und Organisation industrieller Unternehmen*, Schmidt, Berlin.
Picot, A. (1979a) Rationalisierung im Verwaltungsbereich als betriebswirtschaftliches Problem, in *Zeitschrift für Betriebswirtschaft*, **12**, pp. 1145–1165.
Picot, A. (1979a). Organisationsprinzipien, in *Wirtschaftswissenschaftliches Studium*, **8**, pp. 480–485.
Picot, A. (1980) Betriebswirtschaftlicher Nutzen kontra volkswirtschaftliche Kosten? – "Humanisierung des Arbeitslebens?" in ökonomischer Sicht, in Rosenstiel, L. von and Weinkamm, M. (ed.). *Humanisierung des Arbeitslebens – vergessene Verpflichtung?*, Schäffer-Poeschel, Stuttgart, pp. 225–242.
Picot, A. (1981) Der Beitrag der Theorie der Verfügungsrechte zur ökonomischen Analyse von Unternehmensverfassungen, in Bohr, K. *Unternehmensverfassung als Problem der Betriebswirtschaftslehre*, Schmidt, Berlin.
Picot, A. (1982a) Unternehmungsorganisation und Unternehmungsentwicklung im Lichte der Transaktionskostentheorie, in Streissler, E. (ed.), *Information in der Wirtschaft*, Duncker & Humblot, Berlin, pp. 283–286.
Picot, A. (1982b) Transaktionskostenansatz in der Organisationstheorie: Stand der Diskussion und Aussagewert, in *Die Betriebswirtschaft*, **2**, pp. 267–284.
Picot, A. (1985) Integrierte Telekommunikation und Dezentralisierung in der Wirtschaft, in Kaiser, W. (ed.). *Integrierte Telekommunikation*, Springer, Berlin, pp. 484–498.
Picot, A. (1986) Transaktionskosten im Handel: Zur Notwendigkeit einer flexiblen Strukturentwicklung in der Distribution, in *Der Betriebsberater*, Supplement 13 to No. 27, pp. 2–16.
Picot, A. (1989a) Der Produktionsfaktor Information in der Unternehmensführung, in *Thexis*, **4**, pp. 3–9.
Picot, A. (1989b) Zur Bedeutung allgemeiner Theorieansätze für die betriebswirtschaftliche Information und Kommunikation: Der Beitrag der Transaktionskosten- und Principal-Agent-Theorie, in Kirsch, W. and Picot, A. (eds), *Die Betriebswirtschaftslehre im Spannungsfeld zwischen Generalisierung und Spezialisierung*, Gabler, Wiesbaden, pp. 361–379.
Picot, A. (1990) Organisation von Informationssystemen und Controlling, in *Controlling*, 6, pp. 296–305.
Picot, A. (1991a) Ökonomische Theorien der Organisation – Ein Überblick über neuere Ansätze und deren betriebswirtschaftliches Anwendungspotential, in Ordelheide, D., Rudolph, B. and Büsselmann, E. (eds). *Betriebs-*

wirtschaftslehre und ökonomische Theorie, Schäffer-Poeschel, Stuttgart, pp. 143–170.

Picot, A. (1991b) Ein neuer Ansatz zur Gestaltung der Leistungstiefe, in *Zeitschrift für betriebswirtschaftliche Forschung*, **4**, pp. 336–357.

Picot, A. (1991c) Subsidiaritätsprinzip und ökonomische Theorie der Organisation, in Faller, P. and Witt, D. (eds). *Erwerbsprinzip und Dienstprinzip in öffentlicher Wirtschaft und Verkehrswirtschaft, Festschrift für K. Oettle*, Nomos, Baden-Baden, Germany, pp. 102–116.

Picot, A. (1993a) Organisation, in Bitz, M. et al (eds), *Vahlens Kompendium der Betriebswirtschaftslehre*, Vol. 2, 3rd ed., Vahlen, Munich, pp. 101–174.

Picot, A (1993b) Organisationsstrukturen der Wirtschaft und ihre Anforderungen an die Informations- und Kommunikationstechnik, in Scheer, A.-W. (ed.), *Handbuch Informationsmanagement: Aufgaben – Konzepte – Praxislösungen*, Gabler, Wiesbaden, pp. 49–68.

Picot, A. (1993c). Contingencies for the Emergence of Efficient Symbiotic Arrangements, in *Journal of Institutional and Theoretical Economics*, **4**, pp. 731–740.

Picot, A. (1994) Effizienz im Spannungsfeld zwischen Zentralismus und Dezentralismus, Vortrag auf der 32. Kooperationstagung der Evangelischen Akademie Tutzing mit der Allianz AG, 18 January.

Picot, A. and Dietl, H. (1990) Transaktionskostentheorie, in *Wirtschaftswissenschaftliches Studium*, **4**, pp. 178–184.

Picot, A. and Dietl, H. (1993) Neue Institutionenökonomie und Recht, in Ott, C. von and Schäfer H.-B. (eds), *Ökonomische Analyse des Unternehmensrechts*, Physica, Heidelberg, pp. 307–330.

Picot, A. and Franck, E. (1988) Die Planung der Unternehmensressource "Information", Part I and II, in *Das Wirtschaftsstudium*, **17**, pp. 544–549, 608–614.

Picot, A. and Franck, E. (1993) Vertikale Integration, in Hauschildt, J. and Grün, O. (eds), *Ergebnisse empirischer betriebswirtschaftlicher Forschung: Zu einer Realtheorie der Unternehmung, Festschrift für E. Witte*, Schäffer-Poeschel, Stuttgart, pp. 179–219.

Picot, A. and Franck, E. (1995) Prozeßorganisation. Eine Bewertung der neuen Ansätze aus Sicht der Organisationslehre, in Picot, A. and Nippa, M. (eds). *Prozeßmanagement und Reengineering. Die Praxis im deutschsprachigen Raum*, Campus, Frankfurt am Main/New York, pp. 13–38.

Picot, A. and Gründler, A. (1995) Deutsche Dienstleister scheinen von IT nur wenig zu profitieren, in *Computerwoche,* **10**, pp. 10–11.

Picot, A. and Reichwald, R. (1987). *Bürokommunikation. Leitsätze für den Anwender*, 3rd ed., CW-Publikationen, Hallbergmoos, Germany.

Picot, A. and Reichwald, R. (1991) Informationswirtschaft, in Heinen, E. (ed.), *Industriebetriebslehre: Entscheidungen im Industriebetrieb*, 9th ed., Gabler, Wiesbaden, pp. 241–393.

Picot, A. and Reichwald, R. (1994) Auflösung der Unternehmung? Vom Einfluß der IuK-Technik auf Organisationsstrukturen und Kooperationsformen, in *Zeitschrift für Betriebswirtschaft*, **5**, pp. 547–570.

Picot, A. and Wolff, B. (1994) Zur ökonomischen Organisation öffentlicher Leistungen "Lean Management" im öffentlichen Sektor?, in Naschold, F. and Pröhl, M. (eds), *Produktivität öffentlicher Dienstleistungen, Vol. 1, Dokumentation eines wissenschaftlichen Diskurses zum Produktivitätsbegriff*, Bertelsmann Stiftung, Gütersloh, Germany, pp. 511–520.

Picot, A., Bortenlänger, Ch. and Röhrl, H. (1995) The Evolution of Electronic Markets. Observations of the Capital Market, in *Journal of Computer Mediated Communication*, **3**, URL: http://www.usc.edu/dept/annenberg/vol1/issue3.

Picot, A., Dietl, H. and Franck, E. (1995) *Organisation – die ökonomische Perspektive*, in progress.

Picot, A., Laub, U.-D. and Schneider, D. (1989) *Innovative Unternehmensgründungen: Eine ökonomisch-empirische Analyse*, Springer, Berlin.

Picot, A., Neuburger, R. and Niggl, H. (1991) Ökonomische Perspektiven eines "Electronic Data Interchange", in *Information Management*, **2**, pp. 22–29.

Picot, A., Neuburger, R. and Niggl, J. (1994) Wirtschaftliche Potentiale von EDI – Praxiserfahrungen und Perspektiven, in *x-change*, **2**, pp. 32–35.

Picot, A., Neuburger, R. and Niggl, J. (1995) Ausbreitung und Auswirkungen von Electronic Data Interchange – Empirische Ergebnisse aus der deutschen Automobil- und Transportbranche, in Schreyögg, G. and Sydow, J. (eds), *Managementforschung 5*, de Gruyter, Berlin, pp. 47–106.

Picot, A., Reichwald, R. and Behrbohm, P. (1985) *Menschengerechte Arbeitsplätze sind wirtschaftlich!, Das Vier-Ebenen-Modell der Wirtschaftlichkeitsbeurteilung*, RKW, Eschborn, Germany.

Picot, A., Reichwald, R. and Nippa, M. (1988) Zur Bedeutung der Entwicklungsaufgabe für die Entwicklungszeit – Ansätze für die Entwicklungszeitgestaltung, in Brockhoff, K., Picot, A. and Urban, C. (eds), *Zeitmanagement in Forschung und Entwicklung, Zeitschrift für betriebswirtschaftliche Forschung*, Special Issue 23, Verlagsgruppe Handelsblatt, Dusseldorf, pp. 112–137.

Picot, A., Ripperger, T. and Wolff, B. (1996) The Fading Boundaries of the Firm, in *Journal of Institutional and Theoretical Economics (JITE)*, **152**, pp. 65–79.

Pinchot, G. and Pinchot, E. (1993) *The End of Bureaucracy and the Rise of the Intelligent Organization*, Berrett-Koehler, San Francisco.

Pine, B.J. (1993) *Mass Customization. The New Frontier in Business Competition*, Harvard Business School Press, Boston, Mass.

Pomberger, G. and Blaschek, G. (1993) *Grundlagen des Software Engineering – Proto-typing und objektorientierte Software-Entwicklung*, Hanser, Munich.

PonTell, S. et al (1996) The Demand for Telecommuting. Proceedings of the Telecommuting '96 Conference, 25–26 April, Jacksonville, Florida.

Porter, M.E. (1988) *Wettbewerbsstrategien: Methoden zur Analyse von Branchen und Konkurrenten*, 5th ed., Campus, Frankfurt am Main.

Porter, M.E. (1990) *The Competitive Advantage of Nations*, Free Press, New York.

Porter, M.E. and Millar, V.E. (1985) How Information Gives You Competitive Advantage, in *Harvard Business Review*, **4**, pp. 149–160.

Porter, M.E. and Fuller, M.B. (1989) Koalitionen und globale Strategien, in Porter, M.E. (ed.), *Globaler Wettbewerb: Strategien der neuen Internationalisierung*, Gabler, Wiesbaden.

Prahalad, C.K. and Hamel, G. (1990) The Core Competence of the Corporation, in *Harvard Business Review*, May/June, pp. 79–91.

Pratt, J. and Zeckhauser, R. (1985) *Principals and Agents: The Structure of Business*, Harvard Business School Press, Boston.

Pribilla, P., Reichwald, R. and Goecke, R. (1996). *Telekommunikation im Management*, Schäffer-Poeschel, Stuttgart.

Probst, G.J. (1992) Selbstorganisation, in Frese, E. (ed.), *Handwörterbuch der Organisation*, 3rd ed., Schäffer-Poeschel, Stuttgart, pp. 2255–2269.

Probst, G.J. and Büchel, B. (1994) *Organisationales Lernen: Wettbewerbsvorteil der Zukunft*, Gabler, Wiesbaden.

Probst, G.J. and Gomez P. (1991) Die Methodik des vernetzten Denkens zur Lösung komplexer Probleme, in Probst, G.J. and Gomez, P. (eds), *Vernetztes*

Denken: ganzheitliches Führen in der Praxis, 2nd ed., Gabler, Wiesbaden, pp. 3–20.

Raffée, H. and Eisele, J. (1994) Joint Ventures – nur die Hälfte floriert, in *Harvard Business Manager*, **3**, pp. 17–22.

Rau, K.-H. (1991) *Integrierte Bürokommunikation: Organisation und Technik*, Gabler, Wiesbaden.

Rawls, J. (1979) *Eine Theorie der Gerechtigkeit*, Suhrkamp, Frankfurt am Main.

Reber, G. (1992) Lernen, organisationales, in Frese, E. (ed.), *Handwörterbuch der Organisation*, 3rd ed., Schäffer-Poeschel, Stuttgart, cl. 1240–1256.

Reich, R.B. (1991) *The Work of Nations*, Vintage Books, New York.

Reichwald, R. (1977) *Arbeit als Produktionsfaktor*, E. Reinhardt, Munich/Basel.

Reichwald, R. (1979) Zur empirischen betriebswirtschaftlichen Zielforschung, in *Zeitschrift für Betriebswirtschaft*, **6**, pp. 528–535.

Reichwald, R. (1984) Produktivitätsbeziehungen in der Unternehmensverwaltung – Grundüberlegungen zur Modellierung und Gestaltung der Büroarbeit unter dem Einfluß neuer Informationstechnologien, in Pack, L. and Börner, D. (eds), *Betriebswirtschaftliche Entscheidungen bei Stagnation*, Gabler, Wiesbaden, pp. 197–213.

Reichwald, R. (1989) Die Entwicklung der Arbeitsteilung unter dem Einfluß von Technikeinsatz im Industriebetrieb – Ein Beitrag zum betriebswirtschaftlichen Rationalisierungsverständnis, in Kirsch, W. and Picot, A. (eds) (1989) *Die Betriebswirtschaftslehre im Spannungsfeld zwischen Generalisierung und Spezialisierung*, Gabler, Wiesbaden, pp. 299–322.

Reichwald, R. (1990a) EDV-gestützte Werkzeuge der Organisationsanalyse, in Zahn, E. (ed.), *Organisationsstrategie und Produktion*, gfmt, Munich, pp. 389–423.

Reichwald, R. (1990b) Job Design, in Grochla, E. et al (eds.), *Handbook of German Business Management*, Vol. 1, Schäffer-Poeschel, Stuttgart, cl. 1257–1265.

Reichwald, R. (1991a) Management-Report: Vermittelnde Breitbandkommunikation zur langfristigen Sicherung des Unternehmenserfolges, in Ricke, H. and Kanzow, J. (eds), *BERKOM: Breitbandkommunikation im Glasfasernetz. Übersicht und Zusammenfassung 1986–91*, R.V. Decker, Heidelberg, pp. 13–39.

Reichwald, R. (1991b) Innovative Anwendungen neuer Telekommunikationsformen in der industriellen Forschung und Entwicklung, in Heinrich, L.J., Pomberger, G. and Schauer, R. (eds), *Die Informationswirtschaft im Unternehmen*, Linz University, pp. 253–280.

Reichwald, R. (ed.) (1992a). *Marktnahe Produktion*, Gabler, Wiesbaden.

Reichwald, R. (1992b) Die Wiederentdeckung der menschlichen Arbeit als primärer Produktionsfaktor für eine marktnahe Produktion, in Reichwald, R. (ed.), *Marktnahe Produktion*, Gabler, Wiesbaden, pp. 3–18.

Reichwald, R. (1992c) Informationskosten – Ein kostentheoretischer Erklärungsansatz am Beispiel der "lean production", in Scheer, A.-W. (Hrsg.), *Simultane Produktentwicklung*, gfmt, St. Gallen, Switzerland, pp. 335–368.

Reichwald, R. (1993a) *Die Wirtschaftlichkeit im Spannungsfeld von betriebswirtschaftlicher Theorie und Praxis. Arbeitsbericht des Lehrstuhls für Allgemeine und Industrielle Betriebswirtschaftslehre*, Vol. 1, Munich.

Reichwald, R. (1993b) Kommunikation, in Bitz, M. et al (eds), *Vahlens Kompendium der Betriebswirtschaftslehre*, 3rd ed.,Vol. 2, Vahlen, Munich, pp. 447–494.

Reichwald, R. (1993c) *Der Mensch als Mittelpunkt einer ganzheitlichen Produktion. Innovative Organisationskonzepte aus betriebswirtschaftlicher Perspek-*

tive. Arbeitsbericht des Lehrstuhls für Allgemeine und Industrielle Betriebswirtschaftslehre, Vol. 2, Munich.

Reichwald, R. (1994) *Wachstumsmarkt Telekooperation, Arbeitsbericht des Lehrstuhls für Allgemeine und Industrielle Betriebswirtschaftslehre*, Vol. 5, Münich.

Reichwald, R. (1997) Neue Arbeitsformen in der vernetzten Unternehmung: Flexibilität und controlling, in Picot, A. (ed.), *Information als Wettbewerbsfaktor*, Schäffer-Poeschel, Stuttgart, pp. 233–263.

Reichwald, R. and Behrbohm, P. (1993) Flexibilität als Eigenschaft produktionswirtschaftlicher Systeme, in *Zeitschrift für Betriebswirtschaft*, **9**, pp. 831–853.

Reichwald, R. and Bellmann, K. (1991) Optimale Arbeitsteilung in Büroorganisationen – Der Einfluß neuer Informations – und Kommunikationstechniken – Eine kostentheoretische Betrachtung, in *Zeitschrift für Betriebswirtschaft*, **5/6**, pp. 621–639.

Reichwald, R. and Conrat, J.-I. (1994) Vermeidung von Änderungskosten durch Integrationsmaßnahmen im Entwicklungsbereich, in Zülch, G. (ed.); *Vereinfachen und verkleinern – Die neuen Strategien in der Produktion*, Schäffer-Poeschel, Stuttgart, pp. 221–246.

Reichwald, R. and Dietel, B. (1991) Produktionswirtschaft, in Heinen, E. (ed.), *Industriebetriebslehre: Entscheidungen im Industriebetrieb*, 9th ed., Gabler, Wiesbaden, pp. 395–622.

Reichwald, R. and Goecke, R. (1994) New Communication Media and New Forms of Cooperation in the Top Management Area, in Bradley, G.E. and Hendrick, H.W. (eds), *Human Factors in Organizational Design and Management – IV. Development, Introduction and Use of New Technology – Challenges for Human Organization and Human Resource Development in a Changing World.* Proceedings of the Fourth International Symposium on Human Factors in Organizational Design and Management, Stockholm, 29 May–2 June, pp. 511–517.

Reichwald, R. and Goecke, R. (1995) Bürokommunikationstechnik und Führung, in Kieser, A., Reber, G. and Wunderer, R. (eds). *Handwörterbuch der Führung*, 2nd ed., Schäffer-Poeschel, Stuttgart, pp. 164–182.

Reichwald, R. and Hermens, B. (1994) Telekooperation und Telearbeit, in *Office Management*, **10**, pp. 24–30.

Reichwald, R. and Hesch, G. (1993) Der Mensch als Produktionsfaktor oder Träger ganzheitlicher Produktion? – Menschenbilder im Wandel der Betriebswirtschaftslehre, in Weis, K. (ed.), *Bilder vom Menschen in Wissenschaft, Technik und Religion*, Munich, pp. 429–460.

Reichwald, R., Höfer, C. and Weichselbaumer, J. (1993) *Anwenderhandbuch zur erweiterten Wirtschaftlichkeitsbetrachtung, AuT-Verbundvorhaben, Humanzentrierte CIM-Konzepte: Anwendungskonzepte für die rechnerunterstützte integrierte Produktion bei auftragsgebundener Einzelfertigung*, Lehrstuhl für Allgemeine und Industrielle Betriebswirtschaftslehre, Technical University of Munich, Munich.

Reichwald, R., Höfer, C. and Weichselbaumer, J. (1996) *Erfolg von Reorganisations-prozessen. Leitfaden zur strategieorientierten Bewertung*, Schäffer-Poeschel, Stuttgart.

Reichwald, R. and Huber, C. (1996) Mobile Telecooperation in the Construction Industry, in *Just In*, **6**, pp. 10–13.

Reichwald, R. and Koller, H. (1995). Informations- und Kommunikationstechnologien, in Tietz, B., Köhler, R. and Zentes, J. (eds). Handwörterbuch des Marketing, 2nd ed., Schäffer-Poeschel: Stuttgart, pp. 947–962.

Reichwald, R. and Koller, H. (1996) Integration und Dezentralisierung von Unternehmensstrukturen, in Lutz, B., Hartmann, M. and Hirsch-Kreinsen, H. (eds), *Produzieren im 21. Jahrhundert. Herausforderungen für die deutsche Industrie*, Campus, Frankfurt am Main/New York, pp. 225–294.

Reichwald, R. and Möslein, K. (1995) Wertschöpfung und Produktivität von Dienstleistungen? – Innovationsstrategien für die Standortsicherung, in Bullinger, H.-J. (ed). *Dienstleistung der Zukunft: Märkte, Unternehmen und Infrastrukturen im Wandel*, Gabler-FBO, Wiesbaden, pp. 324–476.

Reichwald, R. and Möslein, K. (1996a) Auf dem Weg zur virtuellen Organisation: Wie Telekooperation Unternehmen verändert, in Müller, G., Kohl, U. and Strauß, R. (eds), Zukunftsperspektiven der digitalen Vernetzung.

Reichwald, R. and Möslein, K. (1996b) Telearbeit und Telekooperation, in Bullinger, H.-J. and Warnecke, H.-J. (eds), *Neue Organisationsformen im Unternehmen – Ein Handbuch für das moderne Management*, Springer, Berlin, pp. 691–708.

Reichwald, R. and Nippa, M. (1989) Organisationsmodelle für die Büroarbeit beim Einsatz neuer Technologien, in Institut für angewandte Arbeitswissenschaft e.V. (ed.), *Arbeitsgestaltung in Produktion und Verwaltung*, Wirtschaftsverlag Bachem, Cologne, pp. 423–443.

Reichwald, R. and Rupprecht, M. (1992) Einsatzmöglichkeiten von Informations- und Kommunikationstechnologien im Rahmen zwischenbetrieblicher Kooperation, in Hermanns, A. and Flegel, V. (eds), *Handbuch des Electronic-Marketing – Funktionen und Anwendungen der Informations- und Kommunikationstechnik im Marketing*, Beck, Munich, pp. 407–428.

Reichwald, R. and Sachenbacher, H. (1995) Durchlaufzeiten, in Kern, W., Schröder, H. and Weber, J. (eds). *Handwörterbuch der Produktion*, 2nd ed., Schäffer-Poeschel, Stuttgart, pp. 362–374.

Reichwald, R. and Schmelzer, H. (eds) (1990) *Durchlaufzeiten in der Entwicklung: Praxis des industriellen F&E-Managements*, Oldenbourg, Munich/Vienna.

Reichwald, R., Möslein, K. and Oldenburg, S. (1997) *Telekooperation*, Springer, Berlin (forthcoming).

Reichwald, R., Oldenburg, S. and Schulte, B. (1995) Mobile Telekooperation in der Bauwirtschaft – Reengineering durch Einsatz mobiler Telekommunikation bei Baustellenfertigung, in Reichwald, R. and Wildemann, H. (eds), *Kreative Unternehmen – Spitzenleistungen durch Produkt- und Prozeßinnovationen*, Schäffer-Poeschel, Stuttgart, pp. 339–354.

Reichwald, R., Schulte, B. and Oldenburg, S. (1995) Das mobile Baustellenbüro nimmt Gestalt an, in *Office Management*, **1**, pp. 14–19.

Reid, A. (1994) Teleworking: A Guide to Good Practice, NCC Blackwell, Manchester/Oxford, England.

Reisig, W. (1990) *Petrinetze: Eine Einführung*, Springer, Berlin.

Reiß, M. (1992a) Arbeitsteilung, in Frese, E. (ed.), Handwörterbuch der Organisation, 3rd ed., Schäffer-Poeschel, Stuttgart, pp. 167–178.

Reiß, M. (1992b) Spezialisierung, in Frese, E. (ed.), Handwörterbuch der Organisation, 3rd ed., Schäffer-Poeschel, Stuttgart, pp. 2287–2296.

Reve, T. (1990) The Firm as a Nexus of Internal and External Contracts, in Aoki, M., Gustafsson, B. and Williamson, O.E. (eds), *The Firm as a Nexus of Treaties*, Sage, London, pp. 133–161.

Rice, R. (1992) Task Analysability, Use of New Media and Effectiveness: A multi-site exploration of media richness, in *Organization Science*, **3**, pp. 475–500.

Richter, R. (1994) *Institutionen ökonomisch analysiert*, Mohr, Tübingen, Germany.
Riordan, M.H. (1990) What is Vertical Integration?, in Aoki, M., Gustafsson, B. and Williamson, O.E. (eds), *The Firm as a Nexus of Treaties*, Sage, London, pp. 94–111.
Ripperge, T. (1997) Vertrauen als Organisationsprinzip, Doctoral Dissertation, University of Munich, Munich.
Ritz, D. (1991). Entstehungsmuster elektronischer Märkte. Report Number IM2000/CCEM/8, Institut für Wirtschaftsinformatik, Hochschule St. Gallen, 1991.
Roach, S. (1991) Services Under Siege – The Restructuring Imperative, in *Harvard Business Review*, September/October, pp. 82–91.
Robbins, S. (1990) Organization Theory: Structure, Design and Applications, Prentice Hall, Englewood Cliffs, NJ.
Robbins, S.P. (1994) *Essentials of Organizational Behavior*, 4th ed., Prentice Hall, Englewood Cliffs, NJ.
Robinson, P., Sauvant, K. P. and Govitrikar, V. P. (eds) (1989) *Electronic Highways for World Trade*, Westview Press, Boulder, Colo.
Roethlisberger, F.J. and Dickson, W.J. (1939) *Management and the Worker*, Harvard University Press, Cambridge, Mass.
Rogers, E. M. (1983) *Diffusion of Innovations*, 3rd ed., Free Press, New York.
Rosenbaum, H.R. (1996) Managers and Information in Organizations: Towards a Structurational Concept of the Information Use Environment of Managers. Unpublished Dissertation, School of Information Studies, Syracuse University, May.
Rosenstiel, L. von. (1977) Bedürfnisbefriedigung und Organisationsstruktur, in Macharzina, K. and Oechsler, W. (eds), *Personamanagement I: Mitarbeiterführung und Führungsorganisation*, Gabler, Wiesbaden, pp. 231–246.
Rosenstiel, L. von. (1987) *Grundlagen der Organisationspsychologie*, 2nd ed., Schäffer-Poeschel, Stuttgart.
Rosenstiel, L. von. (1992a) *Grundlagen der Organisationspsychologie*, 3rd ed., Schäffer-Poeschel, Stuttgart.
Rosenstiel, L. von. (1992b) Entwicklung von Werthaltungen und interpersonaler Kompetenz – Beiträge der Sozialpsychologie, in Sonntag, K. (ed.). *Personalentwicklung in Organisationen. Psychologische Grundlagen, Methoden und Strategien*, Hogrefe, Göttingen, Germany, pp. 83–105.
Rosenstiel, L. von, et al (eds) (1993) *Wertewandel als Herausforderung für die Unternehmenspolitik in den 90er Jahren*, 2nd ed., Schäffer-Poeschel, Stuttgart.
Ross, S.A. (1973) The Economic Theory of Agency: The Principal's Problem, in *American Economic Review*, Papers and Proceedings, **63**, pp. 134–139.
Rotering, J. (1990) *Forschungs- und Entwicklungskooperationen zwischen Unternehmen*, Schäffer-Poeschl, Stuttgart.
Rotering, J. (1993) *Zwischenbetriebliche Kooperation als alternative Organisationsform*, Schäffer-Poeschl, Stuttgart.
Royce, W.W. (1970) Managing the development of large software systems: Concepts and Techniques, Proceedings of IEEE WESCON.
Rumbaugh, J. et al (1991) *Object-Oriented Modeling and Design*, Prentice Hall, Englewood Cliffs, NJ.
Rupprecht-Däullary, M. (1994) *Zwischenbetriebliche Kooperation*, Gabler, Wiesbaden.
Sander, P., Stucky, W. and Herschel, R. (1996) *Automaten, Sprachen, Berechenbarkeit*, 2nd ed., Teubner, Stuttgart.

Sattelberger, T. (1991) Die lernende Organisation im Spannungsfeld von Strategie, Struktur und Kultur, in Sattelberger, T. (ed.) (1991) *Die lernende Organisation: Konzepte für eine neue Qualität der Unternehmensentwicklung*, Gabler, Wiesbaden, pp. 11–55.

Savage, C.M. (1990). *5th Generation Management: Integrating Enterprises through Human Networking*, Butterworth-Heinemann, Newton, Mass.

Schanz, G. (1994) *Organisationsgestaltung: Management von Arbeitsteilung und Koordination*, 2nd ed., Vahlen, Munich.

Schanze, E. (1991) Symbiotic Contracts: Exploring Long-Term Agency Structures Between Contract and Corporation, in Joerges, Ch. (ed.), *Franchising and the Law*, Nomos, Baden-Baden, Germany, pp. 68–103.

Scheer, A.-W. (1990) *CIM: der computergestützte Industriebetrieb*, 4th ed., Springer, Berlin.

Scheer, A.-W. (1994) *Wirtschaftsinformatik – Referenzmodelle für industrielle Geschäftsprozesse*, 4th ed., Springer, Berlin, p. 17.

Schein, E.H. (1992) *Organizational Culture and Leadership*, 2nd ed., Jossey-Bass, New York.

Scheller, M. et al (1994) *Internet: Werkzeuge und Dienste*, Springer, Berlin, p. 20.

Schlageter, G. and Stucky, W. (1983) Datenbanksysteme: Konzepte und Modelle, 2nd ed., Teubner, Stuttgart.

Schlicksupp, H. (1992) *Innovation, Kreativität und Ideenfindung*, 4th ed., Vogel, Würzburg, Germany.

Schmid, B. (1993) Elektronische Märkte, in *Wirtschaftsinformatik*, **5**, pp. 465–480.

Schmid, B. (1995) Elektronische Einzelhandels- und Retailmärkte, in Schmid, B. et al (eds), *Electronic Mall: Banking und Shopping in globalen Netzen*, Teubner, Stuttgart, pp. 17–32.

Schmid, B. et al (eds) (1995) *Electronic Mall: Banking und Shopping in globalen Netzen*, Teubner, Stuttgart.

Schmidt-Bleek, F. (1994) Work in a Sustainable Economy: Some irritating Facts, some Questions, and some Hope, in *Proceedings of the European Assembly on Teleworking and New Ways of Working*, 3–4 November, Berlin, pp. 19–34.

Schneider, D. (1988) *Zur Entstehung innovativer Unternehmen – Eine ökonomisch-theoretische Perspektive*, VVF, Munich.

Scholl, W. (1992) Informationspathologien, in Freese, E. (ed.), *Handwörterbuch der Organisation*, 3rd ed, Schäffer-Poeschel, Stuttgart, pp. 900–912.

Scholz, C. (1993) Personalmanagement, 3rd ed., Vahlen, Munich.

Schomburg, E. (1980) *Entwicklung eines betriebstypologischen Instrumentariums zur systematischen Ermittlung der Anforderungen an EDV-gestützte Produktions-, Planungs- und Steuerungssysteme im Maschinenbau*, Technische Hochschule Aachen, Aachen, Germany.

Schöning, U. (1992) *Theoretische Informatik kurz gefaßt*, BI Wissenschaftsverlag, Mannheim, Germany.

Schrader, S. (1990) *Zwischenbetrieblicher Informationstransfer: Eine empirische Analyse kooperativen Verhaltens*, Duncker & Humblot, Berlin.

Schrader, S. (1993) Kooperation, in Hauschildt, J. and Grün, O. (eds), *Ergebnisse empirischer betriebswirtschaftlicher Forschung – Zu einer Realtheorie der Unternehmung, Festschrift für E. Witte*, Schäffer-Poeschel, Stuttgart, pp. 221–254.

Schreyögg, G. (1993) *Unternehmensstrategie. Grundfragen einer Theorie strategischer Unternehmensführung*, de Gruyter, Berlin.

Schulte, B. (1997) *Analyse der Einsatzpotentiale mobiler Kommunikationstechnik*, Munich. (in preparation).

Schulz von Thun, F. (1993) *Miteinander Reden, Part 1, Störungen und Klärungen*, Rowolt, Hamburg.

Schumann, M. (1990) *Abschätzungen von Nutzeffekten zwischenbetrieblicher Informationsverarbeitung, Vortrag auf einer Tagung der Wissenschaftlichen Kommission Wirtschaftsinformatik*, Nuremberg, Germany, March.

Schumann, M. (1992) *Betriebliche Nutzeffekte und Strategiebeiträge der großintegrierten Informationsverarbeitung*, Springer, Berlin.

Schumann, M. (1993) Wirtschaftlichkeitsbeurteilung für IV-Systeme, in *Wirtschaftsinformatik*, **2**, pp. 167–178.

Schumpeter, J.A. (1926) Theorie der wirtschaftlichen Entwicklung, 2nd ed., Duncker & Humblot, Munich.

Schwarzer, B. and Krcmar, H. (1994) Neue Organisationsformen: Ein Führer durch das Begriffspotpourri, in *Information Management*, **4**, pp. 20–27.

Scott Morton, M.S. (1992) The Effects of Information Technology on Management and Organizations, in Kochan T.A. and Useem, M. (eds), *Transforming Organizations*, Oxford University Press, New York/Oxford, pp. 261–279.

Searle, J.R. (1993) Ausdruck und Bedeutung – *Untersuchungen zur Sprechakttheorie*, 3rd ed., Suhrkamp, Frankfurt am Main.

Searle, J.R. (1994) *Sprechakte – Ein sprachphilosophischer Essay*, 6th ed., Suhrkamp, Frankfurt am Main.

Sedgewick, R. (1988) *Algorithms*, Addison-Wesley, Reading, Mass.

Senge, P.M. (1990a) *The Fifth Discipline: The Art and Practice of The Learning Organization*, Doubleday Currency, New York.

Senge, P.M. (1990b) The Leader's New Work: Building Learning Organizations, in *Sloan Management Review*, **1**, pp. 7–23.

Senge, P.M. (1994) *The Fifth Discipline Fieldbook: Strategies and Tools for Building a Learning Organization*, Doubleday Currency, New York.

Shannon, C.E. and Weaver, W. (1949) *The mathematical theory of communication*, University of Illinois Press, Urbana.

Shipley, C., Shipley, D. and Wigand, R.T. (1985) Corporate Transborder Data Flow and National Policy in Developing Countries, in B. D. Ruben (ed.), *Information and Behavior*, Vol. 1, Transaction Publishers, New Brunswick, NJ, pp. 455–480.

Siegel, S. (1957) Level of Aspiration and Decision Making, in *Psychological Review*, **64**, pp. 253–262.

Siegert, H.-J. (1991) *Betriebssysteme: Eine Einführung*, 3rd ed., Oldenbourg, Munich/Vienna.

Simon, H.A. (1955) A Behavioral Model of Rational Choice, in *Quarterly Journal of Economics*, **69**, pp. 99–118.

Simon, H.A. (1978) Rationality as Process and as Product of Thought, in *American Economic Review*, Papers and Proceedings, **2**, pp. 1–16.

Simon, H., Bauer, B. and Jägeler, F. (1993) *Auf der Suche nach Europas Stärken: Managementkulturen und Erfolgsfaktoren*, Moderne Industrie, Landsberg am Lech, Germany.

Sippel, F. (ed.) (1994). *Implementation and Management of Teletraining, Diskussionsbeitrag Nr. 123*, Wissenschaftliches Instituts für Kommunikationsdienste (WIK), Bad Honnef.

Skinner, W. (1974) The Focused Factory, in *Harvard Business Review*, May–June, pp. 114–121.

Smith, A. (1776) An Inquiry into the Nature and Causes of the Wealth of Nations, Strahan and Cadell, London.

Soley, M.R. (ed.) (1990) *Object Management Architecture Guide*, OMG TC Document Number 90.0.1, Framingham, Mass.

Sonntag, K.H. and Schaper, N. (1992) Förderung beruflicher Handlungskompetenz, in Sonntag, K.H. (ed.), *Personalentwicklung in Organisationenen. Psychologische Grundlagen, Methoden und Strategien*, Hogrefe, Göttingen, Germany.

Sorg, S. and Zangl, H. (1986) Vorteile integrierter Bürosysteme für Führungskräfte – Erfahrungen aus einem Pilotprojekt, in *Jahrbuch der Bürokommunikation*, **2**, pp. 117–119.

Spremann, K. (1988) Reputation, Garantie, Information, in *Zeitschrift für Betriebswirtschaft*, **5/6**, pp. 613–629.

Spremann, K. (1990) Asymmetrische Information, in *Zeitschrift für Betriebswirtschaft*, **5/6**, pp. 561–586.

Staehle, W.H. (1973) *Organisation und Führung sozio-technischer Systeme. Grundlagen einer Situationstheorie*, Enke, Stuttgart.

Staehle, W.H. (1990) *Management. Eine verhaltenswissenschaftliche Perspektive*, 5th ed., Vahlen, Munich.

Staehle, W.H. (1991a) *Management. Eine verhaltenswissenschaftliche Perspektive*, 6th ed., Vahlen, Munich.

Staehle, W.H. (1991b) Redundanz, Slack und lose Kopplung in Organisationen, in Staehle, W.H. von and Sydow, J. (eds), *Managementforschung 1*, de Gruyter, Berlin, pp. 313 – 345.

Stalk, G., Evans, P.H. and Shulman, L.E. (1992) Competing on Capabilities: The New Rules of Corporate Strategy, in *Harvard Business Review*, March-April, pp. 57–69.

Starke, P.H. (1990) Analyse von Petri-Netz-Modellen, Teubner, Stuttgart.

Staudt, E. (ed.) (1986) Das Management von Innovationen, Frankfurter Zeitung, Frankfurt am Main.

Staudt, E. and Rehbein, M. (1988) *Innovation durch Qualifikation*, Frankfurter Zeitung – Blick durch die Wirtschaft, Frankfurt am Main.

Steiner, M. (1993) Konstitutive Entscheidungen, in Bitz, M. et al (eds), *Vahlens Kompendium der Betriebswirtschaftslehre*, Vol. 1, 3rd ed., Vahlen, Munich, pp. 115–169.

Steinmetz, R. (1995) *Multimedia-Technologie. Einführung und Grundlagen*, Springer, Berlin.

Sterling, B. (1995) The Hacker Crackdown: Evolution of the US Telephone Network, in Heap, N. et al (eds), *Information Technology and Society: A Reader*, The Open University, pp. 33–40.

Stetter, F. (1988) *Grundbegriffe der Theoretischen Informatik*, Springer, Berlin.

Stewart, T. A. (1994) The Information Age in Charts, *Fortune*, 4 April, pp. 75–78.

Stoetzer, M.-W. (1991) Der Markt für Mehrwertdienste: Ein kritischer Überblick, Diskussionsbeitrag Nr. 69, Wissenschaftliches Institut für Kommunikationdienste (WIK), Bad Honnef, July.

Strassmann, P. (1990) *The Business Value of Computers*, Information Economics Press, New Canaan, CT.

Strautmann, K.-P. (1993) *Ein Ansatz zur strategischen Kooperationsplanung*, VVF, Munich.

Striening, H.-D. (1988) *Prozeß-Management: Versuch eines integrierten Konzeptes situationsadäquater Gestaltung von Verwaltungsprozessen*, Lang, Frankfurt am Main.

Sydow, J. (1991) Strategische Netzwerke in Japan, in *Zeitschrift für betriebswirtschaftliche Forschung*, **3**, pp. 238–254.

Sydow, J. (1992a) Strategische Netzwerke und Transaktionskosten, in Staehle, W.H. von and Conrad, P. (eds), *Managementforschung 2*, De Gruyter, Berlin/New York, pp. 239–311.

Sydow, J. (1992b) *Strategische Netzwerke: Evolution und Organisation*, Gabler, Wiesbaden.

Szyperski, N. (1980) Computergestützte Informationssysteme, in Grochla, E. (ed.), *Handwörterbuch der Organisation*, 2nd ed., Schäffer-Poeschel, Stuttgart, pp. 920–933.

Szyperski, N. and Klein, S. (1993) Informationslogistik und virtuelle Organisationen, in *Die Betriebswirtschaft*, **2**, pp. 187–208.

Tanenbaum, A.S. (1989) *Computer Networks*, Prentice Hall, Englewood Cliffs, NJ.

Taylor, F.W. (1913) *Die Grundsätze wissenschaftlicher Betriebsführung*, Oldenbourg, Munich/Berlin.

Teece, D.J. (1986) Profiting from Technological Innovation: Implications for Integration, Collaboration, Licensing and Public Policy, in *Research Policy*, pp. 285–305.

Telearbeit (1994). Telearbeit und virtuelle Arbeitsplätze: Neue Arbeitsformen als Chance für Unternehmen und Mitarbeiter, Conference on 23–24 August 1994 in Frankfurt am Main, Starnberg, Germany: Management Forum.

Telecommute (1994) Proceedings of the Telecommute '94 Conference, 25–27 October, San Francisco.

Telework (1994) Proceedings of the European Assembly on Teleworking and New Ways of Working, 3–4 November, Berlin.

Texaco (ed.) (1994) Texaco Report – Results of the 1992–1993 Telecommuting Pilot, unpublished report.

Thom, N. (1987) *Personalentwicklung als Instrument der Unternehmungsführung*, Schäffer-Poeschel, Stuttgart.

Thompson, J.D. (1967) *Organizations in Action*, McGraw-Hill, New York, NY.

Thorelli, H.B. (1986) Networks: Between Markets and Hierarchies, in *Strategic Management Journal*, **7**, pp. 37–51.

Thornton, E. (1994) Revolution in Japanese Retailing, *Fortune*, 7 February, p. 144.

Thurow, L. (1992) *Head to Head*, Morrow, New York.

Tietzel, M. (1981) Die Ökonomie der Property-Rights: Ein Überblick, in *Zeitschrift für Wirtschaftspolitik*, **30**, pp. 207–243.

Trist, E.A. et al (1963) *Organizational Choice*, Tavistock Publications, London.

Tröndle, D. (1987) *Kooperationsmanagement. Steuerung interaktioneller Prozesse bei Unternehmenskooperationen*, Eul, Bergisch-Gladbach, Germany.

Uebele, H. (1992) Kreativität und Kreativitätstechniken, in Gaugler, E. and Weber, W. (eds), *Handwörterbuch des Personalwesens*, 2nd ed., Schäffer-Poeschel, Stuttgart, pp. 1165–1179.

Ulich, E. (1991) Gruppenarbeit – arbeitspsychologische Konzepte und Beispiele, in Friedrich, J. and Rödiger K.-H. (eds), *Computergestützte Gruppenarbeit (CSCW)*, Berichte des German Chapter of the ACM 34, Teubner, Stuttgart, pp. 57–77.

Ulich, E. (1994) *Arbeitspsychologie*, 3rd ed., Schäffer-Poeschel, Stuttgart.

Ulich, E., Groskurth, P. and Bruggemann A. (1973) *Neue Formen der Arbeitsgestaltung. Möglichkeiten und Probleme einer Verbesserung des Arbeitslebens*, Europäische Verlagsanstalt, Frankfurt am Main.

Ullmann-Margalit, E. (1977) *The Emergence of Norms*, Oxford University Press, Oxford.

Ulrich, P. (1986) *Transformation der ökonomischen Vernunft. Fortschrittsperspektiven der modernen Industriegesellschaft*, Haupt, Bern/Stuttgart.

Ulrich, H. and Probst G.J. (1991) *Anleitung zum ganzheitlichen Handeln: Ein Brevier für Führungskräfte*, 3rd ed., Haupt, Bern/Stuttgart.

Underwood, L. (1993) *Intelligent Manufacturing*, Wokingham.
US Congress, Office of Technology Assessment. Electronic Enterprises (1994) *Looking to the Future*, US Government Printing Office, OTA-TCT-600, Washington, DC.
Vanberg, V. (1982) *Markt und Organisation*, Mohr, Tübingen, Germany.
Vertretung der Europäischen Kommission in Deutschland (ed.) (1995) *Die Informationsgesellschaft*, EU-Informationen No. 2, Bonn, February.
Vester, F. (1980) *Neuland des Denkens*, Deutsche Verlags-Anstalt, Stuttgart.
Vizjak, A. (1990) *Wachstumspotentiale durch Strategische Partnerschaften*, B. Kirsch, Herrsching, Germany.
Voskamp, U. and Wittke, V. (1994) Von "Silicon Valley" zur "virtuellen Integration" – Neue Formen der Organisation von Innovationsprozessen am Beispiel der Halbleiterindustrie, in Sydow, J. v. and Windeler, A. (eds), *Management interorganisationaler Beziehungen: Vertrauen, Kontrolle und Informationstechnik*, Westdeutscher Verlag, Opladen, Germany, pp. 212–243.
Vroom, V.H. (1964) *Work and Motivation*, John Wiley & Sons, New York.
Wagner, R. (1994) *Die Grenzen der Unternehmung – Beiträge zur ökonomischen Theorie der Unternehmung*, Physica, Darmstadt.
Wagner, D. and Schumann, R. (1991) *Die Produktinsel: Leitfaden zur Einführung einer effizienten Produktion in Zulieferbetrieben*, TÜV Rheinland, Cologne.
Wahren, H.K. (1987) *Zwischenmenschliche Kommunikation und Interaktion in Unternehmen*, de Gruyter, Berlin.
Walke, B. (1992) Technik des Mobilfunks (Dienste und Protokolle digitaler Mobilfunknetze), in Kruse, J. (ed.), *Zellularer Mobilfunk – Neue Märkte mit neuen Netzen für das Funktelefon*, Springer, Berlin, pp. 17–63.
Wallis, J.J. and North, D.C. (1986) Measuring the Transaction Sector in the American Economy, 1870–1970, in Engerman, S.L. and Gallman, R.E. (eds), *Long-Term Factors in American Economic Growth*, University of Chicago Press, Chicago/London.
Warnecke, H.-J. (1992) *Die fraktale Fabrik: Revolution der Unternehmenskultur*, Springer, Berlin.
Warnecke, H.-J. and Hüser, M. (1992) Lean Production – eine kritische Würdigung, in *Angewandte Arbeitswissenschaft*, **131**, pp. 1–26.
Watzlawick, P., Beavin, J.H. and Jackson, D.D. (1967) *Pragmatics of Human Communication*, Norton, New York.
Watzlawick, P., Beavin, J.H. and Jackson, D.D. (1990) *Menschliche Kommunikation: Formen, Störungen, Paradoxien*, 8th ed., Huber, Bern.
Weaver, C.N. (1991) *TQM – A Step-by-Step Guide to Implementation*, ASQC Quality Press, Milwaukee.
Weber, A. (1909) *Über den Standort der Industrien, Part 1: Reine Theorie des Standortes*, Mohr, Tübingen, Germany.
Weber, B.W. (1993) How Financial Markets are going On-line, in *EM Newsletter*, **9–10**, pp. 18–19.
Weber, M. (1972) *Wirtschaft und Gesellschaft*, 5th ed., Mohr, Tübingen, Germany.
Weiser, N. et al (1991) *The Arthur D. Little Forecast on Technology and Productivity: Making the Integrated Enterprise Work*. John Wiley, New York.
Weitzendorf, Th. and Wigand, R.T. (1991) *Cost-Benefit Analysis of Personal Computer Productivity*. Institute for Information Processing Report Series, University of Graz Press, Graz, Austria, 304, pp. 1–16.
Weizsäcker, E.U. von (1972). Erstmaligkeit und Bestätigung als Komponenten der Pragmatischen Information, in Weizsäcker, E.U. von. (ed.) (1974), *Offene*

Systeme I – Beiträge zur Zeitstruktur, Entropie und Evolution, Klett-Cotta, Stuttgart.

Welge, M.K. (1987) *Unternehmensführung, Vol. 2: Organisation*, Schäffer-Poeschel, Stuttgart.

Wenger, E. and Terberger, E. (1988) Die Beziehung zwischen Agent und Prinzipal als Baustein einer ökonomischen Theorie der Organisation, in *Wirtschaftswissenschaftliches Studium*, **10**, pp. 506–514.

Werhahn, P.H. (1989) *Menschenbild, Gesellschaftsbild und Wissenschaftsbegriff in der neueren Betriebswirtschaftslehre*, 2nd ed., Haupt, Bern/Stuttgart.

Wheeler, M. and Zackin, D. (1994) *Work-Family Roundtable: Telecommuting*, **1**, Spring.

White Paper on Growth (1993) Growth, Competitiveness and Employment: The Challenge and Ways forward into the 21st century. *Bulletin of the European Communities*, Supplement No. 6.

Wigand, R. T. (1984) Transborder Data Flow, Informatics, and National Policies, *Journal of Communication*, **34**(1), pp. 153–175.

Wigand, R. T. (1985a) Integrated Communications and Work Efficiency: Impacts on Organizational Structure and Power, in *Information Services and Use*, **5**, pp. 241–258.

Wigand, R.T. (1985b) Transborder Data Flow: Its Impact on Business and Government, *Information Management Review*, **1**(2), pp. 55–65.

Wigand, R.T. (1986) Substituting Communication for Transportation, *Global Mobility*, **3**, pp. 1–8.

Wigand, R.T. (1988a) Fünf Grundsätze für die erfolgreiche Einführung des Informations-Managements, in *Information Management*, **3**(2), pp. 24–30.

Wigand, R.T. (1988b) Integrated Services Digital Networks: Concepts, Policies and Emerging Issues, *Journal of Communication*, **38**(1), pp. 29–49.

Wigand, R. T. (1988c) Integrated Telecommunications, Networking, and Distributed Data Processing, in Rabin, J. and Jackowski, E. (eds), *Handbook of Information Systems and Resource Management*, Marcel Dekker, New York, pp. 293–321.

Wigand, R. T. (1988d) The Witte Report: Restructuring of Germany's PTT, *Telecommunications Policy*, **12**(2), pp. 184–188.

Wigand, R.T. (1994) Electronic Data Interchange in the United States of America: Selected Issues and Trends, in Kilian, W. et al (eds), *Electronic Data Interchange (EDI). Aus ökonomischer und juristischer Sicht*. Nomos Verlagsgesellschaft, Baden-Baden, Germany, pp. 369–391.

Wigand, R.T. (1995a) Doing Business on the Information Superhighway: Are We Adding Value? Paper Presented to the Society for Information Management, Annual Spring Meeting, Syracuse, NY, May, and *The Business Journal*, **9**(24), pp. 3–15.

Wigand, R.T. (1995b) Electronic Commerce and Reduced Transaction Costs: Firms' Migration in to Highly Interconnected Electronic Markets, in *Electronic Markets*, **16/17**, pp. 1–5.

Wigand, R.T. (1995c) The Information Superhighway and Electronic Commerce: Effects of Electronic Markets. Paper presented to the Annual Conference of the International Communication Association, Albuquerque, NM, 25–29 May.

Wigand, R.T. (1995d) Information Technology and Payoff: The Productivity Paradox Revisited. Paper Presented to the Annual Conference of the International Communication Association, Albuquerque, NM, 25–29 May.

Wigand, R.T. (1996) An Overview of Electronic Commerce and Markets. Paper Presented to the Annual Conference of the International Communication Association, Chicago, IL, 23–27 May.

Wigand, R.T. and Benjamin, R.I. (1995) Electronic Commerce: Effects on Electronic Markets, in *Journal of Computer Mediated Communication*, **3**, URL: http://www.usc.edu/dept/annenberg/vol1/issue3.

Wigand, R.T. and Frankwick, G.L. (1989) Interorganizational Communication and Technology Transfer: Industry-Government-University Linkages, *International Journal of Technology Management*, **4**(1), pp. 63–76.

Wigand, R.T., Shipley, C. and Shipley, D. (1984) Transborder Data Flow, Informatics and National Policies, *Journal of Communication*, **34**(1), pp. 153–175.

Wildemann, H. (1994) *Die modulare Fabrik: Kundennahe Produktion durch Fertigungssegmentierung*, 4th ed., TCW, Munich.

Wilensky, H.L. (1967) *Organizational Intelligence, Knowledge and Policy in Government and Industry*, Basic Books, New York.

Wilkens, A. and Ouchi, W. (1983) Efficient Cultures: Exploring the Relationship between Culture and Organizational Performance, in *Administrative Science Quarterly*, **28**, pp. 468–481.

Williamson, O.E. (1975) *Markets and Hierarchies: Analysis and Antitrust Implications. A Study in the Economics of Internal Organization*, The Free Press, New York.

Williamson, O.E. (1979) Transaction Cost Economics: The Governance of Contractual Relations, *Journal of Law and Economics*, **22**, pp. 233–261.

Williamson, O.E. (1981) The Modern Corporation: Origin, Evolution, Attributes, *Journal of Economic Literature*, **19**, pp. 1537–1568.

Williamson, O.E. (1985) *The Economic Institutions of Capitalism. Firms, Markets, Relational Contracting*, 11th ed., The Free Press, New York.

Williamson, O.E. (1990) The Firm as a Nexus of Treaties: an Introduction, in Aoki, M., Gustafsson, B. and Williamson, O.E. (eds), *The Firm as a Nexus of Treaties*, Sage, London, pp. 1–25.

Williamson, O.E. (1991) Comparative Economic Organization: The Analysis of Discrete Structural Alternatives, in Administrative Science Quarterly, **36**, pp. 269–296.

Windsperger, J. (1991) Der Unternehmer als Koordinator, in *Zeitschrift für Betriebswirtschaft*, **12**, pp. 1413–1429.

Winograd, T. (1986) A Language Perspective on the Design of Cooperative Work, in *Proceedings of the ACM Conference on Computer-Supported Cooperative Work*, 3–5 December, ACM, Austin (Texas), New York, NY, pp. 203–220.

Winograd, T. and Flores, F. (1986) *Understanding Computers and Cognition. A New Foundation for Design*, Ablex, Norwood, NJ.

Winograd, T. and Flores, F. (1992) *Erkenntnis, Maschinen, Verstehen – Zur Neugestaltung von Computersystemen*, 2nd ed., Rotbuch, Berlin.

Witte, E. (1984) *Bürokommunikation. Ein Beitrag zur Produktivitätssteigerung*, Springer, Berlin.

Witte, E. (1988) Phasen-Theorem und Organisation komplexer Entscheidungsverläufe, in Witte, E., Hauschildt, J. and Grün, O. (eds), *Innovative Entscheidungsprozesse*, Mohr, Tübingen, Germany, pp. 202–206.

Wittgenstein, L. (1953) *Philosophische Untersuchungen*, Suhrkamp, Frankfurt am Main, 1975.

Wohlenberg, H. (1994) *Gruppenunterstützende Systeme in Forschung und Entwicklung: Anwenderpotentiale aus industrieller Sicht*, Gabler, Wiesbaden.

Wolff, B. (1995) *Organisation durch Verträge*, Gabler, Wiesbaden.

Wolff, B. (1996) Incentive-Compatible Change Management in a Welfare State, Working Paper # 6.4, Center for European Studies, Harvard University, Cambridge, USA.

Wolff, B. and Neuburger, R. (1995) Zur theoretischen Begründung von Netzwerken aus der Sicht der Neuen Institutionenökonomik, in Jansen, D. and Schubert, K (eds), *Netzwerke und Politikproduktion*, Schüren, Marburg, Germany, pp. 74–94.

Wolff, M.-R. (1993) Multimediale Informationssysteme, in Heilmann, H. (ed.), *Multimedia*, HMD No. 169, Forkel, Wiesbaden, pp. 9–26.

Wollnik, M. (1988) Ein Referenzmodell für das Informations-Management, in *Information Management*, **3**, pp. 34–43.

Wollnik, M. (1992) Telearbeit, in E. Frese (ed.), *Handwörterbuch der Organisation*, 3rd ed., Schäffer-Poeschel, Stuttgart, pp. 2400–2417.

Womack, J.P., Jones, D.T. and Roos, D. (1990) *The Machine that Changed the World*, Rawson Ass., New York.

Worch, A. (1994) Rechtliche Rahmenbedingungen, in Godehardt, B. (ed.), *Telearbeit Rahmenbedingungen und Potentiale*, Westdeutscher Verlag, Opladen, Germany, pp. 205–280.

Wunderer, R. and Grunwald, W. (1980) *Führungslehre*, 2 Vols., de Gruyter, Berlin/New York.

Zahn, E. (ed.) (1990) *Organisationsstrategie und Produktion*, GMT, Munich.

Zäpfel, G. (1989) *Taktisches Produktions-Management*, de Gruyter, Berlin/New York.

Zbornik, S. (1995) *Elektronische Märkte, elektronische Hierarchien und elektronische Netzwerke*, UVK-Universitätsverlag Konstanz, Konstanz, Germany.

Zimmermann, H.-D. and Kuhn, C. (1995) Grundlegende Konzepte einer Electronic Mall, in Schmid, B. et al (eds), *Electronic Mall: Banking und Shopping in globalen Netzen*, Teubner, Stuttgart, pp. 33–94.

Zink, K.J. and Ritter, A. (1992) *Mit Qualitätszirkeln zu mehr Arbeitssicherheit*, Universum Verlagsantalt, Wiesbaden.

Zuboff, S. (1988) *In the Age of the Smart Machine*, Basic Books, New York, NY.

Index